Research on Old French: The State of the Art

Studies in Natural Language and Linguistic Theory

VOLUME 88

Managing Editors

Marcel den Dikken, *City University of New York*
Liliane Haegeman, *University of Ghent, Belgium*
Joan Maling, *Brandeis University*

Editorial Board

Guglielmo Cinque, *University of Venice*
Carol Georgopoulos, *University of Utah*
Jane Grimshaw, *Rutgers University*
Michael Kenstowicz, *Massachusetts Institute of Technology*
Hilda Koopman, *University of California, Los Angeles*
Howard Lasnik, *University of Maryland*
Alec Marantz, *Massachusetts Institute of Technology*
John J. McCarthy, *University of Massachusetts, Amherst*
Ian Roberts, *University of Cambridge*

For further volumes:
http://www.springer.com/series/6559

Deborah L. Arteaga
Editor

Research on Old French: The State of the Art

Springer

Editor
Deborah L. Arteaga
Department of Foreign Languages
University of Nevada
Las Vegas, NV, USA

ISSN 0924-4670
ISBN 978-94-007-4767-8   ISBN 978-94-007-4768-5 (eBook)
DOI 10.1007/978-94-007-4768-5
Springer Dordrecht Heidelberg New York London

Library of Congress Control Number: 2012946203

© Springer Science+Business Media Dordrecht 2013
This work is subject to copyright. All rights are reserved by the Publisher, whether the whole or part of the material is concerned, specifically the rights of translation, reprinting, reuse of illustrations, recitation, broadcasting, reproduction on microfilms or in any other physical way, and transmission or information storage and retrieval, electronic adaptation, computer software, or by similar or dissimilar methodology now known or hereafter developed. Exempted from this legal reservation are brief excerpts in connection with reviews or scholarly analysis or material supplied specifically for the purpose of being entered and executed on a computer system, for exclusive use by the purchaser of the work. Duplication of this publication or parts thereof is permitted only under the provisions of the Copyright Law of the Publisher's location, in its current version, and permission for use must always be obtained from Springer. Permissions for use may be obtained through RightsLink at the Copyright Clearance Center. Violations are liable to prosecution under the respective Copyright Law.
The use of general descriptive names, registered names, trademarks, service marks, etc. in this publication does not imply, even in the absence of a specific statement, that such names are exempt from the relevant protective laws and regulations and therefore free for general use.
While the advice and information in this book are believed to be true and accurate at the date of publication, neither the authors nor the editors nor the publisher can accept any legal responsibility for any errors or omissions that may be made. The publisher makes no warranty, express or implied, with respect to the material contained herein.

Printed on acid-free paper

Springer is part of Springer Science+Business Media (www.springer.com)

*Dedicated with love to my daughters,
Rachel and Rebecca Arteaga, and my sisters,
Mary Alice Birk and Denise Meredith*

Contents

1 Introduction 1
   Deborah Arteaga

Part I Diachronic Studies

2 A Diachronic View of Old French Genitive Constructions 19
   Deborah Arteaga and Julia Herschensohn

3 Grammaticalization in Progress in Old French:
   Indefinite Articles 45
   Anne Carlier

4 Null Objects in Old French 61
   Bryan Donaldson

5 Compensatory Lengthening in Historical French:
   The Role of the Speaker 87
   Randall Gess

6 Perception, Production and Markedness
   in Sound Change: French Velar Palatalization 107
   Haike Jacobs and Janine Berns

7 Evolution and Regrammation in the Mood System:
   Perspectives from Old, Middle, Renaissance
   and Modern French 123
   Jan Lindschouw

8 Analogy Among French Sounds 149
   Michael L. Mazzola

9 The Development of the Declension System 167
   Lene Schøsler

| 10 | The Diasystem and Its Role in Generating Meaning: Diachronic Evidence from Old French | 187 |

Harald Völker

Part II   Synchronic Studies

| 11 | Crusaders' Old French | 207 |

Cyril Aslanov

| 12 | The Use of the Future and Conditional in High Medieval Literature | 221 |

Igor Dreer

| 13 | Old French Parataxis: Syntactic Variant or Stylistic Variation? | 243 |

Julie Glikman and Thomas Verjans

| 14 | A Derivational Approach to Negative Polarity Item Licensing in Old French | 261 |

Richard Ingham

| 15 | Theoretical Issues in Old French Inflectional Morpho(phono)logy | 283 |

Jürgen Klausenburger

| 16 | Forms and Functions of Reported Discourse in Medieval French | 299 |

Sophie Marnette

| 17 | The Left-Periphery in Old French | 327 |

Eric Mathieu

| 18 | Grammatical Meaning and the Old French Subjunctive | 351 |

Margaret E. Winters

Index 377

Chapter 1
Introduction

Deborah Arteaga

Old French has been the subject of scholarly research beginning with the Neogrammarians in the nineteenth century. It has been a fruitful ground, given the fact that it is so well-documented, principally from the twelfth century onwards, a solidly attested transition between Latin and Modern French. The present volume contributes to this tradition. This is the first edited volume focusing entirely on the various linguistic facets of Old French. There are several traditional grammars of Old French which are still in print (*inter alia* Buridant 2000; Jensen 1990; Foulet 1982; De Lage 1975; Einhorn 1975; Togeby 1974). There are also scholarly volumes that consider one grammatical aspect of Old French, such as Marchello-Nizia (1985), who traces the evolution of the adverb *si* 'so' from Old French to Modern French. Another such work is that of Pearce (1990), who discusses Old French infinitival complements from a diachronic perspective. Additional volumes which present a narrow study of one or more linguistic features of Old French include Roberts (1993) and Vance (1997); these two scholars address Old French word order, the distribution of null subjects, and the evolution thereof.

There are also a limited number of books (cf. Gess and Arteaga 2006) that devote a few chapters to current theoretical research on Old French within a general Romance perspective. Other volumes that typically contain a chapter (or two) on Old French based on updated linguistic theories are the selected proceedings of *The Linguistic Symposium on the Romance Languages* (e.g., Colina et al. 2010; Herschensohn 2011). However, neither the specialized volumes nor those containing one or more chapters on Old French give a broad overview of its linguistic subdisciplines.

D. Arteaga (✉)
Department of Foreign Languages, University of Nevada,
Las Vegas, NV, USA
e-mail: deborah.arteaga@unlv.edu

Too often in the field of linguistics, edited collections present only research by authors who work in a few theoretical frameworks and who are from a limited geographical region, such as North America or Europe. This divide is unfortunate, as it does not provide an accurate snapshot of the research that is currently being conducted in the field. This volume stands in sharp contrast to this practice. Its breadth is extensive in that the 17 contributors, who hail from 8 different countries, pursue research on a wide variety of topics in Old French focusing on the various subsystems of language. The theoretical frameworks in which they conduct their research are similarly diverse, ranging from Optimality Theory to Minimalism to the Columbia School. Many of the chapters are corpus-based, reflecting a new trend in the field, as more electronic corpora become available. Because of this variety, this volume succeeds in presenting the discipline as it is practiced today, in all of its forms.

The present volume is not only directed at linguists and graduate students who specialize in Old French, but will also be accessible to non-specialists as well, such as linguists who conduct research in historical linguistics in other languages, those focusing on theoretical linguistics, and Romance linguists in general. All examples are carefully glossed and the relevant characteristics of Old French are clearly explained. The chapters in this volume center around two central research questions:

1. How do the diachronic studies in this volume contribute not only to the field of Old French but also to our current understanding of language change *per se*?
2. How do the synchronic studies lead to a better understanding of language systems in general, and specifically, that of Old French?

Three studies in the volume address nominal morphosyntax, including the role of the case system in Old French, yet their focus and theoretical framework are different. Deborah Arteaga and Julia Herschensohn, in their chapter entitled "A Diachronic View of Old French Genitive Constructions" and Lene Schøsler, in her chapter, "The Development of the Declension System," consider, at least in part, the evolution of the case system. The third study by Anne Carlier, "Grammaticalization in Progress in Old French: Indefinite Articles," discusses the development of the article system. Arteaga and Herschensohn frame their research in the Minimalist Program (Chomsky 1995, 2001) and that of Lightfoot (1999), while Schøsler and Carlier consider the role of grammaticalization in language change.

Both Arteaga and Herschenson and Schøsler argue that the case system was used in Old French to identify the syntactic role of NPs. Yet Arteaga and Herschensohn focus only on the case system, specifically its loss, as a means to explain the evolution of Old French genitive structures. Schløsler, on the other hand, seeks to answer broader questions specific to case marking, including the question of why Old French preserved, in part, the Latin case system, and why it was lost. Both studies conclude that the loss of final *s* played a pivotal role, although Schøsler emphasizes that case marking on the determiner and the need to mark plural must be carefully taken into account, in addition to its role within the grammar, in general, of Old French. In their study, Arteaga and Herschensohn note that a variety of genitive structures existed in Latin, including the juxtaposition genitive, (JG) in which no intervening preposition is found between the possessed and the possessor: *unos multorum* 'one (of) many,' because Latin nouns carry the syntactic features of gender, number and definiteness.

With respect to the diachronic evolution of these structures into Old French and beyond, Arteaga and Herschensohn assume the theoretical framework of Lightfoot (1999), who argues that a cue-based analysis can account for language change. His proposal is that language evolution begins with children when they create "new" grammars based on the input that they receive. particularly when it is variable. The Old French genitive could be expressed by five structures, all of which meant 'the duke's niece': *la nièce du duc, la nièce au duc, la nièce le duc, la duc nièce* and *la nièce duc*, and would therefore not lead to the construction of a "new" grammar by children.

Arteaga and Herschensohn argue that two factors contributed to the downfall of the JG, the loss of the case system in the thirteenth century, and the fact that in OF, unlike in Modern French, a definite article was always [+specific]. It was unexpressed otherwise, such as nouns having a generic interpretation *Galois sont tuit par nature plus fol que bestes an pasture.* 'The Gauls are all by nature crazier than animals at pasture.' (cf. Modern French, obligatorily **Les** *Gaulois*, which is not specific). Therefore, in their view, when the plural morpheme [s] also ceased to be pronounced in Old French, the functional load of the definite article, which continues to carry the features gender and number was increased, as it was generalized to [−specific] DPs as well, meaning that the morphological clues for children were at first variable and then ceased to exist.

Schløsler considers the evolution of the Old French declension system from Latin, as well as its role within the grammar of Old French. In Old French, case has been considered as "superfluous" (Detges 2008). Much previous work has viewed the development or loss of a case system as a reorganization of grammar *per se*. Schøsler argues instead that cases are one of several grammatical mechanisms that the medieval language had at its disposal to identify the function of arguments. The theoretical framework in which she grounds her study is variational linguistics; one of her central claims is that diachronic change is due to variation. She argues that diasystemic variation is parametrized so as to allow for differing interpretation of variants. To support her analysis, she considers case variation with respect to text genre, comparing prose texts to those in verse, and narrative texts to non-narrative texts (i.e., charters). She further addresses (fictive) direct discourse compared to narrative, as well as the charters from Luxembourg.

Schøsler argues that a crucial part of her theory, namely case-role indexing, can account for the fact that the Romance used a variety of structural mechanisms to absorb the functions of Latin case. Sometimes, these languages preserved cases outright, such as in the development of pronouns. Her analysis also explains why, in other instances, the Romance languages expanded the use of prepositions and grammaticalized structures to counteract the loss of the case endings.

Finally, she argues that her account is further supported by the fact that the Romance languages have innovated by using both word order and cross-reference to mark the function of arguments.

Like Schøsler, Anne Carlier also views language change as, in part, grammaticalization, although her chapter has a different focus, in that she considers the development of the entire article system in French, not merely case. Carlier notes that cross-linguistically, the grammatical category of articles is not widespread, and, for this reason, in her view, the development of a complete three-term paradigm of articles in French provides an interesting case study.

Her chapter focuses on the emergence of indefinite article *uns* and the partitive article. She argues that at the beginning stage in Old French, *uns* is still very close to its numeral meaning both in its quantitative dimension of uniqueness marker ('only one') and its qualitative dimension of identity marker ('one and the same'). She claims that through pragmatic strengthening, the textual role of *uns* in Old French changed to mark the noun phrase as new for the hearer/reader. In Carlier's view, her analysis accounts for early occurrences of more abstract functions of the indefinite article, such as attributive and even generic uses of *uns,* which are often considered incompatible with a beginning stage of grammaticalization. With respect to the partitive article, she argues that in Old French, it has not even reached the status of an article, but rather has a hybrid status between preposition and determiner.

For Carlier, a comprehensive account of the exact meaning and the specific conditions of the use of *uns* and of the partitive in Old French must be based upon both a correct definition of the source expression, as well as on its evolutionary stage *vis à vis* this structure. In her view, it must further fit into an overall picture of these articles' path towards grammaticalization, which leads to their development into full-fledged articles. In this way, she argues, a synchronic analysis of these grammatical elements is strengthened when combined with a diachronic perspective.

The case system is also discussed by Jürgen Klausenburger in his chapter "Theoretical Issues in Old French Inflectional Morpho(phono)logy," though his focus is on morphophonological alternations, and, in his discussion, he also gives equal consideration to verbal morphology. Michael Mazzola, in "Analogy Among French Sounds," also addresses the interface of morphology and phonology, and, although both Klausenburger and Mazzola consider morphological leveling to be of paramount importance in the evolution of Old French, Mazzola claims that cultural aspects of Latin, not previously considered by researchers, also play a role in suppletive leveling.

Unlike other the studies in the volume, Klausenburger frames his analysis within the theoretical viewpoint of natural morphology of Mayerthaler (1981) ('system-independent') and Wurzel (1984) ('system-dependent'), in which concrete analyses, in accordance with Ockham's Razor, are shown to be superior to abstract ones, which illustrate Chatton's Anti-Razor, and necessitate recourse to arbitrary rules. Klausenburger views as crucial to his account the concepts of iconicity, which he defines as "system-independent naturalness" and system congruity (SC), or "system-dependent naturalness," which operate according to paradigm structure conditions, manifested by invariance and final consonant alternation. These few conditions, he argues, can give a principled account for the language system in Old French as well for as its evolution.

Klausenburger proposes that for the history of French, the Old French synchronic 'slice' manifests an excellent recapitulation of sound changes from Latin to the medieval period, as represented in the data that he presents from inflectional morphology of the noun and the verb. Since Old French constitutes a period closer to the Latin source than does Modern French, he claims that we are able to recover historical change much more readily in the synchrony of the earlier stage of the language. The extensive sound changes between Old and Modern French makes such a distinction uncontroversial, in his view.

Klausenburger considers that morphophonology and morphosyntax, by their very labels, constitute 'transition' components in any language. As a consequence, in his analysis, the interrelation between synchrony and diachrony come to the fore, especially clearly in studies of data within these areas. As he notes, the 'reality' of Old French synchrony has traditionally been seen as linked to the diachronic side, both from Latin to Old French and from Old to Modern French.

The chapter by Michael Mazzola examines the role of three versions of analogy: (1) analogy as structure, (2) analogy as lexical diffusion, and (3) analogy as suppletive leveling. In order to test the relative value of these three approaches to analogy, he examines their relevance to the data from the history of French sounds from the fourth to the sixth centuries. He argues that these data are especially relevant, since the conventional nineteenth-century approach relied heavily on analogy with recourse to allomorphic leveling. He concludes that analogy as suppletive leveling is not suitable for yielding a record of historical accuracy (i.e. Old French begins only after the arrival of the Franks). Accordingly, he provides an alternative analysis, based solely on analogy as structure and as lexical diffusion, which reveals that Old French begins with a continual development of the Latin language, nurtured by Latin culture and early political structure, introduced into Gaul by the Roman armies.

Mazzola seeks to address our current understanding of language change by emphasizing the distinction between structural variants and social variants. In his view, by proposing an innovative, purely regular, phonological change, it can be determined which items are representative of each change. He claims that the interplay between the two types of variants further contributes to our current understanding of language change by leading us to view suppletive leveling as unnecessary. He argues that this perspective on language change contributes to the field of Old French by fixing its origins not on an abrupt and later introduction of Frankish, as is conventionally believed, but rather on a gradual development from a parent language that was neither static nor unchangeable.

Three chapters in the volume address verbal syntax from a Minimalist perspective: "Null Objects in Old French," by Bryan Donaldson, "A Derivational Approach to Negative Polarity Item Licensing in Old French," by Richard Ingham, and "The Left-Periphery in Old French," by Éric Mathieu. Donaldson focuses on the distribution of object drop in the history of French, while Ingham and Mathieu consider the oft-debated question of word order in Old French, specifically questioning whether V2 word order is truly the base word order in the older state of the language. Both Ingham and Mathieu conclude that despite apparent evidence to the contrary, V2 word order is basic; they both explain other word orders, such as V3 and V4, by a detailed analysis of the left periphery.

Donaldson's analysis takes as a point of departure the study by Arteaga (1997) and demonstrates that, as in numerous modern Romance varieties and as in Classical Latin, the grammar of Old French allowed direct objects to be unexpressed. Data from *écrasement* (reduction of a series of two third-person object pronouns to a single pronoun, such as *li le* 'it to him' becoming *li* 'to him'), verb coordination, adjunct clauses, null cognate objects, formulaic expressions, arbitrary human null objects, and left-dislocations with null resumptive pronouns are presented from a variety of Old French prose and verse texts from the eleventh to the fourteenth century. On the basis of available data and diagnostics, he suggests that object drop in Old French involved both null pronominals and null variables.

Donaldson claims that because Classical Latin possessed object drop, and because Old French also allows it, object drop – as a general phenomenon – does not represent an innovation in Modern French. On the other hand, he notes that the specific properties of null objects appear to have changed diachronically, as Old French differed somewhat from Modern French with respect to the contexts in which it licenses null objects. He argues that in Old French, omission of the direct object pronoun in *écrasement* contexts was nearly systematic, whereas in Modern French, *écrasement* is limited to certain registers (and perhaps regional varieties). Similarly, he claims that Old French allowed a single object pronoun to be coordinated across multiple finite verbs, a possibility that is largely absent from the modern language. Finally, in his view, French has extended the use of the third-person arbitrary human null object since the Old French period, which offers only sparse evidence of this construction.

Ingham's chapter focuses on a long-standing problem in Old French syntax, namely the left periphery of main clause structure, which is generally considered to have evolved from a CP V2 grammar to the modern non-V2 system (cf. Adams 1987; Roberts 1993; Vance 1997). However, as he notes, apparent violations of V2 syntax in Old French complicate the picture.

His chapter discusses the fact that V3 and even V4 word orders appear with certain adverbs (*ja* 'ever/indeed' and *onques* 'ever'). He shows that V > 2 word order is also regularly found if preposed PPs contain polarity items. Ingham argues that the explanation for these apparent counterexamples to V2 lies in the fact that such clauses have continued to be TP structures from Old French to Modern French. He provides reasons grounded in recent studies of negative polarity for their exceptional status, and concludes that their systematic status still allows one to posit an otherwise general V2 grammar for Old French main clauses.

In so doing, Ingham gives a Minimalist phase-based account of the syntax of negative clauses in Old French, distinguishing polarity arguments from polarity adjuncts in terms of their ability to raise to Spec CP. In his view, polarity features on arguments in Old French were checked in the vP phase, leaving discourse-linked polarity arguments free to be topicalized in the CP phase, and hence to engage V2. He proposes that polarity time adjuncts, on the other hand, were checked in the CP phase, but within TP: they did not topicalize and hence did not engage V2. Ingham seeks to provide in his chapter a principled account of exceptions to V2 word order, while also strengthening the notion that V2 order was, indeed, found in most OF main clauses.

1 Introduction

Mathieu devotes his chapter to the process known as Stylistic Fronting. He claims that in this syntactic operation, if no overt subject is found in Spec-TP, an XP may be fronted to a position before the finite verb. For example, in *Ce sanc que an mes dras __regart* 'That blood that in my sheets I see.' (*Le Chevalier à la Charrette*, year ~1180, 4800), the XP *en mes dras* 'in my sheet' has fronted to the XP preceding *regart*. He shows that in addition to XPs, a head can be fronted. Mathieu notes that many languages today, such as Icelandic, have Stylistic Fronting as part of their grammars, so that an analysis of and other kind of topicalisation operations in Old French can also help clarify the structure of the left periphery in these languages.

Mathieu adopts the cartographic approach of Rizzi (1997, 2004), Cinque (2002, 2006), and Belletti (2004) and applied to Old Italian and Old Spanish by Benincá (2006), Benincá and Poletto (2002). He proposes that the crucial differentiating factors between languages that have Stylistic Fronting and those that do not are the possibility of null subjects and the presence of a special position (e.g., a split CP) for topics. Old French, in his view, is an ideal testing ground for this theory, as it has both null subjects and special topics positions, which leads him to conclude that the richness of the left periphery varies cross-linguistically and across time. He claims that our knowledge of Germanic syntax and the microvariation among Germanic languages has allowed for a better understanding of languages like Old French because Old French was greatly influenced by German. Finally, Mathieu argues that his analysis can account not only for cases of stylistic fronting, but for also V3 and V4 word orders in embedded clauses in Old French.

Two more contributions consider Old French syntax, specifically parataxis, or the omission of *que* in Old French clauses, although the theoretical frameworks in which they ground their research are quite different. Julie Glikman and Thomas Verjans' study, "Old French Parataxis: Syntactic Variant or Stylistic Variation?" considers parataxis within a variationist perspective, specifically a Coserian theory (Coseriu 1973; Verjans 2009). Sophie Marnette, on the other hand, situates her study within the linguistic analysis of Speech and Thought Presentation (cf. Cerquiglini 1981, 1984; Rychner 1980, 1987). Another difference between the two studies is that Glikman and Verjans mostly present data from *La Chanson de Roland*, because, they argue, focusing on one text can better illustrate the phenomenon of parataxis, while Marnette bases her conclusions on a very large corpus. Both studies view text genre as indispensable to a discussion of parataxis, which, as they show, is an important syntactic phenomenon in the history of French.

Glikman and Verjans note that in Old French, the omission of the complementizer *que* 'that,' in a subordinate clause was widespread, as in *Ço sent Rollant la veüe ad perdue* 'Roland feels (that) he has lost his sight,' although it was never obligatory. It has been previously argued (cf. Marchello-Nizia 1999) that paratactic constructions are only found with certain verbs (e.g., *vouloir* 'to want,' *savoir* 'to know,' and *jurer* 'to swear'). Glikman and Verjans' study is corpus based, using eight texts which run the gamut from highly stylized to oral narratives. Their data reveals that paratactic constructions are far more widespread than has been claimed in the past, and are not only found where the complement clause is in the subjunctive or is subject to a sequence of tense. Their corpus further shows that paratactic constructions are not restricted to certain persons, and that negation of the subordinate clause a trigger for parataxis in Old French.

They argue that the type of text (e.g., *les Chansons de geste* vs. prose) is relevant, as the former are oral narratives. They note that in Modern French, parataxis continues to be found in the informal register, although such structures are not accepted by prescriptivists (Bauche 1920; Gadet 2003). Glikman and Verjans conclude that paratactic constructions, in both Old French and Modern French, are in fact, in free variation with those in which the complementizer is expressed. They conclude that parataxis and the lack thereof can be accounted for if a linguistic system is considered to be a "system of possibilities" particularly of "communicative constraints" (cf. Coseriu 1973; Verjans 2009). This allows us to arrive at a deeper understanding of Medieval literary genres (e.g., their various conceptualizations of reality, history, and fiction), which, in turn, could help us reflect more deeply on Modern genresighlights a well-known phenomenon of Old French, namely parataxis, within a synchronic perspective.

Marnette, building on work by Cerquiglini (1981, 1984) and Rychner (1980, 1987), argues that Medieval French, despite what has been previously thought, does not lack complex discourse structures. In her view, situating her study within the linguistic analysis of Speech and Thought Presentation allows us to arrive at a deeper understanding of Medieval literary genres (e.g., their various conceptualizations of reality, history, and fiction), which, in turn, could help us reflect more deeply on Modern genres.

Marnette suggests that a dynamic view of discourse should be adopted in any analysis, as it represents the nexus of the elaboration of forms and functions. Within such a framework, she argues, we can see not only the evolution of medieval theory genres, but also how the authors conceive of reality, history, and fiction, as well as narrator-audience interrelationships. She notes that structures without the complementizer *que* are found in both Indirect and Direct discourse in Old French.

She bases her discussion on the 39 texts first considered by Marnette (2005). She claims that a corpus-based study is essential for an in-depth understanding of reported discourse categories in general, and of their use in Medieval French in particular. Her analysis argues against traditional definitions that distinguish Indirect Discourse from Direct Discourse based purely on the presence of subordination markers. She claims that by studying language in use (in this case in various literary genres), we are able to understand the language system at that point in time. For Marnette, further generalizations can be drawn, since these particular phenomena are also found in Modern Spoken French (cf. the discussion of Glikman and Verjans above), so that it is possible to make a broader hypothesis regarding the forms and functions of reported discourse in language.

Two diachronic studies contribute to the debate of oft-discussed topics in French phonology, compensatory lengthening, addressed by Randall Gess in his chapter "Compensatory Lengthening in Historical French: The Role of the Speaker," and velar palatalization, the focus of the chapter "Perception, Production and Markedness in Sound Change: French Velar Palatalization," by Haike Jacobs and Janine Berns. In both studies, the authors argue that both production and perception must be taken into account to explain sound change in Old French. Gess's chapter, highlights the role that the speaker plays within the phonological change involving the lengthening of vowels in the evolution of French. Specifically, Gess considers the process of compensatory lengthening (CL), through an in-depth exploration of two major types that occurred in Old French (CVC > CV: [fɛstə] > [fɛːtə]; CVCV > CV:C [krɛjə] > [krɛːj]). The model put forth in this chapter complements the strictly listener-oriented account of CL proposed in Kavitskaya (2002), which Gess argues to be inadequate for explaining CL. For Gess, the speaker, as innovator, is the ultimate source of CL, which he argues to be a gradual process with intermediate forms becoming, through postlexical reductions on the part of the speaker, more and more similar to (confusable with) forms with long vowels. He claims that a central aspect of this more comprehensive view of CL is that the speaker, through innovative reductive articulations that are constrained by articulatory gesture preservation constraints (Gess 2008), crucially feeds listener misperceptions.

Gess claims that his study can account for both the motivation (conservation of articulatory effort) and mechanics (implementation and constraints impinging on it) of phonological change in general, and reduction with CL specifically. With respect to our understanding of Old French phonology, this study suggests that distinct processes of reduction with CL, CVCV and CVC types, which occurred at different stages of the language, had a common motivation and also had a common constraint enforcing the observed lengthening. Gess argues that this commonality demonstrates the importance of the principle of isochrony in the history of the French language, a principle that directly or indirectly shaped the phonological outcomes of the overall reductive change so characteristic of historical French.

Like Gess, Jacobs and Berns consider sound change in the history of French. Specifically, they address the issue of French velarization of the consonant /k/ and /g/ before /a/, which yielded, respectively, [tʃ] and [dʒ] in Old French ([ʃ] and [ʒ] in Modern French), and which is unique to French. They note that whereas the palatalization of /k/ and /g/ before high vowels (i.e., /i/ and i/e) that occurred in all of the Romance languages can be explained by assimilation, French palatalization before /a/ cannot, as the vowel /a/ is low.

In the past, analyses have focused either on production (cf. Ohala 1992; Guion 1998; Plauché et al. 1997) or on perception (cf. *inter alia* Lahiri and Evers 1991; Calabrese 1993; Jacobs 1993; Clements and Hume 1995). Jakobs and Berns argue that in order to properly understand this change, both processes need to be taken into account, given that there is no clear phonetic motivation either from production or from perception as to why low back vowels should have triggered palatalization of preceding velars.

Moreover, in their view, contra Blevins (2004), markedness constraints play a crucial role in analyzing sound change in French. Jacobs and Berns claim that OT-CC (Optimality Theory with Candidate Chains, McCarthy 2007) offers a more principled analysis than a perceptual account when it comes to the question of why some sound changes appear to be irreversible. The authors argue that it is necessary to separate the roles of production, perception, and markedness and to tease out the roles of phonology and phonetics. By proposing an analysis that takes all of these factors into account, Jacobs and Berns seek to further our understanding of general principles underlying language change.

Three chapters in the volume consider the mood and tense system in Old French. Their approaches are different from many previous studies in that all view as important the *meaning* of mood and tense and its role in both the evolution of the system in Old French (Jan Linschouw and Igor Dreer) and in its synchronic state (Margaret Winters). Both Lindschouw and Winters and devote their studies to the subjunctive mood, whereas Dreer discuss the future and conditional tenses.

Lindshow's chapter, "Evolution and Regrammation in the Mood System: Perspectives from Old, Middle, Renaissance and Modern French," discusses the evolution of mood after concessive conjunctions. Lindschouw makes reference to the theory of Andersen (2001a, b), according to which the sequences of language change can generally be predicted. Andersen argues that if a language change is introduced 'from below', (i.e., is linguistically motivated within the language system), it normally first appears in unmarked contexts (e.g. dialogues, correspondence, diaries, theatre plays in prose) and will, in the course of time, spread to marked ones (e.g. poetry, theatre plays written in verse, argumentative texts). By contrast, if a change is introduced 'from above', (i.e., triggered by dominant groups of speakers' perception of style and registers), it is normally introduced in marked contexts and will spread to unmarked ones.

Lindschouw's study therefore focuses on the role of text genres with respect to language change. He argues that the important driving force in diachronic evolution, namely reanalysis, should not always be understood in terms of referential ambiguity in the linguistic sign, but can also be linked to an ambiguity with respect to the sign's distribution across text genres. He claims that since the evolution of the mood system does not take place abruptly from one century to another, it is necessary to adopt a broad diachronic perspective. He shows that through time, the mood system in concessive clauses undergoes a reorganization, passing from a relatively flexible system in Old French in which considerable syntactic and functional alternation between the two moods is found, to a system in Modern French which is highly constrained. Lindschouw describes the evolution of the mood system within the framework of an extended grammaticalization theory, which considers grammaticalization to be a process that changes grammatical systems, and to which he refers as a "regrammation".

Winters, in her chapter, "Grammatical Meaning and the Old French Subjunctive," examines how, in cases of complex synchronic polysemy, a variety of theories may be developed to account for the variety of meaning of a given grammatical construction and, though much less frequently, how it evolves over time. She limits her discussion to the range of approaches which view the subjunctive (and indeed grammar in general) as meaningful; the theories examined fall, then, under the heading of semantics rather than syntax.

She argues that the result is a typology of synchronic theories of the meaning of the subjunctive, some of which apply better than others to the Old French data. More broadly, in her view, her analysis points to the fact that many descriptive theories are unsatisfactory because they are based on limited aspects of some very complex constructions. For Winters, other shortcomings of such theories include the large numbers of counter-examples that can be found and the fact that these previous studies only consider isolated cases of the subjunctive. The author argues that the notion of *irrealis* can help us understand much of the distribution and meaning of the Old French subjunctive, in part because hypothetical constructions take the subjunctive in the earlier stage of the language. She argues that such an analysis also accounts for the fact that a range of other constructions in which the speaker does not commit to the veracity of the facts also can take the subjunctive in Old French. Winter concludes by arguing that an explanatory theory is best based on something as broad and multifaceted as human cognition (functioning to assign salience, compare, categorize, etc.) which can then better account for the multiplicity of synchronic meanings and also for various directions of change.

Dreer's chapter, "The Use of the Future and the Conditional in High Medieval Literature," considers the distribution of the future and conditional moods in Old French within the framework of the Columbia School Theory. As he notes, the basic premise of this theory is that language is a symbolic tool of human communication. This definition implies mainly that language is a communicative device, made up of an inventory of Saussurean signs, (i.e., distinct signals and their invariant meanings), whose use contributes to particular communicative purposes.

Dreer's central claim is that the Old French speaker (encoder) uses the future to indicate to the listener (decoder) that a future event is likely, and the conditional when the possibility of an occurrence is uncertain. He terms these, respectively, Future Occurrence and Future Occurrence Questioned; they represent communicative strategies within the theoretical framework that he assumes. Significantly, in Dreer's analysis, these differences in distribution reflect a difference in meaning, although he notes that these differences may be subtle.

For example, he argues that the future can be found to express an order that the speaker assumes will be fulfilled, or to an outcome that he will do his best to see through, for example: *Seigners baruns, a Carlemagnes irez* 'Lord Barons, you shall go to Charlemagne (Chanson de Roland lines 70–72), *Certes, ja mes ne vus faldrai* 'Rest assured that I will never fail you (Le Fraisne 65:291.298). Even though these outcomes are not guaranteed, they still reflect, in his view, more certainty on the part of the speaker. For Dreer, the conditional, on the other hand, throws the entire claim into doubt: *Ki bien voldreit raisn entendre*, 'Anyone who would want to (i.e., is willing to) listen to reason.' (*Equitan* 52, lines 311–314).

Dreer tests his theory in a detailed statistical study based on 362 examples of the future and 116 of the conditional from *Le roman de Tristan*. He notes that in the first part of the novel, the conditional is found far more frequently than in the second part, which he attributes to the fact that in the first half, the characters either do not control events or their lives are at stake (i.e., they are unsure as to their future). Dreer's conclusion is that the opposition of the OF Future and Conditional constitutes an example of a language system that was used to deal with future occurrences.

There are two chapters that consider semantic aspects of Old French, but their focus is very different. Cyril Aslanov's contribution, "Crusaders' Old French," addresses the issue of language contact, and to that end, considers a broad snapshot of Levantine Old French. Harald Völker, on the other hand, in his chapter "The Diasystem and its Role in Generating Meaning: Diachronic Evidence from Old French," bases his analysis on an in-depth study of the evolution of four words. Yet there is a basic thread for both chapters, as they emphasize the importance of extralinguistic influence.

Aslanov's chapter calls into question the notion of the impermeability of language systems. To this end, he shows that the Cypriot Greeks, who worked as notaries in the court of Lusignan, sometimes hesitated between two forms – one Italo-Romance and the other French. He claims that once transplanted into a place where they stayed in constant contact, Old French and Italian were part of the same ecolinguistic horizon. Under those circumstances, he argues, a grey zone emerged where it was difficult to distinguish between Italianized Old French and Gallicized Italian.

For Aslanov, other unique characteristics of Levantine Old French can be traced back to the process of *koineization* on the basis of dialects pertaining mainly to the continuum stretching from Picardy to Burgundy. He notes that in the Kingdom of Jerusalem, a specific *koiné* emerged with dialectal components that were quite different from the Parisian *koiné*. The latter was a product of more central dialects which produced a specific blend on the basis of which Middle French emerged during the fourteenth century. Thus, he claims that the Levantine *koiné* with its Cypriot continuation, represents an alternative to the processes that occurred in France itself.

Finally, Aslanov argues that the contact between Crusaders' Old French with Armenian, Arabic and Greek displays interesting dynamics of Orientalization/ Occidentalization. He notes that the Middle Armenian used in the Kingdom of Little Armenia in Ciliciam, as it was in contact with Old French, integrated several Old French terms relating to jurisprudence and feudalism. Likewise, he shows that the Demotic Greek of Peloponnesus and Cyprus received a huge importation of Romance words, mostly from Old French. Conversely, Levantine Old French was receptive to the influence of Arabic, especially as far as the lexical items were concerned, some of which of have survived into Modern French.

Völker provides a lexico-semantic contribution regarding diasystematical marking and its dynamics in the lexicon. He argues that the source of diasystematic marking can be either intralinguistic by a *signifié* (Saussure) or extra-linguistic. For his study, he adopts the theoretical framework of variational linguistics, developed by Flydal (1952) and Weinreich (1954). Völker claims that a representation of the native speaker's lexical competence must be included in any principles account of the evolution of the diasystem. This will, in turn, he argues, allow us to better grasp the process of semiosis and to refine a theory of the mental lexicon.

In a language like Old French, Völker notes that it is impossible to present the cultural framework within which native speakers organized their lexicon or its discourse traditions. He points out that we simply cannot determine the contexts of the medieval *parole*. However, it is possible, in his view, to recontextualize texs and formalize the Old French diasystem, and in so doing, capture the malleability of the lexicon. He argues that this is actually easier in a language like Old French (in which only texts are available) than in Modern French, as native speakers of the modern language are unable to pinpoint the role of semiosis in the meaning of cotexts and context.

According to Völker, there is a diachronic filter that stems from either the evolution of French, or from the fact that scholars can only observe, and not directly access, the lexical organization. He argues that the study of historical lexical units can contribute greatly to our understanding of semiosis in general. He concludes by claiming that if we regard the *siginfié* aspect of semantic malleability from a variationist perspective, we are able to take into account the effect of lexical deterioration across time.

In sum, the 17 chapters in this volume further our understanding of language change and language systems in important ways. The studies illustrate unequivocally that historical linguistics can contribute a great deal to the discussion of a broad range of linguistic topics that are currently being debated in the literature. Using Old French as a linguistic laboratory, the studies are devoted to a broad range of topics and grounded within diverse theoretical frameworks. They approach data in very different ways, some considering only a snapshot of grammatical elements, and others basing their study on large corpora. Because of these unique features, this volume not only gives us a more complete picture of the current study of Old French as a discipline, but also provides an overview of ground-breaking linguistic research.

References

Adams, Marianne. 1987. Old French and the theory of pro-drop. *Natural Language and Linguistic Theory* 5(1): 1–32.
Andersen, Henning. 2001a. Markedness and the theory of linguistic change. In *Actualization. Linguistic change in progress*, ed. H. Andersen, 21–57. Amsterdam/Philadelphia: John Benjamins.
Andersen, Henning. 2001b. Actualization and the (uni)directionality of change. In *Actualization. Linguistic change in progress*, ed. H. Andersen, 225–248. Amsterdam/Philadelphia: John Benjamins.
Arteaga, Deborah. 1997. On null objects in Old French. In *Romance linguistics: Theoretical perspectives*, ed. Armin Schwegler, Bernard Tranel, and Myriam Uribe-Etxebarria, 1–11. Amsterdam: Benjamins.
Bauche, Henri. 1920 (1946). *Le langage populaire*. Paris: Payot.
Belletti, Adriana (ed.). 2004. *Structures and beyond: The cartography of syntactic structures*, vol. 3. Oxford: Oxford University Press.
Benincà, Paola. 2006. A detailed map of the left periphery in Romance. In *Negation, tense, and clausal architecture: Crosslinguistic investigations*, ed. Raffaella Zanuttini, Héctor Campos, Elena Herberger, and Paul Portner, 53–86. Georgetown: Georgetown University.
Benincà, Paola, and Cecilia Poletto. 2002. Topic, focus and V2: Defining the CP sublayers. In *The structure of CP and IP. The cartography of syntactic structures*, vol. 2, ed. Luigi Rizzi, 52–75. Oxford: Oxford University Press.
Blevins, Juliette. 2004. *Evolutionary phonology*. Cambridge: Cambridge University Press.

Buridant, Claude. 2000. *Grammaire nouvelle de l'ancien français*. Paris: Sedes.
Calabrese, Andrea. 1993. Palatalization processes in the history of the Romance languages: A theoretical study. In *Linguistic perspectives on the Romance languages*, ed. W.J. Ashby et al., 65–83. Amsterdam: John Benjamins.
Cerquiglini, Bernard. 1981. *La Parole médiévale*. Paris: Minuit.
Cerquiglini, Bernard. 1984. Le Style indirect libre et la modernité. *Langages* 73: 7–16.
Chomsky, Noam. 1995. *The minimalist program*. Cambridge, MA: MIT Press.
Chomsky, Noam. 2001. Derivation by phase. In *Ken Hale: A life in language*, ed. M. Kenstowicz, 1–52. Cambridge, MA: MIT Press.
Cinque, Guglielmo (ed.). 2002. *Functional structure in DP and IP: The cartography of syntactic structures*, vol. 1. Oxford: Oxford University Press.
Cinque, Guglielmo (ed.). 2006. *Restructuring and functional heads: The cartography of syntactic structures*, vol. 4. Oxford: Oxford University Press.
Clements, George Nick, and Elisabeth Hume. 1995. The internal organization of speech sounds. In *The handbook of phonological theory*, ed. J.A. Goldsmith, 245–306. Cambridge, MA: Blackwell.
Colina, Sonia, Antxon, Olarrea, and Ana Carvalho. 2010. *The Romance linguistics continuum: Crossing boundaries and linguistic categories*. Amsterdam: John Benjamins.
Coseriu, Eugenio. 1973. *Sincronía, diacronía e historia. El problema del cambio lingüístico* (tr. fr. T. Verjans, *Texto !* [en ligne] – 2007). Madrid: Gredos Biblíoteca románica hispánica.
De Lage, Guy. 1975. *Introduction à l'ancien français*. Paris: Société d'édition d'enseignement supérieur.
Detges, Ulrich. 2008. How useful is case morphology? The loss of the Old French two-case system within a theory of preferred argument structure. In *The role of semantic, pragmatic, and discourse factors in the development of case*, Studies in language companion series, ed. Jóhanna Barðdal and Shobhana Chelliah, 93–120. Amsterdam: Benjamins.
Einhorn, Esabe Carmen. 1975. *Old French: A concise handbook*. Cambridge: Cambridge University Press.
Flydal, Leiv. 1952. Remarques sur certains rapports entre le style et l'état de langue. *Norsk Tidsskrift for Sprogvidenskap* 16: 241–258.
Foulet, Lucien. 1982. *Petite syntaxe de l'ancien français*. Paris: Librairie Honoré Champion.
Gadet, François. 2003. *La Variation sociale en français*. Paris-Gap: Ophrys.
Gess, Randall. 2008. More on (distinctive!) vowel length in historical French. *Journal of French Language Studies* 18: 175–187.
Gess, Randall, and Deborah Arteaga (eds.). 2006. *Historical Romance linguistics: Retropectives and perspectives*. Amsterdam: Benjamins.
Guion, Susan. 1998. The role of perception in the sound change of velar palatalization. *Phonetica* 55: 18–52.
Herschensohn, Haike. (ed.). 2011. *Romance linguistics 2010*. Amsterdam: Benjamins.
Jacobs, Haike. 1993. La palatalization gallo-romane et la représentation des traits distinctifs. In *Architecture des représentations phonologiques*, ed. B. Laks and A. Rialland, 147–171. Paris: CNRS Éditions.
Jensen, Frede. 1990. *Old French and comparative Gallo-Romance syntax*. Tübingen: Max Niemeyer Verlag.
Kavitskaya, Darya. 2002. Compensatory Lengthening. Phonetics, phonology, diachrony. New York/London: Routledge.
Lahiri, Aditi, and Vincent Evers. 1991. Palatalization and coronality. In *The special status of coronals. Internal and external evidence*, ed. C. Paradis and J.-F. Prunet, 79–100. San Diego: Academic.
Lightfoot, David. 1999. *The development of language: Acquisition, change, and evolution*. Oxford: Blackwell.
Marchello-Nizia, Christiane. 1985. *Dire le vrai: l'adverbe "si" en français médiéval. Essai de linguistique historique*. Genève: Droz.

Marchello-Nizia, Christiane. 1999. *Le Français en diachronie: douze siècles d'évolution*. Gap/Paris: Ophrys.
Marnette, Sophie. 2005. *Speech and thought presentation in French: Concepts and strategies*. Amsterdam/Philadelphia: John Benjamins.
Mayerthaler, Willi. 1981. *Morphologische Natürlichkeit*. Wiesbaden: Athenaion.
McCarthy, Daniel P. 2007. *Hidden generalizations. Phonological opacity in optimality theory*. London: Equinox.
Ohala, John J. 1992. What's cognitive, what's not in sound change. In *Diachrony within synchrony: Language history and cognition*, ed. G. Kellerman and M.D. Morrissey, 309–355. Frankfurt: Lang.
Pearce, Elisabeth. 1990. *Parameters in Old French syntax: Infinitival complements*. Dordrecht: Kluwer.
Plauché, Madeleine, Cristina Delogu, and John J. Ohala. 1997. Asymmetries in consonant confusion. In *Proceedings of Eurospeech'97: Fifth European conference on speech communication and technology*, vol. 4, 2187–2190. New York/London: Routledge.
Rizzi, Luigi. 1997. The fine structure of the left periphery. In *Elements of grammar*, ed. Liliane Haegeman, 281–337. Dordrecht: Kluwer.
Rizzi, Luigi (ed.). 2004. *The structure of CP and IP: The cartography of syntactic structures*, vol. 2. Oxford: Oxford University Press.
Roberts, Ian. 1993. *Verbs and diachronic syntax: A comparative history of English and French*. Dordrecht: Foris.
Rychner, Jean. 1980. La Présence et le point de vue du narrateur dans deux récits courts: *Le Lai de Lanval* et *La Châtelaine de Vergi*. *Vox Romanica* 39: 86–103.
Rychner, Jean. 1987. Messages et discours doubles. In *Studies in medieval French and literature presented to Brian Woledge in honour of his 80th birthday*, ed. S Burch-North, 145–161. Geneva: Droz.
Togeby, Knud. 1974. *Précis historique de grammaire française*. Odense Akademisk Forlag.
Vance, Barbara. 1997. *Syntactic change in medieval French*. Dordrecht: Kluwer.
Verjans, Thomas. 2009. *Essai de systématique diachronique: genèse des conjonctions dans l'histoire du français (9e – 17e siècles)*. PhD, Paris-Sorbonne University Verlag.
Weinreich, Uriel. 1954. Is a structural dialectology possible? *Word* 10: 388–400.
Wurzel, Wolfgang. 1984. *Flexionsmorphologie und Natürlichkeit*. Berlin: Akademie.

Part I
Diachronic Studies

Chapter 2
A Diachronic View of Old French Genitive Constructions

Deborah Arteaga and Julia Herschensohn

2.1 Introduction

As noted by Arteaga (1995), Delfitto and Paradisi (2009, henceforth D and P), Arteaga and Herschensohn (2010, henceforth A and H), Old French (OF) and Modern French (Mod FR) shared certain genitive structures, but not others. For example, OF, like Mod FR, had a wide range of genitive structures including those with *à*, (type *un ami à moi* 'a friend of mine') and those with *de* (type *la tête de la femme* 'the head of the woman'). The most important difference between OF and Mod FR genitive structures was the existence of the so-called juxtaposition genitive (JG) in OF but not in Mod FR, which could be either postnominal (type *la niece le duc* 'the niece of the duke'), or prenominal (*la duc niece* or *le duc niece*).

In this chapter, we adopt the general analysis of OF genitive constructions mapped out by A and H and D and P. Unlike these articles, however, we focus on the diachronic evolution of the genitive from Latin to OF and then to Mod FR. We seek to answer the following questions:

1. Why was the JG lost?
2. What explains the change of distribution of the prepositional genitives?
3. How does the evolution of the genitive from Latin to Mod FR broaden our understanding of language change in general?

D. Arteaga (✉)
Department of Foreign Languages, University of Nevada,
Las Vegas, NV, USA
e-mail: deborah.arteaga@unlv.edu

J. Herschensohn
Department of Linguistics, University of Washington,
Seattle, WA, USA
e-mail: herschen@u.washington.edu

In the following sections we first review the genitive constructions of Latin, Late Latin, OF and Mod FR. We next provide background concerning our theoretical framework, the Minimalist Program (cf. Chomsky 1995) and provide accounts of the possessive constructions in Latin, OF and Mod FR. We then consider the development of the various genitive constructions, including the loss of the juxtaposition genitive (both types). We then discuss the change in distribution of prepositional genitives, and finally, how the evolution from Latin to OF to Mod FR informs our view of diachronic change in general.

2.2 Latin Genitive Constructions

Traditional philologists (Jensen 1990; Ménard 1988; Moignet 1988; Westholm 1899) note that Latin genitive structures are the source for those found in OF. The oldest structure found in Latin is the JG. In such structures, the possessor could either precede or follow the possessed without an intervening preposition (e.g., Ménard 1988:27; Anglade 1965:155) and the possessor (in bold) was marked by genitive case[1]:

(1) ***Regis***   *filius*
king-m-sg-gen son-m-sg-nom

filius   ***Regis***
son-m-sg-nom king-m-sg-gen

'the son of the king'

(2) ***dei***   *gratia*
God-m-sg-gen grace-f-sg-nom

gratia   ***dei***
grace-f-sg-nom God-m-sg-gen

'God's grace'

Compare (3)–(4) below (Westholm 1899:2):

(3) *Illic est* ***Philocomasio*** *custos*
Here is-3sg Philocomasiu-gen-m-sg guardian-nom-m-sg
'Here is Philocomasiu's guardian.'
           (Plautus Mil 272)

---

[1] The following abbreviations are used : m = masculine, f = feminine, neut = neuter, sg = singular, pl = plural, nom = nominative, gen = genitive, dat = dative, obl = oblique, abl = ablative, imp = imperative, def = definite, spec = specific, 1-2-3 = first-second-third person.

(4) *illic   est   **Philocomasii**   custos*
    Here   is-3sg   Philocomasiu-dat-m-sg   guardian-nom-m-sg
    'Here is Philocomasiu's guardian.'
                        (Plautus Mil 1431)

Note that in (3) the possessor, *Philocomasio*, precedes the possessed, *custos*, which is in the nominative case (Ménard 1988). In Later Latin, the possessor noun could also be in the dative case (4). The strong link in Latin between the dative and genitive case is particularly important for the evolution of genitive structures in OF.

The preposition *de* 'from, of' is also found with a genitive use in Popular Latin (e.g., the works of Plautus, Meyer-Lübke 1888) expressing possession (Westholm 1899). An example can be found in (5)–(6) below (Jensen 1990:24):

(5) *unos   **multorum***
    one-nom-m-sg of.many-gen-m-sg
    'One of many.'

(6) *unus   de   **multis***
    one-nom-m-sg of   many-dat-m-sg
    (=5)

As seen by (5) and (6) above, the genitive *multorum* alternated with the structure *de multis* (dative).

Another genitive structure found in Later Latin (Meyer-Lübke 1888:375), was one construed with *a/ad* 'to':

(7) *hic   requiescunt   membra*
    here   lie-3pl   remains-nom-neut-sg

   ad duus   *fratres*   *Gallo et   Fidencio*
   to two-dat-m-pl   brothers-dat-m-pl   Gallo and Fidencio

   qui feorunt   fili   ***Magno***
   who were-3pl the sons-nom-m-pl   Magno-dat-m-sg

   et   vixerunt   in pace.
   and   lived-3pl   in peace-ablat-f-sg
   'Here lie the remains of two brothers Gallo and Fidencio who were sons of Magnus and lived in peace.'

In (7) above the prepositional phrase *ad duus fratres* indicates possession, despite the fact that *duus fratres* is in the accusative. Note further that the proper noun *Magno* is in the dative, not genitive, case.

To summarize, Classical Latin preferred genitives with no intervening preposition (JG). The head noun could precede the possessor or follow it. In Later Latin, prepositional genitives, in which the dative alternated with the genitive to indicate possession, were also found.

2.3 Old French Genitive Constructions

Like Latin, OF evinced several genitive structures.[2] We begin by considering prepositional genitives as described by traditional philologists. We then look at JG genitives, a structure no longer found in Mod FR.

2.3.1 Prepositional Genitives

2.3.1.1 Genitive with à

In OF, possession could be indicated with the preposition *à*, such as in the following:

(8) *les   piés   au   cheval*
    the   feet-obl-m-pl   to the-obl-m-sg   horse-obl-m-sg
    'The feet of (literally 'to') the horse.'

(Renart 1.1498)
(Herslund 1980:84)

(9) *chastel   as   puceles*
    the castle-nom-m-sg   to.the-obl-f-pl   maidens-obl-f-pl
    'The castle of (literally 'to') the maidens.'

(Queste 46.29)

(10) *fille   ad   un   comte*
     daughter-nom-f-sg   to   a-obl-m-sg   count-obl-m-sg
     'She was the daughter of (literally 'to') a count.'

(St. Alexis, 42)

Note that the possessor could be definite, *les* (*à+les=as*) *puceles* as in (9), or indefinite, as in (10) *un comte*.[3] However, in all cases, the possessor is specific

---

[2] An anonymous reviewer notes that the JG is relatively rare and that our analysis is not based on a corpus. However, we have culled examples from scores of philologists, so that our analysis is based on empirical data. The relative rarity of JG does not exempt it from investigation; on the contrary, we find this construction sheds new light on the diachronic development of OF. Another anonymous reviewer, noting Kibler's (1984) suggestion that the JG is limited to possessors represented by kinship, rank profession or "God," indicates that "this could already represent a narrowing down of a previously more general construction."

[3] This is contra D and P who argue that the genitive with *à* was normally used with indefinite articles and could not be iterated (p. 298).

[+spec]. The possessor is not necessarily human [+hum], as (8) indicates. This construction is quite common in Modern Spoken French (see Joseph 1988), as in structures like the following:

(11) *L'ami à ma soeur.*
'My sister's friend.' (literally, 'The friend to my sister.')

However, the distribution of *à* genitives is not identical in Mod FR and OF. In Mod FR the *à* genitive is limited to [+human] possessors (Grevisse 1993:531–533). Unlike Mod FR, OF also evinced genitive with *à* constructions in which the possessor is animate, but not human, as seen in (8) above. To summarize, then, in OF, *à* genitives could be used with definite or indefinite possessors, providing that they were animate.[4] We next turn to the genitive with *de*.

2.3.1.2 Genitive with *de*

It is widely accepted that genitive structures with *de* have the widest distribution in OF. Consider (12)–(13) below[5]:

(12) *la pel du lou*
the-nom-f-sg skin-nom-f-sg of.the-obl-m-sg wolf-obl-m-sg
'The skin of the wolf.'

(Renart 10.1622)

(13) *fiz de sa sorur*
son-nom-m-sg of his-obl-f-sg sister-obl-f-sg
'The son of his sister.'

(Brut 9141)

(14) *sor le bort de la nef*
on the-obl-m-sg bord-obl-m-sg of the-obl-f-sg ship-obl-f-sg
'on board the ship' '(literally 'on the board of the ship')

(Queste 100.31)
(Herslund 1980:84)

These structures could occur before any kind of article and with animate and inanimate possessors. In (12) the possessor *lou* is [+animate, -human]; in (13) the possessor *sa sorur* is [+animate, +human], and in (14) it is [-animate, -human]

---

[4] Philogists (inter alia Togeby 1974; Foulet 1928/1982; Jensen 1990) argue that the genitive with *à* is found when the possessor is indefinite or plural. However, there are counterexamples from the literature that illustrate that this is a tendency only.

[5] Examples (17)–(19) are taken from Herslund (1980:84).

(*la nef*). Therefore, the *de* genitive differed from the *à* genitive in that it could be used with inanimate possessors (14). The two prepositional structures patterned similarly, however, with respect to the feature [+spec]. We next turn to the JG.

2.3.2 The Juxtaposition Genitive

2.3.2.1 The Postposed JG

Like Latin, in OF possession could be indicated by the JG (Arteaga 1995; Delfitto and Paradisi (2009; A and H 2009). Recall that in such structures, there is no intervening preposition between the head noun and the possessor. Yet OF was different from Latin in that it only had two cases (rather than five), nominative (sentential subject) and oblique (all other functions). In OF, while the possessor was obligatorily in the oblique case, the case of the head noun depended on its grammatical function in the sentence. The most common of the JG structures in OF was the DP that was possessed followed by the possessor, as in (15):

(15)   *la*   *chambre*   **son**   ***pedre***
       the-obl-f-sg   room-obl-f-sg   his-obl-m-sg   father-obl-m-sg
       'The room of his father' (Literally, 'the room his father')

(St. Alexis 75)

(16)   *La*   *niece*   ***le***   ***duc***   *manoit*[6]
       the-nom-F-sg niece-nom-f-sg the-obl-m-sg duke-obl-m-sg remained-3sg
       'The duke's niece remained.'
                    (La Chasteleine de Vergi 376)
                    (Foulet 1928/1982:14)

(17)   *des*   *chevaliers*
       some-obl-m-pl knights-obl-m-pl

       le   *roi*   ***Artu***
       the-obl-m-sg king-obl-m-sg Arthur-obl-m-sg
       'Some of King Arthur's knights'

(Mort 5.6)
(Herslund 1980:119)

---

[6] Cited in Arteaga (1995).

(18) et cil   a   prise   et
    and this.one-nom-f-sg has-3sg taken-nom-f-sg and

    recëue   sa   fame
    received-nom-f-sg his-obl-f-sg wife-obl-f-sg

    des   mains   **un abé**
    from.the-obl-f-sg hands-obl-f-sg an abbot-obl-m-sg
    'And this one took and received his wife from the hands of an abbot.'

                    (Guillaume 1293)
                    (Herslund 1980:85)

In (15), the possessor *son pedre* is in the oblique case; the nominative would be *ses pere(s)*. In the example (16), the possessor *duc* is in the oblique case (nominative *li ducs*). In (17), *le roi Artu* is also in the oblique case (nominative *li rois Artus*), and in (18) *abé* is oblique. Note that while the possessor is invariably specific, the DP that is possessed can be either be [+spec(ific)] or [-spec(ific)]. Evidence that the crucial feature is [+specific], rather than definite or indefinite comes from examples such as (18) above, where *un abé* has the sense of *un tel abé* 'one such abbot'.[7] We next consider the prenominal JG structure.

2.3.2.2 The Preposed Juxtaposition Genitive

Another genitive construction was possible in OF, one in which the possessor preceded the DP that was possessed. This form is thought by philologists to be older than the postposed JG discussed above (*inter alia* Jensen 1990; Ménard 1988; Moignet 1988; Tobler 1921; Anglade 1965).[8] Consider the following:

(19) *Mes ne tocha   la   **deu**   merci*
    but not attained-3sg the-obl-f-sg God-obl-m-sg grace-obl-f-sg
    'But he never attained the grace of God.' (literally 'The grace God')
                    (Tobler 1921:70)
                    (Ch. Lyon 5063)

---

[7] D and P claim that the DP that is possessed is always definite in the JG structure. However, counterexamples abound. See Herslund (1980) for discussion. As for the possessor, an anonymous reviewer confirms that there are isolated cases in which it may be indefinite. However, we note that it is always [+specific]. Proper names do not usually show determiners although they are [+spec], as *Dieu* in *l'Hotel Dieu*.

[8] An anonymous reviewer points out that this genitive was far less common in OF (Foulet 1928/1982:18; also Buridant 2000: 95). This is accounted for by our analysis because the structure contains a defective phase, which is necessarily marked, and perhaps less stable for that reason. See Section 3.2.3 for details.

(20) *Car   il   fut   ja*
since he-nom-m-sg was-3sg already

de   son   pere   maisnie]
from his-obl-m-sg father-obl-m-sg household-obl-f-sg

'He was already part of the household of his father. (Literally 'the household his father.')
(Tobler 1921:70)
(Ch. Lyon 948)

In (19), the article is not that of *deu* (masculine), but rather the one corresponding to *merci*, which was feminine in OF. However, in (20), the possessive adjective is masculine oblique, indicating that it belongs to *pere*, and not *maisnie* (feminine). In both cases, the possessor is in the oblique case (cf. nominative *deus, ses pere(s)*). Previous analyses have noted that the JG is used with [+human] possessors, and have claimed that the possessor must be [+def], which cannot account for examples like (19) above. We therefore propose that the essential feature is specificity [+spec]. The JG is usually a single possessed-possessor, but there are instances of multiple instantiations, as (21) shows.[9]

(21) *le   prei*
the-obl-m-sg meadow-obl-m-sg

les   oirs   le   Pelletier
the-obl-m-sg heirs-obl-m-sg the-obl-m-sg Pelletier-obl-m-sg
'Pelletier's heirs' meadow' (literally 'The meadow the heirs the Pelletier')
Lanher (1975:117.5)
Holman (1992:142)

To summarize, in Old French, four genitive structures were found, two of which are not found in Mod FR, namely the preposed and postposed JG (cf 15–21). In the JG, the possessor could precede or follow the possessed without the use of a preposition. The two other structures, the genitive with *à* and with *de*, are found in Mod FR, although the distribution of the former is now limited to [+human] possessors, as opposed to all animate nouns, as was the case in OF. In the discussion that follows, we will return to the research questions outlined in Sect. 2.1 above:

1. Why was the JG lost?
2. What explains the change of distribution of the prepositional genitives?
3. How does the evolution of the genitive from Latin to Mod FR broaden our understanding of language change in general?

---

[9] Contra D and P's claim (p. 297) that "multiple instantiations are excluded."

2.4 Theoretical Framework

2.4.1 *Minimalism*

The program that we adopt is that of Minimalism (Chomsky 1995, 2001), a framework that has grown out of the Principles and Parameters approach (Chomsky 1981), but differs in that it advocates a streamlined computational system. Both frameworks propose an account of syntactic structures of a given language in terms of a grammar capable of generating its sentences. The current program assumes a minimal number of operations, Merge (the combination of two syntactic items) and Move, procedures that are very often triggered by feature-matching. Syntactic categories may carry interpretable (necessary for semantic interpretation to give meaning to the sentence) or uninterpretable (strictly grammatical) features. The latter represent links that are syntactically required but meaningless; they must be "valued" and then eliminated (checked off) during the course of the syntactic derivation.

For example, verbs carry person/number features that are grammatical (hence uninterpretable), while nominative subjects carry those same features as interpretable characteristics of the noun. In this case, the uninterpretable features must "look for" syntactic categories that carry interpretable features to match, value and check off the uninterpretable ones. The result is subject verb agreement, with the verb carrying person-number features that are only interpretable in terms of the subject NP. Another example of uninterpretable features includes case on nouns. Prepositions, on the other hand, which can syntactically determine case, carry the interpretable feature of case. Finally, determiners carry an interpretable [def] feature, while nouns may carry an uninterpretable [*u*def] feature that must be valued by the determiner (Lin 2008). This feature is crucial to the GJ in OF.

2.4.2 *Previous Analyses of OF Genitive Constructions*

Recall that the OF genitive constructions included possessors marked by *à* and *de* as in Mod FR (22)–(23) as well as postnominal (24) and prenominal (25)–(26) JGs.

(22) *chastel as puceles* (=(9) above)
(23) *la pel du lou* (=(12) above)
(24) *la chambre son pedre* (=(15) above)
(25) *mais il ne tocha la deu merci* (=(19) above)
(26) *Car il fut ja de son pere maisnie* (=(20) above)

The prenominal genitive must be preceded by a definite article, but this definite determiner may relate either to the possessor or the possessed as the two examples show.

2.4.2.1 Arteaga (1995)

Within the Government and Binding framework, Arteaga (1995) considers OF genitive constructions. Her conclusion is that their derivation can be explained if the presence of an agreement (AGR) projection in DPs is posited. This lexical AGR (Contreras 1992) assigns a case to genitive complements in the JG without the need for a preposition. She argues that the two JGs in OF have the same base structure. The prenominal JG is explained, in this view, by movement out of the lower NP, after which it adjoins to the AgrP of the higher DP. She further claims that if the lower D is null, the definite determiner is that of the DP that is possessed, whereas if it is the higher D that is null, the definite determiner is that of the raised possessor.

Summing up the views of traditional philologists, Arteaga (1995) notes that the three types of genitive in OF are essentially a function of lexical selection. In the case of the genitive with *à*, it was typically found when the complement noun was plural or lacked a definite determiner. The genitive with *de* was preferred when the possessor was not a person, when a whole class of individuals is designated, with proper nouns, or before a personal pronoun. Finally, the JG occurred when the possessor was human and the article definite or a proper noun. She explains the loss of the JG by the fact that AGR ceased to be available in Middle French, as the language was no longer pro-drop by the fifteenth century. She does not address the evolution of prepositional genitives, i.e., the fact that *à* came to be used with [+human] only.

2.4.2.2 Delfitto and Paradisi (2009)

D and P provide an analysis of genitive structures in OF, Old Italian, and general Romance.[10] They note that in OF, the possessor in genitives may be preceded with the prepositions *à* or *de* (cf. (8–14) above), which assign case (oblique in OF) as one of their lexical properties. The structure of possessive *de/à* constructions that they assume is as in (27), in which the head noun *voiture* 'car' moves from an IP to a position in spec D/PP.[11]

(27)   la[$_{D/PP}$_____ [[$_{IP}$ Jean [AGR° [voiture]$_j$ ... →
    la[$_{D/PP}$voiture$_j$ [de [$_{IP}$ Jean [AGR° [e]$_j$ ... 'Jean's car' (literally, 'the car of Jean')

Following Kayne (1993, 2005), D and P assume preposition insertion of *de* in the above structure to assign case to *Jean*. In fact, as an anonymous reviewer notes, the structures proposed in (27) are not clear. The movements are primarily based on Kayne's earlier proposals and do not correspond to recent assumptions within the minimalist framework (see Arteaga and Herschensohn 2010 for extended discussion).

---

[10] See d'Alessandro and Roberts (2008) for discussion of past participle agreement in defective phases, and Hartman and Zimmerman (2003) on adnominal genitives.

[11] Kayne (1993:102) uses the symbol D/P "to represent a prepositional determiner *de* (comparable to a prepositional complementizer)."

2 A Diachronic View of Old French Genitive Constructions 29

Furthermore, they provide no motivation for adopting the structure in (27) where the possessor is base generated between the D *la* and the head noun *voiture* (an order that looks similar to the prenominal JG that they do not discuss).

They deal mainly with prepositionless genitives, and limit their discussion to the postnominal JG (cf. (15)–(17)), relating it to similar genitives in other Romance and Semitic languages. They adopt Kayne's (1993) antisymmetric structure for DP in which the possessor precedes the head noun and in English can raise to spec DP (from complement of D to specifier of D), giving the Saxon genitive as *the king's horse* (cf. Adger 2003:257–258). For the OF JG, D and P (2008:299) propose the structure in (28) whereby the head N raises from IP, as does AGR/K, the "agreement-case morphology associated with the possessor constituent" into D°.

(28) la [$_{D/PP}$ [[_____ -D°][$_{IP}$ le duc [AGR/K$_k$° [niece]$_j$ ...
→
la [$_{D/PP}$ niece$_j$ [[AGR/K$_k$° -D°][$_{IP}$ le duc [e$_k$ [e]$_j$ ... 'the duke's niece'
(literally, 'the niece the duke') = (16)

The most important points are that D and P assume an AGR/K phrase that assigns objective case to the possessor in the OF JG and that the possessor and possessed leapfrog one another to be placed in the correct order. While their account is a serious attempt to link genitive structures in various Romance languages, both synchronically and diachronically, it has limitations (see A and H 2010 for detailed discussion). A major problem is that their analysis does not extend to the prenominal JG, as in (19)–(20), a shortcoming addressed in A and H.[12]

A and H propose the same structure for all genitive structures (prepositional and JG) in OF, (29):

(29) [$_{DP}$ D [$_{nP}$ ... [$_{NP}$ N [$_{KP}$[K/P [$_{DP}$ D [$_{nP}$ ... [$_{NP}$ **N-possessor**]]]]]]]]

They argue that in OF genitive structures, the possessor nouns in question carry interpretable gender and number features (e.g. [+f, -pl], cf. Bernstein 1991; Longobardi 1994; Mallén 1997) and uninterpretable case and definite features (per Lin 2008) as [$u$case], [$u$def]. The D carries interpretable [def], and there are additional functional projections such as NumP, SpecP between D and nP which likewise carry interpretable features that can value and delete the $u$features (Lin 2008). The gender, number, and case features are the same as in Mod FR. They assume that in OF prepositional genitive structures, the relational character of *à/de* carries an interpretable feature [K] (a case assigning feature) that can value and delete the [$u$case] feature of the oblique N. The head of this "possessor" complement phrase is K/P, a grammatical head that is overt, appearing as a preposition (P, *à* or *de*), or else null, appearing as K, a genitive

---

[12] Furthermore, many of their claims, such as the lack of iteration of JG or genitive with *à*, the notion that *à* genitives are almost always indefinite, and their observation that the possessor in the JG is almost always masculine, can simply not be reconciled with the data, as there are counterexamples. Discussion of these issues is beyond the scope of this paper.

case assigning interpretable feature that grounds the possessor referentially in time and space (Bittner and Hale 1996).[13] In prepositional genitive structures, as we have seen in (8)–(14), the possessor may be definite or indefinite, in which case D carries an interpretable [+/-def] feature. The [*u*def] feature of the possessor N may be valued by [+/-def] on the D, while the SpecP provides interpretable [+spec]. We assume that unlike some languages which allow *in situ* checking of features, OF DP requires a c-command relationship for case checking (e.g. the case assigning K c-commands the possessor DP embedded under it). Recall that the possessed N receives its case from a higher source (nominative through Tense or oblique often from the verb).

For the JG, on the other hand, A and H propose that the K/P head here has no overt reflex (as in overt P), but must also carry the features [*u*hum], [*u*def], [*u*spec] since those features of the JG possessor provide sufficient reference to "ground" the DP complement (cf. Pesetsky and Torrego 2004, 2009). The [hum], [def] and [spec] features of the K/P projections and the features of the possessor DP check and delete, while the interpretable case feature of the null K head deletes the [*u*case] feature of the possessor DP (cf. Pesetsky and Torrego 2004). For the postnominal JG (*la niece le duc* type), A and H adopt the structure of (29), proposing that the K/P head here has no overt preposition, but must carry the features [*u*def], [*u*hum], [*u*spec] to ensure the referentiality of the DP complement. These features of K/P are valued by the [+def] determiner and the necessarily [+hum, +spec] possessor noun *le duc*, while the null preposition of K/P deletes the oblique case of the possessor DP. According to their account, the postnominal JG construction is obtained by the feature checking and valuing of [+def], [+hum], [+spec] of the possessor DP.

For the prenominal JG, A and H assume that either the possessor or the DP that is possessed, is defective, in that it lacks D, and is thus a bare *n*P. It is an incomplete DP functional shell that requires a D to check off the uninterpretable features of the *n*P. In other words, if there is no D in the lower possessor NP, it must raise to prenominal position, as *la deu merci* or *la duc niece* using the [+def] feature of the higher D to check the [*u*def] feature of both the DP that is possessed and the possessor. Recall that in such structures, it is the definite article of the upper DP that is expressed.

In A and H's proposal, when the determiner is that of the lower DP, as *son pere maisnie* or *le duc niece*, it is the upper NP that has no D.[14] In that case, the entire lower possessor DP fronts to check off and value the uninterpretable [*u*def] feature of the upper N as well as that of the originally lower possessor noun that has been subsequently raised. This in turn explains examples like *son pere maisnie*, in which the entire lower possessor DP has fronted.

---

[13] An anonymous reviewer questions this notion, as s/he claims that a possessor may be generic. We have found no examples of generic JGs. However, articles do not appear in Old French generics. See A and H (2010) for discussion.

[14] An anonymous reviewer asks why the [*u*Def] feature of the upper N can't probe down to enter into a checking relationship with the possessor DP, that the order could remain *maisnie son père*. This is explained by our analysis because the upper phase is defective and therefore cannot enter into a checking relationship with a lower D in situ, given the c-command requirement.

2.5 New Proposal

2.5.1 Latin KP

While neither A and H nor D and P discuss Latin genitive structures, we believe that generally speaking, their analyses regarding case assignment apply to Latin as well. Pereltsvaig (2007) argues for the universality of DP whether or not a language has overt determiners or not. As noted by A and H (2010) a special case phrase (KP) is needed for case assignment in Latin within a minimalist framework. The structure we propose is the following:

(30) *filius regis* 'son of a king' (=(1))

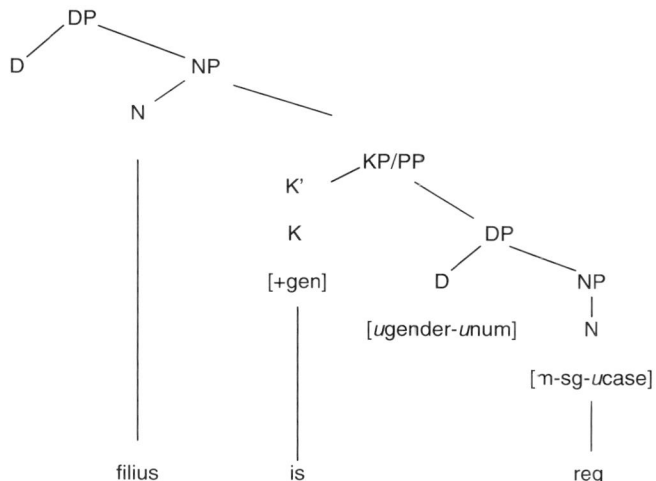

In the above structure, K carries the interpretable feature of genitive which will match and delete the [*u*case] of the possessor noun. The determiner, which is often null in Latin (except for demonstratives, possessives, quantifiers and the like), carries the uninterpretable features of number and gender and the interpretable definiteness that are not realized overtly (cf. Lin 2008 for null D in Chinese). The D feature may be either [+/-def] for it to delete the [*u*def] feature of the noun. The noun, in turn, carries the interpretable features of gender, number, [*u*case] and [*u*def].[15] To generate the correct morphology, *reg-* will raise to precede the genitive suffix *–is* as part of the spelling out of morphology.

In later Latin, however, as noted above, the prepositions *ad* and *de* were also found, suggesting that a PP alternated with KP in Proto Romance, as proposed for

---

[15] We adopt the broadly accepted terminology of [gender] as an interpretable feature of the noun (cf. Carstens 2000, 2003) although it is clearly a grammatical one with semantic interpretation only in terms of animate nouns. See also Bittner and Hale (1996).

OF by A and H (2010) and D and P. We therefore provide the following structure for the example in (7) above:

(31) *ad duus fraters* 'of the two brothers'

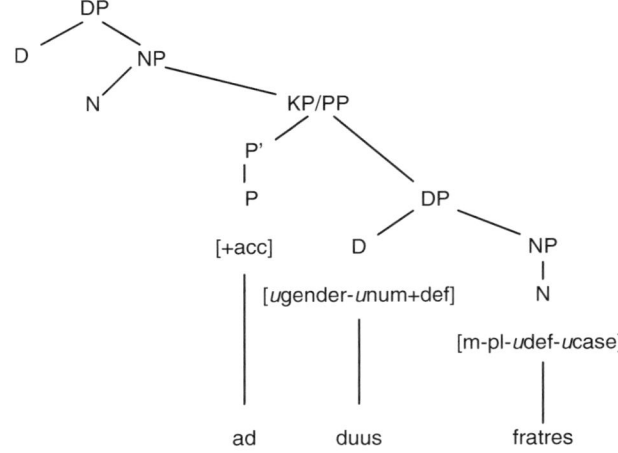

In the derivation of both (30) and (31), contra D and P's analysis of OF, we assume that in Latin genitive structures, the nouns in question carry interpretable gender and number features and uninterpretable case. Note that (30) can mean either 'the son of the king' or 'the son of a king.' This illustrates the fact that the crucial uninterpretable feature is not [+def] but rather [+spec] (cf. Ionin 2006), a feature that is determined by the discourse and speaker intent. In (31), the determiner is overt, checking and deleting [*u*spec] on the noun which, in turn, deletes the uninterpretable features of D. The overt preposition *ad* is able to check [*u*case] of the noun.

As seen by the examples above, one difference between the determiner system in Latin and OF was that the determiner in the former language could be null, yet could nonetheless express [+/-spec] and/or [+def] (Gamillscheg 1957). We therefore assume, following Lin's (2008) analysis for Mandarin Chinese, that a null definite feature could check off [*u*def] in Latin. In later Latin, demonstratives, including *illi* (Classical *ille*, f *illa*, neuter *illud*), the source of Romance articles, came to be used as definite articles expressing specificity, as in (32):

(32) *Cito   proferte   mihi   stolam*
  right.away offer-imp-2sg to.me shawl-obl-f-sg

  illam   *primam.*
  that-obl-f-sg   first-obl-f-sg
  'Offer me right away the (literally, 'that') first shawl.
              (Luke 15 v 22)
              (Grandgent 1934:36)

In the example in (32), demonstrative article *illam* modifies *stolam*, matching it in both gender (feminine) and case (accusative). We interpret this to mean that in later Latin a null determiner was losing its ability to check off and value the feature [+spec]. As the Latin demonstrative lost its deictic value and became grammaticalized into the definite article in OF, it also eventually evolved into a distinctive mark of the JG. The KP case phrase that could license genitive case in Latin evolved into what we designate as K/PP in OF. As argued above, the JG allows a null preposition, but carries the [*u*def] and [*u*spec] features that require a definite article and a [+spec] DP. We will see that by Middle French the [*u*spec] and [*u*hum] features of the K/P and null preposition are no longer sufficient to indicate the possessor relationship, thus leading to the requirement of overt prepositions (*à* or *de*).

2.5.2 Old French KP/PP

2.5.2.1 Prepositional Genitives

As noted above, A and H propose that in OF genitives, the case assigner could either be an overt P (*à* or *de*) or in the juxtaposition genitive constructions, a null preposition. In prepositional genitives, the possessor could be [+/-def] or [+/-hum], but for the JG the possessor had to be [+/-def], [+hum],[+spec] to sufficiently identify the reference of the possessor using a null P.[16] There is independent empirical evidence for A and H's proposal that null prepositions were possible in OF. As noted by Herslund (1980), Togeby (1974), Jensen (1990), among many others, dative verbs may be construed with or without *à*, which is required in Mod FR.[17]

(33) et   le   dist   **le**   **roi**
and it-obl-m-sg said-3sg pro the-obl-m-sg king-obl-m-sg
'He said it to the king.' (literally, 'he said it the king')
(Herslund 1980:25)
(Didot-Perceval 1941)

(34) *Droit* **a mon**   **oncle**   *le*   *dirai*
directly to my-obl-m-sg uncle-obl-m-sg it-obl-m-sg will.tell-1sg pro
'I will tell it to my uncle directly.'
(Togeby 1974:56)

In (33) above, no preposition introduces the dative complement *le roi*, whereas the preposition *à* marks the dative in (34). If, however, the dative complement takes

---

[16] Most frequently the JG is [+def], but there are attested cases of [−def] [+spec].

[17] When dative verbs are construed with an object pronoun, it is invariably the dative that is used, except in North-Eastern and Anglo-Norman varieties, as pointed out by an anonymous reviewer.

an object pronoun, it is invariably the indirect (as opposed to the direct) object, as illustrated by (35):

(35) *De   moie   part   li   dites*
     from my-obl-f-sg   part-obl-f-sg   to.him   say-imp-2sg
     'Tell him from me'
                                    Herslund (1980:25)
                                    (Barbastre 3611)

The fact that in (35) above, only the dative pronoun in francien *li* is possible (as opposed to the accusative pronoun *le*) further demonstrates that dative verbs took a dative complement in OF whether or not an overt preposition (*à*) introduced the full lexical DP.[18] The complement of dative verbs is usually [+human] in OF as in Mod FR.

We assume, therefore, that the OF prepositional genitives were structured as in Latin and Mod FR with *à* and *de*, thus continuing the Proto Romance alternation of a PP with KP. We provide in (36) the structure for the example in (10) above:

(36) *la fille ad un comte* 'the daughter of a count' (=10)

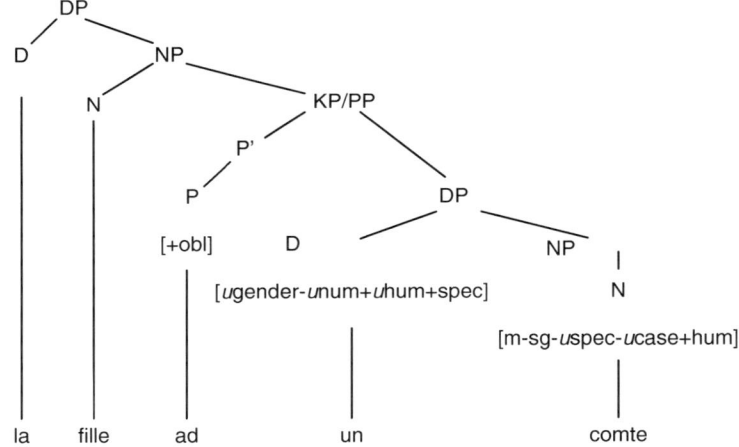

In (36) the uninterpretable features (number and gender) of the D match and are deleted by the interpretable features (masculine singular) of the N, whereas the uninterpretable feature of N (specific) is matched and deleted by the interpretable counterpart of D.

2.5.2.2 Juxtaposition Genitives

For the JG, we assume then—continuing the KP structure seen in late Latin—that OF allowed possessors to be complements of the head (possessed) NP, introduced by either a an overt or null preposition in K/PP. When the P was overt, it could assign case to the possessor; if P were null, the additional stipulations of the

---
[18] An anonymous reviewer notes that Anglo-Norman continued to have the JG even after the decline of the case system. Due to space limitations, we are unable to address dialectal variation in this paper.

2   A Diachronic View of Old French Genitive Constructions   35

human-definite-specific features were required, thus excluding indefinites such as *[ad] un comte*. The JG had a structure similar to (36), but further required that the possessor be [+spec], [+hum] as illustrated by (37):

(37) *La chambre son père* 'the room of his father'

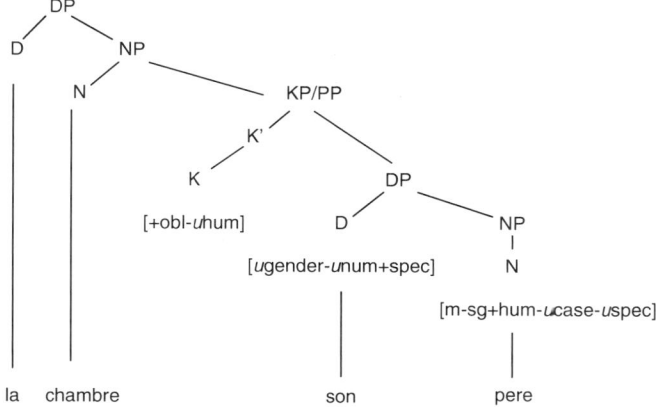

In (37) the uninterpretable features of the D (gen, num) are valued and deleted by the interpretable gender and number of *pere*, while its [*u*spec] feature is matched by the definite determiner. The noun's [*u*case] is matched by the interpretable oblique feature of K/P that is licensed by [+def, +hum]; the uninterpretable K/P feature [*u*human] is valued by the noun.

For the prenominal JG, recall that either the possessor or the possessed is defective, lacking D, which is needs to check off *u*features, as in (38):

(38) *la deu merci* 'the mercy of God' (=25)

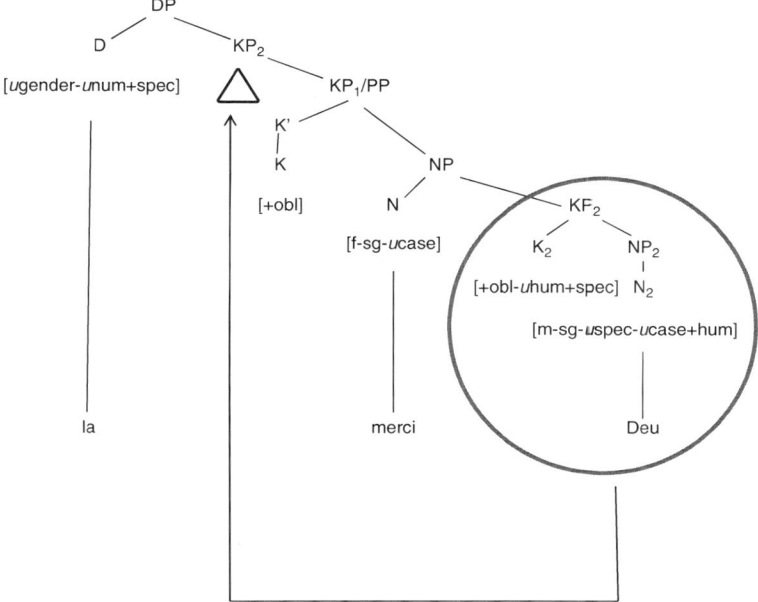

If there is no D in the lower possessor NP_2, it must raise to prenominal position, as *la deu merci*, using the [+def] feature of the higher D to check the [*u*def] feature of both the possessed and the possessor. Recall that in such structures, it is the definite article of the upper DP that is expressed. If the higher NP_1 is defective, the non-defective DP_2 raises to furnish the features [+def+spec] as in *son pere maisnie*.

Our analysis can account for the fact that the prenominal JG is older, because it is part of a defective phase, which is marked as it is not the norm. Our analysis differs from both D and P and A and H, in that the possessor must be [+spec]; it may be either [+-def]. What is crucial to our analysis is that the [*u*spec] feature may be valued by [+spec] on the D. We next turn to our diachronic analysis from Old French to Mod FR.

2.5.3 Modern French

With the loss of the OF dual case system, possessors could no longer be oblique complements of the head (possessed) NP, introduced by a null preposition. Either the preposition *à* or *de* was now required, and their distribution became more specialized. No longer was there a definiteness restriction (as for the JG) on the possessor, and *de* became the general all-purpose genitive marker. The preposition *à* now became limited to [+human] possessors as in *un ami à moi*. In our view, the Mod FR prepositional genitives are structured as in Latin and OF with *à* and *de*, although they only continue the PP. We provide in (39) the following structure for the example *fille d'un comte* 'daughter of a count' (cf. 10 above):

(39) *la fille d'un comte* 'the daughter of a count'   (cf. (10) above)

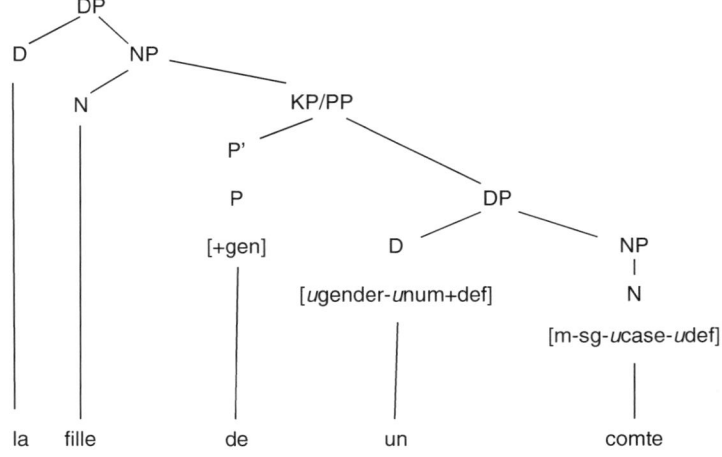

2.6 The Evolution of the OF Genitive as a Window into Language Change

The changes exemplified by the evolution of genitive structures from Latin to Mod FR show from one perspective the development of analytic morphosyntax from synthetic nominal declensions and from another perspective the interplay of morphology, phonology, and syntax. We see these changes as a gradual replacement of minimal features as native speakers reanalyze the underlying structure of their changing language. In the case at hand, the KP case phrase in Latin began sharing its function with PPs with overt prepositions in Late Latin, thus giving the prepositional and juxtaposition genitives found in Classical Latin, Late Latin and OF. The JG of OF, with its requirements of [+spec+hum] possessor, gave way to only the prepositional genitive once case morphology eroded in Middle French. In Mod FR, only prepositional genitives can license possessor complements. Crucial to our analysis, discussed below, is the proposal by Lightfoot (1999) of cue based language change (Lightfoot 1999) in the evolution of genitives in French.

2.6.1 Diachronic Evolution of OF Genitive Structures

2.6.1.1 Loss of the JG

In our view, there are several reasons for the loss of the JG. Recall that while Latin had five nominal cases, these were reduced to two in OF, nominative and oblique. The case difference was not usually seen in the feminine (except in imparisyllabic nouns whose nominative and oblique forms had differing numbers of syllables, and in nouns ending in consonants, Pope 1934:312–313), but rather was evident in the masculine whose nominative singular and oblique plural were distinguished by final –*s*. Consonants (especially [s/z]) were effaced in final and preconsonantal positions certainly by the end of the Middle Ages (in many cases thus rendering the case marking of nominative and oblique masculine ineffective). This, in turn, resulted in the breakdown of the OF case system, at around the time that the JG was lost (Arteaga 1995). Isolated examples of the JG may be found after that time, but they are considered to be archaisms (Grevisse 1993; Herslund 1980; Palm 1977).

The loss of the case system in nominals related to the morphological leveling that resulted in part from the loss of final consonants and in part from a shift from synthetic grammatical marking (inflections on nouns and verbs as in Latin) to more analytical indication of grammatical function (prepositional phrases and word order). As Pope (1934:313) notes, "The gradual effacement of final *s* in pre-consonantal position and even elsewhere rendered the flexional system often inoperative; the increasing fixity of word order made it unnecessary." In our view, the fact that the case system was no longer functional meant that null prepositions were not possible: the generalization of oblique case to both nominative and accusative functions—distinguished now exclusively by word order except in the pronominal system—excluded the use of oblique as the marker of possession.

Thus a native speaker could no longer determine the relationship of a noun adjacent to another noun or as a verbal complement without an intervening preposition. This is confirmed by the fact that null *à* after dative verbs was no longer possible at the same time (Herslund 1980). The features [+spec], [+hum], [+oblique case] no longer sufficed to identify a juxtaposed possessor, so the K/P head could no longer carry a null P with the features described earlier. The overt P, either *à* or *de*, became obligatory to indicate possession, and the order of the possessor with respect to the possessed became fixed to follow the possessed NP (as was the case for all nominal complements). Finally, these changes obviated the restriction of the JG to human definites, and the distribution of prepositional genitives necessarily changed as well.

Our proposal also accounts for the earlier loss of the prenominal JG. Recall that in such structures either the definite article of the upper DP or that of the lower DP is expressed. We have argued that in such cases, the phase is defective. We would expect, therefore, that such a marked structure would be lost earlier than the postnominal JG that followed the same word order as prepositional genitives.

2.6.1.2 Change in Distribution of Prepositional Genitives

As noted above, from OF to Mod FR there has been a change in the use of genitive *à*, namely that it generally refers to [+human] in Mod FR. Grevisse (1993:531–533) provides ample examples of human pronouns and nouns, suggesting that the usage with à may be a reduction of appartenant à 'belonging to.'; Only two non-human examples are given, *l'écurie à la vache* 'the cow's stable' and *la faute à la guerre* 'war's fault.' Our explanation for this has its roots in the dative structure. According to Herslund (1980), the indirect object has always been animate and human. Consider the following example:

(40) *Dist la pucele au chevalier*
Says the-nom-f-sg maiden-nom-f-sg to.the-obl-M-sg knight-obl-m-sg
'The maiden said to the knight.'
                                        (Lancelot 1044)

Historically, *à* has usually been used for [+human] as an indirect object, a practice that is almost exclusive in Mod FR (Herschensohn 1996). The dative can exceptionally be used to individuate/personify inanimate objects and animate beings as in *donner à manger aux animaux* or *donner le nom de Joseph à l'épée*. But generally, speakers came to associate indirect object and possessive constructions headed by *à* with [+human]. The loss of JG in the fourteenth century necessitated the adoption of a preposition, and the default genitive marker for [+/-human] became *de* since it was already positioned to apply to [+/-hum, +/-def]. The preposition *à* was not simply limited to human possessors, but became lexically restricted as well in Mod FR.

2.6.2 Broader Implications: Cue Based Evolution

How does the diachronic change described in this study contribute to our more general understanding of how languages change and what the implications may be for synchronic language variation and acquisition? In order to consider these broader implications, we examine the proposal of Lightfoot (1999). He has argued that children are the vehicles of language change in that they may modify the input they receive in creating what turn out to be "new" grammars of their native language. For example, sixteenth century English, as French, used to be a language in which the inflected verb raised above negation and adverbs as in *thinks not* (cf. MF *pense pas*) instead of *does not think*. Modern English allows raising of only auxiliaries, leaving the main verb *in situ*. Lightfoot argues that young children scan their input for cues to the grammar that they are building, and if they perceive variability, they will select cues that sometimes generalize to a grammar that differs from that of their parents—a non-raising pattern for verbs in English, for example. Why would children construct "new grammars"? According to Lightfoot (1999:202), "children need evidence to establish the category that a lexical item belongs to. That evidence might be distributional, inflectional or paradigmatic." We next explore each of these characteristics with respect to the genitive structures we have examined in the earlier sections, most particularly the total displacement of JG from OF by the prepositional genitive of Mod FR.

In terms of distribution, the JG already had competition from *à* and *de* in late Latin and in OF, so children were exposed to variable input, first in terms of JG and prepositional, but also in terms of the post- and prenominal JG and its variable determiner. The JG was further limited to [+hum+def+spec] DPs, reducing further its generalizability, while *à* genitives were limited to [+animate]. If we look at salience, one must conclude that overt prepositions are more salient than null ones, and the obvious winner in the competition would probably be the most generally used P, *de*. A final note on distribution is that the definite article—along with oblique case, which is the principal overt morphology indicating possession for the JG—was not used in OF for generic (41) and abstract noun phrases (42), both of which are [-spec]:[19]

(41) *Pechiez   le m' a   tolut*
sin-nom-m-sg him to.me has-3sg taken.away-nom-m-sg
'Sin took him away from me' (cf. Mod FR *Le peché*)
(Saint Alexis 108)

---

[19] Although see Gamillscheg (1957:90) who argues that with abstract nouns, the definite article is present from the earliest texts when they refer to "concrete cases." He cites three examples, in all of which the definite article has a possessive function. For example, *Guardez, de nos ne turnez le curage* (Roland 650) 'Watch that you do not turn away from your courage. '

(42) *Galois   sont   tuit   par   nature*
Gauls-nom-m-pl are-3pl all-nom-m-pl by   nature-obl-f-sg

plus fol   que bestes   an   pasture
more crazy-nom-m-sg than beasts-nom-f-pl at   pasture-obl-f-sg
'The Gauls are all by nature crazier than animals at pasture.'
(cf. Mod FR *Les Gaulois*)
(Perceval 241–242)
(Foulet 1928/1982:51)

In (41), the abstract noun *Pechiez* is unaccompanied by an article. Similarly, in (42), there are three generics that are not introduced by a definite article, *Galois*, *bêtes*, and *nature*.[20]

The use of the definite article spread to generics around the fourteenth century, thus eliminating the link between specificity and definiteness. The increased functional load of definite articles in Middle French would further reduce the interpretability of definite articles, making the JG a poor cue for children learning the language.

In terms of inflection, we have already noted that the inflectional systems first of Latin and later of OF experienced morphological erosion that represented a shift from synthetic grammatical marking to analytical (separate grammatical words and fixed word order). The exclusive use of the genitive case with free word order JG in classical Latin was supplemented in later Latin with the prepositional genitives using *ad* and *de*. These same constructions were used in OF, which had two cases (reduced from five in Latin), with oblique serving as direct object, indirect object, and genitive object, all of which permitted null prepositions.

The loss of final consonants in late Old French (cf. Chap. 9 by Schøsler, Chap. 7 by Lindschouw, Chap. 5 by Gess, this volume) led to several changes that influenced the cues that children would have received. Speakers no longer made the distinction between nominative and oblique for masculine and consonant final feminine nouns, since the final –*s* was lost. Similarly, the loss of –*s* obviated the distinction between singular and plural for all nouns so that the burden of marking plurality fell to the determiner (see (41)–(42) above). Partially due to this shift, determiners became obligatory, and thus grammaticalized, in French, and the null determiner which had formerly signaled [-spec] generic DPs gave way to the definite article. The JG then experienced two factors that contributed to its non-distinctness as a means of marking possession by a juxtaposed DP: oblique case was no longer distinctive as an indication of case, and definiteness was no longer a distinct mark of referential specificity. Objective case, the non-nominative case, had to be assigned by either a verb (direct object) or by an overt preposition; the option of a K/PP with a null preposition was lost.

---

[20] In Mod FR either *par la nature* or *par nature* is found, the latter of which is a fixed expression.

Finally, considering paradigmatic data, we see that the converging tendencies described above contributed to paradigm leveling, which in turn further marginalized the JG. The loss of the two case nominal system resulted in the domination of the objective form (generalized to both masculine and feminine as no marker in singular and –s in plural for orthography) for nouns and articles. But because the orthographic –s was lost in spoken French, it was only the articles (e.g. *le/la* singular, *les* plural) that distinguished number. Imparisyllabic nouns—the most saliently marked nouns case-wise—were eliminated since usually only the oblique form survived. Paradigm leveling is not a primary factor in the loss of JG, but it is definitely concurrent. If paradigm identification helps learners to master morphological alternations, then the leveling could be seen as effecting change. Lightfoot's criteria seem to hold, for it certainly appears that the converging morphosyntactic changes engendered by phonological evolution provided children with at first variable and then non-existent cues that led them to restructure the genitive marking of possessor nouns in Middle and Mod FR. Alternately, the same forces might be seen as affecting teenagers or adults in their use of the language; the mechanisms of past language change cannot be known for sure.

2.7 Conclusion

In this paper, we have considered the evolution of genitive structures from Latin to OF. We first introduced Latin data, followed by a presentation of the dative in OF. Our analysis differs from earlier ones in that we argue that the possessor in all genitive structures in OF must be [+spec], not merely [+def], as an indefinite article could occasionally introduce the possessor, provided that the latter was specific. We then proposed an analysis of case marked genitive and dative in Latin and then showed how the KP case phrase of Later Latin evolved into K/PP. It is this structure which OF inherited, using a preposition, null or overt, to mark genitive and oblique case. In our view, null prepositions, which checked the case of the juxtaposition genitive and certain datives, ceased to be possible in Middle French (MidF).

We then discussed genitive structures from a diachronic viewpoint. We argued that once final consonants ceased to be pronounced, leading to the loss of the case system and the concomitant paradigmatic leveling, a child would no longer receive unambiguous input. The upshot of this is that speakers ceased to use the JG. This also explains the fact that the dative pronoun *à* not only became obligatory, but was almost exclusively limited to [+human] complements, meant that the distribution of the à genitive followed suit.

Finally, we addressed the evolution of genitive structures from Latin to OF, discussing how this diachronic development has implications for language change in general.

References

Primary Sources

Chrétien de Troyes. 1912. *Li contes del graal* (Perceval), ed. Gottfried Brisgau. Bibliothèque universitaire de Fribourg.
Chrétien de Troyes. 1967. *Le Chevalier au Lion*, ed. M. Roques. Paris: Champion, CFMA.
Chrétien de Troyes. 1970. *Lancelot, le chevalier de la charrette*, éd. M. Roques. Paris: CFMA 86, Champion.
Documents linguistiques de la France, II, Vosges, ed. Jean Lanher. Paris: Centre National de la Recherche Scientifique, 1975.
La Chasteleine de Vergi, ed. G. Raynaud. Paris: Champion, CFMA, 1963.
La mort le roi Artu, ed. J. Frappier. Paris/Genève: Droz/Minard, 1964.
La Queste de Saint Graal, ed. A. Pauphilet. Paris: Champion, CFMA, 1921.
La vie de Saint Alexis, ed. Gaston Paris. Paris: Champion, CFMA, 1968.
Le siège de Barbastre, ed. J.-L. Perrier, CFMA, 1926.
Plautus *Miles Gloriosus*, 1267, ed. Robert Yelverton Tyrrell, 1844–1914. London: MacMillan.
Renart, Jean. 1962. *Le roman de la rose ou de Guillaume de Dole*, ed. F. Lecoy. Paris: CFMA.
The Didot-Perceval, 1941, ed. W. Roach. Philadelphia: University of Pennsylvania Press.
Wace. 1938–1940. *Le Roman de Brut*, 2 vol., ed. I. Arnold. Paris: SAFT.

Linguistic References

Adger, David. 2003. *Core syntax: A minimalist approach*. Oxford: Oxford UP.
Anglade, Joseph. 1965. *Grammaire élémentaire de l'ancien français*. Paris: Armand Colin.
Arteaga, Deborah. 1995. On old French genitive constructions. In *Contemporary research in Romance linguistics*, ed. Jon Amastae, Grant Goodall, Mario Montalbetti, and Marianne Phinney, 79–90. Amsterdam: J. Benjamins.
Arteaga, Deborah, and Julia Herschensohn. 2010. A phase-based analysis of Old French genitive constructions. In *Romance linguistics 2009: Selected papers from the 39th annual conference of the linguistic symposium on the romance languages*, ed. Sonia Colina, Antxon Olarrea, and Ana Maria Carvalho, 285–300. Amsterdam/Philadelphia: J. Benjamins.
Bernstein, Judith. 1991. DPs in French and Walloon: Evidence for parametric variation in nominal head movement. *Probus* 3: 101–126.
Bittner, Maria, and Ken Hale. 1996. The structural determination of case and agreement. *Linguistic Inquiry* 27: 1–68.
Buridant, Claude. 2000. *Grammaire nouvelle de l'ancien français*. Paris: Sedes.
Carstens, Vicki. 2000. Concord in minimalist theory. *Linguistic Inquiry* 31: 319–355.
Carstens, Viki. 2003. Rethinking complementizer agreement: Agree with a case–checked goal. *Linguistic Inquiry* 34: 393–412.
Chomsky, Noam. 1981. *Lectures on government and binding*. Dordrecht: Foris.
Chomsky, Noam. 1995. *The minimalist program*. Cambridge, MA: MIT Press.
Chomsky, Noam. 2001. Derivation by phase. In *Ken Hale: A life in language*, ed. Michael Kenstowicz, 1–52. Cambridge, MA: MIT Press.
Contreras, Heles. 1992. On the position of subjects. In *Syntax and semantics*, Perspectives on phrase structure: Heads and licensing, vol. 26, ed. Rothstein Susan, 63–79. London: Academic.

D'Alessandro, Roberta, and Ian Roberts. 2008. Movement and agreement in Italian past participles and defective phases. *Linguistic Inquiry* 39: 477–491.
Delfitto, Denis, and Paola Paradisi. 2009. Towards a diachronic theory of genitive assignment in Romance. In *Historical syntax and linguistic theory*, ed. Paola Crisma and Giuseppe Longobardi, 292–310. Oxford: Oxford UP.
Foulet, Lucien. 1928/1982. *Petite syntaxe de l'ancien français*. Paris: Librairie Honoré Champion.
Gamillscheg, Ernst. 1957. *Historische französische Syntax*. Tübingen: Max Niemeyer.
Grandgent, Charles. 1934. *An introduction to vulgar Latin*. New York: Hafner.
Grevisse, Maurice (refondue par André Goosse). 1993. *Le bon usage, grammaire française,* 13e ed. Paris: Editions Duclot.
Hartmann, Katharina, and Malta Zimmermann. 2003. Syntactic and semantic adnominal genitives. In *(A)symmetrien – (A)symmetric*, ed. Claudia Maienborn, 171–202. Tübingen: Stauffenburg Verlag.
Herschensohn, Julia. 1996. *Case suspension and binary complement structure in French*. Amsterdam/Philadelphia: J. Benjamins.
Herslund, Michael. 1980. *Problèmes de syntaxe de l'ancien français. Compléments datifs et génitifs*. Uppsala: Akademisk Forlag.
Holman, Robyn. 1992. The syntax of the genitive structure in thirteenth century Vosgian charters. *Romance Notes* 23: 141–149.
Ionin, Tania. 2006. This is definitely specific: Specificity and definiteness in article systems. *Natural Language Semantics* 14: 175–234.
Jensen, Frede. 1990. *Old French and comparative Gallo-Romance syntax*. Tubingen: Max Niemeyer Verlag.
Joseph, John. 1988. New French: A pedagogical crisis in the making. *The Modern Language Journal* 72: 31–36.
Kayne, Richard. 1993. *The antisymmetry of syntax*. Cambridge, MA: MIT Press.
Kayne, Richard. 2005. *Movement and silence*. Oxford: Oxford UP.
Kibler, William. 1984. *An introduction to Old French*. New York: Modern Language Association.
Lightfoot, David. 1999. *The development of language: Acquisition, change, and evolution*. Oxford: Blackwell.
Lin, Yi-An. 2008. A Probe-Goal approach to parametric variation in English and Mandarin Chinese nominal phrases. In *Proceedings of the 20th North American Conference on Chinese Linguistics (NACCL-20)*, vol. II, ed. M. Chan and Hana Kang, 775–784. Columbus: The Ohio State University.
Longobardi, Giuseppe. 1994. Reference and proper names: A theory of N-Movement in syntax and logical form. *Linguistic Inquiry* 25: 609–665.
Mallén, Enrique. 1997. A minimalist approach to concord in noun phrases. *Theoretical Linguistics* 23: 49–77.
Ménard, Pierre. 1988. *Syntaxe de l'ancien français*. Paris: Bordeaux Éditions Bière.
Meyer-Lübke, Wilhelm. 1888. Die lateinische Sprache in den romanischen Ländern. In *Grundriss der Romanischen Philologie*, ed. Gustav Gröber, 351–382. Strasbourg: Karl J. Truebner
Moignet, Guy. 1988. *Grammaire de l'ancien français*. Paris: Klincksieck.
Palm, Lars. 1977. *La construction li filz le rei et les constructions concurrentes avec à et de étudiées dans des oeuvres littéraires de la second moitié du XIIe siècle et du premier quart du XIIIe siècle*. Uppsala: Almqvist and Wiksell.
Pereltsvaig, Asya. 2007. The universality of DP: A view from Russian. *Studia Linguistica* 6: 59–94.
Pesetsky, David, and Esther Torrego. 2004. Tense, case and the nature of syntactic categories. In *The syntax of time*, ed. Jacqueline Guéron and Jacqueline Lecarme, 495–537. Cambridge, MA: MIT Press.

Pesetsky, David, and Esther Torrego. 2009. Probes, goals and syntactic categories. In *Proceedings of the 7th Annual Tokyo Conference on Psycholinguistics*, ed. Y. Otsu. Tokyo: Hituzi Syobo Publishing Company.

Pope, Mildred K. 1934. *From Latin to Modern French with especial consideration of Anglo-Norman: Phonology and morphology*. Manchester: Manchester UP.

Tobler, Adolf. 1902–1921. *Vermischte Beiträge zur Französischen Grammatik*, vol. 5. Leipzig: S. Hirzel Verlag.

Togeby, Kund. 1974. *Précis historique de grammaire française*. Odense: Akademisk Forlag.

Westholm, Alfred. 1899. *Etude historique sur la construction du type fiz le roi en français*. Unpublished PhD thesis, Vester.

Chapter 3
Grammaticalization in Progress in Old French: Indefinite Articles

Anne Carlier

3.1 Introduction

Grammars of Old French mention the existence of three articles: the definite article, originating from the Latin distal demonstrative *ille*, the indefinite article, which derives from the Latin unity numeral *unus*, and the so-called partitive article, resulting from a contraction of the preposition *de* and the definite article.[1] Although the three forms that constitute the paradigm of articles in Modern French are already attested in Old French, they do not have the same extension as their Modern French counterparts, as can be seen from the Table 3.1.

This table offers a comparison of the relative frequency of the articles in an Old French translation and in a Modern French translation of the same Latin source.[2] The figures show that the definite article is already frequent in Old French and that its extension from Old French to Modern French is relatively modest: it increases with a factor of only 1.3. As to the indefinite article *un(s)*, its evolution is more spectacular: it quadruples in frequency. Finally, there are no clear instances of the partitive article in this late Old French corpus.

---

[1] *Cf.* Foulet (1916/1998: 45–83), Price (1971: 115–120), Ménard (1973: 26–30), Moignet (1976: 100–111), and Joly (2004: 43–44). On the contrary, Revol (2000: 192) argues against giving the status of article to the contracted form "*de* + definite article" and analyzes *de* as a preposition.

[2] The Old French translation was written by Jean d'Antioche in 1282, and the Modern French translation is by Henri Bornecque. The percentages, taken from Goyens (1994: 224), are based on a comparison of the first 2500 NPs in the Old French translation with their equivalents in the Modern French translation. Contrary to most of the medieval translations, this translation is fairly faithful to the source text. Moreover, the figures in the table take into account only the comparable sequences.

A. Carlier (✉)
University of Lille-Nord de France, University of Lille 3, France

CNRS UMR 8094 – LaTTiCe, ENS, Paris, France

CNRS UMR 8163 – STL, Lille, France
e-mail: Anne.Carlier@univ-lille3.fr

Table 3.1 Comparison of the relative frequency of the articles in translation of Cicero's *De Inventione* and of the anonymous *Rhetorica ad Herennium* into Old French and into Modern French (Carlier and Goyens 1998)

Article	Old French (%)	Modern French (%)
le/les	50.4	65.4
un(s)	3.2	12
du/des (de)	0	4.2
Zero marking	46.4	18.4

The evolution of the relative frequency of use of the three articles, from Old French to Modern French, offers at least a rudimentary measure for evaluating their degree of grammaticalization in Old French, since frequency increase is one of the striking features of grammaticalization (Bybee 2003: 602). The definite article, which already emerges in Late Latin (*cf. inter alii* Selig 1992; Vincent 1997; Bauer 2007; Carlier and De Mulder 2010), has reached a certain degree of maturity in Old French. The indefinite article *un(s)*, however, seems to still be in an embryonic stage. As to the partitive, the question has to be raised whether or not it reaches the status of an article.

In this chapter, the focus will be on the two articles that express in Modern French indefiniteness, *viz.* singular (*un*) and non-singular (*du/des*). On the basis of synchronic facts, we will specify their stage of grammaticalization in Old French. In this way, the use of the articles in Old French is not described in a static perspective, but is rather conceived as a stage in the dynamic process of the construction of a new grammatical paradigm.

3.2   *Uns* in Old French: which stage of evolution?

From a typological perspective, the shift from the unity numeral towards the indefinite singular article is conceived as a widespread or even universal grammaticalization process (Givón 1981; Heine 1997). According to Heine (1997), the following stages can be distinguished: starting from its source meaning, *i.e.* the numeral 'one', the emergent article moves on successively to the stages of presentation marker, indefinite-specific marker, and indefinite-nonspecific marker, before reaching the ultimate stage of a generalized article:

Heine (1997: 71–74), moreover, adds that this desemantization is correlated to a contextual expansion:

i   The article does not originally occur within the scope of negation, modality, and interrogation, known as non-specific contexts. It will spread to these contexts only at stage **IV**. This extension of its conditions of use goes on at stage **V**, where it appears also in generic contexts.

ii   In the early stages, the use of the article is confined to singular count nouns, whereas in stage **V** it is extended to plural count nouns and to non-count nouns.

3   Grammaticalization in Progress in Old French: Indefinite Articles

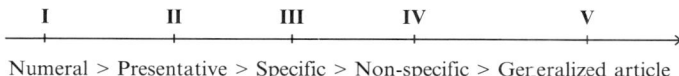

Numeral > Presentative > Specific > Non-specific > Generalized article

Fig. 3.1 From unity numeral to article, according to Heine (1997)

iii The indefinite article derived from the unity numeral can even undergo a neutralization of its opposition with the definite article. This is the case when it extends to generic use, since the meaning differences between (1a), (1b) and (1c) are subtle:

(1) English (Hawkins 1978: 214, quoted by Heine 1997: 70)
   a. *A lion is a noble beast.*
   b. *The lion is a noble beast.*
   c. *Lions are noble beasts.*

The low frequency of *uns* in the Old French translation of *De Inventione* (cf. Table 3.1), which has also been observed by Foulet (1915/1998: 60) in untranslated texts, suggests that *uns* is still in an early stage of grammaticalization. It has indeed been argued by Carlier (2001) and by Herslund (2003), that *uns* in Old French is still close to its source meaning of unity numeral. Evidence for this is provided by translations of the Latin unity numeral *unus*: although *un* in Modern French is still ambiguous between article and unity numeral, the modern translator has to systematically use contextual devices like the discontinuous restriction operator *ne ...que* ('only') in (2c) in order to activate the numeral value. As is shown in (2b), the Old French translator felt no need to do so, because the numeral value is still dominant:

(2) a. **una**=*ne*   **pecunia**   *fuerit* (Cicero, *De Inventione* II, 64)
       one NOM.SG.F=Q   sum-NOM.SG   be-PFCT;FUT.3SG
    b. Fu   ele   **une**   **pecune**?
       be-PST.3PL she   one/a-F.SG   sum?
       'Has there been **one sum**?' (transl. J. d'Antioche, LI [1282])
    c. N'   y   a-t-il eu   qu'   **une**   **somme**?
       RESTR LOC   have-PFCT.3SG   RESTR   one/a-F.SG   sum
       'Has there been only **one sum**?' » (transl. Bornecque [20th C.])

The non-reinforced translations of the Latin unity numeral disappear during the period of Middle French (Carlier 2001), when the article is no longer under the guardianship of the unity numeral value.

Although *uns* still had a strong numeral value in Old French, it also developed article uses. In its role as a presentative marker (stage II in Fig. 3.1), it introduces a new discourse referent (Foulet 1916/1998: 56; Joly 2004: 34), which can be taken up again in the subsequent context:

(3) Atant   i   vint   ***un-s***   ***paien-s***,
    then   LOC   come-PST.3SG   *a*-NOM.SG   *pagan*-NOM.SG
    Valdabrun-s.
    Valdabrun- NOM.SG.

Icil	en vait	al	rei	Marsiliun
DEM.DIST.M.SG	go-PRST.3SG	to-the-REG.M.SG	King-REG.SG	Marsiliun

'Then there came *a pagan* Valdabrun. He went to King Marsiliun.'
(*La Chanson de Roland*, 617–618 [1100])

Its use is, however, not systematic for specific indefinite reference (stage III) (cf. Buridant 2000: 79; Carlier 2001, *contra* Price 1971: 118).

(4) Si ele a   enfanté,   aveuque ***home***   habita.
    If she have-PRST.3SG give-birth-PST.PTCP, with   man.REG.SG live-PST.3SG
    'If she has given birth, she has been living with *a man*.'
    (transl. J. d'Antioche, XXVII [1282])

More surprisingly, *uns* in Old French is compatible with referential values that are associated with advanced stages of grammaticalization according to the grammaticalization path of Heine (1997). Indeed, *uns* is sporadically attested within the scope of modality, yielding a non-specific interpretation (stage IV):

(5) Se il   y   eust   ***un***   ***chat***$_i$
    If it-EXPL.SBJ LOC   have-PST.3SG a-REG.M.SG *cat*-SGFL
    qui   s'   en   fuist
    who   REFL INCHOAT   flee-PST.3SG
    de l' ost des Crestiens, ne peust   il$_i$ mie eschaper
    from the camp of-the Christians, not can-PST.3SG he NEG escape
    que li Sarrasin ne le$_i$ *preissent*
    that the Saracens not him caught.
    'If there were *a cat*$_i$ fleeing from the camp of the Christians, it$_i$ couldn't escape without being caught by the Saracens.' (*Chronique d'Ernoul* 23, 51 [1231])

It occurs also in predicate position (Buridant 2000: 112) and in the complement of a comparison (Marchello-Nizia 2006):

(6) Sire,   je sui ***unn-e***   ***essillie***
    Sir-NOM.SG I   am   *an*-F;sg   exile
    (*Roman de Thèbes*, 2318 [1150])

(7) A la   mort   vai   cum   ***uns***   ***anels***.
    To the-F.SG death-SG go-PRST;3SG like a-NOM;M;SG   lamb-NOM;M;SG
    'He (= Christ) goes to death like *a lamb*.' (*Passion de Clermont*, 156 [950])

3   Grammaticalization in Progress in Old French: Indefinite Articles   49

The following example shows that the Old French *uns* is even compatible with a generic interpretation (stage V):

(8) **Uns   faibles   hons**   porte   la
    A-NOM.M.SG frail NOM.M.SG man- NOM.M.SG bear-PRST.3SG the-F.SG
    some   par us   et par accoutumance
    burden by custom and by habit
    qu'uns autre de greignor puissance ne porte-r-oi-t   pour
    that an other of greater   strength   no bear-FUT-IMPF-3SG   for
    nule rien.
    no   thing.
    '*A frail man* carries the burden out of habit that another man, of greater strength, wouldn't bear on any account.' (Chr. De Troyes, *Yvain* 3582 [1180])

Moreover, *uns* is not restricted to singular count nouns (stage V). There exists a plural form of *uns* (Woledge 1956; Guillaume 1969; Herslund 2003), used mostly to refer to pairs (e.g. *unes eles* 'a pair of wings') or entities composed of identical elements which are inseparable physically (e.g. *unes denz* 'teeth', *unes montaignes* 'a chain of mountains'), or functionally (*unes armes* 'weapon equipment'). Secondly, *uns* is also compatible with non-count nouns, including mass nouns (7) and abstract nouns (8) (Heinz 1982).

(9) le   vaissel [...] est   tailliez a   cisel
    the receptacle   is   carved with chisel

    d'   *un marbre* **fin blanc et   bis   et si bel**
    from a marble   fine, white and greyish and so beautiful...
    que tels ne fu   depuis le temps Abel.
    that such not was since the time Abel

    'the receptacle [...] is carved with a chisel out from (litt. *a*) ***fine, white and greyish marble*** so beautiful that there was no such [marble] since Abel's time.' (Guillaume de Machaut, *Le jugement dou roy de Behaigne*[1340])

(10) Je l'   amoie   d' *une   amour   si tres pure*
     I her-ACC.F.SG love-IMPF.1SG of a.F.SG love-SG so very pure-SG
     qu' onques vers   li   ne pensay   fausseté.
     that never towards her not think-IMPF.1SG falsity.
     'I loved her with ***such a pure love*** that I never had any deceitful thought towards her.' (Guillaume de Machaut, *La loange des dames* [1377])

If we accept that *uns*, given its low frequency, is still in an early stage of the grammaticalization process in Old French, it seems difficult to accommodate the observed facts (examples (5)–(10) above) with the grammaticalization path proposed by Heine (1997). Therefore, a new model of development of the article has to be envisaged, and the meaning of the unity numeral as the starting point of this evolution has to be redefined.

In its numeral meaning, *uns* is a marker of unity both in a quantitative and a qualitative dimension. In its quantitative meaning, *uns* indicates the uniqueness of the referent, whereas in its qualitative meaning, it marks identity. These two meanings can be highlighted by *seul* ('only') and by *meisme* ('same').

(11) **Un   seul   filz** a   de sa moullier
     One-RÉG.M.SG single   son have-PRST.3SG of his wife.
     'He had one single son of his wife.' (*Roman de Thèbes* [1150])

(12) avrons   ambedui **un-e-s   meïsmes armes**
     have-FUT.1PL both   one-F-PL same-PL weapons-PL
     et   couverture-s d'une   maniere
     and   blanket-PL   of one-F.SG sort.
     'Both of us will have the same arms and saddle blankets of the same type.'
     (*Mort le Roi Artu*, 12 [1230])

By pragmatic inference, a textual role is grafted onto this numeral meaning: *uns* in Old French acquires the function of marking the discourse status of the evoked entity and presents it as new or unidentified for the hearer/reader. When this textual role becomes a conventionalized part of the meaning of *uns*, the article status is reached.[3]

– In its **quantitative** meaning, *uns* used as an article introduces a new entity and gives it the status of a prominent discourse referent. It is, however, not strictly limited to indefinite specific reference, e.g.:

(6) Atant i   vint   **un-s   paien-s,**   Valdabruns.
    then LOC come-PST.3SG *a*-NOM.M.SG *pagan*-NOM.M.SG Valdabrun-NOM.M.SG

    Icil   en vait   al   rei
    DEM.DIST.M.SG go-PRST.3SG to-the-REG.M.SG King-REG.SG
    Marsiliun
    Marsiliun
    'Then there came *a pagan* Valdabrun. He went to King Marsiliun.'
    (*La Chanson de Roland*, 617–618 [1100])

Uns can also occur for non-specific reference; as is illustrated by (5), the presence of the article is required when there is an anaphoric expression in the subsequent context:

(5) Se il   y   eust   **un   chat**
    If it-EXPL.SBJ LOC have-PST.3SG *a*-REG.M.SG *cat*FL

---

[3] The early grammaticalization stage of *uns* involves thus pragmatic strengthening rather than semantic bleaching (*Cf.* Hopper and Traugott 2003: 94). On the notion of pragmatic inference and its reanalysis as a semantic meaning, see the "Semantic Change Model" presented by Traugott and Dasher (2002: 34).

qui s'   en   fuist
who REFL INCHOAT   flee-PST.3SG

de   l'ost   des   Crestiens, ne peust   il   mie eschaper
from the camp of-the Christians, not can-PST.3SG he NEG escape-INF

que li   Sarrasin   ne *le preissent*
that the Saracens caught him.

'If there were ***a cat***$_i$ fleeing from the camp of the Christians, it $_i$ couldn't escape without being caught by the Saracens.' (*Chronique d'Ernoul* 23, 51 [1231])

On the contrary, even in the case of specific indefinite reference, *uns* can be lacking when the referent is unimportant and is not mentioned again in the subsequent context, as is exemplified by (4).

(4) Si ele a   enfanté,   aveuque ***home***   habita.
If she have-PRST.3SG give-birth-PST.PTCP with   man.REG.SG live-PST.3SG
'If she has given birth, she has been living with ***a man***.' (transl. J. d'Antioche, XXVII [1282])

– As a marker of **qualitative** identity, *uns* used as an article introduces a new type or new category (13). It occurs with some frequency in the more elaborate form of *une maniere de* ('a sort of/a type of') (Buridant 2000: 116) (14). The newly introduced category is often followed by an explicit denomination (13/14).

(13) assemblé   ot   la   ***un-e-s***   ***gens***   ***barbarian-s***,
gather-PST.PTCP have-PST.3SG LOC a-F.PL   people-PL barbaric-PL

Nommez   furent   Tyberïens
call-PST.PTCP.PL be-PST.3PL Tiberian-PL
'He had assembled there ***barbarian people***. They were called Tiberians.'
(Christine de Pizan, *Le livre de la mutacion de fortune* [1400])

(14) y   envoioit   gens   qui   portoient   ***une manière de pain-s***
there send-PST.3SG people who carry-PST.3PL a-F.SG manner of bread-PL

que l'   en appelle   bequis,
that one call-PRST.3SG biscuits-PL

pour ce que il   sont   cuis   par .II. foiz.
because that they are-PRST.3SG cooked-PL by two times
'he sent people who were carrying ***a sort of bread***-PL that is called "biscuits" because they are baked twice' (Joinville, *Histoire de saint Louis* [1305])

If we accept, on the basis of the low frequency of *uns* in Old French, that the grammaticalization from unity numeral to article is still at an early stage, the more abstract uses of *uns* in predicate position (6), in the complement of a comparison

(7) and even with a generic interpretation (8) cannot be considered as instances of an advanced stage of the grammaticalization process. Rather, they are linked to the article use deriving from its **qualitative** meaning: in this sense, *uns* introduces a new category and can be used to affirm that the referent evoked in the sentence is a member of the category or has at least the salient characteristics of the category.

3.3 The partitive in Old French: which stage of evolution?

In Modern French, indefinite non-singular reference is expressed by the so-called 'partitive' article (15a), composed of *de* (meaning 'from' > 'of') contracted with the definite article. Cross-linguistically, the existence of an article for indefinite non-singular reference is an exceptional feature. As a general rule, even languages that have an article for the indefinite singular leave the indefinite non-singular unmarked (e.g. English (15c)). This is also the case in Old French (15b):

(15) a. Modern French: Il-s boivent du vin.
         They-NOM-PL drink-PRST.3PL of;the;M;SG wine-SG
     b. Old French: Boivent   Ø   vin
                           drink- PRST.3PL   wine-REG.SG
     c. English: They   are drinking Ø   wine.

Hence, the Old French partitive, as illustrated by (16), cannot be considered as an ordinary indefinite article:

(16) Le gastel et le vin   leur   baillent…
     The pastry and the wine them-DAT.PL bring
     Del   vin   volentiers   bev-ai-ent
     of-the-M.SG wine-REG.SG gladly   drink-IMPF-3PL
     'They bring them the pastry and the wine. They drink gladly (some) of the wine.' (Chrétien de Troyes, *Erec*, 3178 [1170])

From a semantic viewpoint, the Old French partitive differs from the Modern French partitive in several respects:

  i It presupposes a contextually defined set and creates a partition within this set (Foulet 1916). Indeed, contrary to the Modern French *du vin* in (15a), which has a properly indefinite interpretation, the use of *del vin* in (16) presupposes that a bottle of wine is on the table.
  ii The Old French partitive is restricted to nouns referring to a concrete referent, be it mass (16) or count (17), but does not occur with abstract nouns (18) (Englebert 1996; Carlier 2004):

     (16) ***Del   vin***   volentiers bevai-ent.   (Old French)
          of-the-M.SG wine-SG gladly   drink-IMPF-3PL
          'They drink gladly (some) of the wine.' (Chrétien de Troyes, *Erec*, 3178 [1170])

(17) prent   li   pedre
    take-PRST.3SG the-NOM.M.SG father-NOM.SG
    de ses   meillours   serjanz (Old French)
    of his-REG.PL best-REG.PL servants-REG.PL
    'then the father takes (some) of his best servants' (*Vie de saint Alexis*, 23 [±1050])

(18) Il   ressent   **de la**   **haine**   envers elle.
    He-NOM.M.SG feels-PRST.3SG of the-F.SG   hatred   towards her.
    (Modern French)

iii The Old French partitive occurs mostly in object position with a very limited number of verbs, the most frequent of which are *boire* ('drink') and *manger* ('eat') (Foulet 1916/1998: 76). Occasionally, however, it is used in combination with other transitive verbs (19) or even in other non-prepositional syntactic functions, such as the predicate of a copulative sentence or the subject (20):

(19) *Encontré a   **de son   seignor***
    Discover-PRF.3SG of his-REG.M.SG lord-REG.SG
    'He discovered the tracks of his lord'
    (Béroul, *Tristan*, v. 1498, quoted by Tilander 1951)

(20) *Blancandrins   fut   **des   plus saives
    paiens***
    Blancandrin-NOM.SG be-PST.3SG of-the.REG.PL more wise-REG.PL
    heathens-REG.PL
    'Blancandrin was amongst the wisest heathens'. (*Chanson de Roland* [1100], 24)

From a syntactic viewpoint, *de* as a constitutive element of the partitive has a hybrid nature. On one hand, it still behaves like a preposition with respect to the NP it governs. This can be shown by examples such as (21), where the NP governed by *de* takes the form of a pronoun[4]:

(21) *Seignors,   du   vin   <u>de</u>   qoi*
    Lord-REG.PL of-the wine-REG.SG   of   which-N
    il   burent   avez   oï
    they drink-PST.3PL have-PST.2PL heard- PST.PTCP
    'Lords, you heard about the wine of which they drank?' (Béroul, *Tristran & Iseut*, v. 2133–2135)

On the other hand, the partitive constituent has the status of a direct object with respect to the verb, which means that *de* is no longer a preposition. Evidence for this can be found in causative constructions. As has been pointed out by Damourette and Pichon (1911–1940), Kayne (1975), and Martineau (1992), in the French causative

---

[4] More syntactic evidence is offered by Carlier (2007: § 1.2.2.2).

"*faire* + infinitive" construction, the subject of the embedded infinitive is normally assigned accusative case (22):

(22) **Infinitive – Direct Object → Subject:** ACCUSATIVE
Il est biaux enfes, bien me plait.
he is beautiful boy well me he pleases
Alez, si   le   faites   mengier.
GO-IMP.2PL   him-ACC.M.SG make-IMP.2PL   eat-INF
'He is a nice boy, I like him, make him [ACCUSATIVE] eat' (*Miracle de saint Jehan Crisothomes* [1340])

However, if the infinitive has a direct object, the subject of the infinitive conveys dative case or is expressed as a PP introduced by *à* 'to' (23), because in French, accusative case cannot be assigned to more than one constituent.

(23) **Infinitive + Direct Object → Subject: DATIVE or PP introduced by *à* ('to')**
Les   gentilz   houmes   preuz
the-REG.M.PL   noble-REG.M.PL   man-REG.M.PL   brave-REG.M.PL
et   biax
and   handsome-REG.M.PL

fet   mengier a   chiens,   a oisiaux!
make-PRST.3SG eat-INF to   dog-REG. PL,   to bird-REG.PL
'He makes dogs and birds[DATIVE] eat noble, brave, and handsome men'
(*Roman de Thèbes* [1150], v. 10097–10098)

When the infinitive has an oblique or prepositional object, the subject of the infinitive is nevertheless normally assigned accusative case (24).[5]

(24) Infinitive + Prepositional object → Subject: ACCUSATIVE
Pompée [...] le   fait   parler   des
Pompeius   him-ACC.M.SG make-PRST.3SG   speak-INF of-the
princes de l' aurore.
princes of the dawn.
'Pompeius makes him[ACCUSATIVE] tell about the princes of the dawn'
(G. de Breboeuf, *Les Guerres civiles de César et de Pompée* [1655])

Crucially for our argument, when the infinitive has a partitive object, its subject is assigned the dative case (26), in the same way as for a direct object (cf. (23) and (25)). Hence, in relationship to the verb, *de* does not behave like a preposition.

---

[5] As pointed out by an anonymous reviewer, there is some fluctuation as to the case marking of the subject of the infinitive in causative constructions. For a detailed discussion, cf. Pearce (1990).

(25) Car   **un**   ***bevrage***   <u>leur</u>   *fait*
because a-REG.M.SG beverage-REG.SG them-DATIVE.PL make-PRST.3SG
boire.
drink-INF
'Because he makes <u>them</u> [DATIVE] drink **a beverage**.'
(Gautier de Coinci, *Miracles de Notre-Dame*, Ed. V.F. Koenig, vol. 1, p.159)

(26) *Boire*   <u>li</u>   *fait...*
Drink-INF him- DATIVE.SG make-PRST.3SG
del   bevraige   qui a   tel force
of-the beverage-REG.SG that has such strength
'He makes <u>him</u> [DATIVE] drink (some) **of the beverage** that has such strength.'
(Gautier de Coinci, Miracles de Notre-Dame, Ed. V.F. Koenig, vol. 3, p. 412)

These empirical facts allow us to define the exact status of the partitive *de*. As pointed out by Lehmann (2002: 67), a full preposition is a two-sided relator. It establishes a relationship with an external element (e.g., the verb), but also with the nominal complement it governs. *De* as a constitutive element of the medieval partitive is one-sided relator and has an intermediate status, between preposition and determiner. It does not behave any longer like a preposition with respect to the verb (see example 26), but it is still a preposition with respect to the NP it governs (see example 21).

The prepositional status of *de* with respect to the NP has a semantic correlate: *de* indicates that the referent of the NP is not wholly affected by the verbal action, but only partially.[6] The very specific interpretation of the medieval partitive, described above, is a result of this semantic dimension of *de*: the medieval partitive presupposes a contextually determined set and creates a partition within this set. This meaning also explains the following distributional constraints:

i. The Old French partitive is restricted to nouns referring to a concrete referent, but does not occur with abstract nouns (see examples (16) to (18)).
ii. It occurs mostly in combination with verbs whose object is affected by movement or by modification of physical properties and is thus more likely to be used with verbs like *boire* 'drink' rather than *voir* 'see'. In so far as the meaning of 'partial affectedness' can be relevant in the context, *de* can nevertheless be used marginally in combination with other verbs and even in other syntactic functions (see examples (19) and (20)).

On the grammaticalization chain from the preposition *de*, denoting a spatial movement of distancing from a source or an origin (e.g. *de digito anulum detraho* 'I remove the ring from the finger' Cato *R.R.* 157,6), towards the full-fledged indefinite

---

[6] *Cf.* the description of the genitive case in Russian (Timberlake 1977; Paykin and Van Peteghem 2002; Fischer 2004), in Homeric Greek (Humbert 1960) and of the partitive case in Finnish (Sands and Campbell 2001).

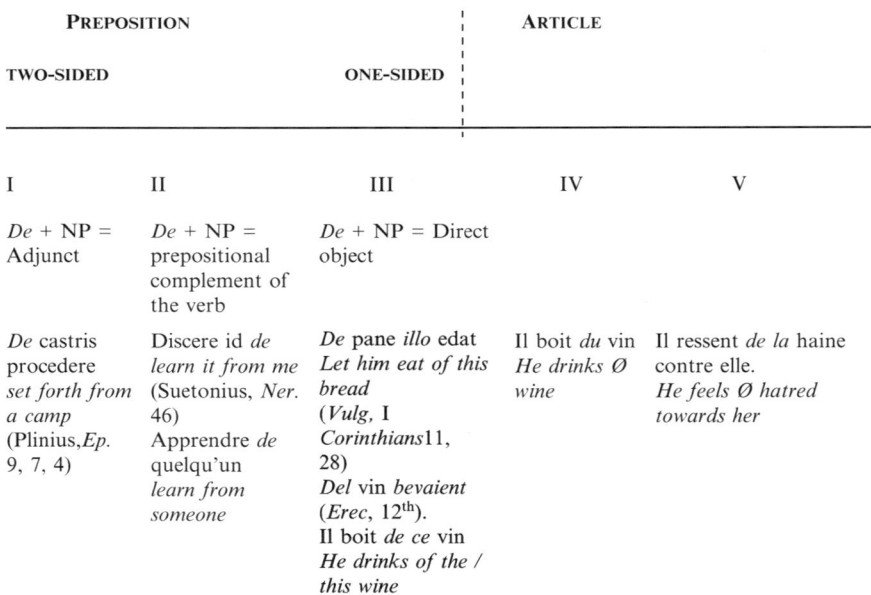

Fig. 3.2 From preposition to article (Carlier 2007)

non-singular article, the medieval partitive corresponds to stage III, *i.e.* the preliminary stage to the status of article.

The partitive corresponding to stage III has a rather low frequency in Old French texts of the twelfth century. It is not a new feature of Old French. It is already attested in the Late Latin popularizing texts of the fourth and fifth century written in Gaul, in those particular by Christian authors (Väänänen 1981, cf. example in Fig. 3.2). Moreover, the occasional use of a case or adposition meaning 'from' for the periphrastic expression of the partitive is, in fact, not cross-linguistically uncommon, as it has been identified as a universally available syntactic construction in any language (Harris and Campbell 1995: 54–56). The partitive has, however, been the object of study by many historians of the French language because it is the precursor of a newly created article. The very beginnings of this use of the partitive as an article, corresponding to stage IV in Fig. 3.2, are already found in Old French dramatic texts, which reproduce a language of conversation and probably adopt a more informal register (Foulet 1916/1998: 83); they become less uncommon in the thirteenth century. Consider the following example:

(27) *Ha! biaus   dous   fiex,   seés   vous   cois,*
       Ha! handsome sweet   son,   seat-IMP.2PL   you-PL   quiet,
       *ou   vous   arés   **des**   **eviaus.***
       or   you-PL   have-FUT.2PL of-the-REG.SG.M hits-REG.PL
       'Ha! Dear sweet son, keep quiet, or you will take hits' (Adam de la Halle, *Jeu de la Feuillée*, 396–397 [1276], quoted by Foulet 1916/1998)

In the example (27) above, *de* is no longer a one-sided preposition but is rather an element of the article. From a semantic viewpoint, the partitive does not create a partition in a presupposed contextually determined set, but rather marks indefiniteness. At the same period in Old French, the partitive remains exceptional in formal registers. For instance, Jean d'Antioche's translation of theoretical work on rhetoric, quoted above (footnote 2), which is written in the late thirteenth century, contains no clear instance of the partitive. The partitive does not attain a significant level of frequency until Middle French. The frequency of the partitive in the written tradition rises sharply in the fifteenth century, thereby attesting to its establishment as the so-called 'partitive' article.[7] In the initial period, it is still restricted to concrete reference (stage IV of Fig. 3.2), but it extends to abstract nouns during the seventeenth century (stage V of Fig. 3.2). This evolution is not entirely accomplished in Modern French: in a prepositional group, the abstract noun is often used without an article, whereas the use of the partitive article is rather systematic in combination with concrete mass nouns, as is shown by the following figures.

(28) Relative frequency of the partitive in the *Frantext* corpus (1900–2010)
 a. *avec amour* : 99,2%   *avec de l'amour*: 0,8%
    with love   with of-the.SG love
 b. *avec lait* : 2%   *avec du lait* : 98%
    with milk   with of-the.M.SG milk

3.4 Concluding remarks

It is well-known that from a typological viewpoint that the grammatical category of the articles is not universal. According to Dryer (1989), only one third of the languages of the world have at least one article, mostly the definite article. Moreover, only 8% of them have both a definite and an indefinite article. Originating from a mother language without articles, French has nevertheless created a paradigm of articles with three distinct etymological sources: the distal demonstrative, the unity numeral, and a contraction of the spatial preposition *de*, meaning 'removal', and the definite article. The early Old French texts already contain the three forms that will constitute the paradigm of articles in Modern French. This chapter has been devoted to the two articles marking indefiniteness in Modern French, the article derived from the unity numeral and the so-called 'partitive' article.

In this chapter, the conditions of the use and the meaning of the indefinite article *uns* and of the partitive in Old French have been extensively studied from a synchronic viewpoint. From a methodological viewpoint, this study shows that a synchronic analysis benefits by being combined with a diachronic perspective: a more

---

[7] Quantitative data are provided in Carlier (2007 : § 3.2).

comprehensive account of the exact meaning and the specific conditions of uses of *uns* and of the partitive in Old French can be offered if the analysis is based upon a correct definition of the source expression, evaluates its evolutionary stage with respect to this source and fits into an overall picture of the grammaticalization path towards the status to full-fledged article. Frequency and frequency increase have proved to be a reliable measure for evaluating the stage of grammaticalization.

As far as *uns* is concerned, its low frequency in Old French with respect to Modern French points to an early stage of grammaticalization. As evidenced by the translations of the Latin unity numeral, it still seems to be strongly associated with its numeral value, both in its quantitative dimension of uniqueness marker ('only one') and in its qualitative dimension of identity marker ('one and the same'). By pragmatic strengthening, *uns* has nevertheless acquired the textual role of marking the entity in question as new for the hearer/reader. As this textual role becomes part of the meaning of *uns*, article status is reached. On one hand, in line with its quantitative numeral meaning, *uns* has the ability to introduce a new discourse referent. On the other hand, in accordance with its qualitative numeral meaning, *uns* can introduce a new category and/or identify an entity as a member of this category. The more abstract uses of *uns* in nominal predicates, in comparisons, and even for generic meaning, are in line with this qualitative numeral meaning and do not reveal, as is suggested by the evolutionary model of Heine (1997), an advanced stage of grammaticalization. On the contrary, the strong discourse-pragmatic motivation of the article use of *uns* confirms that it is still in an early stage of the grammaticalization process.

With respect to the partitive, the question whether it is still a preposition or already an article in Old French has often been raised. It is claimed in this study that it has an intermediate status in Old French, between preposition and article, and that it has not yet reached the status of article. This analysis accounts for its very low frequency, for its hybrid syntactic properties, and for its very specific meaning of partition within a concrete and contextually determined set. As has been pointed out by Harris and Campbell (1995), the occasional use of a genitive or a periphrastic construction using an adposition meaning 'from' for the expression of the partitive is as such cross-linguistically a rather widespread phenomenon. However, what is specific about the Old French partitive is that it grammaticalized into an article. The first attestations of this newly created article occur in Old French sources closer to the oral register, but the article use of the partitive attains a significant level of frequency only in Middle French.

The evolution of *un(s)* and *du/des* from Old French to Modern French is conditioned by the process of further integration within the paradigm or 'paradigmatization' (Lehmann 2002: § 4.2). The feature of indefiniteness, creating a binary opposition with the definite article *le*, is fore-grounded. Other features characteristic of *uns* and the partitive in Old French that do not contribute to binary paradigmatic oppositions are reoriented or eliminated. As to *uns*, the value of unity numeral fades away from Middle French on and evolves towards the grammatical feature of singular number. For the partitive, which refers in Old French to an indefinite quantity taken from a concrete and contextually defined partition set, the notion of partition set disappears during the period of Middle French, but the feature of indefinite and, hence, non-singular quantity remains. This leads to a tightly integrated paradigm, structured in terms of two main parameters, (in)definiteness and number, with only a very restricted place for zero determination, at least in combination with common nouns.

The importance given in this study to the respective source meanings of *uns* and of the partitive can seem self-evident because they correspond in Old French to early stages of the grammaticalization process. However, even when an expression reaches an advanced stage of grammaticalization and seems fully integrated in a paradigm, it can still convey traces of earlier meanings, which are reflected in constraints on use or meaning (Hopper and Traugott 2003: 96). For instance, as has been shown by the frequency rates in (28), in a prepositional group, the Modern French partitive article is still often lacking in combination with abstract nouns whereas its use is nearly systematic with concrete nouns. This can be understood as a phenomenon of "persistence" (Hopper 1991): for the forerunner of the partitive article, the concrete character of the partition set was an absolute distributional constraint.

Acknowledgement I am very grateful to Richard Ingham (Birmingham City University) for his critical reading of the prefinal version of the manuscript and his useful comments. My paper also benefited from the remarks of an anonymous reviewer.

References

Bauer, B. 2007. The definite article in Indo-European: Emergence of a new category. In *Nominal determination*, ed. E. Stark et al., 103–140. Amsterdam: J. Benjamins.
Buridant, C. 2000. *Grammaire nouvelle de l'ancien français*. Paris: SEDES.
Bybee, J. 2003. Mechanisms of change in grammaticization: The role of frequency. In *The handbook of historical linguistics*, ed. B.D. Joseph and R.D. Janda, 602–623. Oxford: Blackwell.
Carlier, A. 2001. La genèse de l'article *un*. *Langue Française* 130: 65–88.
Carlier, A. 2004. Sur les premiers stades de développement de l'article partitif. *Scolia* 18: 115–146.
Carlier, A. 2007. From preposition to article: The grammaticalization of the French partitive. *Studies in Language* 31(1): 1–49.
Carlier, A., and W. De Mulder. 2010. The emergence of the definite article: *ille* in competition with *ipse* in Late Latin. In *Subjectification, intersubjectification and grammaticalization*, ed. K. Davidse et al. Berlin: Mouton de Gruyter.
Carlier, A., and M. Goyens. 1998. De l'ancien français au français moderne: régression du degré zéro de la détermination et restructuration du système des articles. *Cahiers de l'Institut de Linguistique de Louvain-la-Neuve* 24(3–4): 77–112.
Damourette, J., and E. Pichon. 1911–1940. *Des mots à la pensée: essai de grammaire de la langue française*. Paris: d'Artrey.
Dryer, M.S. 1989. Article-Noun Order. *Papers from the 25th Regional Meeting of the Chicago Linguistic Society*, pp. 83–97.
Englebert, A. 1996. L'article partitif: l'évolution des conditions d'emploi. *Langue Française* 109: 928.
Fischer, S. 2004. Partitive vs. genitive in Russian and Polish: An empirical study on case alternation in the object domain. In *Experimental studies in linguistics*, I, LiP 21, ed. S. Fischer, R. van de Vijver, and R. Vogel, 73–89. Potsdam: Universitätsverlag Potsdam.

Foulet, L. 1916. *Petite syntaxe de l'ancien français*, 3rd ed. 1998. Paris: Champion.
Givón, T. 1981. On the development of the numeral 'one' as an indefinite marker. *Folia Linguistica Historica* II(1): 35–53.
Goyens, M. 1994. *Émergence et évolution du syntagme nominal en français*. Bern: Lang.
Guillaume, G. 1969. *Langage et science du langage*, 2nd ed. Paris: Nizet.
Harris, A.C., and Campbell, L. 1995. *Historical Syntax in Cross-linguistic Perspective*. Cambridge: Cambridge University Press.
Hawkins, J.A. 1978. *Definiteness and indefiniteness: A study in reference and grammaticality prediction*. London: Croom Helm.
Heine, B. 1997. Indefinite articles. In Id.: *Cognitive foundations of grammar*. Oxford: Oxford University Press.
Heinz, S. 1982. *Determination und Re-präsentation im Altfranzösischen*. München: Fink.
Herslund, M. 2003. Le pluriel de l'article indéfini en ancien français. In *La Cognition dans le temps*, ed. P. Blumenthal and J.-E. Tyvaert, 75–84. Tübingen: Niemeyer.
Hopper, P.J. 1991. On some principles of grammaticization. In *Approaches to grammaticalization*, vol. I, ed. E. Traugott, 17–35. Amsterdam: Benjamins.
Hopper, P.J., and E.C. Traugott. 2003. *Grammaticalization*. Cambridge: Cambridge University Press, 2nd ed. (1st ed.:1993).
Humbert, J. 1960. *Syntaxe grecque*. Paris: Klincksieck.
Joly, G. 2004. *L'ancien français*. Paris: Belin.
Kayne, R.S. 1975. *French syntax*. Cambridge, MA: MIT Press.
Lehmann, Ch. 2002. *Thoughts on grammaticalization*. München/Newcastle: Lincom, 3rd ed. (1st ed.:1982).
Marchello-Nizia, Ch. 2006. Contextes et étapes d'une grammaticalisation: les articles génériques en français. In Id., *Grammaticalisation et changement linguistique*, 199–229. Bruxelles: De Boeck.
Martineau, F. 1992. Mouvements verbaux et nominaux dans les constructions causatives et de perception. *Travaux de Linguistique* 25: 93–110.
Ménard, Ph. 1968. *Manuel d'ancien français: syntaxe*. Bordeaux: Sodobi, 2nd ed.
Moignet, G. 1976. *Grammaire de l'ancien français. Morphologie – syntaxe*. Paris: Klincksieck, 2nd ed. (1st ed.:1973).
Paykin, K., and M. Van Peteghem. 2002. Definiteness in a language without articles: A case-study of Russian. *Recherches linguistiques de Vincennes* 31: 97–112.
Pearce, Elizabeth. 1990. *Parameters in Old French syntax: Infinitival complements*. Dordrecht: Kluwer.
Price, G. 1971. *The French language: Present and past*. London: Arnold.
Revol, T. 2000. *Introduction à l'ancien français*. Paris: Nathan.
Sands, K., and L. Campbell. 2001. Non-canonical subjects and objects in Finnish. In *Non-canonical marking of subjects and objects*, ed. A. Aikenvald, R.M.W. Dixon, and M. Onishi, 251–305. Amsterdam: Benjamins.
Selig, M. 1992. *Die Entwicklung der Nominaldeterminanten im Spätlatein. Romanischer Sprachwandel und lateinische Schriftlichkeit*. Tübingen: G. Narr.
Tilander, G. 1951. 'De sa fame ne voit mie (point)': un problème syntaxique du vieux français. *Studia Neophilologica* 24: 1–39.
Timberlake, A. 1977. Reanalysis and actualization in syntactic change. In *Mechanisms of syntactic change*, ed. Ch.N. Li, 141–177. Austin: University of Texas Press.
Traugott, E.C., and R.B. Dasher. 2002. *Regularity in semantic change*. Cambridge: Cambridge University Press.
Väänänen, V. 1981. La préposition latine de et le génitif. In Id. *Recherches et récréations latino-romanes*. Napoli: Bibliopolis.
Vincent, N. 1997. The emergence of the D-system in Romance. In *Parameters of morphosyntactic change*, ed. A. Van Kemenade and N. Vincent, 149–169. Cambridge: Cambridge University Press.
Woledge, B. 1956. The plural of the indefinite article in old French. *The Modern Language Review* 51: 17–32.

Chapter 4
Null Objects in Old French

Bryan Donaldson

4.1 Introduction

A number of traits found predominantly in informal spoken modern French—as opposed to the normative standard written variety—have origins that can be traced to earlier stages of the language. Thus, left-dislocations (LDs), for example, which are more characteristic of spoken French than written French (Lambrecht 1981), are found in texts from as early as the beginning of the twelfth century (Marchello-Nizia 1998; Priestley 1955). Null objects—the non-expression or dropping of the object of a verb—are another such trait more characteristic of spoken than written French (Lambrecht and Lemoine 2005; Schøsler 2000; Yaguello 1998, and others). Null objects have been widely discussed in a variety of languages. As with null subjects, languages differ as to whether or not they permit objects to be null. Chinese, for example, licenses null objects freely (Huang 1984), whereas for English and French, the conventional view is that objects must be overtly expressed (Huang 1984; Raposo 1986; Vincent 2000). However, null objects are in fact well documented in modern French (Authier 1989a; Fónagy 1985; Lambrecht and Lemoine 2005; Larjavaara 2000; Schøsler 2000; Yaguello 1998) and have also been found in Old French: Arteaga (1997) and Buridant (2000) give examples beyond the well-documented case of *écrasement* that is presented in most grammars and descriptions of Old French (e.g., Anglade 1941; Einhorn 1974; Foulet 1930; Jensen 1990; Kibler 1984; Raynaud de Lage 1962). Finally, Latin—the source of French and the other Romance varieties—also allowed referential null objects (Luraghi 1997; Pieroni 1999; Pinkster 1990; Schøsler 1999; Vincent 2000).

This paper examines null objects in twelfth- and thirteenth-century Old French. The objectives are twofold: first, to illustrate environments in which Old

B. Donaldson (✉)
Department of French and Italian, University of Texas, Austin, TX, USA
e-mail: bdonaldson@austin.utexas.edu

French permitted null objects and to relate them to the modern language, and second, to propose, on the basis of the data available, that Old French possessed both null pronominals and null variables.

4.1.1 Null Objects

Null objects are a type of syntactic empty category. The exact nature of this empty category has been of central interest in the (generative) literature, where two types of null objects have been described: null variables and null pronominals (or small *pro*). The principal characteristics of each will be described in turn.

Huang's (1984) description of null objects in Chinese and Raposo's (1986) description of null objects in European Portuguese analyzed the empty categories in these languages as null variables. Null variables are bound by antecedents—null or overt—in a non-argument (A-bar) position. That is, null variables receive their identity from a constituent in a non-argument position. As a consequence, null variables cannot be co-referential with an argument (A-position) in the clause. The null variable is bound either by a null topic (Huang 1984), a null operator (Raposo 1986), or a (null) quantifier (Authier 1989a) in a leftward non-argument position. In Raposo's analysis, this is COMP (see Authier 1989b for further discussion of this position). Whether one posits an operator or a null topic, the analysis remains basically the same: as Authier (1988) pointed out, null operators can be indistinguishable from null topics. Under this type of analysis, the identity of the null object (null variable) is pragmatically—rather than syntactically—determined and depends on discourse topic. Other properties that have been identified for null variables include the possibility of non-gap topics (Cole 1987) and the presence of cross-over and subjacency effects. In analyses that posit an operator in COMP, a null variable should be prevented by the doubly-filled COMP filter from appearing in a phrase where there is another overt element in COMP (e.g., a *wh*-element).

Whereas null variables are bound by a non-argument, null pronominals are bound by a sentence-internal argument (Cole 1987). The identity of a null pronominal is thus determined by a constituent in an argument (A) position. The corollary is that a null pronominal cannot take its reference from an element in a non-argument (A-bar) position. Cole analyzed null objects in Imbabura Quechua, Thai, and Korean, all of which may be co-referential with a main clause argument, as instances of null pronominals. As Cole demonstrated, null pronominals (at least in these languages) do not exhibit cross-over or subjacency effects. Finally, in cases of null pronominals, neither non-gap topics nor null topics are allowed.

One of the principal differences between null variables and null pronominals, then, is the nature of the antecedent that binds them—or, in other words, how each type of null object receives its referential identity. In the case of null variables, the binding element is in a non-argument position, whereas null pronominals are bound by an element in an argument position. This criterion will prove more practicable than cross-over and subjacency for historical data.

As Rizzi (1986a) noted, null objects represent a mismatch between meaning and the form(s) onto which that meaning is mapped. In the case of null objects, a constituent is understood despite not being overtly present in the syntax or realized phonetically. For a null object to be licit, its identity must be readily ascertainable and understandable to the interlocutor (Authier 1988; Huang 1984; Lambrecht and Lemoine 1996, 2005; Raposo 1986).

4.1.2 Null Objects in Modern French

Despite its conventional classification as a language that does not permit null objects (e.g., Huang 1984; Raposo 1986; Vincent 2000), numerous studies have documented null objects in modern French in a variety of contexts. Although Yaguello (1998) argued that modern French licenses referential null objects more easily with [−human] than with [+human] referents, both are possible. With an arbitrary human referent, null objects are readily attested: Authier (1989a) discussed examples whose interpretation corresponds to an arbitrary third-person referent 'one,' as in (1), whose interpretation is essentially that of (2), in which the object is overtly expressed.

1. *L'   ambition   mène   à commettre   des   erreurs.*
   the-SG.ambition-F-SG leads-3-SG [e] to commit-INF some-PL errors-F-PL[1]
   'Ambition leads __ to make mistakes.'
2. *L'   ambition   mène   les   gens*
   the-SG.ambition-F-SG leads-3-SG the-PL people-M-PL
   à commettre   des   erreurs.
   to commit-INF some-PL errors-F-PL
   'Ambition leads people to make mistakes.'

To these examples, which involve infinitival complements, one can add examples involving finite verbs like that in (3), made in reference to the fan on a laptop computer:

3. *Ça   affole   juste un   peu,   le   ventilo.*
   it-M-SG bothers-3-SG [e] just a-M-SG bit-ADV the-M-SG fan-M-SG
   'It bothers __ just a bit, the fan.'

In Authier's (1989a) analysis, arbitrary null objects take the quantificational force of the sentence's quantifier; they are free variables bound by an operator. Arbitrary null objects (or their operators) are restricted in modern French to verb tenses that allow a generic time reference (e.g., present, imperfect).

---

[1] Glosses follow the Leipzig glossing rules. A null object is represented with [e] following the verb of which it is an argument; null subjects are not indicated in the morpheme glosses but are indicated by an underlined position in the literal gloss.

In a descriptive study, Fónagy (1985) observed that verbs like *aimer* 'to like' and *connaître* 'to know/be acquainted with' are often used transitively without an expressed object in informal spoken French, as in (4) and (5).

4. *Le cubisme, vous connaissez?*
   the-M-SG cubism-M-SG you-2-PL know-2-PL [e]
   'Cubism, do you know __?'
5. *Qu'est-ce qu'il y a pour dîner?*
   what.is-3-SG.it-3-M-SG that.it-3-M-SG there-OBL has-3-SG for dinner-M-SG
   Sauté de veau.
   sauté-M-SG of veal-M-SG
   On aime.
   one-3-SG-INDF likes-3-SG [e]
   'What is there for dinner?'
   'Sauté of veal.'
   'We like __.'

One of Fónagy's central concerns dealt with the lexical properties of the verbs in question. For Fónagy, the ability of a verb to license a null object depended on its lexical properties. This view was challenged by Lambrecht and Lemoine (2005), who drew on several corpora of spoken French and argued that the verbs attested with null objects in their corpora did not form a natural lexical class. Rather, for Lambrecht and Lemoine, the issue was one of pragmatics. In their view, any transitive verb can permit a null object given the appropriate discourse conditions. Beyond the arbitrary null objects described in Authier (1989a) and the *aimer*-type examples in Fónagy (1985), Lambrecht and Lemoine cited numerous examples of definite referential null objects, such as those in (6) and (7), whose identity depends on a previous discourse referent.

6. *Avant, j' avais mon dossier à Jester, mais*
   before I-1-SG-NOM.had-1-SG my-M-SG file-M-SG at Jester-LOC but
   j' ai enlevé.
   I-1-SG-NOM.have-1-SG removed-PTCP [e]
   'Before, I had my file at Jester, but I removed __.'
7. *Je vais demander si je peux passer ce*
   I-1-SG-NOM go-1-SG ask-INF if I-1-SG-NOM can-1-SG come-INF this-M-SG
   soir prendre.
   evening-M-SG take-INF [e]
   'I am going to ask if I can come by this evening to take __.'

In examples like (8) and (9), the possibility of the null object depends on the use of a particular verb in a specific context (Schøsler 2000). The omission of the object is probably facilitated by the frequency with which the particular verb appears in the context. Expressions of the type in (8) and (9) are formulaic and contextually limited.

8. *Il   n'a   pas encore chaussé.*
   he-3-M-SG-NOM NEG.has-3-SG NEG yet   put.on-PTCP [e]
   'He has not yet put on ___ .' (Always refers to ski boots)
   (Bescherelle 1997, §106)
9. *Pierre   abat.*
   Pierre-3-SG shuffles-3-SG [e]
   'Pierre shuffles ___ .' (Always refers to playing cards)
   (Schøsler 2000, p. 113)

Although the verbs in (6) through (9) are clearly transitive, determining transitivity is often problematic. Cummins and Roberge (2004) proposed a *null cognate object*, whose meaning derives directly from the lexical properties of the verb (see Schøsler 2000 for a similar discussion). Under such an analysis, even conventionally intransitive verbs like *dormir* 'to sleep' contain a null cognate object along the lines of *un somme* 'a sleep.' Verbs such as *manger* 'to eat' and *boire* 'to drink,' which can be transitive but are often used intransitively—or at least without an overt object—can be analyzed as having null cognate objects meaning 'something edible' and 'something drinkable,' as in (10).

10. *Il   mange   et il   boit   tous   les*
    he-3-M-SG-NOM eats-3-SG [e] and he-3-M-SG-NOM drinks-3-SG [e] all-M-PL the-PL
    jours.
    days-M- PL
    'He eats __ and he drinks __ every day.'

Taken together, the data in this brief overview provide evidence of relatively widespread possibilities for object omission in modern (spoken) French.

4.1.3 Old French

This section demonstrates that null objects were attested in a variety of contexts in twelfth- and thirteenth-century Old French. The grammar of Old French during this period licensed null subjects (Adams 1987; Vance 1989, 1997), and word order was governed by a fairly robust verb-second (V2) constraint (Adams 1989; Vance 1997), although V2 was slowly weakening, with word order moving progressively toward the SV(O) order known in modern French (e.g., Vance et al. 2010). The two-case system (nominative and oblique), substantially more visible in the masculine than the feminine, was progressively weakening but still largely intact.

Old French has not generally been considered to allow object drop, and Marchello-Nizia's (1995) position is representative: 'When a verb is transitive, its object is necessarily expressed in early periods of French' (1995, p. 47, my translation), although Marchello-Nizia noted the common—indeed, nearly systematic—exception of *écrasement* (discussed subsequently). Schøsler (1999) studied verb valence in Latin, Old French, Middle French, and modern French. Her analysis led her to hypothesize that Old French avoided object drop because of the possible resulting difficulty of distinguishing between the subject and direct object of the verb: Because the nominative/oblique case distinction was only rarely apparent in the feminine, and because expression of the subject was not obligatory, examples like (11), taken from Schøsler (1999), present a potential ambiguity. Ignoring information from context and the likely position of the initial subordinate clause (see Skårup 1975), the feminine constituent *la pulcela* 'the girl,' whose nominative and oblique forms are indistinguishable, could function either as the subject or the direct object of the verb *esguarda* 'looked at.'

11. *Cum veit   le   lit,   esguarda   la   pulcela.*
    when saw-3-SG the-M-SG bed-M-SG looked-3-SG the-F-SG girl-F-SG
    'When (he) saw the bed, (he) looked at the girl/the girl looked.'
    Vie de Saint Alexis, verse 56

The propensity of Old French to leave the subject unexpressed leads to a preference for the first reading (with *la pulcela* as direct object); Schøsler's claim is essentially that when an argument is left unexpressed, it is typically the subject rather than the object. In other words, Old French avoided leaving a direct object unexpressed. According to Schøsler's hypothesis, object drop became more frequent only in Middle French, when, as the expression of the subject became obligatory and SV word order became fixed, distinguishing subjects from direct object (NPs) presented less difficulty than under a null-subject V2 grammar with flexible word order.

Nevertheless, Old French data evince object drop. Although works in the philological tradition present isolated examples of what I am calling null objects, Arteaga (1997) is the only previous study to my knowledge to assemble a significant number of examples of null objects in Old French and offer discussion from a contemporary theoretical perspective. Arteaga discussed several contexts in which Old French allowed null direct or indirect objects: (a) LDs, (b) coordination structures, (c) *écrasement*, and (d) certain adjunct clauses. Each of these contexts, discussed in more detail subsequently, is illustrated here with examples taken from Arteaga, given in (12) through (15).

12. Left-dislocation
    Cest   nostre   rei   por coi lessas   cunfundre?
    this-M-SG our-SG-POSS king-M-SG-ACC for what let-2-SG [e] flounder-INF
    'This our king why do (you) let __ flounder?'
    Chanson de Roland, line 2583

13. Coordination
    Il   retrait   s'espee   et met
    he-3-M-SG-NOM pulls.back-3-SG his-F-SG-POSS.sword-F-SG and puts-3-SG [e]
    ou   fuerre.
    in-ART-M-SG fire-M-SG
    'He pulls back is sword and puts __ in the fire.'
    Queste del Saint Graal, §111

14. *Écrasement*
    Tient   une   chartre, mais ne   li   puis
    holds-3-SG a-F-SG letter-F-SG   but NEG him-3-SG-DAT can-1-SG
    tolir.
    take.away-INF [e]
    '(He) holds a letter, but (I) cannot take __ from him.'
    Vie de Saint Alexis, line 355

15. Adjunct clause
    On   le   remenroit   en le   vile   por
    one-3-SG-INDF-NOM her-3-F-SG-ACC lead-3-SG-COND in the-F-SG city-F-SG for
    ardoir.
    burn-INF [e]
    'One would lead her to the city to burn __.'
    Aucassin et Nicolette, §16

Arteaga (1997) treated Old French null objects as a unified phenomenon and argued that the examples in (12) through (15) all represented cases of null pronominals and not null variables. First, in the LD examples cited, a *wh*-element appears in COMP, leaving no position available for the null operator or null topic that would be necessary to bind a null variable (see e.g., Raposo 1986). In Arteaga's analysis, the resumptive pronoun that would typically be expected in a LD is null in the Old French examples. Next, in coordination across two conjoined clauses as in (13) and in *écrasement* as in (14), Arteaga observed that the reference of the null object in the second clause appears to always be restricted to co-referentiality with the object of the verb in the first clause. In the case of a null variable bound by a null topic, one would anticipate that the null object could refer to something other than the object of the first clause. Furthermore, a null variable analysis would require that the object of the first clause be a topic, which Arteaga argued to be unlikely. The next argument in favor of a null pronominal analysis comes from a type of coordination that involves adjunct clauses, as in (15). Following Kayne (1994), Arteaga analyzed the null object in the adjunct clause as bound by the object of the main clause, a relation that suggests a null pronominal rather than a null variable. Finally, in *écrasement*, Arteaga noted that the null object can trigger past participle agreement, as in (16).

16. *Uns   siens   chevaliers   qui porvit   la*
    a-M-SG-NOM his-M-SG-NOM knight-M-SG-NOM who deal.with-3-SG the-F-SG
    letre   si   li   a   leüe.
    letter-F-SG thus him-3-SG-DAT has-3-SG read-PTCP [e]
    'One of his knights who was in charge of the letter read __ to him.'
    Roman de la Rose, line 1015

These pieces of evidence led Arteaga (1997) to conclude that null objects of the type in (12) through (15) all constituted examples of null pronominals. As she noted, (12) through (15) are incompatible with a null topic analysis for Old French. Rather, they require an overt antecedent in the sentence.

4.2 Data and Analysis

In this paper, beyond identifying a range of contexts in which null objects are attested in Old French, I will be concerned principally with how the identity of the null object is established—that is, I will consider the nature of the binding antecedent, if there is one. Cases where the null object is unambiguously co-indexed with a sentence-internal main clause argument will be taken as suggestive of a null pronominal. When the null object is not co-indexed with a sentence-internal argument, or no sentence-internal argument is available, and the null object's identity depends on an element in a non-argument position, this will be taken as suggestive of a null variable. Several other common diagnostics found in the null object literature are impracticable when working with Old French data. For example, as Arteaga (1997) noted, the data required to examine cross-over effects are not available. We are also hampered by the inability to convincingly demonstrate ungrammaticality in Old French; we are limited to the available written data, all of which are necessarily understood to be grammatical. The (obvious) lack of native speakers precludes manipulations of the available data (Marchello-Nizia 1995), reducing diagnostics available for analyzing historical data.

The data are taken predominantly from between 1100 and 1300, the period for which the largest number of Old French texts are available. Both prose and verse texts were included, and text genre was not taken into consideration, although Schøsler (1999) noted apparent differences in object omissibility between literary and judicial texts. Further exploration of this issue is beyond the scope of the present inquiry but offers a topic for future research. Data come from the searchable electronic Amsterdam Corpus (Stein et al. 2008), analyses of complete texts not in the Amsterdam Corpus, and previous scholarly work.

4.2.1 Contexts for Null Objects in Old French

This section will illustrate and discuss object omission in Old French in seven contexts: *écrasement*, coordination, adjunct clauses, null cognate objects, formulaic or context-bound expressions, arbitrary human null objects, and the left-periphery. The discussion begins with *écrasement*, the most commonly discussed null object environment in Old French.

4.2.1.1 Écrasement

Écrasement (literally, 'crushing') is a well-documented and systematic phenomenon in Old French in which, given a sequence of two third-person object clitics, the direct object clitic is not expressed. Thus, the sequence of direct object pronoun + indirect object pronoun yields only the indirect object pronoun, as shown in (17) and illustrated in (18).

17. *la/le/les + li —> li*
    la/le/les + lor —> lor

18. *Et   cil   dit   que l'   an   li*
    and he-3-M-SG-NOM said-3-SG that the-SG.one-SG-INDF-NOM him-3-SG-DAT
    aport   ses   armes,   et an
    bring-3-SG-SBJV his-PL-POSS weapons-F-PL and one-3-SG-INDF-NOM
    li   aporte.
    him-3-SG- DAT bring-3-SG [e]
    'And he asked that someone bring him his weapons, and one brought __ to him.'
    Perceval, lines 2138–2139

Importantly, however, the omitted direct object pronoun is syntactically active in the sense of Bouchard (1989). Recall from Arteaga (1997) that it is capable of triggering gender agreement on the past participle. Furthermore, it can be overtly expressed, as in (19).

19. *Celui   qui ses   armes   gardoit   i   vit   e   si*
    he-3-M-SG-ACC who his-PL-POSS weapons-F-PL kept-3-SG there saw-3-SG and thus
    comanda s'   espee   et   cil   la   li
    gave-3-SG his-SG-POSS.sword-F-SG and he-M-SG-NOM it-3-F-SG-ACC him-3-SG-DAT
    garda.
    kept-3-SG
    'He who saw the one who kept his weapons and gave him his sword, and he kept it.'
    Perceval, lines 3182–3184, cited in Foulet (1930)

The identity of the null direct object in *écrasement* invariably comes from an earlier constituent in the sentence, and *écrasement* appears impossible when the antecedent of the null object is different from that of the preceding nominal direct object. The null object in *écrasement* is thus bound by an element in an argument position. Following Arteaga (1997), I analyze instances of *écrasement* as null pronominals. *Écrasement* can still be found in modern colloquial speech (Lambrecht and Lemoine 2005; Yaguello 1998).[2] Traditional accounts (e.g., Martin and Wilmet 1980) suggest that *écrasement* is the result of phonological reduction, although Lambrecht and Lemoine (2005) contested this claim.

4.2.1.2 Coordination

Old French allowed a single object to be coordinated across multiple verb phrases, in which case the object pronoun was expressed overtly only once, as in (20).

---

[2] Yaguello (1998) suggested that écrasement is less likely to occur with a [+human] than a [−human] referent, an observation that remains to be investigated in Old French.

20. *Einsi le   pans   et cuit   et croi.*
    thus it-3-M-SG-ACC think-1-SG and believe-1-SG [e] and believe-1-SG [e]
    'Thus (I) think this and (I) believe __ and (I) believe __.'
    Perceval, line 1044

In (21), the infinitive has been fronted, preceding the object clitic, which has climbed past the finite verb *voil* 'want.' The object clitic is then omitted with the future-tense *occirai* 'will kill.'

21. *Occire, fet   il,   le   voil   je   et*
    kill-INF did-3-SG he-3-M-SG-NOM him-3-M-SG-ACC want-1-SG I-1-SG-NOM and
    occirai.
    kill-1-SG-FUT [e]
    'To kill, said he, him I want and (I) will kill __.'
    Queste del Saint Graal, §191, cited in Vance (1993)

This omission may take place even the overtly expressed object is direct, and the omitted object is indirect, as in (22) and (23), in which *fet* 'makes/gives,' *dire* 'to tell,' and *prometre* 'to promise' all subcategorize for an indirect object.

22. *Si   la   rebeise   et   fet   grant   joie.*
    thus her-3-F-SG-ACC again.kisses-3-SG and makes-3-SG [e] great-SG joy-F-SG
    'So (he) kisses her again and gives __ great joy.'
    Erec et Enide, line 6465, cited in Kibler (1984)

23. *Et   la   comença   a conforter   et   a dire   et   a*
    and her-3-F-SG-ACC begins-3-SG to comfort-INF and to tell-INF [e] and to
    prometre   quant   que il   peut.
    promise-INF [e] everything that he-3-M-SG-NOM can-3-SG
    'And (he) began to comfort her and tell __ and promise __ everything he could.'
    Roman de Troie, §65, cited in Jensen (1990)

Omission may also take place if the antecedent is a full noun-phrase (NP) rather than an object pronoun. Consider (24) and (25):

24. *Li   feist   l'   en   vin   aporter   et*
    him-3-SG-DAT did-3-SG the-SG.one-3-SG-NOM-INDF wine-M-SG bring-INF and
    but   por son   cors   deporter.
    drank-3-SG [e] for his-3-M-SG-POSS body-M-SG distract-INF
    'One had wine brought to him and (he) drank __ to distract himself.'
    Roman de la Rose, lines 6475–6476

25. *Et lors comença   chascuns   à aporter   le   gaieng   et*
    and then started-3-SG each.one-3-M-SG-NOM to carry-INF the-M-SG loot-M-SG and
    à metre   ensemble.
    to put-INF [e] together
    'And then each one started to carry the loot and to put __ together.'
    Villehardouin, *Conquête de Constantinople*, §252

4 Null Objects in Old French   71

In (24), the direct object *vin* 'wine' of the verb *aporter* 'to bring' is clearly the intended object of the following verb *but* 'drank.' Similarly, in (25), *le gaieng* 'the loot' is the object of *metre ensemble* 'put together.' In these examples, if the object were overtly expressed, it would logically appear as an object clitic rather than a full NP.

After the first realization of the object in coordination structures, omission of the object pronouns with subsequent verbs was systematic in Old French, but occasional examples with repetition of the object pronoun exist, such as in (26), where *li* represents the accusative feminine singular, and (27), a passage very similar to (24) but with overtly expressed objects for each use of the verb *bevre* 'to drink.' Foulet (1930) attributed such repetition to stylistic effects.

26. *Je   desir   tant   li   embracier   et   li*
    I-1-SG-NOM desire-1-SG so.much her-3-F-SG-ACC embrace-INF and her-3-F-SG-ACC
    veoir   et   li   oïr.
    see-INF and her-3-F-SG-ACC hear-INF
    'I so desire to embrace her and see her and hear her.'
    Chansons de Colin Muset §41, cited in Foulet (1930)

27. *Car ja nul   jor   ne   li   pleust   bevre   vin*
    for NEG no-M-SG day-M-SG NEG him-3-SG-DAT please-3-SG drink-INF wine-M-SG
    et   s'il   en   beust   il   le
    and if.he-3-M-SG-NOM some drank-3-SG-PST-SBJV he-3-M-SG-NOM it-3-M-SG-ACC
    beveit   mauveis   et aigre.
    drank-3-SG bad-M-SG and sour-M-SG
    'For he never enjoyed drinking wine, and if he drank some he drank it bad and sour.'
    Vie de Saint Martin de Tours, lines 3217–3218

Finally, variation between null and overt objects exists across different manuscripts of the same text. Consider the first passage, from Chrétien de Troyes' *Perceval*, in which Perceval's mother is overcome with joy at the sight of her son. The same passage contains a null object in the version in (28) and an expressed object in the version in (29).

28. *Grant   ioie   ot   en meisme l'   ore   qu'ele*
    great-SG joy-F-SG had-3-SG in self-SG the-SG.time-F-SG that.she-3-F-SG-NOM
    le   uit   et pas ne pot   dire   la   ioie   que
    him-3-M-SG-ACC saw-3-SG and NEG NEG could-3-SG say-INF the-F-SG joy-F-SG that
    ele   en   ot   car   comme mere   qui mout
    she-3-F-SG-NOM of.it had-3-SG because as   mother-F-SG who much
    aime   cort   contre lui   et si   le
    loves-3-SG [e] runs-3-SG toward him-3-M-SG-OBL and thus him-3-M-SG-ACC
    claime   'biax   fils   biax   fils.
    calls-3-SG beautiful-M-SG son-M-SG beautiful-M-SG son-M-SG

'Great joy had (she) all at once when she saw him and (she) could not express the joy she had from it, so as a mother who loves __ greatly (she) runs toward him and calls him 'handsome son handsome son.''
Perceval, lines 342–347, manuscript R

29. *car comme mere   qui mout l'   ainme   cort*
    for as   mother-F-SG who much him-3-SG-ACC.loves-3-SG runs-3-SG
    contre lui
    against him-3-M-SG-OBL
    'for as a mother who loves him greatly she runs toward him'
    Perceval, lines 345–346, manuscript M

In the version in (28), which contains a null object, the identity of the null object is the same as the object of the preceding verb *uit* (*vit*) 'saw,' separated from the null object by more intervening material than in previous examples of coordination. Similarly, in (30) a relative clause separates the clause containing the full NP antecedent *l'autre* 'the other one' from the clause containing a null object with the verb *feri* 'struck.'

30. *Le   clerc   rensui   l'autre,   lequel   cuida*
    the-M-SG cleric-M-SG follow-3-SG the-SG.other.one-M-SG who-M-SG about.to-3-SG
    descendre   en une   estrange meson   la   ou   gent
    go.down-INF in a-F-SG strange-SG house-F-SG there where people-M-SG
    veilloient   encore, et le   clerc   feri   du
    stay.awake-3-PL still   and the-M-SG cleric-M-SG struck-3-SG [e] with-ART-M-SG
    fauchon   parmi   la   teste
    sword-M-SG through the-F-SG head-F-SG
    'The cleric followed the other one, who was about to go into a strange house where people were still awake, and the cleric hit __ on the head with a large knife.'
    Joinville, §117, ms. Paris, Bibl. Nat., fr. 1356

Again, manuscripts differ as to whether or not the object is expressed; example (31) presents the same passage with the object of *feri* 'struck' expressed overtly.

31. *Li   clers   rensui   l'   autre,*
    the-M-SG-NOM cleric-M-SG-NOM follow-3-SG the-SG.other.one-M-SG
    liquels   cuida   descendre   en une   estrange maison,   là
    who-M-SG-NOM about.to-3-SG go.down-INF in a-F-SG strange-SG house-F-SG there
    où   la   gent   veilloient   encore; et   li
    where the-F-SG people-F-SG stay.awake-3-PL still   and the-M-SG-NOM
    clerc   le   feri   dou   fauchon   parmi
    cleric-M-SG-NOM him-M-SG-ACC struck-3-SG with-ART-M-SG sword-M-SG through
    la teste.
    the-F-SG head-F-SG

'The cleric followed the other one, who imagined that he was going into a strange house where people were still awake, and the cleric hit him on the head with a large knife.'
Joinville, §117: ms. not identified, cited in Viollet-le-Duc (1874)

In coordination, the null object is bound by an overt antecedent in an argument position in a preceding verb phrase. The reference of the null object is identical to the overtly expressed object earlier in the clause.[3] As in Arteaga (1997), I adopt a null pronominal analysis.

4.2.1.3 Adjunct Clauses

If a non-finite clause adjoined to a main clause contains a null object, the antecedent of the null object is an argument (nominal or pronominal) in the main clause. In this respect, non-finite adjunct clauses resemble the examples of coordination discussed in Sect. 4.2.1.2. The example in (32) presents a participial adjunct, whereas those in (33) and (34) are infinitival, introduced by *por* 'to/for' and *sanz* 'without,' respectively.

32. *Il   monta   sor son   cheval   et prent*
    he-M-SG-NOM mounted-3-SG on his-M-SG-POSS horse-M-SG and takes-3-SG
    s'   amie   devant   lui,   baisant   et
    his-SG-POSS.friend-F-SG in.front.of him-3-M-SG-OBL kissing-PTCP [e] and

---

[3] In the following example, the antecedent (*la vile* 'the city') of the null object in the second sentence is not the direct object of a prior verb but rather the object of a preposition:

Lors sejorna   l'empereres   Henri par cinq jorz,   et   puis chevaucha
Then stayed-3-SG the-SG.emperor-M-SG-NOM Henry for five days-M-PL and then rode-3-SG
trosque à la   cité   del   Dimot, por savoir   coment ele   ere
until   to the-F-SG city-F-SG of-ART-M-SG Dimot for know-INF how   it-F-SG-NOM was-3-SG
abattue,   et se on   la   porroit refermer. Et se
destroyed-F-PTCP and if one-3-SG-NOM-INDF it-F-SG-ACC could-3-SG repair-INF and 3-SG-REFL
loja   devant   la   vile,   et vit,   et il   et si
camped-3-SG in.front.of the-F-SG city-F-SG and saw-3-SG and he-3-M-SG-NOM and his-3-PL-POSS
baron,   que il   n'estoit   mie leus   de fermer   en
barons-M-PL-NOM that it-3-M-SG-NOM NEG.was-3-SG NEG place-M-SG of secure-INF [e] in
tel   point.
this-M-SG condition-M-SG

'Then the emperor Henry stayed for five days, and then (he) rode as far as the city of Dimot, to see how it had been destroyed, and if one could refortify it. And (he) camped in front of the city and saw, he and his barons, that there was no place to secure __ in this condition.' (Villehardouin, *Conquête de Constantinople*, §449)

By way of contrast, note the expressed object *la* 'it' in the final *se* clause of the first sentence.

acolant.
embracing-PTCP [e]
'He got on his horse and takes his beloved in front of him, kissing __ and embracing __.'
Aucassin et Nicolette, §26, cited in Jensen (1990)

33. *Ja   la   voloient   en feu   metre   por rostir*
    already her-3-F-SG-ACC wanted-3-PL in fire-M-SG put-INF for roast-INF [e]
    et   por greillier.
    and for grill-INF [e]
    'Already (they) wanted to put her in the fire to roast __ and to grill __.'
    Cligès, lines 5936–5937, cited in Troberg (2004)

34. *Car il   les   conquiest   sanz   occirre.*
    for he-3-M-SG-NOM them-3-PL-ACC defeated-3-SG without kill-INF [e]
    'For he defeated them without killing __.'
    Queste del Saint Graal, §54, cited in Jensen (1990)

The adjunct clause may also be fronted, with the result that the null object precedes the overtly expressed co-indexed argument, which suggests that the null object is licensed prior to focus movement or topicalization, as in (35).

35. *Por occierre   le   queroient.*
    for kill-INF [e] him-3-M-SG-ACC looked-3-PL
    'In order to kill __, (they) were looking for him.'
    Roman de la Rose, line 6408, cited in Jensen (1990)

If one follows Lambrecht and Lemoine (2005), who argued that *écrasement* is not phonologically driven, then null objects in coordination structures appear as a parallel structure to *écrasement* in what might be a larger Old French strategy of omitting objects after a sentence-internal first mention. In any case, the examples of null objects in coordination structures, like those in *écrasement* contexts, take their identity from a sentence-internal co-indexed argument, and they are analyzed here, as in Arteaga (1997), as instances of null pronominals.

4.2.1.4 Null Cognate Objects

As Luraghi (1997) pointed out in her discussion of null objects in Latin, it can be difficult to judge the transitivity of certain verbs, and the lack of native speakers eliminates the possibility of judgment data. By following the approach in Cummins and Roberge (2004), which allows for null cognate objects, we can partially avoid this difficulty, at least for some transitive verbs that are often used absolutely. Old French evinces null cognate objects, for example in (36), where the understood null objects are 'something drinkable,' 'something edible,' and 'something speakable,' respectively. Examples of these verbs with overt objects are also frequently attested.

4   Null Objects in Old French   75

36. *Il   fu   bien deux jours   que il   ne*
    it-3-M-SG-NOM was-3-SG well two days-M-PL that he-3-M-SG-NOM NEG
    but,   ne   ne   manja,   ne   ne   parla.
    drank-3-SG [e] NEG NEG ate-3-SG [e] NEG NEG spoke-3-SG [e]
    'For a good two days he neither drank __, nor ate __, nor spoke __.'
    Joinville, §145

A similar situation obtains in (37) with the verbs *prometre* 'to promise' and *doner* 'to give,' neither of which have an overtly expressed object:

37. *Vilenie   est   d'autrui   gaber   et de prometre*
    disgrace-F-SG is-3-SG of.other-INDF make.fun-INF and to promise-INF [e]
    sans   doner.
    without give-INF [e]
    '(It) is shameful to make fun of others and to promise __ without giving __.'
    Perceval, lines 1017–1018

The statement in (37) is general; the understood object of *prometre* and *doner* is 'something that can be promised' and 'something that can be given.' In the continuation of the same passage, the statement is rendered more explicit by the overt object pronoun sequence *rien nule* 'nothing,' given in (38).

38. *Vilanie   est   d'autrui   gaber   et de prometre*
    disgrace-F-SG is-3-SG of.other-INDF make.fun-INF and to promise-INF [e]
    sans   doner.   Prodom   ne   se   doit   antremetre de rien
    without give-INF [e] worthy.man-M-SG NEG 3-SG-REFL must-3-SG commit-INF to NEG
    nule   a autrui   prometre   que doner   ne   li
    nothing-INDF to other-SG.INDF promise-INF that give-INF NEG him-3-SG-DAT
    puise   et voille
    can-3-SG-SBJV and want-3-SG-SBJV
    'It is shameful to make fun of others and to promise __ without giving __. A man of honor should not commit to promising anything to anyone that he cannot do and does not have the intention of doing.'
    Perceval, lines 1017–1021

Following the approach in Cummins and Roberge (2004), I suggest that examples like (36) and (37) contain null (cognate) objects. The analysis here must differ from that offered for the *écrasement*, coordination, and adjunct clause examples discussed previously, in that (36) and (37) contain no sentence-internal argument that is available for co-indexation. The null object must get its identity elsewhere. The null objects are interpretable by virtue of the context and the lexical properties of the verb; an analysis as null pronominals is ruled out because of the absence of a sentence-internal antecedent in argument position, suggesting that these are instances of null variables.

4.2.1.5 Formulaic or Conventional Expressions

Garcia Velasco and Portero Muñoz (2002) demonstrated that null objects are frequent in fixed or conventional expressions. Example (39) presents a common Old French expression involving the verb *tranchier* 'to cut.' Knowing that there existed a member of the court whose duty was to cut the meat at mealtimes (the *maistre queux*), this phrase—found regularly in texts about the court—is readily interpretable when it occurs in an appropriate discourse context.

39. *Devant le   roy   tranchoit   du   coutel   le*
    in.front the-M-SG king-M-SG cut-3-SG [e] with-ART-M-SG knife-M-SG the-M-SG
    bon   conte   Jehan de Soissons
    good-M-SG count-M-SG Jean of Soissons
    'In front of the king, the good count Jean of Soissons cut __ with a knife.'
    Joinville, §94

Similarly, the expression *ferir des esperons* 'to strike with the spurs' is most often used without an overt object as in (40), although 'horse' is understood, given the larger discourse context of military action.

40. *Il   feri   des   esperons   et   tout*
    he-M-SG-NOM struck-3-SG [e] with-ART-PL spurs-M-PL and all-M-SG
    l'ost   aussi.
    the-SG.army-M-SG also
    'He struck __ with the spurs and the whole army (did the same).'
    Joinville, §186

However, as shown in (41) it is also possible to find *cheval* 'horse' as the expressed object, with no apparent change in meaning from (40).

41. *Quant le   quens   de Flandres oi   chou   si*
    when the-M-SG count-M-SG-NOM of Flanders heard-3-SG this-M-SG thus
    feri   cheval   des   esperons   et   tot   li
    struck-3-SG horse-M-SG of-ART-PL spurs-M-PL and all-M-PL-NOM the-M-PL-NOM
    autre   apres
    others-M-PL-NOM after
    'When the count of Flanders heard this, (he) struck (his) horse with the spurs, and the others followed.'
    Conquête de Constantinople, lines 2381–2382

No overt antecedent is explicitly available in (39) or (40), either sentence-internally or in the passages preceding the extracts. Rather, it is the preceding discourse context that establishes the frame that permits the interpretation of the null object. The null object occurs with a precise, lexically constrained use of the verb (Schøsler 2000). Such a situation is compatible with a null variable analysis. The absence of an overt antecedent in an argument position excludes an analysis as a null pronominal.

4.2.1.6 Arbitrary Human Null Objects

Authier (1989a) documented common cases of null objects with the arbitrary human reading in modern French, and comparable examples exist in Old French (but see Schøsler 1999 for discussion of the omissibility of [–human] referents). In (42), the unexpressed object of the verbs *aidier* 'to help' and *plaire* 'to be pleasing to' can only be an arbitrary human referent; no other discourse referent is available or logical.

42. *si   cum ens en la   bible   trueve   en paradis   avoit   un*
    just as in   in the-F-SG bible-F-SG finds-3-SG in paradise-M-SG had-3-SG a-M-SG
    fluive   ki   parmi contreval coroit   dont   tote   plentez
    river-M-SG that through down   flowed-3-SG from.which all-F-SG abundance-F-SG
    acoroit   comme de   pierres   preciouses   mult chieres   et   mult
    sprang-3-SG like   some stones-F-PL precious-F-PL very valuable-F-PL and very
    gratiouses   esmeraudes   rubiz   topazes   et   altres   ki
    beautiful-F-PL emeralds-F-PL rubies-M-PL topazes-M-PL and others-PL that
    ont   bones   grazes   telz   ki   pueent   aidier   et
    have-3-PL good-F-PL elegance-F-PL such-PL that can-3-PL help-INF [e] and
    plaire   si   come jel   truis
    please-INF [e] just like I-I-SG-NOM.it-M-SG-ACC find-I-SG
    'just as, in the Bible, (one) finds (that) in Paradise, (there) was a river that flowed down, from which abundance sprang, like precious stones, very valuable and very beautiful, emeralds, rubies, topazes, and others that have much elegance, which can help __ and please __, like I find it.'
    La Genèse d'Évrat, lines 724–740

Similarly, in (43), the warriors Roland and Oliver strike (*ferir*) and massacre (*capler*) an arbitrary human referent—in this case, members of the opposing army. That *ferir* and *capler* have an object is indisputable because in the last phrase of this passage, the enemy warriors who have been struck down are promoted to topic status and can be counted.

43. *Dur   sunt   li   colps   e   li*
    severe-M-PL are-3-PL the-M-PL-NOM blows-M-PL and the-M-SG-NOM
    caples   est   grefs;   mult grant   dulor   i   ad
    battle-M-SG-NOM is-3-SG fierce-M-SG very great-SG suffering-F-SG there had-3-SG
    de chrestiens.   Ki   puis veïst   Rollant e   Oliver de lur
    of Christians-M-PL who then see-3-SG-SBJV Roland and Oliver of their-PL-POSS
    espees   e   ferir   e   capler!   Li
    swords-F-PL and strike-INF [e] and massacre-INF [e] the-M-SG-NOM

arcevesque   i   fiert   de sun   espiet.   Cels
archbishop-M-SG there strikes-3-SG of his-M-SG-POSS pike-M-SG those-M-PL
qu'ils   unt   mort,   ben les   poet
that.they-3-M-PL-NOM have-3-PL killed-PTCP well they-3-PL-ACC can-3-SG
hom   preiser
one-3-SG-NOM-INDF count-INF

'The blows are severe and the battle is fierce; the Christians had much suffering. What a spectacle to see Roland and Oliver strike __ and massacre __ with their swords. The archbishop strikes in that manner with his pike. Those that they killed, one can count them well.'
Chanson de Roland, lines 1680–1684

In the arbitrary human null object examples, no overt antecedent is present to bind the null object, and a null variable analysis is adopted. In this respect, the analysis of Old French arbitrary human null objects closely resembles Authier's (1989a) treatment of the same phenomenon in modern French.

4.2.1.7 Left-Periphery

Arteaga (1997) analyzed examples like (12)—repeated here as (44)—and (45) as instances of LD with a null resumptive pronoun, which she analyzed as a null pronominal.

44. *Mais or   dites,   si ne   vous   griet,   vostre*
    but   now say-2-PL-IMP, if NEG you-2-PL-DAT torment-3-SG your-SG-POSS
    tere   qui deffendra   quand li   rois
    land-F-SG who defend-3-SG-FUT [e] when the-M-SG-NOM king-M-SG-NOM
    Artus   y   venra?
    Arthur-M-SG-NOM there come-3-SG-FUT
    'But tell now, if it doesn't anger you, your land who will defend __ when King Arthur will come there?'
    Chevalier au Lion, lines 1614–1616, cited in Arteaga (1997)

45. *E! malvais   deus,   por quei nus   fais   tel*
    oh bad-M-SG god-M-SG-NOM for what us-1-PL-DAT do-2-SG such-M-SG
    hunte?   Cest   nostre   rei   por quei lessas
    shame-M-SG this-M-SG-ACC our-SG-POSS king-M-SG-ACC for what let-2-SG [e]
    cunfundre? Ki   mult te   sert,   malvais   luer
    flounder-INF who much you-2-SG-ACC serves-3-SG bad-M-SG reward-M-SG
    l'en   dunes!
    him-SG-DAT\of.it give-2-SG

'Oh cruel god, why do (you) inflict such shame on us? This our king why do (you) let __ flounder? He who serves you well (you) give a bad reward.'
Chanson de Roland, lines 2582–2584, cited in Arteaga (1997)

As Arteaga (1997) pointed out, the constituents *vostre tere* 'your land' and *cest nostre rei* 'this our king' cannot have been fronted by a topicalization process (*wh*-movement) because the COMP position is already filled with a *wh*-word (*qui* 'who' and *por quei* 'why'), hence the analysis as a LD with a null resumptive pronoun. Examples like (44) and (45) have counterparts with overt resumptive pronouns (see Priestley 1955), both in declaratives (46 and 47) and for both yes/no and *wh*-interrogatives (48 and 49).[4, 5]

46. *Cels   qu' ils   unt   mort,   ben les*
    those-M-PL-ACC that.they-3-M-PL-NOM have-3-PL killed-PTCP well they-3-PL-ACC
    poet   hom   preiser.
    can-3-SG one-3-SG-INDF count-INF
    'Those that they killed, one can count them well.'
    Chanson de Roland, line 1683, cited in Priestley (1955)

47. *Ceste   bataille, veriment la   ferum.   La   rereguarde de*
    this-F-SG battle-F-SG truly   it-F-SG-ACC do-1-PL-FUT the-F-SG rearguard-F-SG of
    la   grant   host   Carlun,   il   est
    the-F-SG great-SG army-F-SG Charles-M.SG.ACC it-3-M-SG-NOM is-3-SG
    juget   que nus   les   ocirum.
    pass.judgment-PTCP that we-1-PL-NOM them-3-PL-ACC kill-1-PL-FUT
    'This battle, really (we) will do it. The rearguard of the great army of Charles, it is said that we will kill them.'
    Chanson de Roland, lines 882–884, cited in Priestley (1955)

48. *L'aveir   Carlun   est   il   apareilliez?*[6]
    the-SG.treasure-M-SG Charles-M-SG-ACC is-3-SG it-M-SG-NOM prepare-PTCP
    'Charlemagne's treasure is it ready?'
    Chanson de Roland, line 644, cited in Priestley (1955)

49. *Sa   grant   valor   kil   purreit   acunter?*
    his-F-SG-POSS great-SG worth-F-SG who.it-F-SG-ACC could-3-SG-COND measure-INF
    'His great worth, who could measure it?'
    Chanson de Roland, line 534, cited in Melander (1943)

---

[4] Modern French similarly allows LDs with or without a resumptive pronoun in *wh*-interrogatives, as in *Jean-Claude, quand est-ce que tu l'as vu?* 'Jean-Claude, when did you see him?' and *Le chianti, qui aime?* 'Chianti, who likes?' The second example, however, appears to be less acceptable for some speakers.

[5] Arteaga's (1997) analysis, following Cecchetto (1997), predicts that LDs will not appear with a resumptive pronoun in Old French. Further investigation of this point is left for future work.

[6] I follow Roberts (1993) in analyzing these examples as LDs and not stylistic inversion.

The present analysis of LDs with null resumptive pronouns draws on Benincà's (2004, 2006) model of the left periphery of medieval Romance. In Benincà's model, inspired by Rizzi (1997), the left periphery is composed of a number of fields. A simplified version from Benincà (2004, p. 257) is given in (50), showing the frame, topic, and focus fields.

50. $\{_{\text{Frame}}...[\text{Hanging Topic}]...\}\{_{\text{Topic}}...[\text{Left-Dislocation}]...\}\{_{\text{Focus}}...[wh]\ V\}$

Benincà argues that elements situated in the focus field are generated via movement, whereas elements in the topic and frame fields are base generated. Research on modern Romance data also corroborates the claim that LD is base-generated (Cinque 1997; De Cat 2007; Hirschbühler 1997). Benincà further argues that medieval Romance allowed null topics (but not null focus), a claim that finds support in Authier's (1988) claim that null topics are base-generated.

From a discourse perspective, all the left-dislocated constituents in (44) through (47)—with or without a resumptive pronoun—behave like topics (Lambrecht 1981) rather than focus.[7] In (44), 'your land' is an inferrable referent—and hence able to promoted to topic (e.g., Prince 1981)—and the *wh*-interrogative *qui* 'who' represents the focus. In Benincà's (2004, 2006) analysis, these two elements would be situated in the topic and focus fields, respectively. Similarly, in (45), the topic of the preceding passage has been the king, and the interrogative *por quei* 'why' is situated in the focus field. In both (46) and (47), the left-dislocated constituent represents the topic of the preceding discourse.

Because left-peripheral positions are A-bar positions (Rizzi 1997), I propose that the LDs with null resumptive pronouns should be treated as instances of null variables bound by the topic in the left-periphery, departing in this respect from Arteaga (1997), who analyzed them as null pronominals. If Benincà (2004, 2006) is correct that medieval Romance—and therefore Old French—allowed null topics, then in the present analysis, arbitrary human null objects, formulaic null objects, null cognate objects, and LD with a null resumptive pronoun all share a similar structure in which a null or overt topic in the left periphery serves as the antecedent to a null variable in the main clause.

4.3 Discussion and Conclusion

The data presented here demonstrate that Old French must be included among the Romance varieties in which null objects are attested. The present data do not permit speculation about how frequent object drop was in earlier stages of the language.

---

[7] There need not be an exact correspondence between a constituent's discourse function and the functional projection in which it is situated (e.g., a topic in TopicP); what is important is that the LD is in a leftward (A-bar) position, as evidenced by the presence of a focus element in COMP.

Rather, the claim is that Old French, like modern French, permitted null objects in a wider variety of contexts than has been previously acknowledged, and that the ability to drop objects is not an innovation in later stages of French. These contexts include the well-documented phenomenon of *écrasement* but also encompass coordination across multiple verbs, adjunct clauses, null cognate objects, formulaic or context-bound expressions, arbitrary human null objects, and LDs.

Claims that Romance varieties do not permit null objects (e.g., Huang 1984; Vincent 2000) should be questioned in light of the present data and earlier research that has documented null objects in European Portuguese (Raposo 1986), Brazilian Portuguese (Galves 1989), Italian (Rizzi 1986a), Spanish (Campos 1986), and modern French (Authier 1989a; Cummins and Roberge 2004; Fónagy 1985; Lambrecht and Lemoine 2005; Schøsler 2000; Yaguello 1998). That null objects should be attested in a range of Romance varieties is not surprising, given that null objects were present in their Latin parentage (Luraghi 1997; Pinkster 1990; Schøsler 1999; Vincent 2000), for example in coordination, as in (51). The example is from Luraghi (1997, p. 250).

51. *qua   necessitate   Mithridates   diem*
    which-ABL necessity-F-SG-ABL Mithridates-M-SG-NOM day-M-SG-ACC
    locumque   foederi   accepit
    place-M-SG-ACC.and agreement-NEUT-SG-DAT accept-3-SG-PRF
    castelloque   egreditur   ac primo Radamistus   in
    castle-NEUT-SG-ABL.and go.out-3-SG-DEP and first   Radamistus-M-SG-NOM in
    amplexus   eius   effusus   simulare
    embrace-M-SG-ACC him-M-SG-GEN pour.out-PTCP feign-INF
    obsequium,   socerum   ac parentem
    indulgence-NEUT-SG-ACC father.in.law-M-SG-ACC and parent-M-SG-ACC
    appellare;   adicit   ius iurandum,   non ferro,
    name-INF [e] adds-3-SG oath-NEUT-SG-ACC NEG sword-NEUT-SG-ABL
    non veneno   vim   adlaturum.
    NEG poison-NEUT-SG-ABL violence-F-SG-ACC bring-SG-ACC-PTCP-FUT [e]
    simil   in lucum   propinquum   trahit.
    at.same.time in grove-M-SG-ACC near-M-SG-ACC drags-3-SG [e]
    'Out of necessity, Mithridates accepted the time and place for negotiations and went out of the castle. First, Radamistus embraced him feigning love, calling __ father-in-law and parent; he swears that he will not bring violence (toward) __ either with weapons or by giving __ poison. At the same time, he drags __ to a nearby grove.'
    Tacitus, *Annals*, §12:46–47

In (51), *Mithridates* is expressed overtly as a subject and then as the pronoun *eius* (genitive). *Mithridates* is then the unexpressed object (direct or indirect) of three further verb forms: *appellare* 'to name,' *adlaturum* 'will bring,' and *trahit* 'drags.' Old French could omit objects in verb coordination in precisely the same fashion. Similarly, as in Old French, null objects in Latin—although frequent in coordination structures—were not systematic (Luraghi 1997). Given these parallels, Vincent's

(2000) claim that the rise of the clitic system in Romance marked the end of object omission inherited from Latin seems untenable. The variation noted between overt and null objects in Old French (e.g., in *écrasement*, coordination, and between manuscripts) could plausibly be attributed to stylistic choices, as in modern French (Fónagy 1985) and perhaps in Latin (Luraghi 1997), although this remains a topic for future research.

The data illustrate the omission of the direct object in numerous contexts in Old French. According to Schøsler's (1999) hypothesis, the possibility of object drop was limited in Old French and did not become a widespread possibility until Middle French, when the obligatory expression of the subject eliminated potential confusion about the identification of arguments (i.e., distinguishing nominal subjects from direct objects). It is true that for a large number of full NP constituents (especially in the feminine), the Old French case system and the relatively free word order conspire to render distinctions between potential subjects and direct objects difficult, as in (11), at least in the absence of context.

Consequently, for a transitive verb that subcategorizes for a direct object, omission of the (full NP) object could engender confusion, given that subjects are more easily omitted than objects. In such a (putative) case, guided by the knowledge that subjects—but not objects—are frequently unexpressed, one could be led to misinterpret the expressed subject as the direct object. However, this argument, which depends on the convergence of nominative and oblique case forms in (especially feminine) NPs, is less relevant for null object pronouns. The Old French nominative and oblique pronoun paradigms overlap only partially, in the first- and second-person plural (*nos* and *vos* in both nominative and oblique) and, much less frequently, in the third-person feminine plural, where nominative *eles* matches the oblique strong form *eles* but not the more common weak form *les*.

In examples of null objects in *écrasement*, coordination structures, adjunct clauses, and with LDs, the null object, if it were to appear overtly, would appear as a pronoun rather than a full NP, as evidenced by (19), (26), and (27). To use Yaguello's (1998) term, these null objects are *virtual clitics*. The fact that pronouns typically occur after first mention and have as their anaphor a known discourse referent facilitates their ability to drop in contexts where their identity is unambiguous (see Lambrecht and Lemoine 2005). Old French object drop is nearly systematic in *écrasement*, coordination, and adjunct clauses, where the null object is most frequently in the third-person singular.

No overlap exists between the third-person nominative and oblique paradigms: The omission of a direct object pronoun should have no impact on the ability to distinguish between subject and direct object in such contexts. In the case of null cognate objects and formulaic expressions, the omitted object would most likely surface as a full NP if it were expressed, as seen in (41). I take these observations to suggest that Old French allowed both clitic pronoun and full NP direct objects to be null. Although further research is necessary to determine if the frequency of null objects increased during subsequent stages of the language, the data seem to validate Lambrecht and Lemoine's (2005) suggestion that null objects have always been present in French, although normative grammar has discouraged their use.

The contexts in which Old French and modern French allow null objects are similar but not identical. *Écrasement*, systematic in Old French, remains a possibility in modern French but is restricted to colloquial speech. On the other hand, coordination, also systematic in Old French, is now extremely limited, restricted to a series of past participles linked by a single auxiliary (Rizzi 1986b), as in (52). A series of verbs in the present tense, as in (53), unacceptable for most modern speakers, although in Old French this represented the default situation.

52. *Il   l'   a   acheté   et mangé.*
    he-M-SG-NOM it-SG-ACC.has-3-SG bought-PTCP and eaten-PTCP [e]
    'He has bought it and eaten __.'

53. **Je   le   veux,   paie   et achète.*
    I-1-SG-NOM it-3-M-SG-ACC want-1-SG pay-1-SG [e] and buy-1-SG [e]
    'I want it, pay (for) __, and buy __.'

According to Cummins and Roberge (2004), Modern French allows null objects in what appear to be equivalents of the Old French adjunct clauses discussed in Sect. 4.2.1.3. Modern French also allows null cognate objects, null objects in formulaic expressions, arbitrary human null objects, and null resumptive pronouns with LD. In the case of the arbitrary human null object, the modern usage appears to have expanded beyond the limited possibilities found in the Old French data, where the only attested examples so far involve infinitives.[8] If it turns out that use of the arbitrary human null object has expanded in the course of the development of French, one possible explanation is that it corresponds to a gap in the French object pronoun paradigm. The French third-person subject pronoun *on* 'one,' which admits an arbitrary reading, has no oblique counterpart—this is precisely the context where in many cases the arbitrary human null object is attested, a fact that suggests that nominative *on* has an oblique counterpart that is null (see Lambrecht and Lemoine 2005 for related discussion about null objects and gaps in the pronoun paradigm). The null pronoun posited in this analysis would necessarily be distinct from the one suggested by Schøsler (1999), who argued that modern French object pronoun paradigm possesses a null member restricted to [−human] referents.

On the basis of whether the antecedent of the null object occupied an argument or a non-argument position, it is proposed that Old French evinced two types of null objects: null pronominals (*écrasement*, coordination, adjunct clauses) and null variables (null cognate object, formulaic expressions, arbitrary human null objects, and null objects with an antecedent in a frame or topic position in the left periphery). This analysis of *écrasement*, coordination, and adjunct clauses corroborates the claims made in Arteaga (1997) but differs in the analysis of LDs with null resumptive pronouns by arguing that the left-dislocated antecedent, situated in an A-bar

---

[8] An anonymous reviewer inquires how the arbitrary human null object has evolved diachronically. The present research is restricted to the Old French period; future research is warranted to trace the development of the possibilities attested in Modern French (see examples 1, 3).

position (see Benincà 2004, 2006), provides evidence of a null variable, in line with other an`alyses of LD (e.g., Rizzi 1997). An examination of the discourse behavior of the (admittedly modest) LD data presented here suggests that those with null resumptive pronouns fulfill the same or similar discourse roles as those with overt pronouns. In conclusion, the data in this paper, together with those in Arteaga (1997), provide evidence of object drop in a range of contexts in twelfth- and thirteenth-century Old French.

Acknowledgments I would like to acknowledge Barbara Vance, Laurent Dekydtspotter, Julie Auger, Michael Johnson, the audiences at the 34th Linguistic Symposium on Romance Languages (University of Utah) and the University of Texas at Austin, and the anonymous reviewers for helpful comments and suggestions. All errors and shortcomings are my own.

References

Adams, Marianne. 1987. From Old French to the theory of pro-drop. *Natural Language and Theory* 5: 1–32.
Adams, Marianne. 1989. Verb second effects in medieval French. In *Studies in Romance linguistics*, ed. Carl Kirschner and Janet Decesaris, 1–31. Amsterdam: Benjamins.
Anglade, Joseph. 1941. *Grammaire élémentaire de l'ancien français*. Paris: Armand Colin.
Arteaga, Deborah. 1997. On null objects in Old French. In *Romance linguistics: Theoretical perspectives*, ed. Armin Schwegler, Bernard Tranel, and Myriam Uribe-Etxebarria, 1–11. Amsterdam: Benjamins.
Authier, Jean-Marc P. 1988. Null object constructions in KiNande. *Natural Language and Linguistic Theory* 6: 19–37.
Authier, Jean-Marc P. 1989a. Arbitrary null objects and unselective binding. In *The null subject parameter*, ed. Osvaldo Jaeggli and Kenneth J. Safir, 45–67. Dordrecht: Kluwer.
Authier, Jean-Marc P. 1989b. Two types of empty operator. *Linguistic Inquiry* 20: 117–124.
Benincà, Paola. 2004. The left periphery of medieval Romance. *Studi Linguistici et Filologici Online* 2: 243–297.
Benincà, Paola. 2006. A detailed map of the left periphery of medieval Romance. In *Crosslinguistic research in syntax and semantics: Negation, tense, and clausal architecture*, ed. Raffaella Zanuttini, Hector Campos, Elena Herburger, and Paul Portner, 53–86. Washington, DC: Georgetown UP.
Bescherelle. 1997. *La grammaire pour tous*. Paris: Hatier.
Bouchard, Denis. 1989. Null objects and the theory of empty categories. In *Studies in Romance linguistics*, ed. Carl Kirschner and Janet Decesaris, 33–49. Amsterdam: Benjamins.
Buridant, Claude. 2000. *Grammaire nouvelle de l'ancien français*. Paris: Sedes.
Campos, Hector. 1986. Indefinite object drop. *Linguistic Inquiry* 17: 354–359.
Cecchetto, Carlo. 1997. *The distribution of clitics in dislocation structures*. Paper presented at the 27th Linguistic Symposium on Romance Languages, Irvine, CA.
Cinque, Guglielmo. 1997. Topic' constructions in some European languages and 'connectedness'. In *Materials on left dislocation*, ed. Elena Anagnostopoulou, Henk van Riemsdijk, and Frans Zwarts, 93–118. Amsterdam: Benjamins.
Cole, Peter. 1987. Null objects in universal grammar. *Linguistic Inquiry* 18: 597–612.
Cummins, Sarah, and Yves Roberge. 2004. Null objects in French and English. In *Contemporary approaches to Romance linguistics*, ed. Julie Auger, J.Clancy Clements, and Barbara Vance, 121–138. Amsterdam: Benjamins.
De Cat, Cécile. 2007. *French dislocation: Interpretation, syntax, acquisition*. Oxford: Oxford University Press.

Einhorn, E. 1974. *Old French: A concise handbook*. Cambridge: Cambridge University Press.
Fónagy, Ivan. 1985. Verbes transitifs à objet latent. *Revue Romane* 20: 3–35.
Foulet, Lucien. 1930. *Petite syntaxe de l'ancien français*. Paris: Honoré Champion.
Galves, Charlotte Chambelland. 1989. L'objet nul et la structure de la proposition en portugais du Brésil. *Revue des langues romanes* 93: 305–336.
Garcia Velasco, Daniel, and Carmen Portero Muñoz. 2002. Understood objects in functional grammar. *Working Papers in Functional Grammar* 76: 1–24.
Hirschbühler, Paul. 1997. On the source of lefthand NPs in French. In *Materials on left dislocation*, ed. Elena Anagnostopoulou, Henk van Riemsdijk, and Frans Zwarts, 55–66. Amsterdam: Benjamins.
Huang, C.-T.James. 1984. On the distribution and reference of empty pronouns. *Linguistic Inquiry* 15: 531–574.
Jensen, Frede. 1990. *Old French and comparative Gallo-Romance syntax*. Tübingen: Max Niemeyer Verlag.
Kayne, Richard S. 1994. *The antisymmetry of syntax*. Cambridge, MA: MIT Press.
Kibler, William W. 1984. *An introduction to Old French*. New York: MLA.
Lambrecht, Knud. 1981. *Topic, antitopic, and verb agreement in non-standard French*. Amsterdam: Benjamins.
Lambrecht, Knud, and Kevin Lemoine. 1996. Vers une grammaire des compléments zéro en français parlé. In *Absence de marques et représentation de l'absence: Travaux linguistiques du CERLICO*, ed. Jean Chuquet and Marc Fryd, 279–309. Rennes: Presses Universitaires de Rennes.
Lambrecht, Knud, and Kevin Lemoine. 2005. Definite null objects in spoken French: A construction-grammar account. In *Grammatical constructions*, ed. Mirjam Fried and Hans C. Boas, 13–55. Amsterdam: Benjamins.
Larjavaara, Meri. 2000. *Présence ou absence de l'objet: Limites du possible en français contemporain*. Helsinki: Academia Scientiarum Fennica.
Luraghi, Silvia. 1997. Omission of the direct object in Latin. *Indogermanische Forschungen* 102: 239–257.
Marchello-Nizia, Christiane. 1995. *L'évolution du français: Ordre des mots, démonstratifs, accent tonique*. Paris: Armand Colin.
Marchello-Nizia, Christiane. 1998. Dislocations en ancien français: Thématisation ou rhématisation? *Cahiers de Praxématique* 30: 161–178.
Martin, Robert, and Marc Wilmet. 1980. *Manuel du français du moyen âge*. Bordeaux: SOBODI.
Melander, Jehan. 1943. Le tour français *Cet homme, je le connais*: Sa fréquence et sa syntaxe dans l'ancienne langue. *Studia Neophilologica* 16: 195–200.
Pieroni, Silvia. 1999. Subject properties and semantic roles in Latin. Paper presented at the 10th International Colloquium on Latin Linguistics, Paris.
Pinkster, Harm. 1990. *Latin syntax and semantics*. London: Routledge.
Priestley, L. 1955. Reprise constructions in French. *Archivum Linguisticum* 7: 1–28.
Prince, Ellen F. 1981. Toward a taxonomy of given-new information. In *Radical pragmatics*, ed. Peter Cole, 223–255. San Diego: Academic.
Raposo, Eduardo. 1986. On the null object in European Portuguese. In *Studies in Romance linguistics*, ed. Osvaldo Jaeggli and Carmen Silva-Corvalán, 372–390. Dordrecht: Foris.
Raynaud de Lage, Guy. 1962. *Introduction à l'ancien français*. Paris: Société d'Edition d'Enseignement Supérieur.
Rizzi, Luigi. 1986a. Null objects in Italian and the theory of pro. *Linguistic Inquiry* 17: 501–557.
Rizzi, Luigi. 1986b. On the status of subject clitics in Romance. In *Studies in Romance linguistics*, ed. Osvaldo Jaeggli and Carmen Silva-Corvalán, 391–419. Dordrecht: Foris.
Rizzi, Luigi. 1997. The fine structure of the left periphery. In *Elements of grammar*, ed. Liliane Haegeman, 281–337. Dordrecht: Kluwer.
Roberts, Ian. 1993. *Verbs and diachronic syntax: A comparative history of English and French*. Dordrecht: Kluwer.
Schøsler, Lene. 1999. Réflexions sur l'optionnalité des compléments d'objet direct en latin, en ancien français, en moyen français et en français moderne. *Etudes Romanes* 44: 9–27.

Schøsler, Lene. 2000. Le statut de la forme zéro du complément d'objet direct en français moderne. *Etudes Romanes* 47: 105–129.
Skårup, Povl. 1975. Les premières zones de la proposition en ancien français [Special issue #6]. *Revue Romane.*
Stein, Achim, Pierre Kunstmann, and Martin-D. Gleßgen. 2008. *Nouveau Corpus d'Amsterdam.* Electronic corpus of Old French literary texts c. 1150–1350, originally established by Anthonij Dees. Stuttgart: Institut für Linguistik/Romanistik.
Troberg, Michelle. 2004. Topic-comment resumptive pronouns in Modern French and Old and Middle French. *Toronto Working Papers in Linguistics* 23: 133–156.
Vance, Barbara. 1989. The evolution of pro-drop in medieval French. In *Studies in Romance linguistics*, ed. Carl Kirschner and Janet DeCesaris, 413–441. Amsterdam: Benjamins.
Vance, Barbara. 1993. Verb-first declaratives introduced by et and the position of pro in Old and Middle French. *Lingua* 89: 281–314.
Vance, Barbara. 1997. *Syntactic change in medieval French: Verb-second and null subjects.* Dordrecht: Kluwer.
Vance, Barbara, Donaldson Bryan, and B. Devan Steiner. 2010. V2 loss in Old French and Old Occitan: The role of fronted clauses. In *Selected proceedings of the 39th linguistic symposium on Romance languages*, ed. Sonia Colina, Antxon Olarrea, and Ana Maria Carvalho, 301–320. Amsterdam: Benjamins.
Vincent, Nigel. 2000. Competition and correspondence in syntactic change: Null arguments in Latin and Romance. In *Diachronic syntax: Models and mechanisms*, ed. Susan Pintzuk, George Tsoulas, and Anthony Warner, 25–50. Oxford: Oxford University Press.
Viollet-le-Duc, Eugène. 1874. *Dictionnaire raisonné du mobilier français de l'époque carlovingienne à la Renaissance.* Paris: Librairie centrale d'architecture.
Yaguello, Marina. 1998. La réalisation zéro des clitiques objet dans les constructions di-transitives du français parlé. In *Analyse linguistique et approches de l'oral: Recueil d'études offert en hommage à Claire Blanche-Benveniste*, ed. Mireille Bilger, Karel van den Eynde, and Françoise Gadet, 267–274. Leuven: Peeters.

Chapter 5
Compensatory Lengthening in Historical French: The Role of the Speaker

Randall Gess

5.1 Introduction

Historical French has seen two of the most common types of compensatory lengthening (CL), the well-known process whereby one segment is lengthened as the result of the reduction or deletion of an adjacent or nearby segment. Both of these entailed the lengthening of a vowel – one, the earlier one, triggered by the deletion of an immediately following syllable-final consonant, as shown in (1), and the other by the deletion of a vowel in a following syllable, as shown in (2):

(1) CL triggered by syllable-final consonant loss
    a. *blasmer*   [blazmer] > [blaːmer]   'to blame'
    b. *angle*   [ãnglə] > [ãːglə]   'angel'
    c. *large*   [laʁdʒə] > [laːdʒə][1]   'wide'

---

[1] It has been a rather standard assumption that the rhotic in Old French had a dental or alveolar place of articulation. Gess (1999) points out the quote below cited in Bishop (1968:69), however, suggesting that the rhotic in fact had a uvular articulation, at least in some varieties. Jean de Joinville, the biographer of King Louis IX, attributes this quote to him.

> To restore [*rendre*] is such a hard thing to do that even in speaking of it the word itself rasps one's throat because of the *r*'s that are in it. These *r*'s are, so to speak, like the rakes of the devil, with which he would draw to himself all those who wish to 'restore' what they have taken from others.

Bishop concludes that "the remark indicates that the Parisian, or uvular, *r* was current in the thirteenth century". I adopt the same conclusion here.

R. Gess (✉)
School of Linguistics and Language Studies, Carleton University, Ottawa, ON, Canada
e-mail: randall_gess@carleton.ca

(2) CL triggered by word-final vowel loss
    a. *craie*   [kʁɛjə] > [kʁɛːj]   'chalk'
    b. *sapience*   [sapjãsə] > [sapjãːs]²   'knowledge'
    c. *iustice*   [jystisə] > [jystiːs]³   'justice'
    d. *chambre*   [ʃãbʁə] > [ʃãːbʁ]²   'bedroom'

The data in (1), representative of what we will refer to as CVC CL, are discussed at length in Gess (1998, 1999), the latter of which focuses on the dating of the consonant loss. (1a) illustrates lengthening triggered by the deletion of syllable-final /S/ (=[s] or [z]); (1b) shows lengthening triggered by the loss of syllable-final nasals; and in (1c) the trigger for lengthening is the deletion of syllable-final /ʁ/.⁴ Syllable-final /l/ was also lost through vocalization to [w] during roughly the same period, but the result in this case was a diphthong.

Gess (1999) provides evidence that the changes in (1) took place over two or three centuries, from the eleventh to the fourteenth century, rather than over a much longer period of perhaps as much as ten or eleven centuries that traditional scholarship on OF might have us believe. Gess' analysis suggests either that the sounds were treated as a class, with consonant loss occurring more or less simultaneously, or that the sounds were affected one by one, but in order of increasing sonority, with the least sonorous /S/ being affected first, followed by /N/ , /l/ and finally /ʁ/.

The data in (2) are representative of what we will refer to as CV(C)ə CL. The form in (2a) is mentioned by Morin (1992:139), who explicitly places the change in the Old French period. However, the change appears to have been restricted phonologically and geographically until at least the Middle French period (Pope 1952:116, 118, 205–206). Furthermore, the cases Pope cites as occurring earliest involve the loss of final unstressed vowels immediately following another vowel. If these cases are indeed to be treated as cases of CL (and I know of no good reason why they should not be), then the optionality of the intervening C should be indicated in the label. The forms in (2b–d) are mentioned in the sixteenth century by Estienne (1557). This suggests that word-final vowel deletion and CV(C)ə CL took place gradually over a large span of time, affecting first vowels in hiatus (or following a glide) and then those following consonants. According to Pope (1952:116, 118), the process began earlier and proceeded more rapidly in the north-eastern and eastern region, due to a heavier stress accent.

---

[2] Note that the relevant vowel in these forms was also subject to an earlier process of compensatory lengthening (as illustrated in (1)). The length indicated in these forms is in addition to the inherent length resulting from the earlier process.

[3] Like many words representing abstract concepts, this word was introduced into the language after the deletion of syllable-final /S/- hence the unaffected [s] in the initial syllable.

[4] The deletion of rhotics in syllable-final position was incomplete geographically and in terms of lexical diffusion in those dialects in which it did occur. Furthermore, lost rhotics were largely restored in the course of the seventeenth and eighteenth centuries (Gess 1996:2).

A correlation between the nature of the medial C in CV(C)ə sequences and the likelihood of CL conforms to observed cross-linguistic tendencies. That is, CL may be restricted based on the nature of the intervocalic consonant, such that there may be none (as in the case of OF at the beginning of the process), only glides, only nasals, only sonorants, only liquids and voiced stops, only nasals and voiced fricatives, only nasals, voiced fricatives and voiced stops, or no restrictions (Kavitskaya 2002:121–122, 197–199).

The more restrictive and less widespread nature of CVCV CL, as compared to CVC CL, is also in line with cross-linguistic tendencies. In her Appendix 1, Kavitskaya (2002) lists 58 languages in which CVC CL is manifested, as compared to only 21 languages in her Appendix 2, in which CVCV CL takes place (although she neglects to include Yapese (Jensen 1977) and Skolt Saami (McRobbie-Utasi 1999), where in both cases it appears to be a synchronic process).

The goal of this study is to explore the nature of the changes in (1) and (2) given traditional descriptions of the changes in OF, and within the context of a contemporary challenge to traditional views on CL in general. Traditional descriptions of the changes in OF imply that the process is a speaker-controlled one, with the triggering reduction involving gradual changes in articulation over time. The quote from Morin (1992:139) below is typical of this type of description.

> one can establish that the vowel [in 'CVCə sequences] was lengthened before the complete loss of the post-tonic shwa. The stressed vowel was progressively lengthened, while the following shwa shortened, to the point it became mute when its length reached zero.

Morin goes on to emphasize the gradual nature of CL, saying that, "the stressed vowel was gradually lengthened and the post-tonic schwa simultaneously shortened" (1992:140). Morin's study includes a pointed critique of discrete, non-linear models of CL, which "have not been too concerned with phonetic implementation" and in which he sees "no room [...] for gradual prosodic changes" (Morin 1992:140).

Note that the focus of this study is not on the phonological outcome and subsequent history of the changes illustrated in (1) and (2), but rather on the processes themselves. There is some controversy over whether and for how long the length resulting from these cases of CL was phonologically distinctive. For this issue, the reader is referred to Gess (2001, 2006, 2008), Picard (2004) and Morin (2006).

The focus of this study, then, on is the phonetic implementation of CL. After reviewing previous approaches to CL, I will outline two possible conceptions of a constraint-based, speaker-controlled, phonetic conservation model of the process. This fits into a typology of approaches put forth in Kavitskaya (2002) that includes phonetic conservation approaches, phonological conservation approaches, and non-conservation approaches. An overview of these types of approaches is presented in the following section, describing for each how they might handle the data from historical French. I then describe Kavitskaya's more radical listener-oriented approach, which excludes the speaker from the story of compensatory lengthening. Finally, I present the two possible alternatives in the final section and argue in favor of one of them.

5.2 A Typology of Speaker-Oriented Approaches to CL

This section describes how three previous approaches to CL would handle the data in (1) and (2) and evaluates the relative strengths and weaknesses of each. The approaches, taken in turn in Sects. 5.2.1, 5.2.2, and 5.2.3 are a phonetic conservation approach, a phonological conservation approach, and a non-conservation approach. See also Gess (2011).

5.2.1 A Phonetic Conservation Approach to CL

A phonetic conservation approach to CL is one based on the central assumption that the process is a gradual and goal-oriented one that serves to preserve the phonetic duration of a segment undergoing weakening by associating the lost duration with an adjacent or nearby segment. Drawing on the work of Timberlake (1983), we can schematize the process as shown in (3):

(3) CL as a phonetic process (adapted from Timberlake (1983))

    a. CVC CL

        /CVC/ > [CV$^{1.0+\alpha}$C$^{-\alpha}$]

    b. CV(C)ə CL

        /CV(C)ə/ > [CV$^{1.0+\alpha}$(C)ə$^{-\alpha}$]

Timberlake (1983) treats CL in Late Common Slavic, and therefore deals only with CVCV CL (in his case the final vowel is a weak jer, and there is always an intervening consonant). (3a) is a straightforward extension of his proposal to the case of CVC CL. For CVC CL, as the duration of the final consonant is reduced by amount α, the vowel preceding it is increased by the same amount (pronounced at full duration of a single mora (labeled as 1.0) plus α). Similarly for CV(C)ə CL, the full vowel preceding schwa is increased in duration by the same amount α by which the schwa is reduced. It is obvious from the formalism that lengthening in both cases is entirely compensatory.

This type of approach can easily accommodate the view, like Morin's (1992) quoted earlier and others, that CL in OF was a gradual process. This is schematized in (4), where Timberlake's formalism for CVCV CL (shown in (4b)) is straightforwardly extended to CVC CL (shown in (4a)). For illustration here and throughout, we use /fyst/ *fust* for the earlier, CVC CL, and /kʁɛjə/ *craie* for the later, CV(C)ə CL.[5]

(4) The gradual nature of compensatory lengthening in a phonetic conservation approach (adapted from Timberlake (1983:298))

    a. CVC CL in OF *fust* 'was'
        a. /fyst/ > [fy$^{1.2}$ s$^{-.2}$t]   {α = 0.2}
        b. /fyst/ > [fy$^{1.4}$ s$^{-.4}$t]   {α = 0.4}
        c. /fyst/ > [fy$^{1.6}$ s$^{-.6}$t]   {α = 0.6}
        d. /fyst/ > [fy$^{1.8}$ s$^{-.8}$t]   {α = 0.8}
    b. CV(C)ə CL in OF
        a. /kʁɛjə/ > [kʁɛ$^{1.2}$jə$^{-.2}$]   {α = 0.2}
        b. /kʁɛjə/ > [kʁɛ$^{1.4}$jə$^{-.4}$]   {α = 0.4}
        c. /kʁɛjə/ > [kʁɛ$^{1.6}$jə$^{-.6}$]   {α = 0.6}
        d. /kʁɛjə/ > [kʁɛ$^{1.8}$jə$^{-.8}$]   {α = 0.8}

The formalism in (4) very explicitly reflects the assumption of a gradual and progressive change, from slight erosion of post-vocalic consonants (4a) and final schwas (4b) with a concomitant minor lengthening of preceding vowels, to a drastic reduction in each case, with equally salient compensatory lengthening.

Timberlake (1983) assumes that compensatory lengthening can only take place phonologically once the triggering segment is deleted, which can in principle happen at any stage of reduction. However, if deletion happens at a stage in which reduction is not significant enough (for Timberlake, below 50%), then the lengthened vowel will not be analyzed as phonologically long. This will only happen once the 50% threshold for lengthening has been surpassed, as illustrated in (5):

(5) Schematization of phonological reanalysis (adapted from Timberlake (1983:299))

    a. Phonemic analysis for CVC CL in OF
        a. [fy$^{1.2}$ s$^{-.2}$t]   ⇒ /fyt/   {α = 0.2}
        b. [fy$^{1.4}$ s$^{-.4}$t]   ⇒ /fyt/   {α = 0.4}
        c. [fy$^{1.6}$ s$^{-.6}$t]   ⇒ /fy:t/   {α = 0.6}
        d. [fy$^{1.8}$ s$^{-.8}$t]   ⇒ /fy:t/   {α = 0.8}
    b. Phonemic analysis for CV(C)ə CL in OF
        a. [kʁɛ$^{1.2}$jə$^{-.2}$]   ⇒ /kʁɛj/   {α = 0.2}
        b. [kʁɛ$^{1.4}$jə$^{-.4}$]   ⇒ /kʁɛj/   {α = 0.4}
        c. [kʁɛ$^{1.6}$jə$^{-.6}$]   ⇒ /kʁɛ:j/   {α = 0.6}
        d. [kʁɛ$^{1.8}$jə$^{-.8}$]   ⇒ /kʁɛ:j/   {α = 0.8}

---

[5] An example of CVC CL in a final syllable is chosen for illustration in order to avoid confusion, since many instances of CVC CL in penultimate syllables resulted in forms that later underwent CVCə CL as well. The forms in (1b, c) and (2b, d) are examples of words that would have been available for both rounds of CL.

One problem for the phonetic conservation approach outlined here is that the values for α must refer specifically to percentages of the duration of a full mora, with equivalence therefore implied between vowel and consonant moras and moras associated with full vowels and those associated with schwa. This is likely problematic even for Timberlake's own analysis of CVCV CL in Late Common Slavic, assuming that so-called 'weak' jers and other vowels were not equivalent in duration, but it is certainly problematic for CVC CL in OF (and generally) since consonants, even if moraic, are certainly nowhere near equivalent to vowels in terms of duration. It is also problematic for CV(C)ə CL in OF under the assumption that schwa was shorter than full vowels.

Another problem for this approach, if one agrees in general with the superiority of constraint-based approaches over rule-based ones, is that the motivation for compensatory lengthening is not incorporated into the grammar as a principle operating in it. We will return to this point in Sect. 5.4.

5.2.2 A Phonological Conservation Approach to CL

A phonological conservation approach to CL is one which assumes that the process is goal oriented and functions to preserve the phonological duration associated with a timing slot of some sort (a C or V-slot, an X-slot, or a mora[6]) that forms a part of the phonological representation of the relevant word. In the ensuing discussion we will adopt the moraic framework that has been most successful. Its success lies in its ability to account straightforwardly for the robust cross-linguistic observation that CL occurs when deleted elements are weight-bearing (vowels or moraic coda consonants), but not otherwise, most obviously in the case of onset consonants (although see Hock (1986:443–444) for evidence of intervocalic consonants inducing CL).

In terms of formalism, the standard phonological conservation account represents CL as the result of the delinking of a deleted segment and its associated mora and the subsequent reattachment of the latter to a preceding vowel. This is illustrated in (6) and (7) for OF CVC CL (/fyst/ > [fy:t]) and CV(C)ə CL (/kʁɛjə/ > [kʁɛ:j]), respectively.

(6) Compensatory lengthening in a CVC sequence (adapted from Hayes (1989:262))
 a. /s/-deletion
  $s \rightarrow \emptyset / \_\_\_ C$ (segmental tier only)
 b. CL
  μ μ′   where μ′ is a segmentally unaffiliated mora
  |..--˙
  α

---

[6] For discussion of the choice between these alternatives, see McCarthy (1979), Clements and Keyser (1983), Hyman (1984, 1985), Levin (1985), Lowenstamm and Kaye (1986), McCarthy and Prince (1986), Hayes (1989), and Szigetvári (2009).

5 Compensatory Lengthening in Historical French: The Role of the Speaker   93

c⁷.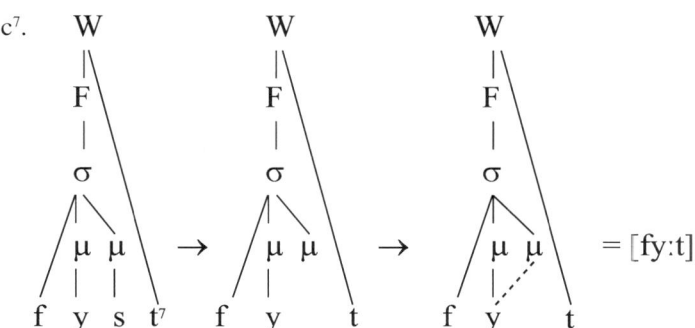

(7) CL in a CCVCə sequence (adapted from Hayes (1989:268–269))

a.  Input

b. σ σ Schwa deletion

   /μ /μ
   kʁ ɛ j

c. σ Parasitic delinking

   /μ μ
   kʁ ɛ j

d. 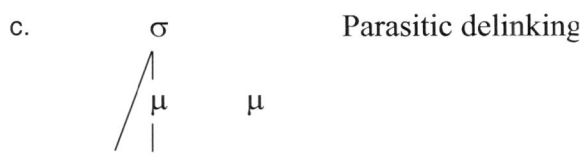 CL

---

[7] For the licensing of word-final consonants and the site of their adjunction, see Gess (1996:98–99).

e. 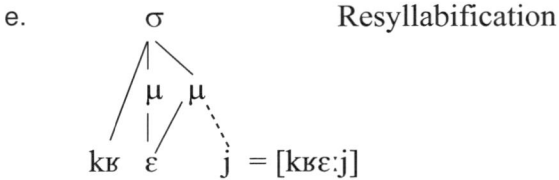 Resyllabification

Hayes (1989) proposes "parasitic delinking" in (7c) as a mechanism that repairs ill-formed syllable structure caused by segmental deletion, by removing relevant association lines as well as the syllable node. Fox (2000) criticizes parasitic delinking as "a radical measure which is not required in most other processes of Compensatory Lengthening". Another aspect of parasitic delinking which appears problematic is the fact that while the syllable node is deleted because of ill-formedness, the mora is permitted to remain under the same circumstances. It is unclear why this should be the case since a mora with no associated segment is just as ill-formed as a syllable with no associated segment.

Fox (2000:100–102) offers two other criticisms of Hayes' (1989) approach to CL. The first of these has to do with the linking of the vowel of the first syllable to the stranded mora in (7d). An equally possible and perhaps even more straightforward outcome would be for the stranded consonant to link to the stranded mora. Indeed, given this alternative, the solution offered by Hayes appears quite circular. In his final criticism of Hayes' (1989) approach to CL, Fox links Hayes' definition of the mora as "the basic unit for syllable weight" to the motivation for CVCV CL. His purpose in making this link is to point out that syllable weight is not maintained in these cases.

A potential problem for phonological conservation approaches generally, for both CVC and CV(C)ə cases, is that they appear ill-equipped to deal with the gradual nature of CL. To see this, consider the representation in (8), where there is an additional association line linking the vowel to the mora of the reduced postvocalic consonant. The representation attempts to suggest that a shared mora would provide additional length to the secondary, vowel host.

(8) Phonological conservation and modeling gradual CL in CVC through double linking

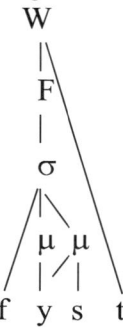

While the shared mora representation in (8) appears adequate for representing an intermediate stage between a fully moraic postvocalic segment and a long vowel with no following consonant, the formalism offers no way to represent any more than a single such stage even if more are assumed. This problem is perhaps mitigated by assuming that a single phonological representation can receive different phonetic interpretations by successive generations. For example, for the first generation with the linked representation in (8), this representation may entail a duration of /s/ only slightly shorter than the duration of original /s/ dominated exhaustively by its mora, with no linking to the latter of the preceding vowel. For the next generation, the same representation may give rise to a production with an even shorter consonantal articulation, and so on. Indeed the principle of conservation of articulatory effort would militate in favor of this, especially if the outcome is determined by the grammar to be perceptually tolerable (see Sect. 5.4.2).

The representation problem might be considered more serious in the case of CV(C)ə, as it involves the crossing of association lines, as illustrated in (9).

(9) Phonological conservation and modeling gradual CL in CV(C)ə through double linking

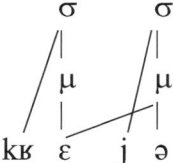

Given the general ban on the crossing of association lines, modeling CV(C)ə CL as mora conservation requires a fully deleted final schwa, or an explicit assumption of separate C and V tiers. Failure to adopt separate C and V tiers would preclude any analysis of the change that assumes gradual erosion of the schwa with concomitant lengthening of the preceding vowel.

5.2.3 *A Non-conservation Approach to CL*

A non-conservation approach to CL is one that denies any connection between the loss of one segment and the lengthening of another. The only major work advocating such an approach is De Chene and Anderson (1979), and it only treats CVC CL. For them, putative cases of this type involve two unrelated processes. The first of these involves the gliding of the consonant through a general process of lenition, resulting in a dipththong. The second process involves the monophthongization of the resulting sequence. This second process, according to De Chene and Anderson, will produce a long vowel only if there is already a distinction in the language between long and short vowels (in other words, CL itself cannot introduce into the language such a distinction). There is much evidence against this claim, although the existence of a general structure-preserving tendency along these lines is of no particular surprise. The reader is referred to Hock (1986), Hayes (1989), Morin (1992), Lin (1997) and Gess (1998) for further discussion of this issue. The latter treats the very data from OF on which de Chene and Anderson rely, showing that what they assume to be pre-existing long vowels are in fact sequences of two separate syllables, as evidenced by their treatment in OF poetry.

There has also been much discussion around the claim that traditionally labeled cases of CL in reality result from two distinct processes (Hock 1986; Poser 1986; Sezer 1986; Gildea 1995). While none of the discussion discounts the possibility of long vowels coming into existence in the way suggested by De Chene and Anderson, all of it questions the claim, convincingly, that all cases of CL can be explained in this way.

In fact, it is difficult to exclude the possibility that CVC CL in OF was not a two-step process, so we illustrate it here.

(10) CVC CL in OF as a two-step process, à la De Chene and Anderson (1979)
  a. Step one: lenition to a glide
     /fyst/ > [fyht]
  b. Step two: monophthongization
     /fyht/ > [fyːt]

The obvious and not particularly controversial assumption in (10) is that [h] is a glide. Nor is the assumption of an intermediate stage particularly controversial, although Pope (1952:151) suggests an intermediate "fricative palatal or velar" sound based on rhyming patterns of relevant French loan-words in German. The spelling with *h* in Walloon manuscripts and the explicit statement in *Orthographia Gallica* (Stürzinger 1884), "Quant *s* est joynt [a la *t*], ele avera le soun de *h*"[8] can be interpreted either way. In any case, even if there was an intermediate stage with a palatal or velar fricative, it is clear that it was subject to lenition itself, and it is well attested that voiceless (and even voiced) fricatives very typically lenite to [h] (Gess 2009).

Although De Chene and Anderson's proposed two-step account of CL in OF is far from unfathomable, it begs one further question. Should not the long vowel resulting from monophthongization (reduction and eventual elimination of the glide gesture) itself be seen as a consequence of CL? Moreover, it is not at all clear why a glide should be treated any differently than any other postvocalic segment in this regard. If its length is kept as the glide weakens, it is because the preceding vowel is lengthened in a compensatory fashion. In the final analysis, all that De Chene and Anderson achieve by breaking the process down is to highlight the gradual nature of CL.

Since OF had no pre-existing vowel length distinction (Gess 1998), it provides strong evidence against De Chene and Anderson's claim that CL can only occur when such a distinction already exists. And of course CV(C)ə CL, not even mentioned by De Chene and Anderson, provides evidence against their claim that CL does not exist independently from general lenition and monophthongization.

---

[8] "When *s* comes with a following *t*, it will have the sound of *h*."

5.3 A Listener-Oriented Approach to CL

Although Kavitskaya (2002) does not go quite as far as De Chene and Anderson (1979) in suggesting that CL does not exist per se, she does propose an equally radical account according to which there is no such *speaker-oriented* process. Rather, Kavitskaya proposes that CL (both CVC and CVCV types) is an entirely listener-oriented phenomenon. According to Kavitskaya CVC CL happens when vowels are lengthened before certain consonants and the latter are subsequently lost. With the loss of a consonant that originally triggered lengthening, the phonetic length is no longer explicable and is therefore interpreted by listeners as a phonological feature of the vowel. Similarly, CVCV CL happens when vowels lengthened in open syllables come to be in closed syllables because of the loss of a following vowel. Since there is no longer a structural explanation for vowel length, it is again interpreted as a phonological feature of the vowel. If Kavitskaya is correct in her analyses of CL, then it is neither speaker-controlled nor compensatory.

Kavitskaya's account of CVC CL can be applied to OF quite straightforwardly. All of the consonants involved are those that can be argued to cause lengthening in the ways suggested by Kavitskaya: liquids; nasals; and fricatives. Let us briefly review the relevant arguments. Kavitskaya suggests that CL arises when liquids are not heard because of the very long transitions between them and the previous vowel (Kavitskaya 2002:51–52). In the case of nasals, Kavitskaya relies on the fact reported by Delattre (1962), Whalen and Beddor (1989), and Beddor (1993) that "nasalized vowels tend to be longer than their oral counterparts. Thus, at least in principle, phonetic length of nasalized vowels can be phonemicized as a consequence of nasal loss" (2002:57). Finally, with respect to /s/, Kavitskaya makes the perfectly reasonable assumption that this fricative, like others, went through a stage of lenition as a glottal glide, as we discussed in the previous section. The relevance, Kavitskaya points out, is that the shape of vocal tract during the production of glottal approximants tends to be the same as for surrounding vowels (Ladefoged and Maddieson (1996:325), citing Keating (1988)). Thus, "the noise after the vowel is interpreted as the vowel itself" (Kavitskaya 2002:67).

While Kavitskaya's analysis of CVC CL is applicable to OF in principle, given the nature of the consonants involved, the problem is that it relies on misperception in each of three individual cases. Indeed OF is rather unusual in her typology of CVC CL cases, covering 58 languages. She lists five categories of segments that trigger CL: glides, liquids, nasals, fricatives, and stops (almost exclusively the glottal stop). Forty-two of these languages have CL in only one category, and of those only a single segment is involved in 33 cases. In ten languages CL occurs in two categories and in four cases, including OF, it occurs in three categories. (No categories are listed for Semitic, presumably because CL in this language is quite different and results from requirements of templatic morphology. No categories are listed for Piro, with no explanation.) The problem with assuming Kavitskaya's analysis for CVC CL in OF, in which it is a highly robust phenomenon, is that it assumes that OF speakers were either terrible listeners in general (a not very satisfactory assumption) or that they were guided in their perception by a very powerful systemic preference. Under the latter assumption, it is difficult to conclude that such a powerful systemic preference, whatever its specific nature (see next section), could not have an effect as well on the production grammar. It is also difficult to exclude the possibility that the preference was not principally a production-oriented one.

Further, there is a substantial argument against Kavitskaya's approach from CVCə CL in OF, and its development in MF (= Middle French) as well. Recall that according to the listener-based approach, phonological CL in such sequences is due to reanalysis of phonetic length occurring in open syllables as phonological once a word-final schwa is deleted and the phonetic length on the previous vowel is no longer explainable on the basis of syllable structure. However, it is a well-known fact that even at the earliest stage of OF, syllable-final segments were limited to sonorant consonants and /S/. Syllable-final stop consonants were lost already in Late Latin. Furthermore, as we have seen, syllable-final sonorants and /S/ were gradually lost over the course of the OF period, with the result that the language came to have a strictly C(C)V syllable structure, except in word-final position where only /s/ and /t/ occurred as inflectional elements on certain verb forms (and these were subject to deletion as early as the thirteenth century (Rickard 1989:63)). As Klausenburger (1970:62) puts it, "a major structural tendency is discernible in all these changes: a tendency toward open syllabicity".

Given this fact, when CVCə CL began, in a CVCə-shape word pronounced without the final schwa, the original syllable structure is recoverable since analysis of the output as a CVC syllable is not permitted by the phonology (except as a possible inflected verb form if the final C is /s/ or /t/). Recall that the beginnings of the process in late OF involved only the loss of final unstressed vowels immediately following another vowel, or a glide (2a). The occurrence of schwa deletion with CL in forms with an intervening consonant (2b–d) is not well attested until the sixteenth century. By this time the deletion of singleton final consonants is well established (Pope (1952:222): "in uneducated speech it is evident that there was already a marked disposition to use the forms with mute consonant in this [word-final] position"). Therefore, final consonants in output forms from CVCə CL themselves serve as a cue to a following vowel so that a lengthened preceding vowel can still be attributable to an underlying open syllable structure. Kavitskaya's approach, which crucially relies on reanalysis, therefore predicts that CL will not occur in CVCə forms. Ironically, closed syllables that would permit reanalysis as predicted by Kavitskaya were eventually produced by the very process that would have entailed CL via reanalysis had such syllables already existed. The fact that CL occurred anyway, without pre-existing closed syllables, suggests that the process was not a listener-oriented one.

Words like *chambre*, with a complex onset in the original final syllable, are even more damning for the listener-oriented approach, since obstruent-liquid sequences are licit in the phonology of the language, at least until the Modern French period, only as syllable onsets. Again, Kavitskaya's approach predicts that CL will not occur in these forms, or at most (if CL in regular CVCə forms could somehow be explained away) that it would occur much later than CL in forms not involving such sequences. And yet CL is attested by for both CVCə and CVCCə (CC = obstruent + liquid) forms in the sixteenth century (Estienne 1557), with no evidence at all to suggest that there was any substantial difference in their relative chronology.

To conclude this section, OF poses a problem for Kavitskaya's listener-oriented approach to CL. In the case of CVC CL, the highly robust nature of the process suggests a powerful systemic preference for maintaining the length associated with lost consonants. Such a preference should be encoded in the grammar. In the case of CV(C)ə CL, the general phonotactics of OF and MF render a listener-oriented account implausible, as consonants made final by the loss of schwa are still interpretable as onsets of underlying final syllables. Gess (2011, in preparation) provides additional evidence against Kavitskaya's approach – a synchronic example from Skolt Saami involving sequences that do not lend themselves to the type of reanalysis suggested by Kavitskaya. In that case, solidly supported by careful phonetic analysis (McRobbie-Utasi 1999), it appears quite clearly that the process is motivated by a principle of isochrony – basically, a preference for temporal uniformity of prosodic units. In the following section, I explore how this principle might be incorporated into an account of CL in OF.

5.4 A Constraint-Based, Speaker-Oriented, Phonetic Conservation Account of OF CL

There are two possibilities for incorporating the principle of isochrony into a speaker-based account of OF CL. These two possibilities, reflecting a direct influence or an indirect one, are explored in the following two sections. Both possibilities are couched in an overall framework that is phonetically based in that it assumes that the reductive change triggering CL is gradual and phonetic (non-categorical), and that this phonetic change eventually comes to have phonological effects. The framework is also constraint-based rather than rule-based, so that it can accommodate the view that functional principles like conservation of effort, assumed to be responsible for the incipient reductive change, are integrated into the grammar rather than being considered extragrammatical.

5.4.1 A Direct Isochrony-Based Account

If the principle of isochrony works directly in the grammar, we might assume that it is encoded as a universal markedness constraint, ISOCHRONY, which penalizes output forms that are not isochronous with input forms. This is illustrated in the tableau in (11):

(11) Tableau illustrating a direct isochrony-based account of CVC CL in OF

/fyst/	ISOCHRONY	CAE	PRES (MAG;DUR(s/_t)#)	*ENHANCE (GESTURE)
a. fyst		*		
b. fyt	*		*	
▶ c. fyːt			*	*

The tableau in (11) makes use of two types of constraints proposed in Gess (2009). CAE (= Conserve Articulatory Effort) is the constraint assumed responsible for the initial reduction that leads to CL. It penalizes any output candidate with no reduction in effort vis-a-vis a canonical target form. Any form that requires effort at or above the canonical target threshold will be penalized as in (11a). The constraint PRES(MAG;DUR(s/_t)) penalizes any forms not preserving the magnitude and/or duration of articulatory gestures associated with /s/ before a final /t/, as in (11b) and (11c). The constraint *ENHANCE(GESTURE) is a novel constraint penalizing any enhancement (of magnitude or duration) of gestures associated with underlying segments, as in (11c), where the duration of the gestures associated with /y/ are enhanced. This constraint is an obvious phonetically-based analog to DEP, and is in shorthand form here. Like the PRES constraint, it will have specific instantiations referring to each segment in the string, with an inherent ranking amongst them with more noticeable enhancements penalized more than less noticeable ones.

The obvious assumption in (11) is that enhancement of /y/ is the least noticeable enhancement in this specific context (less noticeable, for example, than enhancing the duration of /f/). If a form falls too far from the target in terms of effort expenditure, i.e., if there is complete deletion of /s/ with no compensation for duration via /y/, the result will be a form that is perceived as non-isochronic, thus violating the constraint ISOCHRONY, as in (11b). Another necessary assumption in (11) is that it is less effortful to maintain gestures associated with the vowel than to transition into and carry out gestures associated with the following consonant.

The tableau in (12) illustrates the same constraints operating on a CVCə form. In this case the effort threshold relates to the maintenance of full gestures associated with the two vowels, again in relation to a canonical target form. The form in (12a) is ruled out because it represents full effort. The form in (12b) entails full reduction, i.e., elimination, of the final schwa, with no CL of the preceding vowel, and is therefore ruled out by the ISOCHRONY constraint. The successful candidate, in (12c), entails both a reduction of one gesture and an enhancement of another, but these deviations from the input are tolerated in order to satisfy ISOCHRONY.

(12) Tableau illustrating a direct isochrony-based account of CVCə CL in OF

/kʁɛjə/	ISOCHRONY	CAE	PRES (MAG;DUR(ə/VC_#))	*ENHANCE (GESTURE)
a. kʁɛjə		*		
b. kʁɛj	*		*	
▶ c. kʁɛːj			*	*

In this direct isochrony-based account of CL, there is a slight duplication of effort in constraints working to preserve duration. The ISOCHRONY constraint is perceptually based and penalizes any forms with a deviation in overall duration. The PRES constraint, on the other hand, is based on articulation and penalizes forms with reduction specifically in those articulatory gestures associated with the specified segment. See Gess (2009) for a detailed discussion of perception-oriented cue preservation constraints versus articulation-oriented gesture preservation constraints. Note that Gess does not rule out the possibility that both might be required, and this would be a case demonstrating such a need.

5.4.2 An Indirect Isochrony-Based Account

If the speaker participates in CL through speaker-controlled behavior, another possibility is to assume that this behavior is informed by a perceptual knowledge source like Steriade's (2001, 2009) "map of perceptibility effects" (or P-Map). According to Steriade's P-Map hypothesis, articulatory reductions are not random – rather, the speaker seeks "perceptually *tolerated* articulatory simplification" (Steriade 2001:232, citing work by Lindblom et al. (1995), Kohler (1990) and Hura et al. (1992)). Under this view, CL results from the speaker seeking the minimal perceptual deviation from the input in making the triggering reductions. That is, a form with CL is considered a more minimal deviation from the input than a form without CL, on perceptual grounds.

The P-Map hypothesis relies on the notion of confusability. The idea applied in the case at hand is that output forms that are isochronic with respect to the input are more confusable with entirely faithful outputs than are forms that are not isochronic. Isochronic output forms are therefore more tolerated on perceptual grounds than non-isochronic ones, all else being equal. In an account relying on a perceptual knowledge source like the P-Map, the role of isochrony in the process of CL is indirect. Isochrony plays a role in determining confusability and therefore informs the perceptual knowledge source rather than operating directly in the speaker's grammar.

The role of the perceptual knowledge source is to project constraints and determine their ranking (Steriade 2009:151). The constraints that Steriade employs are standard markedness and faithfulness constraints. In the cases she deals with, the P-map comes into play in deciding which element (feature or segment) involved in a given phonotactic problem is subject to modification and in which way. However, the problem of CL is quite different than any of those treated by Steriade. In the case of CL in OF, we can assume that the phonotactic problem is the consonant sequence in the CVC type, (including the C onset of the following syllable) and the number of syllables in the CVCə type (a specific instantiation of the general *STRUC constraint). What the P-map does in these instances is to decide which element in the string is subject to reduction – the first of two consonants in CVC cases, and the weaker of the vowels in CVCə cases (in both cases the element in the string most confusable with zero or, following Gess (2009), with a reduced counterpart).

In a straightforward application of Steriade's P-map hypothesis, the P-map comparisons for CVC and CVCə CL would be as shown in (13), where C stands for a reduced consonant and [ə] for a reduced schwa.

(13) P-map comparisons for CVC and CVCə CL
    a. CVC CL
        $\Delta(VC\text{-}V\emptyset)/\_C > \Delta(VC\text{-}V{:}\emptyset)/\_C$
    b. CVCə CL
        $\Delta(VC[\text{ə}]\text{-}VC\emptyset)/\_\# > \Delta(VC[\text{ə}]\text{-}V{:}C\emptyset)/\_\#$

The statement in (13a) says that the difference between VC and VØ before a consonant is greater than the difference between VC and V:Ø in the same context. The lesser difference between V:ØC and VCC means that V:ØC is more confusable with VCC than is VØC, and is therefore the preferred deviation from VCC, on perceptual grounds. The statement in (13b) says that the difference between VC[ə] and VCØ in word-final position is greater than the difference between VC[ə] and V:CØ in the same context. The lesser difference between V:CØ and VC[ə] means that V:CØ is more confusable with V[ə] than is VCØ. Again, this means that V:CØ is the preferred deviation from VC[ə], on perceptual grounds.

With respect to the formal analysis, we have already ascertained what the phonotactic problems are, and straightforward phonological constraints *C/_C and *V could be invoked for those. But in a phonetically based account we will again assume the CAE constraint and the PRES constraints. The latter will correspond to *C/_C and *V since the relevant segments will be targeted in the strings in which they occur because of their perceptual weakness. The constraint *ENHANCE(GESTURE) is also the same as in the direct isochrony-based account. The difference between the two analyses will be in the constraints specifically projected from the statements in (13), and this is far from clear.

The constraint that we need for the analysis to work is one requiring the preservation of the duration of the reduced segment, in perceptual terms. Let us call this PRES(P-DUR(x)), which requires the preservation of the perceptual duration of a segment x. Crucially, this constraint does not require that the duration of x be maintained specifically via articulatory gestures associated with x. Consider the tableau in (14):

(14) Tableau illustrating an indirect isochrony-based account of CVC CL in OF

/fyst/	PRES (P-DUR(/s/))	CAE	PRES (MAG;DUR(s/_t)#)	*ENHANCE (GESTURE)
a. fyst		*		
b. fyt	*		*	
▶ c. fy:t			*	*

The analysis shown here fares no better than the direct isochrony-based account with respect to duplication. Both constraints refer specifically to duration, one to its perceptual dimension and the other to its articulatory dimension (the maintaining of an articulatory gesture). It is not easy, therefore, to decide which account is superior. Ironically, an alternative approach inspired by Evolutionary Phonology (Blevins 2004, 2006a, b), which informs Kavitskaya's (2002) strictly listener-oriented account, is informative in this regard, and suggests that the direct isochrony account may be the better one.

A proponent of Evolutionary Phonology might suggest that speakers favor isochronic variants because they represent the most common misperceptions of output forms. If this is the case, then speakers do not consider the similarity of misperceived forms to target representations – they rely simply on the frequency of occurrence of the favored variant (Steriade 2009:177). Under this view, for which there appears to be some evidence (Lehiste 1977; Donovan and Darwin 1979, cited in Patel 2008), isochrony acts as a filter on perception. However, if isochrony can act as a filter on perception, there is no principled reason to exclude the possibility that it can have an analogous function with respect to production. Furthermore, if the most common misperceptions of output forms are isochronous ones, this would entail that stored exemplars are largely isochronous – ones with and without reductions. This being the case, it might even be expected that this generalization across exemplars, that they are isochronous, would become encoded somehow in the grammar, i.e., as a markedness constraint like ISOCHRONY.

In conclusion, then, we have argued for a phonetically-based speaker-oriented account of CL in OF, relying on a direct influence of the markedness constraint ISOCHRONY in the production grammar. Isochrony appears to have had an important impact on the language over a large time span, interacting with important processes of consonant and vowel loss to produce the phenomenon known as CL. The in-depth examination of CL provided here gives us a clearer picture of how it manifested itself in OF, i.e., through speaker-controlled behavior, and how it manifests itself generally.

References

Beddor, Patrice. 1993. The perception of nasal vowels. In *Nasals, nasalization, and the velum*, ed. M.K. Huffman and R.A. Krakow, 171–196. San Diego: Academic Press.
Bishop, Morris. 1968. *The middle ages*. Boston: Houghton Mifflin.
Blevins, Juliette. 2004. *Evolutionary phonology: The emergence of sound patterns*. Cambridge: Cambridge University Press.
Blevins, Juliette. 2006a. A theoretical synopsis of evolutionary phonology. *Theoretical Linguistics* 32: 117–165.
Blevins, Juliette. 2006b. Reply to commentaries. *Theoretical Linguistics* 32: 245–256.
Clements, G.N., and Samuel Jay Keyser. 1983. *CV phonology: A generative theory of the syllable*. Cambridge, MA: MIT Press.
De Chene, B., and S.R. Anderson. 1979. Compensatory lengthening. *Language* 55: 505–535.
Delattre, P. 1962. Some factors of vowel duration and their cross-linguistic validity. *Journal of the Acoustical Society of America* 24: 1141–1143.
Donovan, A., and C.J. Darwin. 1979. The perceived rhythm of speech. In *Proceedings of the 9th international congress of phonetic sciences*, vol. 2, 268–274. University of Copenhagen: Institute of Phonetics.
Estienne, Robert. 1557. *Traicte de la grammaire francoise*. Paris: R. Estienne. Reprinted 1972. Geneva: Slatkine.
Fox, Anthony. 2000. *Prosodic features and prosodic structure. The phonology of suprasegmentals*. Oxford: Oxford University Press.
Gess, Randall. 1996. *Optimality in the historical phonology of French*. Ph.D. dissertation, University of Washington.

Gess, Randall. 1998. Compensatory lengthening and structure preservation revisited. *Phonology* 15: 353–366.

Gess, Randall. 1999. Rethinking the dating of Old French syllable-final consonant loss. *Diachronica* 16: 261–296.

Gess, Randall. 2001. Distinctive vowel length in Old French: Evidence and implications. In *Historical linguistics 1999: Selected papers from the 14th international conference on historical linguistics*, ed. Laurel J. Brinton, 145–156. Amsterdam/Philadelphia: John Benjamins.

Gess, Randall. 2006. The myth of phonologically distinctive length in historical French. In Historical romance linguistics: *Retrospective and perspectives*, ed. Randall Gess and Deborah Arteaga, 53–76. Amsterdam/Philadelphia: John Benjamins.

Gess, Randall. 2008. More on (distinctive!) vowel length in historical French. *Journal of French Language Studies* 18: 175–187.

Gess, Randall. 2009. Reductive sound change and the perception/production interface. *Canadian Journal of Linguistics* 54(2): 229–253.

Gess, Randall. 2011. "Compensatory Lengthening." The Blackwell Companion to Phonology. van Oostendorp, Marc, Colin J. Ewen, Elizabeth Hume and Keren Rice (eds). Blackwell Publishing, 2011. Blackwell Reference Online. 09 July 2012 <http://www.companiontophonology.com/subscriber/tocnode?id=g9781405184236_chunk_g978140518423666>.

Hayes, Bruce. 1989. Compensatory lengthening in moraic phonology. *Linguistic Inquiry* 20: 253–306.

Hock, Hans Henrich. 1986. Compensatory lengthening: In defense of the concept 'mora'. *Folia Linguistica* 20: 431–460.

Hura, Susan, Björn Lindblom, and Randy Diehl. 1992. On the role of perception in shaping phonological assimilation rules. *Language and Speech* 35: 59–72.

Hyman, Larry. 1984. On the weightlessness of syllable onsets. In *Proceedings of the tenth annual meeting of the Berkeley Linguistics Society*, ed. C. Brugman and M. Macaulay, 1–14. Berkeley: University of California.

Hyman, Larry. 1985. *A theory of phonological weight*. Dordrecht: Foris.

Jensen, John T. 1977. *Yapese reference grammar*. Honolulu: University Press of Hawaii.

Kavitskaya, Darya. 2002. *Compensatory lengthening. Phonetics, phonology, diachrony*. New York/London: Routledge.

Keating, Patrica. 1988. Underspecification in phonetics. *Phonology* 5: 275–292.

Klausenburger, Jurgen. 1970. *French prosodics and phonotactics. An historical typology*. Tubingen: Niemeyer.

Kohler, Klaus J. 1990. Segmental reduction in connected speech in German: Phonological facts and phonetic explanation. In *Speech production and speech modeling*, ed. W.J. Hardcastle and A. Marchal, 69–92. Dordrecht: Kluwer.

Ladefoged, Peter, and Ian Maddieson. 1996. *The sounds of the world's languages*. Cambridge, MA: Blackwell.

Lehiste, Ilse. 1977. Isochrony reconsidered. *Journal of Phonetics* 5: 253–263.

Levin, Juliette. 1985. *A metrical theory of syllabicity,* MIT dissertation, Cambridge, MA.

Lin, Yen-Hwei. 1997. Syllabic and moraic structures in Piro. *Phonology* 14: 403–436.

Lindblom, Björn, Susan Guion, Susan Hura, Seung-Jae Moon, and Raquel Willerman. 1995. Is sound change adaptive? *Rivista di Linguistica* 7: 5–37.

Lowenstamm, Jean, and Jonathan Kaye. 1986. Compensatory lengthening in Tiberian Hebrew. In *Studies in compensatory lengthening*, ed. Leo Wetzels and Engin Sezer, 97–133. Dordrecht: Foris.

McCarthy, John. 1979. *Formal problems in semitic phonology and morphology*. MIT dissertation, Cambridge, MA.

McCarthy, John, and Alan Prince. 1986. *Prosodic morphology* (RuCCS Technical Report Series TR-3). New Brunswick: Rutgers University.

McRobbie-Utasi, Zita. 1999. *Quantity in the Skolt (Lappish) Saami Language: An acoustic analysis*, University Uralic and Altaic Series, vol. 165. Bloomington, IN: Indiana University Research Institute for Inner Asian Studies.

Morin, Yves Charles. 1992. Phonological interpretations of historical lengthening. In *Proceedings of the 7th international phonology meeting*, ed. W.U. Dressler, M. Prinzhorn, and J. Rennison, 135–155. Turin: Rosenberg and Sellier.

Morin, Yves Charles. 2006. On the phonetics of rhymes in classical and pre-classical French. In *Historical Romance linguistics: Retrospective and perspectives*, ed. Randall Gess and Deborah Arteaga, 131–162. Amsterdam/Philadelphia: John Benjamins.

Patel, Aniruddh D. 2008. *Music, language, and the brain*. New York: Oxford University Press.

Picard, Marc. 2004. /s/-deletion in old French and the aftermath of compensatory lengthening. *Journal of French Language Studies* 14: 1–7.

Pope, Mildred K. 1952. *From Latin to modern French with especial consideration of Anglo-Norman. Phonology and morphology*. Manchester: Manchester University Press.

Poser, William. 1986. Japanese evidence bearing on the compensatory lengthening controversy. In *Studies in compensatory lengthening*, ed. W. Leo Wetzels and Engin Sezer, 167–186. Dordrecht: Foris.

Rickard, Peter. 1989. *A history of the French language*, 2nd ed. London/New York: Routledge.

Sezer, Engin. 1986. An autosegmental analysis of compensatory lengthening in Turkish. In *Studies in compensatory lengthening*, ed. W. Leo Wetzels and Engin Sezer, 227–250. Dordrecht: Foris.

Steriade, Donca. 2001. Directional asymmetries in place assimilation: A perceptual account. In *The role of speech perception in phonology*, ed. Elizabeth Hume and Keith Johnson, 219–250. San Diego: Academic Press.

Steriade, Donca. 2009. The phonology of perceptibility effects: The P-Map and its consequences for constraint organization. In *The nature of the word. Studies in honor of Paul Kiparsky*, ed. Kristin Hanson and Sharon Inkelas, 151–179. Cambridge, MA: MIT Press.

Stürzinger, Jakob. 1884. *Orthographia gallica; ältester traktat über französische aussprache und orthographie*. Heilbronn: Gebr. Henninger.

Szigetvári, Péter. 2011. "The Skeleton." The Blackwell Companion to Phonology. van Oostendorp, Marc, Colin J. Ewen, Elizabeth Hume and Keren Rice (eds). Blackwell Publishing, 2011. Blackwell Reference Online. 09 July 2012 <http://www.companiontophonology.com/subscriber/tocnode?id=g9781405184236_chunk_g978140518423656>.

Timberlake, Alan. 1983. Compensatory lengthening in Slavic 2: Phonetic reconstruction. In *American contributions to the Ninth International Congress of Slavists*, Linguistics, vol. 1, ed. M.S. Flier, 293–319. Columbus: Slavica.

Whalen, Douglas, and Patrice Beddor. 1989. Connections between nasality and vowel duration and height: Elucidation of the Eastern Algonquin intrusive nasal. *Language* 65: 457–486.

Chapter 6
Perception, Production and Markedness in Sound Change: French Velar Palatalization

Haike Jacobs and Janine Berns

6.1 Introduction

Whereas the palatalization of velar consonants before front high and mid vowels is a common process of the historical phonology of the Romance languages and a commonly attested phenomenon in the evolution of the world's languages (Bhat 1978; Guion 1998; Ladefoged and Maddieson 1996, among others), the history of French is intriguing in that it also evinces velar palatalization before the low vowel *a*. In French, velar palatalization took place in two stages, traditionally referred to as the First and Second Velar Palatalization. During the First Velar Palatalization, the voiceless and voiced velar stops [k] and [g] were palatalized and subsequently affricated before the front high and low vowels [i, e, ɛ], resulting in [ts], and [dʒ], respectively. During the Second Velar Palatalization, velars were also palatalized and affricated before the vowel *a*, yielding, respectively [tʃ] and [dʒ].

With respect to the formal analysis of velar palatalization, two types of accounts have been proposed. The first type is perceptually-based, and relies on the phonemic similarity of fronted velars and palatoalveolar affricates (cf. Ohala 1992; Guion 1998; Chang et al. 2001). The accounts of the second type are articulatory-based and assume that a fronted velar acquires a palatal off-glide and then is shifted to a coronal place of articulation (cf. the traditional descriptions in Pope 1934; Fouché 1958; Bourciez and Bourciez 1974, and the feature geometry based descriptions in Lahiri and Evers 1991; Calabrese 1993; Jacobs 1993; Clements and Hume 1995).

Given that there is no clear phonetic motivation either from either production or perception as to why low back vowels should have triggered palatalization of preceding velars, the Second Velar Palatalization is problematic for models that claim that sound change is essentially phonetically motivated and that markedness

H. Jacobs (✉) • J. Berns
Department of Romance Languages and Cultures, Radboud University Nijmegen, Nijmegen, The Netherlands
e-mail: h.jacobs@let.ru.nl; j.berns@let.ru.nl

constraints can be dispensed with (Blevins 2004). Therefore, this sound shift is extremely interesting for a better understanding of general principles underlying language change.

This chapter is organized as follows. In Sect. 6.2, we will briefly present the main facts of the First and Second Velar Palatalization. Section 6.3 discusses the two different (perception/production) accounts. After that, in Sect. 6.4, we will present our view of velar palatalization and address the relevance of markedness constraints. We will argue, contrary to Blevins (2004), that markedness constraints do play a role, and a crucial one, in accounting for sound change in general and for velar palatalization in Old French in particular. We will show that OT-CC (Optimality Theory with Candidate Chains) offers a more principled account than a perceptual account when it comes to the question why some sound changes appear to be irreversible. In Sect. 6.5, we conclude by discussing the different traditional accounts that have been proposed for the velar palatalization before *a*, as well as a more recent one by Buckley (2003). We then provide our own analysis, which is essentially phonological and not phonetic in nature (cf. Buckley 2000).

6.2 French Velar Palatalization

The first process of velar palatalization in the history of French took place in Late Latin. Velar consonants were palatalized before the front vowels [i, e, ɛ], as shown in (1).

(1) | *Latin/Late Latin* | *Gallo-Romance* | *Modern French* |
| --- | --- | --- |
| centum > [kʲentu] | [centu] > [tsentu] | [sã] *cent* |
| mercedem > [merkʲede] | [mercede] > [mertsede] | [mɛʁsi] *merci* |
| placer > [plakʲere] | [placere] > [platsire] | [pleziʁ] *plaisir* |
| gentem > [gʲente] | [ɟente] > [dʒente] | [ʒã] *gens* |
| argentum > [argʲentu] | [arɟentu] > [ardʒentu] | [aʁʒã] *argent* |
| reginam > [reɣʲina] | [rejina] | [ʁɛn] *reine* |

At the time that the Romance languages had already developed independently from each other, a second process of palatalization occurred, which was limited to some of the Gallo-Romance dialects. This time, velars palatalized before Latin *a*, as well as before the diphthong [a]. Although the etymological sequences of [k] and [g] followed by the front vowels [i, e, ɛ] had disappeared from the language after the first process of velar palatalization was completed, a number of such sequences had been reintroduced in Gallo-Romance by borrowings from other languages (and were mainly from Germanic or Arabic origin). These forms were equally involved in the process of palatalization, and showed the same development as velars before Latin *a*.[1]

---

[1] As observed above, the voiceless and voiced velar stops [k] and [g] resulted in [ts] and [dʒ] during the First Velar Palatalization, but in [tʃ] and [dʒ] during the Second Velar Palatalization. The precise outcome of palatalization in the Romance languages is subject to a great deal of dialectal variation (cf. Fouché 1958; Meyer-Lübke 1890). In this paper, we will not address the question of why the results of the First and Second palatalizations were different. We refer the reader Calabrese (1993), among others.

6   Perception, Production and Markedness in Sound Change: French Velar Palatalization   109

(2) a. *Latin/Late Latin*   *Gallo-Romance*   *Old French* *Modern French*
       carrum > [karru]   [kʲarru] > [carru]   [tʃar]   [ʃaʁ] *char*
       arcam > [arka]   [arkʲa] > [arca]   [artʃe]   [aʁʃ] *arche*
       bacam > [baga]   [baɣʲa]   [baje]   [bɛ] *baie*
       buccam > [buk:a]   [buk:ʲa] > [buc:a]   [buttʃe]   [buʃ] *bouche*
       largam > [larga]   [largʲa] > [larɟa]   [lardʒe]   [laʁʒ] *large*
       gardinum > [gardinu]   [gʲardinu] > [ɟardinu] [dʒardn̩]   [ʒaʁdɛ̃] *jardin*
       ligare > [liɣare]   [liɣʲere]   [leiier]   [lje] *lier*
       causam > [kau̯sa]   [kʲau̯sa] > [cau̯sa]   [tʃoz]   [ʃoz] *chose*
       gaudium > [gau̯dju]   [gʲau̯ju] > [ɟau̯ju]   [dʒoie]   [ʒwa] *joie*

  b. *Gallo-Romance*   *Old French   Modern French*
     (e)skina [(e)skʲina] > [escine]   [estʃine]   [eʃin] *échine*
     meskinu [meskʲina] > [mescin]   [mestʃin]   [meʃin] *mechin (mesquin)*

In the following section, we will first describe the major formalizations of velar palatalization that have been proposed in the literature, and consider to what extent these analyses are able to account for the French facts.

6.3   Velar Palatalization: Perception and Production

6.3.1   Approaches to Velar Palatalization: Perception

A number of scholars have challenged the traditional articulatory-based accounts that propose that before a front vowel, a fronted velar acquires a palatal off-glide and then is then shifted to a coronal place of articulation.[2] Instead, they have proposed a perception-based analysis of velar palatalization (Guion 1998; Ohala 1992; Chang et al. 2001). Guion (1998: 18) rejects an account by Grammont (1933) according to which a fronted [k] develops a fricative release and shifts in articulation to a more anterior position, because that account does not "motivate a change from affricated palatal to palatoalveolar. There is no articulatory reason why the sound change could not result in palatal place of articulation. However, this is a typologically rare outcome of velar palatalization" (Guion 1998: 18). A second account (Anttila 1989), which proposes that a fronted velar acquires a palatal off-glide and then is shifted to a

---

[2] In this study, we will limit ourselves to velar palatalization in a vowel context, and will not discuss unconditioned velar palatalization. An example of the latter, as pointed out by an anonymous reviewer, is the French variety of la Champagne et la Brie (département de Seine-et-Marne), cf. Bourcelot (1966–1969–1978), where velars palatalize in all sorts of environments. A related issue, also pointed out by an anonymous reviewer, which we will not address due to space limitations, is the precise interpretation of the release of velars in word-final position, as can be observed in contemporary varieties of Parisian French in for instance *en cloque* 'pregnant'.

coronal place of articulation due to the narrow shape of the vocal tract, is rejected by Guion (1998: 19) as well:

> It remains unclear, however, why a narrowed vocal tract would give rise to fronting. A problem with these accounts is the assumption that palatalization is *purely* an articulatorily motivated change. The two accounts just mentioned begin with a fronted velar, but diverge from there. While it might be possible to imagine a purely articulatory account in which the tongue begins at a velar articulation and gradually creeps up to a palatoalveolar place of articulation, changing the part of the tongue used for the articulation from dorsum to blade as well as acquiring a fricative release along the way, the actual fleshing out of this account is problematic.

Following earlier work by Ohala (1992), Guion defends a perceptual motivation for palatalization. A number of perception experiments show that velar stops before front vowels and palatoalveolar affricates are acoustically very similar, which, as Guion concludes, parallels the sound change of palatalization.[3] Furthermore, these experiments have shown that [k] is heard as [tʃ] more often before high front vowels, that [k] is perceived as [tʃ] more often than [g] is perceived as [dʒ], and that [tʃ] is rarely confused with [k]. The latter fact is consistent with sound change typology: a [k] becoming [tʃ] is quite common, but the reverse, [tʃ] becoming [k] is quite rare, if existent at all.

Chang et al. (2001) take as a starting point the observed [ki]/[ti] confusion asymmetry observed in Plauché et al. (1997), where, in a laboratory setting, [ki] was found to be often confused with [ti], but [ti] almost never with [ki]. This asymmetric confusion was enhanced by filtering out the characteristic mid-frequency spectral peak of the velar burst in [ki]. In a first study, Chang et al. (2001: 89) further motivate this finding, and in second study they show that this asymmetric confusion is specific to a high front vocalic environment. This supports the claim that the acoustic properties of [ki] and [ti] are responsible for the confusion asymmetry and not markedness, given that a simple markedness account "would be unable to explain why the confusion asymmetry is not obtained in all vocalic environments since velars stops are presumably more marked than alveolar stops regardless of the quality of the following vowel" (2001: 89). If in a laboratory setting, [ki] is often confused with [ti], but [ti] almost never perceived as [ki], one might expect [ki] to change into [ti] as a regular common sound change, which as they note is not the case: "Rather [ki] ubiquitously changes to [tʃi] or [tsi] in the languages of the world, not to [ti]" (Chang et al. 2001: 95). They observe that in the previously carried out confusion asymmetry studies, [tʃi] was not offered as an option, but instead a choice was forced between [ki] and [ti]. Furthermore, they note that the stops used in the laboratory studies were unaspirated, which may equally have influenced the judgments of the participants (Chang et al. 2001: 95):

> It is unlikely, we think, that subjects will perceive a change in the manner of articulation as well as a change in the place of articulation for unaspirated stops. We suspect that it is the aspiration noise following the degraded burst of a [kʰi] that is reanalyzed as the [ʃ] of a [tʃ], that is, the listener "hears" an alveolar burst (as demonstrated by the first study) followed by an unusual, incongruous amount of aspiration for an alveolar stop (since velars are known to

---

[3] It is important to keep in mind that the participants in Guion's experiments were American English speakers.

engender the longest VOT, especially before the high, front vowel [i]; Cho and Ladefoged, 1999). Faced with such acoustic cues, we argue, some listeners parse the token as [tʃi].

In a third study, designed to better reflect the actual sound change ki > tʃi, their hypothesis is experimentally confirmed. The material consisted of target words *key* [kʰi] and *chi* [tʃʰi], read five times by three speakers and with two filtered *key* tokens without the characteristic mid-frequency spectral peak of the velar burst. Participants had to rate the similarity of the tokens to the canonical form [tʃʰi] on a seven-point scale. The filtered *key* tokens proved to receive better goodness scores than the natural [kʰi] tokens. Again, the authors conclude that acoustic-auditory factors underlie the perceptual errors and consonant confusion asymmetries and that further, markedness plays no role in these confusions[4]:

> As far as markedness is concerned, affricates such as [tʃ] are rarer in the phonologies of the world than a plain stop like [k]. A markedness account of consonant confusion asymmetries fails to explain how the less marked velar stop could become the highly marked affricate [tʃ] in so many languages. (Chang et al. 2001: 99–100)

A perception-based account of velar palatalization, if extended to French, faces a number of problems. First, to the best of our knowledge, velar plosives in Latin and also in French are unaspirated and were most probably also unaspirated at the time of velar palatalization. Moreover, the fact that the voiced velar [g] also palatalized, a stop typically lacking aspiration, makes an account of velar palatalization based on perception alone an unlikely one. Second, velar palatalization also took place before the vowel *a*, whereas in the laboratory experiments, (unfiltered and filtered) [ka] did not lead to perceptual confusions (cf. Chang et al. 2001: 91). Third, in the last study of Chang et al. (2001), [tʃi] was offered as an additional option, contrary to most previous studies. One can only speculate as to what happened exactly in the historical phonology of French. If the inclusion of [tʃi] as an option is required to trigger misperception of [ki] as [tʃi], then who offered that option in the historical phonology of French, if not a speaker? In other words, if speakers misperceive [ki] as [ti], but not as [tʃi] and only as [tʃi] when [tʃi] is offered as an option, misperception cannot be the entire answer.

The same criticism applies to Blevins (2004: 139) who states, following Guion (1998), that:

> coarticulation is able to account for fronting of the tongue body, producing [kʲ], a palatalized velar, or [c], a pure palatal, but articulatory factors are unable to explain the shift from velar to alveo-palatal, which involves a change in the articulator- from the tongue body for [k] to the tongue blade for [tʃ] [...] Coarticulation is the ultimate source of velar palatalization, but resulting palatalized velars may give rise to coronal percepts.

First, observe that velar palatalization in this sense (coarticulation, followed by misperception as a coronal percept) is different from the direct change [k] to [tʃ] in the studies mentioned above. Second, it is not clear, at least not without a specific definition in terms of features or articulators, why a change from velar [k] to palatal [c] does not involve a change in articulator. Keating (1988) has suggested, on the

---

[4] As a matter of fact, we will argue below that markedness does play a role, but that segmental and contextual markedness must not be confused.

basis of cross-linguistic evidence from the UCLA X-ray database, that palatals are more complex than palatoalveolars in that palatals are simultaneously coronal and dorsal, while palatoalveolars are only coronal. This would explain why Polish palatal, or alveolopalatal affricates [tɕ]/[dʑ], contrary to the other affricates [ts]/[dz] and [tʂ]/[dʐ], cannot be palatalized, given that they are inherently specified as coronal and dorsal (cf. Rubach 2003; Padgett and Zygis 2003; Jacobs 2007 for more discussion).

In the next section, we will turn to approaches that, contrary to Blevins, do try to "explain the shift from velar to alveo-palatal" in articulatory-terms.

6.3.2 Approaches to Velar Palatalization: Production

A number of different ways to account for velar palatalization in terms of an articulatory change have been proposed in the literature. Given the lack of consensus regarding the exact featural representation of segments, the proposals differ in some respects, but share the idea that palatalization is essentially assimilatory in nature. We will not try to provide an exhaustive overview of the different proposals, but will rather review only a few of them. The change from velar [k] to [c]/[tʃ] before front vowels has been described by Clements (1993) and Clements and Hume (1995) as a two-step operation. In their view, front vowels are only specified for a coronal articulator node. First, the coronal V-place node from the front vowel is spread as a secondary articulator node to the preceding velar, creating a fronted or palatalized velar [kʲ], followed by Tier Promotion, by which the original dorsal C-place node is deleted from the velar and by which the secondary coronal V-place node becomes promoted to primary articulator, resulting in [c]/[tʃ].

Following Keating (1988), Jacobs (1993) and Jacobs and Van de Weijer (1992) assume that a front vowel [i], just like the palatal glide [j], is both specified for a coronal and a dorsal articulator, and not only for a dorsal articulator (as originally proposed in Sagey 1986) or only for a coronal articulator (as in Clements and Hume 1995). On the assumption that all vowels are [dorsal] segments and that they are further specified for the tongue body features [+/-high, +/-low, +/-back], back rounded vowels like [u] or [o] are complex in having both a dorsal and labial articulator. Front vowels are complex in having both a dorsal and coronal articulator. The feature analysis of the French vowels at the stage in the language when palatalization applied is provided in (3) below.

(3) French vowel specifications

/i/	/e/	/ɛ/	/a/	/ɔ/	/o/	/u/
[COR]	[COR]	[COR]		[LAB]	[LAB]	[LAB]
[-ant]	[-ant]	[-ant]				
[DOR]	[DOR]	[DOR]	[DOR]	[DOR]	[DOR]	[DOR]
[+high]	[-high]	[-high]	[-high]	[-high]	[-high]	[+high]
[-low]	[-low]	[+low]	[+low]	[+low]	[-low]	[-low]
[-back]	[-back]	[-back]		[+back]	[+back]	[+back]

The view in which front vowels are complex segments consisting of both a dorsal and a coronal articulator allows for a direct articulatory-based description of most of the ingredients of velar palatalization. The fronting or palatalization of [k] to [kʲ] before a front vowel can be seen as the spreading of the dorsal [-back] from the front vowel to the preceding dorsal, as in (4a). The further change from [kʲ] to [c] can be viewed as the spreading of the coronal articulator to the preceding palatalized velar, as in (4b) creating, in line with Keating's proposal, a complex coronal-dorsal segment.

In this view, the change from [kʲ] to a pure palatal [c] is indeed a change in the articulator, or rather the addition of a supplementary articulator (coronal) to the articulator (dorsal) of the velar consonant. There is thus, contrary to Guion and Blevins, a clear articulatory motivation for the fact that a palatalized velar becomes coronalized, as illustrated in (4):

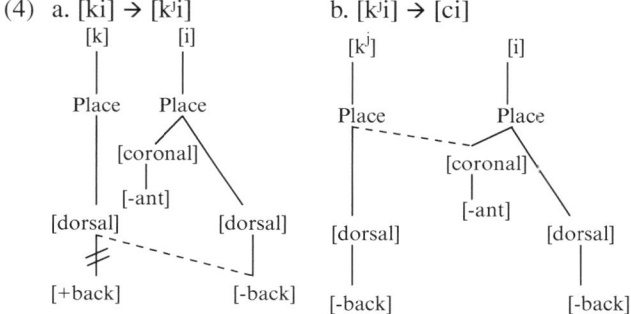

The last step in the palatalization process, by which a palatal plosive [c] is changed into an affricate is, however, less straightforward in an articulatory-based account. Affrication has been described as a contour-creating process in Jacobs (1993). However, the view that affricates are complex segments is no longer widely accepted, as argued among others by Rubach (1994), Clements (1999), and Kim (2001). They have pointed out that if affricates are described as segments specified for both [-continuant] and [+continuant] underlyingly (either ordered or unordered), the wrong prediction is made that affricates pattern with fricatives in processes that target [+continuant] sounds.

In Polish, for instance, affricates fail to participate in fricative assimilation, which led to a description of affricates as strident stops (see Rubach 1994 for more detail). Under this assumption, if affricates pattern with fricatives, it is because of the fact that they share [+strident], and not on the basis of [+continuant]. Clements (1999) and Kim (2001) both point out that treating affricates as simple stops implies that the common process of plosive assibilation before high vowels or a palatal glide cannot be correctly accounted for by the spreading of the feature [+continuant] from the high vocalic segment to the preceding stop, since affricates are not specified for [+continuant]. The assibilation process, which occurs in Canadian French, among others, is illustrated in (5) below (examples are taken from Kim 2001).

(5) *Standard French*   *Québec French*
    pe[ti]t   pe[tˢi]t   'little, small'
    [ti]pe   [tˢi]pe   'type'
    [tj]ens   [tˢj]ens   '(I/you sg.) hold'
    [ty]rc   [tˢy]rc   'Turk'
    [tɥ]er   [tˢɥ]er   'to kill'

Both Clements and Kim propose that affricates resulting from plosive assibilation are created by the insertion of the feature [+strident] onto the plosive. Phonetically, this makes good sense in that the plosive before a high vowel or glide is released into a very narrow constriction generating turbulent airflow. Given that the underlying representation of an affricate is phonetically uninterpretable, the incompatible features [-continuant] (no airflow) and [+strident] (turbulent airflow) have to be ordered in the phonetic realization. Affrication is thus considered the result of a phonology-phonetics mismatch, caused by the insertion of the feature [+strident]. Clements (1999: 272) summarizes it as follows:

> [...] the fact that affricates consist of single segments in the phonology and two segments in the phonetics constitutes a residual case of phonology-phonetics mismatch which cannot be resolved by any further reallocation of phonetic material to phonological segments. In this case, however, the mismatch is a principled one, motivated [...] by the fact that the features [-continuant, +strident] cannot be produced simultaneously [...]. It is just this inherent conflict in feature definitions which [...] requires the incompatible features to be phonetically sequenced.

To summarize the discussion so far, it seems that neither a perceptually-based account nor a purely articulatory-based account are able to fully account for the different steps of velar palatalization. Especially the last step in the process, the change from [c] to [tʃ], seems both perceptually and articulatory-based. Speakers produce turbulent airflow which listeners are likely to perceive as strident stops. In the next section, we will present our own view of velar palatalization, which is partially articulatory and partially perceptually-based. We will also address the role of markedness constraints in sound change.

6.4 Production, Perception and Markedness in Velar Palatalization

As we have seen above, the change from [k] to [kʲ] and then further to [c] can be seen as assimilatory in nature, and can straightforwardly be described as articulatory-based. The change from palatal stop to palatoalveolar affricate, however, cannot be readily motivated in assimilatory terms. In this respect, it is worth mentioning Schane (1973: 115), who observes that "It is inherently more difficult, that is, much more muscular control is needed, to effect complete closure in the palato-alveolar region than in those regions where stops are commonly made". Along the lines of

Clements (1999) and Kim (2001), we assume that the release of a palatal plosive, just as a coronal one, into a narrow constriction (before a high off-glide) creates turbulent airflow which may be misperceived as stridency.

To put it more clearly, the change from palatal stop to palatcalveolar affricate can be motivated in terms of both the speaker and the listener. A speaker may produce a palatal plosive before a high off-glide with turbulent airflow, which can be perceived and interpreted as the feature [+strident] by the hearer. In this respect we are in agreement with Blevins, not in the sense that "resulting palatalized velars may give rise to coronal percepts" (2004: 139), but rather that palatal plosives before a palatal off-glide may give rise to *affricate* percepts. Contrary to Blevins, however, we do believe that markedness plays a role in sound change, especially when it comes to addressing Guion's criticism that an articulatory-based account does not "motivate a change from affricated palatal to palatoalveolar" (1998: 18). In this respect, we follow Padgett and Zygis (2003), who suggest that the strong inherent palatalization of [ɕ]/[tɕ] and the retroflexion of [ʂ]/[tʂ] motivate the universal articulatory markedness ranking in (6).

(6) Articulatory markedness: *tɕ >> *tʂ >> *tʃ

We propose that the ranking in (6) is responsible for the fact that velar palatalization typically results in a palatoalveolar affricate [tʃ] rather than a palatal or alveopalatal one [tɕ]. Given the hierarchy in (6), one would expect that if a speaker produces a palatal with turbulent airflow, the resulting affricate would be [tʃ], instead of, say, [tɕ] or [tʂ]. We also believe that the status of velars as fronted and/or palatalized needs to be expressed by the grammar. Blevins' (2004: 243–244) main criticism of markedness constraints, and for that matter OT, is the fact that it relies "on universal markedness constraints as a means of capturing typological generalizations across phonological systems". A case in point is the [k]>[tʃ] change at hand. As observed above by Guion (1998), Ohala (1992), and Chang et al. (2001), this change is quite common, whereas the reverse [tʃ] turning into [k] is not. The more or less implicit criticism for an OT-analysis would seem to be that any ranking of constraints is possible and that thus any change is possible. This is illustrated in (7), where two brute force markedness constraints, militating against [ki] and [tʃi] respectively, and one faithfulness constraint IDENT (F), requiring feature identity between input and output forms, are used:

(7a) /ki/	*ki	IDENT (F)	*tʃi
[ki]	*!		
☞ [tʃi]		*	*
(7b) /tʃi/	*tʃi	IDENT (F)	*ki
[tʃi]	*!		
☞ [ki]		*	*

Whereas the grammar in (7a) expresses the attested change, the grammar in (7b) incorrectly expresses the reverse change as equally possible. What we would like to suggest here is that the reverse unattested sound changes do not occur, exactly because of markedness. To demonstrate this, we will use the version of OT that makes use of Candidate Chains (McCarthy 2007). Let us first start by providing a more detailed traditional OT account of the relevant assimilatory steps in the velar palatalization process. In order to illustrate this, we propose the constraints in (8).

(8) PALATALIZATION 1:
A velar must develop an off-glide before front vowels.
PALATALIZATION 2:
A velar must assimilate to the coronal articulation of a following coronal vowel/glide.
IDENTITY DORSAL:
A dorsal consonant must not change its dorsal specifications.
MAX-IO PLACE:
A place specification must not be deleted.
DEP-IO PLACE:
No new place specification must be added.

The constraint rankings below straightforwardly account for a language in which there is no palatalization (9a), for one in which velars develop a palatal off-glide (9b), and for one in which a velar is changed into a palatal plosive (9c).

(9a) /ki/	ID DORSAL	PAL 1	DEP-IO PLACE	PAL 2
[kʲi]	*!			*
☞[ki]		*		*
[ci]	*!		*	
(9b) /ki/	PAL 1	ID DORSAL	DEP-IO PLACE	PAL 2
☞ [kʲi]		*		*
[ki]	*!			*
[ci]		*	*!	
(9c) /ki/	PAL 2	PAL 1	ID DORSAL	DEP-IO PLACE
[kʲi]	*!		*	
[ki]	*!	*		
☞ [ci]			*	*

In (9) above, we have assumed that if a velar changes into a palatalized velar or a palatal plosive, it has a violation of the IDENTITY DORSAL constraint, because the feature [+back] changes into [-back] (cf. (4) above). Furthermore, we assume that the palatal plosive, being a complex consonant, has a dorsal [-back] and a coronal [-anterior] specification and does not violate the constraint PALATALIZATION 1, but does entail a violation of the constraint DEP-IO PLACE, because a new coronal specification has been added. We will argue next, that once the palatal plosive is taken as an input to the constraint grammar, there is no possible way of changing it back into a plain velar. To drive this point home, let us first briefly discuss OT-CC (OT with Candidate Chains).

The basic difference with respect to classic OT is that evaluation does not take into account every possible candidate, but only well-formed chains connecting a given input to an output. A candidate is a chain of forms connecting input to output. The first member of every candidate chain is a fully faithful parse, violating no faithfulness constraints. A single faithfulness violation at a specific location is called a LUM (*Localized Unfaithful Mapping*). Successive forms in a chain are required to accumulate all of their predecessor's LUMs and add exactly one LUM. Moreover, every successive form has to be more harmonic than its predecessor according to the constraint hierarchy of the language (cf. McCarthy 2007 for a more detailed account). According to Candidate Chain theory, the well-formed and ill-formed chains for an input form /ɛskina/ 'spine' (from (2b) above), assuming grammar (9c) from above, are illustrated in (10). Following McCarthy's notation, the fully faithful initial form is indexed and a LUM is indexed for the locus of violation.

(10) 1 $<\varepsilon_1 s_2 k_3 i_4 n_5 a_6,$ ɛskina>
    2 $<\varepsilon_1 s_2 k_3 i_4 n_5 a_6,$ ɛskina, ɛskʲina>
    3 $<\varepsilon_1 s_2 k_3 i_4 n_5 a_6,$ ɛskina, ɛskʲina, ɛscina>
    4 $<\varepsilon_1 s_2 k_3 i_4 n_5 a_6,$ ɛskina, ɛscina>

1 = well-formed, no LUM.
2 = well-formed, LUM sequence < ID-DORSAL@3>
3 = well-formed, LUM sequence < ID-DORSAL@3, DEP-IO PLACE@3>
4 = ill-formed, two LUMs between successive forms < ID-DORSAL@3, DEP-IO PLACE@3>

The chains (1–3) connecting input /ɛskina/ to output candidates (1) [ɛskina], (2) [ɛskʲina] and (3) [ɛscina] are well-formed chains. In chain 1 no LUM is added, in chain 2 only one LUM is added and the second form in that chain is more harmonic than its predecessor, given the ranking of PALATALIZATION 1 above ID(ENT)-DORSAL. Chain 3 is well-formed as well: in each successive form only one LUM is added and each of the successive forms is more harmonic than the preceding form in the chain, given the ranking of PALATALIZATION 1 above ID(ENT)-DORSAL and the ranking of PALATALIZATION 2 above DEP-IO PLACE. Chain 4, finally, is ill-formed, given that between two successive forms more than one LUM has been added.

Now let us show why a reverse change is excluded under OT-CC. Let us assume a grammar where velar palatalization is no longer productive at the time when Latin labiovelars [kʷ] and [gʷ] were changed into [k] and [g], which were no longer subject to palatalization. We further need to assume that [ɛscina] then is no longer derived from an input /ɛskina/, but represented as /ɛscina/ underlyingly. A change back, expressed as a chain ([ɛscina] > [ɛskjina] > [ɛskina]) is ill-formed under any of the rankings, given that /ɛscina/ has no harmonic improvement to gain from giving up any faithfulness. This is so, because there are only contextual markedness constraints, PALATALIZATION 1 and PALATALIZATION 2, that militate against velars in a front vowel context. The only possible way of getting the unattested change (from

[c] to [kʲ] and then to [k]) would be by adding opposite contextual markedness constraints (like, for instance, AVOID [kʲ] BEFORE FRONT VOWELS) contrary to what markedness expresses. One might, however, add a segmental markedness constraint (like *[c]), not specific to a front vocalic environment, but which states that a palatal plosive in general is marked relative to a palatoalveolar affricate. This would, for instance, account for a context-free change from palatal plosive to affricate, as in the history of Athabaskan (cf. Blevins 2004).[5]

In this section, we have proposed that in order to adequately account for velar palatalization, both production (articulatory-based) and perception need to be taken into account. We have further argued and motivated that markedness constraints do play an important role in accounting for sound change and that OT with Candidate Chains allows a straightforward alternative (not perception-based) answer for why some sound changes are typically irreversible. In the last section of this chapter, we return to the problematic fact that velar palatalization was also triggered by the low vowel *a*.

6.5 Velar Palatalization Before the Low Vowel *a*

The different views on Gallo-Romance palatalization that have been defended in the literature, can roughly be divided into three groups. The first one assumes a general fronting of Latin *a*. In Pope (1934) for example, front vowels are considered the triggers for velar palatalization. Pope assumes that in early Gallo-Romance, the Latin vowel *a* changed from velar to palatal, causing it to participate in the Gallo-Romance palatalization process, next to [i] and [e].

A second possible analysis that has been put forward does not assume a specific change in the quality of *a* that would have made it a trigger for velar palatalization. Fouché (1958), among others, notes that Latin *a* diphthongized in stressed open syllables only and that the Second Velar Palatalization then took place in a context where it failed to apply during the First, most likely because of the specific characteristics of the Gallo-Romance languages.

---

[5] An anonymous reviewer has pointed out two potential problems for the claim defended here. First, in Picardy and Normandy varieties of French, velars became palatalized, triggered Bartsch's law (i.e. the diphthongization of /a/), and then regressed back into plain velars. However, as the reviewer points out, the claim that [k] was fronted in those dialects is not an empirically attested fact, only a non-necessary hypothesis for Bartsch's diphthongization, under the assumption that diphthongization could only take place after [+high] consonants. Moreover, one could assume, if this traditional hypothesis were accepted, that palatalized [kʲ] was still a surface allophone of /k/ when the regression took place. A second, more problematic, counter-example is offered by the evolution of the verb *tenir* in Canadian French, where the forms *tiens* and *tient* have many variant pronunciations: [tʲẽ, tʃẽ, cẽ, kʲẽ, kẽ]. If the variant [kẽ], as the reviewer points out, arises through a chain of changes [tʲẽ] > [cẽ] > [kʲẽ] > [kẽ], the claim defended here would be invalidated. Further research is needed in order to empirically falsify this claim.

The third view on Gallo-Romance palatalization lies somewhere between the two extremes. Buckley (2003) claims that both phonetic and phonological factors are involved in this process. He assumes that palatalization is primarily phonetically conditioned, by the coarticulation of a velar plosive and the following front vowel: "[…] the second palatalization was in fact triggered by *all* front vowels, and the rule must be understood from that perspective" (Buckley 2003: 7). However, he considers a general fronting of all allophones of Latin /a/ too radical. He argues that in a stressed open syllable, /a/ took a fronted realization [æ], creating the phonetic context for velar palatalization to occur. Palatalization then gradually extended to all contexts where a velar consonant was followed by any instance (both fronted and unfronted) of the phoneme /a/, causing the process to take place also in contexts lacking a phonetic motivation.

Buckley's account appears to be an interesting one, but it is questionable whether (allophonic) fronting of the vowel is really the crucial factor in velar palatalization before /a/. As a matter of fact, it appears to be neither a sufficient nor a necessary conditioning factor. Not sufficient, because as mentioned in Footnote 5 above, in Artois, Normandy and Picardy, velars did not end up as affricates before the low vowel /a/, although in those varieties the same structural conditions did exist: a fronted allophone in stressed open syllables. Thus, *a*-fronting in stressed open syllables and velar palatalization and affrication before /a/ appear to have been two independent phenomena. Allophonic fronting does not seem to be a necessary conditioning factor, either. In earlier work, Buckley (2000) refers to an example of Zuni, where velars were fronted before the front vowels /i/ and /e/. The process was extended to the non-front vowel /a/, and, interestingly enough, after the velar had been palatalized, the non-front vowel itself got fronted to [æ] by the influence of the preceding segment. Furthermore, Buckley (2003: 11) refers to personal communication with Paul Boersma and Yves Charles Morin, who noted that in some contemporary varieties of French, [k] also appears to be fronted before /a/. A word like *quatre* ('four') for instance, may be realized as [kʲatʁ], even though the vowel is still "relatively central".

For the Zuni case, Buckley (2000) proposes a phonological (cognitive) explanation: the desire to include /a/ in any of the existing patterns of velar + vowel interactions (fronting before front vowels and rounding before round vowels). This is what we would like to propose for French as well. We agree with Buckley (2003) that it is the phonological categorization of /a/ that plays a crucial role in understanding its behavior with respect to palatalization before [a], but we will argue that it is independent from its evolution in stressed open syllables.

In our view, there is no phonetic motivation for why the low central vowel /a/ would pattern with either the front or the back vowels as it is inherently neither front nor back, but central. In terms of feature representation this means that /a/ for principled reasons is ambiguous with respect to the Dorsal [+/-back] specification, as illustrated in (11) below (cf. (3) above).

(11)

/i/	/e/	/ɛ/	/a/	/u/	/o/	/u/
[COR]	[COR]	[COR]		[LAB]	[LAB]	[LAB]
[-ant]	[-ant]	[-ant]				
[DOR]	[DOR]	[DOR]	[DOR]	[DOR]	[DOR]	[DOR]
[+high]	[-high]	[-high]	[-high]	[-high]	[-high]	[+high]
[-low]	[-low]	[+low]	[+low]	[+low]	[-low]	[-low]
[-back]	[-back]	[-back]		[+back]	[+back]	[+back]

?
[back]

In the vocalic system, the vowel /a/ thus has a phonologically ambiguous status, given that it is neither front nor back (and hence unspecified). As such, it may pattern with either the front or back vowels of the inventory. In the case of the Second Velar Palatalization, it behaves like a front vowel, triggering palatalization of the velar, just like the vowels that are both phonetically and phonemically front. The Second Velar Palatalization is not an isolated case where /a/ patterns with the front vowels.

Klausenburger (1974) presents two cases, one in which /a/ patterns with the front vowels and one in which /a/ patterns with the back vowels. In the process of diphthongization, the back ([dorsal][labial]) vowels [ɔ] and [o] develop a labial-dorsal glide [w], respectively, before and after the vowel, as in [flore] > [flowre] 'flower', whereas the front ([coronal][dorsal]) vowels [ɛ] and [ə] develop a palatal ([coronal] [dorsal]) glide [j] respectively before and after the vowel, as in [debɛt] > [dejbɛt] 'must PRES 3 SG.'. The vowel /a/ patterns with the front vowels in developing a palatal glide, as in [mare] > [majre] 'sea' (cf. Klausenburger 1974: 20). A case where /a/ patterns with the back vowels is provided by the processes of "Vokalisierung des [l]" ([l]-vocalization) and "[l]-Verlust" ([l]-loss). The consonant [l] develops into a glide [w] after back vowels in oblique case singular plural alternations, such as [kɔl] ~ [kɔws] 'neck, SG/PL'. The same process applies to [a], as in [bal] ~ [baws] 'dance SG. PL.'. In the case of front vowels, the [l] is lost, as in [nyl] ~ [nys] 'nobody SG. PL.' and [fil] ~ [fis] 'son SG. PL.' (cf. Klausenburger 1974: 42–43). Therefore, /a/ undergoes phonological processes of both front and back vowels.

6.6 Summary

In this chapter, we have reviewed perception-based and production-based accounts of velar palatalization in light of the French First and Second Velar Palatalization. We have argued that both production and perception are important factors in accounting for the two French velar palatalizations. Moreover, we have argued that markedness constraints play a crucial role in analyzing sound change in French and that they must be incorporated into any analysis (Blevins 2004). We have shown that OT-CC (Optimality Theory with Candidate Chains) is superior to a perceptual analysis, when it comes to the question why some sound changes appear to be irreversible. Furthermore, we have provided a principled phonological, not phonetic, account of the atypical velar palatalization before *a*. By trying to separate the roles of production, perception and markedness on one hand, and the role of phonology and phonetics on the other, we hope to have contributed to furthering our understanding of general principles underlying language change.

References

Anttila, R. 1989. *Historical and comparative linguistics*. Philadelphia: John Benjamins Publishing Company.
Bhat, D.N.S. 1978. A general study of palatalization. In *Universals of human language*, Phonology, vol. II, ed. J.H. Greenberg, 48–92. Stanford: Sage Publications.
Blevins, J. 2004. *Evolutionary phonology*. Cambridge: Cambridge University Press.
Bourcelot, H. 1966-1969-1978. *Atlas linguistique et ethnographique de la Champagne et de la Brie*. Paris: Editions du CNRS.
Bourciez, E., and J. Bourciez. 1974. *Phonétique française. Etude historique*. Paris: Klincksieck.
Buckley, E. 2000. On the naturalness of unnatural rules. In *Proceedings from the second workshop on American Indigenous Languages. UCSB working papers in linguistics*, vol. 9, 1–14. Santa Barbara.
Buckley, E. 2003. *The phonetic origin and phonological extension of Gallo-Roman palatalization*. Philadelphia: Ms, University of Pennsylvania.
Calabrese, A. 1993. Palatalization processes in the history of the Romance languages: A theoretical study. In *Linguistic perspectives on the Romance languages*, ed. W.J. Ashby et al., 65–83. Amsterdam: John Benjamins Publishing Company.
Chang, S., M. Plauché, and J. Ohala. 2001. Markedness and consonant confusion asymmetries. In *The role of speech perception in phonology*, ed. E. Hume and K. Johnson, 79–101. London/San Diego: Academic.
Cho, T., and P. Ladefoged. 1999. Variation and universals in VOT. Evidence from 18 languages. *Journal of Phonetics* 27(2): 207–229.
Clements, G.N. 1993. Lieu d'articulation des consonnes et des voyelles: une théorie unifiée. In *Architecture des représentations phonologiques*, ed. B. Laks and A. Rialland, 101–145. Paris: CNRS Éditions.
Clements, G.N. 1999. Affricates as noncontoured stops. In *Proceedings of LP'98*, ed. O. Fujimura et al., 271–299. Prague: Karolinum Press.
Clements, G.N., and E. Hume. 1995. The internal organization of speech sounds. In *The handbook of phonological theory*, ed. J.A. Goldsmith, 245–306. Cambridge: Blackwell.
Fouché, P. 1958. *Phonétique historique du français*. Paris: Klincksieck.
Grammont, M. 1933. *Traité de phonétique*. Paris: Delagrave.
Guion, S. 1998. The role of perception in the sound change of velar palatalization. *Phonetica* 55: 18–52.
Jacobs, H. 1993. La palatalization gallo-romane et la représentation des traits distinctifs. In *Architecture des représentations phonologiques*, ed. B. Laks and A. Rialland, 147–171. Paris: CNRS Éditions.
Jacobs, H. 2007. Contrasting coronal sibilants: Polish and Ubykh. In *Université Européenne d'été – Vol. Sciences du langage*, 113–128. Paris.

Jacobs, H., and J. van de Weijer. 1992. On the formal description of palatalization. In *Linguistics in the Netherlands*, ed. R. Bok-Bennema and R. van Hout, 125–135. Amsterdam/Philadelphia: John Benjamins Publishing Company.

Keating, P.A. 1988. *Palatals as complex segments: X-ray evidence. UCLA working papers in phonetics,* vol. 69, 77–91. Los Angeles.

Kim, H. 2001. A phonetically based account of phonological stop assibilation. *Phonology* 18: 81–108.

Klausenburger, J. 1974. *Historische Französische Phonologie aus Generativer Sicht.* Tübingen: Niemeyer.

Ladefoged, P., and I. Maddieson. 1996. *The sounds of the world's languages.* Cambridge: Blackwell.

Lahiri, A., and V. Evers. 1991. Palatalization and coronality. In *The special status of coronals. Internal and external evidence,* ed. C. Paradis and J.-F. Prunet, 79–100. San Diego: Academic.

McCarthy, J.J. 2007. *Hidden generalizations. Phonological opacity in optimality theory.* London: Equinox.

Meyer-Lübke, W. 1890. *Grammatik der Romanischen Sprachen,* Romanische Lautlehre, vol. 1. Leipzig: Fues' Verlag.

Ohala, J. 1992. What's cognitive, what's not in sound change. In *Diachrony within synchrony: language history and cognition,* ed. G. Kellerman and M.D. Morrissey, 309–355. Frankfurt: Lang.

Padgett, J., and M. Zygis. 2003. The evolution of sibilants in Polish and Russian. *ZAS Papers in Linguistics* 3: 155–174.

Plauché, M., C. Delogu, and J. Ohala. 1997. Asymmetries in consonant confusion. In *Proceedings of Eurospeech'97: Fifth European conference on speech communication and technology,* vol. 4, 2187–2190. Rhodes: Greece.

Pope, M.K. 1934. *From Latin to modern French with especial consideration of Anglo-Norman.* Manchester: Manchester University Press.

Rubach, J. 1994. Affricates as strident stops in Polish. *Linguistic Inquiry* 25: 119–143.

Rubach, J. 2003. Polish palatalization in derivational optimality theory. *Lingua* 113: 197–237.

Sagey, E. 1986. *The representation of features and relations in nonlinear phonology.* PhD dissertation, MIT.

Schane, S. 1973. *Generative phonology.* Englewood Cliffs: Prentice-Hall.

Chapter 7
Evolution and Regrammation in the Mood System: Perspectives from Old, Middle, Renaissance and Modern French

Jan Lindschouw

7.1 Introduction

The goal of this contribution is to describe the evolution of the mood system (i.e. the indicative and the subjunctive) of French from the perspective of grammaticalization and language change. Since the evolution of the mood system does not take place abruptly from one century to another, but instead proceeds gradually over several centuries, this study will not be confined to Old French. On the contrary, in order to give a full account of the evolution of the mood system and to show the importance of synchronicity for diachronic studies, a broader diachronic perspective needs to be adopted, beginning with the Old and Middle French periods and ending with Modern French. The evolution of the mood system will be described within the framework of grammaticalization theory, but with reference to an extended version of the concept, whereby grammaticalization does not only apply to the transition from lexical to grammatical items, but can also be considered a process which changes grammatical systems into new grammatical systems (Heltoft et al. 2005; Nørgård-Sørensen et al. 2011). This process will be referred to as *regrammation* (Andersen 2006).

This study is based on the general assumption that the evolution of the mood system is linked to a change in its functional categories. More specifically, it is assumed that the modal value of the mood system can be interpreted in terms of assertion and non-assertion (Hooper 1975; Confais 1995 [1990]; Haverkate 2002; Korzen 2003; Lindschouw 2006, 2008, 2011). It will be shown that during the period from Old to Modern French, the non-assertive potential of the subjunctive is lessened. To put it in terms of regrammation, the subjunctive mood undergoes a paradigmatic reduction (see Lehmann 1995 [1982]), whereby its functional content is reduced (desemantized) (op.cit.: 127) and its variation with the indicative gradually

---

J. Lindschouw (✉)
Department of English, Germanic and Romance Studies, University of Copenhagen,
Copenhagen, Denmark
e-mail: janl@hum.ku.dk

disappears (the subjunctive thus undergoes a process of obligatorification[1] (op.cit.: 139) and specialization (Hopper and Traugott 2003 [1993]: 116–118)).

This contribution is particularly concerned with the way in which the evolution of the mood system contributes to our current understanding of language change *per se*. With this in mind, reference will be made to the theory of Andersen (2001a, b), according to which the sequences of language changes can be predicted. If a language change is introduced *from below*, it is normally introduced in unmarked contexts and will in the course of time spread to marked ones. By contrast, if a change is introduced *from above*, it is normally introduced in marked contexts and will spread to unmarked ones. The evolution of the mood system will be related to Andersen's theory of language change.

In this chapter, it will also be shown that text genres have an impact on the evolution of the mood system. For example, it seems that one of the non-assertive values of the subjunctive, the *irrealis* value, is highly frequent in abstract text genres such as legal documents, medical texts, and religious prose, because these genres favour unreal or hypothetical statements. One could thus hypothesize that since the interlocutors do not know if this value belongs to the linguistic form or to the text genre, the system has created an ambiguity, which might have led to the gradual disappearance of the *irrealis* value within the subjunctive paradigm.

The method used to collect data is on the whole based on corpus linguistics. The vast majority of data come from large electronic corpora containing texts from Old to Modern French: *Base de Français Médiéval, Dictionnaire du Moyen Français,* and *Frantext* (see Sect. 7.4). It should be emphasized that, since the evolution of the entire mood system would require at least a full monograph, the main focus of the present chapter will be on concessive clauses, though this evolution seems to reflect the evolution of the mood system in general. As shown in Winters (1989), Buridant (2000: 333–353), and Lindschouw (2011: 271–272), there seems to be a general tendency in the history of the mood system that the subjunctive loses ground to the indicative, which consequently extends its range. This is, for example, observed in conditional clauses, complement clauses following a verb of opinion, and in indirect interrogative clauses. It is my belief that, though this contribution is only concerned with the evolution of mood in concessive clauses, the results to a large extent reflect the general evolution of the mood system, but further research needs, of course, to be done.

7.2 Regrammation of the Subjunctive Paradigm

The hypothesis of this study is that the evolution of the subjunctive in concessive clauses can be described in terms of grammaticalization. Traditionally, grammaticalization has been considered to be a process that is defined according to a cline of

---

[1] The term *obligatorification* is a neologism introduced by Lehmann (1995 [1982]: 139) to designate a form which loses its variability with other forms and thus becomes obligatory. Since this term has been used in many works on grammaticalization, it will be maintained in this study.

grammaticality, where the lexical item ideally passes from a free content item to a grammatical word, and later to a clitic pronoun, and then an inflectional affix (Meillet 1948 [1912]; Lehmann 1995 [1982]; Traugott 2003; Hopper and Traugott 2003 [1993]). This definition, which is both very narrow and imprecise, moreover does not allow for interpreting the evolution of the subjunctive as a case of grammaticalization, since the subjunctive already displayed a grammatical function in Classical Latin, as it was systematically used in subordinate clauses (cf. Harris 1974). Consequently, in this study, we propose an extended definition of grammaticalization. We will propose that grammaticalization is also a process that reorganizes grammatical systems into new grammatical systems, provided that the relationship between the form and meaning of the grammatical item in question undergoes a change within a closed paradigm (Heltoft et al. 2005; Nørgård-Sørensen et al. 2011), and that the scope of the item is reduced.

This change will be referred to as a process of *regrammation* (Andersen 2006). Note that all of these conditions are met within the diachronic evolution of the subjunctive, as it is organized within a closed paradigm (the mood paradigm) and undergoes a change between its form and meaning. Furthermore, its scope has gradually been reduced. To put it in more traditional terms of grammaticalization theory, it will be argued that the subjunctive undergoes a paradigmatic reduction (Lehmann 1995 [1982]), whereby its functional content is reduced (desemantisized) (op.cit.: 127) and it gradually ceases to be in free variation with the indicative. In other words, the subjunctive thus undergoes a process of obligatorification and specialization (Hopper and Traugott 2003 [1993]: 116–118).[2] These changes are preceded by two reanalyses of the mood system, which is a condition for every instance of grammaticalization (Detges and Waltereit 2002: 190; Hopper and Traugott 2003 [1993]: 59; Heltoft et al. 2005; Marchello-Nizia 2006: 45–46) (see Sect. 7.5.4). Conversely, it is hypothesized that the indicative mood, though reorganized within the mood paradigm, does not undergo a process of regrammation, because it extends its functional domain from a single value to three values.

One could raise the objection that the change affecting the subjunctive in concessive clauses is not a process of grammaticalization, but rather a pure semantic change. However, there are a number of strong arguments in favor of viewing the change of the subjunctive as a case of grammaticalization or regrammation. First of all, the evolution of the subjunctive implies not only a semantic change, but also a formal change, since its more or less free variation with the indicative mood tends to disappear in certain linguistic contexts (Winters 1989; Lindschouw 2011: 271–272). Secondly, the changes in the subjunctive trigger a reorganization of the entire mood system, resulting in a transfer of certain semantic values from the subjunctive to the

---

[2] Note that Lehmann's theory is essentially concerned with the development from lexical to grammatical material, but I contend that it can be extended to reorganizations of grammatical systems, as well, if it is specified that desemantisization concerns a reduction of the grammatical-functional content and that obligatorification or specialization is a reduction of the alternation between items that have already become grammatical.

indicative. This observation is in accordance with Meillet (1948 [1912]: 133), who states that grammaticalization changes the grammatical system as a whole, contrary to, for example, analogy. Thirdly, a core definition of grammaticalization is that the grammaticalized entities undergo a simplification process, leading to a reduction of the paradigm into which they enter (Lehmann 1995 [1982]: 136). This definition also applies to the evolution of the subjunctive, since its formal and functional domain is gradually reduced, which consequently leads to a reduction of the mood paradigm. Finally, as will be shown, some of the crucial changing processes in grammaticalization can be recognized in the evolution of the subjunctive, i.e. desemantisization, obligatorification/specialization, and reanalysis.

7.2.1 Internally and Externally Motivated Language Change

One of the goals of this contribution is to study the way in which the evolution of the mood system contributes to our current understanding of language change *per se*. Here we make reference to Andersen's (2001a, b) theory, according to which the succession of language changes can be predicted. A basic distinction can be drawn between external and internal motivations for language change. External factors are social, including migration, language contact (e.g., peaceful contact situations, invasions, trade), language policy, and dominant groups influencing speakers' perception of style and registers. Internal factors are to be understood as purely linguistically motivated within the language system (e.g. analogy, reorganization of syntagmatic and paradigmatic structures).

Andersen uses the concepts of internal and external change in a traditional way, with the very important exception that external factors need not necessarily be the result of contact situations, but can also stem from language policy and speakers' perception of style and registers. This definition of external change is essential to this study, since, as it will be shown, dominant groups of society contribute to the evolution of the mood system. Another divergence is that Andersen establishes a link between internal and external factors and the actualization process (i.e. introduction) of changes in the language with respect to their markedness status. According to Andersen, if a language change is externally motivated, it is normally introduced *from above* and appears in a marked context, such as poetry, plays written in verse, argumentative genres, or text genres that are close to the distance pole[3] in the continuum of texts proposed by Koch and Oesterreicher (1990, 2001). Externally motivated language changes are expected to extend, in the course of time, to unmarked contexts such as dialogues, correspondence, diaries, or, say, the proximate pole of

---

[3] The distance pole has to do with text genres characterized by e.g. public communication, an unknown addressee, a weak degree of emotionality, planned communication, whereas the proximate pole is characterized by e.g. private communication, a known and/or intimate addressee, a high degree of emotionality, and spontaneous communication. See Koch and Oesterreicher (2001: 586).

Koch and Oesterreicher's continuum. Conversely, if a language change is internally motivated, it is normally introduced *from below*, and appears first in unmarked contexts and later spreads to marked ones.

One could raise the objection that the theory of markedness agreement contains some speculative elements, which are difficult to substantiate in practice. It is true that we cannot be certain regarding the intentions of speakers and the status of grammatical items in diachrony, and we could question whether Andersen's proposal should be considered a method or a theory. In fact, Andersen's hypotheses have been tested on a large amount of data coming from typologically and genetically different languages, for example German, English, French, Russian, and Norwegian (cf. the contributions in the volume that cite Andersen (2001a, b)). Since all of these studies generally confirm Andersen's hypotheses, they should consequently be considered as constituting a theory that enables researchers to predict certain language changes. Yet we are certainly not claiming that all aspects of change can be predicted from this theory.

In this chapter, it will be shown that the evolution of the mood system is, in fact, influenced by both external and internal motivations of language change. In fact, some concessive conjunctions, and thus some values of the mood forms, seem to be externally motivated, while others seem to be internally motivated, as can be seen in Sects. 7.5.1, 7.5.2, 7.5.3 and 7.5.4 below. In addition, the predictive power of Andersen's theory will be evaluated on the basis of the French data examined.

7.3 The Theory of Assertion

As mentioned above, this study is based on the general assumption that the difference between the indicative and the subjunctive mood can be described in functional terms, and that the evolution of the mood system in concessive clauses is linked to a change of its functional categories. Thus, in order to give a full account of the changes of the mood system from Old to Modern French, we must take into account the semantic-pragmatic values of the two modal forms. A purely syntactic approach, such as the one proposed by Sneyders de Vogel (1927), Foulet (1968 [1919]: 204ff) and Harris (1974), is not sufficient, because it cannot explain why the mood system has changed. Rather, it merely enumerates the syntactic contexts in which the subjunctive could appear in Old French and compares these with those of Modern French.[4]

The modal value of the mood system can be interpreted in terms of assertion and non-assertion, where the indicative constitutes the assertive domain (i.e. giving new information) and the subjunctive the non-assertive domain, presenting the propositional content as either presupposed (or known) information or as *irrealis*, i.e., referring to a state of affairs that is not realized at the moment of utterance or is questioned by the speaker for one reason or another (Hooper 1975; Confais 1995 [1990] Haverkate 2002; Korzen 2003; Lindschouw 2006, 2008, 2011).

---

[4] See Lindschouw (2011: 42–44) for further discussion.

At older stages of French, this functional opposition seems to be a relevant descriptive parameter to account for the difference between the indicative and the subjunctive mood, as illustrated by the following occurrences in concessive clauses.

(1) Et quant Saintré entend Madame si haultement parler, ja
 and when Saintré hears-IND Lady so nobly speak, already
 soit que son cuer *estoit* ja conclud
 is-SUBJ that her heart was-IND already won

 'And when Saintré heard the Lady speak so nobly, even though her heart was already won' (Saintré: 146, fifteenth century cit. BFM)

(2) mes il ne se pueent mie granment esjoïr de gaaing (...),
 but they not themselves can-IND not very be happy about victory (...),
 ja soit ce qu' il *aient* plus gent que nos n' avons
 already is-SUBJ it that they have-SUBJ more men than we not have-IND

 'but they cannot be very happy about the victory (...), even though they have more men than we do' (Artu: 148, thirteenth century cit. BFM)

(3) Vanterie est trop vilains vices; qui s' en vante, il
 boasting is-IND too terrible sin ; whoever himself about it boats-IND, he
 fet trop que nices, car, ja soit ce que fet l'
 makes-IND too than poor, for, already is-SUBJ it that done it
 eüssent, toutes vois celer le **deüssent**
 they had-SUBJ, however hide it they should-SUBJ

 'Boasting is a terrible sin; whoever boasts about it is a poor man, for, even if they had done it, they should however have hidden it'(Meun: v5805, thirteenth century cit. BFM)

In (1), by means of the indicative *estoit* 'was', the proposition of the subordinate clause is asserted, because the author is giving an account of an event. In (2), however, by using the subjunctive *aient* 'have', the speaker presupposes the content of the concessive clause, because he presents a state of affairs that the interlocutor is presumed to be aware of (i.e. the explicit reference to the interlocutor by the use of the pronoun *nos* 'we'). In (3), the concessive clause presents a hypothetical state of affairs; the subjunctive *eüssent* 'had' thus expresses *irrealis* modality, which is supported by the non-referential marker *qui* 'who', and the double hypothetical structure consisting of two imperfect subjunctives (*eüssent* 'had' and *deüssent* 'should'), which indicate counterfactuality. Note that the fact that subjunctive *soit* 'is' follows *ja* 'already' in all examples is not taken into account, since it is part of the conjunction *ja soit (ce) que* 'even though/if' and does not carry any specific modal value (see Sect. 7.5.1 below).

In Modern French, however, the distribution of mood in concessive clauses has changed. The more flexible mood system of Old French has been considerably reduced, so that mood selection has become increasingly specialized. In fact, the subjunctive, which primarily occurs after conjunctions like *bien que* and *quoique* 'even though', is no longer able to express *irrealis* modality,[5] but rather only presupposed information (4), whereas the indicative still indicates assertion in concessive clauses introduced by *encore que* 'even though' (5) and *irrealis* in those introduced by *même si* 'even if' (6):

(4) Paul est parti bien que/quoique Mireille *soit* revenue d' un
    Paul is-IND left even though Mireille is-SUBJ returned from a
    long voyage
    long trip

   'Paul left, even though Mireille returned from a long trip'

(5) Mireille s' est beaucoup amusée, encore qu' elle *est* rentrée
    Mireille herself is-IND much amused, even though she is-IND went home
    tôt
    early

   'Mireille had a lot of fun, even though she went home early'[6]

(6) Nous ferons une partie de campagne même s'il *pleut*
    we will make-IND a picnic even if it rains-IND

   'We will go for a picnic, even if it rains'

As mentioned above, we will concentrate here on the evolution of mood in concessive clauses and not on the entire mood system. There are three reasons for this. First the theory of assertion seems almost 'preconstructed' to describe the mood opposition in concessive clauses, at least at an earlier stage of French, as is evident from examples (1)–(3). Secondly, concessive clauses constitute an illustrative example of modal evolution that can be described within the framework of grammaticalization theory, and thus reflect the general evolution of the mood system (Lindschouw 2011: 271–272). Finally, the evolution of concessive clauses contributes to our understanding of language change in general.

7.4 Method

An empirical study was carried out using large text corpora from Old, Middle and Modern French (see *References* for further information). To obtain a representative corpus, we have considered data from a variety of text genres representing both the

---

[5] It is true that in Modern French the subjunctive expresses *irrealis* modality in utterances like *quoi que vous fassiez, je vous aiderai* 'whatever you do, I will help you', but I analyse these concessive relative clauses with *quoi* as the antecedent of *que*, while *quoique* in (4) introduces an adverbial clause. The two structures display important syntactic, semantic and pragmatic differences compared to the fixed conjunction *quoique* and will therefore not be taken into account here.

[6] The subjunctive may also appear in concessives introduced by *encore que* (see Sect. 7.5.3).

distance and the proximate poles in Koch and Oesterreicher's text continuum (1990, 2001) (see Sect. 7.2.1 above). Text genres belonging to the distance pole include argumentative and non-literary prose as well as versified texts (poetry and drama), while the proximate pole is represented by plays in prose, dialogues, and direct discourse. Literary texts have also been included, but, as shown in Lindschouw (2011: 128–129), they cannot easily be defined with respect to the distance and proximate poles, since they display features of both. Consequently, the latter occupy an intermediate position on the continuum.

Two hundred examples were collected in Renaissance and Modern French for each of the conjunctions under consideration. However, for the Old and Middle French periods, only 133 occurrences of the mood forms in concessive clauses relevant to this study were found. This is most likely due to the limited number of texts available for these periods. For example, *La Base de Français Médiéval*, which was consulted for the earlier period, consists of only 80 texts, and even though different text genres are represented in the corpus (e.g. literature, historical, legal and scientific texts, hagiographies) literary texts are dominant. Consequently, the Old and Middle French periods are somewhat underrepresented.

Another methodological issue that must be taken into account is the gradual weakening of preconsonantal [s] in the termination –*st* of the third person singular of the imperfect subjunctive (e.g. *fust* 'was', *eust* 'had' and *conclust* 'concluded'), which implies that some speakers ceased pronouncing –*t* or –*st*. This weakening resulted in confusion with the preterit indicative (e.g. *fut*, *eut* and *conclut*), where –*t* was also lost, meaning that speakers in these periods were not able to distinguish phonetically the indicative from the subjunctive. (Morin 2001: 72; 2006: 142). This evolution began in the last part of the Middle French period, and perhaps earlier (see Chap. 5 by Gess this volume), and continued until the Renaissance and into Pre-classical French, but was not fully realized until the publication of the Dictionary of the French Academy in 1740. The phonetic change finally resulted in the morphological replacement of –*st* by –^*t* (Catach 1995: 1129). In order to avoid untenable conclusions, these ambiguous forms have not been included in the results from the relevant periods.[7]

7.5 Evolution of Mood in the Concessive System

We will now proceed to the empirical part of this contribution. As mentioned in the introduction, this will be divided into a number of synchronic sections, which will ultimately provide data for a diachronic evolution.

---

[7] Note that these ambiguous forms are not of the same nature as those in Modern French, where the subjunctive of verbs ending in –*er* in the infinitive is identical to the indicative in some persons, which is often used as an argument in favour of the general narrowing of the use of the subjunctive. However, in the case of *fut/fust* we are also dealing with a confusion between the moods, as we cannot know for sure the mood of the form even though they formally represent two different moods.

7.5.1 Concession and Mood in Old and Middle French

According to Herman (1963: 233) and Soutet (1990: 33), the concessive connectors of Classical and Post-classical Latin disappeared without leaving any traces in the Pre-roman dialects, which consequently lacked at first an inventory of concessive markers. Sneyders de Vogel (1927: 191) observes that the subjunctive (when not preceded by a conjunction or an adverb) is the only means by which concession could be indicated during the Pre-roman period. It would appear that concessive connectors of the *Romania* are established little by little without any traces of Latin.

At the beginning of the Old French period, concession was expressed by the use of adverbs of the type *ja* 'already', *tot* 'all', *encore(es)* 'still', *or(es)* 'now'. They are polysemous, but, when used concessively, they all take the subjunctive, whose value can be described according to the assertion criterion discussed above in Sect. 7.3. Consider the following examples, which illustrate these points:

(7) Il est   voirs, se li   rois conmande, que bien me püent   faire lait,
    it is-IND true, if the king orders-IND, that really me they can-IND make harm,
    encor ne l' *aie*   ge forfeit
    still   not it have-SUBJ I made mistake
    'It is true, if the king orders it, that they can truly hurt me, even though I have not made any mistake' (Renart I: v1270, twelfth century cit. BFM)

(8) se aucune fame   grosse   se   marie   a autre   persone qu' a
    if some   woman pregnant herself gets-IND married to another person than to
    celui qui l' engroissa   hors   mariage, car, tout *soit*   il nés ou
    he   who her made-IND pregnant out of wedlock, for, all is-SUBJ he born in
    tans de mariage, toutes voies fu   il conceus en bastardie
    time of wedlock, however   was-IND he conceived in illegitimacy
    'if a pregnant woman marries a person other than the one who made her pregnant out of wedlock, for even if he [the child] is born in wedlock, he has still been conceived illegitimately'. (Beaumanoir: 280, thirteenth century cit. BMF)

(9) Ela molt ben sab   remembrar de soa carn cum Deus fu   naz.
    she very well can-IND remember   of her flesh how God   he was-IND born
    Ja.   l *vedes*   ela si   morir, el resurdra.
    already him sees-SUBJ she thus die, he will be-IND resurrected'
    'She [Mary] remembers very well how God let him [Jesus] be born of her flesh, even though she sees him die/even though she will see him die like this, he will be resurrected'(Passion: v335, tenth century cit. BFM)

In (7), the subjunctive of the proposition with *encor* indicates known or presupposed information (note the explicit reference to the speaker *ge* 'I'), whereas the subjunctive in (8) presents a hypothesis, which could be explained by reference to text genres, since it appears in a legal document. This type of text is of an abstract nature, because it lists laws, rules, and exceptions, and focuses on the totality rather than on individual cases. Example (9) is ambiguous, following the assertion criterion. On one hand, the subjunctive of the *ja*-proposition could indicate presupposed information if the utterance is interpreted generically, as the speaker refers to common knowledge (the Bible). On the other hand, the subjunctive could present the information as hypothetical (maybe she will see him die, but she is not certain that she will). This interpretation is supported by the presence of the future *resurdra* 'will be resurrected' in the following phrase.

In the evolution of Old French, more fixed expressions of concession appear, especially semi-conjunctions of subordination consisting of an adverb (*ja* 'already' or *tout* 'all'), a verbal nucleus in the present or the imperfect subjunctive (*soit* 'be' or *fust* 'were'), an optional demonstrative pronoun (*ce* 'this/that') or impersonal pronoun (*il* 'it'), and the complementizer *que* 'that': *ja soit (ce) que, ja fust (ce) que* 'already be/were it that', *tout soit (ce) que, tout fust (ce) que* 'albeit/all were it that'. In cases where *tout* is the introducing adverb, an optional *ainsi* 'so' can follow the impersonal pronoun *il*: *tout soit il ainsi que, tout fust il ainsi que* 'albeit/all were it so that'. They could all be paraphrased as *even though* or *even if*.

These semi-conjunctions can be followed by the subjunctive or the indicative mood, corresponding to the opposition between non-assertion (presupposition (10) or *irrealis* (11)) and assertion (12):

(10) car, tout soit   il ensi que vous *soiiés*   boins cevaliers, si   me
    for, all   is-SUBJ it so   that you are-SUBJ brave knight, however myself
    douteroie   je de vous encontre   cestui
    would-IND doubt I to you meet-IND this one
    'for, even though you are a brave knight, I doubt whether I should let you meet this one' (Trispr:121, thirteenth century cit. BFM)

(11) Vanterie est   trop vilains vices; qui   s'   en   vante,   il
    boasting is-IND too terrible sin ; whoever himself about it boats-IND, he
    fet   trop   que nices, car, ja   soit   ce que fet
    makes-IND too much than poor, for, already is-SUBJ it that done
    l' *eüssent*,   toutes vois   celer le deüssent
    it they had-SUBJ, however   hide it they should-SUBJ
    'Boasting is a terrible sin; whoever boasts about it is a poor man, for, even if they had done it, they should however have hidden it'(Meun: v5805, thirteenth century cit. BFM)

(12) Et quant Saintré entend   Madame si haultement parler, ja soit
    and when Saintré hears-IND Lady   so nobly   speak, still is-SUBJ
    que son cuer *estoit*   ja   conclud
    that her heart was-IND already won
    'And when Saintré heard the Lady speak so nobly, even though her heart was already won' (Saintré: 146, fifteenth century cit. BFM)

In (10), it is most likely that the proposition of the subordinate clause is presupposed, because the author reminds the interlocutor of something that he is assumed already to know, that the knight is courageous (note further the explicit reference to the interlocutor by the use of the personal pronoun *vous* 'you'). This explains why the subjunctive *soiiés* has been translated by *you are*, indicating a fact, and not by *may be*, presenting a hypothesis. Further, the subordinate clause occupies the thematic position in the information structure, which is very often used to indicate known (i.e. presupposed) information (Daneš 1974: 109ff; Winter 1982: 81ff; Thompson and Longacre 1985: 206ff). In Sect. 7.3, examples (11), or (3) above, and (12), or (1) above, were discussed, but we repeat the analysis here for ease of reference. In (11), (cf. (3) above), the interlocutor is presented with a hypothetical statement, and the subjunctive conveys the *irrealis* modality. As discussed above, in this example, the non-referential marker *qui* 'who', and the double hypothetical structure consisting of two imperfect subjunctives (*eüssent* 'had' and *deüssent* 'should'), which indicates counterfactuality, lend support to this hypothesis. In (12), (cf. (1) as above), the author is relating the event, so the role of the indicative is to assert the proposition.

If we consider *tout soit/fust (ce) que* and *ja soit/fust (ce) que* more closely, some striking differences appear, both with respect to their chronological span and their occurrence in genres.[8] Following the principle of markedness agreement (Andersen 2001a), according to which the scope of the marked form is included in that of the unmarked one,[9] *tout soit/fust (ce) que* can be considered the marked conjunction, and *ja soit/fust (ce) que* its unmarked counterpart. This is because the chronological and textual distribution of *tout soit/fust (ce) que* is much narrower than, and therefore included in, that of *ja soit/fust (ce) que*. Indeed, chronologically, the distribution of *tout soit/fust (ce) que* is very restricted, because it is attested in the thirteenth century only, whereas *ja soit (ce) que* is primarily found between the twelfth and the fifteenth centuries.

As far as the distribution of the two conjunctions across genres is concerned, it appears that *tout soit/fust (ce) que* once again has very restricted distribution, since it is found primarily in legal documents and historical texts, a fact which corroborates the findings of Soutet (1992: 197). Of the 86 occurrences of this conjunction in my corpus, including all of its variants, 77 (89.5 %) occur in a legal text by Beaumanoir, and the remaining coming from other genres. By contrast, the 47[10] occurrences of *ja soit/fust (ce) que* are found in 14 different works, mainly literary prose or verse, but also – to a lesser extent – in legal documents. These findings show

---

[8] It could be argued that the following detailed discussion regarding the distribution of these two conjunctions is unnecessary, since, like all other concessive conjunctions of Old French, they disappear during the Middle French period (Soutet 1992: 213). I contend however, that it is very important to take them into account, since the modal values that they introduce by means of the indicative and the subjunctive do not disappear and are, in fact, taken over by conjunctions that have survived into Modern French. See Sects. 7.5.2 and 7.5.3 below.

[9] Andersen (2001a) is particularly concerned with the semantic or grammatical values of linguistic signs or words in his hierarchy of markedness agreement, i.e. the present is the unmarked grammatical counterpart of the past, since the present indicates the *present* and the *(historical) past*, while the past only indicates the *past*. I argue that the markedness opposition is also a useful descriptive parameter on a more general level, including chronological expansion over time and representation of linguistic forms across text genres.

[10] As shown in Table 7.1, 46 occurrences of *ja soit (ce) que* were attested. In addition, one occurrence of *ja fust (ce) que* followed by the subjunctive with *irrealis* value was found. Due to this modest number, no separate table was produced for *ja fust (ce) que*.

Table 7.1 Relative frequency and modal value of the subjunctive and the indicative mood in concessive clauses introduced by *ja soit (ce) que*

	Value	Number of occurrences
Subjunctive		
Total occ.: 36 (78.3 %)	Presupposition	31 (86.1 %)
	Irrealis	5 (13.9 %)
	Assertion	0 (0.0 %)
	Unclassifiable	0 (0.0 %)
Indicative		
Total occ.: 10 (21.7 %)	Presupposition	0 (0.0 %)
	Irrealis	1 (10.0 %)
	Assertion	9 (90.0 %)
	Unclassifiable	0 (0.0 %)
Total (subj./ind.): 46 occ.		

Table 7.2 Relative frequency and modal value of the subjunctive and the indicative mood in concessive clauses introduced by *tout soit (ce) que*

	Value	Number of occurrences
Subjunctive		
Total occ.: 57 (81.4 %)	Presupposition	14 (24.6 %)
	Irrealis	43 (75.4 %)
	Assertion	0 (0.0 %)
	Unclassifiable	0 (0.0 %)
Indicative		
Total occ.: 13 (18.6 %)	Presupposition	0 (0.0 %)
	Irrealis	4 (30.8 %)
	Assertion	9 (69.2 %)
	Unclassifiable	0 (0.0 %)
Total (subj./ind.): 70 occ.		

that the textual extension of *ja soit/fust (ce) que* is much greater than that of *tout soit/fust (ce) que*.

With regard to the modal distribution of *tout soit/fust (ce) que* and *ja soit/fust (ce) que*, some important differences emerge, even though no markedness relation between them exists at this point in time. Instead, each conjunction has a specialized semantic use. Consider Tables 7.1, 7.2, and 7.3.

As can be seen in Tables 7.1, 7.2, and 7.3, both conjunctions *tout soit/fust (ce) que* and *ja soit/fust (ce) que* can be followed both by either the subjunctive or the indicative, with the exception of the variant *tout fust (ce) que*, which only appears with the subjunctive (see Table 7.3). Further, after both conjunctions, the subjunctive allows for a reading as presupposition or *irrealis*, and the indicative for assertion. However, this generalization is too simplistic to account for their distribution and interpretation. Indeed, when *tout soit/fust (ce) que* is followed by the subjunctive, the *irrealis* interpretation is the one favored (*tout soit (ce) que*: 75.4 %, *tout fust (ce) que*: 56.25 %), whereas *ja soit (ce) que* combined with the subjunctive is more

Table 7.3 Relative frequency and modal value of the subjunctive and the indicative mood in concessive clauses introduced by *tout fust (ce) que*

	Value	Number of occurrences
Subjunctive		
Total occ.: 16 (100.0 %)	Presupposition	6 (37.5 %)
	Irrealis	9 (56.25 %)
	Assertion	0 (0.0 %)
	Unclassifiable	1 (6.25 %)
Indicative		
Total occ.: 0 (0.0 %)	Presupposition	0 (0.0 %)
	Irrealis	0 (0.0 %)
	Assertion	0 (0.0 %)
	Unclassifiable	0 (0.0 %)
Total (subj./ind.): 16 occ.		

likely to occur in contexts in which the concessive clause is presupposed (86.1 %). The high frequency of the *irrealis* value of the subjunctive observed in the use of *tout soit/fust (ce) que*, should probably be explained in terms of its semantic value. According to Soutet (op.cit.: 41) the adverb *tout* "véhicule une idée d'intégralité" 'expresses an idea of totality', which is also reflected in its English equivalent *all*. This could explain the reason why *tout soit/fust (ce) que* is primarily employed in legal prose, which, as we have argued above, is abstract, because it details laws, rules, and exceptions. For such purposes, this conjunction is suitable, since this type of writing focuses on the law *per se*, rather than on specific cases. The adverb *ja* does not contain such a value, which could at least explain why *ja soit (ce) que* + subjunctive is only used with a hypothetical sense in few cases (13.9 %), as it favors the presuppositional reading.

As Tables 7.1 and 7.2 reveal, when *ja soit (ce) que* and *tout soit (ce) que* are followed by the indicative (e.g. *ja soit (ce) que*: 90.0 %, *tout soit (ce) que*: 69.2 %), the favored modal interpretation is assertion, as predicted by the theory of assertion that we are assuming (see Sect. 7.3), even though the indicative occurs with a far lower frequency than the subjunctive.[11] However, as Tables 7.1 and 7.2 also show, the indicative mood expresses *irrealis* modality in a few cases.

Since *tout soit/fust (ce) que* seems to be restricted to legal documents and similar argumentative and marked text genres belonging to the distance pole of Koch and Oesterreicher's continuum (1990, 2001) (see Sect. 7.2.1), it is assumed that this conjunction is externally motivated. It could have been introduced in the French language by lawyers, historians, and other dominant groups for certain argumentative and stylistic purposes.[12] However, Andersen's (2001a, b) theory would have

---

[11] The same tendency holds for Renaissance French, where the indicative also occurs with a far lower frequency than the subjunctive (see Sect. 7.5.2).

[12] Recall that, according to Andersen, externally motivated language changes do not necessarily imply language contact, but may also be caused by dominant groups of speakers' perception of style and register (see Sect. 7.2.1.), which is the case here.

predicted that *tout soit/fust (ce) que*, having been externally introduced, would gradually have spread to genres next to the proximate pole, as it becomes common in language usage and accepted by the majority of speakers, but instead it disappears, which might be due to its highly marked status from the beginning. By contrast, *ja soit/fust (ce) que* could have been internally motivated, that is, triggered by purely linguistic motivation, since it is attested from the beginning in a variety of text genres belonging both to the distance pole and to the proximate pole. One might thus hypothesize that this conjunction was originally introduced in informal oral genres before entering the written language and spreading to more formal genres in the twelfth century.

7.5.2 Concession and Mood in Renaissance and Pre-classical French

In Renaissance and Pre-classical French (sixteenth century), *ja soit/fust (ce) que* dies out, as shown by Soutet (1992: 210–213), and new concessive subordinators take over, but the modal system of Old and Middle French survives. In this section, *encore que* and *bien que* 'even though', 'even if' will be examined, as there seems to exist a markedness relation between them. During this period, *quoique* 'although', 'even if' also appears, but will not be dealt with here, since it is derived from the relative domain, *quoi que* lit. 'what that', where *quoi* is the antecedent of the relativizer *que*. As mood selection in complement clauses is driven by a different principle (i.e. the referentiality of the antecedent) from that in adverbial clauses, the data would not have been comparable. Furthermore, it is difficult diachronically to distinguish the relative *quoi que* from the conjunctional *quoique*, since they were used interchangeably by interlocutors until the eighteenth century (Grevisse 1986: 1669).

Neither *bien que* nor *encore que* can be said to originate from *tout soit/fust (ce) que* and *ja soit/fust (ce) que*, as there is no morphological link between them, but interestingly, these two conjunctions display similarity to *tout soit/fust (ce) que* and *ja soit/fust (ce) que* as regards their modal alternation and markedness relation. Soutet (1992: 220) argues in favor of a hypothesis that *bien que* was derived from *combien que* due to the aphesis of the prefix *com-*, which would appear to be a symptom of the loss of the degree value contained in *com-*. However, this hypothesis does not seem to be very plausible. In fact, the coexistence of *combien que* and *bien que* has been observed in several texts, even in Middle French (Lindschouw 2011: 180), and if this hypothesis were correct, one would furthermore have expected aphesis of the adverb *combien* 'how many', 'how much', from which *combien que* must have been derived historically, to the adverb *bien* 'well', but no such process seems to have taken place. In fact, they coexist in Old French and still do today. The appearance of *bien que* could instead be described as an innovation coming *from above* (see below).

The first occurrences of *bien que* and *encore que* were attested in the fourteenth century (op.cit.: 180, 203), but they do not gain in frequency until the middle of the sixteenth century. Generally, *bien que* expresses a concessive relation called strict, simple, or logical (Léard 1987: 166; Soutet 1990: 8; Morel 1996: 6ff). This concessive relation could be considered canonical and is characterized by a coexistence of two propositions that normally do not go together and could be formalized as [if p, then normally ~ q]. Thus in (13), it is normally expected that if Mireille comes home from a long trip, then normally Paul would not leave, but this expectation has been cancelled:

(13) Paul est   parti bien que   Mireille *soit*   revenue d'   un long voyage
Paul is-IND left   even though   Mireille is-SUBJ returned from a   long trip
'Paul left, even though Mireille returned from a long trip'

Encore que, by contrast, indicates a concessive relation called rectificative or restrictive (Léard 1987: 170; Soutet 1990: 11; Morel 1996: 10ff, 25–26). Contrary to *bien que*, this conjunction exploits the implicative relation [if p, then normally ~ q] by modifying the content of the apodosis, which normally requires that the concessive (the protasis) be postposed. In (14) it is first asserted in the apodosis that Mireille had a great deal of fun, but afterwards the concessive rectifies this statement implying that maybe she did not have as much fun as one would have thought in the first place, since she went home early:

(14) Mireille s'   est   beaucoup amusée, encore qu' elle *est*   /*soit*
Mireille herself is-IND much   amused, even though she is-IND/SUBJ
rentrée   tôt
went home early
'Mireille had a lot of fun, even though she went home early'

It should be underlined that the definition of *bien que* as logical concession and of *encore que* as rectificative concession is somewhat simplified. In fact, both connectors are able to express both relations even though *bien que* has a predilection for logical concession and *encore que* for rectificative concession. Moreover, rectification and postposition are not binary relations. It is true that rectification is conditioned by postposition, but rectification is an epiphenomenon, since not every postposed concessive clause rectifies the content of the apodosis. For example, (14) could also be read as non-rectificative in a context in which Mireille had to return early for a different reason rather than boredom, for example, in order not to miss the last train. Finally, a number of linguists observe that rectificative concessives are very likely to be followed by the indicative mood (Soutet 1992: 214 for Renaissance French and Soutet 2000: 98–99 for Modern French), but this statement is not confirmed by my data (see Sect. 7.4 above for the composition of my corpus). In my corpus, even though the indicative is likely to appear in postposed concessive clauses, it does not always contain a value of rectification, and furthermore the subjunctive can also be used with that value.

The flexible mood system observed in Old and Middle French (see Sect. 7.5.1) is also found in Renaissance French. Both *encore que* and *bien que* accept mood alternation and allow for both an assertive (15) and non-assertive (16)–(17) interpretation:

(15) On luy demanda si jamais elle avoit eu affaire à homme;
one her asked-IND if sometimes she had-IND had relation with man;

respondit que non jamais, bien que les hommes quelques foys
she replied-IND that not never, even though the men sometimes

avoient eu affaire à elle
had-IND had relation to her

'She was asked whether sometimes she had had relations with men; she replied that she never had, even though men had sometimes had relations with her' (Rabelais: Tiers livre: 156, sixteenth century cit. BFM)

(16) Encore que ton age ne *soit* pas achevé, ta vie l'est.
Even though your age not is-SUBJ not finished, your life it is-IND
'Even though you are not finished according to your age, your life is' (Montaigne: Essais: 98, sixteenth century cit. Frantext)

(17) Je suis seur qu' elle ne sera point si farouche qu' elle ne
I am-IND sure that she not will be-IND not so shy that she not

permette bien qu' on la baise (…), bien qu'au commencement
permits-IND well that one her kisses-SUBJ (…), even if in the beginning

elle *face* semblant d'y resister
she makes-SUBJ pretext to it resist

'I am convinced that she will not be so shy that she does not allow someone to kiss her (…), even if to begin with, she pretends to resist' (de Turnèbe: Les Contens: 79, sixteenth century cit. Frantext)

In (15), the indicative of the subordinate clause asserts the propositional content, since this example contains a clear assertive marker *respondit* 'replied' by means of which the speaker gives new information to the addressee. Further, the concessive clause occupies the rhematic position, which is often used to indicate new/asserted information (Daneš 1974: 109ff; Winter 1982: 81ff; Thompson and Longacre 1985: 206ff). Example (16) presupposes the content of the concessive clause, because the speaker is stating something already known to the addressee, i.e. as is expressed by the pronouns and articles in the second person. Furthermore, the subordinate clause occupies the thematic position of the information structure, which is often used to indicate known/presupposed information, as we have already seen. In (17) a hypothetical state of affairs, indicating *irrealis* modality, is presented in the concessive clause. It is unknown whether the lady will 'pretend to resist' (note the verb in the future tense, *sera* 'will be').

Tables 7.4 and 7.5 below confirm that the indicative and the subjunctive have a distribution that resembles that between *ja soit/fust (ce) que* and *tout soit/fust (ce) que* (see Sect. 7.5.1 above).

7 Evolution and Regrammation in the Mood System: Perspectives from Old...

Table 7.4 Relative frequency and modal value of the subjunctive and the indicative mood in concessive clauses introduced by *bien que* (sixteenth century)

	Value	Number of occurrences
Subjunctive		
Total occ.: 185 (92.5 %)	Presupposition	158 (85.4 %)
	Irrealis	17 (9.2 %)
	Assertion	0 (0.0 %)
	Unclassifiable	10 (5.4 %)
Indicative		
Total occ.: 15 (7.5 %)	Presupposition	2 (13.33 %)
	Irrealis	5 (33.33 %)
	Assertion	8 (53.33 %)
	Unclassifiable	0 (0.0 %)
Total (subj./ind.): 200 occ.		

Table 7.5 Relative frequency and modal value of the subjunctive and the indicative mood in concessive clauses introduced by *encore que* (sixteenth century)

	Value	Number of occurrences
Subjunctive		
Total occ.: 186 (93.0 %)	Presupposition	122 (65.6 %)
	Irrealis	60 (32.3 %)
	Assertion	0 (0.0 %)
	Unclassifiable	4 (2.1 %)
Indicative		
Total occ.: 14 (7.0 %)	Presupposition	2 (14.3 %)
	Irrealis	1 (7.1 %)
	Assertion	11 (78.6 %)
	Unclassifiable	0 (0.0 %)
Total (subj./ind.): 200 occ.		

As shown by these tables, the subjunctive is by far the most frequent mood, attested in almost 93% of all occurrences, whereas the indicative is found in approximately 7% of cases. The tables also indicate that the subjunctive can be used with two modal values (presupposition and *irrealis*), but these values do not occur with the same frequency in the two types of concessive clauses. In those introduced by *bien que*, the presupposition value is the most frequent (85.4%), while *encore que* concessives are less specialized, since the subjunctive appears with presupposed value in 65.6% of cases compared to *irrealis* value in 32.3% of cases. The preference of *bien que* for combining with the subjunctive of presupposed value is probably due to the semantic content of the adverb *bien*, which, according to Morel (1996: 23), marks the speaker's consent regarding a judgment that he considers known by the addressee. In my view, the reason why *encore que* is less specialized with respect to modal value can be explained both in terms of its semantic content, and also in terms of text genres. Semantically, the adverb *encore* does not indicate that the speaker takes the propositional content for granted, and textually, the *irrealis* use is highly frequent in genres of an abstract nature. See Sects. 7.1 and 7.5.1 above for a definition.

Tables 7.4 and 7.5 also reveal that the indicative mood appears with an assertive value in most cases, though it may also have a non-assertive value. The presupposed value can to a great extent be explained by metric and other stylistic features, whereas the *irrealis* value is generally due to the presence in the concessive clause of the future and conditional forms, which belong to the indicative paradigm, even though they present the content as unreal because of their prospective and/or modal values.

The similarity between *bien que*/*encore que* and *tout soit/fust (ce) que*/*ja soit/fust (ce) que* is very striking because the markedness relation observed between *tout soit/fust (ce) que* and *ja soit/fust (ce) que* also exists between *bien que* and *encore que*. Like *tout soit/fust (ce) que*, *bien que* is the marked concessive conjunction, and, like *ja soit/fust (ce) que*, *encore que* is its unmarked counterpart. This relation is observed at two levels.

At the textual level, *bien que* (as *tout soit/fust (ce) que*) is restricted to genres near the distance pole, since it is most frequent in poetry and plays in verse. By contrast, *encore que* (like *ja soit/fust (ce) que*) does not display any textual preferences, as it is attested in a wide variety of textual genres ranging from those near the distance pole (i.e. argumentative and non-literary genres as well as genres in verse) to those near the proximate pole (i.e. direct discourse and plays in prose). This could be a sign that *encore que* is internally motivated, triggered purely by linguistic motivation (see Sect. 7.2.1 above). Furthermore, as observed for *ja soit/fust (ce) que*, it is not inconceivable that this conjunction was originally introduced in informal oral genres before spreading to the written language and to more formal genres in the sixteenth century (Lindschouw 2011: 221–222). By contrast, *bien que* could have been externally motivated (see Sect. 7.2.1) by authors of the Renaissance period for other stylistic purposes in poetry and plays in verse, such as to characterize the work as intellectual or solemn. It is worth remembering here that the Renaissance introduces a new paradigm and a new way of thinking that breaks with the Middle Ages. Thus, the authors of the Renaissance could have invented *bien que* in order to reflect this new way of thinking.

At the modal level, *encore que* can be considered the unmarked conjunction, as opposed to *bien que*, since the formal and functional scope of *bien que* is included in that of *encore que* (Andersen 2001a). *Encore que* takes either the indicative or the subjunctive and allows for three modal interpretations (assertion, presupposition and *irrealis*). By contrast, *bien que* shows a very strong tendency to combine only with the subjunctive with presupposed value.

7.5.3 Concession and Mood in Modern French

The flexible mood system that was observed both for Old and Middle French and for Renaissance and Pre-classical French is gradually reduced in the course of the following centuries to such a degree that the subjunctive becomes highly constrained

7 Evolution and Regrammation in the Mood System: Perspectives from Old...

Table 7.6 Relative frequency and modal value of the subjunctive and the indicative mood in concessive clauses introduced by *bien que* (twentieth century)

	Value	Number of occurrences
Subjunctive		
Total occ.: 197 (98.5 %)	Presupposition	189 (95.94 %)
	Irrealis	5 (2.54 %)
	Assertion	2 (1.02 %)
	Unclassifiable	1 (0.50 %)
Indicative		
Total occ.: 3 (1.5 %)	Presupposition	0 (0.0 %)
	Irrealis	0 (0.0 %)
	Assertion	3 (100.0 %)
	Unclassifiable	0 (0.0 %)
Total (subj./ind.): 200 occ.		

and loses the possibility of alternating with the indicative. Indeed, such subjunctive/indicative variation is only seen in a limited number of contexts in Modern French, for example with verbs of doubting, such as *croire* 'to think', and in restrictive relative clauses. Since this evolution takes place slowly, I will not present the results for the seventeenth to the nineteenth centuries, in order to concentrate on the twentieth century. For a detailed discussion of the evolution of mood in concessive clauses between the sixteenth and twentieth centuries, see Lindschouw (2008, 2011).

In Modern French, we have arrived at a system where the alternation between the indicative and the subjunctive has almost ceased to exist in concessive clauses. This applies especially to concessives introduced by *bien que*, as shown in Table 7.6.

Here we can see that the subjunctive has virtually developed into the obligatory mood after *bien que*, observed in 98.5 % of the cases, contrary to the indicative, which is only attested in 1.5 % of the instances. As far as the functional distribution of the subjunctive is concerned, the presupposition value has almost entirely replaced the *irrealis* value. Thus in Modern French, *bien que* has become restricted to the subjunctive used with a presupposed value (95.94 % of all occurrences in the subjunctive). Put differently, the tendency to specialization observed in the sixteenth century has been reinforced. Consider Table 7.7 below.

It should be noticed that even though it is not completely clear from Table 7.7, concessive clauses introduced by *encore que* have also undergone a degree of reduction of their modal system. It is true that this conjunction allows mood alternation in Modern French to a much greater extent than *bien que*, and compared with the sixteenth century, the use of the indicative has indeed increased from 7.0 to 12.0 %.[13] Nevertheless, based on my corpus, I maintain that the mood system in concessive clauses introduced by *encore que* has been reduced. First, the *irrealis* use of the subjunctive has been considerably reduced from 32.3 to 6.82 %. Thus the

---

[13] Statistical tests have not been performed on these results, but I contend that they are nevertheless reliable to a large extent, since the results are based on a fair number of samples (14 occurrences in the sixteenth century and 24 occurrences in the twentieth century).

Table 7.7 Relative frequency and modal value of the subjunctive and the indicative mood in concessive clauses introduced by *encore que* (twentieth century)

	Value	Number of occurrences
Subjunctive		
Total occ.: 176 (88.0 %)	Presupposition	162 (92.04 %)
	Irrealis	12 (6.82 %)
	Assertion	0 (0.0 %)
	Unclassifiable	2 (1.14 %)
Indicative		
Total occ.: 24 (12.0 %)	Presupposition	0 (0.0 %)
	Irrealis	10 (41.7 %)
	Assertion	14 (58.3 %)
	Unclassifiable	0 (0.0 %)
Total (subj./ind.): 200 occ.		

Table 7.8 Position of concessive clauses in the indicative mood with respect to the main clause

Encore que – indicative (sixteenth century)
Preposition: 35.7 %
Postposition: 50.0 %
Unclassifiable: 14.3 %

Encore que – indicative (twentieth century)
Preposition: 0.0 %
Postposition: 100.0 %
Unclassifiable: 0.0 %

subjunctive in these clauses also seems to be moving towards a specialization of the presupposed value. Secondly, the indicative has been restricted to concessive clauses postposed the main clause, indicating an autonomous speech act, in contrast with the sixteenth century when it could be pre- or postposed as illustrated by Table 7.8:

My conclusion, based on the above table, is that, despite the increase of the indicative in Modern French, the two moods no longer allow free alternation as was the case in the sixteenth century.

In Sect. 7.5.2 it was proposed that the conjunction *bien que* is externally motivated, since it could have been introduced *from above* by authors of the Renaissance period for stylistic purposes proper to poetry and plays written in verse, while *encore que* is internally motivated, appearing to purely due linguistic reasons, since it could have been introduced *from below*, as it does not display any textual restrictions. From Renaissance French to Modern French, *bien que* spreads to other text genres, but contrary to the predictions made by Andersen (2001a, b) (Sect. 7.2.1), it does not spread to text genres placed at the proximate pole on Koch and Oesterreicher's (1990, 2001) continuum. Rather, it is essentially restricted to those next to the distance pole (argumentative and non-fictional texts) and only spreads to those occupying an intermediate stage (literary prose). However, these result do not necessarily contradict Andersen's theory, since it can be explained by the highly marked nature of *bien que*, whose formal and functional scope, as we have seen above, is included in that of *encore que*, and by the fact that it is in this type of concessives that the regrammation of the subjunctive is the most advanced (see Sect. 7.5.4 below). Conversely, the unmarked nature of *encore que* observed in the sixteenth century also applies to Modern French, as it is still attested in a wide variety of text genres, both in those next to the distance pole and those next to the proximate pole.

7.5.4 Reorganization of the Mood Paradigm in Concessive Clauses

As hypothesized in Sect. 7.2, the modal system, at least in concessive clauses, was reorganized from Old French to Modern French. As a consequence of this reorganization, the subjunctive has undergone a process of regrammation in these clauses (Heltoft et al. 2005; Andersen 2006; Nørgård-Sørensen et al. 2011), since its paradigm has undergone a considerable reduction (Lehmann 1995 [1982]), for several reasons. On one hand, the use of the subjunctive has been restricted with respect to its functional content. In Old, Middle, and Renaissance French, it was able to express two non-assertive values, presupposition and *irrealis*, but in Modern French, it has been reduced to the expression of presupposition. Stated in traditional terms of grammaticalization, the grammatical-functional content of the subjunctive has been desemanticized.

On the other hand, in concessive clauses, the subjunctive no longer alternates with the indicative, meaning that it has undergone a process of obligatorification and specialization. As a consequence of this reduction, it is not inconceivable that the functional opposition between assertion and non-assertion will soon completely disappear from concessive clauses, since the specialization of the subjunctive as an obligatory mood means that speakers will eventually lose the option of presenting the concessive clause as asserted. It is only in postposed clauses introduced by *encore que* that it is currently possible to assert the propositional content by means of the indicative, and, as this context is highly marked, the possibility of asserting the propositional content of concessive clauses will be lost.

As mentioned in the literature on grammaticalization, every instance of the process is preceded by a reanalysis (Detges and Waltereit 2002: 190; Hopper and Traugott 2003 [1993]: 50–59; Heltoft et al. 2005; Marchello-Nizia 2006: 45–46). This also holds true for the regrammation of the subjunctive, if, as we have claimed, reanalysis should first and foremost be understood in semantic-pragmatic terms (Heltoft et al. 2005: 11). According to Heltoft (2005: 26), reanalysis can affect the content of the grammatical item, without necessarily changing its morphosyntactic structure. This also applies to the subjunctive, since its forms do not change considerably during the period from Old French to Modern French, but its content does. It seems that two reanalyses have led to the regrammation of the subjunctive. On one hand, the opposition between assertion and presupposition has been reanalyzed, since these concepts belong to the same notional domain (*realis*), and this has caused a referential ambiguity for speakers. They may have viewed one of these values as superfluous, and consequently the less frequent mood (the indicative) has disappeared.

On the other hand, the opposition between the two modal values of the subjunctive, presupposition and *irrealis*, has been reanalyzed, but – contrary to the first reanalysis – the second is motivated by the influence of text genres. As mentioned in Sects. 7.1, 7.5.1 and 7.5.2, the *irrealis* value is, to some extent, confined to abstract text genres, which favor utterances of an unreal or hypothetical value, especially in the case of *tout soit/fust (ce) que* and *encore que*, whereas the presupposition value is not restricted to any particular text genre. The subjunctive presents an ambiguity, because speakers do not know whether the *irrealis* value belongs to the subjunctive form or to the abstract text genre in which the subjunctive appears. Since the *irrealis* value is at the same time marginal, as opposed to the presupposition value, the conditions for substitution are favorable, since a marginal value is more likely to disappear than a very frequent value.

As stated in Sect. 7.2, even though the indicative has been reorganized in the concessive system, it has not been regrammaticized. This is because the indicative has extended its functional domain. When comparing Tables 7.5 and 7.7, it appears that in the twentieth century the indicative was in fact able to express *irrealis* modality to a much higher degree than in Renaissance French through the future and the conditional, which convey *irrealis* modality because of their prospective nature and/or modal values. This increase can be seen as a consequence of the subjunctive's loss of the *irrealis* value, and one could thus speak of a transfer from one mood to the other. The fact that the indicative mood has enhanced its domain can most clearly be seen if concessive clauses introduced by *même si* 'even if' are considered. This conjunction, almost exclusively followed by the indicative, does not enter the French language until the last part of the seventeenth century (Lindschouw 2011: 230), and its use did not increase noticeably until the nineteenth century. Since concession is generally derived from the conditional domain (König 1985a, b), it is plausible to consider *même si* as deriving from the conditional conjunction *si* 'if,' which could be followed by the subjunctive in Old and Middle French (Buridant 2000: 628), although, according to Grevisse (1986: 1687), the indicative had almost superseded the subjunctive in the sixteenth century. Even though the conjunction *même si* appears very late, I believe that it is essential to take it into consideration in order to present a full overview of the evolution of the concessive system in French.

Due to the presence of *si* as part of the lexical meaning, *même si* has a natural preference for the *irrealis* value, which is clearly seen from its distribution in Modern French (Table 7.9), where the indicative is employed with this value in 75.1 % of the occurrences.

One can thus conclude that in the reorganization of the mood system in concessive clauses, the *irrealis* value does not disappear, but is instead transferred from the subjunctive paradigm (in propositions introduced by *bien que* and *encore que*) to the indicative paradigm (in propositions introduced by *même si*), as is evident from Fig. 7.1[14]:

---

[14] In the counts in Fig. 7.1, only the occurrences of the *irrealis* use of the subjunctive for *bien que* and *encore que* and the *irrealis* use of the indicative for *même si* are given, because these cases are by far the most frequent in the corpus to express *irrealis* modality.

Table 7.9 Relative frequency and modal value of the subjunctive and the indicative mood in concessive clauses introduced by *même si* (twentieth century)

	Value	Number of occurrences
Subjunctive		
Total occ.: 3 (1.5 %)	Presupposition	0 (0.0 %)
	Irrealis	3 (100.0 %)
	Assertion	0 (0.0 %)
	Unclassifiable	0 (0.0 %)
Indicative		
Total occ.: 197 (98.5 %)	Presupposition	42 (21.3 %)
	Irrealis	148 (75.1 %)
	Assertion	0 (0.0 %)
	Unclassifiable	7 (3.6 %)
Total (subj./ind.): 200 occ.		

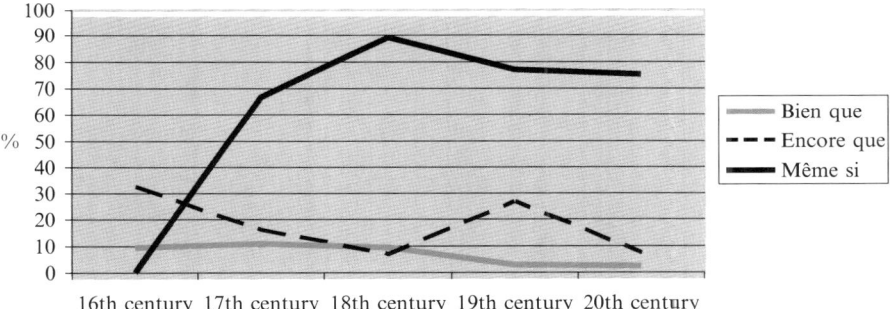

Fig. 7.1 The frequency of the *irrealis* value in propositions introduced by *bien que*, *encore que* and *même si* between the sixteenth and the twentieth centuries

Table 7.10 Reorganization of the mood in the concessive system (Old French – Modern French)

System 1	System 2
Subjunctive: presupposition/irrealis	Subjunctive: presupposition
Indicative: assertion	Indicative: assertion/irrealis/presupposition

However, it should be noted that the *irrealis* use of concessives introduced by *même si* decreases somewhat from the middle of the nineteenth century onwards. In my view, this is due to the fact that another extension of the indicative paradigm is taking place, meaning the use of the indicative mood has spread so that it can now express presupposition, as possibility that was formerly restricted to the subjunctive paradigm, as shown in Table 7.9 above.

The evolution of the mood system in concessive clauses is summarized in Table 7.10.

System 1 refers to the original system (Old, Middle and Renaissance French), while System 2 refers to the reorganized paradigm of Modern French, in which the subjunctive has undergone a process of regrammation, and the use of the indicative has been extended.

7.6 Conclusion

In this chapter, the evolution of the mood system during the period of Old French to Modern French has been examined through the lens of synchronicity, showing the importance of this method in order to give a complete account of the diachronic evolution. It has been shown that the mood system in concessive clauses has passed from a relatively flexible system observed in Old, Middle, and Renaissance French, to a highly constrained system in Modern French. As a result of this reorganization, the subjunctive has undergone a process of regrammation, preceded by two reanalyses, whereby its functional content (non-assertion) has been reduced from two values (presupposition and *irrealis*) to a single value (presupposition). This means that its functional content has been desemantisized, and has therefore ceased to alternate with the indicative. In the framework adopted here, we can conclude that the subjunctive has thus undergone a process of obligatorification and specialization. Even though the indicative has also been reorganized in the concessive system during the periods investigated, it has not been regrammaticized, since its functional domain has changed from a single value (assertion) to three values (assertion, *irrealis* and presupposition). It has been proposed that the values of the subjunctive, at least that of *irrealis*, have been transferred from the subjunctive to the indicative paradigm, especially by means of the introduction of *même si* in the seventeenth century.

This contribution has also illustrated how the evolution of the mood system and of concessive conjunctions contributes to our current understanding of language change *per se* by reference to Andersen's (2001a, b) theory, according to which the sequences of language change can generally be predicted. We have seen that the distinction between externally and internally motivated language changes is a relevant parameter for the prediction of the evolution and propagation of (concessive) conjunctions and mood, and therefore for our understanding of the general mechanisms in language change. We have also seen that the important driving force in language change, i.e. reanalysis, should not always be understood in terms of referential ambiguity in the linguistic sign, but can also be linked to an ambiguity with respect to the sign's distribution across text genres.

Acknowledgement I would like to thank Inger Mees as well as the anonymous reviewers for their helpful comments on an earlier version of this chapter.

References

Andersen, H. 2001a. Markedness and the theory of linguistic change. In *Actualization. Linguistic change in progress*, ed. H. Andersen, 21–57. Amsterdam/Philadelphia: John Benjamins.

Andersen, H. 2001b. Actualization and the (uni)directionality of change. In *Actualization. Linguistic change in progress*, ed. H. Andersen, 225–248. Amsterdam/Philadelphia: John Benjamins.

Andersen, H. 2006. Grammation, regrammation and degrammation: Tense loss in Russian. *Diachronica* 23(2): 231–258.

Buridant, C. 2000. *Grammaire nouvelle de l'ancien français*. Paris: Sedes.

Catach, N. 1995. *Dictionnaire historique de l'orthographe française*. Paris: Larousse.

Confais, J.-P. 1995 [1990]. *Temps, mode, aspect. Les approches des morphèmes verbaux et leurs problèmes à l'exemple du français et de l'allemand*, 2nd ed. Toulouse: Presses Universitaires du Mirail.

Daneš, F. 1974. Functional sentence perspective and the organization of the text. In *Papers on functional sentence perspective*, ed. F. Daneš, 106–128. The Hague/Paris: Mouton & Co.

Detges, U., and R. Waltereit. 2002. Grammaticalization vs. reanalysis: A semantic-pragmatic account of functional change in grammar. *Zeitschrift für Sprachwissenschaft* 21(2): 151–195.

Foulet, L. 1968 [1919]. *Petite syntaxe de l'ancien français*, 3rd ed. Paris: Librairie Honoré Champion.

Grevisse, M. 1986. *Le Bon Usage. Grammaire française*, 12th ed. Paris: Duculot.

Harris, M. 1974. The subjunctive mood as a changing category in Romance. In *Historical linguistics*, vol. 2, ed. J.M. Anderson, and C. Jones, 169–188. Amsterdam/Oxford: North-Holland.

Haverkate, H. 2002. *The syntax, semantics and pragmatics of Spanish mood*. Amsterdam/Philadelphia: John Benjamins.

Heltoft, L. 2005. Ledsætning og letled i dansk. OV-rækkefølgens rester. In *Grammatikalisering og struktur*, ed. L. Heltoft, J. Nørgård-Sørensen, and L. Schøsler, 145–166. Copenhagen: Museum Tusculanum.

Heltoft, L., J. Nørgård-Sørensen, and L. Schøsler. 2005. Grammatikalisering som strukturforandring. In *Grammatikalisering og struktur*, ed. L. Heltoft, J. Nørgård-Sørensen, and L. Schøsler, 9–30. Copenhagen: Museum Tusculanum.

Herman, J. 1963. *La formation du système roman des conjonctions de subordination*. Berlin: Akademie-Verlag.

Hooper, J.B. 1975. On assertive predicates. *Syntax and Semantics* 4: 91–124.

Hopper, P.J., and E.C. Traugott. 2003 [1993]. *Grammaticalization*, 2nd ed. Cambridge: Cambridge University Press.

Koch, P., and W. Oesterreicher. 1990. *Gesprochene Sprache in der Romania: Französisch, Italienisch, Spanisch*. Tübingen: Max Niemeyer.

Koch, P., and W. Oesterreicher. 2001. Langage parlé et langage écrit. In *Lexikon der romanistischen Linguistik (LRL)*, vol. 1, ed. G. Holtus, M. Metzeltin, and C. Schmitt, 584–627. Tübingen: Max Niemeyer.

Korzen, H. 2003. Subjonctif, indicatif et assertion ou: Comment expliquer le mode dans les subordonnées complétives ? In *Aspects de la modalité*, ed. M. Birkelund, G. Boysen, and P.S. Kjærsgaard, 113–129. Tübingen: Max Niemeyer Verlag.

König, E. 1985a. On the history of concessive connectives in English. Diachronic and synchronic evidence. *Lingua* 66: 1–19.

König, E. 1985b. Where do concessives come from? On the development of concessive connectives. In *Historical semantics. Historical word formation*, ed. J. Fisiak, 263–282. Berlin/New York/Amsterdam: Mouton.

Léard, J.-M. 1987. La syntaxe et la classification des conditionnelles et des concessives. *Le français moderne* 3: 158–173.

Lehmann, C. 1995 [1982]. *Thoughts on grammaticalization*, 2nd ed. München/Newcastle: Lincom Europa.

Lindschouw, J. 2006. Grammaticalization, assertion and concession in French and Spanish. In *Change in verbal systems. Issues on explanation*, ed. K. Eksell, and T. Vinther, 139–160. Frankfurt am Main: Peter Lang.

Lindschouw, J. 2008. L'évolution des modes verbaux dans les propositions ouvertes par *bien que* et *encore que* du XVIe au XXe siècle: un cas de grammaticalisation? In *Evolutions en français. Etudes de linguistique diachronique*, ed. B. Fagard, S. Prévost, B. Combettes, and O. Bertrand, 249–267. Bern: Peter Lang.

Lindschouw, J. 2011. *Etude des modes dans le système concessif en français du 16e au 20e siècle et en espagnol moderne. Evolution, assertion et grammaticalisation*. Copenhagen: Museum Tusculanum Press.

Marchello-Nizia, C. 2006. *Grammaticalisation et changement linguistique*. Bruxelles: De Boeck & Larcier.

Meillet, A. 1948 [1912]. L'évolution des formes grammaticales. In *Linguistique historique et linguistique générale*, ed. A. Meillet, 130–149. Paris: Édouard Champion.

Morel, M.-A. 1996. *La concession en français*. Paris: Editions Ophrys.

Morin, Y.C. 2001. La troncation des radicaux verbaux en français depuis le moyen âge. *Recherches linguistiques de Vincennes* 30: 63–85.

Morin, Y.C. 2006. On the phonetics of rhymes in classical and pre-classical French. A sociolinguistic perspective. In *Historical romance linguistics. Retrospectives and perspectives*, ed. R.S. Gess and D. Arteaga, 131–162. Amsterdam/Philadelphia: John Benjamins.

Nørgård-Sørensen, J., L. Heltoft, and L. Schøsler, 2011. Connecting grammaticalisation. *The role of paradigmatic structure*. Amsterdam/Philadelphia: John Benjamins.

Sneyders de Vogel, K. 1927. *Syntaxe historique du français*, 2nd ed. Groningen: Librairie J.-B. Wolters-Groningen.

Soutet, O. 1990. *La concession en français des origines au XVIe siècle. Problèmes généraux. Les tours prépositionnels*. Genève: Librairie Droz S.A.

Soutet, O. 1992. *La concession dans la phrase complexe en français. Des origines au XVIe siècle*. Genève: Librairie Droz S.A.

Soutet, O. 2000. *Le subjonctif en français*. Paris: Editions Ophrys.

Thompson, S.A., and R.E. Longacre. 1985. Adverbial clauses. In *Language typology and syntactic description*, vol. 2, ed. T. Shopen, 171–234. Cambridge: Cambridge University Press.

Traugott, E.C. 2003. From subjectification to intersubjectification. In *Motives for language change*, ed. R. Hickey, 124–139. Cambridge: Cambridge University Press.

Winter, E.D. 1982. *Towards a contextual grammar of English. The clause and its place in the definition of sentence*. London: George Allen & Unwin.

Winters, M.E. 1989. Diachronic prototype theory: On the evolution of the French subjunctive. *Linguistics* 27: 703–730.

Text Corpora

Base de Français Médiéval (BFM). http://bfm.ens-lsh.fr
Dictionnaire du Moyen Français (DMF). http://atilf.atilf.fr/dmf.htm
Frantext. http://www.frantext.fr

Chapter 8
Analogy Among French Sounds

Michael L. Mazzola

8.1 Introduction

In recent years, linguists have turned to focus their attention on a more socially oriented view of the history of the French language (cf. Lodge 1993; Posner 1997; Wright 1982). Within this view, scholars have been influenced heavily by the practice advocated by Malkiel ("… 'reconstructed' … [or] … starred forms deserve to be appealed to only at rare intervals" (1988: 41)). In agreement, others (cf. Herman 2000: 5) have attributed greater importance to documented records and have focused on the irregularities and variations in language change within their broader contexts. Such an approach, they argue, provides a more ample and reliable picture of the diachronic processes of language in use rather than what they consider to be more an artificial reckoning of language development in the abstract. The latter, adhering to the regularity of sound change, takes into account neither the accessibility of written documentation nor the variation in language development and, for that reason, very often appears to present little more than an exercise akin to manuals in bookkeeping. Reconstructions, therefore, can not be considered to fulfill their promise of a full and accurate accounting.

Wright (2002: 297–309) has rightly pointed out the superficiality of reconstructed systems divorced from their social contexts. Yet, since he has also taken care to call attention to the misleading nature of writing with regard to pronunciation, he sees the value in using reconstructions as controls on textual "evidence". In this regard, Posner (1997: 222) clarifies the necessity vividly when she stresses that "we rely … almost wholly on the patchy evidence of written records, without a reliable measure of how they relate to the spoken language." Mindful of this incongruity between speech and writing, the present study (a) calls into question the reliability of written

---

M.L. Mazzola (✉)
Northern Illinois, DeKalb, IL, USA
e-mail: mlm115@hotmail.com

documents; (b) argues that a focus on regular structural accounting gives a more accurate representation of the historical development; (c) demonstrates that that regular progression of change offers a more satisfying background for distinguishing between different types of variants; and (d) calls attention to the unfortunate consequences of an unnecessary reliance on suppletive analogy.

8.2 Morin's Perspective

Probably the most incisive example of this "attested/variationist" orientation for French has been the *prise de position* of Morin (2003), who has presented the case for variation in the history of French and its diachronic consequences in general. In a coherent exposition, Morin has done a service to the field of Historical French Linguistics by calling into question the accounts of the earliest development of French as proposed during the heyday of the neo-grammarian period. These accounts were, of course, firmly devised within the perspective of the regularity of sound change. Morin's paper is all the more noteworthy, because he challenges these studies of the very founders of Romance Philology, who have been revered over a century for their achievements. It is worth repeating that what are at stake in his study are the relative chronologies of the sound changes and the intermediate unattested reconstructions based on the regularity of sound change. The relative chronologies, Morin maintains with reason, are fraught with insurmountable problems. Very much from within a variationist perspective, once again as opposed to a regularist one, he combs carefully through the difficulties entrenched primarily in Straka's efforts (1953, 1956, 1970) to construct, based on the faulty earlier nineteenth century accounts, a relative chronology of the early sound changes from Latin to Gallo-Roman, viz. syncope, voicing, diphthongization, and apocope.

In the course of his paper, Morin, like Straka, carefully focuses on many of the minute details and points out serious shortcomings with Straka's brave attempts to deal with the thicket of varying outcomes for any given change. Given his *a priori* disagreement with the neo-grammarian regularity of sound change and his insistence on documentary evidence, Morin inevitably concludes that those details of Straka's accounting defy the establishment of a relative chronology not only for those data, but indeed for any relative chronology whatsoever. He argues that there are assumptions that underlie each hypothesis in the neo-grammarian attempt, which, when challenged, are seen to lose their validity. The cause of this failure, he concludes, is a persistent adherence to outdated neo-grammarian practice and the consequential neglect of the importance of variants in language change currently in vogue in our day. His study, therefore, presents an "attested-variationist" perspective in accord with the Malkiel/Herman/Wright orientation in order to undermine a "reconstructed-regularist" reckoning represented by the Meyer-Lübke/Straka studies.

8.3 Analogy and Analysis

Placed in a broader context, Morin's position is very much in concert with contemporary work in sociolinguistics which has emphasized that every language has variants and that these variants are indicative of such factors as ethnic identity, economic and educational levels, and other considerations of social consequence. Some linguists have attempted to see how the often-distinct aspects of language structure and language variation interact to effect language change (cf. Labov 1981; Kiparsky et al. 1988; Kiparsky 1995). In his (1995) discussion, Kiparsky has gone further to highlight the analogical role of lexical diffusion in phonological change. Yet another way that proponents of analogy have been intent on showing its effect is by discussing its role in suppletion and the direct and conscious action of speakers on language change especially via the morphology (cf. Venneman and Wilbur 1972). Other linguists, essentially in agreement, have asserted that language structure is by its very nature analogical and consequently that it is primarily through analogy that language change takes place (cf. "Language structure and language use are ... predominantly analogical, and that is why analogy is the backbone of universal grammar" (Antila 2003: 439)). All these have been useful contributions to our appreciation of the role that analogy can play in language development.

However, suppletive analogy, which attempts to explain one kind of variation, emphasizes the conscious role of the speaker and is rarely examined as a bi-product of the cultural bias of linguists. In other words, the issue has yet to be considered whether the social and national preferences of linguists, especially through recourse to suppletive analogy, can be instrumental in creating a *political mysticism* (cf. Beaune 1991; Kantorowicz 1997; Strayer 1957). Thus, it remains to be inquired whether, rather than *reflecting* the history of a language, linguists can be revealed to be complicit in *inventing* the history of a language, which is in turn not immune from the prevalent political, ethnic, economic or class oriented goals of the culture and time in which they live. Accordingly, it will be argued here that procedures derived from the linguistic data themselves should be favored over an orientation derived from prevalent idealistic views of the data. In this way, conclusions regarding diachronic data should be prized more as historical representations than as tools for oligarchic ends. Within the domain of historical phonology, this makes some appeal, therefore, to a more responsive interaction with the data as opposed to a centering either on the speaker or on the linguist as designer of the data. In addressing this point, this paper will attempt to distinguish among the various definitions of analogy cited above: (1) *structure as analogy*, (2) *lexical diffusion as analogy*, and (3) *suppletive leveling as analogy*, as applied to discern the early phonological development of French. The purpose will be to demonstrate, therefore, that (1) and (2), which are derived more intently from the language itself, are more reliable criteria upon which to ascertain phonological development, than (3), which is vulnerable to certain social, cultural, and political aims.

8.4 Political Mysticism and Idealism

In this light, some attention will be given to what has gone largely unnoticed regarding the history of a language even as intensely studied and as prestigious as French; that is, the extent to which the cultural attitudes and national agendas of linguists can shape the methods and color the findings of their diachronic statements. In other words, it will be claimed here that even the intensely debated methods and finely honed theories of linguistics, with all of its scientific claims, can be enlisted to advance political and cultural ends. Thus, diachronic statements regarding sound changes and their relative chronology, in spite of or in concert with the linguist's intent, may make claims that reach beyond themselves to engage in the invention of history through idealism rather than in the *discovery* of history through instruction by the data. Within the orientation of idealism, therefore, diachrony and history come together to represent the linguist's determination not only of the nature of linguistic change, but also of his ideological view of historical events. This issue will be closely examined in this paper especially with reference to the lure of *suppletive leveling as analogy* to use the morphology to determine the phonological changes from Latin to Gallo-Roman during the first five centuries BC before the arrival of the Franks.

In probing the issues raised above, especially important will be my agreement with Morin's claim that the nineteenth century relative chronologies do not afford us with adequate observations upon which to base proposals of linguistic change. I will, however, continue to use a regularist orientation (i.e. *structure as analogy* in conjunction with *lexical diffusion as analogy* as opposed to *suppletive leveling as analogy*) by which I hope to outline a proposed relative chronology which presents statements of change valid enough to correlate with certain characteristics of variation in the history of French. To this end, structural practice can be seen to be indispensable for identifying a relationship between variants, but only against a backdrop of a regular phonological development without recourse to the morphology. In this way, rather than being in conflict and discounting one another, regularity and variation will be considered to complement each other in determining the early history of French from Latin to Gallo-Roman.

8.5 The Issue of Variants

As mentioned previously, therefore, there is a certain agreement between Morin's observation and my own that the conventional accounts are to be set aside for a lack of adequacy. Morin's objection, however, is to the neo-grammarians' neglect of the importance of each of the variants identifiable in any given change. My own objection, in contrast, is to the lack of accuracy in the old neo-grammarian accounting, due not to a lack of sufficient attention to the variants themselves, but rather to a failure to recognize that the variants, in this case the voiced vs. voiceless palatal affricates, were unrelated to an operation in the history of French referred to as Frankish syncope.

A further difference with Morin's discussion deals with a lack of clarity regarding the *nature* of the variants. Unlike Morin, rather than discounting the practice of neo-grammarian relative chronology, I will argue instead that the value of the variants is determined by virtue of their relevance to the revised chronological development sketched below according to the regularity found in the data. In so doing, I will assert that there is a distinction to be made between *structural variants* and *social variants*. Although these latter variants may eventually become more integrated with the rest of the structural development, the introduction into the history of these two types of variants lends greater clarity to the use of the term "variant", in this case the voiced vs. voiceless palatal affricates.

8.6 The Two-Norm Theory

The conventional accounting of phonological change for French, I have argued (cf. Mazzola 2000, 2005, 2006, 2008) gives a rendition of an essentially unaltered Latin until the arrival of the Franks in the sixth century (cf. Muller 1929). The bias behind the traditional analyses is, therefore, that the French language finds its origins only within a Frankish context. The influence of the Franks, according to this conventional view, was then fixed as being the determining factor in the change from Latin to its descendant within the former Gallic province. In support of this claim, I have focused on the periods during the nineteenth and twentieth centuries when these analyses gained prominence, generally during the Franco-Prussian War, the Belle Époque, and the First World War. These were, of course, well recognized periods when tensions between a France in intermittent turmoil and the newly unified German *Länder* were at a heightened level. Although the nationalism of this period throughout Europe has largely escaped the notice of Romance linguists for its possible consequences, scholars of European history have been alert to this excessive infatuation with ethnic pride:

> ... the creative role of the Germanic invaders has been consistently exaggerated. French historians in the nineteenth century were in disagreement as to what perspective they should take. Some saw the French as the descendants of the Gallic race ...; others saw the French monarchy and the French aristocracy, and hence all that was best of French civilization, as being founded by the Germanic Franks and thus were forced to share in the Germanic perspective. On the whole [,] the Germanic view was predominant (James 1982: 89).

I have argued that, although representative of neo-grammarian reconstruction, the "two-norm theory" (cf. Wright (1982) and Lodge (1993), sketched in **(1)** below, was forged by an alliance of two currents which were seemingly at odds especially in Germany during the nineteenth century: (1) science, as implemented in the comparative method; and (2) idealism, as manifested by ethnic pride. Accordingly, the "two-norm theory" proposes two lines or "norms" of development from Latin in Gaul. The first, from which North French is said to derive, remains a fixed and unchanged Classical Latin until the arrival of the Franks. The second, which is comprised of dialects of lesser prestige, follow a line of Vulgar Latin development separating them from the Latin of the first "norm". In order to justify French as a language of greater prestige, it was necessary to preserve the continuation of the first "norm". To accomplish this, an excessive emphasis on *suppletive leveling as analogy* was necessary to account for a disproportionate focus on Frankish syncope (cf. Mazzola 2000, 2006), which was in turn necessary in order to uphold the myth of the Frankish origins of French culture. I maintain that this emphasis was driven by a spirit of nineteenth century nationalism (cf. Mazzola 2005); that analogy and nationalism played a mutually supportive role in inventing history rather than in reflecting it (cf. *ibid.*); and that the two-norm theory bears emblematic value with the ultimate effect of perpetuating a myth of a holy statehood born centuries earlier in the history of Europe (cf. Beaune 1991; Kantorowicz 1997; Poliakov 1996; Strayer 1957).

(1)

The point is then, as shown in (1), that Old French and French are privileged by having developed from a more esteemed source, viz. Classical Latin, while the other dialects of Gaul are said to have found their origin in an "inferior" variety, viz. Vulgar Latin. Although not shown in (1), within this orientation, French is also discussed as having undergone an intermediate stage labeled "Gallo-Roman". However, the use of this label should not be considered as removing French from being derived according to a "two-norm" perspective.

8.6.1 Analogy as Suppletive Leveling and Syncope

The crucial problem which our predecessors needed to resolve in order to reconcile their reckoning with the Frankish bias was the apparent contradiction exemplified by two items: /vindikáre/ > *venger* "to avenge" and /predikáre/ > *prêcher* "to preach." Their conviction regarding the regularity of sound change required them to settle the apparent conflict between the voiced palatal in *venger* with the voiceless palatal in *prêcher*, both from an intervocalic /k/. In order to account for this, they were quick to take advantage of an operation known as *syncope*, most probably, I maintain, because this operation was attributable to Germanic superstratum:

> The Frankish ... accentuation was a strong ... one and it was in the intensifying of the weak Latin tonic stress that the Germanic speech-habits, and in particular the Frankish, exercised their strongest influence on pronunciation. Directly resultant [was] ... the reduction ... of the unstressed vowels ... (Pope 1934: 15).

Their impetus to resort to syncope was doubtless also due to the fact that it is recognized to have occurred in the history of French to a greater extent than in the other Romance languages, as has been observed repeatedly in the manuals (cf. Meyer-Lübke 1890–1906: 287; Pirson 1909: 885–886; Pope 1934: 102–103; Richter 1934: 31, et al.). To illustrate, in these two items (e.g. *venger* and *prêcher*), the unstressed vowel of the pretonic syllable is dropped in the passage from Latin to French. However, to explain the voiceless vs. voiced palatals it was necessary to adopt two stages of syncope: one for the infinitival paroxytones (i.e. items with stress on the penult) and the other for the finite proparoxytones (i.e. items with stress on the antepenult). This illustrated by (2):

(2)	vindikáre	víndikat	prɛdikáre	prédikat
Syncope 1	---------	vén(d)kat	-----------	prɛ́(d)kat
k > g	vendigáre	----------	prɛdigáre	------------
Syncope 2	ven(d)gáre	----------	prɛ(d)gáre	------------
Palatalization	ven(d)ǧáre	vén(d)čat	prɛ(d)ǧáre	prḗ(d)čat
a[> e[	venǧére	-----------	prɛǧére	------------
Čé[> Čié[	venǧiére	-----------	prɛǧiére	------------
	venǧiɛ́r →	vénčəθ	prɛǧiɛ́r ←	prɛ́čəθ

IRREGULARITIES: venǧiɛ́r → vénčəθ   *venger* - *venge*
                    prɛǧiɛ́r ← prɛ́čəθ   *prêcher* - *prêche*

As shown, the syncope of proparoxytones bleeds (i.e. reduces the number of items) voicing upon taking effect (e.g. /víndikat/ > vén(d)kat, prédikat > pré(d)kat). In that way, the voiceless quality of the intervocalic stop in these items could be protected from the voicing that was to follow. This then asserts the operation of Frankish syncope even before the voicing universally shared by the western Romance dialects (e.g. North Italian, Spanish, Portuguese, Catalan), including of course French as well as the dialects of the Midi. A second, remedial stage of syncope was then necessary for paroxytones, which feeds (i.e. increases the number of items) the rule for the palatalization of velars before /a/, but only after voicing has already occurred. This would then give two differing palatals for each example: the voiced palatal in infinitives with penultimate stress and the voiceless palatal in finite forms with antepenultimate stress. This procedure, however, yielded results requiring recourse to further explanation via analogy in order to level the suppletion (i.e. irregularity in the paradigm) by which, for *venger-venge*, the finite form was to be reformed on the basis of the infinitive, whereas for *prêcher-prêche*, the infinitive was to be reformed on the basis of the finite form. The arrows at the end of the derivation given above indicate the direction of this suppletive leveling. From this, we see the operation of the syncope attributed to Frankish and the consequential explanation by analogy put into operation as needed. The conclusion we are to draw is that Latin does not begin to change in Northern Gaul until the sixth century with the advent of the Franks.

8.6.2 Nouns and Adjectives

With regard to nouns and adjectives, this procedure will yield the output intended by the conventional analysis for feminine proparoxytones by adhering unfalteringly to the palatalizaton of/k/before/a/as being pivotal; but, as shown in (3), the derivation of masculine proparoxytones according to this procedure is faulty:

(3) NOUNS:	pértika	pórtiku	mánika	mániku
Syncope 1	pértka	pórtku	mánka	mánku
k > g	-------	-------	----------	----------
Syncope 2	-------	-------	----------	----------
t > d	-------	-------	----------	----------
g > y	-------	-------	----------	----------
Palatalization	pér(t)ča	-------	mánča	----------
á[> é[	-------	-------	----------	----------
Čé > Čié	----------	-------	--------	----------
	pérčə	*pórtkə	mánčə	*mánkə
	perche	*porche*	*manche*	*manche*
			"sleeve"	"handle"

In order to remedy this, and at the same time to graft it onto the mechanism already set up for verbs, there was an insistence on what has come to be called "Neumann's Law", named after Fritz Neumann (1890) who devised it in support of Meyer-Lübke's earlier formulation. This amounts to no more than a casual distinction between k-radicals before /a/ (feminine forms) and k-radicals before/u/(masculine forms). Yet, almost universally after it was proposed, scholars from Meyer-Lübke (1913: 102) to Elise Richter (1934: 31–32) down to a relatively recent article by Georges Straka (1970), have all taken pains to defend it in some way or to follow along in its favor.

In this way, a mechanism was invented on very tenuous grounds for a plausible derivation of masculine forms, but one which was totally different from the procedure for feminines. Reserved for the k-radicals before /u/, on the one hand, was the process of voicing, yod-formation, and palatal affricate development, which I will refer to as *yod-increment*. For k-radicals before /a/, on the other hand, the palatal was derived from the fronting of velars before /a/. Any remaining difficulties as seen for *manicu* "handle," incorrectly derived as *mange* according to this approach, are explained away, as we would expect, by suppletive leveling. The direction of the analogy is shown by the arrow at the bottom line of (4). Given this apparatus, then, it goes without saying that an explanation from *analogy as suppletive leveling* was inevitable, and that it was followed from the insistence upon the use of syncope, a consequence of the Frankish orientation.

(4)	pértika	pórtiku	mánika	mániku
Feminine Syncope	pértka	---------	mánka	---------
Voicing	--------	pórtigu	----------	mánigu
Yod Formation	--------	pórtiyu	----------	mániyu

Masculine Shortening	--------	pɔ́rtyu	----------	mányu
Increment	--------	pɔ́rčə	----------	mánğə
Palatalization	pɔ́rčə	---------	mánğə	---------
	perche	porche	manche →	*mange

The single most important observation, which we are led to draw from this construct is that no change takes place before the operation of syncope, which, as mentioned above, is conventionally attributed to a Germanic superstratum. Consequently, since syncope is supposed to be a characteristic of Germanic and since it is represented more in Gaul than elsewhere, the Latin of Gaul would not have changed in any significant way before the arrival of the Franks in great numbers during the sixth century. I maintain, therefore, that this construct is the formalization of the "two-norm theory", based excessively on a tendentious analogy, a construct, which coincides strikingly with nineteenth century nationalism, referred to above. By this means, we see the Franks ordained and installed as the agents of a very late transformation of Latin in full accord with the sacralizing myths outlined as follows.

8.6.3 Frankish Syncope, Analogy, and Political Mysticism

This analysis then at once affirmed the Germanic bias and was in turn affirmed by two other Frankish legends, reawakened by the Romantic folklore of the nineteenth century. Two important myths, which in my mind are closely connected, come into focus: (1) the quasi-sacred destiny of the Merovingians passed on to the modern state personifying one people united by blood and (2) the consequential special status of French among the Romance languages. The Middle Ages were familiar with legends related to the "origins" of the Franks and to the manner of their arrival in Gaul. Périn and Feffer (1987: 17 ff) and Wood (1994: chapter 3) give an account of Fredegarius' myth whereby he displays more an admiration for Virgil's *Aeneid* than for historic accuracy. Here, we see the Franks, not to be outdone by the Romans, as descendants of Trojans migrating from Asia Minor to Gaul via the Danube.

Further mention is made of the origins and adventures of the Franks giving rise to hypotheses of tawdry fantasy. These have been especially noticeable in popularizing publications of our own time by Baigent et al. (1982, 1986), but also by other purveyors such as Picknett and Prince (1997) whose less sensational, but no less misleading romanticizing has gained a great deal of popular attention. Here, we find, with numerous variations in the details, a daughter of Jesus being born to Mary Magdalene. Moving to the South of France, a descendant of this union is said to have married one of the Merovingian kings. The convenient consequence was that the Blood of Jesus was to flow from then on in the line of the kings of France. Such legends could not fail to appeal to the romanticizing nation building, which was so much in evidence during the nineteenth century in Europe, but no less in France than in Germany. For it is in France that we see this further elaborative legend of the South joining the earlier legend of the North to seal, under the person of the King of

France, the unity of a nation so distinct in local cultures and ethnicities. The Revolution of the end of the eighteenth century had already taken advantage of this myth by simply replacing an anointed King with a revered State, the personification of a holy people in whom by now flowed the Blood of Christ, thereby sealing the challenge of the State to the Church via the Frankish myths.

James (1988: 235–243), citing Poliakov (1996), provides a helpful summary of the back-and-forth among the proponents of one of the peoples of origin: Gauls, Romans, Franks. In doing so, he points out that the issue is clearly related to whatever political debate is current at the time. Early on, the Franks were seen as the aristocratic element of the society from whom were derived all the contributions of greatness to French society. Understandably, this was to be rejected during the time of the Revolution. By then, all sentiment had turned against the nobility in favor of the industrialists and the common people; these latter being regarded as descendants of the Gauls. By the nineteenth century, what was gradually viewed as a conflict of race was being raised to a definition of nationalism. This new science of race led to procedures of exact measurement and classification. Such claims to precision lent to ethnicity a refinement and cachet of being described "scientifically". It was inevitable that such an direction should have led to an unfortunate orientation like that of Gobineau as well as to the intense debate over the superiority of Teutons over Franks or vice versa. The result of such a bleak debate was that idealism, in league by now with romanticism, was to mount its struggle against science and precise measurement. It is by making his way through this intellectual maelstrom that Meyer-Lübke effects his most noteworthy contribution by means of an agile, albeit unlikely alliance between precise measurement and a romanticized idealism.

During the Franco-Prussian War, it is not surprising that in France sympathy was to sway even further from Frankish sentiment. During this time, the Gauls were considered the true founders of France with the Franks regarded as having brought Gallo-Roman civilization to an end. It should be noted that throughout all this debate over the French myth, all attention was devoted to the issue of blood, ethnic descent, and race. Very little of it, however, has centered on the fact that French is a neo-Latin language, and it is this cultural, not racial, heritage that should be at the heart of our discussion. For this to take place, however, it is language that needs to be at the forefront of our attention as opposed to agendas, hidden or otherwise, to resolve debates over ethnic and racial superiority.

8.7 The One-Norm Theory

Following James, and therefore, challenging the changes of those proposals of the nineteenth and early twentieth centuries, I have argued that the wholesale, widespread syncope we know to have taken place in French has been confused with an earlier process of Latin syncope. The later, more intrusive syncope active during a more accurately identified period of Frankish influence, should not be confused with the earlier Latin syncope. It is at this time that we see Latin re-introduced (e.g. tabula>table, seculu>siècle, regula>règle) into the curriculum and regularly syncopated, replacing native forms (e.g. tabula > taule > tôle; seculu > seule; regula > reule). It is in this sense that this Frankish syncopation is a legacy of the Carolingian reforms. In order to distinguish between the two, I have adopted the term "shortening" to indicate the earlier Latin process and its derivative. Examples are given here at **(5)**:

(5) A. VwVC → VwC
    1. Lexical Phonology: ávis + càpis → auceps; nàvi + frágium → naufragium; *júvenior → junior

    2. Surface Phonology: návita → nauta; ávidus → audus; avúnculus → aunculus

    3. Caesar (verb morphology): ennuntiá[ve]rit → enuntiarit Cs I 17; curá[vi]sset → curasset 19; consué[vi]sse → consuesse 43; adpetí[ve]rit → adpetierit 44; consué[vi]ssent → consuessent Cs II 29

  B. Other: láridum → lardum; sólidus → soldus; válide → valde; Hércule → Hercle; manípulos → manuplos; caulículum → coliclo

This has been the basis for my language based support of the "one-norm theory", in agreement with the position adopted by Herman (op. cit.) and corroborated by Wright (op. cit). Here, we see no distinction between Classical Latin, Vulgar Latin, or Late Latin; we see them rather as variations of the same language. Since this distinction, unlike in the "two-norm theory", is absent here, French is thus, of necessity, represented as derived in no way differently from the other Gallo-Romance dialects. See **(6)** as a possible schematization of this view:

(6)
Classical Latin → Vulgar/Late Latin → Gallo-Roman → Gallo-Rom dialects → French

The "one-norm theory" as viewed by Herman and Wright is arrived at by a confidence in the written evidence of language use. I, however, have chosen to adopt another version of the "one-norm theory" which, in agreement with Herman and Wright, derives French along the same line with the other Gallo-Romance dialects. This version, represented in **(6a)**, is based, however, not on documented written attestations of the literate élite, but rather on reconstructions of the spoken language more representative of the underprivileged level of society (cf. Mazzola 2007). This, I maintain, represents a more likely variation which gives rise to the language we know today. Moreover, since we are dealing with a reconstructed system, I have used the label Proto-Romance to distinguish it from Classical Latin and Medieval Latin as different variants of the same language, but not necessarily as different languages.

(6a)
                Classical Latin ------------ → Medieval Latin
          ↗
Latin
          ↘
                Proto-Romance → Gallo-Roman → Gallo-Rom dialects → French

8.7.1 The Proposed Development

Examining the traditional apparatus more critically, I have adopted a totally phonological perspective, requiring no recourse to suppletive analogy, in order to determine whether we can arrive at a different chronology of the changes in question. As shown in (7) below, the analogy claimed to be necessary to level the suppletion for *venger/venge* can be avoided by a different ordering of voicing before the syncope of proparoxytones (Syncope 1), thus having neither a feeding nor a bleeding necessity for syncope. Moreover, by adopting this procedure, we see that the traditional distinction between Syncope 1 and Syncope 2, which held so fast to the morphological traits, is immediately rendered vacuous.

(7) PROPOSED CHRONOLOGY

k > g	vindikáre	víndikat
Syncope 1	vendigáre	véndigat
Syncope 2	----------	vén(d)gat
Palatalization	ven(d)gáre	----------
a[> e[	ven(d)ǧáre	vén(d)ǧat
Čé[> Čié[	venǧére	---------
	venǧiér	---------
	venǧiér	vénǧəθ

Thus, in (7) we see how the voiced palatal can be derived properly. The derivation given in (8), on the other hand, demonstrates how by ordering the rules differently we can derive the items displaying the voiceless palatal. However, as one sees in (8), where syncope bleeds voicing, the distinction between the two types of syncope is also invalidated and voicing is rendered equally unnecessary by this ordering.

(8) ALTERNATE CHRONOLOGY

Syncope 1	prɛdikáre	prédikat
Syncope 2	------------	prɛ́(d)kat
k > g	prɛ(d)káre	-----------
Palatalization	------------	-----------
a[> e[	prɛ(d)čáre	prɛ́(d)čat
Čé[> Čié[	prɛčére	------------
	prɛčiére	------------
	prɛčiér	prɛ́čəθ

Nevertheless, these two orderings still leave us with the issue as to why the rules should be ordered in one way for *venger/venge*, but in another for *prêcher/prêche*. In addressing this issue, our first observation is that neither the ordering given for (7) nor for (8) is sufficient to yield all the forms within the same derivation. The ordering of (7), however, should be considered to be privileged since it posits Western voicing early enough to account for all of the Western dialects. Accordingly, the derivation of the voiced palatal displays a smooth, measured feeding derivation of the dialects of Western Romance. For the voiceless palatal, however, we see the sudden and abrupt intrusion of the "two-norm theory," where Latin remains intact right up to the point where syncope is triggered.

What seems more reasonable to take into account is that in the direction laid out in **(10)** below, all the palatal affricates produced from intervocalic/k/are derived through increment (i.e. a consonant+yod resulting in a palatal consonant). The difference between the voicing of the palatal derived by increment is accounted for solely by the voiced or voiceless quality of the consonant preceding yod. Therefore, we can do away with the distinction between Syncope 1 and Syncope 2, since syncope as a general operation has nothing to do with the preliminary steps of **(9)** and we can eliminate the operation of palatalization of /k/+/a/ so early in the derivation. In **(9)**, we also see the voicing of intervocalic/k/throughout; followed by the weakening of /g/ to /y/, followed by a "shortening" which no longer makes any distinction between proparoxytones and paroxytones. In this way, we also simply eliminate Syncope as determined by the gender of nouns and adjectives.

(10) VERBS:	mastikáre	mástikat	vindikáre	víndikat
Voicing	mastigáre	mástigat	vendigáre	véndigat
g>y	mastiyáre	mástiyat	vendiyáre	véndiyat
Shortening	mastyáre	mástyat	vendyáre	véndyat
Increment	masčáre	másčat	venǧáre	vénǧat
Palatalization	---------	---------	----------	----------
a[>e[	masčére	---------	venǧére	----------
Čé[>Čié[	masčiére	---------	venǧiére	----------
	masčiér	másčəθ	venǧiér	vénǧəθ
	mâcher	*mâche*	*venger*	*venge*

This then is in agreement with Richter's view (1934: 31–32) of the process for masculine nouns and adjectives as opposed to feminine stems. In addressing the derivation of the items at issue, Richter, it will be recalled, insisted on what appears to be a tenuous distinction between syncope and assimilation in connection with the derivation of k-radicals before/u/. In her discussion of the suffix –*átiku*, for example, she simply dismisses syncope as being relevant and insists rather on speaking of her representation of the progression: –átiku>–átigu>átiyu>ádiyu>ádž in terms of a series of assimilatory processes. The voicing of the intervocalic stops, she maintains, and the subsequent fricativization of gy>dž are merely a question of assimilation to the voiced quality of the surrounding vowels. My approach has been to extend this process throughout the lexicon without distinction regarding morphological classification.

Increment can then be applied to all the consonants (not just labials) followed by yod, the voicing of the palatal being determined solely by the voiced quality of the consonant preceding yod as shown in **(9)** above. As a consequence of this chronology, we no longer see any need to level the allomorphy. This would then yield the following variants for which I am reserving the term "structural."

(11) Palatals as Structural Variants

/k/-radicals	→ voiceless palatal	/k/-radicals	→ voiced palatal
collocare	> coucher	carricare	> charger
caballicare	> chevaucher	bullicare	> bouger
fastidiare	> fâcher	manducare	> manger
vindicare	> (re)vencher	vindicare	> venger
excorticare	> écorcher	plumbicare	> plonger
pendicare	> pencher		
impedicare	> empêcher		

The exceptions to this approach involve only voiceless palatals where we would expect to find voiced ones: empêcher instead of *empêger; coucher instead of *couger; pencher instead of *penger; prêcher instead of *prêger, etc.

8.7.2 Borrowing from Frankish-Romance

Turning now to the forms with the voiceless palatals emanating from a voiced consonant before yod (e.g. predicare > prêcher), we see, once again, that these are only forms where we would expect voiced palatals. Exceptions, however, do not run in the other direction, i.e. voiced palatals where we would expect voiceless ones. This prompts considering dialectal borrowing, specifically by Gallo-Romance from Frankish-Romance. This would have been triggered through a process by which Frankish speakers, favoring voiceless palatals, simply devoiced the palatals in question. In addressing individual, troublesome items, Pope considers the voiced palatal to be borrowed: "Divergent forms are sometimes dialectal e.g. basoge, grange (south-western ...)" (1934: 141). Bourciez (1958), in agreement, holds to a voiceless regular development: "[la transformation] de balearica devenu baillarge, et de serica aboutissant à serge ne semble pas normale pour le nord de la France, tandis qu'à côté de grange, on avait régulièrement en afr. granche (=*granica)" (1958: 126).[1] In contrast, Fouché (1966: 938) views the voiced palatal as the regular development and points to Normandy, Champagne and Lorraine as likely areas from which the voiceless palatal was borrowed.

There are, therefore, two possibilities: (1) a regular voiceless palatal with borrowing from the South (necessitated by a strict adherence to the conventional analysis as presented above); or (2) a regular voiced palatal with borrowing from the North. The latter, which will be adopted in this paper, would then have spread from word to word without fully running its course. In this way, through borrowing during this early contact, Frankish-Romance would have had a marginal, but lasting effect on Gallo-Roman. This effect would have been peripheral, but a good

---

[1] [the development] of ballearica to baillarge and of serica to serge does not seem normal for the North of France, whereas alongside grange, granche (=*granica) occurred frequently in Old French.

8 Analogy Among French Sounds

example of Gallo-Roman assimilation of a new fashion. In this way we see that the **structural variants** which consisted of a voiceless palatal resulting from a voiceless consonant + yod and a voiced palatal resulting from a voiced consonant + yod is now superimposed by a new distribution of **social variants**. The social variants are all structured in that they all operate in one direction only. That is to say, that, crucially, only the original **structural variant** is converted over to a new voiceless **social variant**.

(12) Palatals as Social Variants:

	cns-radicals	→	palatal	
	/		\	
voiced radical cns		**voiceless radical cns**		
manducare >	manger		cloppicare >	clocher
plumbicare >	plonger		appropiare >	approcher
iudicare >	juger		masticare >	mâcher
vindicare >	venger	→		(re)vencher
collocare >	*couger	→		coucher
caballicare >	*chevauger	→		chevaucher
pendicare >	*penger	→		pencher
predicare >	*prêger	→		prêcher
impedicare >	*empêger	→		empêcher
granica >	grange	→		granche
basilica >	basoge	→		basoche
manica >	*mange	→		manche
manicu >	*mange	→		manche

As shown in **(10)**, the regular development already yields two palatal variants, which I am calling ***structural variants***, resulting from the voicing of the root consonant of the word involved. In **(12)**, a classification is given of the exceptions to the analysis proposed in **(10)**. In **(12)**, significantly I stress, are represented only items which display voiceless palatals where the regular reflex should be voiced, most probably due to the borrowing of Gallo-Roman from Frankish-Romance. Strikingly absent, therefore, are examples running in the other direction, where voiceless outcomes are replaced by the voiced palatal. These are proposed as examples of lexical diffusion in the history of French and are viewed in accord with Kiparsky's (1995) discussion of *lexical diffusion as analogy*.

8.8 Conclusion

Between the fourth and seventh centuries, what documentation has survived focused on preservation and on imitation. The resultant diglossia between the more prestigious Latin of the clerics and its developing offshoot of the farmer and the shepherdess is the perennial mystery of historical Romance. What is the nature of the latter, given the lack of written documentation especially as to its phonology?

As a result of this, scholars have been content to rely on Meyer-Lübke's *invention* of what transpired between Latin and its continuation before there was a France. This *invention*, however, is usually thought of in artificial terms, given its reconstruction based on inference without written corroboration. In this paper, this *invention* is regarded, rather, as being the result of his joining together German idealism and science during the era in which Meyer-Lübke devised his phonological history. We therefore see a coming together of logical positivism and one of the hallmarks of romantic idealism, i.e. pride in ethnic heritage. For this reason, Meyer-Lübke's contribution can be seen as straddling the opposing two movements by using the scientific methodology of motivated inference in order to delay the birth of the French language until the arrival of the Franks. An alternative, sketched in this paper, also the result of reconstruction, but unconcerned with nation building, outlines rather a *reflection* of history as a continuous development of Gallo-Roman from the mid-fourth through mid-seventeenth centuries before the rise of the Franks to power. This reconstruction has been achieved through a view of analogy not in connection with suppletion, but rather as manifested by regular sound change and lexical diffusion.

References

Antila, Raimo. 2003. Analogy: The warp and woof of cognition. In *Handbook of historical linguistics*, ed. B. Joseph and R. Janda, 425–440. Oxford: Blackwell.
Baigent, M., R. Leigh, and H. Lincoln. 1982. *Holy blood, holy grail*. New York: Dell.
Baigent, M., R. Leigh, and H. Lincoln. 1986. *The messianic legacy*. New York: Dell.
Beaune, Colette. 1991. *The birth of an ideology: Myths and symbols of nation in late-medieval France*. Berkeley: University of California Press.
Bourciez, E., and J. Bourciez. 1958. *Précis de phonétique française*, 9th ed. Paris: Klincksieck.
Fouché, Pierre. 1966. *Phonétique historique du français*, vol. II. Paris: Klincksieck.
Herman, József. 2000. *Vulgar Latin*. University Park: Penn State University Press.
James, Edward. 1982. *The origins of France: From Clovis to the Capetians 500–1000*. London: Macmillan.
James, Edward. 1988. *The Franks*. London: Basil Blackwell.
Kantorowicz, E. 1997. *The king's two bodies*. Princeton: Princeton University Press.
Kiparsky, Paul, et al. 1988. Phonological change. In *Linguistics: The Cambridge survey*, vol. 1, ed. Frederick J. Newmeyer, 363–413. Cambridge: Cambridge University Press.
Kiparsky, Paul. 1995. The phonological basis of sound change. In *The handbook of phonological theory*, ed. John Goldsmith, 640–670. Oxford: Blackwell.
Labov, William. 1981. Resolving the neogrammarian controversy. *Language* 57(2): 267–308.
Lodge, R.Anthony. 1993. *From dialect to standard*. London: Routledge.
Malkiel, Yakov. 1988. *A tentative autobiography*. Special Issue of *Romance Philology* 1988–1989. Berkeley/Los Angeles: University of California Press.
Mazzola, Michael L. 2000. L'analyse à l'encontre de l'analogie. In *Actes du XXIIe Congrès international de linguistique et philologie romanes*, ed. A. Englebert et al., 326. Tübingen: Max Niemeyer.
Mazzola, Michael L. 2005. *Social hypotheses and formal proposals. XVII International Conference on Historical Linguistics*. Madison: University of Wisconsin.
Mazzola, Michael L. 2006. Rhythm and prosodic change. In *Historical Romance linguistics: Retrospective and perspectives*, ed. Deborah Arteaga and Randall Gess, 97–110. Amsterdam/Philadelphia: J Benjamins.

Mazzola, Michael L. 2007. L'analyse soujacente à la diglossie. In *Actes du XXIVe Congrès International de Linguistique et de Philologie Romanes*, ed. David Trotter, 533–539. Tübingen: Niemeyer.
Mazzola, Michael L. 2008. The two-norm theory as an emblem of political power and historical invention. In *Latin Vulgaire – Latin Tardif VIII: Actes du VIIIe colloque international sur le latin vulgaire et tardif, Oxford, 6–9 Septembre 2006*, ed. Roger Wright, 591–599. Hildesheim: Olms-Weidmann.
Meyer-Lübke, Wilhelm. 1890–1906. *Grammaire des langues romanes*. 3 vols. Repr., Geneva: Slatkine, 1974.
Meyer-Lübke, Wilhelm. 1913. *Historische Grammatik der Französischen Sprache*. Heidelberg: Karl Winter.
Morin, Yves-Charles. 2003. Syncope, apocope, diphtongaison et palatalisation en galloroman: problèmes de chronologie relative. In *Actas del XXIII Congreso International de Lingüística y Filología Románica*, vol. I, ed. Fernando Sánchez Miret, 113–169. Tübingen: Niemeyer.
Muller, Henri-François. 1929. *A chronology of vulgar Latin*, Beihefte zur Zeitschrift für Romanische Philologie LXXVIII. Halle: Max Niemeyer.
Neumann, Fritz. 1890. Review of Eduard Schwann. *Grammatik des Altfranzösischen in Zeitschrift für Romanische Philologie* 14: 543–586.
Périn, Patrick, and Laure-Charlotte Feffer. 1987. *Les Francs*. Paris: Armand Colin.
Picknett, Lynn, and Clive Prince. 1997. *The templar revelation*. New York: Simon and Schuster.
Pirson, Jules. 1909. Le Latin des formules mérovingiennes. *Romanische Forschungen* XXVI: 837–944.
Poliakov, Léon. 1996. *The Aryan Myth: A History of Racist and National Ideas in Europe*. Trans. Edmund Howard. New York: Barnes & Noble.
Pope, Mildred K. 1934. *From Latin to modern French*. Repr., Manchester: University of Manchester Press.
Posner, R. 1997. *Linguistic change in French*. New York: Oxford University Press.
Richter, Elise. 1934. *Beiträge zur Geschichte des Romanismen: Chronologische Phonetik des Französischen bis zum Endes des 8 Jahrhunderts*. Max Niemeyer: Halle.
Straka, Georges. 1953. Observations sur la chronologie et les dates de quelques modifications phonétiques en roman. *Revue des langues romanes* 71: 247–307.
Straka, Georges. 1956. La dislocation linguistique de la Romania et la formation des langues romanes. *Revue de linquistique romane* 20: 249–267.
Straka, Georges. 1970. A propos des traitements de -icu et -ica dans les proparoxytons en français. *Travaux de linguistique et littérature* 8: 297–311.
Strayer, Joseph R. 1957. *On the medieval origins of the modern state*. Princeton: Princeton University Press.
Venneman, T., and T. Wilbur. 1972. *Schuchardt, the Neogrammarians, and the transformational theory of phonological change*. Linguistische Forschungen 26. Frankfurt: Athenäum.
Wood, Ian. 1994. *The Merovingian kingdoms*, 450–751. London: Longman.
Wright, Roger. 1982. *Late Latin and early Romance in Spain and Carolingian France*. Liverpool: Francis Cairns.
Wright, Roger. 2002. *A sociophilological study of late Latin*. Turnhout: Brepols.

Chapter 9
The Development of the Declension System

Lene Schøsler

9.1 Introduction

Instead of studying the Old French (OF) declension system in isolation, this chapter takes into consideration the role of the case system with respect to other parts of the grammar. In terms of methodology, it is anchored in variational linguistics. This chapter seeks not only to contribute to a better understanding of OF, but also to enrich our understanding of language change *per se*. It documents how the detailed study of synchronic and diachronic variation contributes to a better understanding of how language systems function in general, and specifically, that of OF.

9.2 Declension from Latin to Modern French, the Problems

The traditional understanding of case systems is that morphological case is needed to mark NPs in order for the speakers to identify their syntactic function (see e.g. Blake 1994: 1–2; Marchello-Nizia 1999: 82; Chaurand 1999: 44 ss). Accordingly, if changes in case systems occur, they are considered to be linked to fundamental reorganizations of the grammatical structure of that language. Studying the loss of nominal case in French is particularly interesting, as it suggests answers to the following questions:

1. Why did French (and Occitan and some Swiss Romance variants) preserve a case distinction (nominative/oblique), whereas Italian, Portuguese and Spanish did not?

L. Schøsler (✉)
Department of English, Germanic and Romance Studies,
The University of Copenhagen, Copenhagen, Denmark
e-mail: schoesl@hum.ku.dk

2. Why was this distinction lost at the end of the Middle Ages (with the exception of Swiss Romance variants)?[1]

The present paper will focus on two main lines of research. One, recently presented by Detges (2008),[2] stresses the fact that morphological case is not necessary for successful communication. This line of thinking is highly relevant, but it studies the function of the case system in isolation, without taking into account other properties of the grammatical system. Moreover, it is unable to address the following three important research questions that should be addressed in any study of declension loss – questions which will be discussed in Sect. 9.5 of this chapter:

- What was the function of the case system in Old French?
- Why was declension preserved for so many centuries? (i.e. ninth to the fourteenth centuries, depending on the dialect)
- Why was declension lost at that particular time? (i.e. between the twelfth and the fourteenth centuries, depending on the dialect)

The line of thinking adopted here differs from the traditional one in particular with respect to the two following points: first, it takes into consideration the role of the case system with respect to other parts of the grammar; second, it is anchored in variational linguistics, implying that synchronic and diachronic variation is both the result of, and the reason for, change.

9.3 Old French Morphology

Before discussing the important questions outlined above in detail, we must consider the morphological facts (see Tables 9.1, 9.2, 9.3, 9.4, and 9.5 below). These reproduce the standard paradigms of OF declension, without the diachronic and diatopic variations that will be touched upon later. Only two cases of the Latin declension system are preserved in Old French. Table 9.1 presents the largest subclass of masculine forms, which distinguishes two cases. Table 9.3 gives the largest subclass of feminine forms, which only distinguishes number and no case. Table 9.2 presents an interesting subclass, in that there is a distinct singular nominative form, which, instead of being distinguished by a final –s, has one syllable fewer than the other forms. There are other subgroups, but these three will suffice for my presentation.

It should be noted that the optional, but nevertheless frequently used definite article (*li, le, li, les*), presents a declension, which permits us to establish the distinction between both case and number of masculine nouns, in spite of just one flexional opposition, namely that between Ø and -s. In principle, the Latin nominative forms

---

[1] Information on Romance morphology can be found in Meyer-Lübke (1894/1972) *inter alia*.
[2] For Latin, a comparable view is presented by Pinkster (1991). Detges' conclusion is that morphological case is "extremely redundant but … not entirely useless".

Table 9.1 Latin > Old French, parasyllabic masculine nouns and adjectives

Case	Singular	Plural
Nominative	murus > (li) murs	muri > (li) mur
Accusative	muru(m) > (le) mur	muros > (les) murs

Table 9.2 Latin > Old French, imparasyllabic masculine nouns (mainly referring to persons)

Case	Singular	Plural
Nominative	latro > (li) lerre	latroni > (li) larron
Accusative	latrone(m) > (le) larron	latrones > (les) larrons

Table 9.3 Latin > Old French, parasyllabic feminine nouns and adjectives

Case	Singular	Plural
Nominative	rosa > (la) rose	rosae > rosas > (les) roses
Accusative	rosa(m) > (la) rose	rosas > (les) roses

Table 9.4 Modern French, masculine nouns and adjectives

No case	Singular	Plural
	le mur	les murs

Table 9.5 Modern French, feminine nouns and adjectives

No case	Singular	Plural
	la rose	les roses

and their OF equivalents[3] are found in the following functions: subject, subject complement, addressee[4]; the Latin accusative forms and their OF equivalents are mainly found in the following functions: object, object complement, and governed by a preposition. However, these rules of use are not fully respected in the OF texts, as important diachronic and diatopic variations occur (see Sect. 9.5).

9.4 From Latin to Romance

9.4.1 Introduction

The Classical Latin declension system was relatively reduced in comparison to the Indo-European declension system and several oppositions no longer existed in some of the paradigms (e.g. the opposition between the dative and the ablative). In spite

---

[3] For convenience, I use the terms nominative and accusative not only for Latin forms, but also for OF forms, although the non-nominative forms assume the form and functions not only of the accusative, but also of the genitive, dative, and the ablative forms. See note 5 for details concerning the modifications of the Latin forms.

[4] The vocative case has no continuation in OF.

of the merger of specific case oppositions,[5] serious case confusion is not found in the texts before the end of the second century. Especially from the third century on, the genitive and the dative are confused, in form as well as in function. From the fourth and fifth century on, the declension system is reduced to two- or three-case systems that differ, to some extent, between the regions. This reduction is general, in spite of the variations found, whereas the subsequent elimination of the declension system is not. Between the sixth and the ninth centuries, nominal (with the exception of pronominal) declension disappears completely in most regions, while declension is preserved in Romanian, Rheto-Romance, and Gallo-Romance dialects. In geographical terms, three zones may be distinguished: a central-southern zone with early disappearance of nominal declension: Africa, Southern and Central Italy,[6] Spain; a north-western zone retaining the distinction between the nominative and oblique cases (still partially found in Rheto-Romance dialects), and an Eastern zone with preservation of a two-case system opposing the nominative-accusative form to the genitive-dative form (still existing in Romanian).[7]

Probably alongside the disintegration of the Latin case system, all the ancestors of Modern Romance languages gradually adopted a continuous noun phrase, which is a prerequisite for the existence of grammatically (rather than pragmatically) motivated word order rules.[8] It has been proposed that the basic order of Latin was SOV, whereas most modern Romance languages have the order SVO. These generalizations have been much debated, and neither Classical Latin nor the modern Romance languages are pure examples of these types. As shown in Schøsler and Skovgaard-Hansen (2007), text types are highly relevant for the presence of discontinuous or continuous NPs in Classical and postclassical Latin. Continuous NPs are a prerequisite for deciding which word order is dominant in a given language. Accordingly, one should not propose just

---

[5] The merger is caused by several changes, which are due to the fact that the distinction of quantity (i.e. short:long vowels) replace the opposition of quality (i.e. high:low vowels) with the resultant fusion of vowels, and due to the disappearance of final –m-. Examples of merger caused by the disappearance of these phonetic distinctions are the opposition between the nominative of the first declension with a short *a*, the accusative with a short *a* followed in writing by *m*, which disappeared (accordingly indicated as (m) in Tables 9.1, 9.2, and 9.3), and the ablative with a long *a*, e.g. nom.sg. *mensa*, acc.sg. *mensam*, abl.sg. *mensa* with a line above the final –*a*. In the third declension, there was confusion of *es* and *is*, accusative plural and genitive singular, respectively, e.g. *montis*, *montes*, and the merger of accusative singular with ablative singular: *montem - monte*. Further examples may be found in Penny (2002:116–117).

[6] It is thought that Italian had a distinction between the nominative and the oblique form (Maiden and Sornicola, personal communication). Only traces are found in Old Italian, and probably in some areas only in the nominative form of plural nouns.

[7] For an excellent short account of the development from Latin to Romance languages, and a balanced analysis of interacting factors, see Herman (1998, 2000). A fine discussion of different approaches to the many problems related to the development of the declension system is found in the Sornicola (2007) Sect. 9.3. A speculative presentation of the development of case and constructions in Proto-Romance is found in Dardel (2001).

[8] In Schøsler and Skovgaard-Hansen (2007), we find in *itinerarium Egeriae* that only 3.2% of all complex NP are discontinuous; but in this text type continuous NPs are the rule, whereas poetry is characterised by discontinuous NPs, e.g. Catullus: 33.3%, Horace 50.9% and Ovid 52.2% discontinuous NPs.

one basic order for Latin. I agree with Pinkster on this point, who affirms that (1990: 188): "...any statement of the type 'Latin was an *X*-language' [is] unfounded...." Indeed, even if one word order was dominant, word order did not have the function of an argument marker, and it is generally accepted that Latin word order does not provide information about argument structure. It is more likely that pragmatic factors and individual stylistic choices (including text type restrictions) determine Latin word order.

In the course of the gradual disintegration of the nominal case system in Late Latin, important changes took place. According to the traditional account of the development from Latin to the Romance languages, case was replaced by prepositions and by word order rules, the latter especially relevant for French. In previous work (see Schøsler 2008 with references therein), I have shown that traditional positions are incorrect, because, among other reasons, of chronological inconsistencies. As I see it, traditional accounts of these changes have wrongly linked two synchronic analyses in an alleged causal relation. Consider, as an illustration, declension and word order. We have seen above that the traditional analysis runs as follows: the first observation is that the main function of the Latin declension system is to identify the syntactic function and the referents of arguments. The second observation is that word order is used to identify the arguments in, say, modern French. The alleged causal link is that the loss of the first caused the appearance of the second. Similarly, the traditional account of the role of the loss of overt final *–s* is incorrect. The traditional analysis runs as follows: final *–s* marks the case in Old French; the loss of overt final *–s* is the cause of the loss of the declension system.[9]

The accounts sketched above are factually incorrect as shown in my previous publications, but need to be discussed further before they can be rejected *in totalis*. The underlying assumption of the traditional accounts is that important functions in grammar, such as the marking of arguments and instructions for the identification of referents, depend upon fragile markers that may deteriorate and vanish, leaving behind a defective grammar in search of new markers. This traditional approach does not seem viable; on the contrary, it is more plausible that important functions are marked by various, connected, grammatical subsystems and that these may gain or lose importance during the history of the language.

A better claim would be that grammatical subsystems are organized in such a way that they collaborate, and that they are best comprehended as connected grammaticalized devices for the marking and identification of arguments. This claim is better for the following three reasons: (1) it is a more general explanation, since they exist in all Romance languages and their relative importance depends on language-specific conditions that should be studied for each language and for each stage of these languages (2) it is non-ad hoc and yet survives falsification that the traditionalist arguments do not, and (3) it provides a better correspondence with the facts.

In the following my main focus will, of course, be on OF. I will draw upon recent research in this field (Schøsler 2001a, b; Detges 2008) and in particular upon ongoing research in the field of grammaticalization and construction grammar (Schøsler 2008; Nørgård-Sørensen et al. 2011).

---

[9] This is a clear example of the well known: *Post hoc ergo propter hoc*-fallacy.

9.4.2 Declension in Latin

Pinkster (1990: 60) puts forward the hypothesis that in Latin: "...the content of the sentence is determined on the basis of the lexical meaning(s) of the predicate and the arguments occurring with it". He exemplifies this statement with the following example: *is illius laudare infit formam virginis* ('he begins to praise the beauty of that girl', Plautus, *Rud*: 51) and states that: "...after all, *forma virginis* is unable to *laudare* a person." Examining his corpus of classical texts from Plautus' time until circa AD 100, Pinkster finds (1990: 62): "...that the marking of the syntactic and semantic function by means of a case is necessary in less than 5–10% of instances." Thus, he concludes that the declension system has a considerably less important function than is normally assumed and that the lexical meanings of predicates and noun phrases should be considered instead (1990: 65).

Although Pinkster's conclusion concerning the *reduced* role of the declension system for marking and identification of arguments is certainly more valid than the traditional account, the data is in no way strong enough to support Pinkster's *minimalistic*[10] view of how communication is maintained (as implied by the adjective "necessary" in the above quotation). In Latin, case undoubtedly contributed to the identification of arguments, without being absolutely "necessary", and functioned as markers on nouns pointing to their function as arguments in the sentence. However, Pinkster is probably right when he suggests that it is not the main function of nominal morphology to identify arguments. Schøsler (1984) arrived at a similar conclusion concerning the role of the declension system in OF and we will return to this point in the following. What then, is the function of the Latin declension system? In Schøsler (2008), it is proposed that an important function of the Latin declension system is to mark the constituents of a noun phrase by means of concord, as Latin is a non-configurative language.[11] That the noun phrase can appear discontinuously through a sentence is one of the typical features of Latin. In order to exemplify this, we may take the following quotation from Cicero: *De inventione* 1–4, where the direct object (marked in bold type) of *video* ('I see') is split into two parts by the predicate *video* and by a prepositional phrase *per disertissimos homines*:

(1)[12]
non **minimam**   *video*
not **little**-SUPERLATIVE-ACC-FEM-SG I see

per disertissimos   *homines* **invectam**
by the most eloquent men   **inflict**-PAST PTCP-ACC-FEM-SG

---

[10] "Minimalistic" in a non-technical sense.
[11] The term proposed in Andersen (2008) for this function is "phrase-internal indexing".
[12] The glosses are conform to the Leipzig Glossing Rules. (http://www.eva.mpg.de/lingua/resources/glossing-rules.php)

partem   incommodorum
part-ACC-FEM-SG **misfortune**-GEN-PL
'I find that it is not **the least part of these misfortunes** that is caused by the most eloquent speakers'

The use of discontinuous nominal NPs is extensive from Early Latin (e.g. Plautus) to Renaissance and Humanist Latin (e.g. Petrarch, Erasmus, Calvin) and its frequency is related to text type, genre and style.[13]

So, if declension was more or less "superfluous", as Pinkster believes, and as the statistics of Latin and OF seem to confirm, we still do not have any answer to the questions asked at the beginning of this chapter, which were: what was indeed the role of case in OF as compared to other parts of grammar and why was declension maintained for several centuries? In most studies on OF declension, these questions have rarely been asked and have certainly not been answered satisfactorily. This will be taken up in Sect. 9.5.

9.4.3 Declension in Old French. Was It "Superfluous"?

Following Pinkster's line of reasoning, but without referring to him, Detges (2008) asks the provocative question: "…how useful is case morphology"? His answer is that inflectional case-marking on full nouns is not necessary for successful communication. Let us recapitulate Detges' argument regarding how successful communication is ensured, keeping in mind that this does not answer the questions raised above, namely, what was indeed the role of case in OF compared to other parts of grammar and why was declension maintained for several centuries?

Detges' paper discusses the loss of the OF case system within the theory of Preferred Argument structure proposed by Du Bois. According to this theory, general preference laws exist, four of which are especially relevant for the analysis of OF. One is the so-called *One lexical Argument Constraint*: "Avoid more than one lexical argument per clause", i.e. avoid more than one core argument realized as an NP containing a full lexical noun. The second is the *Non-Lexical A Constraint*: "Avoid lexical A's", i.e. avoid first arguments of two-place predicates (=A) realized as lexical NPs. The third is the *One New Argument Constraint*: "Avoid more than one new argument per Clause",[14] i.e. avoid more than one argument per clause containing new information. The forth is the *Given A Constraint*: "Avoid new A's", i.e. avoid first arguments of two-place predicates that convey new information.

---

[13] See Schøsler and Skovgaard-Hansen (2007) for a study of discontinuous NPs in selected passages from more than 20 Latin texts.
[14] I believe that the so-called *One New Argument Constraint* should be connected to the One-Chunk-per-Clause processing principle proposed by Chafe (1994:119) and by Givón (1995:358).

Table 9.6 Combinations of the core arguments subject and object, adapted from Detges (2008: Table 10)

Combination and form	Pattern in English	Number of occ.
SØ-OP	Ø greets him	40
SP-OP	he greets him	9
SØ-ON	Ø greets the man	12
SP-ON	he greets the man	1
SN-OP	the knight greets him	15
SN-ON	the knight greets the man	8
patterns with extraposition of O	Ø/the knight greets him, the man	2

According to these so-called preference laws, only the subject *or* the object would normally take the form of a lexical NP. Let us now consider the possible combinations of the core arguments subject and object. Detges refers to Hupka (1982) who studied 100 sentences in the works of Chrétien de Troyes (twelfth century) containing the verb *saluer* ('to greet'). The combination and form of the two core arguments in these sentences are the following (SØ=null subject, SN=lexical subject, SP=pronominal subject; ON=lexical object, OP=pronominal object) (Table 9.6):

Only two combinations are potentially ambiguous: SØ-ON and SN-ON. In these combinations, which total 20% of all occurrences, case may provide the key to identifying the functions of the arguments. However, two issues may be raised here. On one hand, lexical constraints, like the one quoted by Pinkster (1990: 60), or formal constraints, (e.g., difference of number between S and O), may also contribute to understanding the syntactic function of the arguments. On the other hand, the OF declension system does not always provide the key, firstly because feminine nouns hardly have any declension (see Table 9.3 above), and secondly, because the declension system is unstable and many forms do not follow the general rules of use summarized above.

In a study with a corpus of 1494 sentences (i.e. considerably larger than that of Hupka) from the twelfth century chanson de geste *Charroi de Nîmes*, I considered the relative importance of 17 factors including lexical constraints, type and form of constituents, pronominal declension (which is stable throughout the history of French), use of determiners, contextual factors, word order, and nominal case for the identification of the function of arguments (Schøsler 1984). I found that, with only one exception, case always appears in collaboration with other factors that indicate the function of the arguments. In this regard, case is hardly ever "necessary" in the "minimalistic" sense mentioned above, since lexical and grammatical factors present in the sentences indicate the function of the argument. However, this state of affairs does not imply that case is completely without function. As I see it, OF evidence suggests that successful communication employs a number of collaborating

9 The Development of the Declension System

indexes pointing out the function of the arguments. In short, a language - in this case OF - offers its users many collaborating clues to identifying arguments and their referents, including both the lexicon and grammar. Thus, my view is essentially different from the one that calculates the possibility of communication with a minimum of grammar, as Pinkster and Detges do.

Another important way in which this paper differs from Detges' is that it does not consider it possible without caveats to infer OF structures directly from modern spoken Romance language structures. I will return to this issue later in Sect. 9.5. In sum, my approach differs from the "minimalistic" approach of Pinkster and Detges, according to whom grammar provides "useless", i.e. redundant information. Why is grammar redundant in the sense used here? There are at least three reasons for this. First, because most of the factors mentioned above are not obligatory, but optional, e.g. lexical combinations, word order, use of determiners. Second, because the morphological factor of *case* is insufficient in the sense that it is mainly relevant for masculine nouns and hardly for feminine nouns and, moreover, it is unstable. Third, the texts handed over to us are, of course, not oral, but are instead often written in a high literary or administrative style, which must be taken to be more explicit (hence more "redundant" in the sense of displaying a number of collaborating factors) than the spoken language.

This brings us back to Detges' important paper on the "usefulness" of morphological case in OF. As seen above, Detges' arguments concerning morphology not being necessary for successful communication from a strictly grammatical point of view, focuses on the most "economic" form of communication, by which he means how little grammatical information is necessary in order to communicate. This line of argumentation is based on studies of modern oral communication, where gestures etc., provide supplementary information if grammatical information is scarce. This is a fundamentally different situation compared to that of OF, where no informal oral testimony is available.[15] It is indeed plausible that Detges' argument holds for spoken OF, but what we still need to investigate, and what Detges' study does not discuss, are the two questions raised in the introduction of this chapter: what was the function of the "unnecessary" OF declension system,[16] and why was it preserved for so many centuries?

---

[15] Additionally, Detges proposes a comparison between the OF and the corresponding translation of the first 265 verses of the *Chevalier de la Charrette*. But this can hardly be taken as a convincing piece of evidence concerning the relative frequency of lexical S in OF and MF. Moreover, this text represents just one text type, and I am convinced that it is necessary to proceed to a more balanced investigation, based on different text types (see Sect. 9.5.2).

[16] In his conclusion, Detges accepts my view that "morphology is just one of many clues indicating syntactic function and semantic role. In other words, it may be extremely redundant, but not entirely useless". However, Detges does not develop this view in his paper, which focuses on the "uselessness" of morphology.

9.5 The Importance of Variation

9.5.1 Introduction

The morphological system outlined in Tables 9.1, 9.2, and 9.3 above is a generalization masking a wide range of variation. Variation should be included in a diachronic study, in which sense one must agree completely with Andersen (2001: 228):

> Changes are always manifested in synchronic variation, and past changes can commonly be found to be reflected in synchronic alternations, or attested in written records.

9.5.2 Parameters of Variation in Old French

In Schøsler (1984, 2001a, 2006), I have shown that the gradual breakdown of nominal declension progressing from Western to Eastern dialects is a **diatopically** anchored process and these dialectal differences are explicitly recognized by the OF writers. A famous passage showing this is found in (2). It is quoted from the Prologue of *la Vie d'Edouard le Confesseur*, a twelfth century Anglo-Norman translation of the Latin original (verses 1–10), in which the translating nun excuses her deficient understanding of traditional declension rules:

(2) *Si joe l' ordre des cases ne gart*
   'if I the order of the cases not respect'
   Ne ne juigne part a sa part
   'nor not join [a] part to its part'
   Certes n'en dei estre reprise
   'certainly [I] thereof must not be blaimed'
   Ke nel puis faire en nule guise.
   'because [I] not it can do in any way'
   Qu' en latin est nominatif
   'what in Latin is nominative'
   Ço frai romanz acusatif.
   'that [I] will make [in] Romance language accusative'
   Un faus franceis sai d' Angleterre
   'a bad French [I] know from England'
   Ke ne l' alai ailurs quere.
   'because [I] not it went elsewhere find'
   Mais vus ku ailurs apris l' avez
   'but you who elsewhere learnt it have'
   La u mestier iert, l'amandez.
   'where [it] necessary will be, it improve'

(Quoted from Schøsler (1984: 171). Free translation into English: "If I do not respect the case-declension, and do not put together what should go together, I should not be blamed, because I cannot do better. What is in the nominative in Latin, I will make it accusative in French. I know bad French from England, because I never learnt it elsewhere. But you who have learnt it elsewhere, please correct [my grammar], whenever necessary.")

Besides being a diatopically anchored process, the breakdown of the case process proceeds according to lexical, grammatical and pragmatical parameters. **Lexically**, case loss is found earlier in nouns with non-human referents than in nouns with human referents. **Grammatically**, case loss is seen earlier in adjectives than in nouns, earlier in feminine nouns than in masculine nouns, earlier in plural forms than in singular, earlier in nouns than in determiners. Moreover, case is, as stated above, preserved only in personal pronouns in Modern French (MF). The processes of case loss and case preservation therefore conform to the well-known implicational referential hierarchy reproduced below, implying that case is preserved longer in pronouns referring to humans, and with nouns referring to individual humans longer than with nouns referring to non-humans:

Referential hierarchy[17]:
[deix] > [propr] > [pers] > [hum] > [anim] > [discr] > [concr]

Pragmatically, case loss appears to be linked to text types: case loss is earlier in prose than in verse texts, case loss earlier in (fictive) direct discourse than in narrative, as seen, for example, in the OF text *Aucassin & Nicolette*, which combines these four variables. This implies that variation in case, just like variation in other grammatical categories such as tense, aspect, use of pragmatic particles, use of null subjects, etc.,[18] is linked to dialectal, lexical, grammatical, and pragmatic variation.

It has been claimed that case in spoken OF had disappeared relatively early and that what we find in OF texts does not represent actual usage. Instead, it is supposed, (e.g. by Stanovaïa (1993)), that it merely represents the scriptural norms of important cultural centers such as the Monastery of Saint Denis, and that these were elaborated on the basis of Latin norms. For others, the use of the case system was nothing more than an ornament of stylized texts, as proposed by Cerquiglini (1989: 122):

La flexion médiévale, pour autant qu'elle existe, n'a aucune pertinence syntaxique. Elle joue plutôt un rôle rhétorique d'ornementation, marquant un «bon usage» de la langue écrite[19]

---

[17] This is the Silverstein-hierarchy; see Silverstein (1976).

[18] See Schøsler (2006) concerning the relevance of the variational parameters for the use of tense forms, Schøsler (2000), for the use of pragmatic particles, and Schøsler (2002) for the use of personal subject pronouns.

[19] "The medieval inflexion, as far as it exists, has no syntactic relevance. Its function is rather that of rhetorical ornamentation, indicating correctness of the written language" AT

Table 9.7 Forms and functions of the OF two-case system adapted from Völker (2009:55)

	The OF two-case system: forms and functions			
Forms	Accusative forms of nouns		Nominative forms of nouns	
Functions	Used in accordance with the rules	Not used in accordance with the rules	Used in accordance with the rules	Not used in accordance with the rules
Total	5,999 (99.4%)	37 (0.6%)	1,445 (83.8%)	280 (16.2%)
A	1,881 (98.7%)	24 (1.3%)	512 (99.0%)	5 (1.0%)
B	3,490 (99.7%)	11 (0.3%)	882 (99.0%)	9 (1.0%)
C	628 (99.7%)	2 (0.3%)	**51 (16.1%)**	266 (83.9%)

Three types of charters:
A, between partners belonging to the middle class, the clergy, or the gentry
B, between partners belonging to the nobility or higher clergy
C, between partners of which at least one is royal or imperial

Cerquiglini's view coincides entirely with that of Klein (2003: 25), according to whom: "…people do the funniest things to fit in socially…", implying that the mastery of inflectional morphology indicates that the speaker is well-integrated in the speech community.[20]

However, no evidence supports these views, for the following reasons. First, studies on the disintegration of declension clearly demonstrate that gradual loss progresses according to the dialectal, lexical, grammatical and pragmatic parameters mentioned above. This has not only been uncovered in studies performed by the present author, but is now generally accepted.[21] Second, evidence points towards unstable declension being characteristic of the royal chancellery (at least in the thirteenth century) written in the central dialect of Île de France. However, it was respected in other dialects during the same period. Völker (2003, 2009) convincingly demonstrates the importance, not only of the text type, but also of the social position of the partners engaged in written communication. The thirteenth century charters from Luxembourg studied by Völker are written in a north-eastern dialect, which preserves the traditional case forms. In correspondence with the grammar of that dialect, 83.8% of all nouns in the charters take the nominative form as required by the traditional rules of grammar, while the accusative forms are generally used "correctly", in charters between partners using the Luxembourg dialect, whether they belong to the middle class (type A), or to the nobility or higher clergy (type B). However, in the charters addressed to the royal or to the imperial chancellery (type C in my Table 9.7), only 16.1% of the nominative forms are used in accordance with the traditional rules (written in bold letters).

This distribution has the interesting implication that case was not used randomly. On the contrary, declension must have been interpreted by those who wrote in OF

---

[20] Detges (2008) quotes Klein, qualifying his view as "somewhat radical and simplifying".
[21] See e.g., Buridant (2000).

as a distinct marker that had its specific value in diatopic, diastratic and diaphasic terms, as mentioned above.[22] Accordingly, when addressing charters to the royal chancellery, scribes adapted to these standards.

9.5.3 What Was the Function of the Case System?

The preceding Sections and the study of case forms in charters tell us that declension had a number of functions in OF:

- In collaboration with a number of other factors, it contributed to the marking and identification of arguments (Sect. 9.4.3).
- In collaboration with other features, it was a diatopic, diastratic, and diaphasic marker of the text, as demonstrated above (Sect. 9.5.2).

Consequently, and as stated in the introduction, case should not be considered in isolation, but should rather be studied in a way that reveals its interaction with other factors. The preceding sections and further information provided in Sect. 9.5.4 show that a detailed study of synchronic and diachronic variation provide the information needed for a better understanding of how OF functioned.

9.5.4 Why Was Declension Preserved for so Many Centuries and Why Was Declension Lost at That Precise Moment?

Evidence shows that declension rules were no longer entirely respected in western dialects even before the first OF texts, but declension is still partly preserved in writings from the twelfth century. On the other hand, north-eastern dialects preserve declension even after 1300. In Schøsler (1984), I present in detail how the loss of the declension system began in the nominal system, based on the alternation of final $-s$, which tended to disappear at a different pace in the different dialects. In Schøsler (1984), I proposed that an intermediate case system based on the case distinction of articles, which was more complex, seems to have functioned for some time. This case system probably had a vowel difference in nouns due to the compensatory lengthening of the vowel preceding the final $-s$. In Table 9.8, which reproduces the development of the OF paradigm shown in Table 9.1, after the progressive disappearance of final $-s$, this compensatory lengthening is marked as u: or e:. In terms

---

[22] The parameters of variation used here have been shown to be relevant for the study of other languages and other stages of languages; see Völker (2009), Söll (1974), and Koch and Oesterreicher (1985).

Table 9.8 Intermediate OF case paradigm after the disappearance of final −s parasyllabic masculine nouns; pronunciation of the forms

Case	Singular	Plural
Nominative	li mu:r	li mur
Accusative	lə mur	le: mu:r

of morphology, the system outlined in Table 9.8 might have been just as effective as the one presented in Table 9.1.

Thus, simple loss of overt final −s cannot explain the disappearance of the case system. The view that the loss of final −s explains the disappearance of case was, however, generally accepted among scholars until my study on this topic (Schøsler 1984, especially chapter 9). However, the intermediate system presented in Table 9.8 had at least two disadvantages: first, articles were by no means obligatory, implying that the clear morphological oppositions of Table 9.8 between accusative singular and nominative plural, on one hand, and between nominative singular and accusative plural on the other, were not always realized. Second, final −s started weakening before consonants, but was retained before a pause or before a vowel. This implies that the phonetic oppositions of Table 9.8 between the four case forms were not always realized in this way in speech. In other words, there were up to six competing forms for the same function. For the nominative singular, for example: *li murs* [−s] or [−z]/*li mu:r/murs* [−s] or [−z]/*mu:r*, depending on the presence or absence of the article and on the phonetic context (e.g. if adjectives were added), since −s was realized as zero, as [s], or as [z] or as compensatory lengthening of the previous vowel. Thus, the paradigm was indeed less transparent than it appears in Table 9.8, and it violates the principle of one form one function.

In Schøsler (1984), I presented the hypothesis that the OF declension system was preserved – with the functions summarized in Sect. 9.5.3 – as long as it contributed to the identification of the function of arguments. However, due to the increasing loss of transparency of the intermediate OF paradigm in Table 9.8, case no longer functioned as a valid indicator, and the intermediate paradigm was lost. I want to stress the fact that my account of the evolution of the case systems differs from the traditional one in several aspects. First, scholars have not yet discovered the intermediate system that might have continued, if it had not become too complex because of the ongoing phonetic changes. Second, I have highlighted the importance of the increasing presence of determiners, which distinguished number most efficiently when combined with a noun having a clear case form. From the moment that the nominal case form became opaque, the distinction of number was weakened greatly. Third, I have proven that the main function of the case system was not to indicate the function of arguments.

Recall that the OF paradigms presented in Tables 9.1 and 9.8 display the oppositions of case and number based on the alternation of one feature, −s or vowel lengthening. When the markers became less reliable, reorganizations took place in favor of the retention of the morphological distinction of number. This change can be shown to progress in Central French texts during the fourteenth century. In the

9 The Development of the Declension System

Table 9.9 Percentages of "correct" choice of the nominative case in the singular and in the plural

Miracles:	I–X	XI–XX	XXI–XXX	XXXI–XL
	±1340–1350	±1350–1360	±1360–1370	±1370–1380
sg	44,9	42	40,7	37,4
pl	37,7	21,4	12,7	5

Table 9.10 Hybrid paradigm of case/number of masculine nouns

Case	Singular	Plural
Nominative	–s	⎱ –s
Accusative	∅	⎰

Miracles par personnages, composed in Paris every year from 1340 to 1380, case loss calculated as percentages of "correct" choice of the nominative case according to the traditional rules of grammar progresses first in the plural, later in the singular, is seen below in Table 9.9:

Table 9.9 shows that case distinction is partly preserved in the singular, declining from 44.9 to 37.9% of "correct" forms, but is quickly lost in the plural, declining from 37.7 to only 5% of "correct" forms. The result is that around 1370–1380 all plural forms end in –*s*, irrespective of their function, whereas the singular preserves case to a certain degree. Put differently, we here find the hybrid paradigm presented in Table 9.10, and which precedes the MF paradigm without case distinction (Table 9.4):

In principle, the unstable paradigm presented in Table 9.8 could have been simplified in two ways, because either of the two distinctions (case or number) might have disappeared, but as it happened, case was lost. There are at least two observations to be made in this connection. First, morphological marking of number is indeed often retained in Indo-European languages, whereas case is not, and certainly not case at the cost of number. Second, as we have seen above, case was just one of the many ways of identifying argument function, whereas number was only marked morphologically. This suggests that morphological case was only maintained as long as it was not in conflict with another, apparently more important, morphological distinction, the distinction of number. In other words, the unclear nature of the case paradigm was the immediate cause of its simplification. This should not be interpreted as considering phonetics to be the major factor of change; phonetics is here interpreted as a catalytic factor of change. Without the continuous collaboration of the factors referred to in Sect. 9.4.3, which also identify the function of the arguments, the disappearance of the declension system would have had dramatic effects for the correct identification of arguments, which was not the case.

The question why only Gallo-Romance and Swiss Romance dialects preserved case is more difficult to answer. First, it should be observed that this difference between closely related Romance languages clearly supports the view that case in nouns is not absolutely "necessary" for a language to function. Second, it should be noted that the phonetic basis for the morphological case system depended on the preservation of a clear marker, typically the final –s. The final consonant is retained, at least at the outset, in Gallo-Romance and in Swiss Romance.[23] In Italian, final –s disappeared early, so no case marking was available. The languages of the Iberian Peninsula preserved the final –s, but they did not preserve morphological case in nouns. Different reasons for this have been proposed, based mainly on the different grammatical structures of the substratum in the Iberian Peninsula and in Gaul.

9.6 Conclusion

In this paper, I have stressed two main points: first, that the Old French declension system should not be studied in isolation, as it is necessary to take into consideration the role of the case system with respect to other parts of the grammar. Second, I have claimed that the study of synchronic and diachronic variation contributes to a better understanding of the functioning of language and the reasons for change.

With respect to the first point, we have seen in this chapter that grammatical subsystems are organized in such a way that they collaborate. The factors mentioned here, including case, are best comprehended as connected grammaticalized devices for the marking and identification of arguments. Such connected devices exist in all Romance languages, and their relative importance depends on language-specific conditions that should be studied for each language and for each stage of these languages.

As we have seen, the hypothesis concerning changes of grammatical subsystems for marking and identifying arguments and their referents is that these can be described as major shifts in argument marking, or in Andersen's terms (Andersen 2008), as shifts in case-role indexing, since these markers point to specific case-roles.[24] Concerning case-role indexing, the Romance languages preserve, increase, and innovate compared to Latin in the following ways:

1. They preserve the marking and identification of arguments and referents by means of the *lexicon*, but also partially by means of *case*, since it never completely disappeared as argument marker in Romance languages and is still

---

[23] The influence of the germanic super- or ad-stratum has often been proposed to explain the preservation of declension in these dialects

[24] The term *case-role* is used for argument marking and for sub-specification of certain arguments, such as patient, recipient, experiencer, etc.

present in all languages, especially in the pronominal system. A number of grammatical and contextual factors, such as the ones presented in Schøsler (1984) and in Detges (2008), most likely existed from classical Latin;
2. They increase the use of specialized constructions and they increase marking and identification of arguments by grammaticalizing and extending the use of prepositions;
3. They innovate by introducing cross-reference and by introducing word order rules, which have not been discussed here for lack of space.[25]

In sum, my analysis is superior to the traditional one, as well as to recent proposals discussed above, because (1) it takes into account the differences between Romance languages, (2) it is non-ad hoc and yet survives falsification that the traditionalist arguments do not, and (3) it provides a better account of facts.

Returning now to the subject of variation, we have proposed answers to important questions. How should variation be interpreted? Is it a sign of ongoing change or is it "just" variation? During the period in which a new form spread, i.e. the period of actuation, the new and the old systems coexisted. This appears in texts as unclear variation.

In the actual study of old texts, we find clear indications of language change, but we also find variation that we cannot interpret as reflections of changes that have taken place. Indeed, some degree of variation apparently does not lead to a change. One of the difficulties with diachronic linguistics lies in the interpretation of variation, since we are only capable of correctly identifying variations that actually succeed, in the sense that they lead to language change. Looking at synchronic variation, when do we know whether variation should be interpreted as signs of ongoing change? Clearly, our Anglo-Norman nun, translating from Latin into OF (see (2)), was not able to use case in accordance with any system she could identify. She found herself in a chaotic situation, which we are able to analyze because of our knowledge concerning the further development of declension in OF.

I believe that diasystematic variation parameters provide clues for the correct interpretation of variants. I have proposed an interpretation based on diatopic and diastratic variation parameters for cases of variation observed in the preceding sections: the case variation according to the distinctions of prose *vs.* verse texts, (fictive) direct discourse *vs.* narrative, (found, for example, in *Aucassin & Nicolete*), and the case variation observed in the charters from Luxembourg (see Sect. 9.5.2).

Combining two hypotheses, namely that grammar is organized as collaborating devices and that the study of synchronic and diachronic variation reveals ongoing changes of grammar, I hope to have contributed in this chapter to a better understanding of the functioning of language and the reasons for language change.

---

[25] The importance of word order rules has been referred to above; more information can be found in Schøsler (1984). Nørgård-Sørensen et al. (2011) contains an introduction to cross-reference.

Bibliography

Sources

Latin

http://www.thelatinlibrary.com
http://www.fh-augsburg.de
Lewis, Charlton T., and Charles Short. 1879. *A Latin dictionary*. Oxford: Clarendon.

Old and Middle French Electronic Corpora

Lancelot ou le Chevalier de la Charrette Transcriptions (Princeton)
BFM = "Base de Français Médiéval" de l'UMR 8503, composé by Christiane Marquello-Nizia and her research group, http://ccfm.ens-lsh.fr
Le nouveau corpus d'Amsterdam, http://www.uni-stuttgart.de/lingrom/stein/forschung/transcoop/workshop.html
The Middle French electronic corpus ATILF http://www.atilf.fr/atilf/produits/frantext.htm

Old French Manuscripts

Le Charroi de Nîmes, transcription of nine ms. of a 12th century Chanson de geste
A = A1, Paris, Bibliothèque Nationale, f.fr. 774;
E = A2, Paris, Bibliothèque Nationale, f.fr. 1449;
F = A3, Paris, Bibliothèque Nationale, f.fr. 368;
G = A4, Milan, Biblioteca Trivulziana 1025;
H = F (fragment), Paris, Bibliothèque Nationale, nouv. acq.f. 934;
K = B1, London, British Library, Royal 20 D.XI;
L = B2, Paris, Bibliothèque Nationale, f.fr. 24369;
M = C, Boulogne-sur-Mer, Bibl. Municipale 192;
N = D, Paris, Bibliothèque Nationale, f.fr. 1448.

References

Andersen, Henning. 2001. Actualization and the (uni)directionality of change. In *Actualization. Linguistic change in progress*, ed. Henning Andersen, 225–249. Amsterdam and Philadelphia: John Benjamins.
Andersen, Henning. 2008. Grammaticalization in a speaker- oriented theory of change. In *Grammatical change and Linguistictic theory*, ed. Thórhallur Eythórsson, 11–44. Amsterdam: Benjamins.
Blake, Barry J. 1994. *Case*. Cambridge: Cambridge University Press.
Buridant, Claude. 2000. *Grammaire nouvelle de l'ancien français*. Paris: Sedes.
Cerquiglini, B. 1989. *Eloge de la variante. Histoire critique de la philologie*. Paris: Seuil.

Chafe, Wallace. 1994. *Discourse, consciousness, and time*. Chicago/London: The University of Chicago Press.

Chaurand, Jacques. 1999. *Nouvelle histoire de la langue française*. Paris: Seuil.

de Dardel, Robert. 2001. Éléments de rection verbale protoro- mane. *Revue de linguistique romane* 65: 341–368.

Detges, Ulrich. 2008. How useful is case morphology? The loss of the Old French two-case system within a theory of preferred argument structure. In *The role of semantic, pragmatic, and discourse factors in the development of case*, Studies in Language Companion Series, ed. Jóhanna Barðdal and Shobhana Chelliah, 93–120. Amsterdam: Benjamins.

Givón, Talmy. 1995. *Functionalism and grammar*. Amsterdam: John Benjamins.

Herman, József (ed.). 1998. *La transizione dal latino alle lingue romanze*. Tübingen: Niemeyer.

Herman, József. 2000. *Vulgar Latin*. University Park: Pennsylvania State University Press.

Hupka, W. 1982. Zur Funktionalität der altfranzösischen Zwei kasusdeklination. In *Fakten und Theorien: Beiträge zur ro manischen und allgemeinen Sprachwissenschaft*, Tübinger Beiträge zur Linguistik 119, ed. S. Heinz and U. Wandruszka, 95–109. Tübingen: Narr.

Klein, W. 2003. Wozu braucht man eigentlich Flexionsmorphologie? *Zeitschrift für Literaturwissenschaft und Linguistik* 131: 23–54.

Koch, Peter, and Wulf Oesterreicher. 1985. Sprache der Nähe – Sprache der Distanz. Mündlichkeit und Schriftlichkeit im Spannungs feld von Sprachtheorie und Sprachgeschichte. *Romanistisches Jahrbuch* 36: 15–43.

Marchello-Nizia, Christiane. 1999. *Le français en diachronie: douze siècles d'évolution*. Paris: Ophrys.

Meyer-Lübke, Wilhelm. 1894/1972. *Grammatik der Romanische Sprache II: Romanische Formenlehre*. Leipzig: O.R. Reisland; Repr., Darmstadt: Wissenschaftliche Buchgesell schaft.

Nørgård-Sørensen, Jens, Lars Heltoft, and Lene Schøsler. 2011. *Connecting grammaticalisation*. Amsterdam: John Benjamins.

Penny, Ralph. 2002. *A history of the Spanish language*, 2nd ed. Cambridge: CUP.

Pinkster, Harm. 1990. *Latin syntax and semantics*. New York: Routledge.

Pinkster, Harm. 1991. Evidence for SVO in Latin? In *Latin and the romance languages in the early middle ages*, ed. Roger Wright 69–82. London: Routledge.

Schøsler, Lene. 1984. *La déclinaison bicasuelle de l'ancien fran- çais, son rôle dans la syntaxe de la phrase, les causes de sa disparition*. Etudes romanes de l'Université d'Odense, vol. 19. Odense: Odense University Press.

Schøsler, Lene. 2000. The pragmatic functions of the old French particles AINZ, APRES, DONC, LORS, OR, PUIS, and SI. In *Textual parameters in older languages*, ed. With Susan C. Herring, Pieter van Reenen, and Lene Schøsler, 59–105, ISBN: 90-272- 3702-6. Amsterdam: John Benjamins.

Schøsler, Lene. 2001a. The coding of the subject-object distinction from Latin to modern French. In *Grammatical relations in change*, ed. Jan Terje Faarlund, 273–302. Amsterdam/Philadelphia: Benjamins.

Schøsler, Lene. 2001b. From Latin to modern French: Actualization and markedness. In *Actualization. Linguistic change in progress*. Papers from a workshop held at the 14th international conference on historical linguistics. Vancouver, BC, 14 Aug 1999. Current issues in linguistic theory 219, ed. Henning Andersen, 169–185. Amsterdam/Philadelphia: John Benjamins.

Schøsler, Lene. 2002. La variation linguistique: le cas de l'expres-sion du sujet. In *Interpreting the history of French, A Festschrift for Peter Richard on the occasion of his eightieth birthday*, ed. R. Samson and W. Ayres-Bennet, 187–208. Amsterdam/New York: Editions Rodopi B.V.

Schøsler, Lene. 2006. Grammaticalisation et dégrammaticalisation. Etude des constructions progressives en français du type Pierre va/vient/est chantant. In *Sémantique et diachronie du système verbal français*, Cahiers Chronos 16, ed. Emmanuelle Labeau, Carl Vetters, and Patrick Caudal, 91–119. Amsterdam/New York: Rodopi.

Schøsler, Lene. 2008. Argument marking from Latin to modern Romance languages: An illustration of 'combined grammaticalisation processes'. In *Grammatical change and Linguistic theory*, ed. Thórhallur Eythórsson, 411–438. Amsterdam: Benjamins.

Schøsler, Lene, and Michael Skovgaard-Hansen. 2007. Undersøgelse over komplekse nominalsyntagmer i latin. In: *Fra Plautus over klassisk latin, senlatin til humanismen, ALBVM AMICORVM. Festskrift til Karsten Friis-Jensen i anledning af hans 60 års fødselsdag/Studies in Honour of Karsten Friis-Jensen on the Occasion of his Sixtieth Birthday*. Ed. Marianne Pade i samarbejde med/in collaboration with Eric Jacobsen, Hannemarie Ragn Jensen, Lene Waage Petersen, Lene Schøsler, Minna Skafte Jensen, Peter Zeeberg, Lene Østermark-Johansen (39 pages) Renæssanceforum 3 2007 http://www.renaessanceforum.dk/rf_3_2007.htm

Silverstein, Michael. 1976. Hierarchy of features and ergativity. In *Grammatical categories in Australian languages*, ed. R.M.W. Dixon, 112–171. Canberra: Australian Institute of Aboriginal Studies.

Sornicola, Rosanna. 2007. Riflessioni sullo studio del cambia mento morfosintattico dalla prospettiva di un Romanista: sincronia e diacronia rivisitate. *Revue de linguistique Romane* 71: 5–64.

Söll, Ludwig. 1974. *Gesprochenes und geschriebenes Französisch*. Berlin: Schmidt.

Stanovaïa, Lydia A. 1993. Sur la déclinaison bicasuelle en ancien français: point de vue scriptologique. *Travaux de Linguis- tique et de Philologie* XXXI: 163–182.

Völker, Harald. 2003. *Skripta und Variation. Untersuchungen zur Negation und zur Substantivflexion in altfranzösischen Ur- kunden der Grafschaft Luxemburg, 1237–1248*. Tübingen: Niemeyer.

Völker, Harald. 2009. La linguistique variationnelle et l'intralinguistique. *Revue de linguistique Romane*, 73: 27–76.

Chapter 10
The Diasystem and Its Role in Generating Meaning: Diachronic Evidence from Old French

Harald Völker

10.1 Diasystem and Variety

Language variation has been studied by different schools in various ways. Of the schools explicitly dedicated to the study of language variation, structuralism-based variational linguistics and sociolinguistics-based variationist linguistics are the two most important. Despite the differences between these two schools, they share a primary interest in detecting and commenting on the connections between the occurrence of a determined variant, on one hand, and its related extralinguistic (and/or other intralinguistic) context factors, on the other.

Little work has been done on what varying "means", i.e., in how much the fact of being a variant contributes to the genesis of meaning (semiosis).[1] The focus of the present chapter is to discuss the semiosis problem from a variational linguistics perspective. By comparing the changes in the "solidarities"[2] of some Old French lexical variants with other variants, our analysis sheds light on the role of variational information in generating meaning. Looking back to diachrony intensifies the described semiotic effects, and will help us to understand a mechanism which is no less relevant for present day semiosis.

Key theoretical terms are "variety" and "diasystem" – with *variety* meaning 'a bundle (subsystem) of variants co-occurrent with an identical extralinguistic factor,'

---

[1] The semantic importance of diatopic variation has been examined to a major extent only in the framework of perceptual dialectology (see e.g. Anders (2008) as well as Boughton (2005) and (2007)).

[2] "Solidarity" is a word used by Flydal (1952:255) in order to describe the phenomenon of regular co-occurrences of variants forming a subsystem (a *variety*).

H. Völker (✉)
University of Zürich, Romanisches Seminar, Zurich, Switzerland
e-mail: harald.voelker@uzh.ch

and *diasystem* standing for 'the sum of all geographical ('diatopic'), social ('diastratic'), stylistic ('diaphasic') varieties that may, due to little linguistic *Abstand* (distance),[3] be regarded as belonging to one entity'.

10.2 Variational Linguistics: Its Origin and Theoretical Foundations

Major parts of the following arguments are based on concepts and models developed within the framework of structuralism-based variational linguistics. Before beginning the discussion, it is important to emphasize that variational linguistics has evolved as a separate tradition, and must not be confounded with Labovian variationist linguistics. Despite having the same object of interest, i.e., linguistic variation, and at least one common founding father, Uriel Weinreich, the two traditions have developed without major influence on each other.

It is little known that Louis Hjelmslev, despite being a formal linguist, is considered to be the founding grandfather of variational linguistics. In one chapter dedicated to the problem of recognizing and identifying the specific "semiotic system" (=sign system) of glossematically analyzed texts (1953 [1943]), Hjelmslev recognizes the heterogeneity of texts:

> In preparing the analysis we have proceeded on the tacit assumption that the datum is a text composed in one definite semiotic, not in a mixture of two or more semiotics. In other words, in order to establish a simple model situation we have worked with the premise that the given text displays structural homogeneity, that we are justified in encatalyzing one and only one semiotic system to the text. This premise, however, does not hold good in practice. On the contrary, any text that is not of so small extension that it fails to yield a sufficient basis for deducing a system generalizable to other texts, usually contains derivates that rest on different systems. (Hjelmslev 1953:73)

Hjelmslev (1953:73s.) then identifies six levels of distinguishable sign systems ('semiotics'/'semiotic systems', or in less precise terms: 'idioms'): (1) stylistic forms (characterized by various restrictions: verse, prose, various blends of the two); (2) different styles (the creative style, the purely imitative so-called normal style, and the creative and simultaneously imitative archaizing style); (3) different value-styles (higher value-style and the lower so-called vulgar value-style, which is a neutral value-style that is considered neither high nor low); (4) different media (e.g., speech, writing, gesture, flag code); and (5) different tones (e.g., angry, joyful). The last category, (6), includes different idioms, where the following can be distinguished: (a) different vernaculars (the common language of a community, jargons of various cliques or professions), (b) different national languages, (c) different regional languages (e.g. standard language, local dialect), and (d) different physiognomies (as concerns the expression, different "voices" or "organs").

---

[3] See Kloss (1967) and recently Bossong (2008:25–28).

He calls the individual members (variants) of these distinguishable systems connotators:

> The individual members of each of these classes and the units resulting from their combination we will call connotators. Some of these connotators may be solidary with certain systems of semiotic schemata, others with certain systems of semiotic usage, and others with both. (Hjelmslev 1953:74)

Further on, Hjelmslev interprets the relation between connotators and partial systems as a complex sign function:

> Now it seems obvious that the solidarity which exists between certain sign classes and certain connotators is a sign function, since the sign classes are expression for the connotators as content. [...] Not for nothing does the national language stand as a "symbol" for the nation, the local dialect as a "symbol" for the region, etc. Thus it seems appropriate to view the connotators as content for which the denotative semiotics are expression, and to designate this content and this expression as a semiotic, namely a connotative semiotic. (Hjelmslev 1953:76).

On the basis of these observations, it was one of Hjelmslev's pupils, Hans Vogt, who in 1947 sketched out the idea of partial systems in French – one archaic, the other modern – by identifying salient co-stylistical occurrences in the usage of the phonetic variants *[le]* vs. *[lɛ]* for the definite article plural and the morphological ones *que je prenne* 'that I take (present subjunctive) vs. *que je prisse* 'that I took (imperfect subjunctive) (*[lɛ]* and *que je prisse* representing an archaic style).

The first generally quoted[4] founding father of variational linguistics is Leiv Flydal. He takes as a starting point Vogt's case study on French, and identified "regular structural coexistences" (id. 1952:255) within natural languages. These include substructures that differ substantially from "normal" language and that show solidarity effects with extralinguistic factors, the temporal (diachronic) axis (in the case of anachronisms), the spatial (diatopic) axis, and the social (diastratic) axis (Flydal 1952:241–255). In order to describe the construction formed by all of these regular sub-structures within a language, he forged the notion of "architecture" (ib. 245).

Weinreich (1954:389) introduced the notions of "variety" and "diasystem". Within the variational tradition, both notions had more success than Flydal's "regular structural coexistences" (−> variety) and "architecture" (−> diasystem). In order to understand the background of Weinreich's theoretical framework, it is important to know that its purpose was to reconcile dialectology and structuralism and to construe a theoretical bridge between them (see Weinreich 1954:388).

Coseiru (1966) took a decisive step forward in creating a single linguistic tradition. He resumed, unified, modified, and especially promoted, the terminological instruments first proposed by Flydal and Weinreich, by confirming the terms of *diasystem*, *diatopic*, and *diastratic*. However, he rejected the notion of *diachronic* axis, and introduced a new one, which he called *diaphasic*, and whose subcategories consist of various stylistic levels.

---

[4] See, for example, Gleßgen (2007:102).

Unlike the majority of sociolinguistic work, the variational framework has never left behind its structuralist roots. It is true that variational linguistics, like linguistic pragmatics and sociolinguistics, is based on the role of extralinguistic structures. But while most of the work in sociolinguistics and pragmatics seeks, first of all, to analyze correlations with social contexts and the link with the communicative objectives pursued by the speaker, variational linguistics interprets variation as a part of a linguistic (sub)system. Its main concern is the analysis and interpretation of solidarity effects among variants, as well as the definition of groups to which these solidarity effects contribute. It is thus not at all surprising that Flydal's (1952) (see esp. 255) paper is based on Saussure's *Cours de linguistique general* (^{5}1960=CLG).

As we have seen in this section, Hjelmslev (1953 [1943]), Vogt (1947), Flydal (1952), Weinreich (1954) and Coseriu (1966) have established the theoretical framework of variational linguistics. It is most likely due to their disciplinary backgrounds in Romance Studies that the variational framework has been mainly applied to the study of Romance languages, and that most of the subsequent theoretical work has been done in relation to Romance linguistics and/or Romance languages.[5]

10.3 Are Old French Lexical Units More Malleable Than Modern French Ones?

The starting point of the following discussion on diasystem and semiosis is an issue that has been the focus of lexicographical research for 50 years (Imbs 1961; Christmann 1986; Möhren 1997). The question is to what extent Old French lexical units have meaning on their own and to what extent they import meaning from context (the surrounding world) and cotext (the surrounding text). For those about to write a dictionary, this question is crucial because it determines where the line can be drawn between the "stable" semantic content of a lexical unit, and what may be omitted as cotext- and context-induced. Imbs (1961), following Saussure's (^{5}1960) distinction between *langue* vs. *parole*, interprets semiosis as a volatile interplay between the contribution of the lexical unit (on the *langue* level) and its contribution to co- and context (*parole* level). His hypothesis is that Old French words generate a more important part of their meaning from their use than do their Modern French counterparts (see Imbs 1961:138). In order to illustrate this effect, Imbs gives the example of OF *foi* 'fidelity, confidence, loyalty, as well as faith, belief etc.' which, apart from its semantic nucleus, takes on a very different meaning depending on context and cotext (see Imbs 1961:138s).

In a theory orientated paper, Christmann (1986:21) confirmed this observation but expressed some doubt about Imbs' interpretation on the *parole*-level. Instead, he brought into play a third level that he called "not a generally recognized *langue*, but

---

[5] See Völker (2009:28–38) for more information on the more recent development of variational linguistics in Romance Linguistics.

a *langue* belonging to a specific poetical tradition". Without referring explicitly to variational linguistics, Christmann describes an intermediate entity between *langue* and *parole* which is in accordance with Vogt's partial systems.

In contrast to Imbs and Christmann, Möhren (1997:133) denied any fundamental difference between Old French and Modern French words. Möhren argues that the supposed semantic stability of contemporary French words is rather the result of a classical observer's problem, for neither present-day readers of old texts nor modern lexicographers possess the entire cultural knowledge behind the Old French diasystem and its discourse traditions. No one living today has any direct access to concrete, medieval *parole* contexts. The less we are able to compensate for this by recontextualizing their studied texts and reconstructing the relevant Old French diasystem, the greater the malleability of Old French words appears to be.

In reality, the malleability of contemporary French words is no less important, but contemporary speakers and communicators of French seem unaware of the semiosis mechanisms that allow them to arrive at a word's meaning by exploiting both context and cotext, as well as their knowledge of diasystem and discourse traditions. The diachronic filter, either due to real language development or an observation effect, does not allow any type of semantic information to pass in the same way – rendering lexical units from past époques a laboratory for semiosis mechanisms. For in a more theoretical perspective, this observation on semantic malleability vs. stability suggests that the *signifié*-side of the linguistic sign should not be regarded as a homogeneous block, but rather that it might embrace different levels which react to "chronological corrosion" in different ways.

10.4 Multi-level Semiotic Models for the Linguistic Sign

A semantic multi-level model of the linguistic sign can be helpful in specifying the effects of differentiated corrosion in meaning. Tying in with Coseriu's, Gauger's, Heger's and Hilty's reflections on structuralist semantics and semiotic modelling, Raible, Blank and Lebsanft/Gleßgen have developed multi-level models for lexical semiosis operated by a linguistic sign.[6]

Each of these semantic multi-level sign models is fundamentally based on Saussure's distinction between *signifiant* and *signifié* (Saussure [5]1960:99) and is meant to refine it (see Gleßgen 2007:236). Raible (1983:4–7) identifies five levels (illustration see Table 10.1):

1. "nomen": the physical appearance of the sign (phonetic or graphetic)
2. "signans": the phonological or graphematic aspects of the sign

---

[6] See Raible (1983), Blank (1997:96–102), Blank (2001:7–10), Lebsanft and Gleßgen (2004) (with an abstract of the discussion up to then), and Gleßgen (2007:236–242) (with graphical illustrations of the various semiotic models).

Table 10.1 Raible's semiotic pentagon (comment see above – illustration based on Raible 1983:5)

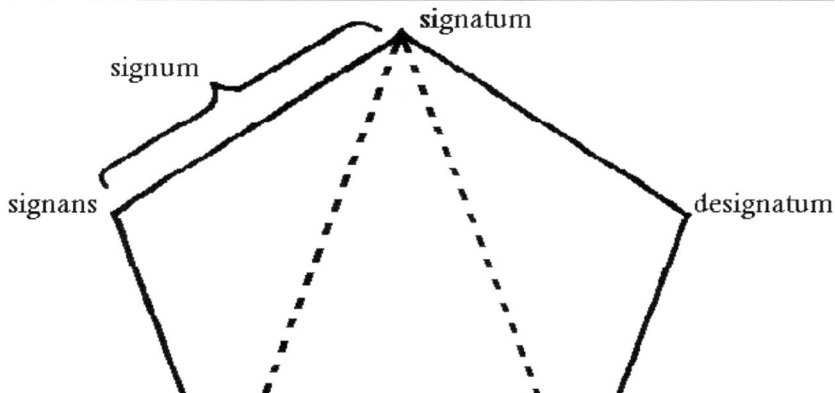

3. "signatum": the lexical meaning in a particular language
4. "designatum": the cognitive category behind the lexical meaning (universal or tied to culture, but not tied to a specific language)[7]
5. "nominandum": the actual referent to which the sign refers

Among these five levels, Raible distinguishes not only a linguistic domain (constituted by 2 and 3, and thus by Saussure's linguistic sign 'signum') from an extralinguistic domain (constituted by 1, 4 and 5), but also an "actual" domain (present here and now, formed by 1 and 5) from a "virtual" one. The latter is formed by entities 2, 3, and 4, represented in the brain and transcending the here and now, which we would currently refer to as a "cognitive" domain. The triangle made with broken lines represents the classical triangle models (see Raible 1983:2 and 6, as well as Ogden and Richards 1923:18) (Table 10.1).

The most recent model was developed by Lebsanft and Gleßgen (see Lebsanft and Gleßgen 2004:14–17) and is graphically presented in Gleßgen (2007:239–242). Although it is called – together with Blank 2001:9 – "carré sémiotique" ('semiotic square'), it also embraces five levels because the second ("langue"-) element is constituted by the sign (signum), in other words, by *signifiant* as well as *signifié*. Its main merit is that it attributes physical places to the five levels.

The advantage of these multi-level models for diachronic studies in semantic change is that they allow us to examine, by means of relevant examples, what happens to the whole sign if a modification initially occurs on only one of these levels. This, in turn, makes it possible to distinguish and to describe different mechanisms

---

[7] "Dingvorstellung" in Freudian terms (see Gauger 1983 and Raible 1983:2–4).

of lexical change and thereby learn more on how semiosis changes if a speaker, researcher, or diachronic corrosion modifies a specific element. Diachrony viewed in this way appears to be a hidden laboratory which contains encrypted reports on experiments that have already been undertaken by millions of invisible hands and are waiting to be interpreted.

In the present paper, our particular interest will be the diachronic evolution of the third level information, especially the first of its component parts. Together with Blank (2001:133–140), these component parts can be detailed as follows:

1. External conception: Information on which variety/ies of the diasystem the sign belongs to.
2. Internal concept: Morphological and syntactical information contained by the sign; information on the lexical relation to other signs.
3. Syntagmatical relations: information on lexicalized phrases and frequent collocations.

10.5 Application of the Multi-level Model to Lexical Change

In this section, we will present a cross-diachronic look at the distribution of semantic elements at the sememe level and at the diasystematic level by means of four examples. The examples given under "attestations in the corpus" are taken from a corpus of Old French charters linked to the county of Luxemburg (Holtus et al. 2003) and have tentatively been discussed in Völker 2004. We will identify the contribution of the sememe-component and the diasystematic one, and will add a comment on that by other component. We will then repeat this operation for the same lexeme in present-day French and compare the results. To facilitate understanding, we present the results in table form. The first column counts the variants discussed here,[8] the second tells us whether and how the variant is diasystematically marked, the third summarizes the sememe information, and the fourth summarizes specific information elements delivered by the marked variant ("diasystematic information"). Finally, the fifth column gives us the opportunity to add remarks of any kind, especially on the role of further information levels. These tables do not represent the whole semantic complexity of the discussed lexemes, but are insead meant to highlight and compare the aspects of interest.

10.5.1 meuble *adj. mobile, movable (minuscule)?*

Etymology: lat. MŌBILIS 'mobile, movable' > mlat. MŌBĪLIS (FEW 6/3:4)

Attestations in the corpus: e.g. *Et ai obligiet et oblige a tenir toutes ces couena(n) ces moi et mes hoirs <u>et to(us) mes bie(n)s meubles</u> et iretages* (1264, wIII465, line

---

[8] As we do not discuss every existing variant here, these lists naturally are not complete.

37: 'and all my goods movable' = 'and all my movables')[9]; *et de ceu a tenír (et) acomplír oblige íe moí (et) mes hoírs · mes biens (et) les biens a mes hoírs meubles (et) No(n)meubles p(re)sens (et) auenír* (1277, wIV425, line 5s.: 'my goods and the goods to my heirs movable and immovable' = 'the movables and the immovables of myself and my heirs)

OF Lexicography: The attestations given under *meuble* 'mobile, mouvant, qui peut changer de place' ('mobile, movable, what may change place'; Gdf 5:318c and Gdf 10 complém.:150c) and *meuble/mueble* 'beweglich' ('movable'; TL 6:400), do not exclusively refer to palpable objects (see for example "Et Ysengrin au cervel moble", 'and Ysengrin with his flexible brain'; TL 6:400) and thus illustrate, besides its diatechnically marked use in legal language (see "nos biens et les biens de nos hoirs, moebles et nonmoebles, presens et a venir", 'our movables and our immovables, those of us as well as those of our heirs, in present and in future'; TL 6:400), the diasystematically unmarked use of meuble adj. in OF.

Further lexicographical comments: FEW (6/3:4) comments on the influence of Latin legal language ("Die juristischen lt. ausdrücke *mobiles res, (bona) mobilia* für 'bewegliche habe' wurden durch das jurist. mlt. verbreitet", 'The juridical Latin expressions mobiles res,), which may help explain the survival of *meuble* adj. in modern juridical French.'

Variant	Diasystematic marking	Sememe	Diasystematic information	Remarks
Multi-level modelling of Old French *meuble* adj.				
(1)	None	Mobile, movable	None	
(2)	Diatechnical: juridical language	Mobile, movable	None	Influenced by juridical Latin: frequent collocation with juridical formulations on the goods pledged by the parties
Multi-level modelling of Modern French *meuble* adj.				
(1)	None	Extinct	Extinct	Replaced by *mobile, portable* etc.
(2)	Diatechnical: juridical language	Mobile, movable	Exclusively referring to the juridical distinction between movable and non-movable things	Frequent collocation with *choses* and *biens*

---

[9] The semantically relevant words of the quotations are underlined. In brackets we add the year of the charter, the identification code of the charter (following Holtus et al. 2003, 45–99 and 259–467), the line (in the charter), a gloss of the semantically relevant words, and a translation (if different from the gloss).

The above tables illustrate that the loss of standard variety *meuble* adj.. Its replacement by *mobile, portable* etc.[10] is certainly a function of the elliptical emergence of *meuble* n., favored by its frequent co-occurrence in the charters with concrete objects that belong to a household. In OF, *meuble(s)* n. 'biens meubles' ('movables'; Gdf V:318) cease to be used. Major changes in lifestyle may have triggered the evolution of *meubles* n. 'movable things/belongings' to *meubles* n. 'furniture'.[11] Although co-occurrence with *biens* et *choses* is even more frequent in juridical French, the latter is characterized by phraseological conservatism and the necessity of producing unambiguous meaning. It further promotes elliptical constructions to a lesser extent. Another contributing factor is certainly the above-mentioned influence of expressions like *mobiles res* and *bora mobilia* in Latin juridical language. The result is that within the juridical language, *meuble* adj. still exists alongside *meuble* n., whereas *meuble* n. has become the only survivor in the standard variety.

Since *meuble* adj. in present day French only exists in one variety[12] (diatechnical: juridical language) it not only takes semantic elements from juridical language, but also actively represents this variety. This means that *meuble* adj. produces the semantic element "legal language/juridical context" by itself even when out of context.

10.5.2   arche *n.f. minuscules?*

Etymology: lat. ARCA 'coffer' (FEW 25/1:92–94)

Attestations: *Je Henris Cuens de lucenborc et de la Roche et marchis de Erlo(n) s Faz sauoir a touz que je doi aquiteir THiebaut conte de bar Enuers Esteueni(n) fauquenel · Citain de mes de q(ua)tre cens l(ivres) de mec(eins) dont <u>li Escriz gist en larche</u>* (1248, wIII025, line 1ss.: 'the document lies in the coffer'); *(et) est a sauoir q(ue) de chascun paiement q(ue) n(ous) ferons on en doit <u>mettre lescrit en larche a mes</u> tant q(ue) n(ous) auerons faiz tous Les diz paimens* (1265, wIII509, line 20s.: 'put the document in the coffer at Metz'). Both attestations geographically refer to Metz in Eastern France.

---

[10] See FEW 6/3:4: "Im fr. übernahm *mobile* zum teil die bedeutungen des af-. *meuble*", 'In present day French *mobile* partially took over the signifié of OF *meuble*'.

[11] See FEW 6/3:4: "Die veränderungen und einschränkungen in der bedeutung von *meuble* 'ganze bewegliche habe' zu 'möbelstück' sind wohl in der zunehmenden stabilisierung der lebens- und reisegewohnheiten begründet" 'The semantic modification and limitation from *meuble* 'movables' to 'furniture' is probably owed to more stable living- and traveling-habits'.

[12] If we leave aside the very particular collocation of *terre meuble* 'terre qui est douce et qui se divise bien d'elle-même' ('soil easy to plough' see Littré 3:548).

OF Lexicography: 'coffer, box' as well as several other specific meanings like 'safe', 'ark' (bibl./rel.) (TL 1:502s., Gdf 1:380 and Gdf 8 complém.:169).

Variant	Diasystematic marking	Sememe	Diasystematic information	Remarks
Multi-level modelling of Old French *arche* n.f.				
(1)	None	Coffer/box, where things can be stored or saved	None	Unspecific; specification by context or frame[13]
(2)	Diatechnical: juridical language	Coffer/box, where things can be stored or saved	Purpose: for storing charters and juridical documents	See corpus attestations. Semantic specification comes from a frame (that is typical for the variety)
(3)	Several other varieties	Coffer/box, where things can be stored or saved	e.g. coffer for the storage of flour, grain etc. (see FEW 25/1:92)	Semantic specification comes from a frame or collocation typical for a variety
Multi-level modelling of Modern French *arche* n.f.				
(1)	None	Extinct[14]	Extinct	
(2)	Diatechnical: juridical language	Coffer/box, where things can be stored or saved	"things"=juridical documents	Fading away or referring to a bygone juridical reality (see TLF 3:420)
(3)	Several: *argot*, religious etc.	Place where things can be stored or saved	Specification in use	In collocations like *aller à l'arche* 'steal, take money' (argot), *arche d'alliance* 'ark of the Covenant' (religious)[15]

In Modern French, *arche* alone is unambiguous enough to specify the purpose of the 'coffer, box', whereas in OF, it could further refer to containers with other purposes.[16] From today's perspective, it is difficult to decide where the specification comes from – from the frame or from the variety. With the diatechnical variety as well as its linguistic realization as being directly linked to the frame (negotiating and writing down a charter), it is virtually impossible to distinguish the contribution of frame from the contribution of diasystem in this case. A solution would be to assume a link between frame and variety, with specific frames being typical for certain varieties.

Another problem is just as interesting: if we could examine the concept-level ("designatum" in Raible's pentagon) of an OF speaker, would it be possible to find

---

[13] "Frame" in the sense of "a data structure for representing a stereotyped situation" (Minsky 1975:212).
[14] See TLF 3:419–421.
[15] See TLF 3:419–421.
[16] See FEW 25/1:92–94.

an abstract entry for *arche*: a sort of "archi-arche" free from any indication about its use, like, for example, in the case of Modern French *récipient* 'container'? Or, is "arche" one of the cases discussed by Imbs, Christmann, and Möhren (see above) where there was never any doubt for a contemporary OF speaker about its specific use? The two quotations at the beginning of this section suggest the latter; otherwise the use of the word alone (as in the first quotation) would be problematic. We can test it by replacing the word with the Modern French *récipient* – which would not be possible in combination with a definite article.

10.5.3 court *n.f.* 'court (cour de justice)'

Etymology: lat. COHORS, COHORTEM > mlat. CORTIS, CURTIS 'courtyard' (FEW 2/1:849–853 and Du Cange 2:585–589)

Attestations: *Et ai renoncie et renonce a toutes autres barres et a <u>tous apeaus de court de crestíjente et de court mondaíne</u>* (1264, wIII468, line 19s.: 'all support by ecclesiastical and by mundane jurisdiction' = 'any support by ecclesiastical and mundane jurisdiction'); *Et promet par foi et par sairement et seur paine de Soissante Mile li(vres) de par(esis) ke ie a nul iour droit ne escheance ne reclamerai <u>en court de crestíjente ne en court seculere</u> ne en autre líu* (1265, wIII524, line 9s.: 'in court of church nor in court mundane' = 'nor in ecclesiastical nor in mundane court'); *(et) por ces choses plus f(er)mem(en)t atenir je man suíz mís desouz <u>La Jurisdition de la Court de T(ri)eures</u> · de mez · de liege (et) de Toul · quil puíssent metre esco(m) íniem(en)t en ma p(er)sone* (1269, wIV111, line 12s.: 'the jurisdiction of the court of Trier' = 'the jurisdiction by the ecclesiatical court at Trier')

OF Lexicography: General meaning 'ferme, exploitation agricole' ('farm'; Gdf 2:318),/'domaine du prince; résidence du souverain et de son entourage; assemblée qui se tenait dans la demeure du souverain; siège de justice où l'on plaide' ('residence of the feudal lord and his entourage; assembly convened in this residence; juridical court'; Gdf 9 complém.:227) as well as several specific meanings in other contexts and varieties (see TL 2:913–915, FEW 2/1:849–851). They all are already attested in middle Latin (DHLF 1:923 and Du Cange 2:585–589).

Variant	Diasystematic marking	Sememe	Diasystematic information	Remarks
Multi-level modelling of Old French *court* n.f.				
(1)	None	Agricultural domain	None	
(2)	None	Place and collaborators of a central, powerful institution	None	
(3)	Diatechnical: juridical language	Place and collaborators of a central, powerful institution	.. of a juridical institution	Frequent collocations like *cour mondaine* or *cour de chrétienté* (see quotations above)

(continued)

(continued)

Variant	Diasystematic marking	Sememe	Diasystematic information	Remarks
Multi-level modelling of Modern French *cour* n.f.				
(1)	Diachronic or diatopic	Agricultural domain	None	See GL 2:1023: "Old and dialectal"
(2)	None	Open place surrounded by walls, hedges, or buildings	None	See TLF 6:331.
(3)	None	Place and collaborators of a central, powerful institution	None	See TLF 6:332–333.
(4)	Diatechnical: juridical language	Place and collaborators of a central, powerful institution	... of a juridical institution	See TLF 6:333–334.

The attestation *en court de crestíjente ne en court seculere* is an example for the sub-level that Blank (2001:133) calls "syntagmatic relation" – the cotext permits the omission of "de justice" – whereas *La Jurisdition de la Court de T(ri)eures* illustrates disambiguation through context. Trier was one of the most important cathedral cities in the old Lotharingian region. These two mechanisms are not mutually exclusive. As in the case of *arche*, the question is, whether in OF we can assume a common abstract concept or whether the concept was always specified by a frame or by its syntagmatical cotext? With the semantic differences within the broad *signifié* of *court* being considerable, a synchronically present common concept of *court* is hard to imagine – both nowadays and in the Middle Ages.

10.5.4 bannal *adj. 'belonging (minuscule)? to the Lord'*

Etymology: Old Low Frankish BAN 'order under threat of punishment' > afrz. *ban* n.m. 'land subjected to the jurisdiction of la seignior' (FEW 15/1:47–53, esp. 51s.)

Attestation: *li bouríois de tyonuill doíent Cuire au four bannal* (1239, wII353, line 16: 'the inhabitants of Thionville have to bake in the common oven')

OF Lexicography: 'appartenant à un ban, à une circonscription féodale' ('belonging to a feudal circumscription'; FEW 15/1:51); 'sujet à la banalité' ('subjected to feudal jurisdiction'; Gdf 1:566); 'appartenant à un ban, à une circonscription seigneuriale; qui est commun à tous les habitants d'un village' ('belonging to a feudal circumscription; what is common to all the inhabitants of a village'; Gdf 8 complém.:282)

Variant	Diasystematic marking	Sememe	Diasystematic information	Remarks
Multi-level modelling of Old French *ban(n)al* adj.				
Only one	None	Belonging to the lord	None	
Multi-level modelling of Modern French *banal* adj.				
(1)	None	Commonplace, uninteresting[17]	None	
(2)	Local dialect and juridical language	Belonging to the local authority[18]	Free for use by all[19]	Fading away
(3)	Diachronic	Belonging to a feudal authority	… to the lord (describing a bygone social order)	Referring to a past reality

In present day French, 'commonplace, uninteresting' is certainly the main, if not the only, meaning of *banal*. In order to explain the great semantic shift from the original seigniorial term to 'commonplace, uninteresting', it might be useful to consider a probable intermediate phase, when feudalism stepped aside to make place for a new (early capitalist) social order that allowed private property. In this phase, the origin of the new meaning is produced by a diastratic differentiation that can be illustrated as follows:

Variant	Diasystematic marking	Sememe	Diasystematic information	Remarks
Intermediate phase *banal* adj.				
(1)	Diastratic: owners of private property	Belonging to the lord/municipality	… and used by all those who don't own	
(2)	Diastratic: non-owners of private property	Belonging to the lord/municipality	… and free for use by all	

Including the reinforcement from 'used by those who don't own' to 'typical for those who don't own,'[20] and finally to 'typical for those who are unschooled,' the

---

[17] See Robert 1:1193.

[18] See DHLF 1:312: "Après la disparition du régime féodal, le mot s'est maintenu comme synonyme pour «communal»" 'After the end of feudality, the word was maintained as a synonym for municipal'.

[19] See TLF 4:111: "Jusqu'au XIXe s., vx, droit admin. des communes [En parlant du bien commun dont les habitants du village ont la libre jouissance] Chasse, forêt, pâture banale; four, moulin, puits banal. Synon. mod. communal"-'Until the 19th century, old, local law [describes the common goods that the inhabitants of a village may use freely] *banal* hunting, wood, pastureland; *banal* .oven, mill, well. Mod. syn. *communal*'.

[20] This evolution might have been spurred on by the fact that OF *banal* could refer to things as well as to persons (see TLF 4:112).

development of *banal* illustrates the dislocation of an information element from one sublevel to another : from the diasystematic sub-level to the sememe-sublevel. This change is originally triggered by a socially differentiated perspective of the same sememe and later by the integration of this perspective in the diasystematic information level.

On the other hand, this example illustrates to what extent semantic development may be based on the loss of an initial standard variant, which later becomes a diastratically lower variant. In this way, a diastratically higher innovation may meet with success and pass into the standard variety, even if the quantitative weight of the social group behind the diastratically high variant is relatively unimportant.

10.6 Conclusion

Focusing on the contribution of diasystematic information to semiosis, the present chapter combines a semiotic multi-level model with diachronic lexical evolution. Before summarizing relevant aspects, we noted that it was important to distinguish diasystematic marking from diasystematic information. As we have seen, the supplementary semantic elements delivered by the affiliation with a specific variety are able to transcend the mere properties of the extralinguistic entities linked to this variety. This distinction (or specification), while yet to be integrated into semiotic modeling, seems relevant for the study of the impact of varieties.

In our analysis, we have described different mechanisms of contributing to semiosis and mechanisms of dislocation among the different semiotic levels, to wit:

1. One of the observed effects of semiosis is that semantic elements may be shifted from one level to another and thus produce lexical change. In the case of *banal*, a decisive semantic element moves from the diasystematic (diastratic) sub-level to the sememe-level. After the end of the Middle Ages, the social distinction which led to the current meaning of 'banal' was only included in *banal* when it belonged to a diastratically "high" variety, whereas *banal* used by the majority of the people did not refer to a social distinction. Today, this social distinction, originally included on the diasystematic sub-level of the designatum, forms the sememe, and is part of the *signatum*.
2. Further, the example of *banal* shows, on the other hand, that the diasystematic information is shaped by its extralinguistic anchoring. If the information about the social distinction moves from the diasystematic sub-level to the sememe-level, it illustrates how linguistic change may be directly linked to extralinguistic development.
3. The study of *La Jurisdition de la Court de T(ri)eures · de mez · de liege (et) de Toul* illustrates the role that cotext plays in disambiguation. This kind of disambiguation was not described as part of the presented semiotic models here. Yet if we understand semiosis to be a concrete *parole*-process *in actu* we should find a way to integrate all of the factors that lead to the concept of semiosis, including cotext effects, into a theory of semiosis,.

Table 10.2 Sign class and connotator in a Hjelmslevian perspective

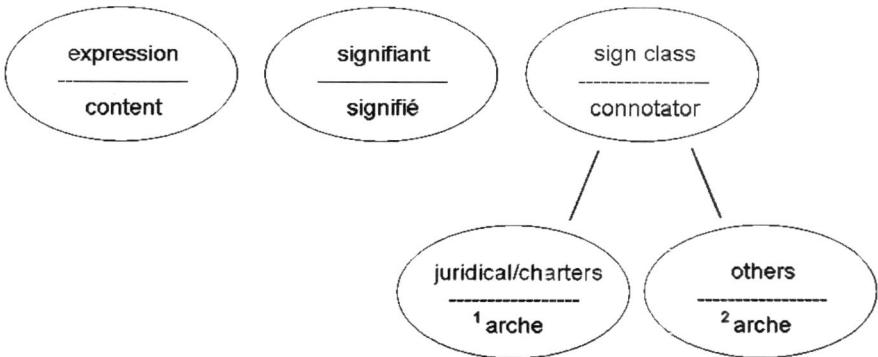

4. We also noted that it is not always easy to distinguish the contribution of *frame* from the contribution of diasystem (see *arche*). But perhaps the problem is not irresolvable. For, after all, aren't frames often typical of specific varieties? But one theoretical problem remains: whereas, in Gleßgen's semiotic square, the diasystem is located in the signifié-part of the sign, a frame, by definition, is independent from a specific language (see Blank 2001:54). If the line between diasystem and frame is, indeed, difficult to draw, what consequences will this have for semiotic sign modelling?
5. Our last observation is concerned with the production of diasystematic marking. Hjelmslev (1953:76; quoted above in Sect. 10.1) writes that the solidarity between certain sign classes and certain connotators is a *sign function*, with the sign classes being an *expression* for the connotators and the connotators being the *content*. In saying this, he suggests that the individual element (the variant) takes its diasystematic information from the diasystematic marking of the sign class. This is certainly one possibility, represented in our paper by *cour* and *arche*, and, to a certain extent, by *banal*. They can all only be well interpreted if one knows in which diasystematic context they come to use. This case is characterized by the fact that an identical *signifiant* exists in more than one variety, and that its semantic differences only become accessible if the reader/hearer is familiar with the variety of the text/discourse. Graphically, this can be represented as follows (Table 10.2):
6 But the opposite case also exists. A lexeme can also be merely part of one and only one variety – here represented by *meuble* adj. (juridical language). In this case, we can say that the lexeme does not import, but rather exports, its diasystematic marking. Inverting Hjelmslev's idea, we could describe it with a phrase like "the connotator is *expression* for the sign class *content*" (Table 10.3).

The question behind these observations is how diasystematic marking is produced. The answer is certainly more complex than indicated here and would go beyond the scope of the present chapter. But it seems that diasystematic marking can be arrived at through different means, i.e.. that it need not be imported from extralinguistical context, but can instead also be induced intralinguistically

Table 10.3 Sign class and connotator in an inverse Hjelmslevian perspective

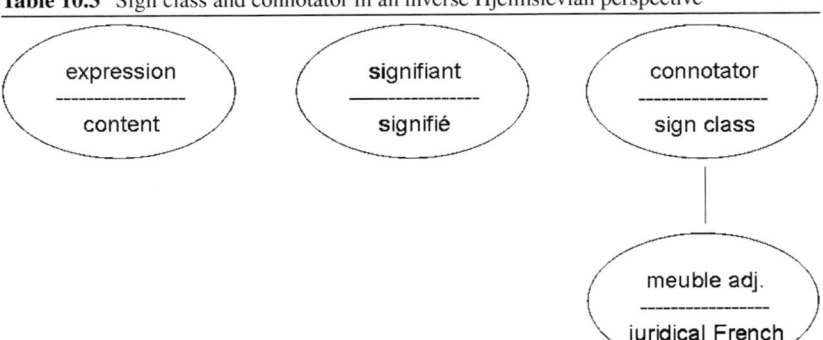

by a *signifié*. If this is correct, the concepts of diasystem and variety could explain the crucial link between the extralinguistic and the (intra-)linguistic universes.

The contribution of Old French to this question of general (diachronic as well as synchronic) concern lies in the diachronicity effects evoked in Sect. 10.2. All of the information that today's speaker contributes, implicitly and unconsciously, to semiosis, must be thoroughly reconstructed by the philologist and the lexicographer when they study Old French lexical units. As we have seen, if we reconsider this "obstacle" by reviewing previous work by philologists and by integrating the structuring potential of variational linguistics, this will allow us to shape the process of semiosis and its relevant factors more precisely, because it forces us to write down explicitly, in a structured way, what our competence in a mother tongue delivers to us automatically. And finally, an improved understanding of how semiosis functions might enable us to refine the theoretical base of the mental lexicon[21] and perhaps even its interaction with grammar.[22]

References

Anders, Christina Ada. 2008. Mental Maps linguistischer Laien zum Obersächsischen. In *Sprechen, Schreiben, Hören. Zur Produktion von Dialekt und Standardsprache zu Beginn des 21. Jahrhunderts*, ed. H. Christen and E. Ziegler, 201–227. Wien: Praesens.

Blank, Andreas. 1997. *Prinzipien des lexikalischen Bedeutungswandels am Beispiel der romanischen*. Tübingen: Niemeyer.

---

[21] See Mensching (2005:27) who, from a minimalist point of view, recently called for more work on the mental lexicon ("En este punto, se podría decir de nuevo que la gramática generativa pudiera querer ignorar todo lo demás, es decir la pregunta de por qué el hablante escoge una vez una variante léxica y otra vez otra. Pero el hecho es que el minimalismo se basa en una parte fundamental en el lexicón, de forma que necesita una teoría elaborada sobre el léxico mental").

[22] I would like to thank Barbara De Angelis, Gabriele Hess, Heike Martens, Charlotte Meisner, and Angela Whale, as well as the editor of this volume and the anonymous reviewers for reading and discussing earlier versions of this paper, and for perspicacious and helpful comments.

Blank, Andreas. 2001. *Einführung in die lexikalische Semantik für Romanisten*. Tübingen: Niemeyer.
Bossong, Georg. 2008. *Die romanischen Sprachen. Eine vergleichende Einführung*. Hamburg: Buske.
Boughton, Zoë. 2005. Accent levelling and accent localisation in northern French. Comparing Nancy and Rennes. *Journal of French Language Studies* 15: 235–256.
Boughton, Zoë. 2007. Ce que prononcer veut dire. The social value of variable phonology in French. *Nottingham French Studies* 46: 7–22.
Christmann, Hans Helmut. 1986. Sprachwissenschaft im Dienst der Mediävistik – Sprachwissenschaft als Mediävistik. In *Zusammenhänge, Einflüsse, Wirkungen. Kongreßakten zum ersten Symposium des Mediävistenverbandes in Tübingen 1984*, ed. J.O. Fichte, K.H. Göller, and B. Schimmelpfennig, 1–26. Berlin: de Gruyter.
CLG = see Saussure. (5th edition) 1960.
Coseriu, Eugenio. 1966. Structure lexicale et enseignement du vocabulaire. In *Actes du premier colloque international de linguistique appliquée. Organisée par la Faculté des Lettres et des Sciences humaines de l'Université de Nancy (26–31 octobre 1964)*, 175–217. Nancy: Mémoires des Annales de l'Est.
DHLF = Rey, Alain. 1998. *Dictionnaire historique de la langue française*. Paris: Robert.
Du Cange, Charles du Fresne. 1883–1887. *Glossarium mediae et infimae letinitatis*. Niort: Favre.
Ernst, Gerhard, Martin-Dietrich Gleßgen, Christian Schmitt, and Wolfgang Schweickard (eds.). 2003–2009. *Romanische Sprachgeschichte. Ein internationales Handbuch zur Geschichte der romanischen Sprachen/Histoire linguistique de la Romania. Manuel international d'histoire linguistique de la Romania*, vol. 3. Berlin/New York: de Gruyter.
Flydal, Leiv. 1952. Remarques sur certains rapports entre le style et l'état de langue. *Norsk Tidsskrift for Sprogvidenskap* 16: 241–258.
Gauger, Hans-Martin. 1983. Bedeutung und Bezeichnung. In Stimm, Helmut, and Wolfgang Raible (eds.). Zur Semantik des Französischen. Wiesbaden:Steiner 25–29.
Gdf = Godefroy, Frédéric. 1881–1902. *Dictionnaire de l'ancienne langue française et de tous ses dialectes du IXe au XVe siècle*. Paris: Vieweg/Bouillon. Repr., Nendeln, Kraus, 1969.
GL = *Grand Larousse de la langue française*. 1971–1978. 7 vol. Paris: Larousse.
Gleßgen, Martin-Dietrich. 2007. *Linguistique romane. Domaines et méthodes en linguistique française et romane*. Paris: Colin.
GR = Robert and Rey (2nd edition) 1985.
Hjelmslev, Louis. 1953. *Prolegomena to a theory of language*. Baltimore: Waverly. [Original Danish version: *Omkring Sprogteoriens Grundlæggelse*, København, Munksgaard, 1943].
Holtus, Günter, Michael Metzeltin, and Christian Schmitt (eds.). 1988–2005. *Lexikon der Romanistischen Linguistik*, vol. 8. Tübingen: Niemeyer.
Holtus, Günter, Anja Overbeck, and Harald Völker. 2003. *Luxemburgische Skriptastudien. Edition und Untersuchung der altfranzösischen Urkunden Gräfin Ermesindes (1226–1247) und Graf Heinrichs V. (1247–1281) von Luxemburg*. Tübingen: Niemeyer.
Imbs, Paul. 1961. La place du vocabulaire ancien dans un thesaurus de la langue française. In *Lexicologie et lexicographie françaises et romanes. Orientations et exigences actuelles (Strasbourg, 12–16 novembre 1957)*, 133–147. Paris: CNRS.
Kloss, Heinz. 1967. Abstand-languages and Ausbau-languages. *Anthropological linguistics* 9: 29–41.
Lebsanft, Franz, and Martin-Dietrich Gleßgen. 2004. Historische Semantik in den romanischen Sprachen. Kognition. Pragmatik. Geschichte. In *Historische Semantik in den romanischen Sprachen*, ed. Franz Lebsanft and Martin-Dietrich Gleßgen, 1–28. Tübingen: Niemeyer.
Littré, Émile (ed.). 1873–1882. *Dictionnaire de la langue française*, vol. 5. Paris: Hachette.
LRL = Holtus, Metzeltin and Schmitt 1988–2005.
Mensching, Guido. 2005. Variación sintáctica, lingüística de corpus y gramática generativa. Teorías, métodos y problemas. In *Variación sintáctica en español. Un reto para las teorías de la sintaxis*, ed. Gabriele Knauer and Valeriano Bellosta von Colbe, 13–33. Tübingen: Niemeyer.

Minsky, Marvin. 1975. A framework for representing knowledge. In *The psychology of computer vision*, ed. Patrick H. Winston, 211–277. New York: McGraw Hill.

Möhren, Frankwalt. 1997. Unité et diversité du champ sémasiologique – l'exemple de l'Anglo-Norman Dictionary. In *De mot en mot. Aspects of medieval linguistics. Essays in honour of William Rothwell*, ed. S. Gregory and D.A. Trotter, 127–146. Cardiff: University of Wales Press.

Ogden, Charles Kay, and Ivor Armstrong Richards. 1923. *The meaning of meaning. A study of the influence of language upon thought and of the science of symbolism*. New York: Harcourt.

Raible, Wolfgang. 1983. Zur Einleitung. In: Stimm/Raible, 1–24.

Rey, Alain (ed.). (2nd edition) 2001. *Le Grand Robert de la langue française*. 6 vol. Paris: Robert.

Robert = Rey (2nd edition)2001.

Robert, Paul, and Alain Rey. (2nd edition) 1985. *Le Grand Robert de la langue française. Dictionnaire alphabétique et analogique de la langue française*, 9 vol. Paris: Robert.

RSG = Ernst, Gleßgen, Schmitt and Schweickard. 2003–2009.

Saussure, Ferdinand de. (5th editiion) 1960. *Cours de linguistique générale*. Paris: Payot.

Stimm, Helmut, and Wolfgang Raible (eds.). 1983. *Zur Semantik des Französischen*. Wiesbaden: Steiner.

TL = Tobler, Adolf, and Erhard Lommatzsch. 1925–. *Altfranzösisches Wörterbuch*. Adolf Toblers nachgelassene Materialien, bearbeitet und herausgegeben von Erhard Lommatzsch, weitergeführt von Hans Helmut Christmann, vollendet von Richard Baum und Willi Hirdt. vol. 1–2: Berlin: Weidmann. vol. 3–: Wiesbaden/Stuttgart: Steiner.

TLF = Imbs, Paul. 1971–1994. *Trésor de la langue française : dictionnaire de la langue du XIXe et du XXe siècle (1789–1960)*. Nancy: Centre National de la Recherche Scientifique/Institut National de la Langue Française.

Völker, Harald. 2004. Bedeutungsebenen und Bedeutungswandel. Mit vier Beispielen aus der altfranzösischen Urkundensprache. In *Historische Semantik in den romanischen Sprachen*, ed. Franz Lebsanft and Martin-Dietrich Gleßgen, 165–179. Tübingen: Niemeyer.

Völker, Harald. 2009. La linguistique variationnelle et la perspective intralinguistique. *Revue de Linguistique Romane* 73: 27–76.

Vogt, Hans. 1947. Språksystem og språkutvkling. *Norsk Tidsskrift for Sprogvidenskap* 14: 293–304.

Wagner, Robert-Léon. 1949. En marge d'un problème de syntaxe (L'ordre de phrase sujet + verbe). In *Mélanges de philologie romane et de littérature médiévale offerts à Ernest Hœpffner, membre de l'Académie des Inscriptions et Belles-Lettres, doyen honoraire de la faculté des lettres de Strasbourg, par ses élèves et ses amis*, 53–62. Paris: Les Belles Lettres.

Weinreich, Uriel. 1954. Is a structural dialectology possible? *Word* 10: 388–400.

Part II
Synchronic Studies

Chapter 11
Crusaders' Old French

Cyril Aslanov

11.1 Historical Background

The linguistic landscape of the Middle East was affected by the arrival of speakers of Western languages, especially Romance languages. Old French, in particular, had great influence, as it was the exclusive and elitist language of the ruling class of the Kingdom of Jerusalem and of other political entities founded by the Crusaders. In this chapter, we will use the term "castolect" to describe this use of French by the aristocrats of the Crusaders' States (first coined in Aslanov 2008). After all, it is certainly not accidental that the generic term for all Westerners in general is "Frank" both in Arabic and Greek, the two main languages that were brought in contact with the Westerners as a result of the Crusades (Arabic *franjī*, Greek Φράγγος). If the Westerners as a whole were called "Franks", it is probably because the French identity and the Old French language played a central and unifying role in the mosaic of people who settled in Syria-Palestine after 1098, in Cyprus after 1191, and in other Greek-speaking countries after 1204.

It seems that each of the political entities founded by the Crusaders produced a language variety of its own, or more exactly a special *koiné*. However, since some of those States were only short-lived, we do not have enough information about the language(s) spoken there. For example, the county of Edessa was destroyed by 1144, less than half a century after its foundation. The county of Tripoli and the Principality of Antioch lasted until 1258 and 1268, respectively. For these reasons, we have little data regarding the specific blend of languages spoken by the ruling class there. Due to the Occitan origin of the Counts of Tripoli, it is most likely that the elites of that county spoke Occitan, which may explain why the variety of Old French spoken in the adjacent Kingdom of Jerusalem (that actually stretched

---

C. Aslanov (✉)
Department of Romance and Latin American Studies, The Hebrew University of Jerusalem, Jerusalem, Israel
e-mail: msaslan@pluto.mscc.huji.ac.il

almost to Beirut) showed great Occitan influence. As for the specific *koiné* that was in use in the Principality of Antioch, we have some indirect information refracted through Arabic or Armenian documents in which it seems obvious that the local dialect was based on Norman (Aslanov 2006b: 39–43).

When Ibn Munqidh (1095–1188) (Ibn Munqidh: 115; 141) quotes the terms *burjāsī* "bourgeois" and *burjāsiyyah* "bourgeoisie", he uses a long *alīf* to represent the phoneme [e] of the Norman forms *burges* and *burgesie*, a dialect in which the reflex of Latin [e:] in a stressed open vowel did not diphthongize as it did in other dialects of Oïl (*bourgeois*; *bourgeoisie*). The Old French loanwords integrated in Cilician Middle Armenian (Karst 1901: 16–40) show a similar feature. Indeed, we find the same *burges* quoted by Ibn Munqidh, as well as forms like *Penet'* for *Benet* (instead of *Benoît*), and *Čoufre* for *Joufré* instead of *Geoffroi* "Jeffrey" (Karst 1901: 18; 21). Another Norman feature reflected in the Old French loanwords adopted into Middle Armenian is the shift [o] > [u] before a nasal consonant, as in *gount'* for *cunte* "earl", *jabroun* for *chaperun* "little hat", *jalounj* for *chalunge* "challenge"; *janoun* for *chanune* "canon" (Karst 1901: 21) and *goundoustapl* / *goundstapl* for *cunstable* "constable" (Dulaurier 1869: lxxv; Hübschmann 1897: 391; Karst 1901: 33).

The data stemming from the Kingdom of Jerusalem, which was actually recentered around Acre after 1191, are the most complete. Thanks to literary documents either written in Acre and in adjacent Cyprus or recopied in the famous scriptorium of Acre, we have a reliable picture of the language spoken there, which is, in turn, confirmed by semi-literary documents (e.g., some juridical texts compiled in Cyprus after the collapse of the Kingdom in 1291). Finally, the spread of the Crusaders' Old French among locals provides valuable confirmation of the data found in Old French documents originating in the Levant. See, for example, Aslanov (2006a), who deciphers an Old French-Arabic glossary in which the Old French lemmas are written with Coptic characters used according to Bohairic (Northern Egyptian) pronunciation of this liturgical language.

11.2 Crusaders' Old French in the Kingdom of Jerusalem: Which Dialects of Oïl Contributed to the Creation of the New *koiné*?

With the exception of the Kingdom of Cyprus that lasted from 1191 to 1473, the Kingdom of Jerusalem, which was first centered around Jerusalem (1099–1187), and then around Acre (1191–1291), was the most lasting entity among the States founded by the Crusaders in the Levant. This may explain why a special blend of local *koiné* was able to exist there. The cross-tabulation of the data provided by Old French texts from Acconitan origin, as compared to the French found in Arabic or Coptic texts (Aslanov 2006a), reveals that the characteristics of the *koiné* were mostly attributable to the dialectal continuum constituted by the northeastern half of the realm of Oïl. In other words, it came from such dialects as Picard, Walloon, Lotharingian, and perhaps even Burgundian (Aslanov 2006a: 149–152; 2007: 52–76).

Among all of these linguistic influences, it seems that those of Walloon are the most important. This is seen, for example, from the shift [s] > [ɹ] before consonants that is attested in two literary texts written in a Levantine context: Philippe of Novara's *Estoire de la guerre des Imperiaux contre les Ibelins*, in which it is quite common, and the anonymous *Chronicle of the Templar of Tyre*, in which it is less so. As a result of this shift, the word *aisné* "firstborn" appears as *aihné* (Philippe de Novare 1200–1270: 72; 210; 288); *masnee* "retinue" as *mahnee* (Ibid.: 72; 82; 204; 226); *mesla* "scramaged" as *mehla* (Ibid.: 118); *asne* "donkey" as *ahne*. The latter word is also found in the above-mentioned Coptic glossary, where it is written *laheneh* (Aslanov 2006a: 66; 130; 147; 2006b: 46–47). Likewise, the shift [ks] > [i̯] may be considered a typical Walloon feature (Pope 1952: 134; 489). It is attested in the Coptic document in words like *tixerant* "weaver" or *cruish* < *crux* (nominative form).

Besides specific Walloon features, one can find many phonetic phenomena that constitute isoglosses between Walloon and adjacent dialects (e.g., Picard and Lotharingian). This is the case of the opening of a closed [e] before [r] in words like *clarc* < *clerc* "cleric", *vart* < *vert* "green" and *vardure* < *verdure* "greenery" (Aslanov 2006b: 56). This opening that is pan-dialectal for open [ɛ] has been extended to closed [e] in an area that stretches from Picardy to Lorraine (Pope 1952: 495). Likewise, the closing countertonic [e] in immediate contact with a palatal consonant that is common to Picard, Walloon and Lotharingian (Pope 1952: 489) is attested in the data transmitted by Coptic scribes. There, the words *cheval* "horse", *peigne* "comb" *seigneur* "sir" and *vieillarz* "old man" appear as *chival*, *pigne*, *signour* (Aslanov 2006b: 57), *villarz* (Aslanov 2006a: 51–52; 120–122; Aslanov 2006b: 91–92).

The *koiné* of the Kingdom of Jerusalem displays another feature characteristic of the area that stretches from the Eastern fringes of Picardy to Burgundia through Wallonia and Lotharingia. It is the reflect of Latin [k] or [s] + [j] as a voiced postpalatal affricate [dʒ], as in *majoun* < *mansione(m)* "house" (cf. Eastern Picard *majon*) or *rajin* < *racemu(m)* "grape" instead of *maison* and *raisin* (cf. Burgundian *raijin*) (Aslanov 2006b: 69–70). Lotharingian in particular evinces the shift [ai] > [a] like in *ragin* (*raisin* "grape"), *majun* (*maison* "house") and in the Levantine toponym *Barut* (< Arabic *Bairūt*) (Aslanov 2006b: 64–65).

However, it is doubtful that this *koiné* was a fixed entity. Some variations within the same Coptic document, the Old French component of which seems to go back to a period preceding 1258 (Aslanov 2006a: 6–7), reveal that the synthesis of languages was perhaps in a process of crystallization. For example, consider the fluctuation between the Coptic digrams <an>, <en>, <in> used to represent the French nasals [ãn]/ [ɛ̃n]. This graphematic instability reflects vacillation between a Picard or Walloon [ɛ̃n] and [ãn], found in other dialects, including Lotharingian. To be sure, this kind of oscillation is also frequently attested in Old French manuscripts. However, there is an important distinction between graphic variationism within a long tradition of writing Old French with Latin characters on the one hand, and the occasional writing down of foreign words by means of an alphabet that is not otherwise used for this specific purpose on the other hand. Unless we assume that Coptic characters might have mechanically transliterated the Latin ones (which is not confirmed by the rather phonetic way of transcribing the Old French items in this document), we must consider this polymorphic spread of Old French words a variation at the phonetic level of the language itself, and not necessarily a graphic variationism at the level of its graphemic representation. Thus, the fact that the word *argent* is written either <*ardjanth*> or <*ardjenth*> may hint at the coexistence of a Walloon or Picard realization of the lexical item with a form where the shift [ɛ̃n]> [ãn] has been completed (Aslanov 2006b: 58–59).

The dialectological identification of this local *koiné* is confirmed by morphological data. Dees (1980, 1985) has clearly demonstrated that the Old French nominal declension survived later in the northeastern half of the realm of Oïl than in the southwestern one (cf. Dees 1980: 36–38). The system that may be reconstructed from the Levantine Old French data reveals that the declension system was preserved almost in its integrity (Aslanov 2006a: 152–156). Old French distinguished the nominative case (subject and vocative) from the oblique case (any other function). We find, for example, a gloss for *litshivels*:

(1) *li   chival-s*
  the-m-sg-Nom horse-m-sg-NOM
  'the horse.'

Here, the agreement between the article *li* of the nominative singular and the ending *-s* is retained. Likewise, a microsyntagma *li chienz,* can be recognized through the gloss *lithsendi*, if it is, as it appears, a copyist's corruption for *lithshends* with a graphemic representation of the affricate [ts], allophone of the case-ending *-s* after a dental consonant, as in (2):

(2) *li   chien-z*
  the-m-sg-Nom dog-m-sg-Nom
  'the dog.'

The fact that case endings were preserved is particularly worth noting if we take into account that, as mentioned above, the Coptic scribes were most likely not influenced by any Latin-based graphematic tradition. Western transmitters, on the other hand, tried to follow rules that tended more and more to become a matter of orthography in the latest phases of the development of Old French (towards the end of the thirteenth century). However, in the material gathered by the Coptic transmitters, part of which probably went back to an earlier period (e.g., end of the twelfth century), one can find evidence showing that the case system was in actual use at the time. Thus, one of the lemmas of the glossary contains both the nominative case and the oblique case of the same microsyntagma (Aslanov 2006a: 13–15):

(3) *noz   sire/*
  our-m-sg-NOM lord-m-sg-NOM

  nostre   seignour
  our-m-sg-OBL lord-m-sg-OBL
'Our Lord; our Lord.'

This lemma does not only display an alternation between the nominative case *sire* and the oblique case *seignour* of the Old French word for "Lord". It also reflects a variation between two forms of the possessive of the 1st person plural *nostre* 'our,' with an interesting alteration of the paradigm, which may be considered a Picardism. In dialects other than Picard, we should have expected the following alternation:

(4) *nostre(s)* sg-NOM; *nostre* sg-OBL; *nostre* pl-NOM / *nostres* or *noz>nos* pl. OBL

Here, however, we find a typically Picard analogical extension of the oblique plural *noz* (> *nos*) to the nominative singular. The chiasmatic alternation -s/ -ø/ -ø/ -s, which is the rule for nominal paradigms such s *li murs* m-sg-NOM/ *le mur* m-sg-OBL/ *li mur* m-pl-NOM/ *les murs* m-pl-OBL, has been systematically extended to the form of the possessive *nostre*:

(5) *noz (nos)* sg-NOM; *no* sg-OBL; *no* pl-NOM; *noz (nos)* pl-OBL

Therefore, the paradigm represented in (5) is actually a combination of the extension of *noz* to the nominative singular found in Picard with features characteristic of dialects other than Picard, that is, use of *nostre* for the singular oblique.

The preservation of the nominal declension, which is attested by the glosses quoted above, may be due to two factors. One is that Levantine Old French originated, in part, from the northeastern region of France, due to historical factors, namely the high proportion of speakers from Flandria, Wallonia and Lotharingia (all places that were French-speaking although not part of the Kingdom of France) who participated in the First Crusades. Of the four polities founded by those crusaders, two – the long-lived Kingdom of Jerusalem and the short-lived County of Edessa – were thus ruled by people stemming from those northeastern areas of the realm of Oïl.

Second, we must take into account the relative isolation of the Kingdom of Jerusalem from the innovative trends that contributed to the collapse of the declension system in France itself. Due to this linguistic conservatism, some features like the preservation of the nominal declension might have existed longer in the Near East.

It is important to note that whereas the Old French *koiné* (King's French/ *francien*) was established around Île-de-France on the basis of several dialects in contact (dialects of the immediate *Hinterland*; Champenois; Picard; Normand and others) (Lodge 2004: 53–79), a different *koiné* developed in the Kingdom of Jerusalem. The two *koinés* differed from each other in several respects. As we have already mentioned above, the basic constituents of Levantine *koiné* came from the north-eastern fringes of the realm of Oïl, whereas the Île-de-France *koiné* combined more central features (Lodge 1993: 98–104, 2004: 58–68; Duval 2007: 131–147).

Another important difference between the two *koinés* is the fact that King's French *francien* eventually developed into Middle French, which, in turn, evolved into Modern French. On the other hand, Levantine *koiné* barely survived the collapse of Crusaders' polities on the Asian mainland. It only persisted in Cyprus, the last stronghold of the Crusaders' presence in front of the Syrian shore, where the survivors of the Kingdom of Jerusalem gathered. On that island, some juridical texts relating to the life in the Kingdom of Jerusalem were compiled, which may be due to the longing of Syro-Palestinian crusaders for their lost country. It may also illustrate culturally and literarily the continuity between the former mainland stronghold that stretched from Jaffa to the vicinity of Beirut and the Cypriot refuge. It seems that the basis of Cypriot Old French was precisely the *koiné* that had been created in the Asian mainland on the basis of the northeastern dialects of Oïl. In the Middle French documents gathered by Jean Richard (Richard 1962), as well as in other monuments related to Cyprus, there is a clearly coloring of the Picard dialect (Aslanov 2006b: 132–136), which is more probably due to the origin of the local Francophony than to a new influx of crusaders from Picardy.

As for the Frankish polities that were created at the expense of the Byzantine Empire, they were related to the West rather than to the last remnants of genuinely Levantine Francophony gathered in Cyprus. The longest lasting entities were the Principality of Achaia (Morea) and the Duchy of Athens. We have only indirect sources of the Old French variety that was in use in Morea. In the *Chronicle of Morea*, a versified narrative of the Frankish Principality of Morea, written towards the end of the thirteenth or the beginning of the fourteenth century, the Old French component held an important place. However, it is difficult in most cases to identify specific dialectal influences on these borrowings. First, there is a considerable variationism in the Romance words in the Greek demotic text. The same Romance etymon could enter Demotic Greek through Italo-Romance, Occitan or Old French proper. If the exact Romance identity of those Romance loanwords in Greek demotic garb is difficult to determine, it is even more difficult to identify the exact dialects of Oïl that contributed to the lexical enrichment of Demotic Greek (Aslanov 2006b: 125–131). In many places, the variationism is complicated by a trend towards hybridization between the various Romance languages that stayed in contact in Frankish-dominated Greece.

Since the Principality of Achaia (Morea) became part of the Angevin possessions of Southern Italy, it is possible to find some common denominators between the language in texts belonging to Southern Italian Francophony and the vestiges of Old French found in Demotic Greek documents. The most striking common denominator is the tendency to blur the boundaries between the various Romance languages, first and foremost Old French and Italo-Romance dialects, and occasionally, Occitan, or Catalan.

Thus, the word καπεροῦνι [kaperúni] (Chronicle of Morea, v. 3437) 'little hut' seems to reflect the Occitan word *caperon* rather than the Old French *chaperon* (unless we consider *caperon* to be a Picard form). Sometimes, there is a hesitation within the text itself between genuine Old French forms and their Occitan equivalent (Aslanov 2006b: 126). Thus, for instance, the term 'provider' appears either as προβεούρην [proveúrin] (< Old French *proveor/ proveour*) (*Chronicle of Morea*, v. 7937, ms. Copenhagen) or as προβεδούρους [provedhúrus] (< Occitan *provedor*) (ms. Paris) (Aslanov 2006b: 127). It is difficult to decide whether this permeability between Old French and Occitan is due to the Greek author/ transmitter of the text or to a hybridization process that took place in the special variety of Old French that was in use in Peloponnesus towards the end of the thirteenth century. The answer to this question may lie in sociolinguistic factors. Perhaps the elite of local Frankish aristocracy tried to maintain a relatively pure variety of Old French, whereas the *gasmouloi*, born from Frankish fathers and Greek mothers, or Greeks in contact with Franks, did not always differentiate between the various Romance languages.

11.3 The Permeability of the Crusaders' Old French to the Other Romance Languages

The Crusaders brought together speakers of various Romance languages who would have otherwise remained separated. We have already mentioned that the County of Tripoli that was bordering the Kingdom of Jerusalem was ruled by an Occitan-speaking aristocracy. In the Kingdom of Jerusalem itself, the lasting presence of Genovese and Pisan traders and seafarers in Acre and in other places of the Kingdom is well-attested historically. It may explain the tendency towards hybridization between Old French and Italo-Romance in literary texts like the aforementioned *Estoire de la guerre des Imperiaus contre les Ibelins* by Philip of Novara or the *Chronicle of the Templar of Tyre*. Documentary texts and other infra-literary sources confirm that the Old French spoken in the Kingdom of Jerusalem or in its Cypriot continuation was strongly Italianized. Thus, Italo-Romance influence may be seen in special terms such as *saracin*, an adaptation of *saracino/ saraceno* used instead of the genuinely Old French term *sarrazin* or *splage*, a cross-formation between *plage* and *spiaggia* 'beach' (Aslanov 2006b: 93).

However, it may also involve basic lexical items, such as the verb 'to read'. In the Coptic glossary mentioned above (Aslanov 2006a), this form appears to be adapted as *legge*, *leç* or *liç*, a cross-formation between *legge* (or its Northern counterpart *leçe*) and Old French *lit* (Aslanov 2006b: 93–95). In the same source, there are even clear examples of intrasentential code-mixing or code-switching, as in the following utterance: *i(l) ne legge (leçe) pas ben* 'he does not read well' (Aslanov 2000). In other cases, a purely Italo-Romance expression appears in a context where Old French should have been expected. Thus, the expression 'keep quiet' is not expressed by *reste coi* or other Old French phrasing, but rather by its Italo-Romance counterpart *stai in pace* with a typically Neapolitan realization *sta'n pašə* (Aslanov 2006b: 95–96).

A similar tendency towards the merging of these two systems appears in *The Chronicle of Morea*, which can be seen to have increased in the fourteenth-fifteenth-century Cypriot documents published by Jean Richard (1962). However, the latter already pertains to the history of Middle French. An example of the former kind of blurring is φρέ 'friar' (*Chronicle*, v. 7), which seems to be a cross-formation between Old French *frere* 'friar' and Italo-Romance *fra*. Examples of the latter is the hesitation between the French forms and their Italo-Romance or Italianized counterparts *scire* and *cere* 'wax'; *dihme* and *dezima* 'tithe'; *houtouvre* and *outovrio* 'October' within the same Cypriot charter redacted by a Greek notary (Richard 1962: 23; 25; 27). By and large, the linguistic situation in Cyprus from 1192 till 1473 was characterized by an intense contact between Old French (which seems to be the continuation of the Levantine *koiné* that evolved in the Kingdom of Jerusalem) or Middle French, on the one hand, and Venetian, on the other. The documents edited by Jean Richard show that at the beginning of the period or in the texts emanating from the High Court (*haute cour*), Old French constituted the matrix language with embedded Italo-Romance words (Aslanov 2006b: 131–141). As in the above-mentioned case of Italo-Romance *leggere* or *leçer* used instead of *lire* 'to read', these Italianisms are not necessarily specialized lexical items. Thus a phrasing like *mia Madame* displays a redundant use of the Italo-Romance possessive *mia* (fem sg) before *Madame* where the French possessive *ma* is implicit (Aslanov 2006b: 137).

The blurring of the differences among the various Romance languages may be due to the influence of the Levantine variety, with the result that the Romance languages spoken in the Crusaders' states hardly differed from each other (Aslanov 2002). As was the case with their speakers, these languages were all called "Frankish". Confronted with local heteroglossia, the speakers of the various Romance languages represented in the area were probably more aware of what was common among their respective languages than of their differences.

In the Coptic glossary, a slight Occitan touch is sometimes felt. Interestingly enough, the Occitan that appears is adapted to the morphophonemic schemes of Old French, according to a process that was at play when a huge quantity of Provençal words integrated Middle French in the fifteenth-sixteenth century (Gebhardt 1974). Thus, for instance, the Occitan word *pena* 'fur; leather' is adapted as *peine* because the speakers of local Old French were probably aware of the phonetic equivalences between Occitan [e] and Old French [ei]/ [oi] on the one hand, between Occitan unstressed [a] and Old French [ə] on the other (Aslanov 2006a: 84; 121; 138; 167; Aslanov 2006b: 105). It is worth noting that in Old French, the word *peine* 'fur; leather' which is an homonym of *peine/ poine* 'penalty; sorrow' is not attested otherwise.

In fact, the hybridization between Old French and other Romance languages is not restricted to Levantine contexts. Due to the intensity of French influence in Italy itself, it is frequently attested in texts composed or recopied in that country where Old French was part of local diglossia before the affirmation of the Italian *volgare illustre*. However, the hybridization processes that characterize Old French, both in the Kingdom of Jerusalem and in the Frankish Polities in Greek lands, always involve at least three languages and not only two as in Italy. For besides Italo-Romance and Old French, there is also an Occitan component. Indeed, it can be said that the contact between Old French and Occitan took place overseas before it happened in France itself. It is the event of the Crusades that permitted the contact between the two languages whose development diverged as long as they were spoken in Europe. For unlike Occitan, a language that was in contact with many Romance languages of *Romania continua* (Italo-Romance; Catalan; Aragonese and even Galician Portuguese if we take into account that Provençal poetry served as a model for the beginning of lyric poetry in Portugal), Old French was land-locked among Germanic languages. The only Romance languages with which it was in contact in its original setting were Franco-Provençal and Occitan. In our view, the venture of the Crusades and the subsequent creation of multicultural polities in the Eastern Mediterranean was responsible for a re-Romanization of a deeply Germanized Romance language.

11.4 The Lexical Impact of the Alloglottic Surroundings on Crusader's Old French

The varieties of Old French that developed in the Near East and in Greek-speaking lands absorbed some local influences. However, the permeability of the language with respect to the alloglottic surroundings varies considerably from place to place. Broadly speaking, the more Old French had been influenced by epichoric languages, the less it left its impact on them. Conversely, the less it was influenced by the local surroundings, the more Old French lexemes penetrated into the lexical stock of the language in contact.

Thus, Old French in Syria-Palestine was quite receptive to Arabic lexemes, part of which even survived in Old French and made their way down to Modern French (Sguaitamatti-Bassi 1974), whereas some others were only short-lived borrowings. As for the impact of Old French on Arabic, it mainly pertains to proper names and toponyms, which cannot be considered part of the linguistic system. On the other hand, both Cilician Armenian (Karst 1901: 16–33; 36–40; Aslanov 2006b: 39–43) and Medieval Demotic Greek (Aslanov 2007), integrated a huge number of Old French words due to the lasting contact with the Franks. Some of these are found in both Armenian and Greek. The aforementioned word καπερῦνι [kaperúni] for *chaperon* 'little hut' is also found in Armenian with a more explicitly Oïl influence: *jabroun* with [dʒ]/ [tʃ] (*jheh*) representing the Old French post-palatal affricate [tʃ] of *chaperon*. An explicit Old French example is *sire* 'lord' reflected in both Armenian and Demotic Greek: *sir* and σίρ.

Conversely, neither Armenian nor Greek left their imprint on the local varieties of Old French. Even in Cyprus, where the contact between Middle French, Venetian, and Greek is well documented in the archives edited by Richard (1962), the presence of Greek phrases or sentences in the hybrid text does not affect the system of Middle French and Venetian. An asymmetric relation can be seen in that Demotic Greek and Middle Armenian were enriched by many Old French lexical items, whereas Old French was quite hermetic to those languages. This may be explained by the hegemonic status of Crusaders' castolect. Highly valorized by Armenians (most of the time close allies of the Franks) and Greeks, Oïl became a high language once transplanted in the Eastern Mediterranean, according to a process of upgrading that is reminiscent of the valorization of Anglo-Norman in Britain (Lusignan 1986).

Let us focus on the Arabization process that took place in the specific variety of Old French that was in use in Crusaders' States. The impact of the Arabic-speaking surroundings consists of an injection of words that refer to local realia or institutions. Thus the function of *muḥtasib* 'market inspector' is expressed by the word *mathessep*, a form that displays an interesting metathesis of [t] and [ḥ] and a devoicing of the last consonant (Aslanov 2006b: 81). This borrowing was short-lived if we consider the development of Old French in general. However, as long as Old French was part of the linguistic horizon of Syria and Palestine, this technical term was fully integrated in the morphophonemic system of the language, as shown by the phonetic adaptations that it underwent.

Another striking example of local Arabic influence in Levantine Old French is the semantic interference as a result of the lasting contact between those two languages. In the aforementioned Coptic glossary, the word *fenestre* 'window' is translated as *ṭāqah*, which means 'little window'. However, *shubbāk*, another Arabic word for window, was integrated into local Old French (as *chubec/ chubbec*) to the extent that it was perceived as the explicandum of the Old French-Arabic glossary. The Arabic word is *rawzan* 'spyhole', a technical term that goes back to a Persian etymon (*rowzan*). Paradoxically enough, in this case an Arabic term of Persian origin was used for elucidating an Old French word of Arabic origin (Aslanov 2006a: 100–102; 162–163; Aslanov 2006b: 78–81).

Some Old French words underwent interesting semantic shifts once confronted with the Levantine linguistic landscape. Thus, the word *bain* is attested with the specialized meaning of *ḥammām* both in the Coptic glossary (Aslanov 2006a: 74–75; 160; Aslanov 2006b: 91) and in the *Chronicle of the Templar of Tyre* (390). Likewise, *jardin* is used to refer to the oriental *bustān* in the two aforementioned texts (*Chronicle of the Templar of Tyre* 1314: 415; Aslanov 2006a: 75–76; 160; Aslanov 2006b: 91).

Another example of the impact of the contact with Arabic on the semantics of Levantine Old French is the use of *vieillarz/ vieillart* 'old man' in the meaning of *sheikh*. This specialization of the word is attested in the Coptic glossary where the word *li villarz* (that is, *li vieillarz* with the aforementioned Picard closing of [ɛ] to [i] in contact with a palatal consonant) is glossed as *al-sheikh al-kabīr* 'the big old man', or even 'the big sheikh' (Aslanov 2006a: 51–52; 120–122; Aslanov 2006b: 91–92). Significantly enough, this equivalence between *sheikh* and *vieillarz* or even *vieus/ viel* is found in the Old French name of the leader of the Isma'ilis (the famous *Hashshāshīn*). In the Old French chronicles where this personality is recorded, the Arabic title *sheikh al-jabal* 'the sheikh of the mountain' is translated as *Li Vieus de la Montaingne* 'the old man of the mountain' (Joinville 1224–1317: 307–308 §§ 98–90). This denomination was conserved as such, which might give the wrong impression that the leader of the Isma'ilis was necessarily an old man. He was actually a *sheikh*, the calque-translation of which was *vieus/ vieillarz* in Crusaders' Old French.

11.5 Identity and Language

In the most lasting polities founded by the Crusaders, there is no doubt that a local dialect existed, influenced by the languages of the region. This linguistic *couleur locale* was part of a broader tendency to develop a special identity, which was neither the western identity transplanted in the East nor the mere adoption of the local civilizations, but rather an eclectic compromise between western and eastern cultural features.

The ruling class of the Kingdom of Jerusalem was quite orientalized, partly because these *poulains* had been there for several generations, and partly because many princesses of the dynasty were of Armenian origin. The gap between *Outremer* 'Overseas', that is, the Levant, and *desa mer* 'on this side of the sea', that is, Europe (these notions being reversible, depending on the standpoint of the author), was so strong that already in 1130, the coming of Foulques V of Anjou, who married Queen Melisenda of Jerusalem, was perceived as an unwelcome intrusion by local Franco-Armenian aristocrats (Aslanov 2008: 4). To be sure, this animosity was mostly due to political reasons. However, it is possible to ascribe part of this to a cultural clash between the local people and the newcomers, whose blend of French might have sounded ridiculous to their ears. Thus, for instance, an Angevin like Foulques most likely spoke a southwestern variety of Oïl. This dialect was quite different from the local *koiné*, which was the result of a synthesis of various northeastern dialects. If we add to this basic difference the fact that the Levantine *koiné* underwent all the aforementioned metamorphosis as a result of its contact with other Romance languages and Arabic, we can imagine the linguistic gap that separated the local aristocracy from Foulques.

These differences of dialects and accents played an important role in the linguistic horizon of Oïl. For example, the famous poem *Mout me semont Amors que je m'envoise* (v. 5–14), was written by Conon de Béthune regarding the reaction that his Picard dialect provoked at the royal court (Wallensköld 1921: 5). Similar reactions most likely happened whenever a newcomer arrived to this area, as his speech was very different from the Levantine variety. Likewise, the Flemings who arrived in the Principality of Achaia (Morea) between 1289 and 1297 provoked reactions of deep antipathy, part of which may have been catalyzed by some cultural and linguistic differences. Not only were these people speaking a different blend of Old French, but unlike the *gasmouloi* and the Franks who had settled a long time ago, they were completely foreign to the Hellenic or Hellenized context (Aslanov 2006b: 122). However, linguistic features of Levantine Old French are not only due to the impact of local influences. The mere fact that a spoken *koiné* had crystallized at least partially already in twelfth-thirteenth century is by itself a remarkable event in the history of the French language.

The dialectal basis for the Levantine *koiné* of the Kingdom of Jerusalem and its Cypriot continuation seems to have been restricted to the northeastern part of the realm of Oïl. It is important to emphasize that in France itself, many centuries passed before a supradialectal *scripta* developed and spread all over the Kingdom. Furthermore, whatever the theory regarding the exact crystallization (Pfister 1973: 253; 1993: 39–40) and diffusion (Dees 1985: 94; Lusignan 1999: 118–124) of the Old French *scripta* in France itself, this supradialectal *koiné* was obviously not a spoken language, but only a written one. At the vernacular level, many different dialects, not yet united in a supradialectal *koiné*, were still spoken in the various regions of Northern France. On the other hand, the *koiné* of the Kingdom of

Jerusalem assumed the sociolinguistical function of a vernacular. In other words, the vernacular of the Kingdom of Jerusalem was unified. Since this political entity was the longest lasting Crusaders' polity on the Asiatic mainland, the Levantine coloring of Old French was probably identified with the specific *koiné* that was in use in the Kingdom of Jerusalem and in its Cypriot extension.

Furthermore, the special blend of Old French that developed in the Levant anticipated the processes of linguistic unification that took place only at the level of Middle French. The relative modernity of this highly dynamic Levantine *koiné* is clearly revealed by several pieces of data that appear in the Coptic glossary (Aslanov 2006a: 151–152; 160–161). Curiously enough, these modern features that anticipate processes which occurred at the level of Middle French (such as the use of the double negation *ne… pas* in the aforementioned phrase *i(l) **ne** legge (leçe) **pas** ben*) coexist with such archaisms as the preservation of the nominal declension. However, as we have already mentioned, this morphological conservatism may be due to the northeastern origin of the main components of Levantine *koiné*.

11.6 Conclusion

On the basis of what may be inferred from literary or documentary texts written in a Levantine context as well as from the witnesses about Old French found in Oriental documents (Greek; Armenian; Arabic and even Coptic), it is possible to state that the Old French of the *poulains* or of the *gasmouloi* was quite receptive to its non-Romance surroundings (Arabic in Syria-Palestine; Greek in Cyprus, Achaia and Morea). However, the most striking features of Levantine Old French may be due to the fact that a new *koiné* arose on the basis of Old French dialects that would not have had contact otherwise in France. The source of the most significant dialectal features is the territorial continuum that stretches from Picardy to Burgundia, particularly Walloon. Moreover, the contact of this *koiné* with Italo-Romance dialects, Occitan, and Catalan, fomented interlingual hybridization, the characteristics of which are perhaps more significant than the occasional borrowing from an Arabic or Greek text.

This Levantine *koiné* that was first and foremost related to the Kingdom of Jerusalem and its Cypriot continuation, became emblematic of Frankish linguistic identity in the Levant. It was the language of prestige of a caste (the aristocrats who were mainly speakers of Oïl). It was also preserved as a component of the new variety of Levantine French that developed in Cyprus during the fourteenth and fifteenth centuries. To be sure, Cypriot Middle French was renewed by linguistic importations from France and Angevin possessions in Italy and Greece. However, the Picardisms that may be found in this variety of Levantine Middle French (as the use of *por my* instead of *por moi*; Aslanov 2006b: 134) may hint at a direct connection that unites the last echoes of Levantine Francophony on the Asiatic mainland (mainly represented by the *koiné* o the Kingdom of Jerusalem) with the renewal of a French-speaking identity in Lusignan Cyprus.

References

Primary Sources

Chronicle of the Templar of Tyre (ca 1314) = Minervini, Laura (ed.). 2000. *Cronaca del Templare di Tiro* (1243–1314). *La caduta degli Stati Crociati nel racconto di un testimone oculare.* Naples: Liguori.

Dulaurier, Édouard. 1869. *Recueil des historiens des Croisades, I.* Paris: Imprimerie impériale.

Ibn Munqidh, Usāmah (1095–1188) = 1999. *Kitāb al-Iḥtibār.* Beirut: Dar al-Kutub al-'Ilmiyyah.

Joinville, Jean sire de (1224–1317) = 1952. *Le livre des saintes paroles et des bons faits de saint Louis.* In *Historiens et chroniqueurs du Moyen Âge*, ed. Albert Pauphilet. Paris: Gallimard.

Philippe de Novare (ca 1200–ca 1270) = 1994. *Guerra di Federico II in Oriente (1223–1242)*, ed. Silvio Melani. Naples: Liguori.

Secondary Sources

Aslanov, Cyril. 2000. Interpreting the language-mixing in terms of codeswitching: The case of the Franco-Italian interface in the Middle Ages. *Journal of Pragmatics* 32: 273–1281.

Aslanov, Cyril. 2002. Quand les langues romanes se confondent…La Romania vue d'ailleurs. *Langage et société* 99: 9–52.

Aslanov, Cyril. 2006a. *Evidence of francophony in mediaeval levant: Decipherment and interpretation*, MS. BnF Copte 43. Jerusalem: The Hebrew University of Jerusalem Magnes Press.

Aslanov, Cyril. 2006b. *Le français levantin, jadis et naguère: à la recherche d'une langue perdue.* Paris: Honoré Champion.

Aslanov, Cyril. 2007. Linguistic Hybridization in the *Chronicle of Morea*. In Η Πελοπόννησος μετά την Δ' Σταυροφορία του 1204 (Πρακτικά διεθνούς συνεδρίου – Μυστράς, 1–3 Οκτωβρίου 2004), ed. Deisis Paraskhou and Aristeas Spendzas, 37–48. Athens-Mystras.

Aslanov, Cyril. 2008. L'ancien français, sociolecte d'une caste au pouvoir: Royaume de Jérusalem, Morée, Chypre. In *Évolutions en français: Études de linguistique diachronique*, ed. Benjamin Fagard et al., 3–19. Bern: Peter Lang.

Dees, Anthony. 1980. *Atlas des formes et constructions des chartes françaises du 13e siècle.* Tübingen: Niemeyer.

Dees, Anthony. 1985. Dialectes et scriptae à l'époque de l'ancien français. *Revue de linguistique romane* 49: 87–117.

Duval, Frédéric. 2007. Le Moyen Age. In *Mille ans de langue française: histoire d'une passion*, ed. Alain Rey, Frédéric Duval, and Gilles Siouffi. Paris: Perrin.

Gebhardt, Karl. 1974. *Das okzitanische Lehngut im Französischen.* Heidelberg: Heidelberger Beiträge zur Romanistik.

Hübschmann, Heinrich. 1897. *Armenische Grammatik.* Leipzig: Breitkopf und Hartel (repr. Hildesheim-New York: Georg Olms, 1972).

Karst, Josef. 1901. *Historische Grammatik des kilikisch-armenischen.* Strasbourg: Trübner (repr. Berlin: Walter de Gruyter, 1970).

Lodge, R.Anthony. 1993. *French from dialect to standard.* London/New York: Routledge.

Lodge, R.Anthony. 2004. *A sociolinguistic history of Parisian French.* Cambridge: Cambridge University Press.

Lusignan, Serge. 1986. *Parler vulgairement. Les intellectuels et la langue française aux XIIIe et XIVe siècles.* Paris/Montreal: Vrin/Presses de l'Université de Montréal.

Lusignan, Serge. 1999. Langue française et société du XIIIe au XVe siècle. In *Nouvelle histoire de la langue française*, ed. Chaurand Jacques, 91–143. Paris: Le Seuil.

Pfister, Max. 1973. Die sprachliche Bedeutung von Paris und der Île-de-France vor dem 13. Jahrhundert. *Vox Romanica* 32: 217–253.

Pfister, Max. 1993. Scripta et koinè en ancien français au XIIe et XIIIe siècle. In *Écritures, langues communes et normes: formation spontanée de koinès et standardisation dans la Gallo-Romania et son voisinage* (Actes du Colloque tenu à l'Université de Neuchâtel du 21 au 23 septembre 1988), ed. Pierre Knecht and Zygmunt Marzys, 17–41. Geneva/Neuchâtel: Droz/Université de Neuchâtel.

Pope, Mildred K. 1952. *From Latin to modern French*, 2nd ed. Manchester: Manchester University Press.

Richard, Jean. 1962. *Documents chypriotes des Archives du Vatican*. Paris: Librairie Orientaliste Paul Geuthner.

Sguaitamatti-Bassi, Suzanne. 1974. *Les emprunts directs faits par le français à l'arabe jusqu'à la fin du XIIIe siècle*. Thèse présentée à la Faculté des Lettres de l'Université de Zurich pour l'obtention du grade de docteur.

Wallensköld, Axel (ed.). 1921. *Les chansons de Conon de Béthune*. Paris: Honoré Champion.

Chapter 12
The Use of the Future and Conditional in High Medieval Literature

Igor Dreer

12.1 Introduction

The sound changes that occurred during the evolution from Latin to Romance resulted in an overlap between the third conjugation paradigms of the Romance Future and Present. Brunot and Bruneau (1969: 304–305) state the following on the matter:

> Il existait, en latin classique, deux types de futur.
> «Ama-bi-s», «tu aimeras», s'opposait à «ama-s», «tu aimes», et à «ama-ba-s», «tu aimais».
> «Leg-e-s», «tu liras», s'opposait à «leg-i-s», «tu lis», et à «leg-a-s», «que tu lises».
> Le futur en –bo semble avoir disparu dans le latin populaire. […]
> Le futur de 3e conjugaison se confondait, en roman commun, avec l'indicatif présent.

	Latin classique	
	Indicatif présent	Futur
	leg-o	leg-a-m
	leg-ĭ-s	leg-e-s
	leg-ĭ-t	leg-e-t
	leg-ĭ-mus	leg-e-mus
	leg-ĭ-tis	leg-e-tis
	leg-ŭ-nt	leg-e-nt

The following abbreviations are used: 1 = First Person, 2 = Second Person, 3 = Third Person, ABL = Ablative, ART = Article, COND = Conditional, FUT = Future, IMP = Imperative, INF = Infinitive, IPFV = Imperfective, LOC = Locative, NEG = Negation negative, OBJ = Object, PFV = Perfective, PL = Plural, PRET = Preterit, PRS = Present, REFL = Reflexive, SBJV = Subjunctive, SG = Singular

I. Dreer (✉)
Department of Foreign Literatures and Linguistics, Ben-Gurion University of the Negev, Beersheba, Israel
e-mail: dreer@bgu.ac.il

En roman commun, ces formes se prononçaient:

leg-o	leg-a-m
leg-e-(s)	leg-e-(s)
leg-e-t	leg-e-t
leg-e-mo(s)	leg-e-mo(s)
leg-e-ti(s)	leg-e-ti(s)
leg-o-nt	leg-e-nt

Les formes du futur, confondues avec celles d'un temps aussi répandu que l'indicatif présent, étaient donc inutilisables.
Une périphrase expressive a remplacé l'ancien futur.

The need for communicative distinctiveness was one of the factors that led Romance speakers and writers (hereafter *encoders*) to replace the Latin Future by new forms. In Old French (hereafter *OF*), the new synthetic form of the Future represents "a unit lexeme, the new stem reflecting the old infinitive and the new ending a reduced form of *habeo*" (Fleischman 1982: 71) 'I have': e.g. *chanter-ai* 'I will sing'. In addition, the Conditional[1] was created by the combination of the infinitive stem and the forms of the Imperfect Indicative of *habere* 'to have': e.g. *chanter-eie > chanter-oie* 'I would sing'.[2]

The next section presents a synchronic sign-oriented analysis of the use of the OF Future and Conditional in medieval texts. It shows that the distribution of both signs is not random, but rather is motivated by their invariant meanings.

12.2 Previous Studies

The first examples of the OF Future (*salvarai* 'I will defend' and *prindrai* 'I will take') appear in *Les Serments de* (cf. de Mourcin 1815: 10). The Conditional appears in the OF as early as the Future. One finds *sostendreiet* 'she would undergo' in *La Cantilène de Sainte* (cf. von Fallersleben 1837: 6).

The evolution of the Future and the Conditional in Romance is discussed by D'Hulst (2004), Fleischman (1982), and Posner (1997: 319–324). Harris (1986) analyzes the evolution of the Conditional modal value from Old to Modern French. Most studies of the OF verb (cf. fn 2) have dealt mainly with the paradigms, not the uses, of the Future and the Conditional. However, it is generally acknowledged that the Future "necessarily involves an element of prediction or some related modalization" (Fleischman 1982: 24) that accounts for its various temporal and non-temporal

---

[1] I realize that the term *Conditional* is improper because the use of this linguistic form does not necessarily imply that the actualization of an event depends on a condition. The term *Conditional* is employed here merely for convenience.

[2] For the detailed analysis of the paradigms to which the terms *the OF Future* and *the OF Conditional* refer, see Brunot and Bruneau (1969: 306–308), Ewert (1943: 206–210), Fouché (1967: 388–412), Moignet (1976: 54–55, 67–70), Nyrop (1967: 156–167), and Pope (1952: 365–368).

uses.³ The Conditional is also considered as performing "both a temporal function of marking an event E as posterior to some past reference point R, and a modal function of expressing contrafaction or hypothetical action in the apodoses of conditional sentences" (ibid: 27).⁴

The studies of Ménard (1973) and Moignet (1976) deserve special attention because they provide lists of the uses of the OF Future and Conditional in diverse linguistic contexts. In their analyses, both researchers apply the sign-oriented Guillaumean theory of the *chronogenesis* (cf. Guillaume 1929, 1971), i.e. the development of the time image towards its realization. According to this theory, the Future attributes an event to a concrete (or determinate) space of time in the future by which the development of a given event will have been completed (actualized). Both Ménard (1973: 144) and Moignet (1976: 254, 261) consider the OF Conditional as part of the Indicative system and refer to the former as the Future action hypothetical '*futur hypothétique*' or the form in *–roie*, because of the ending *–roie* in its morphology. The form in *–roie* attributes an event to an indeterminate space of time, without a clear-cut distinction between the realm of the possible (potential) and the impossible (unreal). The use of this form shows that the development of an event has not been completed (actualized).

12.3 Hypothesis

In this paper, I will use the sign-oriented Columbia School (hereafter *CS*) approach⁵ to analyze the distribution of the OF Future and Conditional. Following this approach, I consider them to be (cf. Saussure 1916: 99), which means that invariant meanings (Saussure's *signifiés*) will be postulated for each of them. In this section, I will not deal with futurity as the system of future reference that, besides tense forms, consists of "aspectuals, modals, temporal qualifiers, or a combination of these devices" (Fleischman 1982: 2). These qualifiers imply a future contextually, whereas both the OF Future and Conditional make a specific claim for future events, actions or states of being (hereafter *occurrences*) that may or may not take place.

---

³ For the analysis of the Future tense as a linguistic category, see Bybee (1985: 156–159), Bybee and Pagliuca (1987), Comrie (1985: 43–48), Tobin (1988, 1989, 1990b), and Ultan (1978).

⁴ The Modern French Conditional has been analyzed by Abouda (1997), Dendale and Tasmowski (2001), Haillet (2002). Caudal and Vetters (2005), and Gobert and Maisier (1995) compare the values of the Modern French Future and Conditional.

⁵ The CS approach is presented in the works of Contini-Morava and Goldberg (1995), Diver (1969, 1981), García (1975), Huffman (1997), Klein-Andreu (1983), Reid (1979, 1991), Reid et al. (2002), and Tobin (1990a, 1993, 1995).

The basic premise of the CS theory is that "language is a symbolic tool whose structure is shaped both by its communicative function and by the characteristics of its users" (Dreer 2007: 258). This definition implies two assumptions: (a) that language is a device of human communication and (b) that language is an instance of human behavior. It follows from the first assumption that the structure and the nature of language are a direct result of its communicative function. Since successful human communication "requires a set of perceptible signals each of which is associated with some conceptual content" (Contini-Morava 1995: 2), CS theory considers concrete Saussurean signs – as opposed to diverse words and sentences – to be basic analytical units. This communicative orientation (or *communicative factor*, in CS terminology) explains the distribution of signs in language: the sign appears where it does because its single invariant meaning conveys information that serves a particular communicative purpose.[6] For the opposition of the OF Future and Conditional, this means that the distribution of both signs in various linguistic contexts (or *contextual messages*, in CS terminology) is not arbitrary, but is rather motivated by their postulated invariant meanings.

The second assumption of the CS definition of language is that the use of language is influenced by the psychological and behavioral characteristics of human beings – its users. The point is that the link between invariant meanings and inferred communicated messages is indirect. If sentences conveyed ideas directly, then the creation of messages, on one hand, and their comprehension, on the other, would be reminiscent of a computational process. Ideas contained in lexical and grammatical components of sentences would be simply summed up. However, it seems far more plausible that the whole message is greater than ideas, conveyed by its component parts. In this case, the abstract invariant meanings of component parts serve as hints by which hearers and/or readers (hereafter *decoders*) infer what is being communicated. The discontinuity between the invariant meanings of signs and their various messages is bridged by human inferential abilities that constitute the *human factor* of "economy of effort" (Diver 1995: 44)[7] of the CS approach. This factor is discussed further below.

As previously stated, the OF Future and Conditional designate occurrences, i.e. "something that is localized in time, that may or may not happen, that involves entities which contribute to a greater or lesser extent to its realization" (Reid 1979: 44). Therefore, both signs belong to a grammatical system, originally proposed by Diver (1969: 47–48) and developed by Reid (1974: 50–51), who refers to it as the *Occurrence system*. The semantic substance of this Occurrence System deals with "*whether* and *how likely* it is that the event did take place" (Diver 1969: 48). Within the Occurrence System, the difference between the OF Future and Conditional is

---

[6] For more details about the communicative factor, see Diver (1995), Huffman (1997), Reid (1979), and Tobin (1990a, 1995).

[7] For more details about the human factor or the human orientation, see Diver (1995), García (1975), Huffman (1997), Reid (1979, 1995), and Tobin (1990a, 1995).

similar to the difference between what Diver (1964: 322) calls the Chronological and Modal Systems, respectively:

> [...] an event associated with the Chronological System (or the 'Indicative', as it will now be called in opposition to the Modal System) is reported as a fact. An event associated with the Modal System is represented as, in the loosest sense of the term, a possibility. Whereas the Indicative deals with events about the certainty of whose occurrence no question has been raised, the Modal System deals with hypothetical events, about whose occurrence there is some question.

The opposition of the OF Future and Conditional can be illustrated by example (1), taken from (cf. Gautiesr 1872: 86). In this example, Olivier expects that Charlemagne's army will come to the rearguard's aid if Roland blows his horn, but Roland is confident that his rearguard will defeat the outnumbering enemy. In both cases, their confidence is expressed by the Future. The Conditional appears when Roland says what he would feel if he called for help, from which decoders infer that the possibility of this occurrence is called into question.[8]

(1) "Cumpainz Rollanz, kar sunez   vostre corn,
    Companion Roland, now blow.IMP.2PL your horn
    'Roland, my companion, blow your horn'

    Si l'ORRAT   Carles, si RETURNERAT   l'oz."
    If it-HEAR.FUT.3SG Charles so RETURN.FUT.3SG the-army.
    'If Charles HEARS it and the army TURN back'

    Respunt Rollanz: "Jo FEREIE   que fols,
    Answers Roland, 'I DO.COND.1SG as fool.PL
    'Roland answers, I WOULD BEHAVE as a fool.'

    En dulce France en PERDREIE   mun lus.
    In sweet France it LOSE.COND.1SG my honor
    'I WOULD LOSE my honor in sweet France.'

    Sempres FERRAI   de Durendal granz   colps,
    Always MAKE.FUT.1SG with Durendal great.PL blows
    'I SHALL STRIKE great blows at once with Durendal.'

    Sanglanz en ERT   li branz entresqu'al or.
    Bloody   it BE.FUT.3SG the blade up to-the gold
    'The blade of it WILL BE bloody up to the gold.'

As shown by example (1), the opposition of the OF Future and Conditional allows the encoder:

- To emphasize an expected or predictable occurrence with the Future.
- To call into question a future occurrence with the Conditional by emphasizing the hypothetical possibility of its realization.

---

[8] In all the examples, the Future is designated as (FUT), and the Conditional as (COND). All the capitalized or italicized forms are mine, as well as the translations from OF into English, unless otherwise indicated.

Therefore, I postulate that the OF Future invariably means FUTURE OCCURRENCE, whereas its Conditional counterpart means FUTURE OCCURRENCE QUESTIONED. The meaning FUTURE OCCURRENCE QUESTIONED emphasizes its opposition to the meaning FUTURE OCCURRENCE and shows that both of them share the Occurrence System. Moreover, this meaning allows us to explain the diachronic development of the Conditional that is discussed below. The meaning FUTURE OCCURRENCE QUESTIONED is also more complex cognitively than the meaning FUTURE OCCURRENCE, as it provides additional information about a future occurrence. From this, I predict that the more specific and complex OF Conditional will be used less frequently than the OF Future.

This appears to be borne out by the data, specifically from a count of the instances of the future vs. the conditional in the texts of *La chanson de Roland* 'The Song of (cf. Gautiesr 1872), *Le roman de Tristan* 'The Romance of Tristan' by (cf. Béroul 1903), written in the twelfth century, *La Vie de Saint* (cf. Paris and Pannier 1872) and a collection of short poems (*lays*) by (cf. de Roquefort 1820). The results are presented in Table 12.1.

The data in Table 12.1 represent a sample of more than 1,200 instances of the OF Future and Conditional. These results strongly confirm my prediction. One can see that in each text, the instances of the OF Future (FUT), meaning FUTURE OCCURRENCE, prevail over the instances of the OF Conditional (COND) with the more specific meaning of FUTURE OCCURRENCE QUESTIONED at a rate of 84.6 versus 15.4 % of the OF Conditional, meaning that the future is five times more prevalent than the latter. Based on these results, I hypothesize that the observed drop in the relative frequency of the OF Conditional is unlikely to have happened by chance, but rather is motivated by its invariant meaning.

As previously claimed, CS theory views language not only as a communicative device, but also as a reflection of human behavior. In other words, the concept of language includes the influence that psychological characteristics of human beings exert on the use of linguistic signs, referred to by CS theory as the human factor that includes the following basic principles:

(1) Human Intelligence – human beings can draw far-reaching conclusions from minimal cues, i.e. through the cognitive process of inference;
(2) Human Efficiency – […] related to the investment of minimal effort for maximal results in the semiotic communication process;
(3) Memory Limitations – human beings have large but limited memories which can be directly related to (1) and (2) above. (Tobin 1990a: 49)

For the opposition of the OF Future and Conditional, human intelligence provides the ability to differentiate between *chanter-ai* (FUT) 'I will sing' and *chanter-oie* (COND) 'I would sing' and to infer what kind of specific message is intended, based on minimal hints provided by both signs. As I have pointed out, the stems of the OF Future and Conditional are identical. Both signs differ only in their endings, expressed by the reduced forms of the verb *habere* 'to have'. The endings of the Future are derived from the Present Indicative of *habere*, while those of the Conditional have as their basis the Imperfect Indicative. Human efficiency

Table 12.1 The predominance of the OF Future over the OF Conditional

	Roland	Tristan	Alexis	Marie de France	Cross totals
FUT	466	362	40	187	1,055
COND	33	116	1	42	192
FUT%: COND%	93.4 : 6.6	75.7 : 24.3	97.6 : 2.4	81.7 : 18.3	84.6 : 15.4

is manifested by producing as many linguistic signs as possible from as few linguistic forms as possible. For example, in Modern French, the Present Indicative stem serves as the base for the Present Subjunctive, the Imperative, the Imperfect Indicative, and the Present Participle of most of French verbs. Relatively limited human memory enables us to store only a finite number of linguistic signs, which facilitates the decoders' intelligence, i.e. the ability to draw conclusions from minimal clues in communication. For the same reason, the stored linguistic signs represent a set of concepts, grammatical interlocks, rather a strict single meaning. Within these interlocks, one signal has meanings in different grammatical systems simultaneously. This differs from the the traditional notion of one form with several meanings or functions. Consider García (1975: 56) on this matter:

> To the extent that such varied functions are mutually contradictory, they point to erroneous analysis [...]; to the extent that the various 'meanings' are not mutually contradictory, they should be traced, and ascribed, to the context to whose influence they are due. It should be clear that the confluence of different meanings from different systems cannot possibly be contradictory, though it may be more or less coherent.

For example, besides the meanings of the Occurrence System, French verbs designate number within the System of Number and person within the System of Person. The System of Number opposes the meanings ONE for the singular and MORE THAN ONE for the plural (cf. Diver 1987; Reid 1991). The System of Person opposes the meanings SPEAKER for the first person, HEARER for the second person and OTHER for the third person (cf. García 1975: 61–71). Within this Occurrence-Person-Number interlock, the signal *fereie* (COND) 'I would do' means FUTURE OCCURRENCE QUESTIONED, SPEAKER, ONE. However, this study will not deal with these meanings, unless their correlation with the meanings of the Occurrence System influences the use of both signs.

12.4 Communicative Strategies of the Use of the OF Future and Conditional

The next step of the analysis is to show that the invariant meanings of the OF Future and Conditional motivate their distribution in diverse messages. I will show that the meaning Future Occurrence contributes to the communicated messages when the OF Future appears and that the meaning Future Occurrence Questioned contributes to the messages when the OF Conditional appears.

The meaningful contrast between the OF Future and Conditional is used in high medieval literature for different communicative purposes, referred to as *communicative strategies* in the CS theory (cf. Diver 1995; García 1975; Reid 1995). Here I mean the regular, standardized, or idiomatic use of both signs to contribute to particular messages. Though OF does not represent a standard language with unified spelling and grammatical norms, one can speak about a growing tendency towards conformity and the systematization of the use of linguistic signs in the eleventh and twelfth centuries. This tendency results from the influence that a social group exerts "on its own members in the direction of a standardized usage" (Diver 1995: 78) that contributes to better communication. The basic communicative strategies are postulated as follows:

- The opposition of the OF Future and Conditional is generally used to (de)emphasize the encoder's expectation of a future occurrence. I will show that the encoder uses the Future to designate expected or predictable future occurrences, whereas the Conditional is used for less probable and uncertain future occurrences that may or may not take place.
- This opposition is used to differentiate volitional messages (e.g., obligation, necessity or even prohibition) from an attenuated request, suggestion or piece of advice. I will show that the former are expressed by the Future, whereas the latter are expressed by the Conditional.
- The opposition of the OF Future and Conditional is used to differentiate the degree of the possibility of occurrences whose realization depends on a condition. I will show that more feasible, reasonably expected occurrences are expressed by the Future, whereas less feasible, more hypothetical occurrences are expressed by the Conditional.

The application of communicative strategies can be explained by the invariant meanings FUTURE OCCURRENCE and FUTURE OCCURRENCE QUESTIONED of both signs. Paraphrasing Reid (1995: 133), I claim that these strategies do not differ grammatically, only pragmatically, i.e. only with respect to what the encoder attempts to convey with (and what the decoder infers from) FUTURE OCCURRENCE or FUTURE OCCURRENCE QUESTIONED in a particular discourse occasion.

12.5 The Data: "Micro-level" Analysis of Individual Examples

The following data represent the "micro-level" analysis of individual examples with the OF Future, used to emphasize expected or predictable future occurrences, and the OF Conditional, used to call into question future occurrences. In order to neutralize the role of intuition in the validation of the invariant meanings, the choice of one sign over another is judged within the wider linguistic context.

12.5.1 The Occurrence System Opposition and the (De) Emphasis of the Encoder's Expectation of an Occurrence

As previously mentioned, the Future is used to make "a clear prediction about some future state of affairs" (Comrie 1985: 44). This allows the encoder to use the Future to express promises, as in the example (2), taken from (cf. de Roquefort 1820: 146). In this example, a female servant uses the Future to promise to her lady to hide an unwanted child in a church.

(2) Jeo vus en DELIVERAI ja,
   I   you of-it RID.FUT.1SG immediately
   'I SHALL RID you of it'

   Si que honie   ne SEREZ
   So that shamed not BE.FUT.2PL
   'So that you WILL never BE ashamed of it'

   Ne   ke james ne la VEREZ.
   Neither that never not her SEE.FUT.2PL
   'Or SEE her ever again.'

   A un mustier la GETERAI,
   To a church her ABANDON.FUT.1SG
   'I SHALL ABANDON her in a church'

   Tut sein e   sauf la PORTERAI.
   Quite sound and safe her CARRY.FUT.1SG
   'I SHALL CARRY her quite safe and sound.'

As opposed to the Future, the OF Conditional indicates that a question has been raised about an occurrence, i.e. that from the encoder's point of view an occurrence may or may not take place. The Conditional often designates a future occurrence perceived from some past moment. In this linguistic context, a question about an occurrence results from the discrepancy between the 'here-and-now' moment of encoding that has become a reality and a future occurrence the realization of which remains potential or hypothetical. The wider the gap is between the reality and the possibility, the less predictable the realization of an occurrence and the more justified the use of the Conditional. Fleischman (1982: 28) states the following on this matter:

> [...] a future removed from its mooring in the speaker's present and reckoned instead from a moment in the past will predictably correlate with modalities implying an even stronger degree of unreality, given the nonactuality (= nonpresent) of the reference point.

Example (3), taken from the *Prologue* to the lays by (cf. de Roquefort 1820: 46), illustrates my point. In this example, the Conditional implies a gap between the fact that the author has collected the lays and the possibility to offer them to the noble king one day.

(3) M'entremis de   Lais assembler,
    Set.REFL   some lays   assemble.INF
    'I set myself to assemble some lays'

    Por rime   faire   e   reconter.
    By rhyme compose.INF and relate.INF
    'To compose and to relate them in rhyme.'

    En mun quoer penseie   e   diseie,
    In my heart   think.IPFV.1SG and say.IPFV.1SG
    'In my heart, I thought and said'

    Sire, ke vus PRESENTEREIE.
    Lord, that you PRESENT.COND.1SG
    'That I WOULD PRESENT them to you.'

12.5.2 The Occurrence System Opposition and (Attenuated) Volitional Messages

As previously stated, the OF Future and Conditional are used in imperative, i.e. "obligative, volitional-desiderative, and intentive" (Fleischman 1982: 133) messages. The choice among these signs is not arbitrary, but rather is motivated by their respective invariant meanings. The invariant meaning FUTURE OCCURRENCE of the OF Future is appropriate for imperative messages "where an immediate and precise fulfilling of the implied request, order or demand is not necessarily of primary importance" (Tobin 1990b: 476). At the same time, as stated by Diver (1964: 331), "we may [...] anticipate that the speaker of the sentence would be somewhat surprised to hear subsequently that the event had not taken place". The invariant meaning FUTURE OCCURRENCE QUESTIONED of the OF Conditional is preferred for attenuated requests, suggestions or advice when the outcome of an occurrence is not necessarily expected. In this case, "the result is a cautious rather than a confident statement, and one can imagine that the speaker would not be particularly surprised if the event did not occur" (ibid). It might be argued that a polite request requires that an outcome be carried out. However, the encoder uses the Conditional precisely in order to allow the decoder the freedom to carry out or to refuse the request (from which OCCURRENCE QUESTIONED), without his/her refusal being discourteous. The set of examples (4)–(5) illustrate the difference between the Future and the Conditional.

Example (4), taken from *La chanson de* (cf. Gautiesr 1872: 6), is an instance of the use of the OF Future to imply an order. In this example, King Marsilla sends messengers to Charlemagne to offer peace. The Future appears to express the king's expectation that his order will be performed:

(4) «Seignurs baruns, a Carlemagne IREZ.
Lords barons, to Charlemagne GO.FUT.2PL
"Lord Barons, you SHALL GO to Charlemagne."

Il est al siege a Cordres la citet.
He is at.ART siege in Cordres the city.
'He is at the siege of the city of Cordres.'

Branches d'olives en voz mains PORTEREZ
Branches of-olives in your hands CARRY.FUT.2PL
'You SHALL CARRY branches of olives in your hands.'

Example (5), taken from *Equitan* by (cf. de Roquefort 1820: 136), presents the use of the Conditional to give advice. In this example, the author suggests learning a lesson from her lay. However, she is not confident that anyone will follow her advice, which explains the use of the Conditional:

(5) Issi mururent ambedui,
Thus die.PRET.3PL both
'Thus they both died'

Li Reis avant, e ele od lui;
The king before, and she with him.
'The king first, and she with him.'

Ki bien VODREIT reisun entendre,
Who very WILL.COND.3SG reason hear.INF
'He who WOULD listen to reason'

Ici PURREIT ensample prendre:
Here CAN.COND.3SG example take.INF
'COULD profit from this example.'

12.5.3 *The Occurrence System Opposition and the Degree of the Possibility of Contingent Occurrences*

Though the Future designates occurrences that may happen, "any prediction we make about the future might be changed by intervening events, including our own conscious intervention" (Comrie 1985: 43). Therefore, it is not by chance that the opposition of the OF Future and Conditional is frequently used to differentiate the degrees of probability of occurrences, whose realization is contingent on the fulfillment of a condition. One usually speaks of the threefold scale of hypothetical occurrences that includes certain, potential, and counterfactual occurrences. We consider certain hypothetical occurrences when "the hypothesis expressed in the protasis [the *if*-subordinate clause] is seen as likely or even certain to be fulfilled, or at least where there is no presupposition that it will not be (or has not been) fulfilled"

(Harris 1986: 408). The protasis of such messages is usually in the Present, and the apodosis (the main or *then* clause) is in the Future. We deal with potential and counterfactual occurrences when "the relevant hypothesis is unlikely to be fulfilled, or indeed incapable of fulfillment" (Harris 1986: 408–409).

In these cases, one finds the Imperfect Subjunctive in both protasis and apodosis.[9] Since the middle of the eleventh century, the Conditional has replaced the Imperfect Subjunctive in the apodosis of potential and counterfactual conditions. Johnston (1901: 134) points out that the "use of the conditional in hypothetical sentences doubtless began in conditional sentences referring to the future", which fits in with the postulated invariant meaning FUTURE OCCURRENCE QUESTIONED of the Conditional. One might argue that the counterfactual use of the Conditional has nothing to do with futurity because this use concerns the past statements. I claim that the communicative purpose of this use of the Conditional is to anticipate that a contingent occurrence might have happened before another contingent occurrence at some point in the future. For this kind of messages, the OF possesses in its inventory the perfective Conditional that means FUTURE OCCURRENCE QUESTIONED, BEFORE. Its use is illustrated by example (6), taken from the lay *Lanval* by (cf. de Roquefort 1820: 214). In this example, a beautiful and rich lady asks his lover, the knight Lanval, to keep their relationship secret, or risk losing her forever.

(6) A tus jurs m'ARIEZ PERDUE,
 To all days me-LOSE.COND.PFV.2PL
 "You WOULD HAVE LOST me forever!"

 Se ceste amurs esteit seue
 If this love.PL be.IPFV.3SG known
 'If this love was (were) known'.

Example (7) illustrates the use of the Future and the Conditional as they appear in the apodosis of hypothetical sentences within the same context. In this example, taken from *Le Freisne* 'Le Fresne' by (cf. de Roquefort 1820: 158), a respected lord tries to convince a poor girl, named Le Fresne, to run away with him. The lord uses the Future to express promises for which he takes responsibility, whereas the Conditional appears to deal with the things beyond his control, such as the wrath that the abbess could show if she discovered the lord's love affair in the abbey and the girl's possible pregnancy:

---

[9] In Dreer (2007), I show that the OF Imperfect Subjunctive with the invariant meaning, postulated as OCCURRENCE QUESTIONED, LESS RELEVANT, is used for all kinds of possible occurrences whose outcome is less relevant to the encoder, including hypothetical occurrences. However, this fact will not be discussed here.

(7) Si vostre Aunte s'aparceveit,
If your aunt notice.IPFV.REFL.3SG
'If your aunt noticed'

Mut durement li PESEREIT,
Very much her GRIEVE.COND.3SG
'This WOULD GRIEVE her deeply'

Encur si feussez enceintez
As well if be.SBJV.IPFV.2PL pregnant;
'If you became pregnant as well'

Durement SEREIT encruciez;
Much BE.COND.3SG angry
'She WOULD BE extremely angry'

Si mun cunseil crere volez,
If my advice believe.INF want.PRS.2PL
'If you accept my advice'

Ensemble od mei vus en VENDREZ.
Together with me you there COME.FUT.2PL
'You WILL COME away with me'

Certes, james ne vus FAUDRAI,
Certainly, never not you FAIL.FUT.1SG
'Certainly, I SHALL never FAIL you'

Richement vus CUNSEILLERAI.»
Powerfully you HELP.FUT.1SG
'I SHALL HELP you powerfully'

12.6 The Data: "Macro-level" Analysis

The "micro-level" analysis alone does not allow us to be sure that the choice between the OF Future and Conditional is not arbitrary. One could argue that this analysis may be "accidents of a few striking examples [or] facile readings of stereotypical sentences out of context" (Davis 2002: 65). Therefore, I will further examine how both linguistic signs are distributed within a text, validating their overall distribution quantitatively. I predict that the non-random use of both signs, observed in examples (1)–(7) above, will also be confirmed within a text where the use of each linguistic form is the choice of the author, in other words, is his/her conscious or subconscious decision to produce a communicative effect. Assuming this, any text can be viewed as an inventory of different ideas (contexts, themes or leitmotifs) consistently built around the major textual message. Consider Davis (ibid, p. 71–72) on this matter:

> A novel is no more a random sample of linguistic forms than a symphony is a random sample of musical notes.

For this analysis, I apply the ascending "from sign to text" approach, developed by Tobin (1990a, 1993, 1995) for the analysis of the distribution of linguistic forms within a larger "macro-level" discourse. This approach is based on the CS assumption that the encoder uses the relatively abstract invariant meaning of a sign(al) to convey concrete contextual messages. Starting with this assumption, one particular sign with its invariant meaning may be more appropriate for the use in particular leitmotifs within a text than other signs found in the same system. Tobin (1995: 62) states the following on this matter:

> The ability to trace the consistent uses of a sign within a system to appear in specific contexts within a particular text is what we call the "from sign to text" approach. It allows us to view the text in the hierarchical ascending order of sign and system to context and text.

As applied to my analysis, the "from sign to text" approach means that the distribution of the OF Future and Conditional is not random, but is rather skewed along thematic lines within a given text. I will divide this text into leitmotifs that may be associated with messages to which the invariant meanings of both signs contribute. This will allow us to speak about the coherent and non-random distribution of the OF Future and Conditional in the chosen text, if one sign appears more frequently than the other in particular leitmotifs.

The text that I have chosen for the "from sign to text" analysis is *Le roman de Tristan* 'The Romance of Tristan' by Béroul, written in the twelfth century. The text deals with the adulterous love between King Mark's wife Isolde and his knight and nephew Tristan. The composition of the manuscript represents a number of episodes of varying length, grouped around cycles, each of which has its own outset, climax and outcome. Consider Lacy (1994: 226) on this matter:

> The narration is cyclical in form, as King Mark repeatedly becomes suspicious of the lovers and acts on those suspicions by threatening or punishing Tristan and Isolde, only to be somehow persuaded that his wife and nephew are guiltless; he then pardons them, and the cycle begins anew.

I claim that the OF Future and Conditional are distributed differently for the different cycles and leitmotifs of the romance. As previously stated, the invariant meaning of the OF Future contributes to messages that express more feasible or predictable future occurrences. Therefore, one could expect that this sign would be more frequent in leitmotifs where the characters feel more or less certain about events that may take place. The invariant meaning of the OF Conditional contributes to messages that express less feasible or uncertain future occurrences. Therefore, one could expect that this sign would appear more in leitmotifs about which the characters feel uncertain.

Following the cycles of the narration, I have conventionally divided Béroul's manuscript into five leitmotifs. The first leitmotif *Under the Tree* (lines 1–573) recounts Tristan and Isolde's date under a tree where King Mark is hiding out to eavesdrop on them. The lovers almost reveal themselves, but finally manage to carry on their conversation in such a manner as to remove all doubts that King Mark has about his wife and nephew's loyalty. Since Béroul's manuscript is missing the beginning, this leitmotif has only one episode. The second leitmotif *Lovers' Escape* (lines 574–2062) includes different episodes in which the enemies of Tristan lure him into a trap (the episode *Flour on the Floor* [lines 574–827]), the lovers are caught together, arrested and condemned to death, but manage to escape (the episode *Condemnation and Escape* [lines 828–1270]). They run away into the forest of Morrois and live there undergoing hardships (the episodes *Forest of Morrois, Hermit Ogrin, Dog Husdant, Governal's Vengeance* [lines 1271–1773]). King Mark discovers the sleeping lovers, and wants to kill them, but sees them wearing their clothes, with a sword lying between them. He thinks that he might have mistaken about their disloyalty (the episode *Lovers' Discovery* [lines 1774–2062]). The next leitmotifs *Isolde's Return* and *Reconciliation* narrate the sequence of events which lead up to Isolde's reconciliation with her husband (the episodes *Love Potion Effect, Ogrin, Return to Mark* [lines 2063–3027]), the emergence of new jealousy and doubts in Mark, and end with Isolde's vindication (the episodes *Isolde's Vindication* and *Ambiguous Oath* [lines 3028–4264]). The last leitmotif *Tristan Revenge* (lines 4265–4485) is the shortest one, because Béroul's narration stops in the middle of a sentence when Tristan kills two noblemen after Isolde's reconciliation with King Mark.

My hypothesis is that these leitmotifs may be associated with the messages, conveyed by the invariant meanings of the OF Future and Conditional. Throughout the first two leitmotifs *Under the Tree* and *Lovers' Escape*, the lovers feel that their lives are in peril due to contingencies beyond their control both when they are at King Mark's court and when they find shelter in the forest of Morrois. Therefore, I predict that the Conditional will be preferred in these leitmotifs, especially in the episodes when the lovers do not control events or their lives are at stake, as in examples (8)–(11). The set of examples (8)–(9) appears in the context of Isolde and Tristan's rendezvous under a tree in the beginning of the manuscript (lines 62–63 and 65–68 respectively). Aware that Mark is eavesdropping on them, Isolde reproaches Tristan for running the risk of inviting her to join in this conversation. Isolde feigns that she feels unsafe because of Tristan's request that she help him to reconcile with King Mark. Her feigned uncertainty is expressed by the Conditional, even after the use of the verb *savoir* 'to know' in example (9).

(8) Je ne SEROIE   pas tant ose
    I not BE.COND.1SG NEG so   daring
    'I WOULD not BE so daring'

    Que je i   osase   venir.
    That I here dare.SUBJ.IPFV.1SG come.INF.
    'That I would dare to come here.'

(9) S'or   en savoit   li rois   un mot,
    If-now it know.IPFV.3SG the king a word
    'If the king knew this'

    Mon cors SERET   desmenbré   tot,
    My body BE.COND.3SG dismembered whole
    'My whole body WOULD BE dismembered'

    Et si SEROIT   a mout grant tort;
    And thus BE.COND.3SG to very big   harm
    'And thus this WOULD BE very much wrong'

    Bien sai   qu'il me DORROIT   la mort.
    Well know.PRS.1SG that-he me GIVE.COND.3SG the death.
    'I know very well that he WOULD KILL me.'

Example (10) appears in the episode when the dwarf Frocin sets a trap to expose the lovers by sprinkling flour between the beds so that they would leave footprints on the floor (lines 712–714). Tristan sees Frocin sprinkling the flour and tries to understand what the dwarf is doing and what could be the consequences of that. His guesswork is represented by the multiple use of the Conditional in example (10).

(10)   Espandroit   flor   por nostre trace
     Sprinkle.IPFV.3SG flower for our   trace
     'He was sprinkling finest flour for our trace'

     Veer,   se l'un   a l'autre   IROIT.
     See.INF if the-one to the-other GO.COND.3SG
     'Being seen if the one WENT to the other'

     Qui IROIT   or, que fous FEROIT
     Who GO.COND.3SG now, what fool DO.COND.3SG
     'He who WOULD GO now, what a foolish thing he WOULD DO'

Example (11) appears in the context of Isolde's trial for treason, i.e. the love affair with Tristan (lines 1175–1179). A leper suggests punishing Isolde by having her raped by a group of lustful lepers, which puts Isolde's life at stake. Her fate depends only on King Mark's decision. Therefore, this uncertainty is implied by the multiple use of the Conditional in example (11).

(11)   Et   que VOUDROIT   mex mort avoir,
     And that WILL.COND.3SG better death have.INF
     'And that she WOULD DIE rather'

     Qu'ele   VIVROIT,   et sanz   valoir,
     Than-she LIVE.COND.3SG and without value
     'Than she WOULD LIVE in disgrace'

     Et   que nus n'en ORROIT   parler
     And that at all not-it HEAR.COND.3SG speak.INF
     'And that he WOULD not HEAR speak about it at all'

     Qui plus ne t'en tenist   por ber.
     Who more no you-it hold.SUBJ.IPFV.3SG for Baron.
     'Who would not consider you any more as a Baron.'

     Rois, VOUDROIES   le faire issi ?»
     King WILL.COND.2SG this do.INF like this
     "King, WOULD you LIKE to do that like this?"

The second half of the manuscript (the leitmotifs *Isolde's Return, Reconciliation* and *Tristan's Revenge*) includes the episodes that deal with Tristan's and Isolde's decision to reconcile with King Mark, who agrees to take back Isolde. Isolde's oath establishes her innocence. Though after the two noblemen's death, Tristan's and Isolde's future is unclear, throughout these leitmotifs the lovers feel more certain and act more decisively. Therefore, my prediction is that the Future will be favored in these leitmotifs, especially in the episodes when the characters exert greater control over the course of events, as in examples (12)–(14). The set of examples

(12)–(13) deals with Tristan's plan to have Isolde reconcile with King Mark (lines 2433–2435, 2438–2445). The hermit Ogrin advises the lovers to write a letter to the king to ask him to forget his anger and to let Isolde return to the court. Tristan makes up his mind to bring this letter to Mark. His decisiveness is expressed by the multiple use of the Future in examples (12)–(13).

(12) «Quil PORTERA ?» dist li hermites.
 Who-it TAKE.FUT.3SG say.PRET.3SG the hermit
 '"Who WILL TAKE it?" said the hermit.'

 – Gel PORTERAI. – Tristran, nu dites.
 I-it TAKE.FUT.1SG – Tristan not-it say.IMP.
 '"I WILL TAKE it." – "Tristan, do not say that!"'

 – Certes, sire, si FERAI bien
 Certainly, sir, like this DO.FUT.1SG well
 '"Certainly, sir, I WILL DO so."'

(13) La roïne REMAINDRA ci;
 The queen REMAIN.FUT.3SG here
 'The queen WILL REMAIN here.'

 Et anevois, en tens oscur,
 And in vain in time obscure
 'And soon, at dark night,'

 Qant li rois DORMIRA seür,
 When the king SLEEP.FUT.3SG surely
 'When the king IS surely asleep,'

 Ge MONTERAI sor mon destrier,
 I MOUNT.FUT.1SG on my horse
 'I WILL MOUNT my horse'

 O moi MERRAI mon escuier.
 With me LEAD.FUT.1SG my squire
 'And I WILL TAKE my squire with me.'

 Defors la vile a un pendant :
 Outside the town at a slope
 'Outside the town, at a slope'

 La DECENDRAI, S'IRAI avant.
 There DISMOUNT.FUT.1SG, GO.FUT.1SG forward
 'I WILL DISMOUNT there and GO on forward'

 Mon cheval GARDERA mon mestre
 My horse KEEP.FUT.3SG my master
 'My master WILL LOOK after my horse'

Example (14) appears in the context of a conversation held between Tristan and Perinis, with whom Isolde sends a secret message to Tristan (lines 3338–3341). The latter promises his help to Isolde, who has to vindicate herself before King Mark and his court. Tristan's decisiveness to help is emphasized by the use of the Future in example (14).

(14) G'IRAI   au   terme, pas n'en dot.
     GO.FUT.1SG to-the term, not not-it doubt
     'I WILL COME in time, no doubt about that'

   Face soi   lie,   saine et baude !
   Face be.SBJV.PRS.3SG happy, healthy and cheerful
   'Let her face be happy, healthy and cheerful'

   Ja   n'AVRAI   mais bain d'eve   chaude
   Already not-HAVE.FUT.1SG more bath of-water warm
   'I WILL never HAVE a bath of warm water'

   Tant qu'a   m'espee   aie   venjance
   Until that-to my-sword have.SBJV.PRS.1SG revenge
   ___ 'Until I have revenge with my sword'

To test my predictions, I have counted all the instances of the OF Future and Conditional used in the manuscript, and have calculated the percentage of the Conditional for the examined leitmotifs. In order to test the significance of the given results, I have calculated the Z-value of the Conditional, used in each leitmotif. The Z-value shows whether the difference between the observed results (value) and the expected results (mean) is large enough to be statistically significant. Following Muller (1992: 91–108), the Z-value is calculated as follows:

- Calculate the expectation (mean) by dividing the overall corpus frequency of the Conditional by the number of all possible outcomes of the Future and the Conditional and then by multiplying the quotient by the number of the outcomes of the Future and the Conditional within a leitmotif: mean = n(outcomes in corpus) / n(corpus) * n(outcomes in leitmotif)
- Calculate the probability q that the Conditional will not occur in the corpus, according to the formula: $q = 1 - (n(\text{outcomes in corpus}) / n(\text{corpus}))$
- Calculate the standard deviation (SD) which is the square root of the product of the calculated mean and the probability q: $SD = \sqrt{mean * q}$
- Calculate Z-value according to the formula: Z = (value – mean) / SD

The results are compared to a standard Z-table in Muller (1992: 175), according to which a significant Z-value must be greater than ±1.645. The probability p of the Z-value ±1.645 is 0.10, i.e. a 90 % confidence level which means that in 90 cases out of 100 the observed result is unlikely to have happened by chance.[10] This level of statistical significance is acceptable for the purpose of my study. The results of the count are presented in Table 12.2.

Table 12.2 present the results of the distribution of the OF Future and Conditional for the examined leitmotifs: *Under the Tree, Lovers' Escape, Isolde's Return,*

---

[10] One might argue that the Z-value is not adding anything to the presentation of the test results and that the percentages alone of the Future and the Conditional show the predicted skewing. However, the two tests have different purposes. A percentage is a relative value, used to express a fraction of the whole. It gives an idea of the relationship between quantities. The Z-value is used to determine whether or not given results differ in a statistically significant manner from calculated results, i.e. to test a suggested hypothesis.

Table 12.2 *Le roman de Tristan*: Non-random distribution of the Future vs. the Conditional for different leitmotifs of the romance

Leitmotifs		FUT	COND	COND (%)	Z[a]
Under the tree	Under the tree	46	29	38.7	2.909
Lovers' escape	Flour on the floor	18	7	30.1	1.707
	Condemnation and escape	48	21		
	Forest of Morrois + Hermit Ogrin	7	3		
	Dog Husdant	11	8		
	Governal's Vengeance	3	1		
	Lovers' discovery	22	7		
Isolde's return	Love potion effect	3	8	16.8	−1.848
	Ogrin	61	8		
	Return to mark	30	3		
Reconciliation	Isolde's vindication	69	13	15.8	−2.155
	Ambiguous oath	32	6		
Tristan's revenge	Tristan's revenge	12	2	14.3	−0.871

[a] Corpus is 478 instances of use: Future – 362 times, Conditional – 116 times. The Z-value for the first leitmotif in this table is calculated as follows:
1. The expectation (mean) for this leitmotif is: mean $= 116/478 * (46+29) = 18$
2. The probability q of the Conditional is: $q = 1 - (116/478) = 0.757$
3. The standard deviation of the calculated variance is: $SD = \sqrt{18*0.757} = 3.691$
4. The Z-value for the first leitmotif is: $Z = (29-18)/3.691 = 2.909$ (In fact, the outcome $Z = (29-18)/3.691$ equals 2.980 because it is based on rounded numbers. The exact Z-value is that which appears in this table, i.e. 2.909)

Reconciliation and *Tristan's Revenge*. These results support my predictions and indicate a preference for the distribution of both linguistic signs for different leitmotifs. The rate of the Conditional drops sharply from 38.7 to 30.1 % in the first two leitmotifs, where the characters mostly feel uncertain, to 16.8, 15.8 and 14.3 % in the three last leitmotifs respectively, where the characters manifest more confidence of the situation. The Z-values (Z) in Table 12.2 are greater than ±1.645 for all the leitmotifs, except for the last one where the manuscript breaks off. The low Z-value may reflect this fact. The results point out the statistical significance of the predicted distribution. The positive Z-values for the first two leitmotifs mean that the Conditional occurs here more than would be expected, whereas the negative Z-values for the other leitmotifs mean that the Conditional appears there less than would be expected.

12.7 Conclusion: Diachronic Meaningful Contrast

I have shown in this chapter that the CS sign-oriented approach, adopted in my analysis, can account for the diachronic development of the French Future and Conditional. I contend that this development results from changes in the invariant meanings of both linguistic signs, such as the diachronic narrowing of the meaning of the Future. The larger meaning FUTURE OCCURRENCE of the OF Future has been narrowed down to imply the abstract idea of futurity in Modern French. This change accounts for the drop in the relative frequency of the Modern French Future in favor of periphrastic forms, expressed by "the 'go' verb with an infinitive: [...] *je vais/ allais chanter*" (Fleischman 1982: 17). This "go-future" designates a specific, inevitable occurrence, "as if it were already a reality [...] to the speaker's point-of-view" (Tobin 1989: 67).

On the other hand, we are faced with the diachronic widening of the invariant meaning of the Conditional, going from a specific uncertain future occurrence (FUTURE OCCURRENCE QUESTIONED) that the Conditional represents in OF to the more abstract and wider modal uncertainty (OCCURRENCE QUESTIONED) that the Conditional means in Modern French. This widening explains the increase in the relative frequency of the Modern French Conditional. The qualitative changes in the meaning, manifested since the seventeenth century, have resulted in the reorganization of the Occurrence System that includes the Indicative, the Subjunctive, and the Conditional in Modern French.[11]

In this chapter, I have presented a functional sign-oriented analysis of the distribution of the OF Future and Conditional. I have shown that the choice and the distribution of both signs in OF are motivated by a semantic distinction between their invariant meanings. The OF Future provides the decoder with an indication that in a given message, a future occurrence *per se* matters, whereas the OF Conditional implies that in a given message, the result of a future occurrence is questioned. The proposed meanings not only account for the consistent use of the Future and the Conditional in individual sentences, but also allow us to make predictions about their distribution within texts.

Acknowledgments I gratefully acknowledge Deborah Arteaga for the opportunity to contribute this paper. I would also like to thank Yishai Tobin for his thorough reading and for his very helpful suggestions. I will claim possible errors of fact and judgment for myself only.

References

Abouda, L. 1997. Recherches sur la syntaxe et la sémantique du conditionnel en français. Thèse de doctorat, Paris VII.

Brunot, F., and C. Bruneau. 1969. *Précis de grammaire historique de la langue française*. Paris: Masson.

Bybee, J. 1985. *Morphology: A study of the relation between meaning and form*. Amsterdam/Philadelphia: Benjamins.

Bybee, J., and W. Pagliuca. 1987. The evolution of future meaning. In *Papers from the VIIth international conference on historical linguistics*, ed. A.G. Ramat, O. Carruba, and G. Bernini, 109–122. Amsterdam: Benjamins.

---

[11] This point, however, needs further research than is possible in this chapter.

Caudal, P., and C. Vetters. 2005. Un traitement conjoint du conditionnel, du futur et de l'imparfait: les temps comme fonction d'actes de langage. In *Temporalité et modalité, Cahiers Chronos 12*, ed. A. Molendijk and C. Vet, 109–124. Amsterdam: Rodopi.

Comrie, B. 1985. *Tense*. Cambridge: Cambridge University Press.

Contini-Morava, E. 1995. Introduction: On linguistic sign theory. In *Meaning as explanation: Advances in linguistic sign theory*, ed. E. Contini-Morava and B. Sussman Goldberg, 1–31. Berlin: Mouton De Gruyter.

Contini-Morava, E., and B.S. Goldberg (eds.). 1995. *Meaning as explanation: Advances in linguistic sign theory*. Berlin: Mouton De Gruyter.

D'Hulst, Y. 2004. French and Italian conditionals: From etymology to representation. In *The syntax of time*, ed. J. Guéron and J. Lecarme, 181–203. Cambridge: MIT Press.

Davis, J. 2002. Rethinking the place of statistics in Columbia School analysis. In *Signal, meaning, and message: Perspectives on sign-based linguistics*, ed. W. Reid, R. Otheguy, and N. Stern, 65–90. Amsterdam: Benjamins.

de Saussure, F. 1916. *Cours de linguistique générale*, publié par Ch. Bally et A. Sechehaye avec la collaboration de A. Riedlinger. Paris: Payot.

Dendale, P., and L. Tasmowski (eds.). 2001. *Le conditionnel en français*. Metz: Université de Metz.

Diver, W. 1964. The modal system of the English verb. *Word* 20: 322–352.

Diver, W. 1969. The system of relevance of the Homeric verb. *Acta Linguistica Hafniensia* XII: 45–68.

Diver, W. 1981. On defining the discipline. *Columbia University Working Papers in Linguistics* 6: 59–117.

Diver, W. 1987. The dual. *Columbia University Working Papers in Linguistics* 8: 100–114.

Diver, W. 1995. Theory. In *Meaning as explanation: Advances in linguistic sign theory*, ed. E. Contini-Morava and B. Sussman Goldberg, 43–114. Berlin: Mouton De Gruyter.

Dreer, I. 2007. *Expressing the same by the different: The subjunctive versus the indicative in French*. Amsterdam/Philadelphia: Benjamins.

Ewert, A. 1943. *The French language*. London: Faber & Faber.

Fleischman, S. 1982. *The future in thought and language: Diachronic evidence from Romance*. Cambridge: Cambridge University Press.

Fouché, P. 1967. *Le verbe français: étude morphologique*. Paris: Klincksieck.

García, E.C. 1975. *The role of theory in linguistic analysis: The Spanish pronoun system*. Amsterdam: North Holland.

Gobert, D.L., and V. Maisier. 1995. Valeurs modales du futur et du conditionnel et leurs emplois en français contemporain. *The French Review* 68(6): 1003–1014.

Guillaume, G. 1929. *Temps et Verbe: théorie des aspects, des modes et des temps; suivi de l'architectonique du temps dans les langues classiques*. Paris: Honoré Champion.

Guillaume, G. 1971. *Leçons de linguistique de Gustave Guillaume [1948–49]. Séries A: structure sémiologique et structure psychique de la langue française I*. Publiées par Roch Valin, avec la collaboration de René Lesage. Québec: Les Presses de l'Université Laval.

Haillet, P. 2002. *Le conditionnel en français: une approche polyphonique*. Paris: Ophrys.

Harris, M. 1986. The historical development of conditional sentences in Romance. *Romance Philology* 39(4): 405–436.

Huffman, A. 1997. *The categories of grammar: French lui and le*. Amsterdam/Philadelphia: Benjamins.

Johnston, O.M. 1901. The French condition contrary to fact. *Modern Language Notes* 16(5): 129–137.

Klein-Andreu, F. (ed.). 1983. *Discourse perspectives on syntax*. New York: Academic.

Lacy, N.J. 1994. Béroul: The Romance of Tristan. In *The Romance of Arthur: An anthology of medieval texts in translation*, ed. J.J. Wilhelm, 225–276. New York: Garland.

Ménard, P. 1973. *Manuel du français du Moyen Age. 1. Syntaxe de l'ancien français*. Bordeaux: Sobodi.

Moignet, G. 1976. *Grammaire de l'ancien français: Morphologie – Syntaxe*, 2ᵉ éd. Paris: Klincksieck.
Muller, Ch. 1992. *Initiation aux méthodes de la statistique linguistique*. Paris: Champion.
Nyrop, K. 1967. *Grammaire historique de la langue française*, vol. II. Copenhague: Gyldendal.
Pope, M.K. 1952. *From Latin to modern French with especial consideration of Anglo-Norman*, 2nd ed. Manchester: Manchester University Press.
Posner, R. 1997. *Linguistic change in French*. Oxford: Clarendon.
Reid, W. 1974. The Saussurian sign as a control in linguistic analysis. *Semiotexte* 1–1: 31–53.
Reid, W. 1979. *The human factor in linguistic analysis: The passé simple and the imparfait*. Ph.D. dissertation, Columbia University, New York.
Reid, W. 1991. *Verb number in English: A functional explanation*. London/New York: Longman.
Reid, W. 1995. Quantitative analysis in Columbia School theory. In *Meaning as explanation: Advances in linguistic sign theory*, ed. E. Contini-Morava and B. Sussman Goldberg, 115–151. Berlin: Mouton De Gruyter.
Reid, W., R. Otheguy, and N. Stern (eds.). 2002. *Signal, meaning, and message: Perspectives on sign-based linguistics*. Amsterdam: Benjamins.
Tobin, Y. 1988. Sign: Context: Text: Theoretical and methodological implications for translation: The dual number in Modern Hebrew a case point. In *Textlinguistik und Fachsprache*, ed. R. Arntz Hildesheim, 449–468. Zurich/New York: Georg Olms.
Tobin, Y. 1989. Space, time and point-of-view in the Modern Hebrew verb. In *From sign to text: A semiotic view of communication*, ed. Y. Tobin, 61–91. Amsterdam: Benjamins.
Tobin, Y. 1990a. *Semiotics and linguistics*. London: Longman.
Tobin, Y. 1990b. The future tense in Modern Hebrew: From sign to text. *Folia Linguistica* 24(3/4): 457–512.
Tobin, Y. 1993. *Aspect in the English verb: Process and result in language*. London/New York: Longman.
Tobin, Y. 1995. *Invariance, markedness and distinctive feature analysis: A contrastive study of sign systems in English and Hebrew*. Amsterdam/Philadelphia: Benjamins.
Ultan, R. 1978. The nature of future tenses. In *Universals of human language*, Word structure, vol. 3, ed. Joseph H. Greenberg, 83–123. Stanford: Stanford University Press.

Corpus

Béroul. 1903. *Le roman de Tristan : poème du XIIe siècle*. Publié par Ernest Muret. Paris: Firmin, Didot et Cie.
de Mourcin, M. 1815. *Serments prêtés Strasbourg en 842 par Charles-le-Chauve, Louis-le-Germanique, et leurs armées respectives*. Paris: P. Didot l'aîné.
de Roquefort, B. 1820. *Poésies de Marie de France, poète anglo-normand du XIIIe siècle, ou recueil de lais, fables et autres productions de cette femme célèbre*, Tome 1ᵉʳ. Paris: Chasseriau.
Gautiesr, Léon. 1872. *La chanson de Roland. Texte critique, accompagné d'une traduction nouvelle et précédé d'une introduction historique*. Tours: A. Mame et fils.
Paris, Gaston, and Leopold Pannier. 1872. *La vie de Saint Alexis: poème du XIe siècle et renouvellements du XIIe, XIIIe, et XIVe siècles*. Paris: A. Franck.
von Fallersleben, August Heinrich Hoffmann. 1837. *Elnonensia. Monuments des langues romane et tudesque dans le IXᵉ siècle, contenus dans un manuscrit de l'abbaye de Saint-Amand, conservé à la Bibliothèque publique de Valenciennes*, avec traduction et remarques par J. F. Willems. Gand: F. et E. Gyselynck.

Chapter 13
Old French Parataxis: Syntactic Variant or Stylistic Variation?

Julie Glikman and Thomas Verjans

13.1 Introduction

Although the existence of parataxis in Old French is frequently mentioned, neither its place in the Old French language system nor how it alternates with its conjunctive variant has been satisfactorily explained.[1] We therefore set out in this paper to investigate the alternation of *que*/Ø,[2] in order to determine whether or not rules can be established for their distribution, either on the syntactic or the stylistic level.

For that purpose, we evaluated widely-held accounts of these constructions that can be found in the literature. Our investigation provides evidence that contradicts the conclusions of most of these previous studies. Based on our data, we will therefore assume that paratactic constructions are syntactic free variants of those introduced by *que*. After having established that the *que*/Ø alternation is syntactically free, we consider other possible explanations for the realization of the Ø variant.

---

[1] The term "parataxis" has two meanings, one considered in the opposition *hypotaxis/parataxis*, in which it is more or less a synonym for *juxtaposition*, and another one, commonly used by the medievalist tradition, in which it means an asyndetic subordination: "a dependent clause may be linked to a main clause paratactically, that is to say without the use of a conjunction or a relative pronoun" (Jensen 1990: 497). In this article, *parataxis* is used in the latter sense.

[2] For ease of reading, we use the sign Ø in this article to signify "non-expression of the morpheme *que*"; it does not imply, however, that an empty element has to be reintroduced in these constructions. The question of the necessity or not of reintroducing an empty element is one worthy of further discussion but will not be addressed here due to space limitations.

J. Glikman (✉)
Lattice & Modyco, CNRS, Paris, France
e-mail: julieglikman@yahoo.fr

T. Verjans
Grelisc, Bourgogne University, Dijon, France
e-mail: thomasverjans@free.fr

We finally propose that the *que*/Ø alternation can be explained by the spoken/written distinction.[3]

Our study is based on constructions of the form *Verb Ø P*,[4] which have a *Verb que P* parallel. This was the criterion used for the data collection.[5] While we have investigated a large corpus, most of the analysis presented here will be based on a smaller data set, taken mainly from the Old French text *La Chanson de Roland*.[6]

13.2 A Syntactic Distribution?

The existence of paratactic constructions in Old French is a well-known fact, observed by almost all grammarians (*cf.* Graeme-Ritchie 1907; Jensen 1990; Moignet 1973; Soutet 1992; Buridant 2000, and many others). In Old French, subordinate clauses are usually introduced by a *qu-* word (Jensen 1990: 500), as in (1), but are also described as having asyndetic variants, as in (2), a phenomenon that is mentioned in the grammars under the name of "*que* deletion" (Buridant 2000: 571) or "parataxis":

(1) Ço sent   Rollant que la mort li   est   pres (*Roland* 2259)
    this feels-IND Roland that the death to.him is-IND near
    Roland feels that death is near

(2) Ço sent   Rollant la veüe ad   perdue ; (*Roland* 2297)
    this feels-IND Roland the sight has-IND lost
    Roland feels [that] he has lost his sight

Previous scholars note that this phenomenon is possible in various kinds of subordinate clauses. In all of these structures, it would appear that the *que* construction can alternate with the Ø realization, as shown in the examples above.

In this section, we will focus on Verb Ø P constructions which have a parallel construction of Verb *que* P. The paratactic constructions will be compared to those introduced by *que*, in order to show that there are no differences between the syntactic contexts of the two constructions. In a discussion of previous studies, we will first consider commonly mentioned criteria such as which verbs can introduce a Ø construction, and the tense of the verbs in the subordinate clause. We then review other aspects of these constructions, such as person or negation, in order to establish whether or not the Ø realization is determined by certain syntactic conditions.

---

[3] This is as described by Koch and Oesterreicher (2001). In our study, we will not consider the paratactic or subordinate status of paratactic constructions, in order to focus on a contrastive analysis of the conditions in which the two structures are manifested. For more specific studies about their syntactic status, see Arteaga (2009), Glikman (2008 a&b). We will use Vmain for the first verb (usually the matrix verb), and Vsub for the second (usually the subordinate verb).

[4] We use P to designate a clause or a proposition which can be introduced by *que* or not.

[5] Most of the results used in this paper can be found in (Glikman 2009b).

[6] We consider it important to study the constructions systematically in small corpora, as one can then see more clearly how the data are integrated in the language system in one particular text.

Our study is therefore based on the most representative verbs in the corpus, namely: *croire* 'to believe', *cuidier* 'to believe', *dire* 'to say', *garder* 'to be watchful, to make sure', *laissier* 'to let', *ne pooir müer* 'to be unable to help doing something', *savoir* 'to know', *voir* 'to see' and *vouloir* 'to want'. Finally, we conclude that since both constructions have the same syntactic distribution, they can be considered as free variants.

13.2.1 Overview of Traditional Distribution Criteria

13.2.1.1 Main Verb (Vmain)

In this section we argue, in contrast to the traditional view, that the paratactic constructions can appear after all verbs which can take a *que*-P construction. This is in contrast to the most widely found description of the conditions of realization of parataxis which claims that it appears only after certain specific verbs. For Buridant, among others, these constructions are limited to the following types of verbs:

> les verbes signifiant la volition, l'ordre, la prière, etc., derrière les verbes signifiant l'inévitabilité, [...] la promesse ; derrière les verbes d'opinion, de connaissance et d'impression, [...] derrière des verbes de perception ; derrière un verbe événementiel. (Buridant 2000: 571)

> 'verbs of volition, order, prayer, etc., after verbs meaning unavoidability, [...], promise, after verbs of opinion, knowledge and impression, [...], after verbs of perception, after event verbs'.

He also mentions another context : " [...] dans l'expression de la préférence [...] derrière des verbes impersonnels" (when expressing a preference [...] after impersonal verbs) (2000: 576). Other philologists make reference to verbs of prevention (Jensen 1990: 497), opinion or declarative verbs such as *promettre* 'to promise', *jurer* 'to swear', *savoir* 'to know', *penser* 'to think', *vouloir* 'to want' (Foulet 1928: 333; Bonnard et Régnier 1997: 212), or structures such as "*ne laier / ne laissier (que) ne*+subjonctif ('not to rest until'...), *garder* ('veiller à')" 'to make sure', 'to be watchful' (Marchello-Nizia 1999: 69).

These assumptions seem to imply that parataxis cannot be found after other types of verbs. While our data confirm that asyndetic constructions do indeed appear mainly after these verbs, this does not imply that the Ø realization cannot occur after other verbs. For example, in *La Chanson de Roland*, the following verbs can be constructed either with or without *que*, such as *cuidier* 'to believe', *dire* 'to say', *laisser* 'to let'. Moreover, most of the verbs in this text that show the presence of *que* can also be found without it in other texts. This is the case, for example, for verbs such as *commander* 'to command' or *connaître* 'to know'. However, some verbs in *La Chanson de Roland*, such as *defendre* 'to defend' or *escrier* 'to cry' never appear with a paratactic construction.

It is important to note that most of these verbs belong to the categories mentioned above by grammarians, even if this is not the case in our restricted corpus. Moreover, the verbs that have only subordinate clauses introduced by *que* are seldom attested in our corpus, suggesting that it is their low frequency that explains the absence of the asyndetic construction. This hypothesis seems to be confirmed when we take into account the *Roman de Renart* (twelfth century), in which the analysis of the first 1,500 lines shows that the three most frequent verbs introducing clauses with *que*, namely *dire* 'to say', *savoir* 'to know' and *cuidier* 'to believe', also introduce an asyndetic clause.[7] This is probably why grammarians have pointed out that verbs like *savoir*, *cuidier*, *garder* 'to be watchful' or *vouloir* 'to want' are often constructed with clause without *que*.

It is thus possible to argue that it is precisely because they are less frequent that these verbs are only employed with a *que*-clause. If we adopt this view, the *que* construction could be perhaps explained by a constraint on interpretation, to facilitate understanding. However, in *La Chanson de Roland*, two verbs are employed only once, each time with an asyndetic clause: *noncier* 'to announce' and *être prêt* 'to be ready', indicating that there is no absolute constraint. We would therefore argue that the two constructions, *que* or Ø, are possible with most verbs, and that it is the alternation itself which can be observed or not, depending on the number of occurrences of the verb in the corpus. This means that the Ø construction, and the alternation with the *que* variant, is not specific to certain verbs, but rather exists in the linguistic system itself as a possibility.[8]

13.2.1.2 Mood and Tense

Another aspect that we focused on in our study is the mood and the tense of Vmain as well as Vsub, in order to see whether or not there is a relationship between parataxis and mood and tense. Results show that regardless of the tense or mood of the subordinate clause, the realization of *que* remains optional.

Vmain

In our corpus, the occurrences of asyndetic constructions show that almost every tense and mood is found. The most frequent verbs in the corpus testify that the indicative as well as the subjunctive or imperative can appear in an asyndetic clause. Moreover, different tenses for each mood occur. For example, for the indicative, either the present, future, preterit, or conditional can appear.[9] Thus, it seems that the realization of an asyndetic clause is unrelated to the choice of tense and modality.

---

[7] See Glikman (2008b).

[8] For the linguistic system as system of possibilities, see Coseriu (1952, 1973 (2007)) and Verjans (2009).

[9] In the example, the sign [/] is used to indicate the end of the line.

The following example illustrates that *laissier* can be used with an indicative future or a conditional clause when the subordinate clause is not introduced by *que*:

(3) La rereguarde des   .XII. Cumpaignuns / Ne   lesserat   bataille ne
    the rearguard of the 12   Lords   / NEG allow-INDfut battle   NEG
    lur   dunt. (*Roland*, 858)
    to-them give-SUBJ
    The rear guard of the 12 Lords will not allow themselves to not combat

(4) "Or ne   leroie,   por   nul home qu' en   sache, / […], /
    so NEG allow-COND   for   no man   that EN know-SUBJ
    A cez glotons   ne   me   voise   combatre." (AB *Louis* 403–05)
    to these bastards NEG   me-REFL go-SUBJ to fight
    I would not allow, for anybody I know, […], myself not to go and fight these bastards

However, the contrast (3–4) with the following example shows that the same tenses are found when the verb introduces a *que* construction:

(5) Ne   laisserat   que n'   i   parolt,   ço dit : (*Roland*, 1252)
    NEG allow-INDfut that NEG here speak-SUBJ this says-IND
    He will not allow him not to speak (= that he doesn't speak)…

The same phenomenon is observed with other verbs, confirming that there is no limitation on mood or tense with the verb *laisser*. The same holds for a verb such as *garder*, which is always used in the imperative, a point also made by Marchello-Nizia (1999: 69). This specific mood is found however both with a paratactic (6) and with a construction introduced by *que* (7):

(6) Tybert, ce   dist   Morans, garde   sor li ne   fier, (*Berte*, 604)
    Tybert this says-IND Moran   make sure-IMP on her NEG hit-SUBJ
    'Tybert, said Moran, make sure (that) you don't hit him.'

(7) Or guart   chascuns que granz   colps i   empleit, (*Roland*, 1013)
    so make sure-SUBJ everyone that big   blows here strikes-SUBJ
    Everyone makes sure that he strikes heavy blows.

Thus, what have been previously claimed to be restrictions on the presence or omission of *que* could be actually linked to certain communicative contexts, rather than by the asyndetic status of the proposition, as we have shown. Conversely, this also means that occurrences of a paratactic construction are not determined by the mood or the tense of the matrix verb, since a construction introduced by *que* can appear in the same contexts.

Vsub

While the tense or mood of the verb in the main clause is not linked to the asyndetic status of the subordinate clause, it could be the mood or tense of the latter that determines whether or not the subordinate clause is introduced by *que*. After all, it is well known that the subjunctive is generally considered to be a subordinate mood. Thus, the presence of a subjunctive in Vsub could therefore be expected to constitute a specific condition for the asyndetic variant. Indeed, some grammarians, do, in fact argue that the subjunctive makes parataxis possible (cf. Buridant 2000: 571).

A contrastive analysis again shows that the mood and tense of Vsub do not determine whether the clause is introduced by *que* or not.[10] For example, three of the verbs in our corpus are always constructed with a subjunctive subordinate clause: *garder, laissier, pooir müer*, but this is not due to whether or not the complement is introduced by *que* (see Marchello-Nizia 1999: 69). Evidence for this is provided by the fact that these verbs are always constructed with a subjunctive, regardless of whether the subordinate clause takes *que*.
Consider the following examples:

With *garder*:

(8) Guardez   de   nos ne turnez   le curage. (*Roland*, 650)
    make sure-IMP from us NEG turn-SUBJ the courage
    Make sure (that) our courage does not fail us.
(9) Guardez,   seignurs, quë il n' en   algent   vif ! (*Roland*, 2061)
    make sure-IMP Lords   that he NEG EN goes-SUBJ alive
    Make sure, Lord, that they don't escape alive.

With *laissier* (cf. (3) above):

(10) Ne   laisserat   qu' Abisme   nen   asaillet (*Roland*, 1659)
     NEG allow-INDfut that Abisme   NEG EN   fight-SUBJ
     He will not allow himself not to fight against Abisme (= that he does not fight against Abisme).

With *pooir* and *müer*:

(11) Pitét en ad, ne   poet   müer   n'   en   plurt. (*Roland*, 2873)
     ...   NEG can-IND prevent NEG EN   cries-SUBJ
     ... he cannot prevent himself from crying (= (that) he cries).
(12) Ne   poet   müer   que de   ses oilz ne   plurt. (*Roland*, 773)
     NEG can-IND prevent that from his eyes NEG   cries-SUBJ
     ... he cannot prevent himself from crying (= that he cries).

In all these cases, Vsub exhibits, with respect to mood, the same behavior with or without the presence of *que*, thus confirming that the *que*/Ø alternation is not determined by the mood or the tense the verb in the subordinate clause.

13.2.2 Other Criteria

In the previous section, we differed from most grammarians' studies by arguing that the presence of absence of *que* cannot be attributed to the tense or mood of either

---

[10] See also Arteaga (2009).

the matrix or subordinate clause. We now consider whether or not other aspects of these constructions play a role.

13.2.2.1 The Subject

It is possible that the conditions for parataxis have to do with the relationship between the subject of the matrix verb and the subordinate one. However, our corpus shows that verbs can be in any person in both constructions, as illustrated by the following examples:

(13) mes je sant moines a si fax / *que je criem   ne   me mesavaingne*,
                                         that I fear-IND NEG me bad-happens-SUBJ
   / se ge faz tant moignes devainne. (*Renart*, 1032–34)
   ... I fear (that) something wrong is happening to me...
(14) Quant   il   chou   virent   ne   se   porent   aidier /
     when   they its   see-IND NEG se-REFL can-IND help-INF...
   Ne lor efforts ne lor aroit mestier, / Trestot lor brans jeterent a lor piés. (*Louis C*, 1666–68)
   When they saw (that) they couldn't help themselves...

The most important point for our purpose is that there is the same distribution in the clauses introduced by *que* or by ø, as the following examples from *Le Roman de Renart* show[11]:

(15) que   bien   sai   qu'   il   avoit   tant   fait
     that   good   know-IND that   he has-IND so much done...
   / vers son saignor de mauvés plet (*Renart*, 2837)
   That I really know that he had made so many...
(16) tuit disoient   que estoit   mort. (*Renart*, 2828)
     all   say-IND   that was-IND dead
   All of them said that he was dead

It is possible that another criterion for a syntactic distribution could be the question of co-reference between the subjects of Vmain and Vsub. In our corpus, this phenomenon concerns in only 25 % of cases, which is a first indication that co-reference is not a specific condition for the use of one or the other construction. Most of the verbs in subordinate clauses in our corpus can be constructed with or without *que* whether or not the two subjects are co-referential. Even when there are restrictions regarding which subjects can occur on both verbs of the complex clause, the same restrictions can be observed in the clauses introduced by *que*. We can therefore assume that these

---

[11] From our review, it is clear that even when some subjects are more frequent with a verb than others, this distribution seems to be governed by textual or communicative rules, such as the discourse/narration opposition. Above all, these restrictions are always the same, either with or without *que*.

restrictions are linked only to the verb itself and not to the Ø/*que* alternation. Consequently, the fact that the subject has the same referent in the two clauses does not constitute a specific condition for the appearance of an asyndetic construction since a similar fact can be observed with clauses introduced by *que*.

13.2.2.2 Negation

Another point that we have examined is whether the presence of an asyndetic construction is linked to the presence of negation in P1 or P2. Our data show that it is not, for several reasons. First, with verbs like *dire* or *cuidier*, we can find the presence or absence of negation:

(17) "De Heudriet mon fil dites   li   pour riens   nee /
                                tell-IMP to-him   for   anything existing
    Ne   seroit   pas   sa mere   un seul jor consirree." (*Berte*, 1650–51)
    NEG be-COND NEG2 his mother one alone day consoled
    ... *tell him... (that) his mother won't be consoled one day ...*
(18) Je ne   di   pas   se   soient / li Frere Prescheeur (Rut. 8; 33–34 IX)
    I   NEG say-IND NEG2 se-REFL be-SUBJ
    I do not say (that) they are...

In our corpus, other main verbs, such *croire, garder, savoir, voir* or *vouloir*, are never negated, although Vsub can appear with or without negation:

(19) "Sire, foi que je doi vo cors, / S'espielus vous estoit li sors, /
    Je croi   ja   ne   vous   sera   bel." (*StNicolas*, 192–194)
    I   believe-IND never NEG to-you be-INDfut good
    ... *I believe (that) it will never be good for you.*
(20) Je croi   bien des   preudomes
    I believe-IND good from gentlemen
    i   ait   a grant   plantei, (Rut.8; 41 XI)
    there have-SUBJ to great number
    I believe (that) there are a lot of courageous men.

This fact could lead us to assume that asyndetic constructions are only possible in contexts where Vmain is not under the scope of a negation.

However, in *Le Roman de Renart*, there are occurrences of these same verbs constructed with a main clause that is negative. It could be that there are not be enough occurrences in our corpus to find asyndetic constructions with negation on Vmain. Moreover, in the case of *savoir*, the following example shows that this verb can be negative with an asyndetic construction:

(21) sire bruns, mais vous ne   savez,   on   dit   à cour... (*Renart*, 527)
    Lord Brun but   you NEG know-IND one says-IND at court
    Lord Brun, you do not know (that) we say at Court...

However, this example could be interpreted in two ways, either as a paratactic construction or as the juxtaposition of two main clauses.

Conversely, verbs such *laissier* or *pooir müer* are always constructed with a negation, as pointed out by grammarians (Marchello-Nizia 1999: 69; Buridant 2000: 575):

(22) Carles li magnes ne poet müer n' en plurt. (*Roland*, 841)
Charles the great NEG can-IND prevent NEG EN cries-SUBJ
Charles the Great cannot prevent himself from crying (= (that) he cries).

(23) "Ja ne leré por nul home que sache /
Never NEG allow for no man that know-SUBJ
Ne vos secore o mon riche barnage." (*Louis* AB, 268–69)
NEG you support-SUBJ...
I won't ever allow, for anybody I know, for myself not to support you ((that) I don't support you...)

This could be interpreted to mean that with these verbs, asyndetic constructions are only possible when the main clause is negated. However, in *La Chanson de Roland*, all the occurrences of these verbs that are introduced by *que* are also constructed with a negation.

It can therefore be concluded that the presence or the absence of negation in either the main or subordinate clause is not a determining factor for the distribution of the paratactic construction. Our study shows that when there are apparent syntactic constraints, they are linked to the construction of the verb itself, since these constraints are identical with a clause introduced by *que*.

13.2.2.3 Phrase Modality

Another aspect that we have taken into account is the modality of the interrelated clauses. Indeed, paratactic constructions occur in declarative sentences, as well as in interrogative or injunctive sentences:

(24) et Roomiax qui le tesmoigne, /
la cort cuidast ce fust mançonge. (*Renart*, 485–86)
the court thought-IND this was-SUBJ lie
… the court thought (that) it was a lie.

(25) Quides tu dont tes Diex ait poësté /
think-IND you so your God has-SUBJ power
Que il te puist en camp vers moi tenser? (*Louis* C, 549–50)
Do you think (that) your God has power…

(26) Sachiés je l' ochirai, s'il anchois ne m'ochist. (*StNicolas*, 411)
know-IMP I him kill
Be sure (that) I will kill him…

The same observation could be made with the non-paratactic constructions, meaning that modality, like the choice of tenses and negation, cannot be considered as a restrictive context for the realization of the Ø variant.

In summary, in this section, a contrastive analysis has shown that the syntactic distribution of the *que* and the Ø variants is the same. Hence we assume that they are not different on the syntactic level, since each can be found in similar contexts and with comparable characteristics.

13.3 Syntactic Free Variants

All the criteria examined above have shown that the non-paratactic and paractactic constructions have the same syntactic distribution. We therefore contend that they are free syntactic variants. In this section, we provide further evidence for this hypothesis, first focusing on textual evidence, and then on the evolution of the complex clause system.

13.3.1 Textual Evidence

Evidence for the syntactic similarity between the paratactic and the clauses introduced by *que* may be found in contexts where both constructions appear. First, on the textual level, this phenomenon can be observed in *La Chanson de Roland*, in which (27) and (28) are separated by only five lines:

(27) Ço set hom ben que jo sui tis parastres, (*Roland*, 287)
 this knows-IND one good that I am-IND your father-in-law
 Everyone really knows that I am your father-in-law.
(28) Ço set hom ben, n' ai cure de manace. (*Roland*, 293)
 this knows-IND one good NEG have-IND care from threats
 Everyone really knows (that) I do not care about threats.

Other examples illustrating this phenomenon may be found in the repetition effects at the beginning of the *laisses* (stanzas), such as in (1) and (2) with the formula *ço sent Rollant*.

Both constructions can also be found at the sentence level, with the same verb in parallel structures. In (29), for example, two coordinated occurrences of *dire* are constructed with a non asyndetic clause in the first case and with an asyndetic one in the second case:

(29) Sire, ele vos a dit ce que li plot, mais ele s'am poïst bien taire. Ne endroit moi ne
 vos en di ge rien, car **ge ne voil** dire ce soit
  because I NEG want-IND to say this be-SUBJ
 voirs, ne **ge [ne] di** que ele mente (Lancelot P., 1220–30)
 true NEG I [NEG] say-IND that she lies-SUBJ
 … because I don't want to say (that) it is true, nor do I say that she lies

In this example, there is no specific factor that explains the choice of a paratactic construction in the former case, and of one introduced by *que* in the latter, which we interpret as meaning that they are in a variant relation. Moreover, both structures are on the same hierarchical level, under the scope of the conjunction *car*.

All these examples show that on the different levels, the two constructions are equivalent and can be viewed as syntactic free variants. Consequently, this means that the *que* realization and the Ø one should be analyzed in the same way.[12]

13.3.2 System Evolution

Evolution of the complex clause system also highlights the free variation between the two constructions.[13] Indeed, some grammarians mention a progressive obsolescence of parataxis in Middle French,[14] closely related to the development of the system of linking of clauses. Conversely, other grammarians argue that parataxis has not disappeared as it still exists in the spoken register (Bauche 1920; Gadet 2003).[15] Whatever interpretation we choose, however, it is also possible to understand this evolution as evidence of the free variant relation of clauses headed by *que* or by ø.[16]

In accordance with Coseriu's modeling of linguistic change, we assume that changes generally do not affect the functionality of language, but rather reinforce it:

> Un changement linguistique commence et se déroule toujours comme le «déplacement» d'une norme. Mais, pour que la norme puisse «être déplacée», il est indispensable : ou que cela soit fonctionnellement opportun et nécessaire, ou que la norme soit ignorée, ou que de l'ignorer n'affecte pas la fonctionnalité de la langue (l'intercompréhension). (Coseriu 1973 (2007): IV, § 6)[17]
>
> *A linguistic change always begins with and takes place as the "transfer" of a norm. But, so that the norm can "be transferred", it is necessary either that it be functionally appropriate or necessary, or that the norm should be ignored, or that to ignore it doesn't hurt the functionality of the language (intercomprehension).*

In this theory, this means that a functional distinction must be replaced before the obsolescence of one or the other variant, or, at least, that both variants must be

---

[12] In the subordinating view of parataxis, this also means that *que* cannot be considered as the exclusive subordinating marker, but only as a linguistic possibility among others existing in the Old French system. Thus, parataxis, in some instances at least, should not be considered as a simple juxtaposition of two clauses, even on a cline of clause-combining constructions (see, among others, Lehmann (1988) or Hopper and Traugott (1993 (2003): 176–184)), but as a kind of subordination (see also Arteaga 2009), making it necessary to take into account other aspects of the subordinating system and of its evolution.

[13] For recent work on the evolution of this system in French, see Verjans (2009).

[14] See, for example, Imbs (1956: 419). The same development has been argued in the evolution of Latin (Ernout and Thomas 1953 (1997): 291).

[15] See also its existence in Canadian French (Wiesmath 2006).

[16] We also argue that parataxis is still possible in Modern French, alongside the *que* variant, but it is not our focus here.

[17] In Coseriu's theory, *norm* is understood as the whole set of non-functional linguistic elements, whereas functional ones constitute the *system*. See Coseriu (1952, 1973 (2007), 1964 (2001)).

already specialized in two different norms or subsystems. Consequently, this change, which could be either the obsolescence of the paratactic structure or its specialization in the spoken register, means that, in Old French, the distribution of the two structures was not functional.

Note that this substitution did not happen only for argumental clauses, but also for other complex clauses such as relative clauses (Ménard 1988: 78; Foulet 1928: 338; Buridant 2000: 575, 580), comparative clauses (Buridant 2000: 645), consecutive clauses, (Buridant 2000: 619 *sqq*), and hypothetical clauses (Buridant 2000: 626, 663), where the *que/Ø* alternation was also possible (see Glikman 2008b, 2009b). That means that the alternation between asyndetic and non-asyndetic clauses could also be considered as free variation, just as in case of argumental clauses, at least in the Old French system. Thus, this allows us to look for other explanations for this alternation on the extralinguistic level.

13.4 A Stylistic Variation?

In this section, we focus on other elements that can explain the *que/Ø* alternation. Considering the genre of the text, we first present the traditional explanations for the frequency of parataxis, in order to show that the distinction between texts written in prose and texts written in verse is not sufficient. Finally, we suggest other hypotheses for this alternation, taking into account the distinction between the spoken and written language.

13.4.1 The Criterion of Genre and Verse/Prose Distinction

Parataxis could also be explained by the generic characteristics of the texts. For example, it has often been pointed out that it is more common in the *Chansons de geste* than in other texts. This difference has often been attributed to the presence of verse in *Chansons de geste*, whereas other texts with less parataxis are written in prose (Marchello-Nizia 1978, 1999). However, it could also be explained by the generic characteristics of *Chansons de geste*, or by the date of the text:

> La juxtaposition des propositions ou parataxe est assez répandue en AF. Comparée à la subordination ou hypotaxe, la parataxe est plus simple, historiquement plus ancienne. Outre ce caractère archaïque, elle relève parfois du style oral, car le langage parlé multiplie les juxtapositions. Elle a enfin un aspect stylistique, car il faut la mettre en rapport avec les genres littéraires, les motifs traités et l'effet recherché. La parataxe est

plus fréquente en vers qu'en prose, plus répandue dans les chansons de geste que dans les romans courtois. [...] Parfois la parataxe tient à des raisons métriques. (Ménard 1988: 188)

The juxtaposition of clauses, or parataxis, is quite common in Old French. Compared with subordination, or hypotaxis, parataxis is simpler, and historically more ancient. In addition to this archaic characteristic, it is sometimes characteristic of oral speech, in which juxtaposition is frequent. Finally, it has a stylistic aspect, and needs to be considered in relation to literary genre, themes and the desired effect. Parataxis is more frequent in verse than in prose, more common in Chansons de geste than in Romans courtois. [...] Sometimes, parataxis exists for metric reasons.

Our study confirms these observations since it is in *La Chanson de Roland* that parataxis is proportionally the most frequent (about seventy occurrences for a 4,000 lines' text).

However, *La Chanson de Roland* exhibits most of the above-mentioned features: it is not only a *chanson de geste*, but it is also one of the older texts and it is written in verse. Thus, it is difficult to know which of these criteria that the presence of parataxis should be attributed to. Moreover, the *Chanson de Roland* is also marked by dialectal particularities, namely those of the Anglo-Norman dialect, which further complicates any explanation of the extensive use of parataxis.

Among all these criteria, the one most frequently mentioned to explain the Ø variant is the verse/prose distinction. Verse is even sometimes viewed as as a necessary condition for its realization:

Ce type de construction est relativement fréquent en vers [...]. Or, toujours, sans exception, la rupture syntaxique entre les deux «propositions» se situe à une coupure rythmique, fin de vers ou hémistiche. Et, il faut insister sur ce point, ces constructions paratactiques sont à peu près totalement absentes de la prose : ce qui tendrait à prouver que la structure du vers est bien une condition nécessaire à leur emploi. (Marchello-Nizia 1978: 37)

This type of construction is quite frequent in verse [...]. Moreover, always, without exception, the syntactic boundary between the two "clauses" takes place at a rhythmic boundary, end of the line or hemistich. And it must be stressed that these paratactic constructions are practically never found in prose, indicating that the structure of verse is a necessary condition for their use.

Along these lines, Marchello-Nizia has shown the relevance of prosodic and syntactic structures:

Les résultats sont clairs : en vers, et dès l'origine, dans plus de 80 % des cas, structure rythmique et structure syntaxique coïncident. (Marchello-Nizia 1978: 36–37)

The results are clear: in verse, ever since the beginning, in more than 80% of cases, rhythmic structure and syntactic structure coincide.

Using this criterion, she therefore considers that in verse, prosodic boundaries sufficed to indicate syntactic boundaries, which would explain the Ø variant, and its obsolescence in prose. However, the *que* variant is also possible in verse, as in:

(30) Carles   comandet   que face   sun servise (Roland, 298)
     Charles   commands-IND   that do-SUBJ   his service
     Charles commands me to do his service (that I do his service.)

In fact, we have shown in Glikman (2009a) that prosodic boundaries can indicate different types of syntactic boundaries, inter- and intra-sentential, between subject and verb, or between two independent sentences. Therefore they are not sufficient to indicate systematically any syntactic relation, meaning that prosody does not encode the syntax in Old French. In our view, the verse/prose distinction does not seem adequate to explain the Ø realization. This is also confirmed by the fact that the Ø construction occurs in prose, as in (31), though less frequently (only six occurrences for the whole text of *La Mort le roi Artu* for example, see also Glikman 2009b):

(31) car   je sai   bien, se je l 'eüsse   mandé, il i
     because I know-IND well if I it would-have-SUBJ ask   he there
     fust   venuz volentiers et debonerement (Artu 186, 45–46)
     be-SUBJ come gladly
     Because I really know (…) (that) he would have come …

While parataxis is more common in the texts in verse than in those in prose, this distinction cannot account for our data. Moreover, this is more a descriptive view with little explanatory power, for it cannot explain the evolution of the phenomenon.

We therefore suggest another explanation for the difference between the frequency among texts of paratactic constructions, which can also account for its diachronic evolution. Rather than explaining the use of these variants by a verse/prose opposition, we hypothesize that the condition of transmission of the text could also be a determining factor, and that the Ø / *que* alternation may be distributed according to the speaking/writing distinction.

13.4.2 The Speaking/Writing Distinction

It seems to us that the spoken/written distinction could better explain the *que/* Ø alternation and its evolution. Most of the arguments for the obsolescence of parataxis are based on its non-attestation in subsequent periods. Admittedly, parataxis is less frequent in prose after the thirteenth century, and practically unattested in data since Middle French. However, parataxis is attested in later texts, albeit seldom, as can be seen in the following example from a play dating from the fourteenth century:

(32) "Alons esprover nostre songe. / Se en monument ne est li cors, /
     Dont   pourrons nous bien dire lors / N'   est   mie   songes
     from which could-IND we   good say then NEG is-IND NEG2 dream
     mais veritez, / **Et que** il   est   resuscitez." (Palatinus, 1746–50)
     but truth   and that he is-IND resuscitated
     …about which we could say (that) it is not a dream but the truth, and that he is resuscitated.

In this example, the paratactic construction is coordinated with the clause introduced by *que*, i.e. they are both governed by the same verb, and thus have the same syntactic distribution. We can therefore assume that asyndetic constructions have always been possible in the language system, with the same syntactic characteristics, although their frequency has declined.

However, this much discussed obsolescence of parataxis is based only on the written register – which is only natural given that this is the only form of documentation available to us for this stage of the language. The loss of parataxis is not attested in the spoken register, for we have no testimony of it.

It should be noted, however, that the Ø variant on Old French is more frequent in direct speech, which provides additional evidence for the oral specificity of parataxis:

> Enfin, on peut également signaler que plus des deux tiers des cas de parataxe dans le texte se trouvent dans du discours direct, alors que la répartition discours direct – narration est à peu près égale pour l'ensemble du texte, ce qui semblerait confirmer certaines théories avançant que la parataxe relèverait plus de l'oralité. (Glikman 2008b: 236)
>
> *A final point to mention is that more than two thirds of the cases of parataxis in the text [Le Roman de Renart] are in direct speech, whereas the direct speech – narrative distribution is well balanced in the text, which seems to confirm certain theories according to which parataxis is more relevant to the oral register.*

Indeed, studies continue to attest occurrences of parataxis in oral varieties of Modern French (Bauche (1920); Gadet (2003) or Avanzi (201_)). This fact is illustrated in (33):

(33) Il a dit j'ai triché (oral<Posner 1997: 76)
He said I cheated

We can therefore hypothesize that parataxis only disappeared from the written register, meaning that it has not disappeared from the French language system when one takes into account the spoken register. A more theoretical argument could be made in order to support these hypotheses: in Coserian theory, a linguistic system is conceived of as a system of possibilities (see Coseriu 1973; Verjans 2009). One or the other possibility may develop different norms which may be linked to a specific medium, that is, the spoken or the written one. In this view, parataxis could be linked only to the spoken norm. The fact that the Ø variant is considered as impossible in Modern French by the normative grammars indicates that the French norm was later probably established on the basis of the written register, a suggestion also put forward by Kristeva (1974).

It can thus be considered that parataxis still exists as a possibility in the system, but is confined to the spoken register (although it is relatively rare). In the case of Old French, despite the lack of oral data, we nonetheless have evidence of asyndetic constructions in early texts, especially the *Chansons de Geste*, a fact that can be explained by the oral features that they are considered to possess: Zumthor, for example, talks of the "exclusively oral characteristic that the genre had, probably until the middle of the twelfth century" "caractère exclusivement oral qu'eut le genre, sans doute jusque vers le milieu du XIIe siècle." (Zumthor 1972 (2000): 539). He adds :

> Un certain nombre de caractères stylistiques, particuliers au genre et qui entrent dans sa définition, s'expliquent par les nécessités propres de la transmission orale de ces longs récits. (Zumthor 1972 (2000): 539)
> *A certain number of stylistic attributes that are characteristic, even defining, features of the genre can be explained by the constraints specific to the oral transmission of these long narratives.*

However, it is important to note that 'oral characteristics' have to be understood not in the physical realization of the spoken/written distinction, but in the communicational constraints that they presuppose. As recent studies have shown, it is not only the medium that makes a difference, but rather a whole set of factors which defines the communicative context (see Biber et al. 1999; Koch and Oesterreicher 1990 (2007), 2001).

The *Chanson de Geste*, as a literary genre, presents some of the characteristics that place it on the oral side. Consequently, as shown in Marnette (1999, 2001), among others, the communicative constraints are not the same in the *Chanson de Geste* as in other texts, and these differences influence the syntax used in the text. This could explain the frequency of parataxis in this genre as well as its low frequency and its progressive obsolescence in prose. Koch also suggests that it is due to the fact that at that time, the "written" register was the Latin variant, whereas the "vulgar" variant, the "oral" one, was Old French, which also could explain why the first Old French texts are not differentiated in terms of speaking/writing distinctions.

We have thus far established that the Ø/*que* alternation can be considered as a speaking/writing variation, but the progressive disappearance of the Ø variant from the written register still needs to be explained. It can be pointed out, however, that this obsolescence seems to be in accordance with a more general change in the syntactic structure of the sentence. Several phenomena lend support to this hypothesis.

13.5 Conclusion

In this paper, we have seen how a contrastive synchronic analysis has led us to a better understanding of the Old French linguistic system. We have argued that there is no syntactic criterion which can satisfactorily explain the Ø/*que* alternation. Thus, we hypothesized that these two types of structures are free variants, which is confirmed by the evolution of the system as well as by textual evidence. Indeed, no differences can be observed between the two constructions, either with respect to the mood/tense variations, the scope of the negation in either clause, or to subject constraints. Rather than explaining the gradual decrease of parataxis by a verse/prose distinction, we put forward the hypothesis that accounting for this difference in terms of communicational constraints sheds a clearer light on the evolution of the phenomenon. We finally surmise that this alternation could be one reflection of the 'speaking/writing' opposition and its communicative constraints.

Acknowledgements We would like to thank an anonymous reviewer and M. Avanzi for their appreciable remarks and suggestions, as well as E. Rowley-Jolivet for her stylistic review.

References

Arteaga, Deborah. 2009. On the existence of null complementizers in Old French. *Romance Linguistics 2007.* Selected papers from the 37th Linguistic Symposium on Romance Languages (LSRL), Pittsburgh, 15–18 March 2007, ed. Pascual José Masullo, Erin O'Rourke and Chia-Hui Huang. Philadelphia/New York: John Benjamins. *Current Issues in Linguistic Theory* 304: 17–32.
Avanzi, Mathieu. 2011. *L'interface prosodie/syntaxe en français, Dislocations, incises et asyndètes.* PhD, Neuchâtel University.
Bauche, Henri. 1920 (1946). *Le langage populaire.* Paris: Payot.
Biber, Douglas, S. Johansson, G. Leech, S. Conrad, and E. Finegan. 1999 *Longman grammar of spoken and written English.* London: Longman.
Bonnard, Henri, and Claude Régnier. 1997. *Petite grammaire de l'ancien français.* Paris: Magnard.
Buridant, Claude. 2000. *Grammaire nouvelle de l'ancien français.* Paris: SEDES.
Coseriu, Eugenio. 1952. Sistema, norma y habla. *Revista de la Faculdad de Humanidades y de Ciencias* VI(9): 113–181.
Coseriu, Eugenio. 1964 (2001). Vers l'étude des structures lexicales. *L'Homme et son langage,* 215–252. Louvain/Paris: Peeters.
Coseriu, Eugenio. 1973. *Sincronía, diacronía e historia. El problema del cambio lingüístico.* Madrid: Gredos Bibliotecа románica hispánica (tr. fr. T. Verjans, *Texto !* [en ligne] – 2007).
Ernout, Alfred, and François Thomas. 1953 (1997). *Syntaxe Latine.* Paris: Klincksieck.
Foulet, Lucien. 1928. *Petite syntaxe de l'ancien français.* Paris: Honoré Champion.
Gadet, François. 2003. *La Variation sociale en français.* Paris-Gap: Ophrys.
Glikman, Julie. 2008a. Les complétives non introduites en ancien français. In *Évolutions en français – Études de linguistique diachronique,* ed. B. Fagard, S. Prévost, B. Combettes, and O. Bertrand, 105–118. Bern: Peter Lang.
Glikman, Julie. 2008b. Les subordonnées asyndétiques en ancien français. In *Congrès Mondial de Linguistique Française – CMLF'08,* ed. J. Durand, B. Habert, and B. Laks, 225–240. Paris: Institut de Linguistique Française.
Glikman, Julie. 2009a. Le rapport entre frontières de propositions et frontières prosodiques en ancien français. In *Grammaire et Prosodie-2,* Travaux linguistiques du Cerlico, ed. D. Roulland, 23–37. Rennes: Presses Universitaires de Rennes.
Glikman, Julie. 2009b. *Parataxe et Subordination en Ancien Français : Système syntaxique, variantes, variation.* PhD, Paris Ouest Nanterre University.
Graeme-Ritchie, Robert Lindsay. 1907. *Recherches sur la syntaxe de la conjonction «que» dans l'ancien français.* Paris: Champion.
Hopper, Paul J., and Elizabeth C. Traugott. 1993 (2003). *Grammaticalization.* Cambridge: Cambridge University Press, coll. *Cambridge Textbooks in Linguistics.*
Imbs, Paul. 1956. *Les propositions temporelles en ancien français. La détermination du moment.* Strasbourg: Publications de la Faculté des Lettres de Strasbourg, fascicule 120.
Jensen, Frede. 1990. *Old French and comparative Gallo-Romance syntax.* Tübingen: Niemeyer.
Koch, Peter, and Wulf Oesterreicher. 1990 (2007). *Gesprochene Sprache in der Romania : Französisch, Italienisch, Spanisch.* Max Niemeyer Verlag: Tübingen, trad. esp. de Araceli López Serena, Lengua Hablada en la Romania : Español, Francés, Italiano, Madrid, Gredos BHC. n° 448.
Koch, Peter, and Wulf Oesterreicher. 2001. Langage parlé et langage écrit. In: *Lexikon der Romanistischen Linguistik,* t. I, 584–627. Tübingen: Max Niemeyer Verlag.
Kristeva, Julia. 1974 (1985). *La Révolution du langage poétique: l'avant-garde à la fin du XIXe siècle, Lautréamont et Mallarmé,* 2 éd. Paris: Éditions du Seuil.

Lehmann, Christian. 1988. Towards a typology of clause linkage. In *Clause combining in grammar and discourse*, Typological studies in language n° 18, ed. John Haiman and Sandra A. Thomspon, 181–225. Philadelphia/New York: John Benjamins.
Marchello-Nizia, Christiane. 1978. Un problème de linguistique textuelle: la classe des éléments joncteurs de propositions. In *Études de syntaxe du moyen-français, Actes du Colloque de Metz*, ed. R. Martin, 33–42. Paris: Klincksieck.
Marchello-Nizia, Christiane. 1999. *Le Français en diachronie: douze siècles d'évolution*. Gap/Paris: Ophrys.
Marnette, Sophie. 1999. Il le vos mande, ge sui qui le vos di: Les stratégies du dire dans les chansons de geste. *Revue de Linguistique romane* 63(251–252): 387–417.
Marnette, Sophie. 2001. Du discours insolite: Le discours indirect sans *que*. *French Studies* 55(3): 297–313.
Ménard, Philippe. 1988 (1994). *Syntaxe de l'ancien français*. Bordeaux: Éditions Bière, coll. *Études Médiévales*.
Moignet, Gérard. 1973. *Grammaire de l'ancien français*. Paris: Klincksieck.
Posner, Rebecca. 1997. *Linguistic change in French*. Oxford: Clarendon Press.
Soutet, Olivier. 1992. *Etudes d'ancien et de moyen français*. Paris: PUF.
Verjans, Thomas. 2009. *Essai de systématique diachronique: genèse des conjonctions dans l'histoire du français (9e – 17e siècles)*. PhD, Paris-Sorbonne University.
Wiesmath, Raphaële. 2006. *Le français acadien. Analyse syntaxique d'un corpus oral recueilli au Nouveau-Brunswick/Canada*. Paris: L'Harmattan.
Zumthor, Paul. 1972. *Essai de poétique médiévale*. Paris: Le Seuil.

Corpus

Adenet le Roi, *Berte aus grans piés*, A. Henry ed., 1963, P U de Bruxelles, PUF, Bruxelles, 272p.; 3487, 13ᵉ **short *Berte***
Jehan Bodel, Le jeu de Saint Nicolas, éd. Par Albert Henri, Droz, Genève, 1981, env. 1200, 1533 vers, premier miracle dramatique en langue vulgaire (d'oil), **short StNicolas**
La Chanson de Roland, Segre C., éd., Genève, Droz, 2003, **short *Roland***
La Mort le roi Artu, Frappier J. éd., Genève, Droz, 1964, éd. 1996, **short *Artu***
La Passion du Palatinus, mystère du (début) XIVe siècle, éd. G. Franck, Paris, Champion, 1972, 1996 vers, **short *Palatinius***
Le Roman de Renart (première branche), éd. Par Mario Roques, Champion, Paris, 2007, 3256 v., éd d'après le manuscrit de CANGE, **short *Renart***
Les Rédactions en vers du Couronnement de Louis, Y. G. Lepage éd., Droz, Paris-Genève, 1978, AB 2671 v., C 2717 v., **short *Louis AB / C*.**
Rutebeuf, *Œuvres complètes*, texte établi, trad., annoté et présenté par M. Zink, 2001, Lettres Gothiques, Classiques Garnier, Paris, 1054p., **short *Rut***

Chapter 14
A Derivational Approach to Negative Polarity Item Licensing in Old French

Richard Ingham

14.1 Introduction

Old French main clause structure has for some time been a subject of debate, especially as to whether constituent order in main clauses is appropriately accounted for in terms of a strict Verb Second grammar, as was proposed by Adams (1987), Roberts (1993), and Vance (1997).[1] It has long been noted that subject-verb inversion was the norm until around 1300 after initial non-subject constituents, but a fully satisfactory theoretical analysis of the observed patterns remains elusive. Kaiser (2002) challenged the idea that Old French was a Verb Second language, though recent work by Mathieu (2006) and Labelle (2007) has restated the argument in favor of its having had Verb Second properties.

A key issue in the debate is the existence of apparent violations of Verb Second (henceforth V2), whereby the verb stands as the third constituent of a main clause (see e.g. Prévost 2001 for discussion), especially following an initial adverbial element. Among such violations is the behavior of clause-initial adverbs *ja* and *onques*, discussed by Ingham (2005), which seems to defy the normal division of Old French adverbs based on Foulet (1930) into 'invertissant', associated with null or postposed subjects, and 'non-invertissant', associated with obligatory preverbal subjects. The latter comprise a small class of initial adverbs such as *certes* ('certainly') and *neporquant*

---

[1] Since Haider and Prinzhorn (1986) a central issue has been the nature of what triggers Verb second. A number of proposals are reviewed by these authors, and also by Vikner (1995), but no definitive picture has emerged of what distinguishes V2 from non-V2 grammars.

R. Ingham (✉)
School of English, Birmingham City University,
Perry Barr B42 2SU, United Kingdom, UK
e-mail: Richard.Ingham@bcu.ac.uk

('nevertheless'). Like them, *ja* and *onques* display SV order with a nominal subject (1a–b). Unlike them, however, they allow null pronominal subjects (2a–b):

(1)a. Onques ma traïson ne vos fist mal
 Ever my betrayal NEG you did-PAST harm
 'Indeed my betrayal did you no harm' Artu 112
(1)b. Car ja cist cors qui ci gist ne sera remuez
 For indeed that body which here lie-pres NEG be-FUT move-PPART
 'For that body lying there will never be removed' *Queste*, 37
(2)a. Ja mes ne seras en si bon point del trouver…
 Ever NEG be-FUT in such good position of-it find-INFIN
 'You will never be in such a good position to find it' *Queste*, 89
(2)b. Onques ne feïstes riens por moi…
 Ever NEG do-PAST-SUBJ anything for me
 'You would never have done anything for me' *Artu,* 160

One might dismiss this as a marginal phenomenon concerning two idiosyncratic adverbs, except that, as shown by Ingham (2005), their behavior when clause-initial is far from unruly. As originally noted by Price (1971), they actually seem to disallow the overt expression of pronominal subjects. They thus display both XSV order and a form of a null subject grammar in which pronominal subjects are not licensed at all, which is puzzling as in Old French null subjects are licensed in a V2 configuration. In fact, these adverbs' distribution is systematic in another respect. Initial *onques* exhibits the above pattern, but initial *ja* does so only in negative clauses, patterning in affirmative clauses with 'invertissant' adverbs such as *ore*. *Onques* is not used in affirmative contexts in main clauses. The question arising is therefore whether the behavior of *ja* and *onques* attests to a structural difference between affirmative and negative clauses, rather than erratic adherence to V2.

The possibility that a special structure is present in Old French negative main clauses is reinforced by the fact that they are peculiar in other ways. Unlike affirmative main clauses, they allowed the subject to be dropped even when no constituent was fronted,[2] e.g.:

(3) «M'aïst Dex, dit ele, nel savoie.
 Me help-SUBJ God said she NEG-it know-IMPERF
 'My God, said she, I did not know that.' LL I 78

A further oddity regarding negative main clauses will be presented in this study, and was discovered while data collection was being carried out for *ja* and *onques*. This was an asymmetry in negative main clauses between initial adjuncts and preposed arguments when they contained polarity items, such as *nul*, to which we return below.

---

[2] By the thirteenth century, however, subjectless negative clauses were quite rare (Skårup 1975).

There are thus good grounds for taking a new look at Old French negation in relation to the V2 property, endeavoring to account for a range of differing phenomena which have not hitherto been given a unified analysis This is the purpose of the present study. The empirical basis is twofold: a follow-up study to Ingham (2005), expanding the enquiry to works of the same genre not considered in that investigation, and a survey of the overt use of subject pronouns in twelfth century Old French epic verse in potential V2 contexts. Both data sources provide very strong motivation for the claim that negative main clauses in Old French allowed non-compliance with V2. As will be shown, their structure permitted not only V1 but also V3 and V4 order.

A structural analysis is presented of the syntactic licensing of polarity items such as *ja* and *onques* in negative clauses which accounts for the distribution of the relevant items. It is framed in terms of current Minimalist conceptions of syntax, in particular those deriving from Chomsky's (2001) notion of derivation by phase. The main proposal will be that the surface positions of polarity items in Old French are explained by a polarity licensing scenario observing the two syntactic phases of feature checking posited by Chomsky (2001) and subsequent work. T-related adjuncts, in particular time adverbs such as *ja/onques*, are added to the derivation after the first (vP) phase, and are therefore checked in the next phase. They remain within TP where they are licensed by the negator *ne*. In other words, they do not front to Spec CP. In common with polarity items in languages such as Hindi (Mahajan 1990), they are thus licensed symmetrically, rather than by an asymmetric approach to polarity licensing relying on structural c-command. Crucially, since they remain within TP, they cannot act as V2 triggers. This analysis of V2 in relation to *ja* and *onques* allows us to achieve a more principled delineation of the main clause sentence types that comply or do not comply with V2 in Old French, and to link work on clausal negation in the history of French with current theoretical approaches to syntax.

The chapter is organized as follow. Section 14.2 outlines the basic analytic assumptions, drawing on previous studies of Old French syntax. In Sect. 14.3 the principal items to be investigated here, the adverbs *ja* and *onques*, are examined in terms of their semantics and their syntactic distribution. Next, in Sect. 14.4, we revisit the empirical basis of the claim made by Ingham (2005) regarding the syntax of these adverbs, making use of a much larger thirteenth century data base. In so doing, we uncover certain other facts relevant to the main issues considered here, one of which, presented in Sect. 14.5, is an asymmetry between argument and adjunct polarity items when in initial position. This leads in Sect. 14.6 to a formal analysis of polarity item licensing in Old French which explicates the observed patterns in terms of polarity licensing by phase. Section 14.7 then investigates whether the analysis is applicable to twelfth century Old French, the earliest period for which we have a substantial textual record, and concludes that the negative clause structure posited may antedate the rise of CP V2 in early Romance.

14.2 Background Assumptions

The key theoretical assumptions made in this study are as follows. First, French was a CP V2 language (Adams 1987; Roberts 1993), in which certain types of initial constituent triggered raising of the finite verb to C in root declarative clauses.[3] These included focused constituents, e.g. *de vous* in:

(4) (Cist autre me dient ce qu'il sevent... mais)
de vous n' ai   je mie oï
from you NEG have-PRES I at-all hear-PPART
ce que vos en savez
that which you of-it know *LL III* 132
'(Those others tell me what they know but) from you I haven't heard what you know of it'

Inversion was regularly triggered by topicalized referential expressions, e.g. *por ce* in:

(5) Por ce li guerredonerai ge de mon povoir
For this her reward-FUT I of my power
'For this reason, I want to reward her as much as is in my power' *LL I* 170

Expressions of illocutionary force such as *mar* and *voirement* also triggered inversion (Buridant 2000: 524), e.g.:

(6)a. Mar conquerron nos l' autre terre
Wrongly conquer-PRES we the other land *Roman de Thebes1*, 99
'We do wrong to conquer the other land'
(6)b. Voirement sont ce des aventures del saint Graal
Truly be-PRES this some adventures of-the holy Grail
'Truly these are the adventures of the Holy Grail' *Queste* 52

The second key assumption we make is that Old French 'forclusifs de la négation', notably *nul*, *onques* and *ja*, were non-assertive polarity items (Foulet 1930; Roberts 2000), i.e. they were neither formally nor semantically negative.[4] The empirical evidence for this claim is that they appeared in irrealis clauses with affirmative polarity, such as conditionals and interrogatives. In Minimalist terms (Roberts 2007), where syntactic relations and operations are seen as determined by uninterpretable features, they had no uninterpretable negative features that needed to be checked when they

---

[3] Axel (2007: 194–8) shows that focused as well as topicalised items triggered V2 in Old High German, as did non-referential adverbs with a strengthening function that contributed to illocutionary force. It seems that finite verb raising to C in the two languages was triggered by much the same factors.

[4] In Modern French, however, the equivalent items are generally restricted to negative contexts (Muller 1991).

appeared in negative clauses.[5] A NegP projection is therefore not adopted in the present study, following the position advocated by Zeijlstra (2004) that NegP was projected iff a negative operator was required to check uninterpretable negative features on n-items.

Thirdly, Old French is assumed to have had two inherently negative elements, *ne* and *non*. Finite clauses were usually negated by an inherently negative particle *ne*, which we take to have been an element proclitic on the finite Verb. *Non* functioned as an inherently negative constituent negator,[6] and also as a negative operator in V2 clauses, e.g.:

(7) (Il ne refusera ja vostre proiere, et se j'estoie chi a cel eure qu'il i venra,)
('He would not refuse your request, and if I were present here at the time when he comes')
non feroit   il la moie
NEG do-CONDIT he the mine
'He would not refuse mine' *HL* 494

Here *non* clearly enjoyed the status of an XP able to satisfy V2 requirement.

Fourthly, our assumptions regarding subject positions in Old French are those of Vance (1997): subject pronouns cliticized to C in subordinate clauses and inverted main clauses. There is good distributional evidence for this, including the fact that subject pronouns appeared in subordinate clauses with preverbal adverbs, but always directly after complementizers such as *que* or *se*, e.g.:

(8) Et   certes   se il onques le pensa,
    And certainly if he ever   it think-PAST
    force d' amors li   fist   fere... *Artu* 5
    force of love   him do-PAST do-INFIN
    'And truly if he ever thought so, the power of love made him do so '

As regards inverted nominal subjects, Vance considered that a nominal subject in inverted clauses could occur in Spec VP. She showed that in inverted clauses with a non-pronominal subject, the Subject NP had to stand after a short adverb such as *ja*:

(9) [$_{TP}$ fronted XP [*ja* [$_{VP}$ subject NP]]]

Since a nominal Subject is analyzable as standing in VP, the position of the fronted XP in an inverted clause could be Spec TP.

The position of the subject in Old French SVO main clauses is controversial. It can be analyzed with the Subject in Spec CP, or else, as argued by Vance (1997), in

---

[5] An interpretable feature in Minimalist syntax is a formal feature on a linguistic item that determines its grammatical behavior, not its semantic interpretation. Thus multiple indefinites with uninterpretable features such as *personne, rien, plus* may appear in a clause expressing single negation such as *Personne ne comprend plus rien* ('no-one understands anything anymore').

[6] E.g. ...*et   non mie vos seulement   LL I* 166.
      And not at all you alone
      'And not only you'

Spec IP. Given this uncertainty over the analysis of SVO clauses, the presence of a CP structure will be taken in what follows as mandated only where there is inversion of a finite verb and a subject pronoun, making it clear that the verb must have left IP.

14.3 Syntax and Semantics of *onques* and *ja*

Before the licensing of *ja* and *onques* in clause-initial position is addressed, their syntactic and semantic properties need to be discussed in more general terms. In negative contexts, they can usually both be translated into English as 'ever', but there is an important semantic difference between them: whereas *ja* modifies future and conditional eventualities, *onques* accompanies past-referring ones (Moignet 1973: 283). Furthermore, in addition to its polarity use, *ja* also functions as an illocutionary force adverb emphasizing the realization of a process (Buridant 2000: 523). Correspondingly, in a negative clause it emphasizes its non-realization, with a meaning of 'in no way', and is virtually equivalent to the negative particles *pas*, *point* (Buridant 2000: 524). Examples of illocutionary force *ja*, in affirmative and negative contexts respectively, are:

(10) Ja   sui   je vostre amie
                                              '*Saisnes* 1197 (cited by Buridant 2000: 524)'
      Indeed be-PRES I   your   friend
      'I am indeed your friend'

(11) Ja   rien   ne   perdissent   si ne   fust   Sagremors
      Indeed anything NEG lose-PAST-SUBJ if NEG be-PAST Sagremos
      'They would definitely not have lost anything if it hadn't been for Sagremor'
                                                                                LL II 270

Syntactically, *ja* and *onques* occur in two linear positions. They may be clause-initial, as in (1)–(2) above, which is the type which will mainly concern us in what follows, or they may be medial. In the latter case, they show up to the left of various other medial adverbs such as *tant, plus* and *gaires*:

(12)a. Je ne   desirrai   onques tant   nule rien
       I NEG desire-PAST ever   so much any thing
       'I never wanted anything so much' *LL I* 362

(12)b. Ge ne   quier   ja   plus vivre   jor
       I   NEG seek-PRES ever more live-INFIN day
       'I do not seek to live another day' *LL II* 454

(12)c. Les armes Hestor   n'   estoient   onques gaires   anpiriees
       The arms Hestor-GEN NEG be-IMPERF ever   hardly damaged-PPART
       'H's armour was hardly ever damaged' *LL II* 292

The immediate postverbal position of *ja* and *onques* when medial indicates that they are to be associated with the tense-aspect-modality field within the clause structure. In non-inverted clauses, this is where, in SVO languages such as Old French, elements marked for tense, aspect and modality are found, not only verbs but also adverbs having temporal semantics. In terms of current generative syntax approaches to adverbs, their structural analysis will depend on whether or not one adopts the cartographical approach of Cinque (1999). If so, medial *ja* and *onques* as in (12) are located within the zone of functional projections associated with TP; if not, they are adjoined to VP like other medial adverbs. In this chapter we do not pursue further the analysis of medial position *ja* and *onques*, other than to note that data presented by Ingham (2005: 122) show that medial position accounted for over twice as many occurrences as initial position, suggesting that it constitutes the unmarked case.

Assertive *ja* can be found in both medial and clause-initial positions. In medial position it often combined with *mais* ('more') yielding the temporal sense 'anymore/ ever', but always in connection with a negated future eventuality: in past-referring contexts *onques* was always used instead. When clause-initial, however, *ja* may modify a past-referring eventuality, e.g.:

(13)a. Ja   vos   avoit   il si   longuement servi
       Indeed you-OBJ have-PAST he so long   serve-PPART
       'Indeed he had served you for so long' *Queste* 119
(13)b. Ja   l'   avez   vos   ocis
       Indeed him   have-PRES   you   slay-PPART
       'Indeed you have slain him' *Artu* 125

We take this as marking illocutionary force rather than temporal use, in line with the semantic distinction drawn between temporal and assertive *ja* by Moignet (1973). Occurrences of initial *ja* in past-referring contexts such as (13) are never accompanied by *mais*, also indicating that they are not temporal uses. Syntactically, they clearly engage the CP system, as shown by the postposed subject pronouns, conforming to the V2 grammar which, as we saw above, requires inversion after other clause-initial discourse particles such as *voirement* and *mar*. However, it remains to be seen whether the same can be said of the subjectless negative clause cases with initial *ja/onques*: this is the issue pursued in the following sections of the study.

14.4 Data Analysis 1: Initial *ja/onques* in Negative Clauses, Thirteenth Century Prose

The analysis of two early thirteenth century prose romances made by Ingham (2005) was conducted using online electronic texts that were generously made available by the Laboratoire de Français Ancien of the University of Ottawa. A total of 40 instances of initial *ja* and *onques* in negative clauses was thus obtained, all of which conformed to the claim made in that study that subject pronouns were absent in this context. However, the size of the sample was clearly modest and could give rise to concern over the generalizability of this result. No other prose texts were available in electronic format that would allow the finding to be replicated on a larger scale, and it was considered possible that Old French poetic works, of which large quantities exist in electronic formats, might be unduly influenced by constraints of versification.

To provide a more reliable basis for analysis, it was therefore decided to expand the evidence base to include four other comparable works written in the first quarter of the thirteenth century. These likewise narrate episodes in the Arthurian knightly tradition, thus exhibiting similar narrative textual properties to the texts originally studied. These were the first three parts of the prose romance *Lancelot du Lac*, and another prose romance, *Le Haut livre du Graal*. As a matter of practical convenience, especially for purposes of annotation, they were examined in the editions published in the *Lettres Gothiques* series.[7] Added to the *Artu* and *Queste* sources, these texts roughly trebled the size of the database examined by Ingham (2005).

The method employed was to hand-count instances from the additional texts, using the following criteria. Instances were entered for analysis if they displayed *ja* or *onques* in initial position in a context having the following properties[8]:

(14) – negated by *ne*
 – independent, i.e. root clauses
 – not coordinated by *et* or *ne*
 – not having an impersonal subject-taking predicate, e.g. *sembler*, as the finite verb

The last two conditions were imposed in order to exclude instances where there might be another reason for the omission of a subject pronoun, rather than the factor which we wished to investigate, the presence of initial *ja* or *onques*. The originally used *Artu* and *Queste* electronic texts were re-checked to ensure conformity with these criteria.

As expected, the target adverbs often appeared accompanied by *mais*, both clause-initially and clause-medially. In general, its presence or absence did not appear to be determined by either of these contexts, so *ja mais* and *onques mais* were included on the same basis as *ja* and *onques* alone. Instances of the target items were tabulated separately for each of the six texts so as to reveal potential differences between the previously analyzed sources and the new ones. Frequencies in each text were entered for whether, with a given adverb, a pronominal subject was preverbal (SpronV), postverbal (VSpron), or null. Although the main focus was on CP V2 contexts as indicated by the syntax of pronouns, instances with full nominal subjects were also collected, for purposes of comparison. They were categorized as preverbal (SnomV), or postverbal (VSnom). Nominal subjects were taken to include all subjects other than personal pronouns, but excluding the borderline case of *hom* (impersonal 'on'), which has sometimes been found to have unusual syntactic properties of inversion in Old French. These procedures gave the results shown in Tables 14.1 and 14.2:

---

[7] The *Lettres Gothiques* texts offer a substantial amount of previously unpublished material. Elspeth Kennedy's edition of *Lancelot* is used for parts I and II, but for part III, the edition by François Mosès of another manuscript is followed. The editor of *Le Haut Livre du Graal*, Armand Strubner, provided a new edition based on a previously unused manuscript from the mid-thirteenth century.

[8] Two instances were discarded where *onques* appeared in initial position as well as being used postverbally. We were not sure how to deal with such cases, and leave open the possibility of scribal confusion.

14 A Derivational Approach to Negative Polarity Item Licensing in Old French

Table 14.1 Subject expression with *ja* and *onques* in negative main clauses, pronominal subjects, thirteenth century prose romances

Text:	LL1	LL 2	LL3	Artu	Queste	HL	Total
Null subj							
ja	18	15	2	12	8	5	60
onques	9	11	3	18	8	19	68
	27	26	5	30	16	24	128 (96%)
SpronV							
ja	0	0	0	0	0	0	0
onques	0	0	0	0	0	0	0
	0	0	0	0	0	0	0
VSpron							
ja	2	1	1	0	0	0	4
onques	0	1	0	0	0	0	1
	2	2	1	0	0	0	5 (4%)
Overall total	29	28	6	30	16	24	133

Table 14.2 Subject expression with *ja* and *onques* in negative main clauses, full nominal subjects, thirteenth century prose romances

Text:	LL1	LL 2	LL3	Artu	Queste	HL	Total
VSnom							
ja	3	2	0	1	1	1	8
onques	1	3	0	3	1	4	12
	4	5	0	4	2	5	20 (22%)
SnomV							
ja	11	5	0	1	8	10	35
onques	2	2	5	6	6	16	37
	13	7	5	7	14	26	72 (78%)
Overall total	17	12	5	11	16	31	92 (100%)

The vast majority of non-nominal instances of initial *ja/onques* were subjectless, as shown in Table 14.1. No preverbal pronominal subjects were encountered, and VSpron was found very infrequently: 5/133 occurrences (3.8%), compared with 20/92 occurrences of inversion with Snom, (21.7%). Just four VSpron cases were found with *ja*, though none from the texts studied by Ingham (2005):

(15)a. Ja ne nos combatons nos por nule querele
JA NEG 1pl-REFL fight–1sg PRES we-SUBJ for any dispute
'Surely we do not fight for any dispute.' *LL I* 498

(15)b. Ja ne sont il, fist il, que autretant comme nos
JA NEG be-3pl they said he but as many as we
'Surely,' he said, 'They are only as many as we are.' *LL I* 496

(15)c. Ja n' a nus d' aus a vos mise main
JA NEG-has any of them to you put hand
'Surely none of them has laid hands on you' *LL II* 282

(15)d. Ja   ne   puis je estre sals se par lui   non
      JA NEG can I be   safe if by him not
      'Surely I cannot be saved except by him' *LLIII* 304

In all these cases, *ja* was used with a present or past-referring tense, not the future or conditional tenses which it generally accompanied. In addition, *ja* appeared in all cases without *mes*. The case for taking these not as temporal polarity items but as assertive markers (glossed as 'JA' and translated as 'surely' in (15a–d) above) thus appears very strong.

The only VSpron instance with *onques* was:

(16) Onques mais ne   fu   il si angoisseus
      Ever   more NEG be-PAST he so anxious
      'He had never been so anxious' *LL II* 492

This single case must be a real counterexample of VSpron with a polarity adverb, since no illocutionary force use counterpart of *onques* apparently existed. This isolated occurrence is discussed further in Sect. 14.6.

With nominal subjects, there were evidently two types of structure in productive operation. VSnom produced 20 instances in Table 14.2, and complies with V2 at least superficially, though such cases can be analyzed with the nominal subject in Spec vP, following Vance (1997), as suggested earlier. The other type, of which there were 72 occurrences, displays SV order with a polarity adverb apparently adjoined to its left, and as such is a clear V2 violation. This latter type is by far the more frequent and probably needs to be taken as the unmarked order for negative clauses with nominal subjects featuring initial *ja/onques*. The prevalence of V3 order in these negative clauses contrasts strongly with the exclusively V2 character of clauses with a nominal subject and an initial adverb such as *ore* or *encore* found by Ingham (2005).

In the course of analyzing the data for Tables 14.1 and 14.2 a number of instances were noted of main clause V4 order, something that is not recorded in any treatment of Old French syntax known to the author, at least as regards prose works. Sometimes a nominal subject together with another complement or adjunct intervened between *ja/onques* and the verb:

(17)a. Mais onques puis Galehoz bele chiere   ne   pot   faire
       But ever   after Galahad fair countenance NEG can-PAST make-INFIN
       'But G. could not look cheerful anymore.' *LL II* 586

Sometimes two non-subject constituents intervened between *ja/onques* and the verb, such as an adjunct and a direct object, or two adjuncts:

(18) Car ja   del   roi Artur secours n'   avra
      For ever of-the king Arthur help   NEG have-FUT
      'For he will never have help from King Arthur.' *LL I* 48

(19) Car ja   aseür une seule hore,
     For ever surely a   single hour
     ne   par nuit ne par jor, n'   i   dormira
     neither by night nor by day NEG there sleep-FUT
     'He will surely never sleep there a single hour, night or day.' *LL I* 244[9]

The limited number of examples does not permit us to generalize as to whether free ordering of constituents is allowed to the left of the finite verb, but there are initial indications here that subjects are ordered first among the constituents in this field between *ja/onques* and the finite verb, while objects stand last before the verb. This is as expected if subjects are in Spec TP and other constituents appear in scrambled orders within the middle field.

In any case, such data with initial *ja/onques* illustrate very clearly that the negative clauses in which they stand disregard the V2 constraint. This indicates that they do not involve a CP projection: if they do not involve CP, and if main clause V2 arises by movement to CP, V>2 orders with preposed *onques* are to be expected. This is indeed what is documented in this section, with evidence not only of the V3 orders discussed by Ingham (2005), but cases of V4 orders as well. Thus, in negative main clauses a different structure is envisaged from that of affirmative main clauses. A negative main clause need not engage an overt CP projection, and where there are initial polarity items, it apparently must not do so. However, other types of initial constituent such as illocutionary force expressions do involve a lexically filled CP projection, as assumed in Sect. 14.2 above. We return in Sect. 14.6 to these issues.

14.5 Argument/Adjunct Asymmetry with Polarity Items and V2

To conclude this part of the study, evidence from the thirteenth century source texts is observed that polarity adverbial expressions behaved differently in Old French syntax from polarity argument expressions. Preposed internal arguments containing *nul* always showed CP V2 syntax, e.g:

(20) Nul si bon   seignor ne   poriez   vos   servir
     Any so good lord   NEG can-CONDIT you-OBJ   serve-INFIN
     'You could not serve any Lord as good as this one.' *HL* 616

---

[9] In this example *ne por nuit ne por jor* does not count as a sentence constituent, being appositional to *une seule hore*.

With adjunct PPs containing polarity items, however, inversion never occurred in our data, resulting in clear V2 violations, e.g.:

(21) Car por nule riens ge ne   voudroie   estre   conneüz
      For for any thing I   NEG wish-CONDIT be-INFIN know-PPART
      'I would not wish to be known for anything.' *Artu* 6

In the texts studied, main clause subjects containing polarity expressions were found to precede the finite verb complex, as in:

(22) Car nus chevaliers ne   se   doit   corrocier   de ...
      For any knight   NEG self should anger-INFIN of
      'For no knight should get angry about...' *Queste* p.118

They were thus compatible with V2 syntax, but as mentioned above, are indeterminate as to whether they are CPs or TPs.

Though data as in (20)–(21) are infrequent, and to our knowledge have not been pointed out before by researchers, the contrast between argument compliance with and adjunct violation of CP V2 structure looks striking, and ought to be integrated into an account of the behavior of polarity items in negative clauses, which the next section provides.

14.6 The Formal Licensing of Negative Polarity Items in Old French

The analysis of polarity items in Old French developed here is framed within a minimalist approach to syntax in which syntactic form is driven by the grammatical feature properties of lexical items, especially semantically uninterpretable but grammatically relevant features which require checking against another element in the derivation (Chomsky 2001). To the extent, therefore, that negative main clauses in Old French may have had a different structure from affirmative main clauses, this must be reducible to characteristics of the elements entering the derivation of a negative clause. A crucial factor documented by the empirical survey in the previous section is the presence of prefinite polarity items, which appeared to block the projection of CP; in this section a detailed account is given of how this operated.

The licensing of polarity items, we claim, functioned in a broadly similar way to the ordinary feature-checking operations of Minimalist syntax. Although polarity items such as *ja, nul*, and *onques* lacked uninterpretable negative features, they did bear an uninterpretable non-assertive polarity feature, which required checking. This featural property was established by Martins' (2000) account of Old Romance indefinites such as Old French *aucun* and *nul*, in which positive and non-assertive polarity features were attributed to the lexical entries of the respective items. In a Minimalist framework, uninterpretable features require to be checked by an interpretable feature on an element they c-command, which would mean the polarity item would have to c-command its licenser. As pointed out by Roberts (2007) this is unworkable for polarity English, which, in languages such as modern English, must be c-commanded by the element licensing them.

In Old French, as we have seen, the situation is somewhat different: taking polarity items in negative clauses to have been licensed by the negator *ne*,[10] they were clearly not sensitive to linear order, since they appeared either before or after the negator, and therefore apparently in higher as well as in lower structural positions. Clearly, a c-command relationship was not required, a not uncommon scenario which Mahajan (1990) proposed to handle on the basis that all negative polarity items were licensed by being c-commanded by Negation at LF. However, once we dispense with the reliance on levels of representation afforded by her GB analysis, we need a different type of account.[11] The crucial notion to be adopted here is that in such languages non-assertive polarity items, henceforth notated by the feature [pol-], are licensed within both specifier and the complement domain of the licenser. Specifically, a negator such as Old French *ne* can license such polarity items in the complement domain of T and also in its specifier(s). The latter includes not only potentially the clause subject but also adjunct constituents left-adjoined to TP. In a language such as Old French, the domain of polarity licensing is thus as follows:

(23) [$_{TP}$ adjunct [pol-] [$_{TP}$ subject [pol-] *ne*+V [$_{vP}$ complement [pol-]]]]

Furthermore, the argument/adjunct asymmetry presented in Sect. 14.5 above suggests that instead of a single-level approach to polarity item licensing, such as that adopted in GB treatments, a non-representational approach is preferable. This is reminiscent of the Binding Theory asymmetry between arguments and adjuncts noted by Lebeaux (1988), which a derivational analysis offers a way of handling. Accordingly, we propose that Old French non-asssertive polarity items are licensed in two phases, approximately corresponding to the phase-based approach to feature-checking in Chomsky (2001, 2008). When merged in the vP phase, polarity expressions must be licensed within vP, that is their polarity feature is checked by a licenser. In the case of Old French, this must be the negative clitic *ne*: polarity features on arguments within vP are checked in this way before the finite verb raises to T. Both internal and external arguments were licensed in this way[12]:

(24)a. [$_{vP}$ *pro* ne[iNEG] +poriez servir   nul[pol-] si bon seignor]   (cf. (20))

(24)b. [$_{vP}$ nus[pol-] chevaliers ne[iNEG]+se+doit corrocier…]   (cf. (22))

---

[10] More precisely a negative operator identified by *ne*, in terms of Zeijlstra (2004). However, in this study we leave open the question of whether a NegP was projected in Old French. Biberauer and Roberts (2011) and Larrivée and Ingham (2012) raise questions for Zeilstra's account of the syntax of negation, under which a language with negative concord, such as Modern French, is supposed to project NegP whereas a non-Negative Concord language, such as Old French, is not.

[11] See also Hoeksema (2000) for a critical discussion of the need for c-command in polarity licensing.

[12] For simplicity, we ignore internal vP structure taking account of the auxiliary verbs, which does not affect the vP phase boundary.

The argument polarity expressions checked within the vP phase were then free to participate in cyclic movement in the CP phase, including movement to Spec TP for Nominative case checking, and movement to Spec CP to satisfy a criterion such as Wh- or Topic, e.g.

(25)

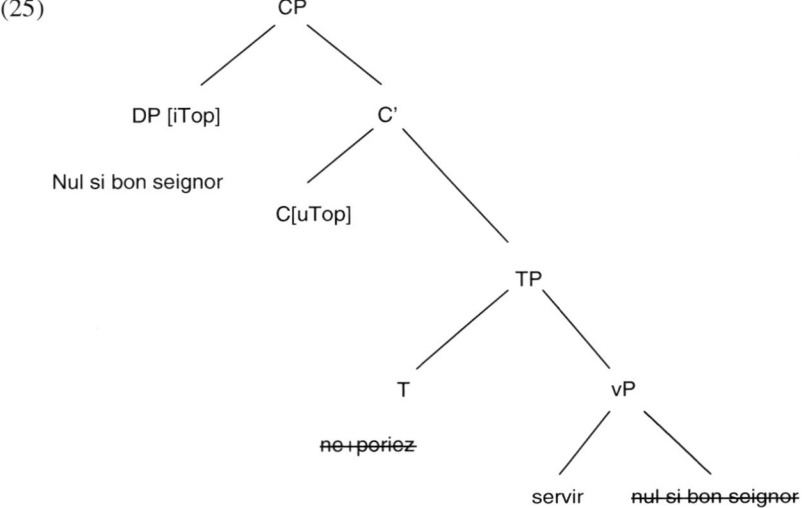

Here, the discourse-linked expression *nul si bon seignor* checks the uninterpretable Topic feature on C.

A T-related adjunct, however, e.g. time adverb, is added to the derivation after the vP phase, and is free to be adjoined to TP. If it bears polarity features, as do *ja* or *onques*, they can only be checked in the next phase, which is CP, following the phase-based approach of Chomsky (2001, 2008). Crucially, polarity items are not topicalized,[13] and thus do not appear in CP, triggering V2. With no XP movement to CP, movement to C of the *ne*+V complex will not occur, so CP will be non-overt. In short, an adjunct polarity expression is checked in the CP phase, but remains within TP where its licenser *ne* resides. The surface result is an uninverted structure with polarity items adjoined to the left of the finite verb, represented in (26):

---

[13] Cf. the inability of the English polarity item *a red cent* to topicalize in the second clause of *I said it wasn't worth a red cent, and a red cent I won't give you.*

(26)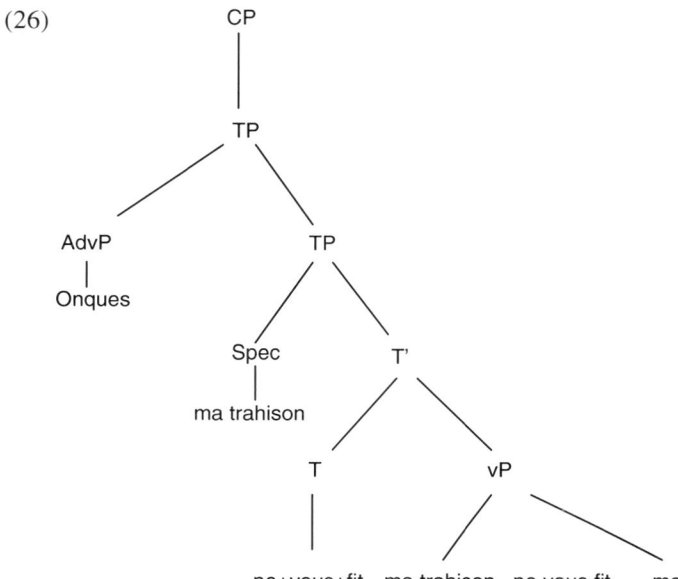

Note that an item with a Force feature triggering V2, such as *ja* in the examples in (15), will do so as a reinforcing adverb, not as a polarity item, so it too will raise to Spec CP, triggering V2.

Support for the analysis proposed comes in the behavior of the negator *non*, as in (7). Unlike polarity adverbs, *non* was able to stand in Spec CP because, as an inherently negative item, it had no polarity feature to be checked. As a marker of Force, however, it raised to the CP domain, triggering V2.

In addition we can now appreciate why no preverbal subject pronoun appears in Old French *ja/onques* initial clauses in Table 14.1 In Old French Spron was either in Spec CP or was a clitic on C. Since the C system was not engaged in *ja/onques*-initial clauses, the absence of Spron follows automatically. The situation was different with nominal Subjects, which appeared in VS order nearly a quarter of the time in the data analysed here, as we saw in Table 14.2. In a non-inverted clause an Snom stood in Spec TP, but a nominal Subject could optionally stand in Spec vP (Vance 1997), giving rise to the VSnom cases. Hence neither pronominal nor nominal subjects involve the CP system in Old French *ja/onques*-initial clauses.

VSpron was possible with initial *ja*, we have claimed, when *ja* was an assertive element rather than a polarity item, but *onques* did not enjoy this alternative status as an assertive element. Mention must now made of the single counter-example noted, example (16), showing *onques* clearly as having raised out of TP, despite its polarity status. Since it was an isolated case, one might treat it as a candidate for performance error, from which texts transcribed in the non-optimal conditions of the medieval environment were surely not immune. Still, let us take it as genuine. It is unusual in occurring in narrative, whereas initial *ja/onques* is normally found in dialogue. Furthermore, it is used at a high point in a particularly dramatic passage where Gawain, one of the central characters in the novel, comes very close to death, as a result of mistaken identity. It is possible that the author was here resorting to some kind of stylistic manipulation of the ordinary syntax of the clause. Perhaps *onques* was being used for rhetorical effect as if it were an illocutionary force item.

Otherwise, however, the analysis offered here accounts for the totality of observed data. Negative main clauses showed two clause structures, one with strict CP V2, and one in which constituents remain within TP. To the former type belonged clauses with an initial argument polarity expression and those with a non-polarity initial constituent, including *non*. To the latter type belonged clauses with initial polarity expressions, which could present V>2 order.

14.7 Analysis 2: Initial Polarity Items in Negative Clauses, Twelfth Century Epic Verse

Having found evidence to suggest that the syntax of negative main clauses with preposed polarity items did not observe the V2 system in the thirteenth century, we may ask whether negative main clauses were structured differently from affirmatives prior to that time. Unfortunately little prose material is currently available that would bear on this question. Large amounts of verse are accessible, however, in epic poems whose date of composition as written text is thought to span more or less the whole twelfth century. Of course, that is not to suggest that versified compositions reflect the ordinary syntax of the French language of the twelfth century. Linguistically, such works are notoriously conservative. Nevertheless, one might reasonably assume that, precisely because they are archaic, the linguistic forms of epic poetry conserve to some extent the usage of an earlier period, even though which period cannot be determined. The question then is whether the earliest substantial body of Old French texts, putatively reflecting the usage of a period earlier than the prose works of thirteenth century, displayed the contrasts shown in Analysis 1.

Thirteen Old French epic poems[14] were analyzed for this purpose. As before, data analysis was carried out to determine whether the presence of an initial non-subject constituent in a negative clause was associated with a null subject, with a prefinite subject pronoun, or a postfinite subject pronoun. A 2,000 line sample of each poem was analyzed (or the complete text if its length was less than this figure). To determine relevant contexts for the variables in question, the same inclusion criteria were observed as for Analysis 1 (see (14) above).

Analysis was performed on pronoun contexts only, excluding nominal subjects, as the main focus was on obtaining evidence for a CP structure, and as discussed above, nominal subjects were indeterminate in this regard.

In view of the fact that Analysis 1 was run using prose while analysis 2 used verse, certain precautions were taken to avoid making unwarranted methodological

---

[14] The texts used were: *Chanson de Roland, Gormont et Isambard, Chanson de Guillaume, Voyage de Charlemagne, Charroi de Nimes, Couronnement de Louis, Moniage Guillaume, Prise d'Orange, Aspremont, Chevalerie Vivien, Aliscans, Raoul de Cambrai*, and *Girart de Vienne*.

Table 14.3 Subject expression with *ja* and *onques* in negative main clauses, pronominal subjects, twelfth century epic verse

	Null subject initial constituent	VSpron	SpronV	Total
ja etc. + *ne*-V	79	1	0	80
ja etc. + XP+*ne*-V	41	0	0	41
NP or PP containing *nul/nient*	9	0	0	9
Total clause-initial polarity items:	129 (99.2%)	1 (0.8%)	0	130
Other items:	119 (73.9%)	42 (26.1%)	0	161

assumptions. It is already well-known (see e.g. Price 1973) that postposed subject pronouns were far less common in twelfth century verse than in the thirteenth century texts, so it was felt desirable to check that subject pronoun expression in these sources did not experience a 'floor' effect. That is, it might be so low in all contexts that no conclusions could be drawn from its absence with clause-initial *ja/onques*. Unlike in analysis 1, therefore, we also included a tally of inversion after ordinary, non-polarity initial expressions. This allowed a comparison to be made between frequencies with polarity and non-polarity expressions in clause-initial position.

Another difference from analysis 1 is that instances of *ja/onques*+XP+*ne*-Vfin were tabulated separately from those without the intervening XP. In the former case there is a manifest V2 violation, whereas the latter is superficially compatible with V2 syntax. Although the thirteenth century data had shown no such contrast between these contexts as regards the expression of postverbal subject pronouns, it was considered advisable to check whether in the earlier period that was also the case.

We also wished to see if the asymmetry between initial arguments and initial adjuncts was already in evidence at this time, so occurrences of NPs or PPs containing polarity items (specifically *nul* or *nient*) were also recorded, as shown below in Table 14.3. Frequencies are displayed on the horizontal axis of the table in terms of whether a subject was omitted, present before the finite verb, or present after the finite verb.

The results from these Old French epics were very much in line with those of data analysis 1. In negative clauses, the availability of inverted subject pronouns differed sharply depending on whether the first element is a polarity item. In the case of *ja, mes, james, onques, ainc, nul, noient, rien,* and *pas,* a subject pronoun was virtually never present, either pre-or post-verbally. There was a single exception, to which we return. In the case of adverbs such as *or, dont, donques, lors,* a postposed subject pronoun occurs 26% of the time, e.g.:

(27) Dont n'   avons   nos nul povre chevalier
      So   NEG have-PRES we any poor knight
      'So we don't have any poor knight.' Aspr 1770

The same applies with other types of initial constituent, such as adjunct PPs, direct objects and predicate complements PPs :

(28) Oliver, frere, vos   ne dei jo faillir
Oliver brother you-OBJ NEG must I fail
'Brother Oliver, I must not fail you' CR 1866

There were only a few initial NP or PP cases with *nul* or *nient*, all lacking an overt Spron, so the argument/adjunct asymmetry regarding inversion that we observed in the thirteenth century data was not discerned here, perhaps because contexts were so infrequent.

The main finding is that, as in the thirteenth century sources, the presence of an initial polarity item in a negative clause affects whether the V2 system is engaged, as evidenced by a postposed subject pronoun. Even when an XP precedes the verb that normally triggers inversion, the subject pronoun is absent if *ja* is initial:

(29)a. Ja de lozenges n'   averas   mais loier
ever of flattery NEG have-FUT-2sg ever reward
'You will never be rewarded for flattery.' CL 139
(29)b. James de nos nen avront   baillie
ever of us NEG have-FUT-3pl power
'They will never have power over us.' Alisc. 517

Of the 41 such sentences identified, none show VSpron. Therefore we take them to be TP structures, not CPs.

A single occurrence of VSpron in the *ja/onques* + *ne*-Vfin condition occurred:

(30) Ja n' ai   je de chevaliers compeigne
JA NEG have-PRES I of knights company
'I surely have no company of knights.' Aliscans 643

Here, we may again be dealing with *ja* as an assertive marker, not a polarity item, since the tense is present, not future or conditional. Thus the position taken in analysis 1 is not challenged by any of the twelfth century findings. In other words, whatever state of the language is transmitted to us by the twelfth century verse, it and the thirteenth century prose both possessed the same structural contrast between negative clauses with initial *ja/onques*, and negative clauses with other types of preposed XPs. The latter, but not the former, was a V2 context throughout the history of Old French.

14.8 Summary

Three types of V2 violation have been identified in previous work on Old French negative clauses. First, negative clauses could have null subjects in the absence of a initial XP. Secondly, *ja/onques* allowed null subjects but also V3 order with nominal subjects. Thirdly, initial adjunct PPs containing polarity items showed V3 order. The aim of this study was to build on these earlier findings and identify properties of negative main clauses in Old French which might offer a structural account of them. The analysis offered here is that polarity adjuncts were licensed in TP, as they were not suitable expressions to satisfy criteria motivating movement to Spec CP. This claim was supported by the tense semantic properties of *ja/onques* in different types of structure. A key aspect of the proposal is that in Old French polarity licensing took place symmetrically within a licensing domain, but by phase: when in vP, the negative polarity licenser *ne* licensed arguments; when in TP it licensed time adjuncts.[15]

Where does this leave the status of V2 in Old French? V2 observance or violation, we believe, may submit to a more principled treatment than critics of the CP V2 analysis have contended. The apparent violations discussed in this study are dealt with once it is recognized that negative clauses were not necessarily V2 contexts. CP was not ordinarily constructed in negative clauses, unless a constituent was displaced there to satisfy a Criterion (Topic, Wh-, or other). Polarity adjunct-initial clauses remained TPs for a principled reason, that of satisfying the licensing requirement on these items. We call such clauses 'TPs' as shorthand for a clause structure in which any CP projection is abstract. In other words, Old French clauses with initial polarity items were like their counterparts in Modern French, such as *Jamais il ne fera une chose pareille*. In terms of overt syntax, such cases are analysable as TP structures with an adjoined initial adverbial expression. On grounds of theoretical uniformity one may posit non-overt CP structure here, these clauses are not V2 contexts, nor were their counterparts in Old French.

In sum, it appears that critics of the CP V2 position are right to the extent that, unlike the modern-day Germanic languages, Old French had major types of main clause structure that were not V2. That is, V2 violation did not just concern a few idiosyncratic adverbs, as it does in German. Another such clause type, found in Old Norse and Old High German, was constituted by V1 affirmative clauses with topicalized verbs (Labelle 2007), at least in twelfth century texts. On the other hand, once we have removed these principled cases from contention, the argument for claiming that CP V2 was a regular feature of Old French is thereby strengthened.[16]

At the same time, much work remains to be done on the properties of Old French negative clauses, exploring further the notion that they normally possessed a TP structure without overt CP material, in addition to those of other kinds of polarity items, especially non-assertive items outside negative contexts. A broader picture of polarity licensing and clause structure from the perspective of current syntactic theory will continue, we believe, to be a goal of future research, to which this study has, it is hoped, provided some useful pointers.

---

[15] Within a CP phase in the sense of an abstract C projection, however, to which no movement took place.

[16] A reviewer asks why Old French differed from Modern German in the respects studied here. The reason would appear to be that as counterparts of *ja* and *onques* and *nul*, German has incorporated n-items (*nie* etc.) which do not need polarity licensing.

Key to Primary Sources Quoted

'Artu': *La mort le roi Artu, roman du XIIIe siècle*, ed. J. Frappier, Geneva, Droz, 1954.
'Queste': *La Queste del Saint Graal*, ed. A. Pauphilet, Paris, Champion, 1949.
'LL I': *Lancelot du Lac I*, text presented by Fr. Mosés, Série Lettres Gothiques Le Livre de Poche, Paris, 1991.
'LL II': *Lancelot du Lac II*, text presented by Marie-Luce Chênerie, Série Lettres Gothiques, Le Livre de Poche, Paris, 1993.
'LL III': *La fausse Guenièvre, Lancelot du Lac III* ed. Fr. Mosès, Série Lettres Gothiques, Le Livre de Poche, Paris, 1998.
'HL'. *Le Haut Livre du Graal [Perlesvaus]* ed. A. Strubel, Série Lettres Gothiques, Le Livre de Poche, Paris, 2007.

References

Adams, M. 1987. Old French and the theory of pro-drop. *Natural Language and Linguistic Theory* 5: 1–32.
Axel, K. 2007. *Studies on Old High German syntax*. Amsterdam: Benjamins.
Biberauer, T., and I. Roberts. 2011. Negative words and related expressions: A new perspective on some familiar puzzles. In *The evolution of negation*, ed. P. Larrivée and R. Ingham, 23–60. Berlin: De Gruyter.
Buridant, C. 2000. *Nouvelle Grammaire de l'ancien Français*. Paris: SEDES.
Chomsky, N. 2001. Derivation by phase. In *Ken Hale: A life in language*, ed. M. Kenstowicz, 1–52. Cambridge, MA: MIT Press.
Chomsky, N. 2008. On phases. In *Foundational issues in linguistic theory: Essays in honour of J.R. Vergnaud*, ed. R. Freidin, C. Otero, and M.-L. Zubizarreta. Cambridge, MA: MIT Press.
Cinque, Guglielmo. 1999. *Adverbs and functional heads – A crosslinguistic perspective*. Oxford: OUP.
Foulet, L. 1930. *Syntaxe de l'ancien français*. Paris: Champion.
Haider, H., and M. Prinzhorn (eds.). 1986. *Verb second phenomena in Germanic languages*. Dordrecht: Foris.
Hoeksema, J. 2000. Negative polarity items: Triggering, scope, and c-command. In *Negation and polarity*, ed. L. Horn and Y. Kato, 115–146. Oxford: Oxford University Press.
Ingham, R. 2005. Adverbs and the syntax of subjects in Old French. *Romania* 123: 99–122.
Kaiser, G. 2002. *Verbstellung und Verbstellungswandel in den romanischen Sprachen*. Tübingen: Niemeyer.
Labelle, M. 2007. Clausal architecture in early Old French. *Lingua* 117(1): 289–316.
Larrivée, P., and R. Ingham. 2012. Variation, change and the status of negatives in peripheral varieties of Old French: The case of néant. In *Le changement linguistique en français: aspects socio-historiques Etudes en hommage au Professeur R. Anthony Lodge*, ed. D. Lagorgette and T. Pooley. Langages (Éditions de l'université de Savoie) no. 10, pp. 99–111.
Lebeaux, D. 1988. Language acquisition and the form of the grammar. PhD thesis. Amherst: University of Massachusetts.
Mahajan, A. 1990. LF conditions on negative polarity licensing. *Lingua* 80: 333–348.

Martins, A.-M. 2000. Polarity items in Romance: Underspecification and lexical change. In *Diachronic syntax: Models and mechanisms*, ed. S. Pintzuk, G. Tsoulas, and A. Warner, 191–219. Oxford: OUP.
Mathieu, É. 2006. Stylistic fronting in Old French. *Probus* 18: 219–266.
Moignet, G. 1973. *Grammaire de l'Ancien Français*. Paris: Klincksieck.
Muller, C. 1991. *La négation en français*. Geneva: Droz.
Prévost, S. 2001. *La postposition du sujet en français aux XVe et XVIe siècles: analyse sémantico-pragmatique*. Paris: CNRS Editions.
Price, G. 1971. *The French language: Present and past*. London: Arnold.
Price, G. 1973. Sur le pronom personnel sujet postposé en ancien francais. *Revue Romane* 8: 476–504.
Roberts, I. 1993. *Verbs and diachronic syntax*. Dordrecht: Kluwer.
Roberts, I. 2000. Some remarks on the diachrony of French negation. *Revista de Documentação de Estudos em Lingüística Teórica e Aplicada (D.E.L.T.A.)* 16: 201–219.
Roberts, I. 2007. *Diachronic sytax*. Oxford: OUP.
Skårup, P. 1975. Les premières zones de la proposition en ancien français. Essai de syntaxe de position. In *Revue Romane*, numéro spécial 6. Études Romanes de l'Université de Copenhague. København: Akademisk Forlag.
Vance, B. 1997. *Syntactic change in medieval French*. Dordrecht: Kluwer.
Vikner, S. 1995. *Verb movement and expletive subjects in the Germanic languages*. Oxford: Oxford University Press.
Zeijlstra, H. 2004. Sentential negation and negative concord. Unpublished PhD dissertation, University of Amsterdam.

Chapter 15
Theoretical Issues in Old French Inflectional Morpho(phono)logy

Jürgen Klausenburger

15.1 Introduction

The purpose of this chapter is to sketch prototypical features of Old French nominal (Sect. 15.2) and verbal (Sect. 15.3) inflectional morphology and to examine them in the framework of the two versions of Natural Morphology, Mayerthaler (1981) ('system-independent') and Wurzel (1984) ('system-dependent'). Such a discussion will involve the theoretical concepts of (degrees of) *iconicity* (system-independent naturalness) and *system congruity* (SC) (system-dependent naturalness), which is created by *paradigm structure conditions* (PSC's). The two principal PSC's are identified as (1) Invariance (INV) and (2) *final consonant alternation* (FCA). In order to make the Old French morphophonological structure more accessible, its major characteristics are traced into their Modern French counterparts (Sects. 15.4 and 15.5). Such an evolution is further examined in Sect. 15.6.

The essence of our account may be considered 'concrete' and 'functional'. Such labels are routinely contrasted with 'abstract' and 'formal' in recent linguistic theorizing. In the last section of this contribution, Sect. 15.7, I will discuss this dichotomy, injecting considerations based on Ockham's Razor (and Chatton's Anti-Razor). Also included will be a review of earlier works on Old French morphophonology, Herslund (1976) and Walker (1981).

J. Klausenburger (✉)
Department of Linguistics, University of Washington, Seattle, WA, USA
e-mail: jklaus@u.washington.edu

15.2 Nominal Inflection

15.2.1 *Invariance*

The first PSC to be analyzed may be illustrated by Old French nouns such as *mur* 'wall' and *porte* 'door', shown in their declensional paradigms as follows:

(1)   Singular   Plural
    Subject case   *murs, porte*   *mur, portes*
    Oblique case   *mur, porte*   *murs, portes*

Leaving out the inflectional suffix *–s* for now, we discover a unique root for both nouns throughout the paradigm, phonetically [myr] and [pɔrtə]. The morphological features of case and number (and gender, indirectly) are signaled in the suffix, since it is fully pronounced in Old French.

In a similar fashion, adjectives like *dur, dure* 'hard' and *bon, bone* 'good' (masculine, feminine) manifest INV, since the root would be transcribed phonetically as [dyr] and [bõn], the suffix *–e* (phonetically a schwa) signaling feminine gender. Adjectives, of course, enter into the same declensional pattern as the nouns.

15.2.2   FCA

There are a number of Old French nouns, exemplified by *champ* 'field' and *cheval* 'horse', which undergo morphophonological alternation of the final consonant inside the complete paradigm:

(2)   Singular   Plural
    Subject case   *chans, chevaus*   *champ, cheval*
    Oblique case   *champ, cheval*   *chans, chevaus*

The assumed pronunciation of the four forms, [čãns], [čəvaws], [čãmp], and [čəval], demonstrates the variation mentioned, as two allomorphs of the root have to be posited, triggered by the inflectional suffix in the subject case singular and the oblique case plural:

the final consonant /p/ is deleted (and homorganic nasal consonant assimilation occurs also) in the noun 'field', while the final /l/ in 'horse' is changed to a glide (traditionally labeled 'vocalization').

An adjective like *bel* 'beautiful' undergoes the following changes:

(3)   Singular   Plural
    Subject case   *beaus*   *bel*
    Oblique case   *bel*   *beaus*

Here, the s-suffix leads to vocalization of the root-final /l/, in addition to epenthesis of the vowel /a/, creating a triphthong in the Old French pronunciation: [beaws].

15.2.3 (Counter)-Iconicity

Let us subject the data under 'INV' for the noun in 2.1 above to an analysis in terms of iconic structure, the basis for establishing 'naturalness' in morphology in Mayerthaler (1981). The following markedness values will be employed:

(4) CASE: subject case = unmarked, oblique case = marked
NUMBER: singular = unmarked, plural = marked
GENDER: masculine = unmarked, feminine = marked

Iconicity is attained when the markedness values given match the overt morphological structure in Old French. When identical signaling for both marked and unmarked members occurs, *non-iconicity* is manifested. Finally, if signaling values hold that are diametrically opposed to markedness values, then *counter-iconicity* must be recognized. Specifically, this is illustrated by 12 pairings, which are extractable from the relationships assumed to exist between the two nouns cited (the most productive two noun declensions only are shown):

(5) Dominant patterns of noun declensions in Old French
  a. <u>subj</u>/sing/masc vs. <u>oblique</u>/sing/masc (*murs/mur*) = counter-iconic
    (s – ø) CASE
  b. subj/<u>sing</u>/masc vs. subj/<u>pl</u>/masc (*murs/mur*) = counter-iconic
    (s – ø) NUMBER
  c. subj/sing/<u>masc</u> vs. subj/sing/<u>fem</u> (*murs/porte*) = counter-iconic
    (s – ø) GENDER
  d. oblique/<u>sing</u>/masc vs. oblique/<u>pl</u>/masc (*mur/murs*) = iconic (ø – s)
    NUMBER
  e. oblique/sing/<u>masc</u> vs. oblique/sing/<u>fem</u> (*mur/porte*) = non-iconic (ø – ø)
    GENDER
  f. <u>subj</u>/pl/masc vs. <u>oblique</u>/pl/masc (*mur/murs*) = iconic (ø – s) CASE
  g. subj/pl/<u>masc</u> vs. subj/pl/<u>fem</u> (*mur/portes*) = iconic (ø – s) GENDER
  h. <u>subj</u>/sing/fem vs. <u>oblique</u>/sing/fem (*porte/porte*) = non-iconic (ø – ø)
    CASE
  i. subj/<u>sing</u>/fem vs. subj/<u>pl</u>/fem (*porte/portes*) = iconic (ø – s) NUMBER
  j. oblique/<u>sing</u>/fem vs. oblique/<u>pl</u>/fem (*porte/portes*) = iconic (ø – s)
    NUMBER
  k. <u>subj</u>/pl/fem vs. <u>oblique</u>/pl/fem (*portes/portes*) = non-iconic (s – s) CASE
  l. oblique/pl/<u>masc</u> vs. oblique/pl/<u>fem</u> (*murs/portes*) = non-iconic (s – s)
    GENDER

Although counter-iconicity appears to be in the minority in the above overview of possible connections, it may, in fact, be considered the pivotal factor contributing to the loss of the case system in later Old French.[1] This is so because the case structure of Old French evolved primarily in the masculine noun, of which the *mur*-type is by far the dominant one. For this noun, triple counter-iconicity, of case, number, and gender (the first three connections listed above), destabilized the system, leading (plausibly) to its demise. For a while during the Old French period, the dominance of the *mur*-type was made overt by well-known analogical shifts: the noun 'father' changed from (etymological) *pere* to *peres* in the singular subject case, and the (etymological) *peres* to *pere* in the plural subject case, by adding or subtracting the final /s/ by the replication of the model *mur/murs*. This is an excellent example of how *system-congruity* (SC), the basis of naturalness for Wurzel (1984), was established in the subsystem of nominal inflection in Old French.

Since the attraction of the *mur*-model created parallel forms in other masculine nouns, the counter-iconicity inherent in the *mur*-paradigm spread more widely in Old French. Therefore, the destabilizing effect of counter-iconicity became even more potent.[2]

15.3 Verbal Inflection

15.3.1 INV

The unique root *chant* [čănt] 'sing' is easily detachable within the present indicative paradigm:

(6)	Singular	Plural
First person	*chant*	*chantons*
Second person	*chantes*	*chantez*
Third person	*chante*	*chantent*

On the other hand, 'sell' may seem to have allomorphy of the root, but this is due to general pronunciation rules of Old French, final consonant (obstruent) devoicing and voicing assimilation (for *vent* [věnt] and *venz* [věnts]), respectively:

(7)	Singular	Plural
First person	*vent*	*vendons*
Second person	*venz*	*vendez*
Third person	*vent*	*vendent*

---

[1] There are also, of course, morphosyntactic factors involved, which led to a gradual loss of case inflection dating back to the Latin period.

[2] In Klausenburger (1990), I suggest that the 12 markedness connections for the Old French noun may have operated inside a cube constellation. If so, the 'destructive' impact of counter-iconicity on the overall system could be considered even more directly and transparently.

The present subjunctive paradigms illustrate root INV clearly, although the two verbs given have different sets of suffixes in the singular, belonging to two different conjugations in Latin:

(8) | | Singular | Plural |
     |--------------|------------------|----------------------|
     | First person | *chant, vende* | *chantons, vendons* |
     | Second person| *chanz, vendes* | *chantez, vendez* |
     | Third person | *chant, vende* | *chantent, vendent* |

15.3.2 FCA

The variety of allomorphic variation of the verbal roots in Old French may be illustrated by four verbs, 'speak', 'love', 'drink', and 'come', as shown in the following:

(9) Present indicative:

	Singular	Plural
First person	*parol, aim, beif, vieng*	*parlons, amons, bevons, venons*
Second person	*paroles, aimes, beis, viens*	*parlez, amez, bevez, venez*
Third person	*parole, aime, beit, vient*	*parolent, aiment, beivent, vienent*

(10) Present subjunctive:

	Singular	Plural
First person	*parol, aim, beive, viegne*	*parlons, amons, bevons, vegnons*
Second person	*parous, ains, beives, viegnes*	*parlez, amez, bevez, vegnez*
Third person	*parout, aint, beive, viegne*	*parolent, aiment, beivent, viegnent*

In these examples, we see vocalization once again, in *parous* [parows] and *parout* [parowt], and homorganic nasal assimilation in *ains* [ãjns] and *aint* [ãjnt]. The other two morphophonological processes, however, do not strictly have to do with a 'final consonant alternation'. First, we may posit a rule of syncope to explain the root allomorph *parl-* [parl], opposed to the unsyncopated *parol* [parol]. Second, three instances of Old French diphthongization are found in the allomorphs: *aim* [ãjm], opposed to *am-* [ãm], in *beiv-* [bejv] opposed to *bev-* [bəv], and in *viegn-* [vjẽñ] opposed to *vegn-* [vəñ]. In order to complete the derivations, one also has to factor in the rule of final obstruent devoicing (to generate *beif* [bejf]), as well as final consonant deletion before the suffixes /s/ and /t/ (to arrive at *beis* [bejs] and *beit* [bejt]). With respect to the verb 'drink,' we find three allomorphs of the root, [bejv], [bəv], and [bej]. Finally, for the verb 'come', a third allomorph, ending in the palatal nasal consonant /ñ/, must be posited. In summary, these are the results of an ('extended') verbal FCA[3]:

(11) 'speak': [parol], [parow], [parl]
     'love':   [ãjm], [ãjn], [ãm]
     'drink': [bejv], [bej], [bəv]
     'come':   [vjẽñ], [vjẽn], [vən], [vəñ]

---

[3] The data on Old French has been gleaned from Einhorn (1974) and Walker (1987a, b).

15.4 Nominal Inflection (Modern French)

15.4.1 INV

The two nouns of this PSC in Old French continue in this category in Modern French, and they are joined by one from the variable category of Old French, the noun for 'field'. With the case system of Old French no longer in existence in Modern French, the only inflectional categories signaled today are number and gender; the latter is actually lexical, without an obvious marker in Modern French (at least in the noun). Therefore, the following represent the overwhelmingly dominant, invariant, PSC of Modern French nouns:

(12)		Singular	Plural
Orthography	*mur, porte, champ*	*murs, portes, champs*
Pronunciation	[myR], [pɔRt], [šã]	[myR], [pɔRt], [šã]

As can be seen, there is total identity between singular and plural oral forms of these nouns, which represent the huge majority of French nouns. The final *–s*, of course, is almost never pronounced, the only exceptions found in (optional) liaison occurrences: *des portes ouvertes* [depɔRt(z)uvɛRt] 'open doors'. It must be added, however, that the plural is signaled by the article *des*, the liaison /z/ functioning redundantly in plural marking.

Similarly, the great majority of modern adjectives have a single pronunciation for both genders, but of the Old French invariant (root) examples listed, only *dur, dure*, both phonetically [dyR], continues in this category. Many others may be added, however, some with identical spelling also:

(13)		Masculine	Feminine
Orthography	*dur, joli, jeune*	*dure, jolie, jeune*
Pronunciation	[dyR], [žɔli], [žœn]	[dyR], [žɔli], [žœn]

Joli,e 'pretty' and *jeune* 'young' differ from *dur,e* in that the first ends in a vowel phonetically and the second has the same spelling for both genders. Statistically, the latter type which manifests identity of genders in both spelling and pronunciation, is the most common in Modern French. It is understood, of course, that the final letter *–e* has no phonetic realization in the standard language, with the exception, perhaps, of pre-*h-aspiré* position: *(une) jolie hausse (des prix)* [žɔli(ə)os] '(a) pretty rise (of prices)' (said likely in a sarcastic tone?). One could claim that in this highly exceptional case. the final schwa of *jolie* actually signals feminine gender.

Total nominal INV is established for the root of all of the given nouns and adjectives of Modern French. It is extended to the noun singular / plural opposition and the adjectival masculine / feminine pairs, if the exceptional circumstances mentioned are set aside.

15.4.2 FCA

In Modern French, this category includes 'irregular' pluralization nouns, like the one for 'horse', *cheval / chevaux*, 'work', *travail / travaux*, and the 'most irregular' noun, for 'eye', *oeil / yeux*. Their phonetic equivalents are:

(14)		Singular	Plural
	'horse'	[šœval]	[šœvo]
	'work'	[travaj]	[travo]
	'eye'	[œj]	[jø]

Their plurals are due to various modifications (at least historically) of the final consonant of the singular, triggered by the final /s/ of the plural. These could be considered morphophonological rules in Old French, but no longer in Modern French, since their transparency has been obliterated. It is most reasonable to consider these pairs as suppletively related today, with no distinction possible between root and full noun form.

Among the adjectives of this category, two distinct classes can be identified. On the one hand, a clear 'final consonant alternation' is visible in the gender pairs *bon / bonne* 'good', *petit,e* 'little', and *grand,e* 'big', as brought into focus by their pronunciation:

(15)		Masculine	Feminine
	'good'	[bõ]	[bɔn]
	'little'	[pœti]	[pœtit]
	'big'	[gRã]	[gRãd]

The final consonants /n,t,d/ may be isolated as the feminine morpheme of the given adjectives and in that sense there is gender variance by FCA for them. However, if the root is considered only, one could claim an invariant root, at least for [pœti] and [gRã], with a zero marker for masculine gender. The adjective for 'good' is complicated for such an analysis, since nasal vs. oral vowel variance remains for its root: [bõ] vs. [bɔ].

The other type of adjective in this category follows the noun given above. *Beau / belle* 'beautiful', *vieux / vieille* 'old', *mou / molle* 'soft' are best seen as suppletions, as their phonetic respresentation underlines:

(16)		Masculine	Feminine
	'beautiful'	[bo]	[bɛl]
	'old'	[vjø]	[vjɛj]
	'soft'	[mu]	[mɔl]

The suppletive nature of such adjectives is supported by the existence of 'special' masculine forms in pre-vocalic pre-nominal position, pronounced identically to the feminine counterpart: *bel, vieil, mol*.

15.5 Verbal Inflection (Modern French)

15.5.1 INV

Three of the six verbs included in the Old French account belong in the invariant category in Modern French, *chanter, parler,* and *aimer*. The single roots for these are:

(17) 'sing'   *chant-*   [šãt]
     'speak' *parl-*   [paRl]
     'love'   *aim-*   [ɛm]

To these roots are added the following suffixes, in both the present indicative and subjunctive:

(18)

	Indicative	Subjunctive
First person singular	–	–
Second person singular	–	–
Third person singular	–	–
First person plural	[-õ]	[-jõ]
Second person plural	[-e]	[-je]
Third person plural	–	–

Such phonetic transcriptions bring into focus the fact that verbal endings have only graphic value (except in the 1st and 2nd persons plural):

(19)

	Indicative	Subjunctive
First person singular	*-e*	*-e*
Second person singular	*-es*	*-es*
Third person singular	*-e*	*-e*
First person plural	*-ons*	*-ions*
Second person plural	*-ez*	*-iez*
Third person plural	*-ent*	*-ent*

15.5.2 FCA

The allomorphic variation of Old French continues in the verbs *boire* and *venir*, and it is also found in *vendre*, which was considered invariant previously:

(20) Present indicative:

	Singular	Plural
First person	*bois, viens, vends*	*buvons, venons, vendons*
Second person	*bois, viens, vends*	*buvez, venez, vendez*
Third person	*boit, vient, vend*	*boivent, viennent, vendent*

(21) Present subjunctive
	Singular	Plural
First person	boive, vienne, vende	buvions, venions, vendions
Second person	boives, viennes, vendes	buviez, veniez, vendiez
Third person	boive, vienne, vende	boivent, viennent, vendent

The most significant variation of the root is created by FCA, as the final consonant of the root in these verbs is not pronounced in the indicative singular forms:

(22) Pronunciation of the Present indicative
First singular   *bois* [bwa], *viens* [vjẽ], *vends* [vã]
Second singular   *bois* [bwa], *viens* [vjẽ], *vends* [vã]
Third singular   *boit* [bwa], *vient* [vjẽ], *vend* [vã]

There is also, however, the continuation of the Old French diphthongal allomorphy in 'drink' and 'come', resulting in this complete picture[4]:

(23) 'drink': [bwa], [bwav], [byv]
     'come': [vjẽ], [vjɛn], [vœn]
     'sell': [vã], [vãd]

FCA is actually much more pervasive in the case of the two-root verbs, such as *vendre*, as it occurs, in addition to the present tense, in the imperfect indicative, future, conditional, and the past participle:

(24) Imperfect (3rd singular): *vendait* [vãdɛ]
     Future (3rd singular): *vendra* [vãdRa]
     Conditional (3rd singular): *vendrait* [vãdRɛ]
     Past participle: *vendu* [vãdy]

All of these forms contain the 'long' root. Therefore, the alternation that we are dealing with essentially opposes a 'short' root, found in the singular of the present indicative, to the long root found everywhere else, in the plural of the present indicative, the present subjunctive, and all the other tenses and moods listed. The past participle represents the complete set of periphrastic tenses, such as the *passé composé*.[5]

---

[4] For the verb *boire*, the continuation of the Old French diphthong is not really a diphthong, but the glide plus vowel combination [wa]. In addition, the 1st and 2nd persons of the plural underwent the unusual change of rounding the root vowel to [y]. In the verb 'come', the palatal root of Old French has been lost, and the completion of the nasalization process has produced the nasal vowel vs. oral vowel plus nasal consonant alternation.

[5] This markedness approach between the present indicative (short root) and all the other tenses (long root) is reminiscent of the role of the velar insert in some Romance languages (cf. Klausenburger 1984), although different oppositions are actually involved.

15.6 More Analysis

15.6.1 PSC's and Diachrony

Let us give a global overview of the correspondences in the nominal and verbal roots included in the preceding presentation:

(25)   Old French   Modern French

Nominal invariance [myr]=(a)   [myr]=(a)
                   [pərtə]=(b)   [pəRt]=(b)

                                                    [šã]=(e)
                   [dyr]=(c)   [dyR]=(c)
                   [bõn]=(d)

Nominal FCA   [čãmp]/[čãn]=(e)
                   [čəval]/[čəvaw]=(f)   [šœval]/[šœvo]=(f)
                   [bɛl]/[beaw]=(g)   [bɛl]/[bo](=g)
                                                    [bə (n)]/[bõ]=(d)

Verbal invariance [čãnt]=(h)   [šãt]=(h)
                   [vɛ̃nd]=(i)
                                                    [paRl]=(j)
                                                    [ɛm]=(k)

Verbal FCA   [parl]/[parol]/[parow]=(j)
                   [ãm]/[ãjm]/[ãjn]=(k)
                   [bəv]/[bej]/[bejv]=(l)   [byv]/[bwa]/[bwav]=(l)
                   [vən]/[vəñ]/[vjẽn]   [vœn]/[vjẽ]/[vjɛn]=(m)
                   /[vjẽñ]=(m)   [vã]/[vãd]=(i)

What is most interesting about this table is the set of change-overs from Old to Modern French in terms of INV or FCA. Five of the original Old French forms undergo changes (cf 25 above):

(26)   Old French   Modern French   Reason
  (d)   INV   FCA   P-change
  (e)   FCA   INV   P-change
  (i)   INV   FCA   P-change
  (j)   FCA   INV   Analogy
  (k)   FCA   INV   Analogy

15 Theoretical Issues in Old French Inflectional Morpho(phono)logy   293

The change-overs listed raise the issue of the role of PSC's in historical evolution. One can, according to Wurzel, distinguish two types of changes. First, PSC's may be altered, most likely by way of phonological change. Thus, examples (d), (e), and (i) manifest transformations from INV to FCA, or vice versa, due to:

(d) deletion of final /n/ as part of the history of vowel nasalization into Modern French;
(e) final consonant deletion, both of N (/m/ and /n/) and /p/;
(i) final deletion of /d/.

Second, PSC's may change, but their form is determined by a replication of a 'stronger' PSC. This has traditionally been called (morphological) analogy, and it is present in (26j) and (26k). What we find in this case is the move of two of the FCA verbs of Old French, 'speak' and 'love', to invariant ones today. We can claim that this happened because for these verbs, which belong to the 1st conjugation, the most productive class in Latin and all the Romance languages, the PSC of INV came to be dominant, meaning that the modern forms replicate a verb like 'sing.' The strength of a PSC is also involved in the other cases, although perhaps only secondarily to the phonological changes alluded to above. Thus, the verb 'sell' moves into the FCA category, apparently the class where non-1st conjugation verbs belong. In addition, the noun of (5) becomes integrated into the unquestionably dominant invariant category for nouns in Modern French. Finally, the adjective 'good' may appear to be more difficult to describe in such terms. As already mentioned, INV characterizes Modern French adjectives, as exemplified by [dyR], [žɔli], and [žœn]. However, FCA seems to dominate for certain high frequency prenominal adjectives, among which [bõ] / [bɔn].

15.6.2   PSC's and Iconicity

The two versions of Natural Morphology mentioned in the Introduction may now be combined in the following equivalencies:

(27) PSC of INV = non-iconic structure
      PSC of FCA = iconic structure

Such correspondences are particularly transparent for verbal structure in Modern French. The unique root in first conjugation verbs means that the relevant grammatical oppositions all relate non-iconically, illustrated by the verb 'speak':

(28)   Inside the present tense:

   a. Person / number opposition: *il parle* [paRl] vs. *ils parlent* [paRl]
   b. Mood opposition: indicative *elle parle* [paRl] vs. subjunctive *qu'elle parle* [paRl]

(29) Present tense vs. other tenses:

    a. Present vs. imperfect: *il parle* [paRl] vs. *il parlait* [paRl-ε]
    b. Present vs. future (conditional): *il parle* [paRl] vs. *il parlera, -ait* [paRl-œRa, -ε]

In most nominal inflections, non-iconicity dominates in Modern French. Most adjectives have one form for both genders:

(30) Masc. *joli* [žəli] vs. fem. *jolie* [žəli]

Further, most nouns have one form for both singular and plural:

(31) Sing. *mur* [myR] vs. plural *murs* [myR]

The same inflectional oppositions of person / number, mood, tense, gender, and number are, on the other hand, reflected iconically in the following examples:

(32) Verbs: Inside the present tense

    a. Person / number opposition: *il vend* [vã] vs. *ils vendent* [vãd]
    b. Mood opposition: indicative *elle vend* [vã] vs. subjunctive *qu'elle vende* [vãd]

(33) Verbs: Present tense vs. other tenses:

    a. Present vs. imperfect: *il vend* [vã] vs. imperfect *il vendait* [vãd-ε]
    b. Present vs. future (conditional): *il vend* [vã] vs. *il vendra, -ait* [vãd-Ra,-ε]

(34) Adjectives:

    a. Masc. *grand* [gRã], *petit* [pœti], *bon* [bõ]
    b. Feminine *grande* [gRãd], *petite* [pœtit], *bonne* [bɔn]

The FCA, or iconic, nouns are not completely transparent for our analysis. Let us take the word for 'horse'. There is, of course, a distinction between singular and plural, sing. *cheval* [šœval], pl. *chevaux* [šœvo]. It is unclear, however, whether the plural form is 'additive' compared to the singular. As a matter of fact, it could be considered 'subtractive', since there is a final /o/ vs. a final /al/ in the singular. The only certainty is that such 'irregular' nouns are NOT non-iconic. The final segments are best not considered suffixes in these, in any case, since a suppletive analysis, which takes both the complete forms as roots of the singular and the plural, seems to be called for here.

The question now arises whether considerations of iconic structure should be subordinated to PSC's or whether a PSC is subordinated to iconic structure. In other words, which one of the two versions of Natural Morphology takes 'precedence'? It seems most appropriate to incorporate the concept of iconicity into PSC's, and thus to consider, in a way, system-independent naturalness as part of system-dependent naturalness. As a consequence, one may claim that the system congruity of Modern

French inflections is principally characterized by non-iconicity, its major PSC. A secondary PSC, though also crucial for today's language, involves iconic structure.

15.7 Theoretical Discussion and Conclusion

15.7.1 Previous Work on Old French Morphophonology

15.7.1.1 Herslund (1976)

This study was written in the wake of the publication, and subsequent prominence, of two 'trailblazing' works in generative phonology, Schane (1968) and Chomsky and Halle (1968). It accepts one of the crucial aspects of this theory, the need to posit single underlying forms, from which the allomorphs occurring 'on the surface' would be generated / derived by a multitude of 'phonological' rules. With respect to Old French, a generative approach, such as Herslund's, following Schane and Chomsky and Halle, clearly emphasized (phonological) base structure. The latter could be represented by one of the surface allomorphs, but it did not have to be. In that case, some of the underlying forms could resemble historical (Latin) roots – a very common occurrence in Schane's account of Modern French vowels.

Therefore, in such a view, the verbal allomorphy we dealt with above, in Sect. 15.3.2., would have to be most likely traced back to 'bases' like the following:

(35) Abstract verb bases
   a. 'speak' /parol/
   b. 'love' /am/
   c. 'drink' /bev/
   d. 'come' /vɛn/

Globally, we have been focusing on the surface allomorphy of the selected verbs, which were explained by 'rules' in our sections on nominal and verbal FCA, above. However, no emphasis was put on 'underlying forms', and care was taken that the rules could be motivated synchronically, by concrete factors such as the suffix trigger /s/.

For the small amount of data introduced in the FCA sections of this paper, it is in particular the diphthongal allomorphy in the verb which is at issue. Herslund (1976: 59–60) includes phonological rules of diphthongization, which, in our examples, would generate the Old French diphthongal allomorphs for 'love', [ãjm], 'drink', [bejv], and 'come', [vjẽñ]. We feel that this alternation is best captured as a historical remnant, no longer 'alive' as a synchronic rule of Old French. In other words, the forms of the surface allomorphy involving Old French diphthongs in the verbal roots should be listed as such with no goal of uncovering their 'base'. The determination of the 'underlying' representation by generative phonologists often became quite arbitrary as different criteria were used. In addition, the transition from the base to the surface utterance was accomplished by means of 'phonological' rules, sometimes of extreme complexity, as Herslund's Phonological Rule 23 (Herslund 1976: 59) illustrates:

(36)
$$\begin{bmatrix} + \text{syll} \\ + \text{moyen} \\ + \text{haut} \\ + \text{Acc} \end{bmatrix} \rightarrow \begin{bmatrix} + \text{syll} \\ \begin{bmatrix} + \text{syll} \\ \alpha \text{ post} \\ + \text{Acc} \end{bmatrix} \begin{bmatrix} - \text{syll} \\ \alpha \text{ post} \end{bmatrix} \end{bmatrix} / \begin{Bmatrix} [- \overline{\text{post}}] \begin{bmatrix} C \\ - \text{haut} \end{bmatrix}_0^1 (+) \\ [+ \overline{\text{post}}] \begin{bmatrix} C \\ - \text{nasal} \\ - \text{haut} \end{bmatrix}_0^1 \end{Bmatrix}$$

This rule, in fact, is said to derive surface [bejv] from underlying /bev/, a copy of the historical sound change from Latin to Old French.[6]

15.7.1.2 Walker (1981)

Although also based on the generative model of 1968, mentioned for Herslund's study, Walker's account of Old French morphophonology attempts to transition to a (more) concrete analysis. The diphthongal samples we have dealt with, for the verbs 'love', 'drink', and 'come' find their place in data headed by (1) 'underlying *a*, stressed *æ*' (for *aj*), (2) 'underlying *ɛ*, stressed *jɛ*', and (3) 'underlying *e*, stressed *ej*' (Walker 1981: 26–7). Three rules are then proposed, Fronting, Diphthongization I, and Diphthongization II (pp. 28–9). Diphthongization II generating the diphthong [ej] from underlying /e/, resembles Herslund's Phonological Rule R 23 (Walker 1981: 29):

(37)

$$\begin{bmatrix} V \\ 3 \text{ height} \\ \alpha \text{ back} \\ + \text{ stress} \end{bmatrix} \quad C_0^1 + \rightarrow 1 \begin{bmatrix} G \\ \alpha \text{ back} \\ \alpha \text{ round} \end{bmatrix} 2 \quad 3$$
$$\qquad\qquad 1 \qquad\qquad 2 \quad 3$$

---

[6] Although resemblance to history is acknowledged, analysts in generative phonology claim not to be swayed by such criteria: only synchronic factors are said to be involved in the formulation of the necessary phonological rules (cf. Herslund 1976:14).

"Stressed /e/ and /o/ diphthongize to *ej* and *ow* respectively, when followed by no more than one consonant at a morpheme boundary"

The crucial modification of generative phonology which Walker makes in this contribution is to propose that such synchronic rules of Old French must be considered 'minor' rules, so that "forms to which they apply ... must carry a specific lexical mark adding to their lexical complexity, and the normal status of these rules will be to fail to apply" (Walker 1981: 32). This constitutes the essence of the morphologization of a phonological rule, which also avoids the possible recapitulation of historical sound change. Nevertheless, Walker's approach still focuses on 'underlying' forms as bases for the roots with diphthongal allomorphy in the data before us. It may therefore be considered a true 'bridge' leading to the view expressed and illustrated in this paper.[7]

15.7.2 Ockham's Razor (and Chatton's Anti-Razor)

I would like to conclude this analysis of some features of Old French morph(phono)logy by framing the position taken here in the larger context of linguistic theorizing, making use of the well-known principle of Ockham's Razor to account for the synchronic data in OF. In its essence, I will claim that my account follows the spirit of Ockham's Razor, while the abstract view fits more accurately into what may be called an 'Anti-Razor' methodology, in line with the ideas of a Franciscan colleague and opponent of Ockham's, Walter of Chatton.

Ockham's Razor's essence may be captured by saying that in theoretical formulations, care should be taken to posit as few entities as possible'. In the lesser-known Anti-Razor of Chatton's, on the other hand, this principle states that one ought to 'posit as many entities as necessary'.[8]

Although, on a certain level, both approaches have 'parsimony' as their goal, the Anti-Razor seems to qualify in this respect only counter-intuitively. In any case, I would now like to apply briefly these two principles to the subject of this paper.

One may say that the abstract generative account of Old French morphophonology contains more entities than the concrete version, as this succinct juxtaposition demonstrates:

(38)

ABSTRACT	CONCRETE
Underlying forms	–
Phonological rules	Morphologized rules
Surface forms	Surface allomorphy

---

[7] I am not aware of any study on Old French morphophonology within the most recent 'incarnations' of (abstract) phonological theory, such as non-linear phonology and optimality theory. It is well known, of course, that many traditional philological works on the language exist.

[8] Chatton's Anti-Razor is thoroughly discussed in Maurer (1984).

At least in the positing of underlying bases, the abstract / generative analyses propose one extra entity than their counterparts. However, it is also the nature of the rules needed in each version of morphophonology which must be taken into account in this discussion. It is clear that the kind of derivations manifested in the generative model violates the spirit of Ockham's Razor by their complexity and 'forced' phonological nature. In other words, the greater the 'distance' between underlying structure and surface allomorphy, the closer one comes to an Anti-Razor methodology. This is not to say that proponents of 'abstract' analyses want to proliferate entities. They simply believe, as Chatton did, that "if three things are not enough to verify an affirmative proposition about things, a fourth must be added, and so on" (Maurer 1984: 464). I would conclude that such a point of view has given analysts the false belief that they are following Ockham's Razor when, in fact, their practices have been guided by the Anti-Razor.[9]

References

Chomsky, Noam, and Morris Halle. 1968. *The sound pattern of English*. New York: Harper and Row.
Einhorn, E. 1974. *Old French. A concise handbook*. Cambridge: CUP.
Herslund, Michael. 1976. *Structure phonologique de l'ancien français*. Copenhague: Akademisk Forlag.
Klausenburger, Jurgen. 1984. The morphology of the velar insert in Romance verbs. In *Romanitas: Studies in Romance linguistics*, ed. Ernst Pulgram, 132–151. Ann Arbor: University of Michigan.
Klausenburger, Jurgen. 1990. Geometry in morphology: The Old French case system. *Zeitschrift fur Phonetik, Sprackwissenschaft, und Kornmunikationsforschung* 43: 327–333.
Klausenburger, Jurgen. In preparation. Ockham's Razor in linguistics. An application to studies in French phonology over the past half century.
Maurer, Armand. 1984. Ockham's Razor and Chatton's anti-Razor. *Mediaeval Studies* 46: 463–475.
Mayerthaler, Willi. 1981. *Morphologische Natürlichkeit*. Wiesbaden: Athenaion.
Schane, Sanford. 1968. *French phonology and morphology*. Cambridge, MA: MIT.
Walker, Douglas. 1981. *Old French morphophonology*. Ottawa: Didier.
Walker, Douglas. 1987a. Patterns of analogy in the Old French verb system. *Lingua* 72: 109–131.
Walker, Douglas. 1987b. Morphological features and markedness in the Old French noun declension. *Canadian Journal of Linguistics* 32: 143–197.
Wurzel, Wolfgang. 1984. *Flexionsmorphologie und Natürlichkeit*. Berlin: Akademie Verlag.

---

[9] Regarding the application of Ockham's Razor to linguistic theory, see Klausenburger (in preparation).

Chapter 16
Forms and Functions of Reported Discourse in Medieval French

Sophie Marnette

16.1 Introduction

Two seminal books mark the study of reported discourse in medieval French: Bernard Cerquiglini's *La Parole médiévale* (1981) and Jean Rychner's posthumous *La Narration des sentiments, des pensées et des discours dans quelques oeuvres des douzième et treizième siècles* (1990).[1] The rich online bibliography available on my research group website (www.ci-dit.com) shows that numerous insightful articles were also written, often within the framework of the French theories de l'énonciation (see Marchello-Nizia, Marnette, Perret).[2] Unsurprisingly, all of these works have to contend with two concerns. The first is how to account for some peculiar forms of reported discourse present in Medieval French and absent from modern literature (but possibly not from spoken French; more on this below). The second is whether to examine reported discourse broadly across all literary genres or to make meaningful connections between reported discourse strategies and specific genres, as Cerquiglini (1981) did brilliantly for verse and prose romances. In the present

---

[1] The term 'reported discourse' is more appropriate than 'reported speech' as it encompasses both speech and thought (Marnette 2005: 49–63). This allows me to talk about reported discourse (Direct Discourse, Indirect Discourse, etc.) in general, and to use reported speech (direct speech, indirect speech, etc.) more specifically when I want to distinguish it from reported thought (direct thought, indirect thought, etc.). I employ 'reported discourse' both as a generic noun to refer to the process of reporting discourse, as well as a count noun to refer to particular occurrences (e.g. there are five reported discourses in this text).

[2] For a description in English of what is meant by "théories de l'énonciation", see Marnette 2001b, 2005: 19–38. The present article is a revised, shortened version of Marnette (2005: 179–223) that includes later work such as Marnette (2006a, b, 2008).

S. Marnette (✉)
Balliol College, University of Oxford, Oxford, UK
e-mail: sophie.marnette@balliol.ox.ac.uk

chapter, I will endeavor to address both of these problems by showing how the investigation of reported discourse enables us to better grasp the elaboration and evolution of medieval literary genres while also shedding light on our general understanding of reported discourse categories.

The first section of this chapter will briefly present the main categories of reported discourse existing in Medieval French. The second section will discuss the relationship between the various forms of reported discourse that developed in medieval literature. It will also examine how the range of 'functions' associated with specific 'forms' of reported discourse can be assembled into particular strategies that determine distinct literary genres (notably *chansons de geste*, verse romances, prose romances and chronicles). Speech and thoughts presentation strategies will thus be shown to affect aspects as diverse as the connection between the narrator and the audience or the apparent 'control' of the narrator over the discourse of his/her characters, as well the representation of notions such as 'truth' or 'history'. The third section will show that the study of unusual but overlooked phenomena such as 'Indirect Discourse without *que*' and 'Direct Discourse with *que*' (occurring both in Medieval French and in Modern French) is essential for an in-depth understanding of reported discourse categories in general. My analysis will call into question traditional definitions that distinguish Indirect Discourse from Direct Discourse purely based on the presence of subordination markers. Indeed, I will show that these markers are not specific to Indirect Discourse or necessary for it.

The 39 texts composing the corpus studied here are the same as for my book (Marnette 2005) and are listed in appendix: 8 *chansons de geste* (epics in decasyllabic verses), 3 *vies de saint* (hagiographical narratives in decasyllabic verses), 9 verse romances (octosyllabic verses), 9 prose romances, 9 prose chronicles (historical narratives) and 1 *chantefable* (text alternating paragraphs in verse and in prose).[3]

16.2 Reported Discourse Categories

16.2.1 *Direct Discourse (In Bold in All Examples)*

In Direct Discourse, the reporting speaker evokes the original[4] speech/thought situation and conveys, or rather claims to convey, the exact words [ideas] of the original

---

[3] For the purpose of the present study, I will consider the collection of short verse stories called *Les lais de Marie de France* and the short verse narrative called *Le lai de l'Ombre* under the heading of verse romances.

[4] The term 'original' should not be interpreted as 'real' and 'anterior': reported discourse, whether direct or indirect, can refer to a future (and thus hypothetical discourse) and it can also summarize several discourses at once.

locutor. The pronouns, tenses and deictic words of the original discourse stay the same: they are not transposed. Direct Discourse can appear after a *verbum dicendi/sentiendi* [1a] and/or with an *inquit* formula [1b]. It can also be used without any introductory clause [2] (Free Direct Discourse).

(1) *Perceforest*, § 9, lines 339–42
Lyonnel, qui estoit le plus entreprenant, escria au chevalier et dist: '**Sire, attendez un petit, et que nous puissons parler a vous. – Beaux seigneurs,** respondy le comte, **aucunement je ne doy point attendre, ains vous hastés se vous voulez parler a moy.**'
[Lyonnel, who was the most enterprising, called the knight and said: '**Sir, wait a little so that we might speak to you. – Good lords,** answered the count, **in no way should I wait, on the contrary, hurry up if you want to speak to me.**']

(2) *Raoul de Cambrai*, 6120–1
Ele le voit, cel recognuct molt bien.
'**Dont viens, amis, por le cors saint Richiel?**'
[Seeing him, she recognized him perfectly. '**Where do you come from, friend, by St Riquier?**']

16.2.2 *Indirect Discourse (Underlined in All Examples)*

In Indirect Discourse, on the other hand, the reporting speaker expresses the original utterance in his/her own words. The reported discourse is subordinated to a reporting verb and is introduced by a subordinating conjunction (e.g. *que*). The pronouns, tenses and deictics of the reported discourse are switched to the reporting situation of enunciation. However, since in Old French literature, the story is often partly told in tenses linked to the present (indicative present, present perfect and future), Indirect Discourse can retain these tenses instead of using the past (Fleischman 1990).[5]

(3) *Le Chevalier au Cygne*, 4512–4
Mais ele set tres bien et pense en son corage
<u>Qu'ele a par son mesfait eü cest destorbage</u>
<u>Et perdu son segnor qui tant ot vaselage.</u>
[But she knows well and thinks in herself <u>that she has brought that trouble about because of her wrongdoing and thereby lost her lord who was so valiant.</u>]

---

[5] This is, of course, also the case in Modern Spoken French, as opposed to most written press or literary fiction. On tense and Indirect Discourse in French, see, among others, Bauer (1996) and Landerweerd and Vet (1996).

Indirect Discourse can also be expressed in an infinitival clause with or without a preposition:

(4)   Commynes, *Mémoires*, lines 160–3
La conclusion dudit duc Philippes fut fort humble et saige, suppliant au roy <u>ne vouloir legierement croire contre luy ne son filz et l'avoir tousjours en sa bonne grace.</u>
[The aforementioned Duke Philip's conclusion was very humble and wise, pleading with the <u>king not to believe lightly anything said against him or his son and to always keep him in his good grace.</u>]

16.2.3   Free Indirect Discourse (In Italics in All Examples)

Free Indirect Discourse is characterized by the presence of features of Direct Discourse (direct questions, exclamations, deictics, colloquialisms, etc.) reported in the fashion of Indirect Discourse, i.e. with shifted pronouns and tenses but without being syntactically dependent on a reporting clause (i.e. without being directly subordinated to a *verbum dicendi* or *sentiendi* and without being co-ordinated to a previous reported clause). As with Indirect Discourse, the tenses of medieval Free Indirect Discourse are not necessarily in the past because the narration itself is partly told in the present tenses [5].[6] Moreover it is important to remember that Free Indirect Discourse does not always follow an instance of Indirect Discourse, but can instead appear on its own [5]. There are also cases where the Free Indirect Discourse does follow an Indirect Discourse but could not semantically be subordinated to its *verbum dicendi* [6].

(5)   *Le Chevalier au Cygne*, 3129–3136
Mirabels de Taburs et Foucars de Riviers
Offrent l'empereor raencon et deniers
D'or quit et de mangons et de bons pailes ciers
Et si seront si home a tos jors volentiers.
Mais il en jure Deu, qui est vrais Justiciers,
<u>Qu'il n'en prendroit Orliens ne Cartres ne Peniers.</u>
Ans .II. les fist detraire a cevals de somiers
Et les autres fist pendre sor les mons es loriers.
[Mirabels de Taburs and Foucars de Riviers offer the emperor ransom and deniers of cooked gold and coins and nice expensive silken brocades. *And they will be his men always willingly.* But he swears by God, the true dispenser of justice, <u>that he would not take Orleans nor Chartres nor Peniers for it.</u> On the contrary he had these two torn apart by pack horses and he had the others hung on the hills, up the bay trees.]

---

[6] See Marnette (1996, 1998: 116–117, 128–129, 144–151, 1999a: 390–392, 2005). Note also the now classic articles by Cerquiglini (1984), Rychner (1980, 1987, 1989) and Bruña-Cuevas (1988, 1989).

(6) *Le Roman du Graal* (prose), p 36, lines 2–8
Ensi envoia l'emperere des plus sages homes de sa cort por ceste cose savoir <u>s'il estoit ensi com li pelerins li avoit conté</u>. *Et si li prophetes estoit mors, c'on li aportast aucune cose a quoi il eüst atoucié por le garison de son fil.* Ensi se partirent li mesage a l'empereor de Rome et vinrent en le terre de Judee.
[So the emperor sent some of the wisest men of his court to inquire about this, <u>if it was as the pilgrim had told him</u>. *And if the prophet was dead, one should bring him back any thing that he might have touched in order to cure his son.* So the messengers of the emperor of Rome left and they arrived in the land of Judea.]

16.2.4 Direct Discourse with que

What I call 'Direct Discourse with *que*' mixes Direct Discourse features (non-transposed spatio-temporal deictics, tenses, persons) with Indirect Discourse features: subordination with *que* (or similar conjunction) and/ or transposition of part of the quoted discourse within the quoting speaker's *hic et nunc*.[7]

(7) *Le Roman du Graal* (prose), p 66, lines 29–33
Et Joseph respont <u>que</u>: '**Miels vous counoist il que vous meïsmes ne vous conissiés. Mais tant vous prions nous par amor et par compagnie que vous nous dites quel part vostre cuers vous trait a aler.**'
[And Joseph answers <u>that:</u> '**He knows you better than you know yourselves. But we pray you, by love and friendship, that you tell us where your heart impels you to go.**']

16.2.5 Indirect Discourse Without que

In my study, 'Indirect Discourse without *que*' is a reported discourse that is transposed within the reference frame of the quoting speaker and dependent on a *verbum dicendi* but without a specific marker of subordination such as *que*, etc. (Marnette 1999a, 2001a).

(8) *La Vie de Saint Alexis*, Ms M2, 116–7
Dont crïent il mout <u>s'ame se soit perdue</u>
<u>Et al juïse devant Dieu confondue</u>.
[Then he is very afraid <u>[that] his soul might be lost and disgraced in front of God, on Judgement Day</u>.]

---

[7] For discussions and examples of mixed discourses in Modern French, see Marnette (2005: 93–104, 283–320).

It is important to note that this category is not similar to that of Free Indirect Discourse (which is sometimes wrongly called 'ID without *que*') since in the case of 'ID without *que*', the *verbum dicendi* can clearly not stand on its own, e.g. **dont crient il mout* in [8]. So although the subordination is not expressed syntactically, it is expressed morphologically (transposition of persons and sometimes of tenses) and semantically. There are only a few cases where hesitation might occur because a verb such as *menacer* [9] can both stand on its own (Narrated Discourse describing a speech act) or introduce a completive (Rychner 1990: 200). In the first case, we are dealing with Free Indirect Discourse (following a Narrated Discourse), in the second, with 'ID without *que*'.

(9)   Béroul, *Le Roman de Tristan*, 1949–50
S'il les trove, molt les MENACE
<u>Ne laira pas ne lor mesface</u>
[Were he to find them, he THREATENS them: <u>he will not fail to kill them</u>.]

16.3 Reported Discourse Strategies and Medieval French Genres

16.3.1 Speech and the Rhetoric of Truth in 'chansons de geste', Chronicles and Prose Romances[8]

We cannot be sure that the *chansons de geste* that have come down to us in manuscripts were actually composed orally, but they were obviously supposed to be performed (sung) in front of an audience.[9] The performer's voice (the *jongleur*) is very present in these texts and often addresses the listeners while telling them about the grand deeds (and occasional love stories) of their epic heroes. In *chansons de geste*, the narrator endeavours to report the characters' discourses in their own words, in order to offer as much direct access as possible to the listeners-readers. In order to do so, he uses a majority of Direct Discourses as a hearer-based strategy that places the listener-reader on an equal footing with the narrator, in the position of a witness who must evaluate the represented speech event (Collins 2001: 68).[10] Thus, the characters' speeches, reported in Direct Discourse, and their actions, recounted in a complex

---

[8] For an in-depth analysis and detailed references to other relevant works, see Marnette (1998, 1999a, b, 2001a, 2002b, 2005).

[9] My corpus contains 8 *chansons de geste*. The *Chanson de Roland* is said to date from late eleventh century The *Pelerinage de Charlemagne* and two versions of the *Prise d'Orange* (manuscripts AB and CE) are dated twelfth century. *Raoul de Cambrai*, *Le Chevalier au cygne*, *Huon de Bordeau* are all three dated from late twelfth century to early thirteenth century. *Tristan de Nanteuil* is a fourteenth-century text.

[10] Direct Discourse represents more than 90 % of the overall number of reported discourses in most *chansons de geste*, with the exception of 73 % for *Cygne* and 81 % for *Nanteuil*. In comparison, the number of Direct Discourses is lower than 80 % in all the other texts of the corpus, except for

mix of present tenses (foregrounding) and past tenses (backgrounding), are told as if they were happening in front of the audience, as the jongleur's performance goes along.

(10)   *Raoul de Cambrai*, 6279–83
Li rois parole con ja porrés oïr:
**'Venés avant, H[erchambaus] de Pontis;
prenés la dame, que je la vos ostri.'**
Et sil respont: **'Sire, vostre mercit.'**
Passa avant, par la main la saisit:
Il fist que fox quant il s'en entremist.
[The king speaks as you will now hear: **'Step forward, Erchambaut of Ponthieu; take the lady for I give her to you.'** And he replies: **'I thank you sir.'** He stepped forward and took her by the hand – fool that he was to undertake it.]

There is no doubt that the extensive use of Direct Discourse, and occasionally of 'DD with *que*' in *chansons de geste* is firmly linked to the staged orality of this type of texts, in the same line as the many narratorial addresses to the listeners-readers and the commentaries about the future fate of the characters (prolepses, wishes, questions, imprecations) and about the inherent good or evil of certain characters. The historical events told in the *chansons de geste* are thus re-lived by the community formed by jongleurs and their audiences, united behind the battles and the destiny of 'our emperor Charles,' 'our Frenchmen,' and 'our barons'.[11] The fact that these events are actually mostly fictive is irrelevant here because what makes them historical and 'true' is that they are presented as such by the story and experienced as such by the audience.[12] It is obvious that Direct Discourse participates in that feeling of authenticity, in the same way as any historical re-enactment would.

While history is seen as re-lived, re-presented in *chansons de geste*, it is put at a distance in the chronicles.[13] This difference is clearly illustrated in the way chronicles

---

Froissart 2 (89 %, see explanations infra). The high amount Direct Discourses in *chansons de geste* tends to be connected to their quality of 'oral performances' and thus to their direct link with the spoken language, whereas Direct Discourse is indeed the principal type of reported discourse in narratives. It is important to note that an in-depth analysis reveals a more complex picture: if epic narrators (*jongleurs*) use Direct Discourses to report their characters' speeches, these characters mostly use (Free) Indirect Discourses to report their own words or the speeches of other characters. These highly organised reported discourse strategies can be shown to be determined by prosody, pragmatics and narratology (see Marnette 1999a, 2005: 189–97).

[11] We find these expressions even in later texts, e.g. *Huon* 8711, etc. *Cygne* 3913, 3923, 3965, etc. *Nanteuil* 1241, 1246, 1267, etc.

[12] For a discussion of the historicity of these events, see Fleischman (1983), Duggan (1987), and Kay (1987, 1995).

[13] I am not discussing whether the events presented in the chronicles are historically true in the modern sense of the term. What is of interest here is that they are presented as true by the narrative. In fact, as Beer (1981) shows, references to eye-witness or insistence on sincerity are rhetorical *topoi* borrowed from ancient Latin texts. For a reflection on the notions of truth and fiction in medieval chronicles and their links with other genres, see, among others, Fleischman (1983), Levine (1985, 1991, 1998), Marnette (1998, 2002a, b), and Zumthor (1975).

use reported discourse.[14] Not only do they generally employ fewer reported discourses than the other texts of my corpus, they also largely prefer Indirect Discourse to Direct Discourse.[15] This predilection can be explained in several ways. First, most chronicles of my corpus were composed (often dictated) by authors who had directly witnessed a good part of the events narrated in their stories. Sometimes, chroniclers also told events that they had learned from intermediary sources. They thus personally guarantee the truth of their stories, and they are referred to in the third person in earlier chronicles (Clari, Villehardouin) and in the first person in subsequent chronicles. These narrators-authors aim at presenting themselves as credible witnesses both in terms of their competence ('I was there', 'I heard this said by trustworthy people') but also in terms of their abilities to recognize the 'finiteness' of their own memory. So they prefer to use Indirect Discourse instead of repeating most discourses in Direct Discourse and giving the impression that they could, in fact, remember everything that was said and how it was said, or that they could reconstruct some things they did not personally hear.

(11)   Clari, § 120, lines 4–10.
[…] chis qui i fu et qui le vit et qui l'oï le tesmongne, Robers de Clari, li chevaliers, et a fait metre en escrit le verité, si comme ele fu conquise; et ja soit chou que il ne l'ait si belement contee le conqueste, comme maint boin diteur l'eussent contee, si en a il toutes eures le droite verité contee, et assés de vérités en a teutes qu'il ne peut mie toutes ramembrer.
[Robert de Clari, the knight, who was there and saw it and heard it, bears witness to it and he has put in writing the truth, how [Constantinople] was conquered; and although he has not narrated the conquest as nicely as many good poets might have, he has always told the straight truth, and he has said nothing about a few truths because he cannot remember all of them.]

---

[14] There are 9 prose chronicles in the corpus: two accounts of the sack of Constantinople, one by Clari and one by Villehardouin (around 1210), the story of Saint Louis' life by Joinville (1309). There are also three excerpts taken from three different books of Froissart's chronicles (volume 1 composed around 1380, volume 3 (ca 1400) and volume 4 (ca 1400)), one excerpt of Monstrelet's chronicle (book 2, ca 1450), one excerpt taken from *Les Chroniques du roi Charles VII* by Gilles Le Bouvier dit Le Héraut Berry (ca 1455) and one excerpt of Commynes' *Mémoires* (volume 1, ca 1490). As will be shown *infra*, the three excerpts taken from Froissart's chronicles behave very differently in terms of reported discourse, which justifies their treatment as separate texts (see Marnette 2002b). Note that verse chronicles also existed in Medieval French, although they were rarer than the prose ones.

[15] The number of Direct Discourses accounts for less than 40 % of the overall number of reported discourses in the chronicles (except Froissart 2, see *infra*). Another way to look at it is to say that chronicles use at least 1.5 Indirect Discourse for every Direct Discourse. It is the exact reverse from *chansons de geste*: one finds at least 3.5 Direct Discourses for every Indirect Discourse in the *Cygne* and *Nanteuil*, and more than 12 Direct Discourses per one Indirect Discourse in all the other *chansons*. It is also important to note that Indirect Discourse is used in less than 1.5 % of the text space in most *chansons de geste* (*Cygne* 2 % and *Nanteuil* 3 %) but in more than 6 % in each of the chronicles (except Froissart 2, 0.6 %, see *infra*). These ratios are obtained by dividing the space (verses or lines) used by reported discourses by the total space (verses or lines) of the text (see Marnette 1998: 16).

(12) Joinville, § 19, lines 1–5
En nom de Dieu le tout puissant, je, Jehan sire de Joyngville, seneschal de Champaigne, faiz escrire la vie nostre saint [roy] Looÿs, ce que je vis et oÿ par l'espace de sis anz que je fu en sa compaignie ou pelerinage d'outremer, et puis que nous revenimes.
[In the name of Almighty God, I, Lord of Joinville, am having the life of our saint king Louis written down, what I saw and heard during the 6 years I spent in his company in the pilgrimage across the sea and after we came back.]

Furthermore, the deferred quality of Indirect Discourse allows chroniclers to ground the events firmly in the past, as any other events narrated in their story where there is very little mixing of present and past tenses, even for the oldest chronicles. The narrators of the chronicles are not re-living the past as they are telling it, nor do they let the listeners-readers experience the 'true' voices of history. They do not even give them access to their own thoughts at the time of the events (except very rarely for Joinville). The distanced objectivity of their historical narration is however influenced by the moral judgments that they are not afraid to add here and there, as well, of course, as their very choice of events told.

As can be seen in example [13] taken from a thirteenth-century chronicle, even a seemingly most objective third-person text may express the chronicler's opinion. Fourteenth and fifteenth-centuries chronicles are sometimes more explicit, since, rather than using exclamative expressions only, they use Indirect Discourses in reflexive formulas that put the author's opinions on stage via the narrator's voice.

(13) Clari, § 112, lines 31–35 [death of the emperor, of Louis count of Flanders and army is fleeing]
Ensi faitement se venja Damedieus d'aus pour leur orguel et pour le male foi qu'il avoient portee a le povre gent de l'ost, et les oribles pekiés qu'il avoient fais en le chité, aprés chou qu'i l'eurent prise.
[So did God take his revenge on them because of their arrogance and for the bad faith they had shown to the poor people of the army, and the awful sins they had perpetrated in the city, after they had overtaken it.]

(14) Froissart 2, p 534, line 7
Le comte Gaston de Foix, dont je parle, en ce temps que je fus devers lui, avoit environ cinquante-neuf ans d'âge. Et vous dis <u>que j'ai en mon temps vu moult de chevaliers, rois, princes et autres; mais je n'en vis oncques nul qui fût de si beaux membres, de sui belle forme ni de si belle taille et viaire, bel, sanguin et riant</u>, …
[The count Gaston of Foix, whom I am speaking about, was around 59 years old when I met him. And I am telling you <u>that in my time I have seen many knights, kings, princes and others, but I never saw one who had such beautiful limbs, of such fine shape, of such a good looking waist, face, handsome, full of life and joyful</u>,…]

(15) Commynes, lines 1831–42
Ledict de Contay hayait ledict Guillaume Bische; toutesfois il disoit ce que plusieurs autres disoyent comme luy; et croy <u>que sa suspicion ne l'en faisoit parler, mais seulement la necessité de la matière</u>.
[The aforementioned de Contay hated the aforementioned Guillaume Bische; however he was saying what many others said like him, and I believe <u>that his mistrust did not cause him to speak, but rather the urgency of the matter</u>.]

In expressions such as *je vous dis que* ('I am telling you that') and *je crois que* ('I believe that'), the pronoun *je* refers both to the narrator *qua* narrator (who tells the story) and to the narrator as a person of the world that holds a specific discourse and expresses certain opinions (see Marnette 2005: 64–77). These 'reflexive' reported discourses entail a certain amount of 'dramatization' of the narrator's speech and thoughts, enabling him to exhibit his own discourse *vis à vis* that of the Other.[16]

An apparent exception to the preference for Indirect Discourse in the chronicles is to be found in Froissart's *Voyage de Bearn* (Froissart 2 in my corpus), which uses a very high percentage of Direct Discourses (89 % of the overall number of reported discourses and more than 8 Direct Discourses per one Indirect Discourse). In that particular excerpt of Book III of his chronicle, Froissart narrates his trip to the court of Gaston Phoebus and his different encounters with informants who told him stories relating to the countryside and to the count Phoebus himself. He reports all these stories in Direct Discourse, i.e. supposedly in the words of his informants and even explains how he jotted all these anecdotes down as soon as he arrived at his hostel at the end of a day's travelling.

(16) Froissart 2, chapter XII, lines 1–7
Des paroles que messire Espaing de Lyon me contoit étois-je tout réjoui, car elles me venoient grandement à plaisance, et toutes trop bien les retenois, et sitôt que aux hostels, sur le chemin que nous fesismes ensemble, descendu étois, je les escripvois, fût de soir ou de matin, pour en avoir mieux la mémoire au temps à venir; car il n'est si juste retentive que c'est d'écriture.

---

[16] Expressions such as *je dis que* are used in the following amounts: Joinville 0.2%, Froissart 2 0.5%, Froissart 3 0.2%, Commynes 0.4%; expressions such as *je crois que* appear with the following frequency: Clari 0.1%, Joinville 0.1%, Froissart 1 0.4%, Monstrelet 0.1%, Commynes 1.4%. While these frequencies seem rather low, they are in fact substantially higher than in the other texts of the corpus. Notice the relative importance of these reflexive expressions in Commynes' text (1.4%), which shows that it is a personal reflection on the story told, i.e. the work of a memoirist. On references to the first-person narrator in the chronicles, see Marnette (2006a).

[The words that Messire Espaing de Lyon was telling me, would fill me with joy because they were very pleasing to me. And I would memorise all of them very well. And as soon as I would arrive at our hostel, on the journey we were taking together, I would write them down whether at night or in the morning, in order to remember them for the times to come, because there is no better memory than in writing.]

This indicates how a chronicler like Froissart is aware of the inherent difficulty in quoting people in their own words. In fact, he is not so much letting us participate to specific past historical events as to the actual composition of his opus: he is using Direct Discourse to chronicle ... the making of his chronicle (Diller 1998: 57).

Prose romances constitute the third medieval genre that could be described as historiographical. However, this is not because they speak of events that really happened but rather because they present their stories as based on a unique source which is both historically and even religiously true. As Zink (1995: 71) notes, the fact that "the first prose romances in French were Grail romances [...] was probably not or not only due to chance". Indeed, these romances use a linguistic medium that had long been associated with the notion of religious and historical truth in Latin and they tell a story that is clearly paralleled to the Bible: revealing the veritable events that happened after Jesus' death and the ensuing creation of the fellowship of the Grail. They are all told in a specific way, with the disappearance of references to the *je*-narrator to the benefit of an impersonal narrative voice performatively referring to itself as *le conte* or *l'histoire*.

(17)   *Lancelot du Lac*, p 233, line 25
Mais or se taist un petit LI CONTES de lui et de sa compaignie, et parole del roi Artu et de monseignor Gauvain.
[Now though THE TALE falls silent about him and his company for a while and speaks of King Arthur and Sir Gawain.]

This expression refers both to the source from which the story is told, and to the story as it is unfolding.[17] Later prose romances, while departing from the Grail thematic and in certain cases from the monological impersonal voice, still present themselves as based on specific historical sources that are translated or transposed by the *je*-narrator.[18]

(18)   *Perceforest*, Prologue of the 4th Book, p 1

---

[17] There are several possible explanations for the unique origin of the narrative (see among others Baumgartner 1995: 82; Burns 1985; Marnette 1998: 45). In the *Lancelot* Cycle, King Arthur's clerks supposedly put into writing the knight's accounts of their quests and adventures, a story subsequently transposed from Latin to French by Gautier Map.

[18] Sometimes the story refers to real persons. In *Le roman de Jehan de Saintré*, for example, the narrator speaks about characters that truly existed (Saintré, Boucicault), while other characters are mentioned only with a formula that keeps them anonymous: *une dame des belles cousines* ('a lady among the beautiful cousins').

Ainsi que dit est ou second et ou tiers voulume des Anciennes CRONICQUES de la Grant Bretaigne qui sont de convenable grandeur, et aussi pour ce que l'istoire est encoires de longue narration, JE encommenceray le quart voulume de ceste noble matière [...].
[As it is said in the second and third volumes of the Ancient CHRONICLES of Great Britain, which are sizeable, and also because the story is yet long to narrate, I will begin the fourth volume of this noble topic [...]]

This *je*-narrator is thus neither the creator nor the guarantor of the story's truth, but instead he is a link on the chain of transmission going from the source of the story to the finished product, the narrative. Interestingly, although prose romances go to great lengths to present themselves as 'chronicles' (ex: *Perceforest* [18]), they easily betray that pretense by their use of reported discourse. Indeed, far from preferring Indirect Discourse as 'real' chronicles do, they tend to employ Direct Discourse, thus giving the story 'psychological realism' if not 'historical truth'.[19] The strategies at work in *chansons de geste*, chronicles, and prose romances thus illustrate the inherent ability of medieval genres to draw on specific tools such as reported discourse to construct themselves both in parallel to, and in opposition to, other genres.

16.3.2 Thought Presentation and the Expression of Point of View in Romances[20]

Contrary to *chansons de geste*, verse romances were not sung. Some were recited from memory and others might have been read aloud from books (some *chansons de geste* probably were read as well and prose romances most definitely were). While verse romances did keep strong links with orality, notably the switching between

---

[19] The number of Direct Discourses in the prose romances is always higher than 64% of the overall number of reported discourses (except for *Guillaume* 50% and *Artois* 37%). They use at least 1.8 Direct Discourse per one Indirect Discourse (except for *Guillaume* 1/1 and *Artois* 0.6/1). A text like *Le Roman du Comte d'Artois* presents interesting mixes, beginning like a chronicle with a very dry account of the hero's military exploits, with more Indirect Discourses than Direct Discourses (68% Indirect Discourses versus 28% Direct Discourses) and then develops into a love story with more Direct Discourses than Indirect Discourses (51% Direct Discourses versus 48 % Indirect Discourses). These Direct Discourses are lovers' monologic complaints or witty dialogues, full of mutual misunderstandings that form the basis of the plot.

[20] See Marnette (1998) for more detailed references on the evolution of verse and prose romances. My corpus contains one romance using the Antiquity's background: *Eracle*, by Gautier d'Arras, takes place in Rome and Constantinople (composed around 1170–5). I included four texts using Briton material, all from the last quarter of the twelfth century): *Erec et Enide* and *Yvain ou Le Chevalier au lion* ('The Knight with the Lion') both by Chrétien de Troyes, Béroul's *Tristan et Iseut*, the *Lais de Marie de France*. The *Estoire dou Graal* by Robert de Boron introduces the story of the Grail, starting from Christ' death (composed around 1200, see *infra*). Three romances take place in a more contemporary courtly atmosphere: *Ipomedon* by Hue de Rothelande (1180–8), *Le Roman de la Rose ou de Guillaume de Dole* and the *Lai de l'Ombre*, both by Jean Renart (1st quarter of thirteenth century).

present tenses for foregrounding of events and past tenses for backgrounding as well as the vivid presence of the narrative voice, they mentioned their author's names more often than *chansons de geste* did and the first-person narrator was also more prominent, with less importance given to the listeners-readers.[21] What was thus underlined was the composition and recitation of the text by the first-person narrator rather than the perception of the events from the listeners'-readers' perspective. The audience was required to believe the narrator and to accept his/her choices of narrated events (i.e. shortcuts or lengthy descriptions of specific events rather than others). In short, the narrator did not describe himself/herself only as a good teller of pre-existing stories (as in *chansons de geste*), but also as an excellent composer and the master of his/her tale (see first person in bold in the following example).

(19)   *Ipomedon*, 7187–202 (the narrator explains why he is undertaking a detour)

Seignurs ke de rime entendez,	Lords, who understand about rimes,
Si **jo mesprenc**, ne **me** blasmez,	If **I make mistakes**, don't blame me,
A escïent pas nel **ferai**.	I won't do it knowingly.
Al plus brefment ke **jo purrai**	As briefly as **I will be able to**,
Vus **irrai** ultre od resun bele,	**I will continue** [this narrative] with a nice matter
Kar ren ne valt lunge favele,	Since nothing is worth a long discourse,
Ne favele ne lung sermun,	Nor a tale, nor a long speech,
Kar ki ist hors de sa resun,	Because whenever one strays from one's matter,
Jol sai mut ben, si savez vus,	**I know** it well, so do you,
Le livre en est meins delitus.	It makes the book less enjoyable.
Pur ço n'i **voil** cunter ne dire	Because of that, **I do** not want to relate or say
Fors tut dreit avant la matire ;	Anything but what goes right into the matter ;
Se vus vers **mei** ben escutez	If you listen to **me** well,
De plus sages en partirez.	You will leave from here wiser.
Ipomedon ne se est targés,	Ipomedon did not delay,
Vers sun païs est aprochez ;	He went towards his country ;

As already noted, the first prose romances (early thirteenth century) were transpositions of romances linked to the Grail, namely the trilogy of *L'estoire dou Graal, Merlin,* and *Perceval,* which are attributed to Robert de Boron.[22] This step towards prose was not fortuitous since the Grail stories were permeated with a religious

---

[21] In Béroul's *Tristan*, there are more references to the listeners-readers than to the first-person narrator. This is one of the factors that make it very close to the *chansons de geste* (see Marnette 1998: 203).

[22] The two other earliest vernacular prose texts were the chronicles of Constantinople by Clari and Villehardouin. The Grail itself is a mysterious object that first surfaced in Chrétien de Troyes' story of the knight Perceval (*Le Conte du Graal*). In that text, it is a precious dish where Christ's blood was collected after his death and it appears to Perceval in a magic castle. Later the focus was shifted from Perceval to Lancelot, a character that first appeared in another of Chrétien's romances (*Le Chevalier de la charette* 'The Knight of the Cart').

atmosphere that was clearly reminiscent of the Bible. Subsequently, the lengthy cycle of six prose romances usually called the *Lancelot-Grail* cycle (or the Vulgate, 2nd quarter of thirteenth century), was marked by an almost complete disappearance of the first-person narrator, as if the religious and historical truth of Grail-related stories could only rhetorically be expressed through an impersonal instance such as performative formulae *le conte* ('the tale') or *l'histoire* ('the story') that refer both to the source-story and to the story unfolding itself, as illustrated in example [17] above. Later prose romances starting with the prose *Tristan* reintroduced references to the first person, but continued to use expressions such as *le conte* or *l'histoire*. In parallel, the view of the chivalric world given in the prose *Tristan* is much more critical and multifaceted than in the previous Grail romances (Marnette 1998: 43–51). The prose *Tristan* was composed shortly after the *Lancelot-Grail* Cycle, which it partly recycles. Another lengthy prose romance, *Perceforest* (fourteenth century), purports to tell the story of King Arthur's ancestors. Afterwards, other prose texts were transposed from pre-existing verse romances (e.g. *Jehan de Paris*, fifteenth century) or *chansons de geste* (e.g. *Roman de Guillaume*, fifteenth century). Others used more 'contemporary' material: the *Roman du Comte d'Artois* (fifteenth century) and the *Roman de Jehan de Saintré* (fifteenth century).

Verse romances and prose romances share common points. Both genres use more Indirect Discourses than *chansons de geste* but fewer than the chronicles.[23] This might be explained by the omnipotence and omnipresence of the narrative voice, be it the first-person narrator or an impersonal narrative voice such as *le conte*. The characters' words are thus transposed within the narrative discourse, in which case they are not represented as such to the listeners-readers. Moreover, a substantial number of these Indirect (and Free Indirect) Discourses are reporting thoughts and not speech, which is also very different from *chansons de geste*. This link between Indirect Discourse and the reporting of thoughts is clearly illustrated in my analysis of spoken French, which underscores the fact that rather than presenting thoughts as pure 'internal speech', Indirect Discourse also often expresses non-verbal attitudes (Marnette 2005: 151–5). Indeed, *chansons de geste* do not often express character's thoughts since they are mainly about great deeds and actions (including great words) rather than about psychological development. The same can be said about chronicles. As I have shown above, chronicles use Indirect Discourses for the sake of authenticity since they cannot pretend to remember every specific word that was uttered and they can only report what the witness has seen or heard, not what people thought at the time of the events.

---

[23] One finds an average of 1 to 4.5 Direct Discourses for every Indirect Discourse in the romances. This number is higher in the *chansons de geste* (except *Cygne* 3.4) and lower in the chronicles (except Froissart 2 8.4). In some romances like *Guillaume, Artois* and the *lais*, Indirect and Free Indirect Discourses account for more than 50 % of the overall number of reported discourses. In other romances, the average is between 20 and 40 %, in comparison to the *chansons de geste* (less than 20 %, except Cygne 27 %) and to the chronicles (more than 62 %, except Froissart 2 11 %). The differences are the same if we look at the space occupied by transposed discourse (Indirect Discourse and Free Indirect Discourse) in the different genres.

In any case, thoughts are more often presented in both types of romances than in any other genre. What is at stake is the personal development of the main characters, notably through the emergence and evolution of their love. Although this is especially noticeable in the use of (Free) Indirect Discourse, it is also true for the use of Direct Discourse. It can, however, be slightly difficult to clearly distinguish between internal speech and external speech in medieval texts since most texts were oralized (i.e. sung or read aloud). So when characters are said to speak to themselves, that discourse can be presented as being uttered aloud. This is clear in expressions such as 'speaking softly so that nobody can hear' or 'speaking between one's teeth'.[24] All in all, romances use more self-addressed monologues in Direct Discourse than other genres, and some of these examples can be described as 'internal speech' rather than 'external speech'. Moreover, next to expressions such as *dire a soi-même* or *en soi-même* ('to speak to oneself' or 'within oneself'), I also found more specific verbs such as *penser* ('to think') followed by Direct Discourse.[25] Obviously, *verba sentiendi* such as *penser* and *être d'avis* ('to think'), *cuidier* ('to think', 'to believe'), *s'apercevoir* ('to realise') are common with Indirect Discourses.

Of course, there are also some important differences opposing the two genres, both in terms of form and content of reported discourse. Indeed, some of these differences are very obvious even in the very first prose romances. As Cerquiglini (1981) first noted (and I confirmed in Marnette 1998: 131–5), the prose transposition of the *Estoire dou Graal* differs from its verse version in that it rarely uses Free Direct Discourse or Free Indirect Discourse. This trend is reflected in most prose romances.[26] Actually, the *verbum dicendi* (or *sentiendi*) is not only almost mandatory in prose romances, but it can also be reinforced by a second one (a very frequent feature in the prose work *Guillaume*).

---

[24] In some texts, the self-addressed monologues must be uttered aloud in order for the plot to unfold. In Béroul's romance, Tristan is said to lament to himself (verse 237: *demente soi a lui tot sol*), but he is actually holding this monologue because he knows that King Marc is hidden in the tree above him. Tristan can therefore convince the king that he is not in love with Iseut. In the prose *Roman du Comte d'Artois*, the count's wife (disguised as his squire) discovers that he loves another woman because he speaks his thoughts aloud during the night (line 3391). Similarly, in Chrétien's *Erec and Enide*, it is because Enide unwittingly expresses her worries aloud that Erec thinks that she regrets having married him and therefore sets out for a trying journey with her (verse 2469). During their journey, Erec forbids Enide to speak to him. However when danger arises, she cannot stay quiet. In a first case, she is said to speak quietly to herself so that he does not hear her (2744–56). In subsequent similar episodes, it is not clear whether or not she is speaking aloud (see verses 2795, 2928, 3070, and 3699).

[25] There are no examples of Direct Thought monologues in the *Graal* texts, or in *Lancelot* and *Jehan de Paris*. I found the verb *penser*+Direct Discourse only in *Ipomedon, Eracle, Ombre, Artois* and *Saintré*. Other texts mostly use expressions with the verb *dire* ('to say').

[26] Free Indirect Discourses account for <1% of the overall number of reported discourses in the prose romances (except *Artois* 2.3% and prose *Tristan* 2.7%), compared to more than 2% in verse romances.

(20) Guillaume, lines 418–9
Ainçois disoit en parlant a soy meesmes: '**Haÿ! Vray Dieux**, fet il, **comme est cellui en grant peinne qui traveillie pour aultruy.** […].'
[On the contrary, he was saying, speaking to himself, '**Ha True God,** says he, **how painful it is for he who suffers for the sake of somebody else.** […].']

Furthermore, the *verbum dicendi* (or *sentiendi*) can also be 'intensified' by the use of a subordination marker such as *que* since the use of 'Direct Discourse following *que*' is higher in prose romances than in any other text. Conversely, prose romances contain almost no examples of 'Indirect Discourse without *que*' (see *infra*).

On the other hand, verse romances use more Free Direct Discourses than any other texts, especially in dialogues, which makes them very lively [21], compared to prose romances [22]. Note that in the following example, there would probably be no helpful punctuation in the medieval manuscript.[27] Moreover, two discourses can appear within the same verse, which never happens in the *chansons de geste* of my corpus.

(21) *Ombre* 789–805 [the lady wants the knight to take his ring back]

Fet ele: '[…]	She says: '[…]
- Si ferez ! – Je non ferai voir!	**- Yes you will! – I will not indeed!**
- Volez le me vos fere avoir	**- Do you want to make me have it**
A force? – Nenil voir , amie:	**By force? – Not at all, my friend:**
Bien sai ce pooir n'ai ge mie […]'	**I know that I don't have that power. […]'**

(22) *Mort Artu* § 31 line 20–32
- **Et ge vos di,** fet la reïne, **que il i ala au plus covertement qu'il pot.** – **Et ge vos di, dame,** fet messire Gauvains, **que se il I fu, ce fu cil as armes vermeilles qui veinqui le tornoiement.** – **Ce ne fu il pas,** fet la reïne, **ce sachiez veraiment;** […].'
- **And I am telling you,** says the queen, **that he went there as secretly as he could.** – **And I am telling you, Lady,** says Gauvain, **that if he was there, he was the one with the crimson weapons, who won the tournament.** – **He was not,** says the queen, **this you should truly know;** […].'

Verse romances also use more 'Indirect Discourses without *que*' (see *infra*). Moreover, in verse romances, *verba dicendi* rarely introduce Direct Discourses immediately following an Indirect Discourse. Indeed, these Direct Discourses sometimes follow a Free Indirect Discourse, therefore easing the transition from the narrator's discourse to the character's discourse.

---

[27] For a discussion of punctuation and reported discourse in medieval manuscripts and a list of useful references, see Marnette (2006b, 2008). The colon and the quotation marks signaling Direct Discourse in the above example would thus be entirely dependent on the modern editor's understanding of the passage. In a sense, it is the modern punctuation that puts pressure on us as readers to make a choice about where we are on the *continuum*, something that would not have been so acute for the medieval listener/reader.

While both genres express more thoughts than other texts, they do not do so in the same way. Prose romances tend to use Indirect Thoughts only, while verse romances also use Free Indirect Thoughts as well as Direct Thoughts (i.e. self-addressed monologues).[28] According to Leech and Short (1981: 324), the norm for representing speech is the direct mode, while the norm for representing thought is the indirect mode since the thoughts of others cannot be directly observed. Therefore, with regards to the respective norms, the free indirect mode implies a movement in the direction of greater narrator control of the discourse in the case of speech, while in the case of thought the reverse situation occurs. Free indirect thought thus involves a movement towards language (however fictional, since we are dealing with thoughts) as does, of course, Direct Thought. By using both, verse romances clearly give more room for the characters' own perspectives and do so more vividly than their prose counterparts.

In summary, prose romances show a very strong tendency to formally identify the various locutors present in the text and to distinguish clearly between the various discourses. Indeed, this can be considered parallel to the structuring role of the formula *le conte dit que* ('the tale says that') that helps identify the many episodes of the text. On the contrary, verse romances allow for flexibility (and even in some cases some ambiguity) as to who is speaking (or thinking). These findings can be linked to the ideology underlying the two genres. Without going into too much detail, one could say that they envisage truth and reality in essentially different ways.

As I have shown in Sect. 16.3.1 above, the first prose romances aimed to represent a unique religious truth based on a specific source (God's voice, witnesses' stories, etc.) and thus a unique reality. Later romances, while not based on a religious topic such as the Grail, were nonetheless often presented as chronicles and thus once again as historical.[29] Historical (and/or religious) truth must rely on clearly identifiable discourses and allow (in principle) only for one point of view, that of the narrative voice, to which the characters' discourses are clearly subordinated (hence the strong marking of reported discourses, the rarity of Free Direct Discourse and Free Indirect Discourse, etc.).

Verse romances present truth not as a reflection of historical and religious events, but rather as based on the verisimilitude of the events told. As often announced in the prologues, this truth relies on the compositional skills of the author and on the

---

[28] In verse romances, Direct Thoughts represent more than 1% of the overall number of reported discourses (except *Graal* 0 %, *Yvain* 0.4%), in comparison to less than 1% for prose romances (except *Guillaume* 2.8%). Verse romances also use more Free Indirect Thoughts (0.9% and above, except *Graal* at 0.6%) compared to prose romances (less than 0.8%, except prose *Tristan*, which is at 1.8%).

[29] The great length of prose romances also gives them an historical and encyclopedic flavor since they are supposed to tell the story of an entire family from their earlier ancestors on (e.g. the *Lancelot-Grail* cycle, the Prose *Tristan, Perceforest*). Obviously, as shown in the previous section and in Marnette (2002b), prose romances that call themselves *chroniques* or *histoires* do so as a rhetorical ploy and do not use the same reported discourse strategies as real chronicles.

way he or she will describe feelings and situations that are coherent with the expectations of the genre. One such expectation is that the description of love should be relevant to the listeners-readers' anticipation of what courtly love should be. Moreover, prologues of texts such as Chrétien's *Erec* and Marie's *Lais*, indicate that the authors give a certain meaning to their texts, which must in turn be interpreted by their listeners-readers.[30] The path to interpretation is undoubtedly challenged by a considerable amount of intricacy between the presentation of characters' thoughts, the narrator's own comments, and some allegorical passages. Indeed, there is doubt as to whether there is any one unique interpretation possible, considering the amount of irony present in verse romances. What we are presented with is several layers of reality and several levels of interpretation, all of which depend on the skills and the will of the first-person narrator. For example, the use of Free Indirect Discourse allows the narrator to blur the boundaries between his/her discourse and that of the characters. Through Free Indirect Thoughts, we are passing from the external point of view of the narrator (standing, as it were, outside of the story) to the internal perspective of the character.[31] In other words, we are dealing with two different realities and this opposition can lead to irony since it opposes what the character thinks and believes to what the listeners-readers and/or the other characters know.

(23) Ipomedon, p 493 [the heroin La Fiere does not know that she is actually fleeing her lover, who has taken a disguise]

La Fiere ad tut sun cunseil pris ;	La Fiere has made her decision;
Meulz veut guerpir tut le païs,	*She would rather leave the entire region,*
Ses chasteaus e tute sa hunur,	*Her castle and her renown,*
Ke prendre celui a seignur.	*Than take this man as her husband.*
Mut est tost del chastel eissu	She has quickly left the castle
E est deske as bateaus venu, (…)	And gone to the boat (…)

Free Direct Discourse also allows for ambiguity and certainly calls for the utmost attention on the part of the listeners-readers since it is not always easy to know who speaks and when [23]. In addition, some characters' monologues in Direct Discourse are, in fact, seemingly schizophrenic discussions between two *personae*, e.g. the reasonable side of the character (Reason) and the unreasonable one (Love). In certain cases, one could even argue for interpreting this dialogic monologue as an actual discussion between the character and the narrator. What is important here is not the authenticity of monologues, but rather the narrator's skill in accurately portraying the different forces at work within the character's mind. Once again, the truth is not referential but rather topical (Kelly 1992: 145, 210).[32]

---

[30] For more details, see Kelly (1992), Marnette (1998: 89–96), and Zink (1995: 55–7).

[31] For a discussion of focalization in romances, see Marnette 1998, chapters 5 and 6.

[32] Other such dialogic monologues are *Ipomedon* p 108, 117, 447, *Eracle* 3543, 3736, 3869, *Yvain* 1432–1510, *Ombre* 684. In *Yvain*, there is also a monologue where the character, Laudine, imagines her argument with her husband's murderer (v 1761). In *Erec et Enide*, Enide's monologues are also similar to a dialogue since she speaks to herself in the second person.

In conclusion, reported discourse strategies in verse and prose romances differ both in form and content, and more importantly they answer very distinct narratological needs.

16.4 Peculiar Forms of Reported Discourses

'Direct Discourse with *que*' and 'Indirect Discourse without *que*' are two 'hybrid' forms of reported discourse found in medieval French. Both have been studied by philologists in ways that were hardly ever contextual or co-textual and definitely lacked statistical data. In fact, as I have shown in great detail (Marnette 2005: 183–8), these forms are better understood if one looks at their use with regards to particular literary genres while also paying attention to the other categories of reported discourse with which they do or do not co-occur. Furthermore, these forms have seldom been connected to similar forms found in contemporary French (i.e. mainly the press for 'DD with *que*' or spoken French for 'ID without *que*'). This is unfortunate since the study of medieval occurrences can shed light on the study of modern ones (and vice versa). Moreover, taking a broader view of the phenomena also helps us to re-consider and possibly re-define the apparently unproblematic category of Indirect Discourse.

On the one hand, philologists traditionally agree to say that 'DD with *que*' appears simply because Indirect Discourse tends to drift back towards Direct Discourse. On the other hand, while aware of the existence of 'ID without *que*', they rarely describe it as a special type of reported discourse but include it instead among the paratactical features characteristic of medieval texts, especially older ones.[33] This is a rather oversimplified view of the strategies at work in medieval literature. In fact, both types of reported discourses are better understood as possible alternatives to Free Indirect Discourse. If one envisions the use of reported discourse as part of a *continuum*, there are possibilities for switching progressively from the narrator's discourse (narration) to a first situation of reported discourse still under the high narrator's control. (Indirect Discourse or even the introductory verb followed by *que* [7]) towards a reported discourse that takes away some control from the narrator and moves towards the pole of the character. This can be done either by switching tenses, deictics, and/or grammatical persons ('DD with *que*'), or by keeping the tenses and grammatical persons of the quoting discourse while leaving unexpressed the subordination marker ('ID without *que*' and/or Free Indirect Discourse). Most texts (or rather genres of texts) show preference for one type of 'hybrid' discourse or another.

In my corpus, a majority of prose romances use 'DD with *que*' rather than Free Indirect Discourse and they tend to offer more occurrences of *que* + Direct Discourse

---

[33] See Marnette (2005: 216–7) for a detailed list of references.

with an *inquit* formula than most other texts.[34] When they use constructions without any introductory verb, they overwhelmingly use a strong connective link to the preceding Indirect Discourse (e.g. *et, car, mais*). The prose texts contain only 3 instances of Direct Discourses following an Indirect Discourse without an *inquit* formula and without a clear syntactical link (one in *Perceforest*, one in *Saintré* and one in Joinville). This means that, as a whole, they keep a strong distancing between quoted discourse and quoting discourse, and they clearly identify who is speaking, which is in line with the general characteristics of prose texts (see *supra*).[35] This 'overmarking' might be, in some ways, comparable to the numerous examples of 'DD with *que*' present in contemporary press, mostly in newspapers (6–10 % of overall reported discourses in the press corpus studied in Marnette 2005).[36]

(24)   *Paris Match*, 17-07-2002, Le S.O.S. des bijoutiers, p 105
Isabelle Guichot, P.-d.g. de Van Cleef & Arpels et présidente du Comité Vendôme, souligne que **"s'il le faut, nous fermerons nos boutiques sur la Côte d'Azur"**.
[Isabelle Guichot, CEO of Van Cleef & Arpels and president of the Vendôme Committee, stresses that **"if necessary, we will close our boutiques on the Côte d'Azur"**.]

---

[34] Based on my own corpus of 39 texts, containing a total of 16,447 reported discourses, the use of 'DD with *que*' is fairly rare. Eight of the 39 texts do not contain any: *Alexis* ms H, ms M2, and ms S, *Charlemagne, Huon, Guillaume*, Villehardouin, Commynes, Monstrelet and Berry. As a whole the corpus, contains 184 'DD with *que*' (i.e. Direct Discourse following an Indirect Discourse, 1.1 % of the overall number of reported discourses), which is similar to the number of Free Indirect Discourses following an Indirect Discourse (201, 1.2 % of the total of reported discourses).

[35] Verse romances, except for the *Graal*, use more Free Indirect Discourses than 'DD with *que*'. They all use more than 0.8 % 'DD with *que*' (with regard to the total amount of reported discourses) and more than 1.7 % Free Indirect Discourse following Indirect Discourse (12 % in the Lais!). In general, the *chansons de geste* do not use many 'DD with *que*' (15 examples, 0.5 % of reported discourses) or many Free Indirect Discourses after Indirect Discourses (13 examples, with 1.2 % in *Roland* and 1.9 % in the *Cygne* being exceptions rather than the norm). *Charlemagne* uses neither of these constructions. Of course, this goes hand in hand with the fact that *chansons de geste*' narrators do not often use Indirect Discourse: less than 8 %, (i.e. less than in any other text of the corpus, except for two later *chansons, Cygne* 22 %, *Nanteuil* 18 %). Finally, the chronicles are quite varied in character. Villehardouin's *Prise de Constantinople* uses neither 'DD with *que*' nor Free Indirect Discourse after Indirect Discourse. Clari, Joinville and Froissart 2 use more 'DD with *que*' than Free Indirect Discourses, while Commynes, Monstrelet, Berry, Froissart 1 and 3 do the contrary.

[36] In newspaper articles, deictics do not always necessarily vary between Direct Discourse and Indirect Discourse, for example, in cases where the third person and the present tense would be possible in both [25]. The segments can thus also be indicated through quotation marks and/or italics only and would therefore not be interpreted as such if these marks were removed. Actually, these more 'neutral' occurrences are more widespread than the former (5–9 % in newspapers versus 1–1.4 %). Rosier (2002) notes that the 'neutral' occurrences are especially used when the quoted sources are written documents or official discourses (e.g. spokesperson, anonymous diplomatic sources, etc.) while the segments are more likely to be explicitly transposed if they originate from known people, which also makes the article more lively.

(25) *Le Figaro*, 11-07-2002, Projet Sarkozy, p 6
Sur le même registre, le responsable syndical remarque <u>que</u> "**les policiers sont vaccinés contre les promesses non tenues**".
[In the same tone, the union representative notes <u>that</u> "**police officers have seen their fair share of broken promises**".]

Journalists use these devices in order to do two things at the same time. On one hand, they can distance themselves from the quoted discourse through the Indirect Discourse apparatus, therefore emphasizing their position as 'objective reporters'. On the other hand, they can use quotation marks to keep the vividness and authenticity of the original discourse, therefore highlighting their skills as storytellers and insisting upon the faithfulness of their story (Rosier 1993, 1995, 1999, 2002, 2009; Maingueneau 1998: 130). For these examples in journalism, Rosier (2002) speaks very cleverly about discours surmarqué ('over-marked discourse').[37]

As opposed to the 'over-marking' of 'DD with *que*', one could say that 'Indirect Discourse without *que*' is 'under-marked' (since it lacks a subordination marker, see [8, 9] above) and in some cases it is even 'neutralized', when there is no difference between Direct Discourse and Indirect Discourse because the pronouns and tenses would be the same in both situations, as is shown in [26]:

(26) La Prise d'Orange, Ms CE, 1196
Mahomet jurent <u>vengement en ert pris</u>;
Or
Mahomet jurent "**vengement en ert pris**."
[By Mohammed they swear vengeance will be had.]

The use of 'ID without *que*' is very much restricted to the *chansons de geste* and verse texts, and almost absent from prose texts (1 occurrence in Graal, Commynes and Monstrelet).[38] Moreover, since one finds it even in later *chansons de geste* (*Cygne, Huon, Nanteuil*), it seems that it is not linked to chronology but instead to genres.[39] As with ordinary Indirect Discourse and Free Indirect Discourse, there are

---

[37] 'DD with *que*' is also possible albeit rare in my corpus of Spoken French conversations (6 occurrences for 1,727 reported Discourses = 0.3 %). See Marnette (2005: 349–51) for a description of the corpus.

l'infirmière elle m'a dit <u>que</u>: **il faut que vous /partez, partiez/ avec l'ambulance /qui, il/ vous attend** + elle m'a amené ici [the nurse she told me <u>that</u> **you must leave with the ambulance that is waiting for you she brought me here**] (Frank 1, p 1, l 6–8)

Note that in Medieval French and in Spoken French, 'DD with *que*' is necessarily signaled by the non-transposition of some markers, since neither medieval manuscripts nor the oral medium rely on punctuation to signal DD, as opposed to the (possibly) more neutral examples found in contemporary press.

[38] It is also absent in *Charlemagne, Erec* and *Yvain*.

[39] There are a total of 86 occurrences of 'ID without *que*', i.e. 0.5 % of the overall number of discourses reported by the narrator (less than 'DD with *que*' or Free Indirect Discourse). As we saw *supra*, there are not many Indirect Discourses in the *chansons de geste* and on average 10 % of them are 'ID without *que*', which is a higher percentage than verse romances (4 %).

many occurrences where the tenses of the completive are linked to the present and not to the past.[40] Furthermore, one quarter of 'ID without *que*' are followed either by Free Indirect Discourses or by Direct Discourses (classified as 'DD with *que*'). It is more likely to be Free Indirect Discourse in the case of verse romances and Direct Discourse in the case of *chansons de geste*. This shows the trend towards a progressive shift from the narrator's discourse (narration) to that of the characters. It is especially true when looking at the use of Free Indirect Discourse in combination with other 'mixed discourses' in verse romances, which therefore tends to allow for a smoother progression and for more ambiguities as to the point of view of the narrator and of the characters (Marnette 1998: 174–84; Perret 1997: 17, see *supra*). As we saw above, *chansons de geste* tend to prefer the use of Direct Discourse or more rarely 'DD with *que*' when the narrator quotes characters, but in reality they use more Free Indirect Discourses and 'ID without *que*' when characters quote other characters, denoting a highly complex hierarchization of voices (see note 10 *supra*, Marnette 1999a).[41] The quasi absence of 'ID without *que*' in prose texts can be linked to their restricted use of Free Direct Discourses (i.e. Direct Discourse without any *verbum dicendi*), and of Free Indirect Discourses, as well as to their higher ratio of 'DD with *que*' that are strongly introduced (i.e. '*verbum dicendi*+que+DD' [7] or 'ID+Direct Discourse with *inquit formula*'). In other words, prose texts, whether romances or chronicles, must clearly identify who is speaking in the text in order to differentiate the sources of speech and thought presentation within the narration, as opposed to the source of the narrative. The latter is presented as unique and truthful, be it a book in the case of prose romances or an individual in the case of chronicles (see *supra*).

Note that while absent from modern literary French, 'ID without *que*' is well represented in informal spoken French (Marnette 2001a, 2005: 156).[42]

(27) Franke 2, p 41 [An alcoholic patient speaks to his doctor]
euh+je me sens en pleine forme c'est ça qui est le pire+vous direz **oui je suis tout gaga ou euh ±perds la tête**
[euh+I feel great that's what is worst+you'll say **yes I am going completely gaga or euh ±loosing my mind**]

The Spoken French corpus also contains examples that do not have a marker of subordination and are not necessarily transposed. In other words, the personal pronouns, verbal endings, tenses and deictics of the quoted utterances would be the same whether in the direct or indirect mode (bold and underlined).

---

[40] 57 % of the *verbum dicendi* introducing 'ID without *que*' are conjugated in a tense linked to the present, and the first verbs of the completives are mostly in the present indicative (36 %), future indicative (27 %) or present subjunctive (19 %).

[41] 'ID without *que*' is also used in the characters' quoted discourses in the verse romances but less than in *chansons de geste* (4 versus 17 % of Indirect Discourse). The category is absent from *Alexis* ms H, M2, S, *Charlemagne, Orange* ms AB, *Orange* ms CE and *Erec*. It is pretty much absent from all prose texts.

[42] In Marnette (2005: 159), the analysis of the spoken French corpus yielded 155 Neutral Discourses (9 %) which is more than Free Indirect Discourses (4 %, 71 occurrences).

(28)   Tricon, p 64 [The speaker is talking to a writer about her last novel, on a literary TV-show]
et alors vous avez dit oh c'est très vrai tout ce que vous dites mais il y a une chose qui m'a frappée et vous dites **elle ne pensait plus en français**
[then you said oh it is very true everything you say but one thing struck me and you say **she wasn't thinking in French any more**]

Since the absence of *que* cannot, in itself, vouch for the presence of a Direct Discourse, we are dealing with what I term a 'Neutral Discourse'. Only mimicking (imitation of accent or gestures) could be a strong indicator of Direct Discourse (Vincent and Dubois 1997: 34–36). However it is doubtful whether the speaker wants or needs to make a difference here. What is important is the content of the reported discourse, because most examples of Neutral Discourses are used in an argumentative context. This is similar to 'typical' Indirect Discourse, but Neutral Discourse has a higher number of first-person examples (72%, 99 occurrences versus 49% in Indirect Discourse) and it appears with speech rather than with thoughts (78% of speech, 119 occurrences versus 46% of speech in Indirect Discourse, see *supra*).

(29)   Nevchehirlian, p 56 [conversation about unions' politics]
et puis je vais te dire bon **si je serais pas d'accord euh je serais pas . à la CGT** hein + bon tu me tu vas me dire **ouais mais euh avec tout tu es d'accord** +
[and then I will tell you **if I did not agree euh I would not be a CGT member** + well you will say **yes but euh you agree with everything** +]

The use of first person and speech is significant because it does not involve a change of voice. So in cases where the quoted utterance is referring to the first-person speaker [29] or to a third-person referent, there is no need to signal the 'quoting process' by strong mimicking or by a strong subordinating marker. We are here on the evidential side of speech and thought presentation, which Vincent and Dubois (1996, 1997) describe as the assertive pole of the *continuum* between reproduction and assertion. There is a strong connection here to what we have observed in *chansons de geste*, since they embed 'ID without *que*' within characters' discourse, using reflexive formulas in the first person [29], a case in which a change of voice is not needed, and more importantly, where the illocutionary force is most prevalent. Here the use of Indirect Discourse signals that, contrary to Direct Discourse, the emphasis is not on the form of the reported discourse (mimicking, exact vocabulary, etc.), but rather on its content. In the case of *verbum dicendi* in the first person indicative present, it is the illocutionary force of the discourse that is highlighted through the creation of a performative expression (e.g. I swear).

(30)   *Tristan de Nanteuil*, 1934, 1949–51
'Sire, dist Aiglantine, nen soiés plus parlans;
[…]
**Et se vous m'espousés, sur sains vous SUIS JURANS,
Ja bien ne vous feray, ne ne seray couchans
Avec vous nu a nu;** […]'
['Sir, said Aiglantine, do not speak about this any longer; […] **And if you marry me, I SWEAR by the Saints, I will never do you any good, nor will I sleep with you naked;** […]']

The study of 'hybrid' discourse in medieval French and contemporary French definitively shows that the use of a subordination marker is not inherent to the category of Indirect Discourse. Indeed, if the absence of *que* does not preclude the advent of Indirect Discourse, its presence does not guarantee it, either, since *que* can appear in what has been described as a 'Direct Discourse with *que*'. The potential lack of differences between the tenses of quoted and quoting discourse and the absence of subordinating marker show that Indirect Discourse is essentially defined by the transposition of deictics and persons. Indeed, some occurrences of 'ID without *que*' in the narrative discourse are what I have called 'neutral discourses': there is no difference between Direct Discourse and Indirect Discourse because the pronouns and tenses would be the same in both situations, as is shown in [26, 28] above. This discussion thus indicates that the relationships between Direct Discourse and Indirect Discourse are best viewed as a *continuum*.

16.5 Conclusion

As this chapter has shown, to examine the evolution of reported discourse in the Middle Ages is to describe complex discourse strategies at work in a language that has sometimes been seen by linguists and literary scholars as lacking in any kind of sophistication. Intrinsically, speech and thought presentation in the Middle Ages can only be studied in a dynamic view. This is due to the fact that it links internal phenomena (elaboration of forms) to external phenomena (elaboration of functions) through the very evolution of medieval literary genres and their various conceptualizations of reality, history and fiction, their distinct depictions of the narrator-audience relationships, and the differences in apparent 'control' of the narrator over his/her characters' discourse. Moreover, as we saw in Sect. 16.4, the study of unusual but overlooked phenomena such as Indirect Discourse without *que* and Direct Discourse with *que* is essential for an in-depth comprehension of reported discourse categories in general as it calls into question traditional definitions that distinguish Indirect Discourse from Direct Discourse purely based on the presence of subordination markers. Indeed, these markers are not specific to Indirect Discourse nor are they necessary for it.

Appendix: Corpus of Medieval French Literature

1. Chansons de geste

La Chanson de Roland. Ed. Gérard Moignet. Paris: Bordas. 1989.
Le Voyage de Charlemagne a Jerusalem et a Constantinople. Ed. Paul Aebischer. Geneva: Droz. 1965.
La Prise d'Orange. Ed. Claude Régnier. Paris: Klincksieck. 1966. Version AB based on manuscripts A and B and version CE based on manuscripts C and E.

Le Chevalier au Cygne. Ed. Jan A. Nelson. Alabama: University of Alabama Press. 1985.

Raoul de Cambrai. Ed. Sarah Kay. Oxford: Clarendon Press. 1992.

Huon de Bordeau. Ed. Pierre Ruelle. Brussels: Presses Universitaires de Bruxelles. 1960. Excerpt verses 1-4078 and 8550-10553.

Tristan de Nanteuil. Ed. K. V. Sinclair. Assen: Van Gorcum. 1971. Excerpt verses 1-2004 and 21316-23361.

2. Verse Romances and Lais

Erec and Enide. Chrétien de Troyes. Ed. W. C. Carleton. New York & London: Garland. 1987.

Yvain ou Le Chevalier au Lion. Chrétien de Troyes. Ed. William W. Kibler. New York & London: Garland. 1985.

Lais de Marie de France. Ed. Karl Warnke. Paris: Le Livre de Poche. "Les Lettres gothiques". 1990.

Eracle. Gautier d'Arras. Ed. Guy Raynaud de Lage. Paris: Champion. 1976.

Le Roman de Tristan. Béroul. Ed. Alfred Ewert. Oxford: Basil Blackwell. 1939.

Ipomedon. Hue de Rothelande. Ed. A. J. Holden. Paris: Klincksieck. 1979.

Le Roman de l'Estoire dou Graal. Robert de Boron. Ed. William A. Nitze. Paris: Champion. 1927.

Le Lai de l'ombre. Jean Renart. Ed. Félix Lecoy. Paris: Champion. 1979.

Le Roman de la Rose ou de Guillaume de Dole. Jean Renart. Ed. Félix Lecoy. Paris: Champion. 1979.

3. Hagiography

La Vie de Saint Alexis. Manuscript H. Ed. Charles Storey. Oxford: Basil Blackwell. 1946.

La Vie de Saint Alexis. Manuscripts M2 and S Ed. Alison G. Elliott. Chapel Hill: University of North Carolina Press. 1983.

4. Prose Romances

Le Roman du Graal. Robert de Boron. Ed. Cerquiglini. Paris: 10/18. 1981.

Lancelot du Lac. non cyclical version. Ed. Kennedy. Oxford: Clarendon. 1980. excerpt p. 154–257.

La Mort le roi Artu. Ed. Frappier. Geneva: Droz. 1964.

Le Roman de Tristan. Ed. Ménard. Geneva: Droz. excerpt 1987. p. 247–277 and 1990. p. 65–190.

Le Roman de Perceforest. Fourth part. Ed. Gilles Roussineau. Geneva: Droz. 1987. excerpt p. 1–200.

Le Roman de Jehan de Saintré. Antoine de la Sale. Ed. Jean Misrhai & Charles A. Knudson. Geneva: Droz. 1965.

Le Roman de Guillaume. Ed. Carl Weber. Halle: Vereinigten Friedrichs-Universität Halle-Wittenberg. 1912 (under the title Die Prosafassungen des "Couronnement de Louis". des "Charroi de Nîmes" und der "Prise d'Orange").

Le Roman du Comte d'Artois. Ed. Charles Sei¬gneuret. Geneva: Droz. 1966.

Le Roman de Jehan de Paris. Ed. E. Wickersheimer. Paris: Champion. 1923.

5. Chronicles

Villehardouin. *La Conquête de Constantinople*. Ed. R. Faral. Paris: Les Belles lettres. 1961. Volume 1.

Robert de Clari. *La Conquête de Constantinople*. Ed. P. Lauer. Paris: Champion. 1924.

Jehan. Seigneur de Joinville. *La Vie de Saint Louis. Le témoignage de Jehan. Seigneur de Joinville*. Ed. N. Corbett. Québec: Naaman. 1977.

Froissart. *Chroniques*. Ed. G. T. Diller. Geneva: Droz. 1991. Volume 1. §§ 1–100. p. 1–131. [= excerpt 1]

Froissart. *Chroniques*. 'Le voyage de Bearn'. In A. Pauphilet and E. Pognon. *Historiens et Chroniqueurs du moyen âge*. Paris: Gallimard. 1952. p. 486–565. [= excerpt 2]

Froissart. *Chroniques*. In A. Pauphilet and E. Pognon. *Historiens et Chroniqueurs du moyen âge*. Paris: Gallimard. 1952. p. 605–647. [= excerpt 3]

Enguerran de Monstrelet. *Chronique*. Edited by L. Douët-D'Arq. Paris: Société de l'histoire de France. 1857. Book II. chapters 258–278.

Gilles Le Bouvier dit Le Héraut Berry. *Les Chroniques du roi Charles VII*. Edited by H. Courteault and L. Celier. Paris: Klincksieck. 1979. p. 3–4. p. 122–99

Commynes. Mémoires. Edited by J. Calmette. Paris: Belles Lettres. 1964. volume 1.

6. Other

Aucassin et Nicolette. Chantefable du XIIIesiècle. Edited by Mario Roques. Paris: Champion. 1975.

References

Bauer, Brigitte L.M. 1996. The verb in indirect speech in Old French: System in change. In *Reported speech: Forms and functions of the verb*, ed. T. Janssen and W. Van der Wurff, 75–96. Amsterdam/Philadelphia: John Benjamins.

Baumgartner, Emmanuèle. 1995. *Le Récit médiéval*. Paris: Hachette.
Beer, Jeanette M. 1981. *Narrative convention of truth in the Middle Ages*. Geneva: Droz.
Bruña-Cuevas, Manuel. 1988. Le Style indirect libre chez Marie de France. *Revue de Linguistique Romane* 52: 421–446.
Bruña-Cuevas, Manuel. 1989. Changer l'appelation 'Style Indirect Libre'? *Romania* 110: 1–39.
Burns, Jane E. 1985. *Arthurian fictions, rereading the vulgate cycle*. Columbus: Ohio State University Press.
Cerquiglini, Bernard. 1981. *La Parole médiévale*. Paris: Minuit.
Cerquiglini, Bernard. 1984. Le Style indirect libre et la modernité. *Langages* 73: 7–16.
Collins, Daniel E. 2001. *Reanimated voices. Speech reporting in a historical-pragmatic perspective*. Amsterdam/Philapdelphia: John Benjamins.
Diller, George T. 1998. Froissarts 1389 travel to Béarn: A voyage narration to the center of the Chroniques. In *Froissart across the genres*, ed. D. Maddox and S. Sturm-Maddox, 50–60. Gainesville: University press of Florida.
Duggan, Joseph J. 1987. Appropriation of historical knowledge by the vernacular epic. In *Grundriss des Romanischen Literaturen des Mittelalters*, vol. 2, ed. H.U. Gumbrecht et al., 285–311. Heidelberg: Carl Winter.
Fleischman, Suzanne. 1983. On the representation of history and fiction in the Middle Ages. *History and Theory: Studies in the Philosophy of History* 23(3): 278–310.
Fleischman, Suzanne. 1990. *Tense and narrativity: From medieval performance to modern fiction*. Austin: University of Texas Press.
Kay, Sarah. 1987. Le Passé indéfini, problèmes de la représentation du passé dans quelques chansons de geste féodales. *Senefiance* 21: 697–709.
Kay, Sarah. 1995. *The chansons de geste in the age of romance: Political fictions*. Oxford: Clarendon.
Kelly, Douglas. 1992. *The art of medieval French romance*. Wisconsin: University of Wisconsin Press.
Landeweerd, Rita, and Co Vet. 1996. Tense in (free) indirect discourse in French. In *Reported speech: Forms and functions of the verb*, ed. T. Janssen and W. Van der Wurff, 141–164. Amsterdam/Philadelphia: John Benjamins.
Leech, Geoffrey, and Michael Short. 1981. *Style in fiction, a linguistic introduction to English fictional prose*. London/New York: Longman.
Levine, Robert. 1985. Myth and Anti-Myth in Cuveliers' *La Vie Vaillante de Bertrand Du Guesclin*. *Viator* 16: 259–275.
Levine, Robert. 1991. Deadly Diatribe in the *Récits d un ménestrel de Reims*. *Res Publica Litterarum* 14: 115–126.
Levine, Robert. 1998. The Pious Traitor: Rhetorical Reinventions of the Fall of Antioch. *Mittellateinisches Jahrbuch*. 33:59–80.
Maingueneau, Dominique. 1998. *Analyser les textes de communication*. Paris: Dunod.
Marnette, Sophie. 1996. Réflexions sur le discours indirect libre en français médiéval. *Romania* 114: 1–49.
Marnette, Sophie. 1998. *Narrateur et points de vue dans la littérature française médiévale: Une approche linguistique*. Bern: Peter Lang.
Marnette, Sophie. 1999a. Il le vos mande, ge sui qui le vos di: Les stratégies du dire dans les chansons de geste. *La Revue de linguistique romane* 63(251–252): 387–417.
Marnette, Sophie. 1999b. Narrateur et points de vue dans les chroniques médiévales: une approche linguistique. In *The medieval chronicle, proceedings of the 1st international conference on the medieval chronicle, Utrecht 13–16 July 1996*, ed. E. Kooper, 174–190. Amsterdam/Atlanta: Rodopi.
Marnette, Sophie. 2001a. Du discours insolite: Le discours indirect sans *que*. *French Studies* 55(3): 297–313.
Marnette, Sophie. 2001b. The French *théorie de l'énonciation* and the study of speech and thought presentation. *Language and Literature* 10(3): 243–262.
Marnette, Sophie. 2002a. *Je dis que ... Je pense que ...* Le je narrateur, auteur, témoin et personnage des chroniques. *LYNX* 32: 271–284.

Marnette, Sophie. 2002b. Sources du récit et discours rapportés: L'art de la représentation dans les chroniques et les romans français des 14e et 15e siècles. In *Le Moyen Français* 51-52-53, 435–459.
Marnette, Sophie. 2005. *Speech and thought presentation in French: Concepts and strategies.* Amsterdam/Philadelphia: John Benjamins.
Marnette, Sophie. 2006a. Experiencing self and narrating self in medieval French chronicles. In *The medieval author in medieval French literature*, Studies in Arthurian and Courtly Cultures, ed. Virginie Greene, 115–134. New York: Palsgrave-Mc Millan.
Marnette, Sophie. 2006b. La Signalisation du discours rapporté en français médiéval. *Langue Française* 149: 31–47.
Marnette, Sophie. 2008. La Ponctuation du discours rapporté dans quelques manuscrits de romans en prose médiévaux. *Verbum* 28(1): 29–46.
Perret, Michèle. 1997. Le discours rapporté dans *Le bel inconnu*. *L'Information grammaticale* 72: 13–18.
Rosier, Laurence. 1993. De la stylistique sociologique suivie d'une application pratique: discours direct, presse et objectivité. *Revue belge de philologie et d'histoire* 71(3): 625–644.
Rosier, Laurence. 1995. La Parataxe: Heurs et malheurs d'une notion linguistico-littéraire. *Travaux de Linguistique* 30: 51–64.
Rosier, Laurence. 1999. *Le Discours rapporté; Histoire, théories, pratiques.* Paris/Bruxelles: De Boeck/Duculot.
Rosier, Laurence. 2002. La Presse et les modalités du discours rapporté: l'effet dhyperréalisme du discours direct surmarqué. *L'information grammaticale* 94: 27–32.
Rosier, Laurence. 2009. *Le Discours rapporté en français.* Paris: Ophrys.
Rychner, Jean. 1980. La Présence et le point de vue du narrateur dans deux récits courts: *Le Lai de Lanval* et *La Châtelaine de Vergi*. *Vox Romanica* 39: 86–103.
Rychner, Jean. 1987. Messages et discours doubles. In *Studies in medieval French language and literature presented to Brian Woledge in honour of his 80th birthday*, ed. S. Burch-North, 145–161. Geneva: Droz.
Rychner, Jean. 1989. Le Discours subjectif dans les *Lais* de Marie de France. A propos d'une étude récente. *Revue de Linguistique Romane* 53: 57–83.
Rychner, Jean. 1990. *La Narration des sentiments, des pensées et des discours dans quelques oeuvres des douzième et treizième siècles.* Geneva: Droz.
Vincent, Diane, and Sylvie Dubois. 1996. A study on the use of reported speech in spoken language. In *Sociolinguistic variation. Data, theory and analysis*, ed. J. Arnold et al., 361–374. Stanford: CLSI Publications.
Vincent, Diane, and Sylvie Dubois. 1997. *Le discours rapporté au quotidien.* Québec: Nuit Blanche.
Zink, Michel. 1995. *Medieval French literature: An introduction.* Binghamton: Pegasus paperbooks.
Zumthor, Paul. 1975. *Langue, texte, énigme.* Paris: Seuil.

Chapter 17
The Left-Periphery in Old French

Eric Mathieu

17.1 Introduction

The cartographic enterprise initiated by Rizzi's (1997) seminal paper has led to a better understanding of the syntactic mapping of focus and topics at the left periphery of the clause in natural languages (Cinque 2002, 2006; Belletti 2004; Rizzi 2004). The overall goal of the present chapter is to show that this type of synchronic research can contribute directly to the study of Old French discourse phenomena. In particular, by focusing on the older stage of the French language, this study is in the tradition of Benincá and Poletto's work (e.g. Benincà 2006; Benincà and Poletto 2002) which, following the cartographic approach, has contributed greatly to the understanding of the architecture of the left periphery of the clause for older stages of Romance languages, including Old Italian and Old Spanish.

In this chapter, I give a general account of the distribution of the elements appearing at the left periphery in Old French. In particular, I show that the Old French CP appears to consist of a rich array of functional projections, most notably a series of topic phrases that surface in the pre-verbal area. Four topic positions are identified. In addition to the traditional topic position associated with V2 (Adams 1987a; Vance 1997, among many others), I argue that the Old French CP contained a special topic position that hosted Stylistically fronted elements and two other topic positions: one for Left Dislocated phrases and the other for Hanging Topics. I show that the topic positions for the latter two existed (at least for a while) alongside the V2 and the Stylistic topic position and that the emergence of left-dislocated and Hanging Topics arises much earlier than previously thought. By breaking down the C domain into

E. Mathieu (✉)
Department of Linguistics, University of Ottawa, Ottawa, ON, Canada
e-mail: emathieu@uottawa.ca

several projections, we come to understand why Old French permitted V3 and V4 order, which were very common in the early stages of the language.

Second, in reaction to Labelle's (2007) recent claim according to which embedded V2 examples in Early Old French (twelfth century and before) did not result from Stylistic Fronting in contrast to Late Old French (thirteenth century), I give arguments in favor of the view that inversion in Old French embedded clauses was always a case of Stylistic Fronting (i.e. in both the early and the late period). Occupying a special topic position, Stylistically fronted elements were extremely common, but never obligatory, a property which sets this construction apart from V2.

The paper is organized as follows. Section 2 discusses the V2 status of Old French and introduces examples of Stylistic Fronting. Section 3 argues against Labelle's (2007) claim that embedded clauses in Early Old French did not involve Stylistic Fronting. I make a case instead for the idea that Stylistic Fronting was productive in Early Old French and that because it was never obligatory, inversion in embedded clauses in that period was not generalized V2. Section 4 reviews the advantages of a Stylistic topic position. In particular, I predict and explain V3 and V4 orders in Old French. Section 5 introduces examples of Left Dislocated and Hanging Topics in Old French. These, it seems, appeared much earlier than traditionally thought. I conclude that there are at least four topic positions in the preverbal area and that the left periphery of the clause in Old French is more complex than previously believed.

17.2 V2 and Embedded Clauses

There is a long linguistic tradition that views Old French as a V2 language (Foulet 1928; Adams 1987a; Dupuis 1989; Roberts 1993; Vance 1997), and more specifically as an asymmetric V2 language: V2 is claimed to be possible in main clauses (1a), but not in embedded clauses (1b) (* indicates "not possible")[1]:

(1) a. Einsi demora   Perceval tout le   jor en la   roche
       thus remain.PAST.3SG Perceval all the day on the rock
       'Thus Perceval stayed all day on the rock.'
       (*La Queste de Saint Graal*, year ~1220, p. 111)
    b. *Je cuit que einsi demora Perceval tout le jor en la roche
       Literally: 'I think that thus stayed Perceval all the day on the rock.'

I follow the traditional generative analysis of V2 languages according to which the verb appears in C while an XP sits in Spec-CP. The XP in Spec-TP is either a topic or a focus and the XP movement operation is compulsory, although, of course, the element in Spec-CP varies. It can be an argumental NP or an adjunct, depending on what receives topic or focus status in the sentence. In embedded clauses, V2 is not possible because a complementizer occupies the C position. There are, however, languages that have been argued to be symmetric V2 languages because V2 applies in all kinds of clauses (main and embedded).

A case in point is Old French. There appear to be cases where inversion is possible in embedded contexts after all, which has led some researchers (e.g. Lemieux and Dupuis 1995; Sitaridou 2004) to argue that Old French was, in fact, a symmetric V2 language. In particular, Adams (1987a, b) shows that V2 is possible in the complements of bridge verbs. Since there is a connection between V2 and null subjects (Hirschbühler 1989), it is predicted that null subjects will be possible in such environments, and it is exactly what we find (see also Arteaga 2009). (2a) and (2b) are given as illustration. The null subject is represented by a gap __.[2]

(2) a. Or   voi   ge   bien, plains __   es   de   mautalant
       now see.1SG   I   well   full   be.2SG of   bad-intentions
       'And now I see clearly that you are full of bad intentions.'
       (*Le Charroi de Nîmes*, twelfth century, 295 in Cardinaletti and Roberts 1991/2002:128)
    b. Je   cuit   plus   sot   de   ti   n'__ i   a
       I   think.1SG   more   stupid   than you   not-there   have.3SG
       'I think that there is no one more stupid than you.'
       (*Le Jeu de la Feuillée*, year 1276, 341, in Adams 1987b:17)

However, it has been noticed that the class of bridge verbs in question is comparable to the class which, in V2 Germanic languages, typically allows complements with matrix properties. A case in point is German, as shown by (3).

(3) Er   glaubt   diesen Film   haben   die   Kinder   gesehen
    he   think.3SG   this   movie   have.3PL   the   children   seen
    'He thinks that the children have seen this movie.' (Vikner 1995:66–67)

As argued by Cardinaletti and Roberts (1991/2000) and Roberts and Roussou (2002), since the complementizer *que* is not present in the kind of examples illustrated in (3), these must be cases of German-style embedded V2. I thus assume that embedded sentences in examples like (2) are in fact root clauses, since the complements of bridge verbs can have root properties independently of V2. The examples in (3) are thus taken care of.

There are nevertheless a residual few examples of bridge verbs taking embedded clauses beginning with a conjunction in which V2 word order is also found. In (4a), the adverb *bien* 'well' has been inverted with the verb *soient* 'be'. In (4b) the PP *de legier* 'of light' has been inverted with the verb *antre* 'enter' (*n'i* 'not there' is a clitic complex, which does not enter in the V2 calculus). Following Vance (1997), I take these clauses to have the structure of main clauses, with CP recursion [$_{CP}$ ... [$_{CP}$ ...]].[3] In these cases, we have an overt subject (which appears in bold).

(4) a. et   dit   que   bien   soient   **il**   venu
        and   say.3SG   that   well   be-SUBJ   they   come
        'and he/she says that they are welcome.' (Vance 1997:144, ex. 18)
   b. ... que   de   legier n'i   antre   **an**   pas ,
      ... because of   light   not-there   enter   one   FORC
        'because one does not enter it easily.'
        (*Le Chevalier à la Charrette*, year ~1180, 654)

Importantly, these examples are very rare: embedded clauses are almost always SVO in the unmarked case (I am abstracting away from the OV parameter in German). (4a–b) are thus exceptional; they are the only type of embedded clauses where postverbal pronominal subjects are found.

Remaining cases of V2 in embedded clauses appear, at least at first, to be more problematic because they are, in fact, very common. In addition, this type of example is not found in Modern German. In (5a) the PP *an mes dras* 'in my sheet' has been fronted before the verb *regart* 'see'. In (5b) the adjective *nues* 'bare' has been fronted before the verb *tienent* 'hold. In both cases we have a null subject, which is how (5a–b) differ from (4a–b). While it is rare to have inversion in embedded clauses when a full subject is present, it is very common for inversion to be triggered when the subject is null. The gap indicates the position of the subject (i.e. Spec-TP).

(5) a. Ce   sanc   que   an   mes   dras   __   regart
        that   blood   that   in   my   sheet   see.1SG
        'That blood that I see in my sheets.'
        (*Le Chevalier à la Charrette,* year ~1180, 4800)
   b. As   espees   que   nues   __   tienent
       their   swords   that   bare   hold.3PL
        'Their swords that they hold bare in their hands.'
        (*Le Chevalier à la Charrette*, year ~1180, 5025)

Mathieu (2006) notes that this type of inversion is possible only if the subject is not overt. Following earlier suggestions made by Dupuis (1989), Cardinaletti and Roberts (1991/2002) and Roberts (1993), he argues that this type of inversion is very similar to Stylistic Fronting, an operation where an XP or a head can be shifted into a position that precedes the finite verb, provided that Spec-TP (the canonical subject position) is not occupied by an overt subject DP. Mathieu (2006) concludes that Old French had Stylistic Fronting as part of its grammar and thus that Old French cases of inversion in embedded clauses are not instances of V2, but are instead examples of Stylistic Fronting.

In order to illustrate further what Stylistic Fronting is, I will provide a few additional examples. Beginning with relative subject clauses (the ideal context for Stylistic Fronting since it always involves a subject gap), (6a) shows Stylistic Fronting of an intensifier (*mout* 'very'), (6b) an adverb *autrement* 'otherwise' and (6c) an adjective (*perilleuse* 'perilous'). The trace indicates movement while the gap indicates the subject position (which I assume to be Spec-TP).[4] In contrast with V2 contexts, the verb remains in T (it does not move to C).

(6) a. Cardonnereuls et pinçons
    goldfinches and chaffinches
    Qui mout$_i$ __ cantent t$_i$ joliement
    That very   sing.3PL   beautifully
    'Goldfinches and chaffinches that sing very beautifully.'
    (*Li Gieus de Robin et de Marion*, year 1275, 30)
  b. Car cil qui autrement$_i$ __ assamblent t$_i$,
    for those who otherwise gather.3PL
    de Nostre Signor se dessamblent
    of Our Lord self distance.3PL
    'For he who gathers differently, distances himself from God.'
    (*Le Roman de Mahomet*, year 1258, 908)
  c. Bien ot les cos de la bataille,
    well have.PAST.3SG the causes of the battle
    Qui perilleuse$_i$ __ est t$_i$ et vilainne,
    that perilous be.3SG and ugly.'
    'Going into battle was justified, a battle which was perilous and ugly.'
    (*Yvain, le chevalier au lion*, year 1179, 5608–5609)

In (7), extraction of PPs is illustrated. *De tiules* 'of tiles' has fronted in (7a) while *avec le reine* 'with the Queen' has raised in (7b). Stylistic Fronting of PPs is very common; of the dozens found, only a few examples are given:

(7) a. S'ont trovee la sale overte
    self-have.3PL found the room open
    Qui [de tiules]$_i$ __ estoit coverte t$_i$
    that of tiles be.PAST.3SG covered
    'They found the room open whose roof was covered with tiles.'
    (*Le Chevalier à la Charrette*, year ~1180, 991–992)
  b. Quant les dames et les damoiselles
    when the ladies and the young-girls
    qui [avec le reine]$_i$ __ estoient assises t$_i$
    who with the queen be.PAST.3PL sat
    'When the ladies and the young girls who sat with the queen.'
    (*La Queste del Saint Graal*, year ~1220, 17, p. 18)

The following two examples illustrate Stylistic Fronting in object relatives. In (8a), which is (5a) above, a PP *an mes dras* 'in my sheets' has been Stylistically Fronted while in (8b), which is (5b) above, it is a past participle *nues* 'bare' that undergoes the Stylistic Fronting operation.

(8) a. Ce   sanc que [an   mes   dras]$_i$ __   regart t$_i$
       that   blood that   in   my   sheets   see.1SG
       'That blood that I see in my sheets.'
       (*Le Chevalier à la Charrette*, year ~1180, 4800)
    b. As   espees que nues$_i$ __   tienent   t$_i$
       their   swords that bare   hold.3PL
       'Their swords that they hold bare in their hands.'
       (*Le Chevalier à la Charrette*, year ~1180, 5025)

Mathieu (2006) notes that two elements can undergo Stylistic Fronting in Old French at the same time. In (9a) both a PP *avoec lui* 'with him' and an infinitival verb *aler* 'to go' front to the left periphery. In (9b), both a DP *l'anel* 'the ring' and a past participle *doné* 'given' undergo Stylistic Fronting.

(9) a. Se   lieve   sus,   et   cil   le   voient
       self   get-up.3SG quickly   and   those him   see.3PL
       Qui [avoec lui]$_j$ aler$_i$ __   devoient   t$_i$ t$_j$;
       who   with   him   go.INF   must.PAST.3PL
       'He gets up quickly and they, who should have gone with him, see him.'
       (*Le Chevalier à la Charrette*, year ~1180, 2203–2205)
    b. Cele   dame une   fee   estoit
       that   lady a   fairy be.PAST.3SG
       Qui   [l'anel]$_j$ doné$_i$ __   li   avoit   t$_i$ t$_j$,
       who   the-ring   given   to-him   have.PAST.3SG
       'That woman was a fairy who had given him the ring.'
       (*Le Chevalier à la Charrette*, year ~1180, 2357–2358)

Mathieu (2006) argues that Old French Stylistically Fronted elements raise to a dedicated position at the left periphery of the clause. That position is a topic phrase with one specifier and a head. This category was labeled Top+ to differentiate it from the Topic position associated with the kind of topicalization found in German (i.e. Germanic Topicalization). The structure in 0 is the representation for embedded clauses. Complementizers sit in Force^0, Stylistically Fronted XPs surface in Spec-Topic+^{0} (10a) while Stylistically Fronted heads appear in Top+^{0} (10b). The main (inflected) verb remains in T^0 (and never raises to Force^0, since that position is occupied by a complementizer). The subject position Spec-TP must be empty for XPs to raise to Spec-Top+^{0}. The account predicts that both an XP and a head can raise to the special topic position. This is when double Stylistic Fronting occurs (cf. 10c).

(10) [$_{ForceP}$ Spec Force^0 [$_{Top+P}$ Spec   Top+^{0} [$_{TP}$ Spec T^0]]]
       a.   que   an mes dras   regart   (cf. 8a)
       b.   que   nues   tiennent   (cf. 8b)
       c.   qui   avoec lui   aler   devoient   (cf. 9a)

In contrast with Holmberg's (2000) original proposal for Stylistic Fronting in Icelandic, Mathieu (2006) assumes that Stylistically Fronted elements do not move to the specifier of TP, but only *through* that position. The idea that Stylistically Fronted elements move to the specifier of TP is problematic for heads. Holmberg (2000) allows raising of heads to that position despite the fact that this is not normally an operation that is permissible in Universal Grammar. In Mathieu's account, only Stylistically Fronted XPs need to raise to Spec-TP; Stylistically Fronted heads can move directly to Top+^{0}.

In main clauses, the verb raises to Fin^0 while a topicalized or focalized XP raises to Spec-Top (cf. Labelle and Hirschbühler 2005). Consider the representation in (11).

(11) [$_{TopP}$ Spec Top^0 [$_{FinP}$ Spec Fin^0 [$_{TP}$ Spec T^0]]]

      Or   voi   ge   ~~voi~~   bien   (cf. 2a)

As we will see in Sect. 4, nothing prevents the Stylistic Fronting category from being projected in main clauses as well. This will explain the possibility of V3 and V4 orders in Old French which are otherwise problematic in the traditional view that the Old French left periphery consists merely of a CP category with only one specifier and only one head position. Note that Labelle and Hirschbühler's (2005) idea that the Old French CP is split between TopP and FinP, it makes it is possible a priori to explain V3 and perhaps even V4 orders, since the Fin projection makes an additional specifier available. However, I want to argue that topics raise to special topic positions. The specifier of FinP is not a topic position and the default hypothesis is that no topic raises to that position. Fin has to do with modality (e.g. choice of complementizer) and looks inward to the clause rather than outward as topic and focus do (see Rizzi 1997).[5] In fact, under minimalist assumptions we can simply claim that, since it is not needed, the specifier of FinP is not projected in this instance.

To conclude Sect. 2, we have seen that there is no reason to consider Old French a generalized or symmetric V2 language.[6] Inversion in Old French embedded clauses is generally not possible when a subject is present. In order for inversion to take place in embedded contexts, the subject position must be phonologically empty. Such cases are instances of the Stylistic operation rather than Germanic Topicalization.[7]

17.3 Stylistic Fronting: Early Old French Versus Late Old French

In recent work, Labelle (2007) makes a distinction between Early Old French and Late Old French, arguing that while inversion in embedded clauses was truly Stylistic Fronting in Late Old French, this was not the case in Early Old French. She claims that Early Old French involves V2 in embedded clauses because it is very common. In particular, Labelle (2007:304) argues that 'If one sees Stylistic Fronting simply as a means of filling a preverbal position not already filled by a subject, it is unclear under what criteria it can be distinguished from V2 (where the preverbal constituent is either a subject or some other element).' The idea is that since inversion of the Germanic type is often accompanied by null subjects in Old French (V2 is a prerequisite for the licensing of null subjects in Old French, cf. Adams 1987a; Hirschbühler 1989) and since null subjects are not uncommon in embedded clauses in the early French period, it is therefore difficult to distinguish Stylistic Fronting from Germanic Topicalization.

However, in my view, there are significant differences between the two constructions. Since Mathieu (2006) makes no distinction between Early Old French and Late Old French, it is important to address Labelle's (2007) claim. The crucial difference between Stylistic Fronting and Germanic inversion is that the first type of operation is always optional while the second type is always obligatory. For the period that Labelle describes (1100–1150), she concludes that inversion in Early Old French embedded clauses was not Stylistic Fronting, despite apparent counterexamples. Because of these, she is forced to admit that Early Old French is atypical from the point of view of the generalized V2 languages discussed in the literature, e.g. Yiddish (Santorini 1995), in that there was in fact never any requirement in Old French that the embedded clause be V2 (in fact, one wonders whether Yiddish, Faroese and Icelandic are really generalized V2 languages – see footnote 4 – but this question is beyond the scope of the present paper).[8]

Labelle (2007) claims that in Early Old French, embedded V2 appears to be freely available in all types of embedded clauses, meaning that V2 is obligatory in both main and embedded clauses. In her view, Early Old French is not a symmetric V2 language (as claimed by Lemieux and Dupuis 1995 and Sitaridou 2004) in that main clauses involve a layered CP with movement of the verb to Fin and inverted elements in the specifier of a discourse projection (as in the traditional V2 account). In embedded clauses, V2 is derived by the verb in T with the pronominal subject or clause initial constituent under the specifier of the highest inflectional head (bearing a [D] feature) and a scrambled constituent within an FP projection. Despite these differences, however, she argues that V2 is nevertheless generalized: V2 order applies to both main and embedded clauses. V2 order in main clauses is CP-related but V2 order in embedded clauses is IP-related (see footnote 6). This means that for Labelle, inversion in embedded clauses is not Stylistic fronting.

However, Labelle's (2007) hypothesis cannot be correct because inversion in Old French embedded clauses is not obligatory. Labelle herself provides a few examples reproduced here as (12) that illustrate that Stylistical Fronting does not have to occur.

(12) a. U   que   __   trove   **tes**   **chevalers**,   sis   prent,
       where   that   finds   your   knights,   si   take
       'wherever he finds your knights, he takes them'
       (*La Chanson de Guillaume*, year ~1140, 966)
   b. Puis   qu'out   **ço**   dist,   plus   n'i   targe;
       after   that-had   this   said,   no-more   neg-there-stay
       'having said this, he didn't stay any longer'
       (*Le voyage de Saint Brandan*, year ~1120, 519)
   c. Puis   vunt   ferir   des   espees   qu' __ unt   **ceintes**.
       Then   go   battle   of-the swords   that   have   girded
       'then they go to battle with the swords that they have girded'
       (*La chanson de Roland*, year 1100, 3598, p. 252)
   d. E   ne   sevent   qu'   __   est   **devenuz** /
       and   neg   know-3p   what   is   become
       Ne   en   quel   leu   est   detenuz
       nor   in   which   place   is   held
       'and they don't know what has become of him nor in which place he is
       held captive' (*Le voyage de Saint Brandan*, year ~1120, 1495–1496)

In the above sentences, I have once again added the position of the empty subject by using a gap __. This helps situate the verb and highlight the potential element to undergo fronting (marked in bold). Crucially, in these cases, nothing is fronted. In situ examples like those, where Stylistic Fronting *could*, but has *not* applied, are numerous, and I agree with Labelle (2007) that they are problematic for a Holmberg type of analysis, since on his account the subject position *must* be filled by overt phonological material. This non-obligatory nature of Stylistic Fronting continues in Later Old French as the following examples illustrate:

(13) a. L'amor   que   __   vos   ai   **demandee**.
       the-love   that   you   have   asked
       'The love that I asked (from) you.'
       (*Le Chevalier à la Charrette*, year ~1180, 5508)
   b. Oiez,   seignor   chevalier   de   la   Table   Reonde
       listen   Sir   knight   of   the   Round   Table
       qui __   avez   **[juree] [la   Queste del   Saint   Graal]**
       who   have.2PL   sworn the   Quest of-the Sain   Graal
       'Listen, Knight of the Round Table who has sworn in the Quest of the Graal.'
       (*La Queste del Saint Graal*, year ~1220, 12–14, p. 19)

It is worth noting that Labelle also fails to recognize the importance of an empty subject in the possibility of Stylistic Fronting. Inversion in embedded clauses in the period that she describes is possible generally only if an empty subject is available in the embedded clause. For example, in (13a), the subject pronoun *je* 'I' is not expressed. Inversion of the Germanic type is not tied to empty subjects and if Early Old French were truly a generalized V2 language, then we would expect inversion to occur even with overt subjects. Although there are a few cases where this appears to be possible (cf. 4a–b), these are not, in my view, numerous enough for a generalized V2 analysis to be warranted.

Other examples with inversion in embedded clauses with full subjects can be analyzed as Stylistic Fronting cases. If the subject remains in its base position (assumed to be within the verbal domain), then it is possible for another element to raise to the subject position and then move to the specifier of Top+P. This is exactly the case in the following examples. In (14a) *le rois* 'the king' has remained in the verbal domain (a case of Free inversion, an operation quite common in Romance languages such as Spanish and Italian) freeing the canonical subject position Spec-TP. The PP *a eus* 'to them' has raised to the subject position. In (14b) *mon pere* 'my father' is the subject that has remained in the verbal domain freeing the higher subject position. The PP *a la vostre bonté* 'against your good will' has raised to that position:

(14) a. quant [_PP a   eus]   __   est   li   rois   venus, ...
         when   to   them   be.3SG   the   king   come, ...
         'When the king came to them, ...' (Dupuis 1989:148)
     b. s'[_PP a   la   vostre bonté] __   vousist   mon pere
         if- against the your good-will   want.PAST.3SG   my father
         prendre   garde
         take.INF   precaution
         'If against your good will my father wanted to take precautions.'
         (*Huon le Roi – Le Vair Palefroi*, in Adams 1987b:19)

These constructions are rare probably because they are marked: the subject has to remain internal to the predicate for the subject position to be free. This is due to a rule (i.e. Free inversion) not common at the time and which most likely involves detopicalization of the subject, a possibility that was new at that stage.

Let us now turn to Labelle's (2007) list of criteria that she uses to distinguish Stylistic Fronting from Germanic Topicalization. Although she notes that the two are difficult to distinguish, (see the discussion above) – an argument she makes for Early Old French in relation to the availability of empty subjects – she nevertheless clearly separates the two constructions for Late Old French. The criteria that she puts forward also help set Early Old French apart from Late Old French in relation to Stylistic Fronting. Some of the criteria that she uses are well-known in the literature (cf. Maling 1980/1990), but she ignores others, which means that her characterization of Stylistic Fronting is incomplete (Labelle 2007: 305).

(A) Stylistic Fronting is an exceptional construction in a language where embedded clauses are normally SVO. As a result of Stylistic Fronting, Spec-IP is filled, i.e. the verb remains in second position of the clause.

(B) Stylistic Fronting requires a subject gap. It occurs: (a) in subject relative clauses; (b) in embedded subject questions; (c) in impersonal sentences where the subject remains within *v*P (Fischer and Alexiadou 2001:117); (d) in stylistically

17 The Left-Periphery in Old French   337

marked constructions like extraposition where the subject is right-adjoined to
the clause.
(C) Stylistic Fronting involves mainly X^0 categories – negation, adverbs, predica-
tive adjectives, untensed verbs – (Jónsson 1991; Maling 1990:76), although
XP's are apparently not totally excluded (Holmberg 2000). Jónsson claims that
only heads are affected and that Stylistic Fronting of bare nouns is always very
marginal (1991:13).
(D) Stylistic Fronting is subject to an accessibility hierarchy: negation (& sentence
adverbs) > adjective > verb & particle. This hierarchy appears to stem from the
fact that Stylistic Fronting tends to affect the element closest to Spec-IP.
(E) Stylistic Fronting is clause-bound. By contrast, embedded V2 is not subject to
these constraints.[9]

With regard to (A), referring to Stylistic Fronting as exceptional is a bit odd,
because it is no more exceptional than, say, Left Dislocation. It appears that she puts
forth this hypothesis in order to situate inversion cases in Early Old French embedded clauses under the Germanic Topicalization umbrella, since inversion in such
contexts is so common in Early Old French. I want to argue that Old French seems
to allow Stylistic Fronting much more frequently than Old Scandinavian languages
or present day Icelandic, because, as argued by Roberts (1993), null subjects were
more freely available in Old French. Modern Icelandic, for example, tolerates null
subjects only in impersonal clauses. I do not think it is controversial to say that as
null subjects disappeared in Old French, the more restricted Stylistic Fronting
became ((B) follows from this).

With regard to (C), although it is true that the original literature on Stylistic
Fronting mainly described the operation as applying to heads, later works on the
topic described the possibility of Stylistically Fronting XPs as well (cf. Holmberg
2000, and especially Hrafnbjargarson 2003, 2004). The examples in (15) show that
a wide range of nominals (modified nouns, bare nouns) can undergo Stylistic
Fronting in Old French[10]:

(15) a. Cil   qui   [toute   rikeche]$_i$ __   avoit t_i.
        the-one   who   all   richness   have.PAST.3SG
        Pour homme   povres   devenoit.
        for man   poor   became.PAST.3SG
        'He who was rich became poor.' (*Le Roman de Mahomet*, year 1258, 892)
     b. Cuers   qui   [tel   compaignie]$_i$ __   pert t_i
        heart   that   such   company   lose.3SG
        Doit   bien   plourer   le   dessevrance.
        must.$_{3SG}$ well   cry.INF   his   separation
        'A heart that loses such company must be crying over his separation.'
        (*Le Roman de Mahomet*, year 1258, 96)
     c. cil   qui   compaignon$_i$ __   en   doivent   estre t_i
        those   who   comrade   of-it   must.3PL be.INF
        'Those who must be knight of it (of the Round Table).'
        (*La Queste del Saint Graal* 6, year ~1220, p. 18)

As we have already mentioned, Stylistic Fronting of DPs is not unique to Old French, but can also be found in Modern Icelandic. According to Falk (1993), Stylistic Fronting of DPs can be found in Old Swedish, and according to Barnes (1987), it also occurs in Faroese. Apparently, the possibility of Stylistic Fronting is more frequent in Icelandic if the DP is non-specific/abstract. If the DP is specific, the sentence is not fully grammatical (Holmberg 2004). As noted by Holmberg (2006) himself, this is an exception to his (2000) generalization that Stylistic Fronting has no semantic effect. The non-specific/abstract constraint does not seem to apply in Old French. For instance, in (15c) the DP that undergoes Stylistic Fronting, i.e. *compaignon*, is not abstract (*rikeche* 'richness' in (15a) and *compaignie* 'company' in (15b) might be argued to be abstract).[11]

With respect to (D) above, Labelle (2007), claims that inversion in the following examples cannot be cases of Stylistic Fronting, because the accessibility hierarchy would lead us to expect that the negative adverb *pas,* which is ranked high in her hierarchy, fronts in (16a), blocking the raising of the PP *a Gormund* 'to Gormund.' Moreover, in her view, in (16b) one would expect the infinitive *desfendre* 'defend' to raise instead of the PP complement of that infinitive:

(16) a. Huelin dist une novele [qui [a Gorm[un]d]$_i$ ne fut pas bele t$_i$]
Huelin said a piece-of-news [which to Gormund neg was not good]
'Huelin brought news which didn't please Gormund.'
(*Gormont et Isembart*, year ~1130, 239–240)
b. [Se [de ce]$_i$ vous volez desfendre t$_i$], alez en tost voz armes prendre
if of this you want defend-INF, go loc soon your weapons take
'if you want to defend yourself, go get your weapons now.'
(*Le Roman de Thèbes* 1, year ~1150, p. 96)

The second example is technically not problematic even if we do not postulate a special category like Top+, because, as shown by Holmberg, it is possible to skip one element for the Stylistic Fronting calculus provided that the two candidates for Stylistic Fronting are sisters. The example in (17) is Holmberg's (2000) implementation of Maling's (1980) Accessibility Hierarchy and his revised version Minimal Link Condition (Chomsky 1995).

(17) *Minimal Link Condition*
A feature F attracts the closest feature that can check F.
Closeness is defined in terms of c-command: in a configuration [α. ... β ... γ] where α c-commands β and γ, β is closer than γ to α, if β asymmetrically c-commands γ.

This allows a verb or a complement PP to undergo Stylistic Fronting as shown for Icelandic by (18a) and (18b) respectively, since they are sisters, and thus equally close to the target.

(18) a. Peir   sem   buið$_i$ __   hafa   t$_i$ í   Ósló   (Icelandic)
       those   that   lived   have.3PL   in   Oslo
    b. Peir sem [í Ósló]$_i$ __ hafa buið t$_i$
    'Those that have lived in Oslo.' (Holmberg 2000:464)

As for (16a), we know independently that it is possible to Stylistically front *pas* 'not' together with another element, as shown by (19). In this case, a DP *sa boche* 'his mouth' has raised, but so has the negative element *pas*, since under normal circumstances it appears after the verb (the verb has raised to T⁰). Since in embedded contexts only one specifier and one head position are available for fronting at the left periphery, I am assuming that *sa boche* 'his mouth' has raised to the specifier of Top+⁰ while *pas* 'not' has raised to the head position Top+⁰ (note that this makes negative reinforcers in Old French heads rather than XPs).

(19) Quant   la   pucele   le   salue,   Qui   [sa   boche]j   pas$_i$__
     when   the   young-girl   him   salute.$_{3SG}$ who   his   mouth   FORC
     n'en   palue   t$_i$ t$_j$ Ne   ne   li   a   neant   costé.
     not-EN   turn-white.$_{3SG}$ neither   not   to-him   have$_{.3SG}$ nothing   cost
    'The young girl's greeting which was not unpleasant did not cost him anything.'
    (*Le Chevalier à la Charrette*, year ~1180, 1570–1573)

To conclude Sect. 3, we have seen that there is no motivation for claiming that Early Old French was a generalized V2 language (Labelle 2007) or even a symmetric V2 language (Lemieux and Dupuis 1995; Sitaridou 2004). Inversion in main clauses in both Early Old French and Late Old French was of the Germanic Topicalization type, while inversion in embedded clauses was of the Stylistic Fronting type.

17.4 V3, V4

The introduction of a special topic position at the left periphery for Stylistic Fronted elements makes interesting predictions for Old French main clauses. For example, it predicts that V3 and V4 orders should be possible in such environments. This prediction is indeed borne out as we shall see in the present section.

On the grounds that Old French freely allowed V3 and V4 orders rather than strictly V2, Kaiser (2000) makes the claim that Old French was not a V2 language. This section will argue against this idea. Consider the following examples of matrix clauses that do not show V2 word order:

(20) a. [Aprés la biere]_PP [venir]_V voient —
behind the coffin come.INF see.3PL
Une rote, et devant venoit...
an escort and in-front-of come.PAST.3SG
'Behind the coffin they see an escort coming and in front of it came...'
(*Le Chevalier à la Charrette*, year ~1180, 560–561)
b. [Parmi le flanc]_PP [l'espié]_DP li mist —
among the side the-sword him put.PAST.3SG
'He put the sword through his side'
(*Gormont et Isembart*, year ~1130, 170)
c. [As pez le abét]_PP [mercit]_N atent —
at-the feet the priest forgiveness await.3SG
'At the feet of the priest, he is asking for forgiveness'
(*Le voyage de Saint-Brandan*, year ~1120, 338)

In (20a) the verb *voient* 'see.3PL' is in third position: a PP *après la biere* 'behind the coffin' and a verb *venir* 'come.INF' have been fronted. In (20b), the verb *mist* 'put' again appears in third position (the object pronoun *li* is a clitic and therefore does not enter into the V2 calculus, as it attaches to the verb forming one unit). A PP *par mi le flanc* 'through his side' and a DP *l'espié* 'the sword' have been fronted and appear side by side. In (20c), the verb *atent* also appears in third position: a PP *as pez le abet* 'at the feet of the priest' (a noun construct) and a noun *mercit* 'forgiveness' have been fronted.

Labelle (2007) also introduces many examples of matrix clauses in Old French in which the verb is not in second position. Some of her examples appear in (21).

(21) a. [Ma longe atente]_DP [a grant duel]_PP est venude
My long wait to great pain is come
'My long wait has ended in great pain.'
(*La Vie de Saint Alexis*, 11th c., LXXXIX, 443)
b. [Je]_DP qu'en diroie?
I what-of.it say.COND.1SG
'Me, what should I say about it?'
(*Le Roman de Thèbes* 1, year ~1150, p. 37)
c. [La bone enseine qu'il tint]_CP, /[de l'autre part]_PP en fit eissir
the good spear that-he held / on the-other side gen made come.out
'He made the good spear that he held come out on the other side (of his opponent).' (*Gormond et Isembart*, year ~1085, 171–172)

In (21a), the verb *est* 'is' is in third position: a DP *ma longe atente* 'my long wait' and a PP *a grant duel* 'to great pain' have been fronted. In (21b), a DP *je* 'I' has been fronted while the verb *diroie* 'say.COND.1SG' is not in second position, since an interrogative word *que* 'what' appears to the right of *je* 'I'. In (21c), a CP *la bone enseine qu'il tint* 'the good spear that he held' and a PP *de l'autre part* 'on the other side violate V2 order, as the verb *est* 'is' is in third position. (Some of Labelle's (2007) examples, e.g. 21c, are cases of Left Dislocation rather than Stylistic Fronting. We will come back to the distinction between the two kinds of fronting operations below).

Although not possible for Modern German, the presence of several XPs before the finite verb is not unusual for Old Germanic languages (Kiparsky 1995; Tomaselli 1995; Fuss 1998; Axel 2002). Indeed, in Old English and Old High German, the position of the finite verb was more variable than it is in modern V2 languages. Main and embedded clauses could be V1, V2, V3 and V-final. Two XPs could front before the finite verb. Axel (2002) attests this for Old High German. According to her analysis, V1 occurs frequently in Old High German prose documents (Old French also allows V1 freely), and so do XP XP sequences before a finite verb.

Therefore, Old French shares with Older Germanic V2 languages (and with Older Romance languages, e.g. Old Italian, cf. Benincá 2006) a richer left periphery than do Modern Germanic V2 languages, suggesting that it would be too premature to place Old French outside the group of languages with V2. Older Germanic V2 languages were V2 despite the fact that they allowed V3 and V4 orders. It is thus wrong to compare Old French V2 with Modern German V2 (as does Kaiser 2000 and many others recently, e.g. Sitaridou 2004; Elsig 2008, 2009).

I want to argue that V3 and V4 orders are possible in main clauses because the elements that appear just before the verb are Stylistically Fronted. As mentioned earlier, the fact that at least two elements can undergo Stylistic Fronting in Old French (an XP and a head, in that order) led Mathieu (2006) to propose that Stylistically Fronted elements in that language moved to a dedicated position at the left periphery of the clause with one specifier and a head. I called this category Top+to differentiate it from the Topic position associated with Germanic Topicalization (see (10)). Since there is no reason to assume that Top+P is unavailable in main clauses, this projection is added in the representation of main clauses in (11), giving us (22):

(22) [$_{TopP}$ Spec   Top^0 [$_{Top+P}$ Spec Top+^{0} [$_{FinP}$ Spec Fin^0 [$_{TP}$ Spec T^0]]]]
     Par mi le flanc   l'espié   li mist (cf. (18a))

The special topic position is sandwiched between the projection hosting Germanic Topicalized elements and FinP, which contains Fin^0 where the verbs sits. Note that this is similar to what is proposed by Labelle and Hirschbühler 2005, except that I add Top+P in between the Top position and the Fin position.

In embedded clauses, V3 orders are of course possible, since both a specifier and a head position are available (those of the Top+category). However, it is predicted that V4 orders will not be possible. Indeed, I have found no such examples in my corpus.

It must be noted that although Stylistically Fronted elements are topics, they are not topics in the traditional sense. The literature identifies two main kinds of topics: a topic can be a background element (already mentioned in the discourse or accommodated) or it is an element that indicates what the sentence is about. Stylistic Fronted elements have neither of these properties. In general, the sole reason why they seem to undergo raising is to make sure that the focused element in the clause is in final position (an operation akin to P-movement, cf. Zubizarreta 1998). This operation is common in verse because the element that is focused is also the element that rhymes with the final element appearing in the next verse. In other words, the Stylistic Fronting operation does not seem to have to do with truth-conditional semantics.

I believe that these "topics" should thus not be confused with Left Dislocated or Hanging Topics. The examples of Stylistic Fronting that I have introduced are strictly topics that are neither presupposed nor foregrounding. This does not mean, however, that Old French had no such topics. As already mentioned, some of the examples introduced by Labelle (2007) are cases of Left Dislocation, e.g. (21c). Typically, these introduce old information. That Old French also allowed Left Dislocated elements is clear not only for main clauses, but also for embedded clauses as in 0 shows. The difference between (23) and (8) above is that in (23) there is an overt subject, whereas in (8), there is none. I assume that in order to obtain Left Dislocation, a subject is needed, with a possible pause between the Left Dislocated element and the subject; no such pause should appear in Stylistic Fronting, an operation which systematically makes use of empty subject positions)[12]:

(23) … que par mon chief je vos ferrai
 that by my head I you make-FUT.1SG
 '… that by my head I shall strike you.' (*Le Chevalier à la Charrette*, year ~1180, 761)

This example contains an overt subject *je* 'I' and although there is no comma indicating we might be dealing with a Left Dislocated element, there is every reason to believe that this element is not a Stylistically Fronting element. First, the subject position is not phonologically empty. Second, *par mon chief* 'by my head' is an expression that emphasizes the speaker's attitude towards the comment made. It is clearly emphatic. In the next section, we turn to Left Dislocation and Hanging Topics and study their exact position in the sentence.

To summarize Sect. 4: I have shown that Stylistically Fronted elements in Old French were topics, albeit of a different kind than the traditional notion of topic. They appear at the left periphery of the clause in addition to more traditional topics, accounting for the fact that V3 and V4 orders were possible in the language. Old French (Early and Late) was an asymmetric V2 language not, despite the facts that apparent V2 orders were possible in embedded clauses (See Section 3), and a strict V2 order was not always found.

17.5 Left Dislocation and Hanging Topics

In the previous sections, we saw that Old French had two different positions for two different kinds of topics: one position (the traditional Topicalization position at the left periphery) for topics and focused elements, and another for non-presupposed topics (Stylistic Fronting). In this section, I turn to two other kinds of topics: Left Dislocation and Hanging Topics. Left Dislocation is often called Clitic Left Dislocation in the Romance languages, since it is possible only with a clitic that doubles the subject or object that has been topicalized. On the other hand, Hanging Topics are found in English: they appear without a clitic.

It is traditionally thought that, as a productive construction, the general displacement of an object to the left periphery of the clause surfaces quite late in the history of French: "P. Ruelle (1966) qui leur a consacré une étude, n'a même pas pu en rassembler une dizaine d'attestations avant le XIVe siècle. C'est en fait à partir du moyen français que ce tour va devenir moins rare [...]"[13] (Marchello-Nizia 1995:54) or "cette construction est très rare"[14] (Marchello-Nizia 1995:54). However, I want to show in this section that there exist more examples than have been traditionally believed. Indeed, both Left Dislocation and Hanging Topics are possible early in the history of Old French (see also Priestley 1950, 1955).

Starting with Left Dislocated elements, Labelle (2007:303) introduces a few examples from the Early Old French period. These examples are introduced in (24); they are both from the eleventh century.

(24) a. Icoste fole gent de Francei,/ mut par unt ili fole
 these mad people of France, very much have they unreasonable
 esperance
 hope
 'these mad people of France, they have a very unreasonable hope'
 (*Gormond et Isembart*, year ~1085, 78–80)
 b. Sed a mei soule vels une feiz parlasses,/
 if to me only want one time speak /
 Ta lasse medrei si lai reconfortasses.
 your poor mother thus her comfort
 'If you had spoken to me at least once/ you would have thus comforted your poor mother'. (*La Vie de Saint Alexis*, eleventh century, XC, 449)

Rouveret (2004:219) introduces the following examples from the twelfth century. I give many examples here in order to show that Left Dislocated elements/topics are not that rare in Early Old French.

(25) a. Li quens Rollant, il est mult irascut
 The king Rollant he is very angry
 (*La Chanson de Roland*, year 1100, 777)
 b. Li niés Marsilie, il est venuz avant
 the nephew Marsilie, he is come avant
 'Nephew Marsilie, he came.'
 (*La Chanson de Roland*, year 1100, 860)
 c. "le cumandement Deu jó l'oï, si l'ai furni..."
 the commandment God I it-heard, thus it-have provided
 'God's will, I heard it, and I have obeyed it.'
 (*Li Quatre Livres des Rois* 30, twelfth century, 20)
 d. Les batailles nostre Seignur, tu les meintienz é furnís ;
 the battles our Lord you them mantain and provide
 'Our Lord's battles, you maintain and obey them.'
 (*Li Quatre Livres des Rois*, twelfth century, 51, 28)
 e. "Cest chevalier, je ne l'aim pas."
 this knight, I NE him-like not
 'This knight, I don't like him.' (*Erec*, year 1170, 602)

Other authors have given examples of Left Dislocated topics in their studies of Old French discourse properties, some of which date back as early as *La Chanson de Roland*. Here is a representative sample (for details see the study from Priestley (1950, 1955) where it is shown that such examples occur early and in large numbers):

(26) a. Ses dras, il les ostad […].
 his clothes he them took-off
 'His clothes, he took off.'
 (*Livre des Reis*, 39,76, in Härmä 1990: 163)
 b. Les deuxiesmes, on les doit aussi ouyr,
 the second ones we they must also hear
 'The second ones, we must also hear.'
 (*Écrits politiques I* 456, 25, in Troberg 2004:138)
 c. [Cels qu'ils unt mort], ben les poet hom priser.
 [those that-they have killed] well they could one to-praise
 'Those that they killed, one could praise indeed.'
 (*La Chanson de Roland*, year 1100, 1683, in Priestley 1955:10)

In fact, Left Dislocation is not uncommon in *La Chanson de Roland* (year 1100). I have found additional examples which appear below:

(27) a. Reis Corsalis, il est de l'altre part:
 King Corsalis, he is from the-other part
 'King Corsablis is from the other part.' (*La Chanson de Roland*, year 1100, 885)
 b. Li nies Marsilie, il ad a num Aelroth;
 the nephew Marsilie he has as name Aelroth
 'Marsilie's nephew, his name is Aelroth.'
 (*La Chanson de Roland*, year 1100, 1188)
 c. E Berenger, il fiert Astramariz:
 and Berenger he strikes Astramariz
 'and Berenger, he strikes Astramariz.' (*La Chanson de Roland*, year 1100, 1304)

It is clear that we are dealing with a Left Dislocated kind of topic, since we have a comma after the topic, a typical written marking that corresponds to the introduction of a pause in discourse. With V2 and Stylistic Fronting no such pause is necessary (or in fact possible).

Some structures which appear to be left-dislocated are in fact Hanging Topics. Hanging Topics are topics which appear without a pronoun or a clitic, which is how they differ from Left Dislocated topics. What is interesting is that Hanging Topics also appear in Old French earlier than has been traditionally thought. Here is a collection of relevant examples, mostly from the twelfth century.

(28) a. [Vostre   terre]   qui   defandra ?
       your   land   who   will-defend
       'Who will defend your land?' (*Chanson de Lyon* 1617, in Arteaga 1997:2)
   b. [Cest   nostre rei],   por coi   lessas   cunfundre?
       this-one   our king   why   let   flounder
       'Why do you let our king flounder?'
       (*La Chanson de Roland*, year 1100, 1.2583, in Arteaga 1997:2)
   c. Et   ce   conseil   nous   vous   donnons.
       and this   counsel   we   to-you   give
       'And this counsel, we give you.'
       (*Chroniques XII*, 152, 16, in Adams 1987a:195)
   d. Un   grail   entre   ses ii.   mains / Une   dameisele tenoit...
       a   grail   between   her two   hands   a   demoiselle hold.PAST.3SG
       'A demoiselle was coming forward, holding a grail in her two hands.'
       (*Perceval ou le Conte del Graal*, year ~1181, 3208)
   e. « Les citez   que   mis peres   prist   sur le   tun,   jos te   rendrái;... »
        the cities   that my father   took   on the   yours I you give.back-FUT
       'The cities that my father took from you, I will give back.'
       (*Li Quatre Livres des Rois*, twelfth century, 164, 34)

All the examples above show that, like other Old Romance languages, Old French had a series of topics before the zone dedicated to Germanic style topicalization. The left periphery thus must have consisted of something akin to what has been proposed by Benincà and Poletto (2002) and Benincà (2006) for other languages as in (29).

(29) [Hang. Topic [Scene Sett. [DeclForce[Left disl. [List interpr [[Focus CP] [Wh-op CP]]
     |FRAME | |THEME | |FOCUS |

However, we must add one layer between the topics to the left and Focus CP, namely the one corresponding to Stylistic Fronting. As discussed in Sect. 4, Stylistically Fronted elements are topics, albeit of a special kind: they are neither what the sentence is about nor are they presupposed. They appear to undergo dislocation simply so that the focus of the sentence falls on the most embedded element (Zubizarreta 1998). This metric explains why Stylistic Fronting was so common in verse: the emphasis and main stress would fall on the last word in the verse. In this type of text, in order to target a certain word in the sentence, other material made way for the focused and rhymed element to appear in the position where main stress and rhyming surfaced. This type of process is typical is contemporary poetry.

The representation in (30) gives the skeleton of the clause at the left periphery for Old French.

(30) Hang. Topic/Left dislocation [$_{TopP}$ Spec Top^0 [$_{Top+P}$ Spec Top+^{0} [$_{FinP}$ Spec Fin^0 [$_{TP}$ Spec T^0]]]]

Four different kinds of topics are available: Hanging Topics, Left Dislocated elements, Germanic/V2 topicalized elements, Stylistically Fronted elements. This concludes Sect. 5.

17.6 Conclusion

In this paper, I have argued that the Old French CP should be split into several projections. In addition to the familiar FinP and TopicP that occupy the pre-verbal area in V2 languages, I have proposed that that the French CP should be further decomposed into a special topic position hosting Stylistically Fronted elements. The decomposition of the CP layer in Old French gives a rationale to the possibility of V3 and V4 order in the language, so that there is no need to claim that Old French was not a V2 language as Kaiser (2000), Sitaridou (2004) and Elsig (2008, 2009) have recently claimed. I have claimed that Stylistic Fronting was available throughout the Old French period (both the Early and the Late period), making Old French consistently a non-generalized V2 language (contra Labelle 2007). Finally, it was argued that the Old French CP consisted of two additional topic positions: one for Left Dislocated elements, the other for Hanging Topics. These topics were argued to have appeared much earlier than traditionally thought in the literature.

Notes

1. An asymmetric V2 language is one where V2 is possible only in main clauses; a symmetric V2 language is one where V2 is possible in both main and embedded clauses.
2. The reason why I use a gap rather than *pro* is that I believe that the postulation of *pro* has theoretical underpinnings that are best avoided. For example, if *pro* is considered to be a syntactic element (as is the case in traditional Government and Binding) then the subject position is technically not empty. However, as will become clear later in this paper, I do not want to assume that the subject position is filled by anything when the subject does not occupy the subject position. On the contrary, I will argue that Stylistic Fronting occurs precisely because there is nothing in the subject position. In addition, according to Minimalism, it is best not to postulate empty categories when it can be avoided (nothing can license empty categories anymore since the notion of Government has disappeared from the theoretical framework).
3. An alternative is to assume, following Roberts and Roussou (2002), that there is a higher complement projection which acts like an embedded clause (ForceP), and a lower one which acts like a main clause (FinP). This is similar to what has

been proposed by Vikner (1995) and Holmberg and Platzack (1995) with the difference that distinct feature specification is attributed to the relevant C heads. The complementizer in Force⁰ is in complementary distribution with verbs in first position.
4. Traditionally, subject clauses are claimed to contain a gap or a null operator. The null is base-generated in Spec-TP and then raises to Spec-CP. I use a gap instead of an empty operator since the latter has theoretical underpinnings. I therefore want nothing in the subject position (see footnote
5. According to Benincà (2001), topic is always higher (to the left of) focus and focus is higher than Fin. Therefore, the specifier of FinP can simply not count as a topic position.
6. By 'generalized V2' I mean V2 order in both main and embedded clauses, but not necessarily through the same process (e.g. CP-related V2 for main clauses versus IP-related V2 for embedded clauses, e.g. Labelle 2007) and by symmetric V2, I mean V2 order in both main and embedded clauses through the same process (e.g. CP-related V2 for both main and embedded clauses or IP-related V2 for both types of clauses).
7. It is in fact doubtful that languages such as Yiddish (Diesing 1990; Santorini 1995), Faroese and Icelandic (Rögnvaldsson and Thräinsson 1990; Sigurðsson 1990), which have been described as symmetric V2 languages, are really symmetric V2 languages, since these languages also appear to have Stylistic Fronting as part of their grammars. In particular, with respect to Icelandic, Maling (1980/1990) shows that embedded V2 clauses in that language result from an operation of Stylistic Fronting. Consequently, Icelandic is now often, if not always, described in the literature as an asymmetric V2 language.
8. It is not easy to find a truly uncontroversial symmetric V2 language. The reason behind this state of affairs might be because there is a general universal constraint against V2 in embedded clauses: it simply does not exist (see previous footnote).
9. Labelle (2007) does not really discuss criterion E. I will not discuss it either, since there are not many data that can be used to show the difference between Stylistic Fronting and V2 when it comes to extraction phenomena. This criterion is in fact not directly relevant to the discussion at hand.
10. I assume (uncontroversially) that subject relative clauses contain a null subject.
11. Interestingly, the restriction does not apply to Old and Middle Danish either, see Hrafnbjargarson (2004).
12. Modern French has not lost the ability for topics to appear in embedded contexts. Although this is not traditionally taken to be possible in English, such topics are possible in Modern French, (cf. de Cat 2007).
13. "P. Ruelle (1966) who has studied this construction could not even gather ten examples before the 14th century. It is in fact only from the Middle French period that this construction becomes less rare [...]" (my translation)
14. "this construction is very rare" (my translation)

References

Adams, Marianne. 1987a. Old French, null subjects, and verb second phenomena. Doctoral dissertation. University of California, Los Angeles.
Adams, Marianne. 1987b. From Old French to the theory of pro-drop. *Natural Language and Linguistic Theory* 5: 1–32.
Arteaga, Deborah. 1997. On null objects in old French. Paper presented at LSRL 27, University of California, Irvine.
Arteaga, Deborah. 2009. On the existence of null complementizers in old French. In *Romance linguistics: Structure, interfaces, and microparametric variation*, ed. Pascual Masullo, Erin O'Rourke, and Chia-Hui Huang. Amsterdam: John Benjamins.
Axel, Katrin. 2002. The syntactic integration of preposed adverbial clauses on the German Left periphery: A diachronic perspective. Manuscript, University of Göttingen.
Barnes, Michael. 1987. Some remarks on subordinate-clause word-order in faroese. *Scripta Islandica* 38: 3–35.
Belletti, Adriana (ed.). 2004. *Structures and beyond: The cartography of syntactic structures*, vol. 3. Oxford: Oxford University Press.
Benincà, Paola. 2001. The position of topic and focus in the left periphery. In *Current studies in Italian syntax. Essays offered to Lorenzo Renzi*, ed. Guglielmo Cinque and Giampaolo Salvi, 39–64. Amsterdam: Elsevier-North Holland.
Benincà, Paola. 2006. A detailed map of the left periphery in romance. In *Negation, tense, and clausal architecture: Crosslinguistic investigations*, ed. Raffaella Zanuttini, Héctor Campos, Elena Herberger, and Paul Portner, 53–86. Georgetown: Georgetown University.
Benincà, Paola, and Cecilia Poletto. 2002. Topic, focus and V2: Defining the CP sublayers. In *The structure of CP and IP. The cartography of syntactic structures*, vol. 2, ed. Luigi Rizzi, 52–75. Oxford: Oxford University Press.
Cardinaletti, Anna, and Ian Roberts. 1991/2002. Clause structure and X-second. Ms. University of Venice and University of Geneva. [Now printed in *Functional Structure in DP and IP: The Cartography of Syntactic Structures*, vol. 1, ed. Guglielmo Cinque, 123–166. Oxford: Oxford University Press].
Chomsky, Noam. 1995. *The minimalist program*. Cambridge, MA: MIT Press.
Cinque, Guglielmo (ed.). 2002. *Functional structure in DP and IP: The cartography of syntactic structures*, vol. 1. Oxford: Oxford University Press.
Cinque, Guglielmo (ed.). 2006. *Restructuring and functional heads: The cartography of syntactic structures*, vol. 4. Oxford: Oxford University Press.
De Cat, Cécile. 2007. French dislocation without movement. *Natural Language and Linguistic Theory* 25: 485–534.
Diesing, Molly. 1990. Verb movement and the subject position in Yiddish. *Natural Language and Linguistic Theory* 8: 41–79.
Dupuis, Fernande. 1989. L'Expression du Sujet dans les Subordonnées en Ancien Français. Doctoral dissertation, Université de Montréal.
Elsig, Martin. 2008. Verb second effects in old French: Evidence for a verb second grammar? Ms., Hamburg University.
Elsig, Martin. 2009. Verb second effects in old French: A result of contact-induced or language change? Talk presented at NWAV. October 24.
Falk, Cecilia. 1993. Non-referential subjects in the History of Swedish. Ph.D. dissertation, University of Lund.
Fischer, Susann, and Artemis Alexiadou. 2001. Stylistic fronting: Germanic vs. Romance. *Working Papers of Scandinavian Syntax* 68: 117–145.
Foulet, Lucien. 1928. *Petite Syntaxe de l'Ancien Français*. Paris: Éditions Champion.
Fuss, Eric. 1998. Zur Diachronie von Verbzweit: Die Entwicklung von Verbstellungs-varianten im Deutschen und Englischen. Master thesis, Johann Wolfgang Goethe-Universität, Frankfurt (am Main).

Härmä, Juhani. 1990. Les Constructions Disloquées en Ancien Français: Problèmes de Définition et de Délimitation. In *L'Anaphore et ses Domaines. Recherches Linguistiques XIV*, eds. Georges Kleiber and Jean-Emmanuel Tyvaert, 159–182. Metz: Centre d'Analyse Syntaxique, Université de Metz.

Hirschbühler, Paul. 1989. On the existence of null subjects in embedded clauses in old and middle French. In *Studies in Romance Linguistics*, ed. Carl Kirschner and Janet De Cesaris, 155–175. Amsterdam: John Benjamins.

Holmberg, Anders. 2000. Scandinavian stylistic fronting: How any category can become an expletive. *Linguistic Inquiry* 31: 445–483.

Holmberg, Anders. 2006. Stylistic fronting. In *The syntax companion (SynCom)*, ed. Martin Everaert and Henk van Riemsdijk. Oxford: Blackwell.

Holmberg, Anders, and Christer Platzack. 1995. *The role of inflection in Scandinavian syntax.* Oxford: Oxford University Press.

Hrafnbjargarson, Gunnar Hrafn. 2003. On stylistic fronting once more. *Working Papers in Scandinavian Syntax* 72: 153–205.

Hrafnbjargarson, Gunnar Hrafn. 2004. Stylistic fronting. *Studia Linguistica* 58: 88–134.

Jónsson, Jóhannes G. 1991. Stylistic fronting in Icelandic. *Working Papers in Scandinavian Syntax* 48: 1–43.

Kaiser, Georg. 2000. Dialect contact as a prerequisite of parametric change: A case study on French Word Order Change. In *Arbeiten zur Mehrsprachigkeit* – Folge B, Nr. Sonderforschungsbereich 538, Universität Hamburg.

Kiparsky, Paul. 1995. Indo-European origins of Germanic syntax. In *Clause structure and language change*, ed. Adrian Battye and Ian Roberts, 80–109. Oxford: Oxford University Press.

Labelle, Marie. 2007. Clausal architecture in early Old French. *Lingua* 117: 289–316.

Labelle, Marie, and Paul Hirschbühler. 2005. Changes in clausal organization and the position of clitics in Old French. In *Grammaticalization and parametric change*, ed. Montse Batllori and Francesc Roca, 60–71. Oxford: Oxford University Press.

Lemieux, Monique, and Fernande Dupuis. 1995. The locus of verb movement in non-asymmetric verb second languages: The case of middle French. In *Clause structure and language change*, ed. Andrew Battye and Ian Roberts, 80–109. Oxford: Oxford University Press.

Maling, Joan. 1980. Inversion in embedded clauses in modern Icelandic. *Íslenskt mál* 2: 175–193. [Reprinted in *Syntax and Semantics 24: Modern Icelandic Syntax*, ed. Joan Maling and Annie Zaenen, 71–91. San Diego, CA: Academic Press. 1990]

Marchello-Nizia, Christiane. 1995. *L'Évolution du Français: Ordre des Mots, Démonstratifs, Accent Tonique*. Paris: Armand Colin.

Mathieu, Eric. 2006. Stylistic fronting in Old French. *Probus* 18: 219–266.

Priestley, Leonard. 1950. Reprise constructions in the «Song of Roland». *Archivum Linguisticum* 2: 144–157.

Priestley, Leonard. 1955. Reprise constructions in French. *Archivum Linguisticum* 7: 1–28.

Rizzi, Luigi. 1997. The fine structure of the left periphery. In *Elements of grammar*, ed. Liliane Haegeman, 281–337. Dordrecht: Kluwer.

Rizzi, Luigi (ed.). 2004. *The structure of CP and IP: The cartography of syntactic structures*, vol. 2. Oxford: Oxford University Press.

Roberts, Ian. 1993. *Verbs and diachronic syntax. A comparative history of English and French.* Dordrecht: Kluwer.

Roberts, Ian, and Anna Roussou. 2002. The extended projection principle as a condition on the tense dependency. In *Subjects, expletives and the EPP*, ed. Peter Svenonius, 125–155. Oxford: Oxford University Press.

Rögnvaldsson, Eiríkur, and Höskuldur Thráinsson. 1990. On Icelandic word order once more. In *Modern Icelandic syntax*, ed. Joan Maling and Annie Zaenen, 3–40. San Diego: Academic.

Rouveret, Alain. 2004. Les Clitiques Pronominaux et la Périphérie Gauche en Ancien Français, *Bulletin de la Société de linguistique de Paris*, t. XCIX, fasc. 1: 181–237.

Ruelle, Pierre. 1966. L'Ordre Complément Direct-sujet-verbe dans la Proposition Énonciative Indépendante. *Mélanges Grevisse*, 307–322. Gembloux, Duculot.

Santorini, Beatrice. 1995. Some similarities and differences between Icelandic and Yiddish. In *Verb movement*, ed. David Lightfoot and Norbert Hornstein, 87–106. Cambridge: Cambridge University Press.

Sitaridou, Ioanna. 2004. The Licensing of Null Subjects in Old French. Talk given at University of Ottawa, September 13.

Sigurðsson, Halldor. 1990. V1 declaratives and verb raising in Icelandic. In *Syntax and semantics 24: Modern Icelandic syntax*, ed. Joan Maling and Annie Zaenen, 41–69. New York: Academic.

Tomaselli, Alessandra. 1995. Cases of verb third in Old High German. In *Clause structure and language change*, ed. Adrian Battye and Ian Roberts, 80–109. Oxford: Oxford University Press.

Troberg, Michelle. 2004. Topic-comment resumptive pronouns in modern French and old and middle French. *Toronto Working Papers in Linguistics* 23: 133–156.

Vance, Barbara. 1997. *Syntactic change in medieval French*. Dordrecht: Kluwer.

Vikner, Sven. 1995. *Verb movement and expletive subjects in the Germanic languages*. Oxford: Oxford University Press.

Zubizarreta, Maria-Luisa. 1998. *Prosody, focus and word order*. Cambridge, MA: MIT Press.

Chapter 18
Grammatical Meaning and the Old French Subjunctive

Margaret E. Winters

18.1 Introduction

It is fair to say that certain grammatical constructions seem to attract a great deal of attention. Often complex, they are described and analyzed in a succession of theoretical frameworks, more usually synchronic than diachronic, and may even become the subject matter of pedagogical papers. This is certainly the case of the French subjunctive, which has been approached from many directions, both syntactic and semantic, with a literature as well on how to teach it to second language learners. Perhaps more than many constructions, it has stimulated much debate as to what – if anything – it means, as well as how to formulate any meaning attributed to it. What is largely missing in these many considerations of the subjunctive, however, is much discussion of earlier linguistic stages including Old French, as well as much consideration of how the mood may have changed over time. I will return to the subjunctive – both early and modern – below, but it is worth first considering more generally the role of meaning as applied more abstractly to grammar.

Articulating precise grammatical meaning is often a difficult task. There are several reasons for this state of affairs, not the least of which is the very basic question of whether or not grammatical constructions can indeed be assigned meaning.

The following abbreviations are used: ACC=accusative, COND=conditional, f=feminine, IND=indicative, INF=infinitive, n=neuter, NOM=nominative, OBJ=oblique, m=masculine, pl=plural, sg=singular, SUB=subjunctive

M.E. Winters (✉)
Office of the Provost, Wayne State University, Detroit, MI, USA
e-mail: mewinters@wayne.edu

This debate has given rise to intense periods of discussion, with the most famous debate referred to as a 'war' (cf. Harris 1993), the crux of which was the possibility of equating meaning with Chomskyan formal Deep Structure. Other versions of the debate continue today, although with less heated discussion (and virtually nothing that might be called warfare). The division can be at least roughly characterized as a split between those who see structure as the basis for Language and those who look to meaning. For this paper, given that establishing further the details of the debate and motivating a personal stance would take us far afield, I simply follow Langacker (1987:2) in stating that many – if not all – constructions arise, flourish, and eventually evolve from stage to stage as symbolic of meaning.[1]

The difficulty of the task does not vanish as a result of coming down on the side of semantic analyses of grammar. If anything, more questions arise, some on the nature of meaning and some methodological. To begin, should grammatical meaning be treated like lexical meaning? Can one, for example, argue for primitives here as one can for lexical items (cf. Wierzbicka 1988 on the semantics of grammar)? Should grammatical meaning rather be treated as entirely – or mostly – different? Finally, how do we deal with polysemy within a construction? This last question is of particular interest when it comes to characterizations of the French construction at question here since at any time in its history the subjunctive is used in a wide variety of contexts. Although the range of contexts is somewhat narrower in Modern French, more complications arise from the fact that some uses appear in all registers, some are restricted to formal speech, and some only in writing. It is not the claim here that variation in register is a modern phenomenon, but rather that relatively direct knowledge of the data (as opposed to conclusions drawn from textual analysis via rare clues or by extrapolation backwards in time) is much easier to acquire with contemporary speakers. Although it has rarely if ever been stated quite this way to my knowledge, the many attempts at assigning meaning to the subjunctive are based in general on the notion that the different uses and contexts in which it appears constitute different – though usually seen as somehow related – meanings. Many descriptions, are, however, still simply lists of uses of the mood arranged variously to convey the tacit understanding that these lists are indications of different (although probably related) meanings.

The purpose of this paper is to consider some of the most salient attempts to assign meaning to the subjunctive. It must be said that this particular exercise has been done many times (citations will follow below); however the point here is to introduce a diachronic point of view. The project of assigning meaning to grammatical constructions is valuable in itself, although the Modern French subjunctive has yet to be adequately and completely described in semantic terms. What is of further interest is to consider to what extent descriptions of the modern subjunctive may be valid for earlier stages of the language and, conversely, to what extent the relatively rare semantic descriptions of those earlier stages may shed light on the modern construction. The paper will be organized in the following way: after

---

[1] As a result of this stipulation, I shall not discuss theories of the subjunctive coming from formal grammar (for example, Progovac 1993) based on syntactic criteria rather than meaning.

this introduction, the first part will be a rather brief reminder of the range of subjunctive meanings which have not changed substantially between medieval and contemporary French. We will then focus on changes, looking in particular at uses which are no longer in play and those which have developed in recent relatively French. The next section will consider the theories of meaning (as opposed to lists of uses) which have been proposed for the modern mood, followed by a consideration of which among them might also apply to the Old French data and what modifications to those theories would then be called for. Finally, the paper will conclude with some more general comments on theories of grammatical meaning and their diachronic behavior.

18.2 French Subjunctive Data

18.2.1 *"Panchronic" Observations*

The uses of the subjunctive which have persisted from early French (and indeed many of them even further back in time, from Latin) will look very familiar. Most of the uses are those which are taught today in elementary and intermediate language courses and may have figured as well in early French textbooks for English-speakers (Kibbee 1991 is a study of such guides). A few examples will suffice here; they are meant to provide a sense of the range of uses which have been more or less constant and are not meant to be inclusive.

18.2.1.1 Independent Clauses

Independent uses were far more frequent in older French, but have not become totally unproductive in Modern French. In addition to such fixed forms as *Dieu vous bénisse* 'May God bless you,' *soit* 'so be it,' and the pragmatically rarer *vive le roi/la reine* 'long live the king/queen, are somewhat more productive constructions (1a, b).[2]

(1) a. Qu'il pleuve/neige (SUB),[3] il sort!
    Let it rain/snow, he goes out!
 b. Qu'il parte (SUB).
    Have him leave.

---

[2] Examples of contemporary subjunctive uses will be drawn from the secondary literature (here Soutet 2000) without further attribution unless such attribution is germane to the discussion.

[3] The following abbreviations are used in glossed texts: ACC=accusative, COND=conditional, f=feminine, IND=indicative, INF=infinitive, n=neuter, NOM=nominative, OBJ=oblique, m=masculine, pl=plural, sg=singular, SUB=subjunctive; with the exception of *oblique* (used in various traditions to designate globally all cases other than the nominative), the other terms are standard grammatical nomenclature and have not been defined.

One could argue that even here we are in the realm of fixed expressions in (1a), and the argument in favor of productivity cannot indeed be pushed too far, but there is somewhat more productivity here than in the truly fixed expressions above. The construction in (1b), an indirect order in the form of a causative, is still more productive. It is worth noting, however, that both (1a) and (1b) start with the conjunction *que*; we will return to this observation below.

In Old French the subjunctive in independent clauses is rather more frequent[4] and appears as often without *que* as with:

(2) a. Voillet   o nun,
 wants-3sg-SUB or not,
 tut   i   laisset   sun   tens[5]
 each.one-m-sg-NOM there leaves-3sg his-m-sg-OBL time-m-sg-OBL
 Whether he wants to or not, each gives up his life (*C Roland*, 1419)

b. Vilain,   dist   il,   tu   me
 peasant-m-sg-NOM said-3sg he-NOM you sg-NOM me-OB
 mesdiz,   mais   tu   aies   honte
 speak ill-2sg forever you-sg-NOM have-2sg-SUB shame-f-sg-OBL
 touz   diz.
 all-m-pl-OBL days-m-pl-OBL
 Peasant, he said, you speak ill to me forever may you be ashamed of it.
                                                    (*Male Honte* 2,41–42)

c. Douce   dame,
 sweet-f-sg-NOM   lady-f-sg-NOM
 pregne   vos   en pitiez!
 take-2sg-SUB   you-2pl-NOM of it pity-f-sg-OBL
 Sweet lady, take pity! (C. Muset *Chansons* VIII, ii)

We can compare the first two Old French examples to those in (1); first, (2a) corresponds to 1a. in that they are both concessive in power ('although it might rain or not', 'although one might wish it or not'). Both (1b) and (2b) have some degree of imperative power (in (1b). as an indirect order and in the Old French as a an expression of desire or hope). Finally (2c) illustrates a more direct request, a construction which appears in Old French in various contexts and not just in fixed expressions such as the modern type exemplified by *vive la France* as mentioned above.

---

[4] Examples from Old French are, as here, largely from Foulet (1967), Martineau (1994), and Dreer (2007). I have provided the Old French source on the same line as the Old French with a word by word gloss below specifying gender, number, and case (NOM = nominative, OBL = oblique/non-nominative) for nominals and person, number, and subjunctive mood for verbs; if tense and other moods (indicative, imperative) are clear from the translation, they has not been otherwise specified.

[5] I thank an anonymous reviewer for this example.

18.2.1.2 Dependent Clauses

In subordinate clauses, the uses of the subjunctive are even less changed from Old to Modern French. They express various modalities - cognitive and emotional – which a speaker might bring to an utterance; the labels used for (3)–(6) are meant to be as theory-neutral as possible and derive more from textbooks than from linguistic analyses.[6]

(3) Necessity
  a. Il faut que Paul parte (SUB).
     It is necessary that Paul leave.
  b. Carles comandet
     Charles-NOM commands-3sg
     que face sun service.
     that do-3sg-SUB his-m-sg-OBL service-m-sg-OBL
     Charles commands that he serve him.
(4) Doubt, including uncertainty of outcome
  a. Pierre doute que Paul soit (SUBJ) parti.
     Peter doubts that Paul has gone out.
  b. Souventez feiz a lui parlerent
     often-m-pl-OBL times-m-pl-OBL to him-m-sg-OBL spoke-3pl
     qu' une gentil dame esposast
     that a-f-sg-OBL noble-f-sg-OBL lady-f-sg-OBL marry-3sg-SUB
     e de cele se delivrast
     and of this (one)-f-sg-OBL himself m-sg-OBL be rid-3sg-SUB
     Often they said to him that he should marry a noble woman and be rid of this one.
     (Marie de France, *Fraisne*, 326–28)
(5) Volition
  a. Il veut que je parte (SUB).
     He wants me to leave (that I leave).
  b. car je vouldroie que je ne alasse jamés
     for I- NOM would like-1sg that I-NOM not go-1sg-SUB ever
     hors de nostre meson (*15 Joyes de Mariage* 176)
     out of our-f-sg-OBL house-f-sg-OBL
     since I would like never to go (that I never go) outside our house
(6) Emotion
  a. Nous regrettons qu'il parte (SUB).
     We're sorry that he is leaving.
  b. Molt criem que ne t' en perde (*St. Alexis*, 60)
     much fear-1sg that not you-sg-OBL for it lose-1sg-SUB
     I fear greatly that I might lose you.

---

[6] In the following examples, a. version is in Modern French and b. in Old French.

(7) Cognition
  a. Elle ne croit pas qu'il ait (SUB) raison
     She doesn't believe that he is right.
  b. Or ne quidiés   mais que j'   atendi
     now not think-2pl ever that I-NOM wait-1sg-SUB
     Now don't think ever that I would wait. (*Aucassin et Nicolette,* 14)

In each of these pairs the Old French and the Modern French constructions are quite similar, with each (roughly constructed) semantic category expressed by a verbal expression followed by *que* and a second clause containing a verb in the subjunctive. In addition to these similarities, many conjunctions as well have continued to serve as triggers of the subjunctive, semantically if not always with the same lexical item: *ainz que, ainçois que* 'before', *conment que, con que, que que* 'although', *mais que* 'provided that', *por ce que* 'so that', *por que* 'provided that', *quelque .. que* 'whatever', *sanz ce que* 'without', *tant que* 'until'.[7]

18.2.2 Changes in Usage Across Time

The above section provides a brief description of subjunctive uses which have persisted from Old to Modern French, allowing all along for a general semantic (as opposed to morphological) equivalence in respect to the triggers of this mood. The description does not contain any discussion of what changes have taken place within these very general categories of uses, in particular the extent to which subjunctive use varies with the indicative (along a wide number of continua including tense, on the one hand, and dialect and other sociolinguistic factors, on the other) and, increasingly over time, with the conditional. For the purposes of this study, it is sufficient to note in very general terms that the continuation of these modal functions is expressed – at least part of the time today – by subjunctive morphology. What follows, still in general fashion, are the most obvious changes in broad usage, first the larger group of modal uses in Old French which are no longer expressed by the subjunctive today, and then the rather smaller group of uses which now trigger this mood at least occasionally, but did not do so in the earliest French.

18.2.2.1 Losses from Old to Modern French

The range of expressions of mood using the subjunctive in Old French was much richer than the current range and indeed remained much richer through the French

---

[7] Of course not all conjunctions with *que* take the subjunctive (pace Foulet 1967 discussed below); there has never been a time, for example, when *parce que* 'because' triggered anything but the indicative.

of the Seventeenth Century (Wagner et Pichon 1962; Martineau 1994). This section will touch on four striking changes and then briefly discuss two other crucial ones. The first construction to be noted is the mood in contrary-to-fact hypotheticals, so-called conditional sentences.[8] In each case the language of a. is Old French with b. including the modern French equivalent as well as a translation into English:

(8) a. Se je   ne fusse   en   tel   prison,
       if I-NOM   not were-1sg-SUB in   such-m-sg-OBL prison-m-sg-OBL
       bien   achevaisse   cest   afere... (*Vair Palefroi* 612–13)
       well   complete-1sg-SUB this-m-sg-OBL matter-m-sg-OBL
    b. Si je n'étais (IND) pas en pareille prison
       je mettrais (COND) fin à cette affaire
       If I weren't in such a prison,
       I would put an end to this matter.

(9) a. Molt en   fusse   baus   et cointes
       much for it be-1sg-SUB noble-m-sg-NOM and valiant-m-sg-NOM
       se je   a li   parlé   eüsse
       if I-NOM to her-3-sg-OBL spoken had-1sg-SUB
       et les   granz   biens   aperceüsse
       and the-m-pl-OBL great-m-pl-OBL good-m-pl-OBL perceived-1sg-SUB
       de qoi   ele   a   grant   renommee (*Vair Palefroi*, 290–93)
       of which she-NOM has-3sg great-f-sg-OBL fame-f-sg-OBL
    b. J'aurais été (COND) noble et courageux
       si je lui avais parlé (IND)
       et je me serais aperçu (COND)
       pourquoi elle était bien connue.
       I would have been noble and valiant
       if I had spoken to her
       and I would have perceived
       why she was well known.

Both (8) and (9) illustrate the change in mood from earlier French to the present in contrary-to-fact hypothetical sentences. The Old French verbs in both clauses of the conditional sentence were in the subjunctive, either imperfect (*achevaisse* and *fusse* (8a); *aperceüsse* (9a)) or the pluperfect (*eüsse parlé* 8a); the alternating tenses of the subjunctive in the result were used with very subtle differences in their meaning. The Modern French sequences of imperfect and conditional or pluperfect and conditional perfect reflect, respectively, a present or past hypothetical.

---

[8] By the seventeenth century, the use of the subjunctive was an archaism, although it appeared:
  i. Et une main si habile eût sauvé (SUB) l'Etat, si l'Etat eût pu (SUB) être sauvé.
     And such a capable hand could have saved the State, if the State could have been saved.

Old French differs from the modern language as well in its choice of mood after verbs of cognition (most often statements of belief) in positive declarative (not interrogative) sentences. Here it contrasts with Modern French in that positive statements of belief are now stated in the indicative, with questions and negative beliefs in the subjunctive. The modern contrast is found in (10):

(10) a. Il croit que la fleur est (IND) jolie.
       He believes that the flower is pretty.
    b. Il ne croit pas que la fleur soit (SUB) jolie.
       He doesn't believe that the flower is pretty.
    c. Croit-il que la fleur soit (SUB) jolie?
       Does he believe that the flower is pretty?

In Old French, all three of these contexts are followed by the subjunctive; only the positive declarative is cited here since the other contexts have not changed in respect to the mood they govern.

(11) Je   cuidoie   que plus loiaus
     I-NOM used-to-think-1sg that more loyal-m-sg-NOM
     me   fussiez   se Dieus   me   conseut,
     me-OBL were-2pl-SUB if god-m-sg-NOM me -OBL counsel-3sg-
     que ne fu   Tristan   a Yseut.
     than not was-3sg Tristan-NOM to Yseut-OBL
     I thought that you were more loyal to me, may God help me,
     than Tristan was to Isolde. (*Chastelaine de Vergi* 758–60)

Two other constructions take the subjunctive in Old French where now they are found with the indicative. The first of these is in the context of indirect questions:

(12) a. Je   ne sai   que je   doie   dire
        I-NOM not know-1sg what I-NOM must-1sg-SUB say-INF
        Ne que   je   puisse   devenir.
        nor what I-NOM am able-1sg-SUB become-INF
                                         (*Chastelaine de Vergi,324–25*)
    b. Je ne sais ni ce que je dois (IND) dire
       ni ce que je peux (IND) devenir.
       I don't know what I must say
       nor what I may become.

The subjunctive also appears in Old French in comparative constructions:

(13) a. Je   vos   aim   plus que
        I-NOM you-pl-OBL love-1sg more than
        vos   ne faciés   mi
        you-2pl not do-2pl-SUB me-OBL (*Aucassin et Nicolette*, 14)
    b. Je vous aime plus que vous ne m'aimez (IND).
       I love you more than you (ever) love me.

18 Grammatical Meaning and the Old French Subjunctive 359

There is some variation, however, and the indicative is found in the same constructions in the Medieval period:

(14) Plus sui jolis
more am-1sg pretty-f-sg-NOM
de je n' avoie ainz esté,
than I-NOM not have-1sg-IND ever been
ce vos plevis
this-n-sg-NOM you-2-pl-OBL swear-1sg (C. Muset *Chansons*, II, 23–4)
I am prettier
than I have ever been, I swear to you

The same variation is still found in modern literary French:

(15) a. Madame de Rênal voulut travailler et tomba dans un profond sommeil; quand elle se réveilla, elle ne s'effraya pas autant qu'elle l'aurait dû (IND). Madame de Rênal wanted to work and fell into a deep sleep; when she woke up, she was not as afraid as she should have been.
  b. Elle aurait pu cependant contempler Mme Morani autant qu'elle l'eût voulu (SUB).
     She could however have contemplated Mme Morani as much as she might have wanted to.

Interestingly, the first of these examples in the indicative (both cited in Wagner and Pichon 1966:609), is nineteenth century and the second in the subjunctive is from the twentieth century.

Before turning to new subjunctive uses in Modern French, two structural remarks are pertinent. First, it should be remembered that Old French – and really most varieties until relatively recently – actively used four tenses of the subjunctive, the present and compound past, both in contemporary use, as well as the now mostly archaic imperfect and pluperfect. The result is a much more complex sequence of tenses based, roughly, on an absolute rather than a relative expression of temporality. Today the present subjunctive indicates that what is designated by the verb is contemporaneous or in the future in relationship to the time of the triggering expression while the compound past is used for a previous time:

(16) a. Je regrette/je regrettais qu'il parte (present SUB).
       I am/was sorry that he is/was/will be will be leaving.
  b. Je regrette/regrettais qu'il soit parti (past SUBJ).
     I am/was sorry that he left/had left.

In older French, the imperfect subjunctive was used more often for prior time after a present tense trigger and the pluperfect after a past trigger (example (11) repeated)[9]:

(17) a. Je   cuidoie   que   plus   loiaus
       I-NOM   used-to-think-1sg   that   more   loyal-m-sg-NOM
       me   fussiez   se Dieus   me   conseut,
       me-OBL were-2pl-SUB if god-m-sg-NOM me-OBL counsel-3sg-SUB
       que ne   fu   Tristan   a Yseut.
       than not was-3sg Tristan-NOM to Yseut-OBL (*Chastelaine de Vergi* 758–60)
       I thought that you were more loyal to me, may God help me, than Tristan was to Isolde.

   b. quida (perfect IND) qu' alkuns   les
      believed-3sg   that someone-m-sg-NOM   them-m-pl-OBL
      eüst   pris
      had-3sg-SUB taken
      en larrecin   e   iluec mis
      in theft-m-sg-OBL and there placed (Marie de France, *Fraisnes*, 185–86)
      he believed that someone had stolen them
      and (had) put them over there

Example (17a). is an instance of contemporaneous time in the past with the imperfect subjunctive functioning to indicate that the speaker's belief is apropos of the present loyalty of the person being contemplated. In the second one, the belief follows the time of the theft and hiding of what was stolen. While the imperfect and pluperfect subjunctive are recognizable today to an educated speaker of French (one who would attend a performance of a play by the seventeenth century dramatist, Racine, for example), it would be an exaggeration to say that they are still used orally or in casual writing and, as a consequence, can still be said to enter into a sequence of tenses. We will see below, however, some examples of the imperfect in literary texts of the nineteenth and twentieth century which would still be understandable.

The second structural remark which will complete this section is that older French allowed much more frequently for the co-indexing of the subject in the triggering clause and the subject in the subordinate, subjunctive clause. Modern French (see below for some nuances) much prefers an infinitival complement to the trigger:

---

[9] The distinction is blurred in sentences expressing comparisons (cf. (14) and (15) above).

(18) a. car je   vouldroie
        for I-NOM wanted-1sg
        que je   ne alasse   jamés hors   de nostre
        that 1-NOM not go-1sg-SUB ever outside of our-f-sg-NOM
        meson
        house-f-sg-NOM (*15 Joies de Mariage,* 11)
    b. car je voudrais ne jamais sortir (INF) de notre maison
        for I would like that I never go/never to go outside the house

Not all modern constructions, however, disallow coindexing of subjects; verbs expressing emotional states, for example, allow both constructions:

(19) a. Je regrette que je sois jamais sortie (SUB) avec eux.
    b. Je regrette d'être jamais sortie (INF) avec eux.
       I'm sorry I ever went out with them.

It has been argued (Ruwet 1984, taken up in Martineau 1994) that such contrasting pairs allow for the expression of distancing between the regret (in this case) and what causes it. Example (19a). under that reading contains a sense of action contemplated from some later perspective; the speaker is looking back at an earlier decision and expressing a more reasoned – and hence less emotional – reaction to it. The general situation, however, is that coindexed subjects with the subjunctive were far more frequent in Old French than they are today.

18.2.2.2 Extensions in Modern French

All of the above section concerns subjunctive uses which have disappeared or have, at the least, been relegated to literary or archaic registers. It is undeniable that there are many more constructions of this sort than ones which have expanded in use since Old French. There are, however, a few which should be considered. The first is the use of this mood after *espérer* 'to hope'[10]: This usage dates most generally from the nineteenth century and, as will be seen below, is still controversial.

(20) a. Si vous espérez que je me sois trompé (SUB), vous allez perdre des illusions.
       If you hope that I made a mistake, you are going to lose your illusions.
    b. Je n'espérais plus qu'elle vînt (SUB).
       I no longer was hoping that she would come/be coming.
    c. Il n'espère pas qu'il entendra (IND) de nouveau l'ordre mystérieux.
       He did not hope to hear again/that he would hear again the mysterious order.

---

[10] Examples in this series are drawn from http://www.etudes-litteraires.com/forum/sujet-7843-2.html and ultimately from handbooks including Grevisse *Le Bon Usage*.

Any use of the subjunctive after 'to hope' is considered suspect, if not entirely wrong, by many French speakers, specifically those who adhere to the prescriptive rule that *espérer* is to be followed by the future. It is found, however, with verbs in the subordinate clause in many tenses of the indicative as well as the subjunctive, and there are, non surprisingly, complex gradations of acceptability. The examples in b. and c. contrast in that b. triggers the subjunctive (and is, one would imagine, drawn from a literary text since *vînt* is the somewhat archaic imperfect subjunctive of *venir* 'to come'). On the other hand c., also in a negative context, illustrates the modern prescriptively dictated rule, that is, that *espérer* calls for a complement clause in the future. Negation and interrogation, interestingly, are more apt to trigger the subjunctive than simple declarative uses, much along the model of other expressions of cognitive activity such as *croire* 'to believe' and related terms. A subjunctive after *espérer* with negation or interrogation is still not universally accepted as grammatical although many speakers consider it better than this trigger in the simple declarative.

When it comes to positive and declarative contents for *espérer*, we still find examples (as in 19a.), although at least one commentator, a native-speaker on a discussion list who is quite clearly not a linguist but is struggling to verbalize her/his intuitions (http://www.etudes-litteraires.com/forum/sujet-7843-2.html) suggests that we find the subjunctive after this verb when its meaning is closer to that of *souhaiter* 'to wish'. There is a danger of circularity in this reasoning (*espérer* may seem closer to *souhaiter* precisely because the latter verb governs the subjunctive), but the statement does underline the semantic content of the relationship between the trigger and verb in the subordinate clause. In the examples in (21a) and (21b) are positive/declarative statements of hope followed by the subjunctive, while c. instantiates the far more usual use of the indicative and, indeed, the future.

(21) a. On pourrait espérer que sa malchance le quittât (SUB).
One could hope that his bad luck would abandon him.
b. Tout mon espoir était qu'Albertine fût partie (SUB).
My entire hope was that Albertine had left.
c. Dans l'espoir qu'il s'en souviendra (IND).
In the hope that he will remember it.

The second relatively innovative use of the subjunctive mood is its appearance after the conjunction *après que* 'after':

(22) on peut y aller tout de suite *après* qu'il ait mangé (SUB)
we can go there immediately after he has eaten

Again, this construction is criticized by prescriptivist grammarians and there is quite a bit of alternation in spoken French between the indicative and the subjunctive. The logic behind its being proscribed is that one can be sure of what happens *after* something else (as in (22) where the speaker can know if the subject has eaten or not) and therefore an expression of doubt about the reality of an action is not appropriate. Like *espérer*, *après que* with the subjunctive is probably a matter of its similarity (in shape and, through polarity, in meaning) to another expression which regularly governs the subjunctive, here *avant que* 'before' and perhaps reinforcement from *jusqu'à ce que* 'until'. This point will be taken up again below.

While *espérer* and even *après que* have certain semantic affinities with other expressions which prompt the subjunctive, some other triggers of the mood in Modern French seem to be counter-intuitive (cf. Dreer 2007: xvii–xxiv). Although it is a marginal, quite literary use, *le fait que* 'the fact that' is, for example, a trigger which seems quite difficult to justify in any semantically orderly view of the mood. In the next section we will discuss the various meanings, both specific and schematic, which have been ascribed to the Modern French subjunctive; the goal is to establish a set of theories which then can be tested against the data of Old French.

18.3 Proposals on the Meaning of the Modern French Subjunctive

The focus of most linguistic work on the French subjunctive has been descriptive, carried out with the aim of grasping the meaning of this mood. In most cases this has been done by seeking ways in which its extremely varied triggers might be seen as all exemplifying some abstract notion which sets them off from the triggers of the indicative in dependent – and by extension the rare independent – clauses. Most of the literature, therefore, has simply presupposed that the meaning of the subjunctive is a meaning – at whatever level of abstraction – which is shared by the verbs, adverbs, conjunctions and nouns which somehow govern it.

This presupposition has generated a full continuum of proposals as to what this meaning might be, summed up by Harris (1978:169) as falling into three possible classes: a range of meanings, one meaning overall, or purely formal status for the morphological mood. This typology provides a good place to begin a survey of theories, to be supplemented below by other work in semantic description.

The arguments for the subjunctive as a meaningless category which serves, at best, as a stylistic marker (Harris 1978:169) rest on the idea that when something is automatic, and therefore predictable, there is a necessary implication that it has no meaning. Weinreich (1980:388) gives most credit for this notion to information theory, which, through a rather specialized computational view of the nature of data, defines meaning as that which emerges from uncertainty. As he further explains, the view is that where there is no uncertainty, there is no information (read by linguists as semantic content) to be transmitted. Meaning, in short, comes with novelty. Mailhac (2000) takes up this point and adds to it other, not contradictory sources of this notion, specifically, the influence of phonology on semantics. It is easy to see where this fundamentally structuralist notion of the phoneme would, rightly or wrongly, introduce this point of view via those trained primarily or exclusively in Prague School or even Saussurean linguistics; just as the structural phoneme is discerned through its contrastive properties and lack of predictability, so too a form (or structure) must show opposition and non-automaticity in order to be considered meaningful.

Following this reasoning, Harris (1978:171–173, *inter alia*) argues that the Romance subjunctive is largely meaningless and has been since Classical Latin, since its presence in a clause can be predicted by the trigger or context in which it appears. This stricture covers virtually all the traditional Latin categories of uses of the subjunctive, in dependent clauses invariably (23a), and in jussive (23b) and optative (23c) main clauses:

(23) a. Impero   ut venias.
        order-1sg that come-2sg-SUB
        I order that you come
   b. Sed maneam   opinor.
        but stay-1sg-SUB think/believe-1sg
        But I should stay, I think.
   c. Valeant   cives   mei!
        Be well-3pl-SUB citizens-m-pl-NOM. my-m-pl-NOM
        May my citizens be well!

Both R. Lakoff (1968:157), whose work is the source of the examples in (23), and Harris (1978:173) argue that independent clauses like those in (23b) and (23c) have underlying abstract verbs (that is, meaning which does not appear in the surface morphology of the sentences) expressing, respectively, command and volition; like the overt expression of command in (23a), these underlying verbs again force an automatic and hence meaningless subjunctive form. Lakoff (1968:161), in fact, goes further than Harris in that she claims that there are no exceptions to this statement: "The markers of mood ... are always devoid of meaning of their own..."

In contrast, Harris (1978:173–174) identifies exceptions in the category of potential subjunctives of two kinds, the first exemplified in (24) in a fully independent clause, contrasted with (25) (my invented but grammatical example) in the indicative:

(24) Velim   hoc   facere.
     like/desire-1sg-SUB this-n-sg-ACC do-INF
     I would like to do this.
(25) Volo   hoc   facere.
     Desire-1sg this-n-sg-ACC do-INF
     I want to do this.

The subjunctive in (24), then, serves to mark tentativeness, both for politeness and uncertainty. What we have here, Harris seems to be arguing, is more or less a minimal pair (note the parallels with phonology) where the mood of the free-standing verb is the variable which changes the meaning of the sentence. In this one context, then, the Classical Latin subjunctive can be said to be meaningful. The difference between (24) and (25). is certainly meaningful (to Harris and to this author) since the former sentence with *velim* 'I would like' expresses a tentative desire unlike (25). where *volo* 'I want' is at least in pragmatic terms a stronger expression.

18 Grammatical Meaning and the Old French Subjunctive   365

Harris's second instance of a meaningful subjunctive is found in the result clause of conditional sentences; (26) is an example:

(26) Non venissem   si id   fecissit
  not come-1sg- SUB if it-n-sg-ACC do-3sg-SUB
  I would not have come if he had done it.

It is not necessary to belabor the fact that Latin had a wide range of conditional expressions, some in the subjunctive (hypotheticals are only one type) and some, considered more certain in terms of the reality of the result, in the indicative. It is not clear, however, that the contrasting modality in these constructions or in (24) as compared to (25), (i.e., 'I would like to do this' vs. 'I want to do this') is any more meaningful than the difference between (23c), a 'meaningless' subjunctive for Harris, which expresses a wish and example (27) where we have a statement of fact. ('May my citizens be well' (23c) vs. 'My citizens are well.' (27)).

(27) Valent   cives   mei.
   be well-3pl-IND citizen-m-pl-NOM my-m-pl-NOM
   My citizens are well.

Depending on the point of view with which one starts out, one can argue that both (25) (contrasted to (24)) and (27) (compared with (23c)) both show either stylistically marked variants or, a conclusion which I would find preferable, meaningful differences.

Conners (1978) makes a similar argument for Modern French. She too posits a subjunctive mood which has a dual nature, with a split between the automatic (and meaningless) uses and those which are optional, therefore having semantic content. Her crucial examples come from relative clauses with indefinite antecedents where one finds pairs such as:

(28) a. Il cherche quelqu'un qui sache (SUB) parler russe.
     He is looking for someone who knows how to speak Russian.
   b. Il cherche quelqu'un qui sait (IND) parler russe.
     He is looking for someone who knows how to speak Russian.

In (28a), the outcome of the search is unsure; there may or may not be anyone at all who fulfills the stated criterion of knowing how to speak Russian. In (28b), on the other hand, that criterion is sure to be fulfilled and the only uncertainty is whether this already known Russian speaker is to be found.[11]

---

[11] One could make an argument that *quelqu'un* 'someone' is semantically ambiguous between a definite and indefinite reading in the same way that the indefinite article of (i):

(i) I am looking for a Russian speaker can be read as referring to a uniquely identified Russian speaker or a true indefinite. In that case Conners and Harris can claim that even here the subjunctive is automatic in (28) and that the indicative/subjunctive choice in French is simply a morphological manifestation of a distinction which is (morpho)phonologically empty in English. I thank Carolyn Heycock for this comment.

What Harris and Conners both seem to be proposing is a kind of massive meta-homonymy, where every subjunctive form is used in two distinct ways which diametrically oppose each other, in one way as a meaningful unit and the other as the marker of a semantically empty distinction. The evidence for this split comes from these linguists' interpretation of the various contexts which govern this mood, an interpretation which in turn is based on the relationship discussed above between novelty and semanticity. What results is a very wide-spread exception to Humbolt's Universal[12] since here the one form – one meaning rule of thumb is violated by *all* the forms of every paradigm. The way one of these two uses fully and systematically contradicts the other would lead to the conclusion that we have widespread homonymy rather than polysemy; the lack of connection between the meaningful and meaningless forms is more central to these analyses than is the shared morphology.

At the other end of the spectrum from those who claim essential meaninglessness are those who, while not denying the semanticity of the subjunctive, have, so to speak, given up on finding any unifying meaning. Both Imbs (1953) and Glatigny (1976) provide extensive lists of contexts which call for the subjunctive, either obligatorily or optionally, but state that this multiplicity of meaning is the essence of the mood. Imbs (1953:50) sees a unity which emerges from the history of its uses and which cannot be seen synchronically as anything but an illogical grab bag of uses. Objections to this strategy can be couched, of course, in terms which are very similar to the objections to the theory of automaticity linked to lack of meaning set out just above. Here again the continued existence of the category *qua* category over time and space suggests that there is some unity of meaning to be sought; speakers still know, for example, whether a morphologically ambiguous verb form is a subjunctive or an indicative in the case of the most central modern triggers.

Between the extremes of (almost) total automaticity and rampant, non-unifiable polysemy (perhaps better identified as homophony), there have been many attempts to find some kind of semantic order in the uses of the subjunctive, most of which have posited some small number of abstract meanings which are meant to subsume all the uses of the mood. These range from one (Damourette and Pichon 1911–1927; Guillaume 1929; Clédat 1932; Hanse 1960), to two (van Wartburg and Zumthor 1947; Wierzbicka 1988), to three organizing meanings (Rothe 1967; Nordahl 1969). Rather than review the contents of all these works (and they are only representative of a larger field), let us look at a few examples.

Among those who posit a single meaning for the subjunctive are the French linguists Damourette and Pichon whose multivolume grammar (1911–1952) is based on a study of the structures of mind as reflected in morphology and syntax. For them the subjunctive is the mood of 'non-judgment', expressing intent, hypotheses, possibilities, empathy, volition, and, with negation, the quite literal denial of any judgment by the subject about the proposition in the subjunctive clause. Despite the

---

[12] The 'Universal' in question states (in my paraphrase) that speakers of languages will tend, over time, to establish an isomorphism of form and meaning so that for every meaning there is one form and for every form there is one meaning.

multiple examples and wide-ranging discussion throughout their work, we are left with a feeling that this is a counter-intuitive way of capturing the meaning of the mood, since there are explicitly judgmental contexts, called subjunctives of empathy (29a) or negation (29b), such as:

(29) a. Nous sommes contents que tu viennes (SUB) avec nous.
We are happy that you are coming with us.
b. Il est douteux qu'elle sache (SUBJ) le faire.
It is doubtful that she knows how to do it.

The example in (29a) is a directly evaluative statement by most accounts, while (29b), somewhat more indirectly, provides the chances (a matter of judgment, one would say) of her knowing (or not knowing) something. Waugh (1979:181) points out correctly that in such cases the authors seem to have confused non-judgment and judgment-that-not. In addition, and this is more central to the whole idea of a single meaning for the mood, there are cases which are simply not captured by this single, all-encompassing meaning. A salient case in point is the use of the subjunctive in fronted clauses, whatever the trigger. It is hard to see where in the following examples judgment (or the lack of it) is at all at all involved, except in the sense that some speaker felt called upon to make the pronouncement:

(30) a. Que Paris soit (SUB) la capitale de la France, c'est un fait.
That Paris is the capital of France, that's a fact.
b. Que le travail soit (SUB) un trésor, vous le savez.
That work is a treasure, you know that.

But if the simple act of stating something provides a necessary degree of judgment or non-judgment, all utterances are judgmental and the subjunctive – indicative dichotomy is consequently not captured by this metric.

Guillaume (1929) starts from a different point of view, based on the number of tenses which are morphologically expressed by each mood, but also finds one unifying meaning to the subjunctive in French, that of time *in fieri*, time as becoming rather than time in existence (*in esse*). The work of Moignet (notably 1959), both diachronic and synchronic, is influenced by Guillaume's views and also posits the subjunctive as a unity through the way it expresses time and, in a limited sense, tense. Hewson (1990/1991), also starting from a Guillaumien bias, sees the essence of the mood in its limited temporal expression as well, resulting, for him, in its use for value judgments of all sorts, brought to bear on the idea of an event rather than the event itself as situated in time (1990/1991:163–164).

Hewson's reasons (1990/1991:157) for positing a single, unifying meaning are worth reviewing: first, child language acquisition needs reasonable simplicity. Secondly he cites the minimal pair sentences like those in (28a) and (28b) above (Conners 1978) which indicate, he argues, an underlying systematic difference. Lastly, he brings cognitive indications to bear, stating that the modal differences between subjunctive and indicative show a regular and coherent cognitive contrast. The second and third reasons, it seems to me, are not arguments necessarily for a unitary meaning, but certainly for a profound semanticity, whatever its complexity.

The first justification that Hewson offers is, however, of a different sort. First of all, "reasonable simplicity" is a relative term and children do acquire quite a lot of polysemy, while, secondly, the evidence seems to point to the late mastering of the subjunctive, an indication that it is of somewhat greater complexity than many other constructions acquired earlier in first language acquisition.

Clédat (1932) offers the "mode de l'action envisagée" 'the mood of envisioned/ imagined action' (1932:19) as his overarching meaning and, like others, then shows how it applies to a wide range of uses. Hanse (1960), in a variant of Clédat's (and others') work, proposes that the meaning of the subjunctive be grasped as the expression of some action or state which is "trop incertaine pour qu'on le situe sur le plan du réel sans qu'il soit question cependant de la présenter comme hypothétique or irréel"[13] (1960:11).

Wartburg and Zumthor (1947), along the same lines as Conners (1978), divide the subjunctive between those senses which express strong psychological energy and those where it is weakened. They see the subjunctive in independent clauses as being of the former type, while those in dependent clauses have a much weakened modal meaning (although not, as Conners would have it, no meaning at all). It is in the dependent clauses, for example, that the verb is more apt to be expressed in the indicative, especially in popular speech, precisely where it marks merely a social or stylistic variant. Wierzbicka (1988), on the other hand, does not consider the stability of the mood in one or another use, but rather sees it as a double expression, that of mental imagination and that of distancing. The choice of mood is motivated variously by one of these abstractions or by the other.

Lastly, in this overview, are the works of Rothe (1967) and Nordahl (1969[14]), both of whom see three meanings to be extracted from the uses of the subjunctive. Nordahl (1969:22) lists them as *volitif* 'volitional', *subjectif* 'subjective', and *dubitatif* 'dubative'. Rothe (1967:42 and throughout) proposes the three subcategories of contrast, variation, and automaticity. As a result, he aligns himself to some extent with Harris (1978) and Connors (1978) although he never claims, like them, that there is ever a full lack of semanticity. Rather – and rightly – he sees many exceptions to such a flat statement.

To summarize, there is, clearly, no consensus about the subjunctive in French. Even if we set aside the various purely syntactic theories, generative or other, the array is impressive and even frustrating. Several questions serve to focus the discussion. Is the subjunctive meaningful or meaningless? If meaningless, do we surrender to chaos or, as has been stated, grasp it as the mood governed by (or at least closely

---

[13] That is, 'too uncertain to be situated on the level of reality without there being, however, a question of presenting it as hypothetical or unreal'.

[14] Nordahl (1969:18) provides a summary of several other attempts to define the subjunctive as a mood, with particular emphasis on French scholars, while Rothe (1967:3–28) does the same, although the first part of this overview discusses primarily German contributions to the question. Moignet (1959) is another excellent source of descriptions of previous work, as is Dreer (2007).

associated with) *que*[15] (Foulet 1928/1967: 207)? If meaningful, how many meanings does it have? Can they only be represented as a list? If not, where do they overlap or how otherwise do they interact?

The brief overview of theories, by no means complete but representative, gives rise not only to questions, but to many immediate problems. These ranges, depending on the number of uses proposed, from those which emerge from excessively abstract unitary meanings to an equally inappropriate refusal to assign any meaning at all. The single abstract meaning, in the cases which were discussed above and others, seems to me to be too abstract, standing by itself, to do justice to the multiplicity of subjunctive uses either synchronically or over time. At the other end of the range of interpretations, the mood cannot be dismissed as a historical relic or as a stylistic variant which adds an air of education or higher social status to the speaker's delivery. It is used, to varying degrees, by all speakers of French in clearly discernible patterns (expressions of doubt, for example, trigger it consistently while certain temporal conjunctions give rise to a great deal of variation). It is also being extended, albeit not widely, to other contexts in ways which show clear patterns of analogical thought; this too would be impossible if we were only dealing, on the one hand, with a relic form or, on the other, with one abstract meaning. In either case, there would be no way to account for the very changes which take place in relatively modern times (subjunctive after *espérer* 'to hope') or to explain why certain ones do not (subjunctive after *parce que* 'because' although it too is a subordinating conjunction).

One last remark about this array of theories is called for: while they are all semantic in the sense of proposing a meaning (or lack of meaning) for the subjunctive, they are not necessarily alike. Moignet's work, in the tradition of Guillaume, for instance, approaches the mood through the interplay of tenses in the subjunctive as contrasted with the indicative. Other theories (Connors 1978, among others) do not necessarily posit a meaning, but emphasize a more metatheoretical notion, that real meaningfulness can only exist in contrast. Yet others pick out a notion which would be recognized as truly semantic, a more usual approach to meaning.

18.4 Theories Applied to the Old French Subjunctive

Let us set aside the Latin examples, furnished by Harris (1978) and Lakoff (1968), which opened Sect. 18.3, on the grounds that the line of transmission from Latin to Romance is not a clear one.[16] We can rather safely, however, state that Modern

---

[15] Foulet points out (1967) (1928, 1967:207) that grammar books describing modern French will actually use *que* in setting out the conjugation of the subjunctive: *que je sois, que tu sois* etc.

[16] cf. Wright 1982 for extensive discussion of the problems in deciding what kind of Latin is the direct ancestor of Romance.

French is the successor of Old French, a claim supported by an unbroken line of documentation from approximately 1100 to the present.[17] In that case, what can be said about the unity (or lack thereof) of the subjunctive across time? In what ways has the meaning remained constant? The last section set forth an array of proposals for what that meaning is today; in what follows some illustrative proposals will be examined as to their suitability for the Old French expression of mood.

18.4.1 Unworkable Proposals

To return to Harris's typology (1978), we can quickly eliminate two of the three approaches to meaning he sets out, here for the earlier form of the language as we did above for contemporary French. First, the Old French subjunctive is not a series of meaningless forms; if anything (and we will return to this below), it is more transparently meaningful than in the modern language. Secondly, for many of the same reasons as for French today, we must reject the idea of unbridled polysemy or homonymy, without even attempting to differentiate between them. As was said above, the evidence of patterns of language, usage, and change point to a system, neither to coincidence nor unconstrained and random variation around morphologically identical forms.

Among the other more focused proposals, I would reject two as being inappropriate for the Old French data. The first of these is Damourette and Pichon's (1911–1927) notion that the core of the mood exists in non-judgment or the related idea of the expression of non- or extra-assertion (Bybee et al. 1994; Aboud 2001:11–12). In both cases, the Old French expressions produce more counter-examples to this proposal than do those in Modern French. The notion of non-judgment was discussed above for Modern French. As was said there, it seems at first glance to be counter-intuitive since so many triggers of the subjunctive can be interpreted as judgments (emotional responses and reports on cognition in the form of beliefs in particular), while the subjunctive clauses in Modern and Old French often display a degree of factivity (*Je suis contente que tu sois guérie* 'I am happy that you are cured' asserts the cure). If we look at non-judgment and non-assertion together, however, some clarity may emerge; in both cases there is a lack of finality in what is uttered and it is perhaps this lack of finality – rather than lack of reaction – that is meant by non-judgment. We can understand Old French hypothetical clauses – as well as indirect statements and questions in the subjunctive – as non-assertive and even uncertain, for example. With cognitive verbs, on the other hand, Old French authors can be understood to assert the content of the subjunctive clause more than in the modern language since that clause can be triggered by a positive statement followed by the subjunctive as was exemplified in (11) above (repeated here as (31)):

---

[17] We will return to this idea below in Sect. 18.5.

(31) Je   cuidoie   que plus loiaus
     I-NOM used-to-think-1sg that more loyal-m-sg-NOM
     me   fussiez   se Dieus   me   conseut,
     me-OBL were-2pl-SUB if god-m-sg-NOM me-OBL counsel-3sg-SUB
     que ne fu   Tristan   a Yseut.
     than not was-3sg Tristan-NOM to Yseut-OBL
                                    (*Chastelaine de Vergi* 758–60)
     I thought that you were more loyal to me, may God help me,
     than Tristan was to Isolde.

Although the above example expresses a belief and not a declarative statement, the degree of certainty is strengthened by the form of the triggering verb (*cuidier* 'to believe') which is neither negative nor interrogative.

The second theory to be set aside is Guillaume's (1929) notion of the subjunctive being the mood of time *in fieri* 'becoming' or 'emerging' rather than *in esse* 'in existence'. An argument of this sort can be made for the modern subjunctive, given that only two sets of forms exist. Such a characterization is perhaps a better way of referring to the simple and compound morphology exemplified respectively by *que je fasse* 'that I do', *que j'aie fait* 'that I have done' than would recourse to the category of *tense* used, as was set out above, to delineate the relationship between the verb of the triggering expression and the verb of the subjunctive clause. When they are contemporaneous, the simple form is used, while for the past of the subjunctive clause relative to the main clause, the compound is found:

(32) a. Elle est/était contente que tu fasses (SUB) un voyage avec elle.
        She is/was happy that you are/were taking a trip with her.
     b. Elle est/était contente que tu aies fait (SUB) un voyage avec elle.
        She is/was happy that you took/had taken a trip with her.

In Old French, however, there are four temporal expressions of the subjunctive, each with distinctive morphology: a present, a past, a perfect, and a pluperfect. It is harder to maintain, therefore, that the mood is one of time in emergence; the tense of the trigger and the tense of the subjunctive clause do enter into a construction showing temporal sequence, this is true, but the choice of tense is also an absolute one depending on a present and past of both clauses as independent of each other. Finally, one aspect of continuation should be mentioned here: at no point in the evolution from Old to Modern French (or in Latin for that matter) is there a morphological expression of the future in the subjunctive; it is invariably to be inferred from the context in which present/simple tense morphology is found.

18.4.2 More Promising Proposals

Many of the other proposals for the modern subjunctive are much more directly semantic and/or psychological in nature. Nordahl (1969) furnishes what might be considered a list of uses with subcategories organized around the major headings of 'volition', 'subjectivity', and 'doubt'. Volition and doubt are certainly core functions expressing the speaker's interaction with the content of the clause in the subjunctive; these specific interactions persist from early usage to today. Subjectivity, on the other hand, is a different kind of proposal. It has to do not with the content of the trigger, but is rather an abstraction over many of these states of mind pointing to the very fact of some interaction other than simple declaration. Others analyses (Clédat 1932; Hanse 1960; Wierzbicka 1988) also focus on the speaker's attitude. When 'envisioned action' (Clédat 1932), 'mental imagination' (Wierzbicka 1988) or 'degrees of psychological energy' (Wartburg and Zumthor 1947) become the explanations for mood choice, we have descriptions which might be seen as panchronic and would as a consequence defeat any study of contrast between two systems or of change itself.

Interestingly, the notions of *irrealis* and the various broadly cognitive summary meanings can be applied, if anything, with greater felicity to Old French than to Modern French, although they were proposed in terms of contemporary data and very broadly fit most instances of modern usage. Hypothetical constructions, for example, no longer take the subjunctive (see the discussion around examples (7) and (8)) but are usually those which come to mind as the most central expressions of *irrealis*. In addition to all the uses of the subjunctive which are largely the same across time, Old French allows it after positive statements of belief (examples under (9) and (10)), in indirect statements (11.), and in comparisons where the speaker is unwilling or unable to be sure of his facts (12). All of these uses speak again to a greater degree of mental activity on the part of the speaker (or the subject) than does the indicative in the modern equivalents of these constructions.

Recent work by Dreer (2007) is a rare look at both the Old and Modern French mood. He proposes that the earlier use of the subjunctive indicated that a given occurrence was being questioned, while the modern mood "has the narrower meaning of 'alternative to occurrence' that expresses a more specific instance of a questioned occurrence" (2007:252). The Old French 'occurrence questioned' is not unlike my belief that the mood at that time was best captured as an expression of uncertainty of outcome (Winters 1989). 'Uncertainty of outcome', however, as developed within the context of Cognitive Grammar, is to be understood as capturing either the central meaning from which others extended or, more probably, a schematic meaning which served as an overarching sort of summary to this complex prototype-based category of related meanings. Dreer's 'alternative to occurrence' is not quite the same as my proposal (also in Winters 1989) of subjectivity at the core of the Modern French mood; both views would have to be explored at greater length to see if there is the possibility of reconciling them. Overall, Dreer's account, unlike mine, is still a claim of a unitary sense, while the prototype-based category posits a multiplicity of uses extending from the central instance rather than insisting on any one (or two or three) fixed meanings. These meanings may be extensions of each other and transparently related or may be extended in various directions and understood only through this central notion of 'uncertainty of outcome'.

What then can be concluded about theories of meaning of the subjunctive when they are applied to Modern and Old French? First, it is certainly the – somewhat obvious – case that there are changes to the meaning emerging from the somewhat different array of uses attested to between 1100 and the present. There is a clear narrowing in the way the mood functions today. The new uses discussed above (with *espérer* and after *après que*) are both somewhat controversial as to acceptability (and therefore marginal) and clearly a matter of analogical extension of other uses; the overall inventory of triggers in any case is smaller than in the past. Although there are many clear continuations in usage, some of the excessively abstract labels discussed above are too broad to capture this overall narrowing. Others are too restricted (Moignet 1959 on tense configuration) and do not apply well either. It can be concluded, then, that no single theory of the meaning of the subjunctive which has been developed solely to account for modern uses is completely adequate for the Old French mood. The fault seems to lie in one or two forms of overstatement. On the one hand, there are cases of very rigid definitions of the mood, formulated with an insistence on a single, double, or – rarely – triple meaning(s) which do not allow for flexibility in looking backward at what is clearly a different earlier meaning since they do not take into account the full range of nuances and their shifting degrees of centrality. On the other hand, we find equally overstated claims that meanings are not at all related and can only be listed; this view leads to a view of change as another, not very illuminating list of differences across time. To repeat what was proposed above, it is by viewing the mood as a semantic category of related uses that one can fruitfully look from the present to the past and thus gain insight on the developments from the past to the present.

18.5 Conclusions: The Nature of Grammar Change

In this paper, we have examined some of the many ways in which the Modern French subjunctive has been characterized. This examination has not, however, been carried out for the sake of a survey alone; many such have already been published (among them Nordahl 1969; Dreer 2007). Rather, the goal has been to evaluate the application of these theories to the Old French uses of this mood. The result has not been satisfactory in one sense; it has become apparent that the theories, when shifted from one stage of French to another, no longer have the same degree of validity they have when applied at the stage for which they were developed.[18]

Stated this way, this conclusion seems at first to be very obvious: why should the meaning of a grammatical construction remain static over time when language is demonstrably in a constant state of flux? On the other hand, we might ask, why should

---

[18] It is certainly the case that the theories examined in this paper can be seen as being more or less satisfactory when they are compared one to another. A full critique of their usefulness to a description of Modern French is beyond the scope of this paper.

we expect change in meaning when so many of the functions of the construction have persisted? The question becomes yet less odd and the answer less obvious if we do not address the entire construction taken as an unanalyzed monolith, but rather look at the construction as a compound of its constituent parts. It is here that the theory of Cognitive Grammar (Lakoff 1987 and Langacker 1987 are basic sources) becomes valuable, not just for grasping the evolution of the subjunctive but also more generally for identifying and explaining change in the semantics of a grammatical construction. In this framework meaning emerges from categorization; we form semantic sets, or categories, with respect to the most salient unit (known also as the prototypical or best instance of the category) and to the relationship of other members of the set to this central member.

Given this view of semantics, a theory of subjunctive meaning would be able to account for all the contexts in which the mood is used at any moment of time. Since categories are structured, information on membership in the set would not just be the fact that some use belonged to the category, but also how close or distant from the central meaning that particular use might be. Finally, cognitive linguistics posits a second kind of meaning which is schematic, both emerging from the polysemy of the category and shaping what might become of the category over time. Many of the theories examined in this paper would become candidates for the schematic meaning of the subjunctive under this theory but, because they do not take into account the various meanings which are more or less related to the central meaning, they are not flexible enough to apply diachronically.

The primary purpose of this paper is not solely or even centrally to promote Cognitive Grammar, although that theory allows for the flexibility of meanings in a networked configuration which, I believe, best captures the intricacies of the subjunctive mood. Rather it is proposed that most of the theories of the meaning of the subjunctive have been focused exclusively on what in cognitive semantics is either the schematic or the central, prototypical meaning. While these theories are, as was said above, successful to some extent in capturing the modern construction, they cannot be transferred to earlier periods because they do not account for changes in the array of meanings extending to varying degrees from this center.[19] With a view of language which allows for more or less central (and hence more or less robust) units within a semantic category like the French subjunctive, we can, I believe, most profitably balance the need to recognize continuity across time and measure change from earlier to later periods. The contractions and expansions in the number and type of uses certainly count as change and negate statements (Foulet 1928/1967 in particular) of identity of meaning from one period to another, but there is still a core which has not disappeared or even altered much in its centrality. To conclude, if we as linguists are to examine theories of meaning as applied to more than one time

---

[19] The metaphors of cognitive grammar tend to be very physical, referring to linguistic entities as if they were arranged in space; I use them because they are the terms of my own work, but they are not necessary for the point being made here; leaving aside the underlying commitments of another theory, an OT tableau of better or worse candidates, as defined by shifting the ranking of constraints, might serve the same purpose.

period, it behooves us to keep track specifically of how these meanings might interact with each other in different ways at any given moment, thus adding nuance to how much persists and how much disappears.

References

Aboud, Lofti. 2001. Négation, Interrogation et Alternance Indicatif - Subjonctif. *Journal of French Language Studies* 12: 1–22.
Bybee, Joan, Revere Perkins, and William Pagliuca. 1994. *The evolution of grammar: Tense, aspect, and modality in the languages of the world*. Chicago/London: University of Chicago Press.
Clédat, Léon. 1932. Les modes et particulièrement le subjonctif. In *En marge des grammaires*, 2–44. Paris: Champion.
Conners, Kathleen. 1978. The meaning of the French subjunctive. *Linguistics* 211: 45–56.
Damourette, J., and E. Pichon. 1911–1927. *Des Mots à la pensée*, vol. V. Paris: Ed. d'Artrey.
Dreer, Igor. 2007. *Expressing the same by the different. The subjunctive vs the indicative in French*. Amsterdam/Philadelphia: John Benjamins.
Foulet, Lucien. 1928/1967. *Petite syntaxe de l'ancien français*. Paris: Champion.
Glatigny, Michel. 1976. Remarques sur le subjonctif. *Le Français dand le Monde* 122: 17–25.
Guillaume, Gustave. 1929. *Temps et verbe*. Paris: Champion.
Hanse, Joseph. 1960. *La valeur modale du subjonctif*. Brussels: Palais des Académies. (rpt. from Académie royale de langue et de littérature de Belgique, 1960).
Harris, Martin. 1978. *The evolution of French syntax. A comparative approach*. London/New York: Longmans.
Harris, Randy A. 1993. *The linguistic wars*. New York/Oxford: Oxford University Press.
Imbs, Paul. 1953. *Le subjonctif en français moderne*. Strasbourg: Publications de la faculté des lettres de l'université de Strasbourg.
Kibbee, Douglas. 1991. *For to Speake French trewly. French language in England, 1000–1600 - Its status, description and instruction*. Amsterdam/Philadelphia: John Benjamins.
Lakoff, Robin. 1968. *Abstract syntax and Latin complementation*, Research monograph no. 49. Cambridge, MA: MIT Press.
Lakoff, George. 1987. *Women, fire, and dangerous things. What categories*. Chicago: University of Chicago Press.
Langacker, Ronald W. 1987–1992. *Foundations of Cognitive grammar*. 2 vols. Palo Alto: Stanford University Press.
Mailhac, Jean-Pierre. 2000. Sens, choix, et subjonctif. *Journal of French Language Studies* 10: 245–271.
Martineau, France. 1994. The expression of the subjunctive in older French. *Catalan Working Papers in Linguistics* 3(2): 45–69.
Moignet, Gérard. 1959. *Essai sur le mode subjonctif*. Paris: Presses universitaires françaises.
Moignet, Gérard. 1984. *Grammaire de l'ancien français*. Paris: Klincksieck.
Nordahl, Helge. 1969. *Les systèmes du subjonctif corrélatif: Etude sur l'emploi des modes dans la subordonnée complétive en français moderne*. Bergen/Oslo: Universitetsforlaget.
Progovac, Ljiljana. 1993. Subjunctive: The (Mis)behavior of anaphora and negative polarity. *The Linguistic Review* 10: 37–59.
Raynaud de Lage, Guy. 1968. *Manuel pratique d'ancien français*, Collection Connaissance des Langues, II. Paris: Editions Picard.
Rothe, Wolfgang. 1967. *Strukturen des Konjunktifs im Französischen*. Tübingen: Niemeyer.
Ruwet, Nicolas. 1984. Je veux partir/*je veux que je parte. A propos de la distribution des complétives à temps fini et des compléments à l'infinitif en français. *Cahiers de grammaire* 7: 75–138.

Soutet, Olivier. 2000. *Le Subjonctif en français*. Paris: Ophrys.
Wagner, Robert L., and J. Pichon. 1966. *Grammaire du français classique et moderne*, 2nd ed. Paris: Hachette.
Wartburg von, Walter, and Paul Zumthor. 1947. *Précis de syntaxe du français contemporain*. Berne: A. Francke.
Waugh, Linda R. 1979. The context-sensitive meaning of the French subjunctive. In *Contributions to grammatical studies: Semantics and syntax*, ed. L.R. Waugh and F. van Coetsem, 179–238. Leiden: E. J. Brill.
Wierzbicka, Anna. 1988. *The semantics of grammar*, Studies in language companion, vol. 18. Amsterdam/Philadelphia: John Benjamins.
Winters, Margaret E. 1989. Diachronic prototype theory: On the evolution of the French subjunctive. *Linguistics* 27: 703–30.
Wright, Roger. 1982. *Late Latin and early Romance in Spain and Carolingian France*. Liverpool: Francis Cairns.

Index

A
Abstract, 40, 49, 51, 58, 88, 124, 131, 135, 140, 144, 149, 191, 197, 198, 224, 240, 279, 295, 298, 338, 363, 364, 366, 369, 373
  vs. concrete, 4, 39, 52, 55, 57, 59, 234, 283, 297
Acconitan, 208
Acre, 208, 213
Adjective, 26, 156–157, 161, 169, 172, 177, 180, 284, 288, 289, 293, 294, 330, 337
Adjunct, 6, 66–68, 73–75, 81–83, 262, 263, 270–274, 277–279, 328
Adverb, 1, 6, 39, 131, 132, 135, 136, 139, 261–268, 270, 274, 275, 277, 279, 329, 330, 337, 338, 363
AdvP, 275
Affirmative, 262, 264, 266, 271, 272, 276, 279, 298
Africa, 170
AGR, 28
Analogy, 4, 5, 126, 149–164, 292, 293
Analytic, 263
  vs. synthetic, 37, 40
Angevin, 212, 217, 218
Antioch, principality of, 207, 208
Arabic, 12, 108, 207–209, 215–218
Aragonese, 214
Argument, 3, 6, 54, 62, 63, 66–69, 73–76, 82, 83, 97, 98, 125, 130, 171–175, 179–183, 188, 256, 257, 261–263, 271–274, 276–279, 316, 328, 336, 354, 363, 365, 367, 371
Armenian, Middle, 12, 208, 215

Article
  definite, 3, 27, 28, 30, 32, 33, 36, 38–40, 45–47, 52, 57, 58, 168, 189, 197
  indefinite, 2, 4, 22, 41, 45–59, 365
Artois, 119, 310, 312, 313
Asia, 157
Assertion, 128, 129, 131, 134, 135, 139–142, 145, 146, 321
  vs. non-assertion, 123, 127, 132, 143
Asyndetic construction, 245, 246, 250, 251, 257

B
Backgrounding, 305, 311
Bohairic, 208
Burgundian, 208, 209
Burgundy, 12

C
Candidate chains, 9, 108, 116–118, 121
Case
  assignment, 31
  confusion, 170
  dative, 21, 54
  genitive, 20, 21, 33, 40, 55
  nominative, 21, 25, 181, 210, 211, 274, 354
  oblique, 24–26, 28, 30, 37–41, 46, 82, 120, 170, 210, 211, 284, 285
  system, 2–4, 34, 36, 37, 41, 82, 167, 168, 170, 171, 173, 177, 179, 180, 182, 210, 286, 288
Castolect, 207, 215

Catalan, 155, 212, 214, 218
Chansons de geste, 8, 254, 255, 257, 300, 304–312, 314, 318–321
Charter, 3, 178, 179, 183, 193–196, 214
Chatton's Ani-Razor, 4, 283, 297–298
Chinese, 31, 32, 61, 62
Chronogenesis, 223
Chronology, relative, 98, 150, 152, 153
Cilician, 208, 215
CL. *See* Compensatory lengthening (CL)
Clause
    adjunct, 6, 66–68, 73–75, 81–83
    concessive, 10, 124, 125, 127–130, 134, 135, 137–146
    conditional, 124, 247
    dependent, 243, 355–356, 364, 368
    embedded, 7, 328–337, 339, 341, 342, 346, 347
    independent, 353–354, 363, 364, 368
    initial, 261, 262, 266–268, 275, 277, 334
    interrogative, 124
    main, 6, 62, 67, 68, 73, 80, 142, 243, 247, 250, 251, 261–263, 265, 269–272, 276, 277, 279, 328, 329, 333, 334, 339, 341, 342, 346, 347, 364, 371
    relative, 72, 129, 141, 254, 336, 347, 365, 371
    root, 268, 329
    subjunctive, 360, 366, 370, 371
    subordinate, 7, 8, 66, 125, 128, 132, 133, 138, 231, 244, 246–249, 251, 265, 355, 362
Clitics, 68, 70, 71, 82, 125, 273, 275, 329, 340, 342, 344
Coarticulation, 111, 119
Cognate, 6, 65, 68, 74–75, 80–83
Cognition, 11, 356, 358, 370
Cognitive grammar, 372, 374
Columbia School, 2, 11, 223
Communicative
    factor, 224
    strategies, 11, 227–228
Compensatory lengthening (CL), 8, 9, 87–103, 179, 180, 278
Complementizer, 7, 8, 28, 132, 265, 329, 332, 333, 347
Concession, 131–144
Concrete, 58, 191, 195, 200, 223, 224, 295, 296
    vs. abstract, 4, 39, 52, 55, 57, 59, 234, 283, 297

Conditional, 10, 11, 140, 144, 221–240, 246, 264, 266, 270, 278, 291, 294, 351, 353, 356, 357, 365
Connotators, 189, 201, 202
Conservation
    vs. non-conservation, 89, 90, 95–96
    phonetic, 89–92, 99–103
    phonological, 89, 90, 92–95
Constraints, 8, 9, 55, 59, 65, 89, 92, 99–103, 108, 114–118, 121, 173, 174, 246, 251, 258, 267, 271, 337, 338, 347, 374
    faithfulness, 101, 115, 117
Contrary-to-fact, 357
Coordination, 6, 66–75, 81–83
Coptic, 208–210, 213, 214, 216, 218
Corpus, 2, 7, 8, 22, 45, 57, 68, 124, 129, 130, 133, 137, 141, 144, 172, 174, 193, 196, 238, 239, 244–246, 248–250, 300, 304, 306, 308, 310, 314, 317–320, 341
CP, split, 7
Crusaders, 11, 12, 207–218
Cue-based
    evolution, 39–41
    learning, 40
Cyprus, 12, 207, 208, 211, 212, 214, 215, 218

D

Dative, 20, 21, 33, 34, 38, 41, 54, 55, 169, 170
Declension
    Latin, 167–169, 171, 172
    romance, 167–176, 182, 183
Definite
    article, 3, 27, 28, 30, 32, 33, 36, 38–40, 45–47, 52, 57, 58, 168, 189, 197
    feature, 25, 29, 30, 32, 33, 35
Desemantization, 46
Determiners, 2, 4, 25, 27, 28, 30–33, 35, 39, 40, 55, 174, 175, 177, 180
Diasystem, 12, 187–202
Diasystematic parameters
    diachronic, 198–200
    diaphasic, 179, 188, 189
    diastratic, 183, 200
    diatopic, 183, 198
Diphthong, 88, 108, 291, 295, 296
Discourse
    direct, 3, 8, 130, 140, 177, 183, 299–306, 308–310, 312–322
    indirect, 8, 299–308, 310, 312–322

Index

with que, 300, 303, 317, 322
reported, 8, 299–322
without que, 300, 303–304, 314, 317, 319, 322
Dislocation, left, 6, 61, 66, 67, 78–84, 337, 341–346
Distant pole, 126, 130, 135, 136, 140, 142, 143
DP, 3, 24, 25, 28–31, 33, 34, 36, 38–40, 330, 332, 338–340

E
Écrasement, 6, 61, 65–69, 74, 75, 81–83
Edessa, county of, 207, 211
Egyptian, Northern, 208
English, 29, 39, 47, 52, 61, 110, 127, 135, 174, 177, 225, 266, 273, 274, 299, 341, 342, 347, 353, 357, 365
Enunciation theory, 301
Expression, formulaic, 6, 64, 68, 76, 81–83
Extralinguistic, 12, 187, 189, 190, 192, 200, 202, 254

F
Faroese, 334, 338, 347
FCA. *See* Final consonant alternation (FCA)
Feature
checking, 30, 263, 272, 273
interpretable, 27, 29–31, 34, 265, 272
uninterpretable, 27, 30–32, 34, 35, 264, 265, 272
Fiction, 8, 301, 305, 322
Final consonant alternation (FCA), 4, 283–285, 287, 289–295
Finite, 6, 7, 63, 70, 155, 227, 264–266, 268, 271–274, 277, 330, 341
Finnish, 55
FinP, 333, 341, 346, 347
Flandria, 211
Frame, 2, 4, 76, 80, 83, 196, 198, 201, 303, 345
France, 12, 153, 157, 158, 162, 164, 178, 195, 211, 214, 217, 218, 225, 227, 300, 310, 343, 354, 355, 360, 367
Franco-Provençal, 215
Frank, 5, 152, 153, 155, 157, 158, 164, 207, 213, 215, 217, 319
French
Medieval, 8, 299–322
Middle, 12, 28, 33, 37, 40, 41, 47, 57–59, 66, 82, 88, 98, 123, 130–136, 138, 140, 144, 211–215, 218, 253, 256, 347

Modern, 1, 3, 5, 6, 8–10, 12, 13, 19, 36, 45–47, 52, 53, 57–59, 61, 63–66, 77–79, 81–83, 98, 108, 109, 123–146, 167–169, 171, 177, 190–191, 194, 196–199, 211, 215, 222, 223, 227, 240, 253, 257, 264, 273, 279, 283, 288–295, 300, 303, 337, 347, 352, 353, 355–373
Parisian, 109
Future
occurrence, 11, 225–230, 234, 240
occurrence questioned, 11, 226–228, 230, 232, 240

G
Gallo-Romance, 108, 109, 118, 119, 159, 162, 170, 182
Gaul, 3, 5, 40, 56, 153–155, 157, 158, 182
Gender
feminine, 33, 284, 288
masculine, 285, 289
Genitive
with à, 19, 22–23, 26, 28, 29, 36, 38
with de, 19, 23–24, 26, 28, 34, 36
juxtaposition
postposed, 24–25
preposed, 25–27
prepositional, 19–24, 26, 28–30, 33–34, 36–40
Genre, 3, 7, 8, 10, 68, 124, 126, 129–131, 133, 135, 136, 139, 140, 142–144, 146, 173, 254–258, 263, 299, 300, 304–317, 319, 322
German, 7, 96, 127, 153, 164, 264, 279, 329, 330, 332, 341, 368
Gesture preservation, 9, 101
Government and binding, 28, 346
Grammaticalization, early stages, 47, 49, 58, 59
Greece, 212, 218
Greek, demotic, 12, 212, 215

H
Human, 11, 23, 26, 28, 34–36, 38, 41, 63, 68, 69, 77–78, 80, 81, 177, 224, 226, 227
null object, 6, 68, 77–78, 80, 81, 83
Hypothetical constructions, 11, 372

I

Icelandic, 7, 333, 334, 337–339, 347
Iconicity, 4, 283, 285–286, 293–295
Idealism, 152, 153, 158, 164
Imparisyllabic, 37, 41
Indefinite
    article, 2, 4, 22, 41, 45–59, 365
    feature, 25, 30, 35, 52, 59, 265, 272
Indicative, 123–130, 132–135, 137–146, 151, 222, 223, 225–227, 240, 246, 247, 286, 287, 290, 291, 293, 294, 301, 320, 321, 351, 353, 354, 356, 358, 359, 362–369, 372
Infinitive, 54, 70, 83, 130, 155, 221, 222, 240, 338, 351, 353
Interpretable feature, 27, 29–31, 34, 265, 272
Intralinguistic, 12, 187
Invariance
    nominal, 292
    verbal, 292
Inversion
    Germanic, 334
    subject-verb, 261
Irrealis, 11, 124, 127–129, 132–135, 138–146, 264, 372
Isochrony, 9, 99–103
Italo-Romance, 12, 212–214, 218
Italy
    Northern, 155
    Southern, 170, 212

J

Jerusalem, Kingdom of, 12, 207–214, 217, 218
Jongleur, 304, 305
Juridical language, 194–199, 201

K

Koiné, 12, 207–214, 217, 218
KP, 31–37, 41

L

Latin
    classical, 6, 21, 37, 40, 125, 153, 154, 159, 169, 170, 183, 364
    late, 20, 34, 37, 39, 46, 56, 98, 108, 109, 159, 171
    vulgar, 153, 154, 159
Left periphery, 5–7, 68, 78–80, 83, 327–347
Levantine, 12, 209–212, 214, 216–218
Lexical diffusion, 5, 88, 151, 152, 163, 164
Lexicography, 194, 196–198
Lexicon, 12, 13, 161, 175, 182, 202
Listener, 9, 11, 89, 97–99, 102, 110, 111, 114, 115, 304, 305, 307, 311, 312, 314, 316
Localized unfaithful mapping (LUM), 117
Lotharingia, 209, 211
Lotharingian, 198, 208, 209
LUM. *See* Localized unfaithful mapping (LUM)
Luxemburg, 193

M

Markedness, 8, 9, 99, 101, 103, 107–121, 126, 127, 133, 134, 136, 140, 285, 286, 291
Marker, presentative, 47
Meaning, invariant, 11, 222–224, 226–228, 230, 232, 234, 235, 239, 240
Mediterranean, Eastern, 215
Microsyntagma, 210
Minimalism, 2, 27, 346
Minimal link condition, 338
Modality, 46, 48, 128, 129, 133, 135, 138, 144, 229, 246, 251–252, 266, 333, 355, 365
Modern French, 1, 19, 45, 61, 98, 108, 123, 167–168, 190–191, 211, 222, 253, 264, 283, 300, 337, 352
Monophthongization, 95, 96
Mood
    conditional, 11
    indicative, 125, 132, 134, 135, 137, 139–142, 144, 145
    subjunctive, 10, 123, 127, 128, 354, 362, 365, 374
Mora, 90, 92, 94, 95
Morphology, 4, 5, 29, 31, 37, 39, 97, 151, 152, 159, 168–169, 172, 173, 175, 178, 180, 223, 283, 285, 293, 294, 356, 364, 366, 371
Morpho-phonology, 5, 283, 295–298
Mysticism, political, 151, 152, 157–158

N

Narrator, 8, 300, 304–308, 311, 312, 314–320, 322
Natural morphology
    system-dependent, 4, 283, 294
    system-independent, 4, 283, 294
Negation, 8, 39, 46, 218, 221, 244, 250–251, 258, 263, 265, 273, 337, 362, 366, 367
Negative, 5, 6, 221, 239, 250, 261–279, 338, 339, 358, 362, 371

Neogrammarians, 1, 150, 152, 153
Neumann's Law, 156
Non-assertion, 146, 370
  vs. assertion, 123, 127, 132, 143
Non-conservation, 89, 90, 95–96
  vs. conservation, 89, 90
Norman, 208
Normandy, 118, 119, 162
Noun, 3, 5, 21, 24, 26–32, 35, 37–41, 46, 49, 52, 55, 57, 59, 156–157, 161, 168–170, 172–175, 177–182, 284–286, 288, 289, 293, 294, 299, 337, 340, 363
Noun phrase (NP), 4, 27, 28, 30, 34, 36, 38, 39, 53, 55, 56, 70–72, 82, 170, 172–174, 265, 277, 278, 328
Null
  cognate, 6, 65, 68, 74–75, 80–83
  objects, 5, 6, 61–84
  pronominal, 6, 62, 67–69, 73–76, 78, 80, 83, 262
  subjects, 1, 7, 61, 63, 65, 66, 174, 177, 262, 276–278, 329, 330, 334, 337, 347
  variable, 6, 62, 67, 68, 75, 76, 78, 80, 83, 84

O
Object
  arbitrary, 6, 63, 64, 68, 77–78, 80, 81, 83
  human, 6, 63, 68, 77–78, 80, 81, 83
  null, 5, 6, 61–84
  pronouns, 6, 71, 82
Obligatorification, 124–126, 143, 146
Occitan, 167, 207, 208, 212–215, 218
Occurrence
  questioned, 11, 226–228, 230, 232, 240, 272
Ockham's Razor, 4, 283, 297–298
Oïl, 208–213, 215, 217, 218

P
Palestine, 207, 215, 216, 218
Paradigmatizaion, 58
Parasitic delinking, 94
Parataxis, 7, 8, 243–258
Paris, 72, 181, 212, 226, 312, 313, 318, 367
Peloponnesus, 12, 213
Perception, 8, 10, 97, 101, 103, 107–121, 126, 135, 245, 311
  vs. production, 9, 107–118
Perception-based analysis, 109
Periphery, left, 5–7, 68, 78–80, 83, 327–347

Persistence, 59
Phonological change, 5, 9, 151–153, 293
Phonology, 4, 8, 9, 37, 98, 102, 103, 107, 111, 114, 121, 151, 159, 163, 295–297, 363, 364
Picard, Eastern, 209
Picardy, 12, 118, 119, 209, 212, 218
P-map, 101, 102
Poems, 217, 226, 276
Polarity, 5, 6, 261–279, 362
Political mysticism, 151, 152, 157–158
Polysemy, 10, 352, 366, 368, 370, 374
Portuguese
  European Portuguese, 62, 81
  Galician Portuguese, 214
Possessor
  animate, 23, 26, 31, 38, 39
  inanimate, 23, 24
  vs. perception,
Pragmatic strengthening, 4, 50, 58
Pre-classical French, 130, 136–140
Preposition, 2–4, 20–22, 24, 26–34, 36–41, 45, 53–58, 73, 142, 169, 171, 183, 302
Production, 8, 9, 95, 97, 98, 103, 107–121, 201
Pronominal, null, 6, 62, 67–69, 73–76, 78, 80, 83, 262
Prose
  chronicles, 300, 306
  romances, 267–269, 299, 300, 304–315, 317, 320
  vs. verse, 254–256, 258
Prototype, 372
Proximate pole, 126, 130, 136, 140, 142, 143

Q
Que
  alternation, 250, 256, 258
  deletion, 244

R
Register
  formal, 57
  informal, 8, 56
  spoken, 253, 254, 257
  written, 257, 253
Regrammation, 10, 123–146
Renaissance, 10, 123–146, 173
Rheto-Romance, 170
Romance, 1, 28, 61, 107, 150, 167, 190, 207, 221, 263, 291, 299, 327, 364
Russian, 55, 127, 365

S

Scandinavian, 337
Schwa, 89–92, 95, 98–101, 284, 288
Semantics, 10, 11, 13, 27, 31, 50, 52, 55, 57, 125, 129, 133–135, 139, 172, 175, 187, 190–193, 195, 196, 198–201, 216, 224, 240, 263, 265–267, 279, 338, 341, 351, 352, 356, 362, 363, 365, 366, 369, 371, 373, 374
Sememe, 193, 194, 196–200
Semiosis, 12, 13, 187, 190, 191, 193, 200, 202
Semiotic sign modelling, 201
Signifiant, 57, 58, 66, 91, 157, 218, 238, 291, 321, 334
Signifié, 12, 191, 192, 195, 198, 201, 202, 223
Slavic, 90, 92
Sound change, 4, 5, 8, 9, 107–121, 149, 150, 152, 154, 164, 221, 296, 297
Spain, 170
Speaker, 8–13, 32, 37, 38, 40, 41, 68, 74, 79, 83, 87–103, 110, 111, 114, 115, 126–128, 130–132, 135, 136, 138, 139, 143, 144, 151, 162, 167, 173, 178, 190, 191, 193, 196, 197, 202, 207, 211, 213, 214, 218, 222, 227, 229, 230, 240, 300, 301, 303, 321, 342, 352, 353, 355, 360–362, 365–367, 369, 372
Specific, 2–4, 6, 12, 20, 22, 25, 34, 35, 41, 48, 50, 51, 55, 58, 64, 98, 100, 101, 110, 111, 117, 118, 135, 170, 171, 179, 182, 188, 191–193, 196, 197, 200, 201, 207–209, 212, 215, 218, 223, 226, 234, 240, 244–250, 252, 257, 258, 297, 299, 300, 303, 308–313, 315, 322, 338, 363, 372
Specifier, 29, 273, 332–334, 336, 339, 341, 347
Speech, 7, 8, 69, 83, 98, 142, 149, 154, 178, 180, 188, 217, 255, 257, 299, 300, 304–313, 315, 320–322, 352, 368
Split CP, 7
Stylistic fronting, 7, 328, 330–339, 341, 342, 344–347
Subjunctive, 7, 123, 189, 221, 246, 287, 320, 351
Suppletion, 151, 155, 160, 164, 289
Suppletive leveling, 4, 5, 151, 152, 154–156
Swedish, old, 338
Swiss Romance, 167, 168, 182
Syllable, 37, 87, 88, 91, 94, 96–99, 101, 118, 119, 155, 168
Syncope, 150, 152, 154–158, 160, 161, 287
Syntactic, change, 167, 253, 258
Syntax, 5–7, 10, 37, 63, 256, 258, 263, 265–268, 270–273, 276, 277, 279, 366
Synthetic, 222
  vs. analytic, 37, 40
Syria, 207, 215, 216, 218

T

Tense
  future, 70, 138, 223
  past, 305, 307, 311
  present, 83, 291, 293, 294, 302, 305, 311, 318, 360
  sequence of, 7, 359, 360
Text types, 170, 171, 173, 175, 177, 178
Thought, 7, 8, 25, 49, 137, 164, 170, 230, 251, 265, 276, 299, 300, 307, 308, 310–317, 320–322, 327, 328, 342, 344, 346, 358, 360, 369, 371
Topic, 2, 7, 8, 13, 62, 67, 68, 77, 80, 82, 83, 180, 274, 279, 310, 315, 327, 328, 332, 333, 337, 339, 341–347
Topicalization, 74, 79, 332–334, 336, 337, 339, 341, 342, 345
TP, 6, 7, 263, 265, 267, 271, 273–276, 278, 279, 328, 330–333, 336, 347
Tripoli, county of, 207, 213
Turbulency, 114, 115

U

Uninterpretable, feature, 27, 30–32, 34, 35, 264, 265, 272

V

V1, 263, 279, 341
V2
  generalized, 328, 334, 336, 339, 347
  non-generalized, 346
V3, 5–7, 263, 270, 271, 278, 328, 333, 339–342, 346
V4, 5–7, 263, 270, 271, 328, 333, 339–342, 346
Variant
  social, 5, 153, 163
  structural, 5, 153, 162, 163
  stylistic, 368, 369
Variational linguistics, 3, 12, 167, 168, 187–191, 202
Velar palatalization
  first, 107, 108
  second, 107, 108, 118, 120

Venetian, 214, 215
Verb, 5, 27, 53, 61, 98, 118, 124, 156, 174, 213, 222, 244, 261, 287, 301, 328, 354
Verse, 3, 6, 10, 66, 68, 126, 133, 140, 142, 177, 183, 188, 263, 276–278, 299, 300, 306, 310, 312–320, 341, 345
  vs. prose, 254–256, 258
Vowel
  initial, 88
  length, 96, 97, 180
  nasalized, 97
  stressed, 89
  syncope, 154, 155, 161
  tense, 291

W
Walloon, 96, 208–210, 218
Word order

V1, 263, 279, 341
V2, 5, 6, 65, 66, 261–268, 270–272, 274–279, 327–331, 333, 334, 336, 337, 339–341, 342, 344, 346, 347,
V3, 5–7, 263, 270, 271, 278, 328, 333, 339, 341, 342, 364
V4, 5–7, 263, 270, 271, 328, 333, 339, 341, 342, 346

X
XP, 7, 265, 274, 277, 278, 328, 330, 332, 333, 337, 341

Z
Zuni, 119

Printed by Printforce, the Netherlands